The World
Economic
Factbook 1996/97

The World
Economic
Factbook 1996/97

EUROMONITOR plc 60-61 Britton Street, London EC1M 5NA

The World Economic Factbook 1996/97
Fourth edition

Researched and published by:

EUROMONITOR plc
60-61 Britton Street
London EC1M 5NA
United Kingdom
Telephone: 0171-251-8024
Telex: 2262433
Fax: 0171-608-3149

EUROMONITOR INTERNATIONAL INC
122 South Michigan Avenue
Suite 1200
Chicago
Illinois 60603, USA
Tel: (312) 922 1115
Fax: (312) 922 1157

3 2280 00541 1590

British Library Cataloguing in Publication Data
A CIP catalogue record for this book is available from the British Library

ISBN 0 86338 682 2

© Euromonitor 1996

Printed in Great Britain by Antony Rowe Ltd., Chippenham, Wiltshire

Contents

Introduction

The World Economic Factbook 1996/97 (4th edition) represents a unique compilation of hard-to-get political and economic information on over 200 countries from all parts of the world, laid out in a concise and above all completely regular format which allows not only ease of access but also the maximum degree of comparability.

Countries are arranged in alphabetical order, with each country presented as a two-page section, the first page of which is a textual summary while the second contains statistical information for the years 1993 to 1995, organised according to a regular grid.

The information is supplemented by a series of specially commissioned maps showing the different continents with the location of each country.

Rankings

The uniformity of coverage is a key feature of the book. The individual country sections have been designed in order to allow the compilation of a series of unique rankings, showing the relative position for each country measured by a variety of criteria, such as geographical area, population, inflation, GDP, and so on. Thus each country can be ranked from 1 to 207 to show its relative position according to a wide variety of different benchmarks.

In order to compile the rankings it has been necessary to standardise and convert the basic data in many cases, particularly where economic material is concerned. It is inevitable that fluctuations in exchange rates and inflation have caused a considerable amount of distortion to the basic data, and as a result the rankings may contain some anomalies, although the editors have taken every care to cross-check the listings.

Where no data was available for the ranking criteria in each case some individual countries have been omitted.

Country Coverage

The 207 countries covered in this Handbook include all of the states for which standardised data is available. They include all the 15 member states of the former Soviet Union, each of which is listed in its own right; but not, conversely, micro-states such as the Vatican or San Marino, where no significant amount of comparable data is available, and where most of the economic data is in any case subsumed within the economy of a larger state (ie Italy in both these cases).

The relatively peaceful break-up of the former Soviet Union has made it possible to compile an extensive amount of data for the constituent republics for the period from 1992. This much cannot be said for the former Yugoslavia, where the chaotic wartime conditions continue to stand in the way of any serious compilation of recent data in much of the region. However, we have decided for this third edition of the book to show statistics relating to each of the newly-independent republics where available.

Sources and Methodology

This book is the result of an extensive research programme carried out during the early part of 1996, involving contact with a wide-ranging set of sources and contacts to gather together as much comprehensive material as possible.

The data have been drawn wherever possible from national sources, including official figures from national statistical agencies.   This primary data has been supplemented where necessary from multilateral sources such as the International Monetary Fund, United Nations, International Labour Organisation, and so on. (See below for further details by sector). In addition information has been drawn from the national press and specialist publications, or collated from Euromonitor's extensive international statistical database.

The availability of data is inevitably somewhat uneven, since some countries are far better documented than others. In many cases figures were unavailable for the latest year from published sources, and it has therefore been necessary in these cases to include estimates based on the best available external data. It was also necessary in many cases to undertake some degree of standardisation of the available data, since the information presented by some countries does not conform reliably with the international norms; there would, after all, be no point in attempting any international comparisons or rankings without having first established a high degree of standardisation.

Euromonitor estimates have mainly been used for 1995 economic data where official figures were unavailable. Data have been compiled using a mathematical model, which is based on data from national statistical agencies and calculated by taking into account economic and inflationary trends, current spending trends, demographic patterns, and so on. Political events and statistical material have been updated as far as July 1996 wherever possible.

Subject Coverage and Definitions

Inflation

This refers to annual average inflation, and is based mainly on figures provided by the *International Monetary Fund*.

Exchange rate

This refers to annual average official exchange rates, and is drawn mainly from figures provided by the *International Monetary Fund*.

GDP

Data for gross domestic product have been drawn wherever possible from national statistical sources, supplemented with data collected by the *International Monetary Fund* or, where necessary, Euromonitor estimates for the latest year.

GDP growth rate figures have also been included wherever they are reliably available. They refer, as one would suppose, to the rate of overall economic growth which is recorded by a country after stripping out the distorting effects of inflation. There is, however, more to this apparently simple task than meets the eye. In some countries, notably those where no proper statistical information has been available since perhaps 1988, it was felt that the foundation for such an estimate was not available, and real growth figures have accordingly been omitted. In certain high-inflation countries, on the other hand, the distortions caused by fluctuating currencies sometimes become so extreme that even the best and most accurate information from independent sources fails to produce a satisfactory result; in these cases, Euromonitor estimates have been supplied.

Consumption

These figures, which refer to private final consumption expenditure, have also been drawn wherever possible from national statistical sources, supplemented with data collected by the *International Monetary Fund* or, where necessary, Euromonitor estimates for the latest year.

Tourism Receipts and Spending

Tourism receipts refers to revenue from foreign nationals ie payments from visitors within the destination country and to the national carriers, while tourism expenditure refers to the reciprocal expenditure by that country's nationals in foreign countries, as collected by government agencies such as national statistical bodies and customs and excise bodies.

The main sources for this section have been national statistics, supplemented wherever necessary by data from the *World Tourism Organisation* and the *Organisation for Economic Co-operation and Development.*

Demographic Data

Population figures, drawn wherever possible from national statistics, refer to national estimates at mid-year. Birth rates refer to live births per '000 inhabitants in the given year. Figures for number of households, and average household size, are generally based on the latest official census material.

Foreign Trade

Import and export data are mainly sourced from *IMF Direction of Trade Statistics.* Figures refer to imports cif (cost, insurance and freight) and exports fob (free on board). Re-exports where relevant (eg in Hong Kong and other transhipment centres) are not included. Percentages of imports and exports for major export destinations and import sources are provided for the leading four major trading partners in each case.

Per capita and dollar conversions

Data for each year have been converted to US dollars, for the sake of ranking and comparability, using the exchange rate quoted on each page. The relevant rate for back years is used for previous years' data. Similarly, per capita calculations are based on population figures for preceding years each time, to arrive at an accurate three-year trend.

Disclaimer

Every effort has been made to ensure accuracy, and great care has been taken during the compilation of **The World Economic Factbook 1996/97**, but it is possible that omissions and errors may have occurred, for which Euromonitor cannot accept responsibility.

Maps

1　World

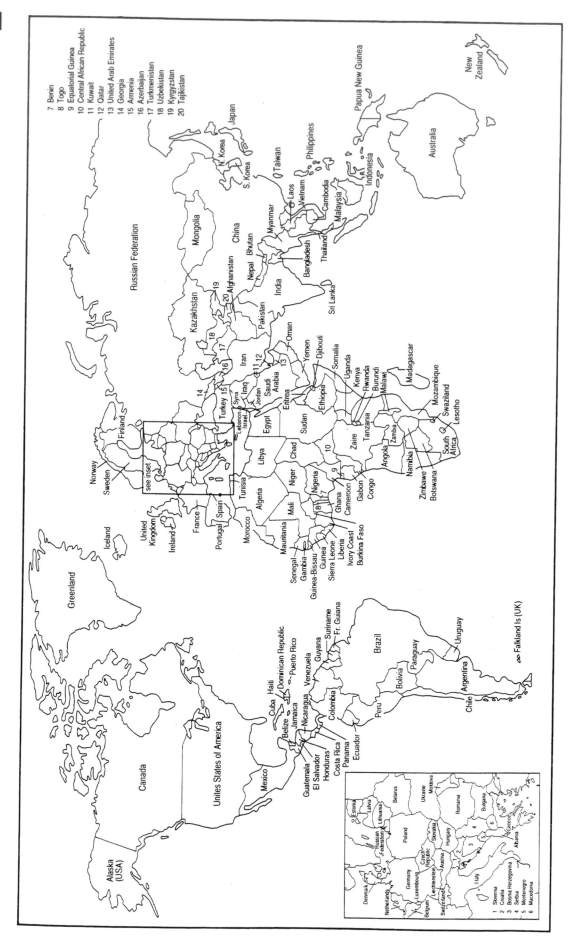

2 Europe

1 SLOVENIA
2 CROATIA
3 BOSNIA-HERZEGOVINA
4 SERBIA
4a Vojvodina
4b Kosovo
5 MONTENEGRO
6 MACEDONIA

3 Middle East and Asia

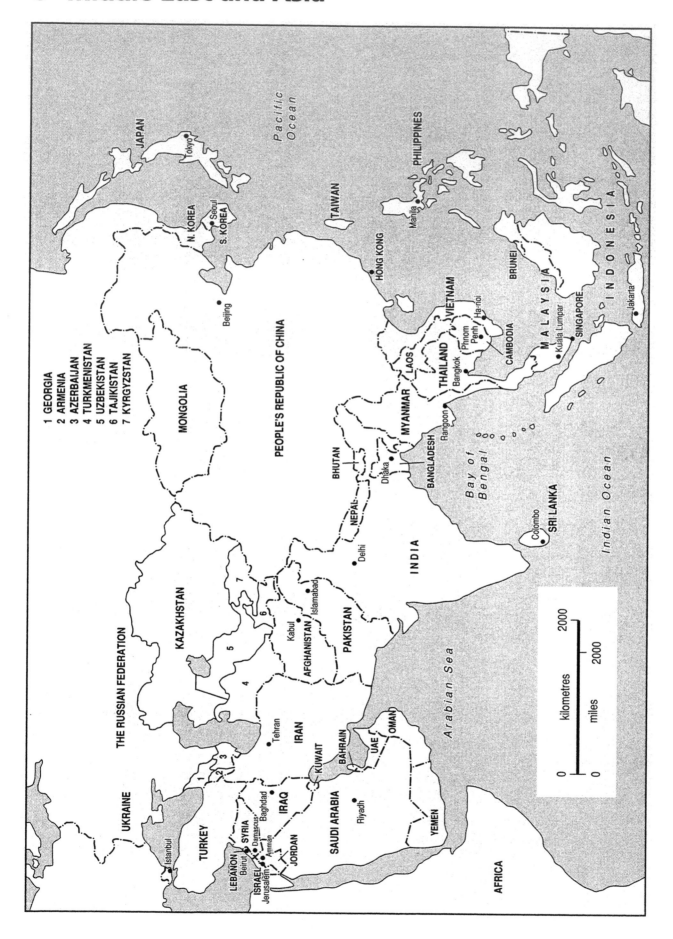

4 Africa

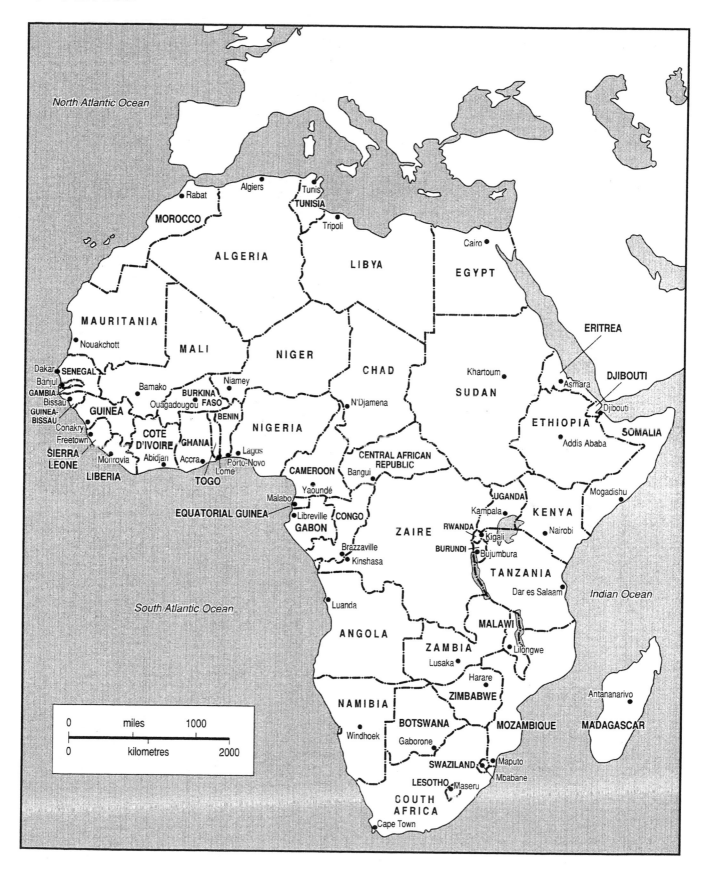

North Atlantic Ocean

Rabat •   Algiers •   Tunis •

MOROCCO   **TUNISIA**

Tripoli •

ALGERIA   **LIBYA**   Cairo •   **EGYPT**

MAURITANIA

Nouakchott •

ERITREA

Dakar •   **SENEGAL**   **MALI**   **NIGER**   **CHAD**   Khartoum •   Asmara •

Banjul •

GAMBIA   Bamako •   Niamey •   **SUDAN**   **DJIBOUTI**

Bissau •   **BURKINA**

GUINEA-   Ouagadougou • **FASO**   N'Djamena •   Djibouti •

BISSAU   **GUINEA**   **BENIN**   **NIGERIA**   **ETHIOPIA**

Conakry •   **COTE**   **SOMALIA**

Freetown •   **D'IVOIRE** **GHANA**   Lagos   Addis Ababa •

SIERRA   Monrovia •   Abidjan •   Accra •   Porto-Novo

LEONE   **CENTRAL AFRICAN**

LIBERIA   **TOGO**   Lomé   **REPUBLIC**   Mogadishu •

CAMEROON   Bangui •

Yaoundé •   **UGANDA**   **KENYA**

Malabo •   Kampala •

EQUATORIAL GUINEA   • Libreville   **CONGO**   Nairobi •

GABON   **ZAIRE**   **RWANDA**

Brazzaville •   Kigali •

BURUNDI   Bujumbura •

• Kinshasa

TANZANIA

Dar es Salaam •   Indian Ocean

Luanda •

South Atlantic Ocean

MALAWI

ANGOLA   **ZAMBIA**   Lilongwe •

Lusaka •

Harare •

Antananarivo •

NAMIBIA   **ZIMBABWE**

BOTSWANA   **MOZAMBIQUE**   **MADAGASCAR**

Windhoek •   Gaborone •

SWAZILAND   Maputo •

Mbabane •

LESOTHO • Maseru

SOUTH AFRICA

Cape Town •

0	miles	1000	
0	kilometres		2000

5 Oceania

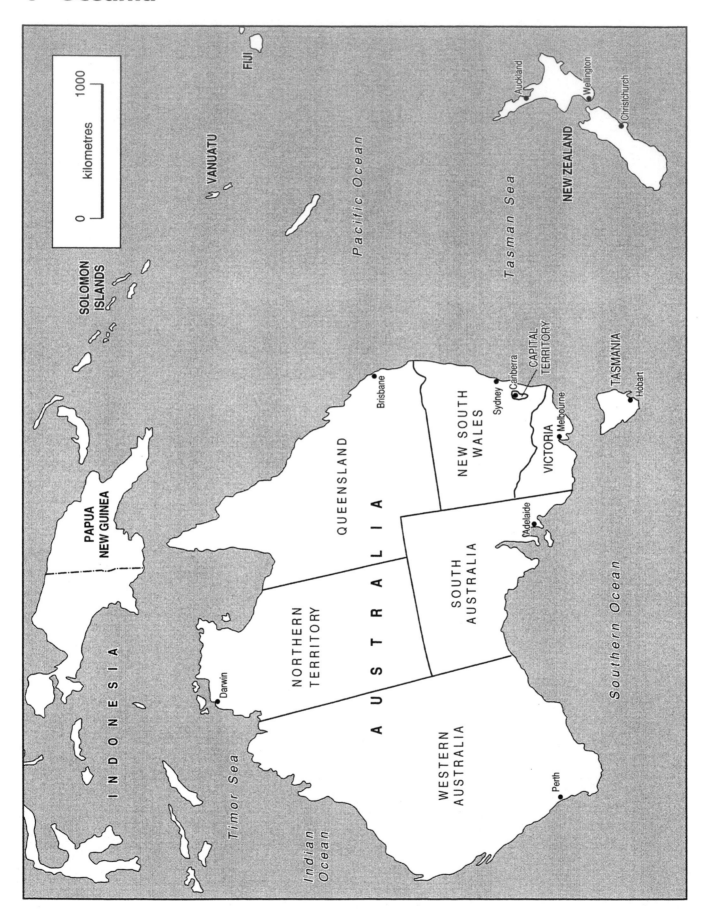

6 North and Central America

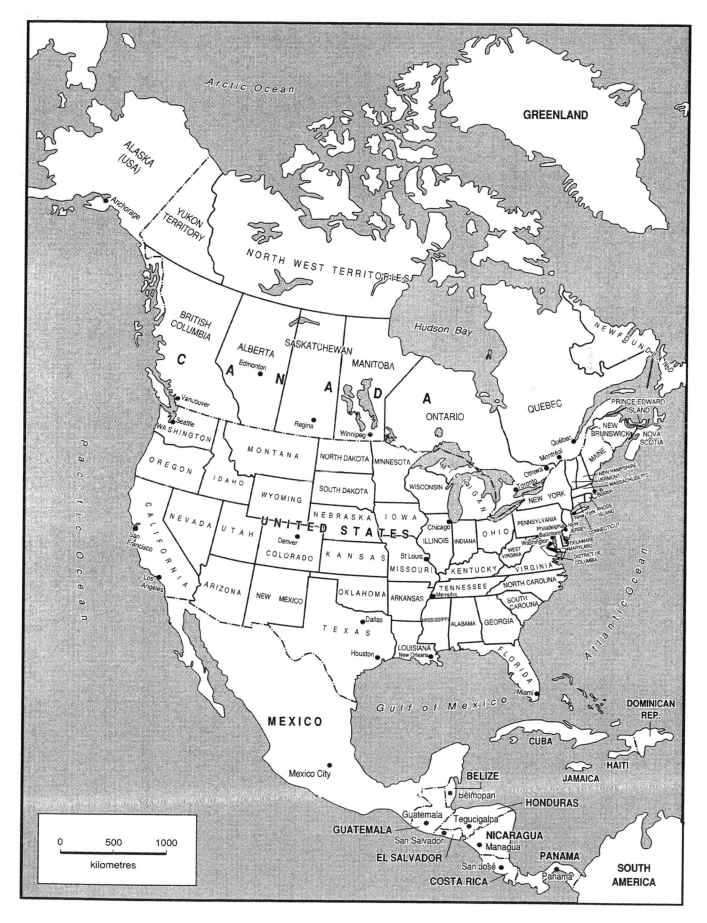

7   South America

Comparative
World
Rankings

Ranking by Area (km²)

1	Russia	17,075,400	53	Cameroon	465,500
2	Canada	9,922,385	54	Papua New Guinea	462,840
3	China	9,597,000	55	Morocco	458,730
4	USA	9,363,130	56	Sweden	449,790
5	Brazil	8,511,965	57	Uzbekistan	447,400
6	Australia	7,682,300	58	Iraq	438,445
7	India	3,166,830	59	Paraguay	406,750
8	Argentina	2,777,815	60	Zimbabwe	390,310
9	Kazakhstan	2,717,300	61	Japan	369,700
10	Gabon	2,667,665	62	Germany	356,840
11	Sudan	2,505,815	63	Congo	342,000
12	Saudi Arabia	2,400,900	64	Finland	337,030
13	Algeria	2,381,745	65	Malaysia	332,965
14	Zaire	2,345,410	66	Vietnam	329,565
15	Mexico	1,972,545	67	Norway	323,895
16	Indonesia	1,919,445	68	Côte d'Ivoire	322,465
17	Libya	1,759,540	69	Poland	312,685
18	Iran	1,648,000	70	Italy	301,245
19	Mongolia	1,565,000	71	Philippines	300,000
20	Peru	1,285,215	72	Burkina Faso	274,122
21	Chad	1,284,000	73	Oman	271,950
22	Angola	1,246,700	74	New Zealand	265,150
23	Mali	1,240,140	75	Ecuador	263,950
24	Niger	1,186,410	76	Yugoslavia (former)	255,805
25	South Africa	1,184,825	77	Guinea	245,855
26	Colombia	1,138,915	78	United Kingdom	244,755
27	Bolivia	1,098,575	79	Ghana	238,305
28	Mauritania	1,030,700	80	Romania	237,500
29	Ethiopia	1,023,050	81	Laos	236,725
30	Egypt	997,739	82	Uganda	236,580
31	Tanzania	939,760	83	Guyana	214,970
32	Nigeria	923,850	84	Belarus	207,595
33	Venezuela	912,045	85	Kyrgyzstan	198,500
34	Namibia	824,295	86	Senegal	196,720
35	Pakistan	803,940	87	Uruguay	186,925
36	Mozambique	784,755	88	Syria	185,680
37	Turkey	779,450	89	Cambodia	181,000
38	Zambia	752,615	90	Tunisia	164,150
39	Chile	751,625	91	Suriname	163,820
40	Myanmar	678,030	92	Nicaragua	148,000
41	Afghanistan	636,265	93	Bangladesh	144,000
42	Somalia	630,000	94	Tajikistan	143,100
43	Central African Republic	624,975	95	Nepal	141,415
44	Ukraine	603,700	96	Greece	131,985
45	Madagascar	594,180	97	North Korea	122,310
46	Kenya	582,645	98	Cuba	114,525
47	Botswana	575,000	99	Benin	112,620
48	France	543,965	100	Honduras	112,085
49	Yemen	527,968	101	Liberia	111,370
50	Thailand	514,000	102	Bulgaria	110,910
51	Spain	504,880	103	Guatemala	108,890
52	Turkmenistan	488,100	104	Iceland	102,820

105	South Korea	98,445	157	Vanuatu	14,765
106	Malawi	94,080	158	Bahamas	13,865
107	Eritrea	93,679	159	Montenegro	13,812
108	Hungary	93,030	160	Qatar	11,435
109	Portugal	91,630	161	Jamaica	11,425
110	French Guiana	91,000	162	Gambia	10,690
111	Jordan	90,650	163	Lebanon	10,400
112	Serbia	88,361	164	Cyprus	9,250
113	Azerbaijan	86,600	165	Puerto Rico	8,960
114	Austria	83,855	166	Brunei	5,765
115	Czech Republic	78,864	167	Trinidad and Tobago	5,130
116	Panama	78,515	168	Cape Verde	4,035
117	United Arab Emirates	75,150	169	French Polynesia	3,940
118	Sierra Leone	72,325	170	Western Samoa	2,840
119	Georgia	70,000	171	Luxembourg	2,585
120	Ireland	68,895	172	Réunion	2,510
121	Sri Lanka	65,610	173	Mauritius	1,865
122	Lithuania	65,300	174	Comoros	1,860
123	Latvia	64,589	175	Guadeloupe	1,780
124	Togo	56,785	176	Martinique	1,079
125	Croatia	56,538	177	Hong Kong	1,062
126	Bosnia-Herzegovina	51,129	178	Netherlands Antilles	993
127	Costa Rica	50,900	179	Sao Tomé e Príncipe	964
128	Slovakia	49,035	180	Dominica	751
129	Dominican Republic	48,440	181	Tonga	699
130	Bhutan	46,620	182	Kiribati	684
131	Estonia	45,226	183	Bahrain	661
132	Denmark	43,075	184	Singapore	616
133	Switzerland	41,285	185	St Lucia	616
134	Netherlands	41,160	186	Andorra	465
135	Guinea-Bissau	36,125	187	Seychelles	455
136	Taiwan	35,990	188	Guam	450
137	Moldova	33,700	189	Antigua	442
138	Belgium	30,520	190	Barbados	430
139	Lesotho	30,345	191	St Vincent & the Grenadines	389
140	Armenia	29,800	192	Grenada	345
141	Solomon Islands	29,790	193	Malta	316
142	Albania	28,750	194	Maldives	298
143	Equatorial Guinea	28,050	195	St Kitts	261
144	Burundi	27,835	196	Cayman Islands	259
145	Haiti	27,750	197	American Samoa	197
146	Rwanda	26,330	198	Aruba	193
147	Macedonia	25,713	199	Liechtenstein	160
148	Kuwait	24,280	200	British Virgin Islands	153
149	Djibouti	23,000	201	Anguilla	91
150	Belize	22,965	202	Bermuda	54
151	El Salvador	21,395	203	Tuvalu	25
152	Israel	20,770	204	Nauru	21
153	Slovenia	20,254	205	Macau	16
154	New Caledonia	19,105	206	Gibraltar	6
155	Fiji	18,330	207	Monaco	2
156	Swaziland	17,365			

Ranking by Mid-Year Population 1995 ('000)

1	China	1,294,400.0	53	Ghana	17,350.0
2	India	933,170.0	54	Kazakhstan	16,590.0
3	United States of America	263,030.0	55	Netherlands	15,450.0
4	Indonesia	193,750.0	56	Madagascar	14,775.0
5	Brazil	155,820.0	57	Syria	14,310.0
6	Russia	147,860.0	58	Côte d'Ivoire	14,230.0
7	Pakistan	130,250.0	59	Chile	14,200.0
8	Japan	125,359.0	60	Cameroon	13,280.0
9	Bangladesh	120,311.0	61	Yemen	13,058.0
10	Nigeria	111,666.0	62	Zimbabwe	11,530.0
11	Mexico	94,780.0	63	Ecuador	11,460.0
12	Germany	81,944.0	64	Cuba	11,051.6
13	Vietnam	73,648.9	65	Angola	10,674.1
14	Philippines	68,420.0	66	Guatemala	10,620.0
15	Turkey	61,640.0	67	Serbia	10,575.2
16	Iran	61,178.1	68	Mali	10,560.0
17	Thailand	60,210.0	69	Greece	10,442.0
18	Egypt	59,230.0	70	Czech Republic	10,347.2
19	United Kingdom	58,576.0	71	Belarus	10,345.0
20	France	58,030.0	72	Belgium	10,222.3
21	Italy	57,316.0	73	Hungary	10,220.0
22	Ethiopia	56,680.0	74	Burkina Faso	10,200.0
23	Ukraine	51,640.0	75	Portugal	9,928.0
24	Myanmar	45,000.0	76	Cambodia	9,837.7
25	South Korea	44,850.0	77	Malawi	9,790.0
26	Zaire	44,469.8	78	Zambia	9,370.0
27	South Africa	41,240.0	79	Niger	9,200.0
28	Spain	39,190.0	80	Somalia	9,131.7
29	Poland	38,590.0	81	Tunisia	8,984.7
30	Colombia	35,100.0	82	Sweden	8,830.0
31	Argentina	34,590.0	83	Bulgaria	8,316.7
32	Kenya	30,520.0	84	Senegal	8,200.0
33	Tanzania	30,340.0	85	Austria	8,070.0
34	Sudan	29,792.2	86	Dominican Republic	7,910.0
35	Canada	29,610.0	87	Rwanda	7,850.0
36	Algeria	28,550.0	88	Azerbaijan	7,500.0
37	Morocco	27,110.0	89	Bolivia	7,410.0
38	North Korea	23,937.2	90	Haiti	7,180.0
39	Peru	23,530.0	91	Switzerland	7,040.0
40	Uzbekistan	22,850.0	92	Guinea	6,690.8
41	Romania	22,680.0	93	Chad	6,347.3
42	Nepal	21,988.7	94	Burundi	6,310.0
43	Venezuela	21,638.0	95	Hong Kong	6,189.8
44	Uganda	21,343.0	96	Honduras	5,950.0
45	Taiwan	21,200.0	97	Tajikistan	5,840.0
46	Iraq	20,367.3	98	El Salvador	5,713.1
47	Malaysia	19,690.0	99	Israel	5,653.5
48	Afghanistan	19,035.0	100	Benin	5,560.0
49	Saudi Arabia	18,133.7	101	Georgia	5,460.0
50	Sri Lanka	18,078.6	102	Jordan	5,460.0
51	Australia	18,050.0	103	Slovakia	5,360.0
52	Mozambique	17,420.0	104	Denmark	5,230.0

105	Finland	5,110.0	157	Réunion	660.5
106	Libya	5,107.8	158	Comoros	645.0
107	Laos	4,880.0	159	Montenegro	626.0
108	Paraguay	4,830.0	160	Qatar	605.1
109	Kyrgyzstan	4,670.0	161	Bahrain	590.0
110	Croatia	4,572.0	162	Djibouti	583.2
111	Nicaragua	4,540.0	163	Guadeloupe	425.0
112	Sierra Leone	4,518.2	164	Suriname	422.6
113	Bosnia-Herzegovina	4,480.0	165	Macau	410.0
114	Norway	4,360.0	166	Luxembourg	403.0
115	Moldova	4,360.0	167	Equatorial Guinea	398.1
116	Turkmenistan	4,099.7	168	Cape Verde	390.7
117	Papua New Guinea	4,070.0	169	Martinique	380.0
118	Togo	4,036.7	170	Solomon Islands	364.0
119	Armenia	3,760.0	171	Malta	360.0
120	Puerto Rico	3,750.0	172	Brunei	285.5
121	Lithuania	3,710.0	173	Bahamas	271.0
122	Ireland	3,580.0	174	Iceland	268.0
123	New Zealand	3,540.0	175	Maldives	260.0
124	Albania	3,439.0	176	Barbados	256.0
125	Eritrea	3,295.0	177	Belize	215.4
126	Central African Republic	3,290.0	178	French Polynesia	212.6
127	Uruguay	3,190.0	179	Netherlands Antilles	210.0
128	Costa Rica	3,141.5	180	New Caledonia	180.0
129	Lebanon	3,010.0	181	Western Samoa	175.0
130	Singapore	2,990.0	182	Vanuatu	165.0
131	Liberia	2,760.0	183	Guam	150.0
132	Panama	2,630.0	184	French Guiana	145.0
133	Congo	2,580.0	185	St Lucia	140.0
134	Jamaica	2,530.0	186	Sao Tomé e Príncipe	120.0
135	Latvia	2,510.0	187	St Vincent & the Grenadines	110.0
136	Mongolia	2,405.0	188	Tonga	98.0
137	United Arab Emirates	2,310.0	189	Grenada	90.0
138	Mauritania	2,265.9	190	Kiribati	82.0
139	Macedonia	2,160.0	191	Aruba	71.0
140	Oman	2,158.2	192	Dominica	70.0
141	Lesotho	2,050.0	193	Seychelles	70.0
142	Slovenia	1,950.0	194	Bermuda	62.0
143	Kuwait	1,690.0	195	Antigua	60.0
144	Bhutan	1,630.5	196	American Samoa	60.0
145	Namibia	1,539.8	197	Andorra	53.0
146	Estonia	1,485.0	198	St Kitts	40.0
147	Botswana	1,460.0	199	Monaco	31.0
148	Gabon	1,295.0	200	Liechtenstein	30.5
149	Trinidad and Tobago	1,270.0	201	Cayman Islands	30.0
150	Mauritius	1,125.2	202	Gibraltar	30.0
151	Gambia	1,090.0	203	British Virgin Islands	20.1
152	Guinea-Bissau	1,068.6	204	Nauru	12.1
153	Swaziland	910.0	205	Tuvalu	11.1
154	Guyana	825.0	206	Anguilla	10.0
155	Fiji	780.0			
156	Cyprus	743.3			

Ranking by Population Density (persons/km^2)

1	Macau	25,625.0	53	Nepal	155.5
2	Monaco	15,500.0	54	Seychelles	153.8
3	Hong Kong	5,828.4	55	St Kitts	153.3
4	Gibraltar	5,454.5	56	Tonga	140.2
5	Singapore	4,853.9	57	Antigua	135.7
6	Bermuda	1,148.1	58	China	134.9
7	Malta	1,139.2	59	Czech Republic	131.2
8	Bahrain	892.6	60	British Virgin Islands	131.1
9	Maldives	872.5	61	Moldova	129.4
10	Bangladesh	835.5	62	Armenia	126.2
11	Mauritius	603.3	63	Sao Tomé e Príncipe	124.5
12	Barbados	595.4	64	Poland	123.4
13	Taiwan	589.1	65	Denmark	121.4
14	Nauru	576.2	66	Nigeria	120.9
15	South Korea	455.6	67	Kiribati	119.9
16	Tuvalu	444.4	68	Serbia	119.7
17	Puerto Rico	418.5	69	Albania	119.6
18	Netherlands	375.4	70	Thailand	117.1
19	Aruba	367.9	71	Cayman Islands	115.8
20	Martinique	352.2	72	Andorra	114.0
21	Comoros	346.8	73	Anguilla	109.9
22	Japan	339.1	74	Hungary	109.9
23	Belgium	334.9	75	Slovakia	109.3
24	Guam	333.3	76	Portugal	108.3
25	American Samoa	304.6	77	France	106.7
26	Rwanda	298.1	78	Malawi	104.1
27	India	294.7	79	Gambia	102.0
28	Lebanon	289.4	80	Indonesia	100.9
29	St Vincent & the Grenadines	282.8	81	Guatemala	97.5
30	Sri Lanka	275.5	82	Cape Verde	96.8
31	Israel	272.2	83	Cuba	96.5
32	El Salvador	267.0	84	Slovenia	96.3
33	Réunion	263.1	85	Austria	96.2
34	Grenada	260.9	86	Romania	95.5
35	Haiti	258.7	87	Dominica	93.2
36	Trinidad and Tobago	247.6	88	Uganda	90.2
37	United Kingdom	239.3	89	Bosnia-Herzegovina	87.6
38	Guadeloupe	238.8	90	Azerbaijan	86.6
39	Germany	229.6	91	Ukraine	85.5
40	Philippines	228.1	92	Macedonia	84.0
41	St Lucia	227.3	93	Croatia	80.9
42	Burundi	226.7	94	Cyprus	80.4
43	Vietnam	223.5	95	Greece	79.1
44	Jamaica	221.4	96	Turkey	79.1
45	Netherlands Antilles	211.5	97	Georgia	78.0
46	North Korea	195.7	98	Spain	77.6
47	Liechtenstein	190.6	99	Syria	77.1
48	Italy	190.3	100	Bulgaria	75.0
49	Switzerland	170.5	101	Ghana	72.8
50	Dominican Republic	163.3	102	Togo	71.1
51	Pakistan	162.0	103	Kuwait	69.6
52	Luxembourg	155.9	104	Lesotho	67.6

105	Myanmar	66.4	157 Kyrgyzstan	23.5
106	Sierra Leone	62.5	158 Mozambique	22.2
107	Costa Rica	61.7	159 Laos	20.6
108	Western Samoa	61.6	160 Sweden	19.6
109	Jordan	60.2	161 Bahamas	19.5
110	Egypt	59.4	162 Zaire	19.0
111	Malaysia	59.1	163 Chile	18.9
112	Morocco	59.1	164 Peru	18.3
113	Lithuania	56.8	165 Brazil	18.3
114	Ethiopia	55.4	166 Uruguay	17.1
115	Tunisia	54.7	167 Finland	15.2
116	Cambodia	54.4	168 Somalia	14.5
117	French Polynesia	54.0	169 Equatorial Guinea	14.2
118	Honduras	53.1	170 Norway	13.5
119	Qatar	52.9	171 New Zealand	13.4
120	Swaziland	52.4	172 Argentina	12.5
121	Kenya	52.4	173 Zambia	12.4
122	Ireland	52.0	174 Solomon Islands	12.2
123	Uzbekistan	51.1	175 Algeria	12.0
124	Belarus	49.8	176 Sudan	11.9
125	Brunei	49.5	177 Paraguay	11.9
126	Benin	49.4	178 Vanuatu	11.2
127	Mexico	48.0	179 New Caledonia	9.4
128	Iraq	46.5	180 Belize	9.4
129	Montenegro	45.3	181 Papua New Guinea	8.8
130	Côte d'Ivoire	44.1	182 Russia	8.7
131	Ecuador	43.4	183 Angola	8.6
132	Fiji	42.6	184 Mali	8.5
133	Senegal	41.7	185 Turkmenistan	8.4
134	Tajikistan	40.8	186 Oman	7.9
135	Latvia	38.9	187 Niger	7.8
136	Burkina Faso	37.2	188 Saudi Arabia	7.6
137	Iran	37.1	189 Congo	7.5
138	Eritrea	35.2	190 Bolivia	6.7
139	Bhutan	35.0	191 Kazakhstan	6.1
140	South Africa	34.8	192 Central African Republic	5.3
141	Panama	33.5	193 Chad	4.9
142	Estonia	32.8	194 Guyana	3.8
143	Tanzania	32.3	195 Canada	3.0
144	Colombia	30.8	196 Libya	2.9
145	United Arab Emirates	30.7	197 Iceland	2.6
146	Nicaragua	30.7	198 Suriname	2.6
147	Afghanistan	29.9	199 Botswana	2.5
148	Guinea-Bissau	29.6	200 Australia	2.3
149	Zimbabwe	29.5	201 Mauritania	2.2
150	Cameroon	28.5	202 Namibia	1.9
151	Guinea	27.2	203 French Guiana	1.6
152	Djibouti	25.4	204 Mongolia	1.5
153	Madagascar	24.9	205 Gabon	0.5
154	Liberia	24.8		
155	Yemen	24.7		
156	Venezuela	23.7		

Ranking by Child Population, Latest Year (% aged 0-14)

1	Kenya	51.3	53	Puerto Rico	44.8
2	Libya	49.7	54	Congo	44.7
3	Uzbekistan	49.6	55	Kyrgyzstan	44.6
4	Uganda	49.6	56	Iraq	44.5
5	Syria	49.2	57	Sierra Leone	44.5
6	Ethiopia	48.8	58	St Lucia	44.5
7	Azerbaijan	48.6	59	Mozambique	44.3
8	Turkmenistan	48.6	60	Western Samoa	44.3
9	Tajikistan	48.6	61	Mauritania	44.1
10	Malawi	48.3	62	Sudan	44.0
11	Burkina Faso	48.3	63	Algeria	44.0
12	Jordan	48.1	64	Bangladesh	43.8
13	Tanzania	47.8	65	St Vincent & the Grenadines	43.8
14	Zimbabwe	47.7	66	Gambia	43.8
15	Niger	47.7	67	Laos	43.6
16	Dominican Republic	47.6	68	Guinea-Bissau	43.3
17	Yemen	47.5	69	Liberia	43.2
18	Swaziland	47.4	70	Lesotho	43.1
19	Solomon Islands	47.3	71	Honduras	42.8
20	Zambia	47.3	72	Botswana	42.8
21	Côte d'Ivoire	47.2	73	Equatorial Guinea	42.6
22	Nicaragua	47.2	74	Nepal	42.3
23	Comoros	47.2	75	Tuvalu	42.0
24	Somalia	47.0	76	Suriname	41.7
25	Pakistan	46.9	77	Mongolia	41.3
26	Cambodia	46.9	78	American Samoa	41.1
27	Maldives	46.9	79	Kiribati	41.1
28	Egypt	46.8	80	Tonga	40.9
29	Guinea	46.7	81	Guyana	40.8
30	Sao Tomé e Príncipe	46.7	82	Papua New Guinea	40.4
31	Armenia	46.6	83	Jamaica	39.7
32	Zaire	46.6	84	Haiti	39.2
33	Benin	46.6	85	Albania	39.1
34	Angola	46.5	86	Vietnam	39.0
35	Oman	46.5	87	Grenada	38.6
36	Afghanistan	46.1	88	North Korea	38.6
37	Burundi	46.0	89	Fiji	38.2
38	Mali	45.9	90	Antigua	38.0
39	Namibia	45.8	91	Tunisia	37.9
40	Rwanda	45.6	92	Turkey	37.5
41	Kazakhstan	45.6	93	Chad	37.4
42	Vanuatu	45.6	94	Philippines	37.3
43	Iran	45.5	95	Myanmar	37.3
44	Guatemala	45.4	96	Ecuador	36.9
45	Togo	45.4	97	Peru	36.7
46	Ghana	45.4	98	Kuwait	36.6
47	Saudi Arabia	45.3	99	Costa Rica	36.6
48	Senegal	45.2	100	Malaysia	36.4
49	Cameroon	45.2	101	Belize	36.4
50	Madagascar	45.1	102	Bolivia	36.3
51	Cape Verde	45.0	103	Venezuela	36.2
52	Central African Republic	45.0	104	El Salvador	36.1

#	Country	Value	#	Country	Value
105	Indonesia	36.0	157	Gibraltar	23.8
106	Lebanon	36.0	158	Poland	23.6
107	India	36.0	159	New Zealand	23.2
108	Morocco	36.0	160	Belarus	23.1
109	French Polynesia	35.9	161	Martinique	23.1
110	Nauru	35.1	162	Singapore	23.1
111	Dominica	35.0	163	Romania	22.8
112	Seychelles	35.0	164	Cuba	22.6
113	South Africa	34.6	165	Lithuania	22.3
114	Brunei	34.5	166	Australia	22.1
115	Colombia	34.4	167	USA	21.9
116	Panama	34.2	168	Cayman Islands	21.5
117	St Kitts	33.3	169	Russia	21.5
118	Paraguay	33.0	170	Ukraine	21.4
119	Mexico	33.0	171	Bulgaria	21.2
120	Brazil	32.8	172	Hungary	21.1
121	New Caledonia	32.7	173	Latvia	20.7
122	French Guiana	32.6	174	Estonia	20.7
123	Taiwan	32.6	175	Slovenia	20.6
124	Bahamas	32.2	176	Canada	20.2
125	Réunion	31.8	177	Andorra	20.1
126	Guam	31.7	178	Sweden	20.0
127	Bahrain	31.7	179	Bermuda	19.9
128	Trinidad and Tobago	31.3	180	Liechtenstein	19.6
129	Thailand	31.3	181	United Kingdom	19.5
130	Israel	31.1	182	France	19.4
131	Chile	30.6	183	Switzerland	19.2
132	Anguilla	30.5	184	Spain	19.2
133	Nigeria	30.2	185	Hong Kong	19.0
134	Mauritius	29.6	186	Finland	19.0
135	British Virgin Islands	29.0	187	Norway	18.9
136	Argentina	29.0	188	Netherlands	18.2
137	Sri Lanka	28.2	189	Belgium	18.1
138	Moldova	27.9	190	Luxembourg	17.5
139	Qatar	27.7	191	Austria	17.4
140	China	26.8	192	Japan	17.3
141	Ireland	26.8	193	Portugal	16.7
142	Guadeloupe	26.4	194	Greece	16.7
143	United Arab Emirates	26.3	195	Denmark	16.7
144	Netherlands Antilles	26.0	196	Germany	16.3
145	Uruguay	25.8	197	Italy	15.1
146	Aruba	25.4	198	Monaco	12.5
147	Cyprus	25.3			
148	Barbados	25.1			
149	Iceland	25.0			
150	Georgia	24.8			
151	South Korea	24.4			
152	Macau	24.4			
153	Malta	24.3			
154	Slovakia	24.1			
155	Czech Republic	24.1			
156	Yugoslavia (former)	23.8			

Ranking by Elderly Population, Latest Year (% aged 65+)

1	Sweden	18.0	53	Israel	9.2
2	Cayman Islands	17.2	54	Yugoslavia (former)	9.2
3	Norway	16.1	55	Guadeloupe	8.8
4	Italy	15.9	56	Georgia	8.8
5	United Kingdom	15.8	57	Cuba	8.8
6	Denmark	15.6	58	Dominica	8.3
7	Austria	15.4	59	Moldova	8.1
8	Germany	15.3	60	Sri Lanka	7.6
9	Belgium	15.1	61	Anguilla	7.4
10	Greece	14.8	62	Grenada	7.3
11	France	14.6	63	Netherlands Antilles	6.9
12	Portugal	14.3	64	Jamaica	6.9
13	Finland	14.3	65	Seychelles	6.8
14	Luxembourg	14.2	66	Botswana	6.7
15	Switzerland	13.8	67	Paraguay	6.6
16	Andorra	13.8	68	Aruba	6.6
17	Spain	13.5	69	Macau	6.6
18	Latvia	13.4	70	British Virgin Islands	6.5
19	Netherlands	13.1	71	Singapore	6.3
20	Hungary	13.1	72	Chile	6.3
21	Estonia	13.1	73	China	6.2
22	Japan	13.0	74	Turkey	6.2
23	USA	12.7	75	Nicaragua	6.0
24	Bulgaria	12.4	76	Honduras	5.9
25	Ukraine	12.3	77	Haiti	5.9
26	Canada	11.9	78	St Vincent & the Grenadines	5.8
27	Russia	11.8	79	Cape Verde	5.8
28	Czech Republic	11.7	80	Central African Republic	5.8
29	Malta	11.7	81	Taiwan	5.8
30	Slovakia	11.7	82	El Salvador	5.8
31	New Zealand	11.7	83	St Lucia	5.6
32	Uruguay	11.6	84	Mauritius	5.5
33	Libya	11.6	85	Trinidad and Tobago	5.5
34	Iceland	11.5	86	Cambodia	5.4
35	Ireland	11.4	87	South Korea	5.4
36	Lithuania	11.4	88	Nigeria	5.3
37	Barbados	11.4	89	Réunion	5.2
38	Liechtenstein	11.2	90	Brazil	5.1
39	Slovenia	10.9	91	Tonga	5.0
40	Poland	10.7	92	Yemen	5.0
41	Gibraltar	10.5	93	Lebanon	5.0
42	Australia	10.4	94	Antigua	5.0
43	Belarus	10.4	95	Congo	5.0
44	Cyprus	10.3	96	Panama	4.9
45	Puerto Rico	10.2	97	Tunisia	4.9
46	Martinique	10.1	98	Sao Tomé e Príncipe	4.9
47	Bangladesh	10.0	99	Morocco	4.8
48	Romania	9.7	100	French Guiana	4.8
49	Hong Kong	9.5	101	Vietnam	4.8
50	Argentina	9.5	102	Bahamas	4.7
51	Bermuda	9.4	103	Belize	4.7
52	St Kitts	9.2	104	Costa Rica	4.5

© Euromonitor 1996

105	Albania	4.4	157 Mongolia	3.2
106	New Caledonia	4.4	158 Guatemala	3.2
107	Syria	4.4	159 Zimbabwe	3.1
108	Comoros	4.3	160 French Polynesia	3.1
109	Colombia	4.3	161 Dominican Republic	3.1
110	Tajikistan	4.3	162 Sierra Leone	3.1
111	Armenia	4.3	163 Iran	3.1
112	South Africa	4.3	164 Guinea-Bissau	3.1
113	Kyrgyzstan	4.3	165 Ethiopia	3.0
114	Turkmenistan	4.3	166 Western Samoa	3.0
115	Azerbaijan	4.3	167 Nepal	3.0
116	Ecuador	4.3	168 Laos	3.0
117	Mexico	4.2	169 Madagascar	3.0
118	Philippines	4.2	170 Sudan	3.0
119	Liberia	4.1	171 Rwanda	2.8
120	Indonesia	4.1	172 Ghana	2.8
121	Burkina Faso	4.1	173 Brunei	2.7
122	Suriname	4.1	174 Somalia	2.7
123	North Korea	4.1	175 Maldives	2.7
124	Nauru	4.1	176 Chad	2.6
125	India	4.1	177 Jordan	2.6
126	Thailand	4.1	178 Guinea	2.6
127	Tuvalu	4.0	179 Zambia	2.6
128	Algeria	4.0	180 Saudi Arabia	2.6
129	Equatorial Guinea	4.0	181 Oman	2.6
130	Burundi	4.0	182 Vanuatu	2.6
131	Angola	4.0	183 Zaire	2.6
132	Guam	3.9	184 Mozambique	2.5
133	Guyana	3.9	185 Malawi	2.5
134	Peru	3.9	186 Uganda	2.5
135	Malaysia	3.9	187 Niger	2.5
136	Venezuela	3.9	188 Benin	2.5
137	Mauritania	3.9	189 Papua New Guinea	2.5
138	Myanmar	3.9	190 Uzbekistan	2.3
139	American Samoa	3.9	191 Bahrain	2.2
140	Swaziland	3.8	192 Egypt	2.2
141	Mali	3.8	193 Côte d'Ivoire	2.2
142	Kiribati	3.7	194 Kenya	2.1
143	Cameroon	3.7	195 United Arab Emirates	1.6
144	Afghanistan	3.7	196 Kuwait	1.2
145	Gambia	3.7	197 Qatar	1.0
146	Lesotho	3.7		
147	Bolivia	3.5		
148	Iraq	3.4		
149	Pakistan	3.4		
150	Kazakhstan	3.3		
151	Namibia	3.3		
152	Solomon Islands	3.3		
153	Fiji	3.3		
154	Senegal	3.3		
155	Tanzania	3.2		
156	Togo	3.2		

Ranking by Birth Rate 1994 (per '000)

1	Niger	55.0	53	Gabon	38.5
2	Mali	51.8	54	Nepal	37.6
3	Yemen	50.7	55	Zimbabwe	37.2
4	Malawi	50.4	56	Eritrea	36.7
5	Rwanda	49.2	57	American Samoa	36.6
6	Uganda	48.8	58	Guatemala	35.4
7	Burkina Faso	48.4	59	Sao Tomé e Príncipe	35.2
8	Zaire	48.4	60	Saudi Arabia	35.1
9	Benin	47.7	61	Bangladesh	35.0
10	Togo	47.3	62	Honduras	35.0
11	Comoros	46.5	63	Tajikistan	34.8
12	Côte d'Ivoire	46.5	64	Iraq	34.1
13	Gambia	46.4	65	Lesotho	34.0
14	Cape Verde	46.2	66	North Korea	33.8
15	Zambia	46.0	67	Papua New Guinea	33.5
16	Somalia	46.0	68	Mongolia	33.0
17	Tanzania	45.5	69	El Salvador	32.8
18	Mauritania	45.4	70	Western Samoa	32.4
19	Angola	45.4	71	Bolivia	32.2
20	Libya	45.3	72	Vanuatu	32.2
21	Madagascar	45.2	73	Paraguay	32.0
22	Sierra Leone	45.1	74	Kiribati	31.6
23	Cambodia	45.1	75	Turkmenistan	30.4
24	Mozambique	45.0	76	Grenada	30.3
25	Ethiopia	45.0	77	Egypt	29.7
26	Guinea	44.1	78	Algeria	29.7
27	Ghana	44.1	79	Uzbekistan	29.0
28	Burundi	44.0	80	Syria	28.8
29	Maldives	43.6	81	Peru	28.7
30	Nigeria	43.5	82	Morocco	28.6
31	Liberia	43.5	83	India	28.5
32	Afghanistan	43.5	84	Myanmar	28.5
33	Namibia	43.4	85	United Arab Emirates	28.3
34	Senegal	43.2	86	Nauru	28.0
35	Laos	43.2	87	Lebanon	27.9
36	Swaziland	43.1	88	Philippines	27.3
37	Djibouti	42.9	89	Jordan	27.0
38	Iran	42.4	90	Malaysia	26.8
39	Kenya	42.4	91	Mexico	26.8
40	Central African Republic	42.3	92	Costa Rica	26.2
41	Pakistan	42.2	93	Brunei	26.2
42	Botswana	42.2	94	French Guiana	25.8
43	Chad	42.1	95	Tuvalu	25.7
44	Sudan	42.0	96	Guam	25.7
45	Guinea-Bissau	40.8	97	Venezuela	25.6
46	Equatorial Guinea	40.7	98	Suriname	25.3
47	Cameroon	40.5	99	Réunion	25.1
48	Oman	40.4	100	Dominican Republic	24.9
49	Congo	40.3	101	Fiji	24.7
50	Haiti	39.7	102	Bahrain	24.7
51	Bhutan	39.3	103	Kyrgyzstan	24.6
52	Solomon Islands	38.9	104	Indonesia	24.5

105	Antigua	24.3	157 Armenia	14.2
106	Kuwait	24.0	158 Canada	14.1
107	Jamaica	23.7	159 Malta	13.6
108	New Caledonia	23.2	160 Norway	13.6
109	Azerbaijan	23.0	161 Luxembourg	13.6
110	Brazil	22.9	162 Ireland	13.4
111	Colombia	22.6	163 Denmark	13.4
112	Albania	22.5	164 Bosnia-Herzegovina	13.3
113	Tunisia	22.5	165 Andorra	13.3
114	French Polynesia	22.2	166 Macedonia	13.2
115	Belize	22.0	167 Yugoslavia (former)	13.2
116	Seychelles	21.9	168 Serbia	13.2
117	Ecuador	21.8	169 Montenegro	13.2
118	Panama	21.7	170 Liechtenstein	13.1
119	Israel	21.2	171 United Kingdom	12.9
120	Chile	20.6	172 Finland	12.9
121	Dominica	20.5	173 Sweden	12.8
122	British Virgin Islands	20.3	174 Poland	12.5
123	Guyana	20.0	175 Slovakia	12.4
124	Thailand	20.0	176 France	12.3
125	Netherlands Antilles	19.7	177 Netherlands	12.1
126	Trinidad and Tobago	19.6	178 Switzerland	11.9
127	Mauritius	19.6	179 Hong Kong	11.8
128	Kazakhstan	19.4	180 Belgium	11.7
129	Bahamas	18.9	181 Portugal	11.7
130	Argentina	18.6	182 Lithuania	11.5
131	Martinique	18.0	183 Austria	11.5
132	Qatar	17.8	184 Hungary	11.3
133	Uruguay	17.7	185 Spain	11.1
134	China	17.7	186 Romania	11.0
135	Guadeloupe	17.7	187 Belarus	10.7
136	Puerto Rico	17.5	188 Monaco	10.7
137	Anguilla	17.2	189 Czech Republic	10.3
138	Cayman Islands	17.0	190 Croatia	10.2
139	Singapore	16.9	191 Japan	10.1
140	South Africa	16.7	192 Greece	9.9
141	Cuba	16.6	193 Slovenia	9.8
142	Iceland	16.3	194 Germany	9.5
143	New Zealand	16.3	195 Russia	9.5
144	Georgia	16.1	196 Latvia	9.5
145	South Korea	16.0	197 Estonia	9.5
146	USA	15.6	198 Bulgaria	9.4
147	Barbados	15.6	199 Italy	9.3
148	Taiwan	15.6		
149	Gibraltar	15.4		
150	Macau	15.2		
151	Bermuda	15.1		
152	Aruba	15.0		
153	Tonga	14.8		
154	Australia	14.5		
155	Moldova	14.3		
156	Cyprus	14.3		

Ranking by Number of Households 1995 ('000)

1	China	357,064	53	Belgium	3,754
2	India	190,864	54	Greece	3,635
3	United States of America	100,308	55	Portugal	3,571
4	Russia	52,107	56	Cameroon	3,566
5	Indonesia	43,065	57	Afghanistan	3,560
6	Japan	40,548	58	Czech Republic	3,395
7	Brazil	38,434	59	Sri Lanka	3,294
8	Germany	35,140	60	Austria	3,276
9	France	22,793	61	Chile	3,261
10	Italy	22,260	62	Kazakhstan	3,244
11	Bangladesh	22,237	63	Belarus	3,136
12	Nigeria	21,850	64	Mozambique	3,131
13	United Kingdom	21,453	65	Serbia	3,116
14	Pakistan	19,400	66	Côte d'Ivoire	3,052
15	Mexico	19,015	67	Ghana	3,019
16	Vietnam	15,760	68	Bulgaria	3,019
17	Spain	15,055	69	Zimbabwe	3,018
18	Turkey	14,655	70	Syria	2,950
19	Egypt	14,397	71	Switzerland	2,898
20	Myanmar	13,950	72	Saudi Arabia	2,890
21	South Korea	13,300	73	Cuba	2,770
22	Thailand	13,014	74	Madagascar	2,723
23	Philippines	12,750	75	Ecuador	2,626
24	Argentina	12,577	76	Angola	2,436
25	Iran	11,966	77	Burkina Faso	2,323
26	Ethiopia	11,911	78	Denmark	2,312
27	Zaire	11,800	79	Zambia	2,285
28	Poland	11,578	80	Yemen	2,283
29	Canada	10,808	81	Cambodia	2,225
30	Ukraine	9,100	82	Guatemala	2,203
31	Colombia	8,482	83	Finland	2,142
32	South Africa	8,190	84	Mali	1,987
33	Romania	7,685	85	Slovakia	1,856
34	Yugoslavia (former)	7,592	86	Norway	1,847
35	Australia	6,768	87	Bolivia	1,803
36	Netherlands	6,371	88	Hong Kong	1,797
37	Kenya	6,252	89	Somalia	1,741
38	Algeria	6,177	90	Malawi	1,651
39	Morocco	5,900	91	Dominican Republic	1,646
40	Taiwan	5,698	92	Niger	1,580
41	Tanzania	5,655	93	Azerbaijan	1,513
42	Peru	5,057	94	Israel	1,438
43	Nepal	5,015	95	Senegal	1,416
44	Sudan	4,864	96	Tunisia	1,403
45	Malaysia	4,028	97	Haiti	1,401
46	Hungary	3,979	98	Rwanda	1,370
47	North Korea	3,950	99	Benin	1,338
48	Uganda	3,914	100	El Salvador	1,291
49	Iraq	3,900	101	Georgia	1,288
50	Venezuela	3,888	102	Chad	1,267
51	Sweden	3,880	103	Tajikistan	1,265
52	Uzbekistan	3,870	104	Nicaragua	1,238

105	New Zealand	1,230	157 Fiji	144
106	Guinea	1,214	158 Luxembourg	138
107	Honduras	1,168	159 Macau	127
108	Jordan	1,131	160 Qatar	127
109	Moldova	1,120	161 Djibouti	117
110	Burundi	1,089	162 Réunion	114
111	Albania	1,028	163 Malta	114
112	Paraguay	1,020	164 Iceland	113
113	Lithuania	1,007	165 Comoros	108
114	Libya	999	166 Equatorial Guinea	97
115	Kyrgyzstan	899	167 Cape Verde	95
116	Laos	880	168 Guadeloupe	90
117	Ireland	865	169 Suriname	83
118	Singapore	815	170 Martinique	83
119	Sierra Leone	790	171 Belize	78
120	Croatia	789	172 Brunei	61
121	Armenia	785	173 Bahamas	56
122	Turkmenistan	750	174 Solomon Islands	55
123	Costa Rica	745	175 Barbados	54
124	Papua New Guinea	692	176 Maldives	45
125	Uruguay	683	177 Netherlands Antilles	43
126	Lebanon	665	178 New Caledonia	37
127	Togo	663	179 French Polynesia	36
128	Latvia	625	180 Western Samoa	36
129	Central African Republic	618	181 St Lucia	29
130	Puerto Rico	618	182 Vanuatu	28
131	Bosnia-Herzegovina	613	183 French Guiana	26
132	Mauritania	569	184 St Vincent & the Grenadines	26
133	Oman	560	185 Guam	24
134	Panama	525	186 Andorra	22
135	Jamaica	521	187 Sao Tomé e Príncipe	21
136	Slovenia	521	188 Tonga	20
137	Liberia	515	189 Antigua	18
138	Mongolia	500	190 Grenada	17
139	United Arab Emirates	461	191 Aruba	17
140	Congo	426	192 Dominica	16
141	Estonia	413	193 Kiribati	14
142	Botswana	381	194 American Samoa	14
143	Bhutan	356	195 Monaco	14
144	Lesotho	354	196 Bermuda	14
145	Namibia	322	197 Liechtenstein	12
146	Trinidad and Tobago	265	198 Seychelles	12
147	Cyprus	250	199 St Kitts	9
148	Kuwait	226	200 Gibraltar	7
149	Mauritius	221	201 Cayman Islands	6
150	Gambia	205	202 British Virgin Islands	5
151	Guinea-Bissau	203	203 Nauru	2
152	Montenegro	198	204 Anguilla	2
153	Gabon	180	205 Tuvalu	1
154	Guyana	178		
155	Bahrain	153		
156	Swaziland	145		

Ranking by Average Household Size 1995 (persons)

1	Kuwait	7.10	53	Grenada	5.11
2	Gabon	6.93	54	Iraq	5.10
3	Bosnia-Herzegovina	6.90	55	Philippines	5.10
4	Tuvalu	6.60	56	Tanzania	5.10
5	Pakistan	6.38	57	Liberia	5.10
6	Solomon Islands	6.29	58	Mali	5.05
7	Tunisia	6.08	59	Haiti	5.01
8	Nauru	6.05	60	Iran	4.99
9	Saudi Arabia	5.96	61	Afghanistan	4.99
10	Swaziland	5.95	62	Somalia	4.98
11	Congo	5.94	63	Honduras	4.98
12	Anguilla	5.94	64	Kyrgyzstan	4.93
13	Guam	5.86	65	Chad	4.89
14	Sudan	5.82	66	Djibouti	4.87
15	Togo	5.78	67	Kazakhstan	4.86
16	Seychelles	5.78	68	Libya	4.86
17	Puerto Rico	5.76	69	Nigeria	4.86
18	North Korea	5.76	70	Mauritius	4.84
19	French Polynesia	5.69	71	Azerbaijan	4.83
20	Burundi	5.66	72	Suriname	4.81
21	Ghana	5.64	73	Bahamas	4.79
22	Malawi	5.63	74	South Africa	4.78
23	Comoros	5.62	75	India	4.78
24	Vanuatu	5.62	76	United Arab Emirates	4.76
25	Uzbekistan	5.61	77	Panama	4.76
26	Papua New Guinea	5.59	78	Mexico	4.74
27	Niger	5.53	79	Dominican Republic	4.72
28	Maldives	5.53	80	Tonga	4.71
29	Kiribati	5.51	81	Guatemala	4.71
30	Lesotho	5.51	82	Western Samoa	4.67
31	Réunion	5.50	83	Netherlands Antilles	4.66
32	Senegal	5.50	84	Ethiopia	4.65
33	Rwanda	5.44	85	Malaysia	4.64
34	Croatia	5.44	86	Kenya	4.64
35	Yemen	5.43	87	New Caledonia	4.63
36	Sierra Leone	5.43	88	St Lucia	4.62
37	Ukraine	5.39	89	Jamaica	4.61
38	Guinea	5.38	90	Syria	4.61
39	Fiji	5.35	91	Cayman Islands	4.60
40	Sao Tomé e Príncipe	5.33	92	Guadeloupe	4.60
41	Gambia	5.29	93	Jordan	4.59
42	Bangladesh	5.29	94	Barbados	4.58
43	Venezuela	5.29	95	Mongolia	4.57
44	French Guiana	5.29	96	Côte d'Ivoire	4.56
45	Mozambique	5.29	97	Trinidad and Tobago	4.55
46	Laos	5.27	98	Namibia	4.54
47	Sri Lanka	5.21	99	Guyana	4.54
48	Turkmenistan	5.19	100	Brunei	4.53
49	Uganda	5.18	101	Qatar	4.53
50	Central African Republic	5.16	102	Paraguay	4.50
51	Madagascar	5.15	103	Bhutan	4.47
52	Guinea-Bissau	5.13	104	Uruguay	4.44

105	Vietnam	4.44	157	Singapore	3.49
106	Armenia	4.43	158	Nicaragua	3.48
107	Peru	4.42	159	Estonia	3.43
108	Thailand	4.40	160	Hong Kong	3.31
109	Tajikistan	4.39	161	Albania	3.27
110	Indonesia	4.38	162	Belarus	3.22
111	Martinique	4.37	163	Serbia	3.22
112	Morocco	4.37	164	Antigua	3.22
113	Algeria	4.36	165	South Korea	3.20
114	Bermuda	4.35	166	Poland	3.17
115	St Kitts	4.34	167	Myanmar	3.06
116	Burkina Faso	4.33	168	Macau	3.06
117	Ecuador	4.32	169	Montenegro	3.00
118	Cambodia	4.31	170	Malta	3.00
119	El Salvador	4.30	171	Japan	2.94
120	Lebanon	4.30	172	Cyprus	2.91
121	Chile	4.25	173	Czech Republic	2.84
122	Angola	4.21	174	Romania	2.80
123	British Virgin Islands	4.20	175	Luxembourg	2.77
124	Nepal	4.17	176	Slovakia	2.74
125	Georgia	4.14	177	Greece	2.74
126	Aruba	4.13	178	New Zealand	2.73
127	Costa Rica	4.12	179	Russia	2.70
128	Dominica	4.11	180	Belize	2.66
129	St Vincent & the Grenadines	4.10	181	Bulgaria	2.66
130	Colombia	4.04	182	Portugal	2.64
131	Benin	4.03	183	Canada	2.64
132	Cape Verde	4.02	184	Argentina	2.61
133	Bolivia	4.02	185	United Kingdom	2.59
134	Gibraltar	4.01	186	Belgium	2.56
135	Turkey	4.00	187	Australia	2.55
136	Equatorial Guinea	3.99	188	USA	2.49
137	China	3.99	189	Spain	2.47
138	Egypt	3.96	190	Hungary	2.46
139	Ireland	3.93	191	Italy	2.44
140	Cuba	3.90	192	France	2.44
141	Zambia	3.90	193	Liechtenstein	2.43
142	Brazil	3.89	194	Andorra	2.43
143	Botswana	3.85	195	Austria	2.35
144	Latvia	3.81	196	Iceland	2.32
145	Mauritania	3.78	197	Switzerland	2.31
146	Israel	3.75	198	Netherlands	2.30
147	Bahrain	3.75	199	Finland	2.28
148	American Samoa	3.71	200	Norway	2.24
149	Moldova	3.70	201	Germany	2.21
150	Oman	3.66	202	Sweden	2.16
151	Zimbabwe	3.63	203	Denmark	2.15
152	Cameroon	3.63	204	Monaco	2.10
153	Zaire	3.58			
154	Slovenia	3.56			
155	Taiwan	3.53			
156	Lithuania	3.50			

Ranking by Urban Population, Latest Year (% of total population)

1	Gibraltar	100.0	53	Lithuania	72.1
2	Nauru	100.0	54	Trinidad and Tobago	71.8
3	Monaco	100.0	55	Jordan	71.5
4	Singapore	100.0	56	Belarus	71.2
5	Cayman Islands	100.0	57	Bulgaria	70.7
6	Bermuda	100.0	58	Ukraine	70.3
7	Guadeloupe	99.4	59	Estonia	70.0
8	Macau	98.8	60	Netherlands Antilles	69.5
9	Belgium	97.0	61	Aruba	69.5
10	Kuwait	97.0	62	Latvia	69.1
11	Hong Kong	95.0	63	Turkey	68.8
12	Martinique	93.3	64	Armenia	68.7
13	Venezuela	92.9	65	Réunion	67.8
14	Iceland	91.6	66	Italy	66.6
15	Qatar	91.4	67	Czech Republic	65.4
16	Israel	90.6	68	Greece	65.2
17	Bahrain	90.3	69	Hungary	64.7
18	Uruguay	90.3	70	Dominican Republic	64.6
19	United Kingdom	89.5	71	Croatia	64.4
20	Malta	89.3	72	Slovenia	63.6
21	Luxembourg	89.1	73	Finland	63.2
22	Netherlands	88.9	74	Nicaragua	62.9
23	Argentina	88.1	75	Andorra	62.5
24	Lebanon	87.2	76	New Caledonia	62.1
25	Germany	86.6	77	Poland	61.9
26	Bahamas	86.5	78	North Korea	61.3
27	New Zealand	86.1	79	Mongolia	60.9
28	Libya	86.0	80	Switzerland	60.8
29	Denmark	85.2	81	Bolivia	60.8
30	Australia	85.0	82	Macedonia	59.9
31	United Arab Emirates	84.0	83	Kazakhstan	59.7
32	Chile	83.9	84	Iran	59.0
33	Sweden	83.1	85	Slovakia	58.8
34	Djibouti	82.8	86	Congo	58.8
35	South Korea	81.0	87	Georgia	58.5
36	Saudi Arabia	80.2	88	Ecuador	58.4
37	Brazil	78.3	89	Brunei	57.8
38	Japan	77.6	90	Ireland	57.5
39	Canada	76.7	91	Tunisia	57.3
40	Spain	76.5	92	Serbia	57.0
41	French Guiana	76.5	93	Yugoslavia (former)	56.5
42	USA	76.2	94	French Polynesia	56.4
43	Cuba	76.0	95	Algeria	55.8
44	Mexico	75.3	96	Austria	55.5
45	Taiwan	75.0	97	Romania	55.4
46	Iraq	74.6	98	Seychelles	54.5
47	Puerto Rico	73.4	99	Cape Verde	54.3
48	Norway	73.2	100	Philippines	54.2
49	Russia	72.9	101	Cyprus	54.1
50	France	72.8	102	Mauritania	53.8
51	Colombia	72.7	103	Malaysia	53.7
52	Peru	72.2	104	Jamaica	53.7

105	Panama	53.3	157	Angola	32.2
106	Paraguay	52.7	158	Haiti	31.6
107	Syria	52.4	159	Benin	31.3
108	Moldova	51.7	160	Swaziland	31.2
109	South Africa	50.8	161	Togo	30.8
110	Suriname	50.4	162	Comoros	30.7
111	Gabon	50.0	163	China	30.3
112	American Samoa	49.8	164	Guinea	29.6
113	Costa Rica	49.7	165	Zaire	29.0
114	Bosnia-Herzegovina	49.0	166	Botswana	28.1
115	Montenegro	49.0	167	Kenya	27.7
116	Morocco	48.4	168	Burkina Faso	27.2
117	St Lucia	48.1	169	Madagascar	27.1
118	Barbados	47.4	170	Mali	27.0
119	St Vincent & the Grenadines	47.0	171	Maldives	26.8
120	Belize	46.8	172	India	26.8
121	Sao Tomé e Príncipe	46.7	173	Myanmar	26.2
122	Tuvalu	46.0	174	Somalia	25.8
123	El Salvador	45.1	175	Gambia	25.5
124	Liberia	45.0	176	Sudan	24.6
125	Turkmenistan	44.9	177	Tanzania	24.4
126	Cameroon	44.9	178	Lesotho	23.1
127	Egypt	44.8	179	Sri Lanka	22.4
128	Honduras	43.9	180	Guinea-Bissau	22.2
129	Côte d'Ivoire	43.6	181	Laos	21.7
130	Zambia	43.1	182	Liechtenstein	21.4
131	St Kitts	42.4	183	Chad	21.4
132	Senegal	42.3	184	Western Samoa	21.0
133	Equatorial Guinea	42.2	185	Vietnam	20.8
134	Zimbabwe	42.0	186	Cambodia	20.7
135	Guatemala	41.5	187	Thailand	20.1
136	Uzbekistan	41.3	188	Afghanistan	20.0
137	Tonga	41.1	189	Vanuatu	19.3
138	Fiji	40.7	190	Bangladesh	18.3
139	Mauritius	40.6	191	Eritrea	17.2
140	Central African Republic	39.3	192	Solomon Islands	17.1
141	Nigeria	39.3	193	Niger	17.0
142	Kyrgyzstan	38.9	194	Papua New Guinea	16.1
143	Guam	38.2	195	Nepal	13.7
144	Namibia	37.4	196	Malawi	13.5
145	Albania	37.3	197	Ethiopia	13.4
146	Ghana	36.3	198	Oman	13.2
147	Guyana	36.2	199	Uganda	12.5
148	Sierra Leone	36.2	200	Grenada	8.0
149	Antigua	35.8	201	Burundi	7.5
150	Kiribati	35.7	202	Azerbaijan	7.0
151	Portugal	35.6	203	Bhutan	6.4
152	Indonesia	35.4	204	Rwanda	6.1
153	Pakistan	34.7			
154	Mozambique	34.3			
155	Yemen	34.0			
156	Tajikistan	32.2			

Ranking by GDP 1995 (US$ million)

#	Country	GDP	#	Country	GDP
1	USA	7,080,000.0	53	Iraq	45,456.0
2	Japan	5,089,310.8	54	Algeria	42,514.6
3	Germany	2,126,223.8	55	Puerto Rico	40,638.1
4	France	1,538,701.9	56	Cuba	40,502.0
5	United Kingdom	1,103,945.1	57	Syria	39,000.0
6	Italy	1,038,867.7	58	United Arab Emirates	37,149.4
7	Iran	730,000.0	59	Morocco	35,012.9
8	China	690,586.1	60	Romania	33,699.6
9	Russia	684,392.0	61	Libya	30,441.6
10	Canada	562,356.9	62	Sudan	28,302.6
11	Spain	559,431.9	63	Bangladesh	28,055.9
12	Brazil	550,000.0	64	Vietnam	26,150.7
13	South Korea	455,570.5	65	Kuwait	25,828.2
14	Netherlands	383,850.9	66	Azerbaijan	23,075.2
15	Australia	344,380.2	67	Uzbekistan	23,060.0
16	India	338,673.8	68	Slovenia	21,229.1
17	Argentina	306,055.3	69	Croatia	19,951.8
18	Switzerland	305,593.2	70	Ecuador	18,395.4
19	Belgium	261,092.3	71	Tunisia	18,164.2
20	Mexico	238,489.1	72	Slovakia	17,400.1
21	Taiwan	237,659.5	73	Kazakhstan	16,350.0
22	Sweden	219,947.1	74	Uruguay	15,796.1
23	Austria	197,468.4	75	Guatemala	15,789.6
24	Turkey	175,893.3	76	Sri Lanka	12,587.6
25	Denmark	171,071.4	77	Luxembourg	12,437.2
26	Indonesia	170,684.9	78	Oman	12,011.7
27	Thailand	166,479.9	79	Dominican Republic	11,669.5
28	Norway	145,984.2	80	Brunei	11,494.0
29	Hong Kong	143,591.7	81	Bulgaria	11,113.9
30	South Africa	133,504.4	82	North Korea	11,028.5
31	Saudi Arabia	126,517.8	83	Costa Rica	9,700.0
32	Finland	125,871.9	84	El Salvador	9,590.3
33	Greece	110,332.5	85	Belarus	9,108.0
34	Poland	104,388.4	86	Paraguay	8,920.6
35	Portugal	97,863.6	87	Cyprus	8,577.8
36	Ukraine	90,370.0	88	Zaire	8,500.0
37	Malaysia	84,054.1	89	Qatar	8,399.2
38	Israel	83,743.9	90	Kenya	8,012.7
39	Singapore	81,308.0	91	Panama	7,756.7
40	Colombia	76,384.1	92	Côte d'Ivoire	7,626.3
41	Venezuela	75,831.1	93	Cameroon	7,236.9
42	Myanmar	75,100.0	94	Ghana	7,052.2
43	Philippines	74,136.2	95	Iceland	7,030.4
44	Chile	67,332.6	96	Bolivia	6,958.4
45	Nigeria	65,570.5	97	Jordan	6,587.0
46	Egypt	60,294.1	98	Lithuania	6,114.5
47	Pakistan	58,592.8	99	Zimbabwe	6,106.4
48	New Zealand	58,393.6	100	Lebanon	6,039.4
49	Ireland	58,281.2	101	Albania	5,849.4
50	Peru	57,986.9	102	Uganda	5,833.0
51	Hungary	45,757.1	103	Gabon	5,814.0
52	Czech Republic	45,632.5	104	Macau	5,696.9

105	Turkmenistan	5,631.0	157	Somalia	928.5
106	Réunion	5,537.7	158	Malawi	895.6
107	Trinidad and Tobago	5,532.2	159	Kyrgyzstan	855.5
108	Papua New Guinea	5,475.3	160	Swaziland	847.6
109	Senegal	5,428.7	161	Sierra Leone	837.2
110	Ethiopia	5,394.4	162	Lesotho	836.1
111	Bahrain	5,021.9	163	French Polynesia	771.7
112	Jamaica	4,793.2	164	Aruba	698.2
113	Armenia	4,522.7	165	French Guiana	697.5
114	Botswana	4,479.8	166	Guadeloupe	634.5
115	Latvia	4,471.9	167	Belize	579.7
116	Nepal	4,139.1	168	St Lucia	550.5
117	New Caledonia	4,053.4	169	Guyana	535.9
118	Honduras	3,994.7	170	Monaco	526.3
119	Mauritius	3,916.0	171	Seychelles	495.3
120	Tanzania	3,596.8	172	Cape Verde	436.9
121	Haiti	3,554.8	173	Antigua	418.3
122	Estonia	3,523.6	174	Gambia	338.9
123	Madagascar	3,520.8	175	Djibouti	330.3
124	Zambia	3,450.0	176	Comoros	318.5
125	Burkina Faso	3,344.4	177	American Samoa	311.1
126	Namibia	3,232.0	178	Grenada	275.7
127	Malta	3,205.2	179	Bhutan	253.7
128	Congo	2,698.0	180	Gibraltar	240.6
129	Martinique	2,657.5	181	St Vincent & the Grenadines	233.6
130	Bahamas	2,583.5	182	Guinea-Bissau	227.9
131	Tajikistan	2,516.4	183	St Kitts	219.7
132	Liberia	2,312.3	184	Dominica	209.7
133	Guinea	2,271.8	185	Vanuatu	195.2
134	Benin	2,118.7	186	Nauru	186.5
135	Niger	2,115.9	187	Solomon Islands	184.4
136	Togo	2,060.8	188	Tonga	169.4
137	Mali	2,030.9	189	British Virgin Islands	167.6
138	Fiji	2,021.3	190	Maldives	135.3
139	Bermuda	1,966.9	191	Western Samoa	133.6
140	Nicaragua	1,921.0	192	Equatorial Guinea	129.0
141	Netherlands Antilles	1,856.3	193	Anguilla	55.9
142	Barbados	1,822.1	194	Kiribati	32.9
143	Suriname	1,817.3	195	Sao Tomé e Príncipe	22.3
144	Laos	1,754.3	196	Tuvalu	5.8
145	Central African Republic	1,597.4			
146	Andorra	1,548.4			
147	Macedonia	1,538.0			
148	Mozambique	1,370.1			
149	Liechtenstein	1,269.4			
150	Chad	1,221.3			
151	Burundi	1,165.0			
152	Mongolia	1,155.0			
153	Mauritania	1,127.9			
154	Cayman Islands	1,049.0			
155	Guam	1,027.0			
156	Rwanda	961.0			

Ranking by GDP per capita 1995 (US$)

1	Switzerland	43,408.1		53	British Virgin Islands	8,355.3
2	Liechtenstein	41,621.0		54	Gibraltar	8,021.5
3	Japan	40,597.9		55	Barbados	7,116.7
4	Brunei	40,260.2		56	Seychelles	7,075.3
5	Belize	36,947.1		57	Martinique	6,993.5
6	Cayman Islands	34,965.1		58	Saudi Arabia	6,977.0
7	Norway	33,482.6		59	Antigua	6,971.5
8	Denmark	32,709.6		60	Guam	6,846.5
9	Bermuda	31,724.2		61	Libya	5,959.8
10	Luxembourg	30,861.7		62	Anguilla	5,594.9
11	Andorra	29,214.8		63	Oman	5,565.5
12	Singapore	27,193.3		64	St Kitts	5,493.6
13	USA	26,917.1		65	American Samoa	5,185.2
14	France	26,515.6		66	Uruguay	4,951.7
15	Iceland	26,232.7		67	French Guiana	4,810.1
16	Germany	25,947.3		68	Chile	4,741.7
17	Belgium	25,541.4		69	Russia	4,628.6
18	Sweden	24,909.1		70	Gabon	4,489.6
19	Netherlands	24,844.7		71	Hungary	4,477.2
20	Finland	24,632.5		72	Czech Republic	4,410.2
21	Austria	24,469.4		73	Croatia	4,363.9
22	Hong Kong	23,198.1		74	Trinidad and Tobago	4,356.1
23	New Caledonia	22,519.0		75	Suriname	4,300.0
24	Australia	19,079.2		76	Malaysia	4,268.9
25	Canada	18,992.1		77	St Lucia	3,932.0
26	United Kingdom	18,846.4		78	Cuba	3,664.8
27	Italy	18,125.3		79	French Polynesia	3,629.5
28	Monaco	16,978.6		80	Brazil	3,529.7
29	New Zealand	16,495.4		81	Venezuela	3,504.5
30	Ireland	16,279.7		82	Mauritius	3,480.3
31	United Arab Emirates	16,082.0		83	Slovakia	3,246.3
32	Nauru	15,410.3		84	South Africa	3,237.3
33	Kuwait	15,283.0		85	Costa Rica	3,087.7
34	Israel	14,812.7		86	Azerbaijan	3,076.7
35	Spain	14,274.9		87	Botswana	3,068.4
36	Macau	13,894.8		88	Grenada	3,063.8
37	Qatar	13,880.9		89	Dominica	2,995.3
38	Iran	11,932.4		90	Panama	2,949.3
39	Cyprus	11,540.9		91	Turkey	2,853.6
40	Taiwan	11,210.4		92	Thailand	2,765.0
41	Slovenia	10,886.7		93	Syria	2,725.4
42	Puerto Rico	10,836.8		94	Poland	2,705.1
43	Greece	10,566.2		95	Fiji	2,591.4
44	South Korea	10,157.6		96	Mexico	2,516.2
45	Portugal	9,857.3		97	Peru	2,464.4
46	Aruba	9,834.5		98	Estonia	2,372.8
47	Bahamas	9,533.2		99	Iraq	2,231.8
48	Malta	8,903.3		100	Colombia	2,176.2
49	Argentina	8,848.1		101	St Vincent & the Grenadines	2,123.5
50	Netherlands Antilles	8,839.6		102	Namibia	2,099.0
51	Bahrain	8,511.8		103	Tunisia	2,021.7
52	Réunion	8,384.1		104	Lebanon	2,006.4

105	Jamaica	1,894.5	157	Comoros	493.8
106	Paraguay	1,846.9	158	Central African Republic	485.5
107	Latvia	1,781.6	159	Mongolia	480.2
108	Ukraine	1,750.0	160	North Korea	460.7
109	Tonga	1,729.0	161	Pakistan	449.8
110	Albania	1,700.9	162	Tajikistan	430.9
111	El Salvador	1,678.7	163	Nicaragua	423.1
112	Myanmar	1,668.9	164	Lesotho	407.8
113	Lithuania	1,648.1	165	Ghana	406.5
114	Ecuador	1,605.2	166	Kiribati	401.1
115	Guadeloupe	1,493.1	167	Benin	381.1
116	Algeria	1,489.1	168	Zambia	368.2
117	Guatemala	1,486.8	169	India	362.9
118	Romania	1,485.9	170	Laos	359.5
119	Dominican Republic	1,475.3	171	Vietnam	355.1
120	Turkmenistan	1,373.5	172	Guinea	339.5
121	Papua New Guinea	1,345.3	173	Burkina Faso	327.9
122	Bulgaria	1,336.3	174	Equatorial Guinea	324.2
123	Morocco	1,291.5	175	Gambia	310.9
124	Jordan	1,206.4	176	Uganda	273.3
125	Armenia	1,202.8	177	Kenya	262.5
126	Vanuatu	1,183.3	178	Madagascar	238.3
127	Cape Verde	1,118.4	179	Bangladesh	233.2
128	Philippines	1,083.5	180	Niger	230.0
129	Congo	1,045.7	181	Guinea-Bissau	213.3
130	Egypt	1,018.0	182	Chad	192.4
131	Uzbekistan	1,009.2	183	Mali	192.3
132	Kazakhstan	985.5	184	Zaire	191.1
133	Sudan	950.0	185	Nepal	188.2
134	Bolivia	939.1	186	Sao Tomé e Príncipe	185.9
135	Swaziland	931.5	187	Sierra Leone	185.3
136	Indonesia	881.0	188	Burundi	184.6
137	Belarus	880.4	189	Kyrgyzstan	183.2
138	Liberia	837.8	190	Bhutan	155.6
139	Western Samoa	763.5	191	Rwanda	122.4
140	Macedonia	712.0	192	Tanzania	118.6
141	Sri Lanka	696.3	193	Somalia	101.7
142	Honduras	671.4	194	Ethiopia	95.2
143	Senegal	662.0	195	Malawi	91.5
144	Guyana	649.6	196	Mozambique	78.7
145	Nigeria	587.2			
146	Djibouti	566.3			
147	Cameroon	544.9			
148	Côte d'Ivoire	535.9			
149	China	533.5			
150	Zimbabwe	529.6			
151	Tuvalu	525.1			
152	Maldives	520.5			
153	Togo	510.5			
154	Solomon Islands	506.6			
155	Mauritania	497.8			
156	Haiti	495.1			

Ranking by Inflation Rate 1995 (% increase)

1	Angola	3,700.0	53	Cameroon	13.9
2	Zaire	542.0	54	Pakistan	13.0
3	Uzbekistan	325.0	55	Slovenia	12.6
4	Suriname	235.9	56	Dominican Republic	12.5
5	Russia	197.4	57	Namibia	11.9
6	Brazil	84.4	58	Peru	11.1
7	Turkey	78.0	59	Nicaragua	11.0
8	Venezuela	59.9	60	Ethiopia	10.7
9	Ghana	59.5	61	Botswana	10.5
10	Iran	49.6	62	India	10.2
11	Madagascar	49.1	63	Bolivia	10.2
12	Nigeria	45.0	64	El Salvador	10.0
13	Uruguay	42.2	65	Slovakia	10.0
14	Sao Tomé e Príncipe	41.7	66	Israel	10.0
15	Central African Republic	41.6	67	Rwanda	9.9
16	Lithuania	39.7	68	Eritrea	9.4
17	Mexico	35.0	69	Indonesia	9.4
18	Guinea-Bissau	34.3	70	Greece	9.3
19	Bulgaria	32.9	71	Hong Kong	9.2
20	Romania	32.2	72	Czech Republic	9.1
21	Latvia	30.0	73	Macedonia	9.0
22	Algeria	29.8	74	South Africa	8.7
23	Niger	29.5	75	Uganda	8.5
24	Honduras	29.5	76	Lesotho	8.4
25	Estonia	28.9	77	Djibouti	8.3
26	Hungary	28.2	78	Cape Verde	8.3
27	Tanzania	27.4	79	Chile	8.2
28	Poland	26.8	80	Philippines	8.1
29	Chad	26.7	81	Senegal	7.9
30	Armenia	26.7	82	Sri Lanka	7.7
31	Sierra Leone	26.0	83	Burkina Faso	7.4
32	Haiti	25.5	84	Gambia	7.0
33	Myanmar	25.2	85	Togo	7.0
34	Malawi	25.0	86	Syria	7.0
35	Costa Rica	23.2	87	St Lucia	7.0
36	Ecuador	22.9	88	Macau	6.4
37	Gabon	22.8	89	Tunisia	6.2
38	Zimbabwe	22.6	90	Morocco	6.1
39	Paraguay	21.3	91	Mauritius	6.0
40	Colombia	21.0	92	Thailand	5.7
41	Jamaica	19.9	93	French Polynesia	5.5
42	Laos	19.6	94	Trinidad and Tobago	5.3
43	Burundi	19.3	95	Malaysia	5.3
44	Guatemala	18.6	96	Italy	5.3
45	Papua New Guinea	17.0	97	Lebanon	5.0
46	China	16.9	98	Egypt	4.9
47	Comoros	15.8	99	Saudi Arabia	4.9
48	Vietnam	15.3	100	Spain	4.7
49	Swaziland	14.7	101	Maldives	4.6
50	Benin	14.5	102	Australia	4.6
51	Solomon Islands	14.4	103	South Korea	4.5
52	Côte d'Ivoire	14.2	104	Kuwait	4.3

105	Portugal	4.1	157	Belgium	1.5
106	Croatia	4.1	158	Guadeloupe	1.5
107	Guinea	4.0	159	French Guiana	1.5
108	St Kitts	4.0	160	Bhutan	1.5
109	Malta	4.0	161	Netherlands Antilles	1.2
110	Nauru	4.0	162	Western Samoa	1.1
111	Gibraltar	3.8	163	Bangladesh	1.0
112	Taiwan	3.7	164	Panama	1.0
113	Mali	3.5	165	Tonga	1.0
114	Argentina	3.4	166	Finland	1.0
115	United Kingdom	3.4	167	Kenya	0.8
116	Aruba	3.4	168	Martinique	0.8
117	Bermuda	3.3	169	United Arab Emirates	0.5
118	Cambodia	3.0	170	Liechtenstein	0.4
119	British Virgin Islands	3.0	171	North Korea	0.2
120	Antigua	3.0	172	New Caledonia	0.0
121	Grenada	3.0			
122	Anguilla	3.0			
123	Belize	2.9			
124	United States of America	2.8			
125	American Samoa	2.8			
126	Guam	2.8			
127	Cyprus	2.6			
128	Sweden	2.5			
129	Puerto Rico	2.5			
130	Norway	2.5			
131	Ireland	2.5			
132	Jordan	2.4			
133	Austria	2.3			
134	Fiji	2.2			
135	Andorra	2.2			
136	Vanuatu	2.2			
137	Oman	2.1			
138	Denmark	2.1			
139	Bahamas	2.0			
140	Canada	2.0			
141	Brunei	2.0			
142	Kiribati	2.0			
143	Tuvalu	2.0			
144	Cayman Islands	2.0			
145	Iraq	2.0			
146	Netherlands	1.9			
147	New Zealand	1.9			
148	Luxembourg	1.9			
149	Barbados	1.9			
150	St Vincent & the Grenadines	1.9			
151	Nepal	1.8			
152	Germany	1.8			
153	Switzerland	1.8			
154	France	1.8			
155	Iceland	1.7			
156	Singapore	1.7			

Ranking by Total Imports 1995 (US$ million)

1	United States of America	771,272.0	53	Bahrain	3,581.0
2	Germany	445,660.0	54	Costa Rica	3,252.0
3	Japan	335,975.0	55	Lithuania	3,010.0
4	France	274,566.0	56	Dominican Republic	2,976.0
5	United Kingdom	261,061.3	57	Uruguay	2,867.0
6	Hong Kong	192,774.0	58	El Salvador	2,853.0
7	Netherlands	174,898.0	59	Malta	2,792.0
8	Canada	168,426.0	60	Zimbabwe	2,749.7
9	China	129,113.0	61	Jamaica	2,709.3
10	Singapore	124,507.0	62	Kenya	2,700.0
11	Spain	115,056.0	63	Panama	2,482.0
12	Switzerland	76,985.0	64	Latvia	1,916.0
13	Malaysia	76,612.0	65	Mauritius	1,878.7
14	Mexico	72,453.1	66	Angola	1,805.0
15	Sweden	64,438.0	67	Iceland	1,756.0
16	Australia	61,286.0	68	Botswana	1,676.0
17	Russia	57,965.0	69	Trinidad and Tobago	1,606.0
18	Brazil	53,783.0	70	Bolivia	1,424.0
19	Denmark	43,161.0	71	Tanzania	1,404.0
20	Indonesia	40,918.0	72	Papua New Guinea	1,375.0
21	India	34,399.0	73	Nepal	1,374.0
22	Norway	32,702.0	74	Honduras	1,219.0
23	Portugal	32,455.0	75	Afghanistan	1,123.5
24	South Africa	30,555.0	76	Swaziland	1,060.0
25	Israel	29,632.0	77	Uganda	1,051.0
26	Poland	27,762.7	78	Nicaragua	949.0
27	Philippines	27,288.0	79	Fiji	864.0
28	Czech Republic	26,527.0	80	Barbados	763.0
29	Turkey	23,270.0	81	Benin	697.3
30	Argentina	20,123.0	82	Haiti	697.0
31	Chile	15,914.0	83	Laos	587.0
32	Hungary	15,073.0	84	Turkmenistan	537.6
33	New Zealand	13,958.0	85	Zaire	388.0
34	Ukraine	13,922.1	86	Togo	384.0
35	Colombia	13,853.0	87	Myanmar	348.0
36	Venezuela	11,977.0	88	Maldives	260.0
37	Pakistan	11,461.0	89	Belize	258.0
38	Slovakia	10,248.9	90	Burundi	234.0
39	Slovenia	9,452.0	91	Central African Republic	189.0
40	Romania	9,424.0	92	Solomon Islands	145.8
41	Peru	9,225.0	93	Sierra Leone	135.0
42	Morocco	8,521.0	94	St Vincent & the Grenadines	134.0
43	Algeria	8,303.0	95	Western Samoa	95.0
44	Tunisia	7,903.0	96	Vanuatu	93.3
45	Croatia	7,582.0	97	Tonga	76.0
46	Kuwait	7,139.0			
47	Bangladesh	6,496.0			
48	Sri Lanka	5,185.2			
49	Syria	4,480.0			
50	Ecuador	4,193.0			
51	Jordan	3,698.0			
52	Cyprus	3,694.0			

Ranking by Total Exports 1995 (US$ million)

1	United States of America	583,863.0	53	Papua New Guinea	2,665.0
2	Germany	509,421.0	54	Costa Rica	2,577.0
3	Japan	443,125.0	55	Trinidad and Tobago	2,514.0
4	France	286,480.0	56	Colombia	2,311.0
5	United Kingdom	237,365.3	57	Zimbabwe	2,104.3
6	Netherlands	194,498.0	58	Uruguay	2,089.0
7	Canada	192,197.0	59	Jordan	1,769.0
8	Hong Kong	173,754.0	60	Malta	1,765.3
9	China	148,797.0	61	Kenya	1,722.0
10	Singapore	118,265.0	62	Mauritius	1,464.0
11	Spain	91,714.0	63	Latvia	1,283.0
12	Sweden	79,908.0	64	Cyprus	1,229.0
13	Mexico	79,541.5	65	Bolivia	1,101.0
14	Russia	79,045.0	66	Jamaica	1,099.0
15	Switzerland	77,649.0	67	Honduras	1,061.0
16	Malaysia	74,045.0	68	El Salvador	998.0
17	Australia	53,067.0	69	Myanmar	846.0
18	Denmark	48,973.0	70	Swaziland	833.0
19	Brazil	46,506.0	71	Turkmenistan	809.1
20	Indonesia	45,417.0	72	Dominican Republic	765.0
21	Norway	41,746.0	73	Tanzania	637.0
22	India	30,539.0	74	Fiji	607.0
23	South Africa	27,860.0	75	Panama	596.0
24	Portugal	22,628.0	76	Nicaragua	525.0
25	Poland	22,320.0	77	Guyana	467.0
26	Czech Republic	21,613.0	78	Uganda	461.0
27	Argentina	20,967.0	79	Zaire	436.0
28	Turkey	20,280.0	80	Nepal	348.0
29	Israel	19,028.0	81	Laos	348.0
30	Venezuela	18,543.0	82	Afghanistan	342.4
31	Philippines	17,106.7	83	Barbados	235.0
32	Chile	16,039.0	84	Togo	209.0
33	New Zealand	13,736.0	85	Central African Republic	187.0
34	Kuwait	13,036.0	86	Solomon Islands	158.7
35	Ukraine	12,754.0	87	Haiti	153.0
36	Algeria	12,695.0	88	Belize	139.0
37	Hungary	12,540.0	89	Sierra Leone	125.0
38	Slovenia	8,286.0	90	Benin	102.6
39	Slovakia	8,019.6	91	Maldives	52.0
40	Pakistan	7,992.0	92	Vanuatu	28.0
41	Romania	7,548.0	93	Tonga	14.0
42	Peru	5,572.0	94	Western Samoa	9.0
43	Tunisia	5,475.0			
44	Croatia	4,633.0			
45	Morocco	4,584.0			
46	Ecuador	4,307.0			
47	Syria	4,044.0			
48	Bahrain	3,930.0			
49	Sri Lanka	3,798.0			
50	Angola	3,691.0			
51	Bangladesh	3,174.0			
52	Lithuania	2,698.0			

Ranking by Tourism Receipts 1994 (US$ million)

1	USA	75,060.0	53	Chile	833.3
2	France	25,630.4	54	Colombia	793.7
3	Italy	21,341.8	55	Slovenia	782.3
4	Spain	19,835.1	56	Syria	742.0
5	United Kingdom	14,728.0	57	Malta	722.9
6	Austria	13,125.0	58	Cuba	687.1
7	Germany	11,308.3	59	Costa Rica	626.0
8	Switzerland	9,357.7	60	Jordan	598.1
9	Hong Kong	8,318.1	61	Barbados	522.8
10	China	7,323.0	62	Kenya	519.3
11	Singapore	7,069.3	63	Venezuela	512.9
12	Mexico	6,396.2	64	Bermuda	491.8
13	Canada	6,309.8	65	Uruguay	473.4
14	Poland	6,151.0	66	Aruba	468.4
15	Australia	5,957.5	67	Slovakia	460.9
16	Paraguay	5,812.1	68	Guadeloupe	401.5
17	Belgium	5,182.6	69	Antigua	387.3
18	Netherlands	5,047.6	70	Martinique	360.3
19	Portugal	4,295.9	71	Mauritius	354.8
20	Argentina	3,969.3	72	Guatemala	353.1
21	Japan	3,922.7	73	Peru	318.6
22	South Korea	3,920.0	74	Cayman Islands	255.9
23	Greece	3,687.8	75	Fiji	252.0
24	Taiwan	3,608.0	76	St Lucia	232.2
25	Denmark	3,175.4	77	Ecuador	232.0
26	Indonesia	3,129.0	78	Panama	231.7
27	Philippines	3,110.0	79	Bulgaria	230.2
28	Turkey	2,858.8	80	Senegal	226.7
29	Sweden	2,821.2	81	Sri Lanka	214.0
30	Macau	2,553.1	82	Ghana	210.8
31	Israel	2,294.2	83	French Polynesia	205.9
32	Malaysia	2,099.2	84	Nepal	204.9
33	Czech Republic	1,996.1	85	Pakistan	185.0
34	Norway	1,978.0	86	Tanzania	159.2
35	Ireland	1,829.4	87	Maldives	147.4
36	India	1,752.0	88	Iceland	134.9
37	Puerto Rico	1,721.6	89	El Salvador	124.3
38	Romania	1,504.0	90	British Virgin Islands	122.0
39	Cyprus	1,457.1	91	Bolivia	120.8
40	Finland	1,435.6	92	Seychelles	120.0
41	Hungary	1,427.0	93	Gibraltar	101.7
42	New Zealand	1,357.6	94	Zimbabwe	100.4
43	Brazil	1,352.0	95	New Caledonia	98.0
44	Egypt	1,351.6	96	Namibia	93.5
45	Nicaragua	1,337.4	97	Trinidad and Tobago	83.4
46	Bahamas	1,332.4	98	Serbia	80.8
47	Morocco	1,267.0	99	Kuwait	77.3
48	South Africa	1,227.5	100	Belize	75.6
49	Tunisia	1,211.8	101	St Kitts	71.9
50	Dominican Republic	1,147.8	102	Uganda	70.4
51	Jamaica	988.7	103	Côte d'Ivoire	67.2
52	Guam	973.9	104	Haiti	60.9

105	St Vincent & the Grenadines	60.3
106	Estonia	60.1
107	Madagascar	58.3
108	Yemen	48.9
109	Cambodia	47.5
110	Algeria	46.0
111	Papua New Guinea	45.0
112	Grenada	44.8
113	Zambia	44.4
114	Anguilla	43.2
115	Benin	41.1
116	Guyana	38.9
117	Cameroon	38.8
118	Togo	37.7
119	Brunei	35.7
120	Iran	34.0
121	Myanmar	31.9
122	Swaziland	31.8
123	Vanuatu	31.1
124	Nigeria	30.3
125	Honduras	29.7
126	Dominica	29.6
127	Gambia	27.0
128	Sierra Leone	23.0
129	Western Samoa	22.7
130	Angola	22.0
131	Niger	21.8
132	Chad	18.2
133	Malawi	18.1
134	Lesotho	17.3
135	Bangladesh	16.3
136	Mauritania	14.9
137	American Samoa	14.1
138	Djibouti	13.6
139	Suriname	12.1
140	Mali	11.5
141	Tonga	11.4
142	Comoros	9.5
143	Burkina Faso	7.1
144	Solomon Islands	6.6
145	Guinea	6.1
146	Gabon	5.3
147	Libya	4.7
148	Sudan	4.0
149	Bhutan	3.8
150	Albania	3.1
151	Burundi	2.9
152	Rwanda	2.2
153	Congo	2.1
154	Afghanistan	1.4
155	Kiribati	1.1
156	Tuvalu	0.3

Ranking by Tourism Expenditure 1994 (US$ million)

1	USA	53,085.0	53	Tunisia	220.8
2	Germany	40,367.2	54	Ecuador	218.5
3	Japan	29,621.7	55	Côte d'Ivoire	209.1
4	United Kingdom	19,085.8	56	Poland	199.8
5	France	13,747.5	57	Bahamas	199.2
6	Italy	13,575.1	58	Bulgaria	192.7
7	Canada	9,940.1	59	Cameroon	185.7
8	Netherlands	9,658.2	60	Pakistan	169.0
9	Austria	8,914.3	61	Bangladesh	166.1
10	Switzerland	8,036.5	62	Paraguay	165.2
11	Taiwan	7,915.2	63	Bahrain	164.5
12	Belgium	6,914.4	64	Bolivia	158.6
13	Mexico	5,768.7	65	Guatemala	154.6
14	Spain	4,805.3	66	Philippines	151.8
15	Sweden	4,752.4	67	Mauritius	150.9
16	Australia	4,731.2	68	Algeria	142.7
17	Norway	3,813.6	69	Gabon	140.4
18	Denmark	3,529.3	70	Libya	139.2
19	Singapore	3,368.0	71	Senegal	138.9
20	China	3,036.0	72	Cyprus	138.8
21	Argentina	2,724.0	73	Uruguay	136.6
22	Israel	2,514.9	74	Bermuda	135.4
23	Thailand	2,395.0	75	Panama	131.1
24	Malaysia	2,193.2	76	Sri Lanka	128.0
25	Brazil	1,947.2	77	Dominican Republic	125.5
26	Finland	1,903.5	78	Nepal	121.4
27	Portugal	1,899.0	79	Trinidad and Tobago	119.9
28	Kuwait	1,758.8	80	Tanzania	110.4
29	South Africa	1,648.3	81	Angola	101.1
30	Ireland	1,401.9	82	Zimbabwe	94.6
31	New Zealand	1,151.4	83	Congo	85.4
32	Nicaragua	1,151.4	84	Namibia	83.2
33	Greece	1,123.3	85	Macau	72.5
34	Egypt	1,063.4	86	Jamaica	67.2
35	Colombia	1,002.7	87	Aruba	65.1
36	Puerto Rico	818.0	88	Mali	63.6
37	Hungary	806.0	89	El Salvador	62.7
38	Turkey	674.4	90	Kenya	60.4
39	India	661.0	91	Madagascar	60.1
40	Chile	650.8	92	Uganda	56.3
41	Czech Republic	606.5	93	Zambia	52.3
42	Jordan	367.2	94	Haiti	47.5
43	Peru	361.4	95	Oman	47.5
44	Slovenia	324.0	96	Togo	46.4
45	Syria	318.0	97	Barbados	46.3
46	Slovakia	309.6	98	Sudan	42.0
47	Costa Rica	284.6	99	Fiji	41.6
48	Romania	279.6	100	Niger	39.6
49	Iceland	269.8	101	Honduras	36.1
50	Morocco	266.3	102	British Virgin Islands	35.0
51	Malta	233.6	103	Mauritania	34.0
52	Nigeria	228.4	104	Burkina Faso	30.9

105	Estonia	30.7
106	Botswana	29.7
107	Maldives	29.3
108	Guinea	28.7
109	St Lucia	24.1
110	Antigua	22.0
111	Belize	21.7
112	Cape Verde	20.9
113	Burundi	19.2
114	Rwanda	18.2
115	Swaziland	18.0
116	Ghana	15.6
117	Solomon Islands	15.1
118	Benin	14.1
119	Suriname	14.0
120	Gambia	13.6
121	Chad	9.5
122	American Samoa	8.0
123	Djibouti	7.3
124	Lesotho	7.1
125	St Vincent & the Grenadines	5.3
126	Albania	5.2
127	St Kitts	5.2
128	Dominica	5.1
129	Sierra Leone	5.1
130	Cambodia	4.0
131	Central African Republic	3.4
132	Tonga	3.4
133	Malawi	3.3
134	Myanmar	2.5
135	Western Samoa	2.4
136	Afghanistan	1.3
137	Vanuatu	1.2
138	Anguilla	1.0

World
Economic
Database

Afghanistan

Area (km²) 636,265

Currency Afghani (= 100 puls)

Location Afghanistan divides the Middle East from the Indian subcontinent. It borders on China in the north-east, Pakistan in the east and south, Iran in the west and the former Soviet Union republics of Turkmenistan, Uzbekistan and Tajikistan in the north. It is this central location that has largely accounted for the successive invasions of the country over the centuries. The capital is Kabul.

Head of State President Burhanuddin Rabbani (December 1992)

Head of Government Arsalan Rahamani (Acting, November 1994)

Ruling Party No ruling party

Political Structure Afghanistan's political situation has steadily deteriorated since the removal of the Soviet-backed President Najibullah in 1992. First, the Jamiat-i-Islami Islamic mujaheddin faction which replaced Najibullah was overturned in 1993 by its bitter rival, Hezb-i-Islami, led by Gulbuddin Hekmatyar. A year later the government of Arsalan Rahamani was facing serious political and military threat from the groups of Taliban ("religious scholars") who quickly gained control over the south of the country. By September 1995 the Taliban resistance had overrun the southern provincial capital of Herat and posed a serious threat to the authority of the provisional central government. While legislative authority rests technically with the National Assembly (Meli Shura), it is clear that normal legal processes no longer function in Afghanistan. March 1996 brought the first sign of peace when the Taliban announced that they were ready to hold direct talks with President Rabbani.

Last Elections No elections have been held since 1988 when the only candidates for the National Assembly were those were members of the ruling National Front of Afghanistan. Mujaheddin delegates refused an invitation to enter the polls.

Political Risk The war in Afghanistan has raged for years with the south of the country now under the control of the Taliban and Kabul itself frequently under attack. Human rights abuses are widespread and tensions with Pakistan, a traditional mujaheddin supporter, are frequent.

International Disputes Afghanistan is still in dispute with Pakistan over the ownership of a large part of the border region, populated by the Pathan tribes who were engaged in much of the rebel fighting during the civil war of the 1990s. The fact that Pakistan gave the tribes logistical support in their struggle and helped in negotiations for a settlement of the war has not improved the situation.

Economy The country has experienced continuous suffering since the late 1980s and its economy is in complete disarray. Most of the Government's plans for reconstruction have been stalled, though it continues to hold out hope for international assistance. The average wage of a government employee in Kabul is estimated to be only about $15 per month. People rely on wood for heating and cooking but this, alone, costs $1 per day for the average family. Only the richest can afford to buy the necessities which people in other developing countries take for granted.

Main Industries Afghanistan's rough and elevated terrain means that opportunities for farming are limited to dry-weather crops.The country's main products are wheat, lentils and cotton, although there is also sugar beet and rice. Sheep are bred for export while carpets and rugs are among the major manufactured exports. The industrial base was always very limited and much of it has been destroyed during the civil war. The mining sector is also underdeveloped but has the most potential for growth. Afghanistan has silver, copper, iron, gold, chrome, lapis lazuli and talc.

Energy Having no domestic oil resources, Afghanistan remains dependent on its neighbours for most of its energy needs. There are coal-burning power stations, but natural gas provides the bulk of the country's energy requirements.

	1993	1994	1995
Inflation (% change)	40.0	5,250.0	
Exchange rate (per US$)	50.60	50.60	50.60
Interest rate			
GDP (% real growth)	3.0		
GDP (Million units of national currency)	2,319,326.3	1,836,370.0	
GDP (US$ million)	45,836.5	36,291.9	
GDP per capita (US$)	2,591.1	1,922.2	
Consumption (Million units of national currency)	1,774,457.9	1,404,959.6	
Consumption (US$ million)	35,068.3	27,766.0	
Consumption per capita (US$)	1,982.4	1,470.7	
Population, mid-year ('000)	17,690.0	18,880.0	19,035.0
Birth rate (per '000)	50.9	43.5	43.0
Death rate (per '000)	22.0	18.9	18.2
No. of households ('000)	3,468.0	3,595.6	3,560.0
Total exports (US$ million)	265.5	320.0	342.4
Total imports (US$ million)	793.3	1,050.8	1,123.5
Tourism receipts (US$ million)	1.3	1.4	1.4
Tourist spending (US$ million)	1.2	1.3	1.3

Average household size 1995 (persons)	4.99				
Urban population 1995 (%)	20.0				
Age analysis (%) (1988)	*0-14* 46.1		*15-64* 50.2		*65+* 3.7
Population by sex (%) (1988)	*Male* 51.3		*Female* 48.7		
Life expectancy (years) (1990)	*Male* 48.6		*Female* 47.1		
Infant mortality (deaths per '000 live births) (1992)	165.0				
Adult literacy (%) (1995)	31.5				

TRADING PARTNERS

Major export destinations 1995 (% share)		Major import sources 1995 (% share)	
China	19.1	Japan	26.7
Pakistan	15.5	Pakistan	7.5
Russia	11.1	Singapore	7.2
Belgium/Luxembourg	11.0	China	6.7

Albania

Area (km²) 28,750

Currency Lek (= 100 quindarka)

Location Albania is situated on the eastern Adriatic coast, with the former Yugoslavian provinces of Montenegro, Serbia and Macedonia marking its northern and eastern boundaries and with Greece to the south. Southern Albania faces the Greek island of Corfu across the Straits of Corfu. The climate is temperate and warm in summer with little rainfall. The capital is Tiranë.

Head of State President Sali Berisha (1992)

Head of Government Aleksandr Meksi

Ruling Party Democratic Party (DP). The Head of Government, however, has no party affiliations.

Political Structure Albania is run under an executive Presidency answerable to a 140-member People's Assembly elected by popular vote. Beset by fractional in-fighting, the DP was defeated in a national referendum on a new constitution in 1995 and appears to be losing some of its popular support. The DP's previous coalition partners, the Social Democrats and the Republican Party, also split away in December 1995 after the failed referendum vote.

Last Elections Albania held its third free elections in May 1996 since the fall of a repressive Stalinist regime in 1990. The first round of the poll proved to be a chaotic one when five opposition parties withdrew while voting was going on. A large turnout gave the ruling Democratic Party of Sali Berisha a victory over its main rival, the Socialist Party of former Communists. However, widespread evidence of election fraud and violence has led international observers to reject the results and demand a new poll.

Political Risk The installation of a stable parliamentary democracy has substantially improved the prospects for Albania. However, the leaders of the DP have inevitably proved to be very short of political experience. Disputes have arisen over the handling of the judiciary, the sacking of the chairman of the Supreme Court and the imprisonment of Fatos Nona, the former prime minister and leader of the Socialist Party. Albania has nevertheless emerged as an area of relative tranquillity in the cauldron of the Balkans. It is building close economic, political and military ties with the USA, which already uses northern Albania for reconnaissance flights and logistical support for NATO's Partnership for Peace programme.

International Disputes The possibility that war will resume in the former Yugoslavia and the repression of the ethnic Albanian population in neighbouring Kosovo in southern Serbia dominate Albania's international agenda. The country's relations with Greece, though improved, also remain fragile. Greece harbours an estimated 100,000 ethnic Greek Albanians that it claims have been systematically mistreated by Albania. Some diplomats fear that a West preoccupied with bringing peace to Bosnia will underestimate the wider threats in the Balkans, many of which involve the security of Albania.

Economy Albania is the poorest country in Europe but has made one of the most rapid transitions to a market economy over the past three years. Growth is coming from small companies in the private sector (whose fortunes have been boosted by greater private control over real estate) and strong income gains in agriculture. Large-scale foreign aid and remittances from Albanians working abroad provide important boosts to the economy and allow the country to live beyond its means. Nearly $400 million in foreign aid is being devoted to infrastructure development. This includes the construction of adequate roads, airports, water and power supplies and improvements in banking and telecommunications.

Main Industries Although chronically short of investment capital, Albania possesses the potential for wealth in the form of its massive mineral resources. The country has some of the world's richest deposits of chrome, molybdenum and copper, as well as nickel and limestone. Agriculture has been traditionally geared to meet only domestic needs, with wheat, maize, potatoes and fruit being the main crops. The nature of the farming sector is changing rapidly, thanks to the almost total privatisation of the Albania's agricultural land, where about 60% of the population lives. This element of the reform programme is judged to be the country's greatest success story so far. Agriculture's share of GDP has risen from about 33% in the late 1980s to over 55% today.

Energy Albania relies on imported crude oil for almost half of its modest energy requirements, but international oil companies are showing increased interest in exploring for offshore oil and gas. These companies are spending over $140 million and are committed to drilling at least four exploratory offshore wells by the end of 1996.

	1993	1994	1995
Inflation (% change)	91.0	10.0	
Exchange rate (per US$)	95.00	94.30	
Interest rate			
GDP (% real growth)	5.0	-2.7	-3.6
GDP (Million units of national currency)	486,333.8	520,377.2	551,599.8
GDP (US$ million)	5,119.3	5,518.3	5,849.4
GDP per capita (US$)	1,510.1	1,618.3	1,700.9
Consumption (Million units of national currency)	56,312.8		
Consumption (US$ million)	592.8		
Consumption per capita (US$)	174.9		
Population, mid-year ('000)	3,390.0	3,410.0	3,439.0
Birth rate (per '000)	22.0	22.5	
Death rate (per '000)	5.6	5.3	
No. of households ('000)	977.0	990.2	1,027.6
Total exports (US$ million)			
Total imports (US$ million)			
Tourism receipts (US$ million)	3.0	3.1	
Tourist spending (US$ million)	5.0	5.2	

Average household size 1995 (persons)	3.27		
Urban population 1995 (%)	37.3		
Age analysis (%) (1995)	*0-14* 39.1	*15-64* 56.5	*65+* 4.4
Population by sex (%) (1995)	*Male* 51.5	*Female* 48.5	
Life expectancy (years) (1990)	*Male* 69.6	*Female* 75.5	
Infant mortality (deaths per '000 live births) (1992)	32.9		
Adult literacy (%) (1983)	75.0		

Algeria

Area (km²)   2,381,745

Currency   Algerian dinar (= 100 centimes)

Location   Algeria, one of the largest countries in Africa, occupies most of the western Mediterranean coast of North Africa, and faces Spain and Italy across the Mediterranean at a distance of no more than 150 km. It is bordered to the west by Morocco and Mauritania, to the south by Mali and Niger, and to the east by Tunisia and Libya. The climate is warm and has a dry desert character. The capital is Algiers.

Head of State   President Brig. Gen. Lamine Zeroual (January 1994)

Head of Government   Mkhdad Sifi (April 1994)

Ruling Party   The five-member High Council of State (HCS) governed the country until January 1994 when it was then replaced by the executive Presidency of Brig. Gen. Zeroual. A non-party government rules with military backing.

Political Structure   Algeria has an executive presidency which is technically answerable to an elected parliament (Majlis). However, considerable unrest has occurred since the virtual collapse in 1991 of the National Liberation Front, which had been the sole political party since 1962 under President Benjedid Chadli. The cancellation of elections in January 1992 was followed by the assassination of Chadli's successor, Mohammed Boudiaf. After a short period of interim rule, Brig.-Gen. Zeroual was appointed President. Islamic rebels have wrecked havoc since Zeroual assumed power, destroying oil installations and killing foreigners, journalists and Algerian intellectuals.

Last Elections   Algeria's troubles began in earnest following the general elections in December 1991. The militant Islamic Salvation Front gained an unexpectedly large majority over the ruling socialist National Liberation Front (FLN). Zeroual was returned to power in the general elections held in November 1995, though both the outlawed Islamic Salvation Front (FIS) and the FLN boycotted the poll. The main parties may now believe that they erred in boycotting the latest presidential election. Neither the FLN (which has changed its secretary-general) nor the other political parties are unlikely to stand aloof again. But for a political revival, it will be vital that the FIS play an active role. A group of eight political parties known as the "National Charter group" has drafted a peace plan and is calling for a negotiated settlement to the civil war.

Political Risk   The continuing rise of religious fundamentalism, along with the collapse of socialist rule, greatly increase the risks associated with the country. Now that terrorists' attention have turned to tourists, the implications for foreign investment are regarded as grave. In 1996, the country's Armed Islamic Group (GIA) moved against crucial export industries by threatening to kill oil and gas workers. Another group of Islamic fighters controls large swathes of the country, particularly in the mountainous regions of eastern Algeria.

International Disputes   Algeria has been in conflict with Morocco (and initially Mauritania as well) over occupation of the Western Sahara territories in 1976 which Spain had withdrawn. Meanwhile, Algerian terrorists are charged with having set off several bombs in France and oppose any ties with that country.

Economy   A wave of strikes and constant violence has derailed the government's attempts to reform the economy which, until mid-1994, had seemed to be doing better than its political system. Hopes of economic growth have disappeared as the security situation has worsened. International investors are now worried that Islamic law may eventually be introduced if the current tide toward militant Islam continues. Algeria's economy is dominated by state-owned enterprises, many of which were expropriated in the 1960s. The government can do little to shed these assets so long as the civil war continues.

Main Industries   Algeria's dominant industries depend on the extraction of crude oil and natural gas, much of which is exported to France, Spain and Italy. There are also a number of downstream, oil-using industries, as well as plants producing steel, chemicals, paper products, metal manufactures and even motor vehicles. Agricultural development is limited to the coastal regions, where wheat, maize and sugar beet are grown; there is, however, a flourishing trade in oranges and other fruit.

Energy   Algeria meets all of its energy requirements from its indigenous supplies of oil and natural gas. It is, indeed, the world's third largest consumer of gas after Canada and the United States.

	1993	1994	1995
Inflation (% change)	20.5	29.0	29.8
Exchange rate (per US$)	23.35	35.06	46.69
Interest rate (% per annum)	13.0	12.5	12.0
GDP (% real growth)	2.0	-2.0	-1.0
GDP (Million units of national currency)	1,166,000.0	1,470,400.0	1,984,922.4
GDP (US$ million)	49,946.5	41,940.7	42,514.6
GDP per capita (US$)	1,856.7	1,521.8	1,489.1
Consumption (Million units of national currency)	594,700.0	772,907.5	1,003,233.9
Consumption (US$ million)	25,474.4	22,045.9	21,488.0
Consumption per capita (US$)	947.0	799.9	752.6
Population, mid-year ('000)	26,900.0	27,560.0	28,550.0
Birth rate (per '000)	28.8	29.7	
Death rate (per '000)	6.4	6.2	6.6
No. of households ('000)	5,846.9	6,005.2	6,176.8
Total exports (US$ million)	10,230.0	11,127.2	12,695.0
Total imports (US$ million)	7,770.0	8,432.0	8,303.0
Tourism receipts (US$ million)	55.0	46.0	
Tourist spending (US$ million)	170.7	142.7	139.1

Average household size 1995 (persons)	4.36		
Urban population 1995 (%)	55.8		
Age analysis (%) (1987)	*0-14* 44.0	*15-64* 52.0	*65+* 4.0
Population by sex (%) (1987)	*Male* 50.5	*Female* 49.5	
Life expectancy (years) (1990)	*Male* 63.0	*Female* 65.0	
Infant mortality (deaths per '000 live births) (1993)	55.0		
Adult literacy (%) (1990)	57.4		

TRADING PARTNERS

Major export destinations 1995 (% share)		Major import sources 1995 (% share)	
Italy	18.6	France	31.0
USA	15.8	Spain	9.8
France	11.4	Italy	8.9
Germany	8.6	USA	8.6

American Samoa

Area (km²)   197

Currency   US dollar (US$ = 100 cents)

Location   American Samoa is a cluster of islands within the Samoan group, to the east of the state of Western Samoa. Apart from Tutuila, Tau, Aunu'u, Ofu, Olosega, and Rose, American Samoa includes the more northerly Swain's Islands, which are closer to Tokelau, a dependent territory of New Zealand. The climate is warm, with limited rainfall but occasional danger of cyclones. The capital is Pago Pago.

Head of State   President Bill Clinton (1993)

Head of Government   Governor: A P Lutali (November 1992)

Ruling Party   None

Political Structure   American Samoa is an unincorporated territory of the United States, whose executive authority rests in the Governor, appointed for a four-year term. Legislative authority lies with the House of Representatives, part of which is elected every two years. The Senate (Upper House) is directly appointed by the island's tribal elders (Matai). One observer is sent to the US Congress in Washington. The US voted in 1986 to revise the country's Constitution, but this decision has still not been ratified by Congress.

Last Elections   The last governatorial elections were held in November 1992, when A P Lutali ousted Peter Coleman, gaining 52% of the vote against the latter's 36%.

Political Risk   With a modestly wealthy population and a stable political structure, American Samoa poses little risk to businesses and investors. However, the gradual withdrawal of US defence interests from the Pacific raises some doubt about the willingness of Washington to continue to provide the islands with aid.

Economy   American Samoa remains highly dependent on the United States. It not only receives US aid but enjoys certain tax advantages and some immunity from that country's import restrictions. A government scheme is in place to encourage further foreign investment. The islands' heavy dependence on the USA is nevertheless a problem in a period when Washington is withdrawing its defence activities in the Pacific region.

Main Industries   With no natural mineral resources and limited scope for manufacturing exports, the country depends heavily on its agricultural industries. The greater part of the farm land is owned by smallholders producing crops such as yams and pineapples. The largest export crops are copra and tree fruits (mainly bananas). Equally important is the country's fishing industry, which contributes as much as a third of GDP; the main catch is tuna. There are two large American-owned tuna canneries which comprise the greater part of the country's industrial base. With strong government backing, services have been developing in recent years. The tourist sector has also added a number of new hotels and the banking sector shows considerable promise.

Energy   American Samoa has at least twice as much generating capacity as it actually needs at present. Apart from geothermal sources and natural sources such as timber, the country has ready access to oil supplies from the USA.

	1993	1994	1995
Inflation (% change)	2.7	3.0	2.8
Exchange rate (per US$)	1.00	1.00	1.00
Interest rate			
GDP (% real growth)	-3.0	-4.0	-3.0
GDP (Million units of national currency)	315.0	312.0	311.1
GDP (US$ million)	315.0	312.0	311.1
GDP per capita (US$)	6,300.0	5,672.7	5,185.2
Consumption (Million units of national currency)	208.5	208.5	207.9
Consumption (US$ million)	208.5	208.5	207.9
Consumption per capita (US$)	4,170.0	3,790.9	3,465.2
Population, mid-year ('000)	50.0	55.0	60.0
Birth rate (per '000)	37.8	36.6	36.0
Death rate (per '000)	4.2	4.0	4.0
No. of households ('000)	14.1	14.1	14.1
Total exports (US$ million)			
Total Imports (US$ million)			
Tourism receipts (US$ million)	14.0	14.1	14.1
Tourist spending (US$ million)	8.0	8.0	8.0

Average household size 1995 (persons)	3.71				
Urban population 1995 (%)	49.8				
Age analysis (%) (1990)	*0-14* 41.1		*15-64* 55.0		*65+* 3.9
Population by sex (%) (1990)	*Male* 50.4		*Female* 49.6		
Life expectancy (years) (1990)	*Male* 62.8		*Female* 67.1		
Infant mortality (deaths per '000 live births) (1992)	12.4				
Adult literacy (%) (1980)	97.3				

Andorra

Area (km²)   465

Currency   Spanish peseta/French franc

Location   The Principality of Andorra lies in the central Pyrenees between Spain and France, where its position on a mountain pass has always served its function as a trade and transhipment centre. Despite its southern position, its high altitude (3,000 metres) means that its climate is often cool. The capital is Andorra la Vella.

Head of State   President Jacques Chirac (France) and Joan Marti Alanis (Bishop of Urgel) are Co-Princes

Head of Government   Marc Forné Molné (December 1994)

Ruling Party   The Liberal Union (UL) leads a five-party coalition.

Political Structure   Andorra became an associate member of the EU in 1991, although its interests in the Community are always represented by France and Spain, which appoint its two co-princes. Under the 1993 Constitution, legislative authority is exercised by the 28-member Consell Général de las Valls, which is elected by Andorran nationals and serves for a period of four years. The government is led by the President of the Executive Council, but the co-princes have some powers of veto.

Last Elections   The country's first multi-party elections to the Consell Général de las Valls were held in December 1993, when over 80% of the 7,250 registered voters went to the polls (the 42,000 foreign residents have no vote). The result was a victory for the government of Oscar Ribas Reig, who had won the previous 1989 elections by a slim majority. Ribas Reig's National Democratic Grouping (AND) won eight of the 28 seats, compared with five for the Liberal Union, five for the New Democracy Party, and six seats for small parties and independents. In December 1994 Reig lost a vote of confidence in his administration and left office, to be succeeded by Marc Forné Molné.

Political Risk   Thanks to its sheltered political climate, its prosperity and traditionally positive orientation toward foreigners, Andorra is perceived as an extremely low-risk region for investment.

Economy   Andorra's economic well-being is unusually dependent on its ability to offer continued financial advantages to outsiders, since it has virtually no domestic industries. The offshore banking system is among the most developed in Europe. However, membership of the EU may temper these advantages in the coming years.

Main Industries   Apart from financial services, Andorra's main sources of income are the provision of duty-free goods and the increasingly important tourist industry. Andorra's altitude makes it ideally placed to exploit the growing enthusiasm for skiing holidays.

Energy   The country's modest electricity needs are met mainly from hydro-electric sources, although it also receives solid fuel and oil and gas from Spain and France.

	1993	1994	1995
Inflation (% change)	2.2	2.2	2.2
Exchange rate (per US$)	5.66	5.55	5.20
Interest rate (% per annum)	10.0	10.0	10.0
GDP (% real growth)	2.0	2.9	3.0
GDP (Million units of national currency)	7,273.2	7,648.8	8,051.6
GDP (US$ million)	1,285.0	1,378.2	1,548.4
GDP per capita (US$)	24,711.9	26,003.1	29,214.8
Consumption (Million units of national currency)	4,307.3	4,575.0	4,512.1
Consumption (US$ million)	761.0	824.3	867.7
Consumption per capita (US$)	14,634.8	15,553.3	16,372.0
Population, mid-year ('000)	52.0	53.0	53.0
Birth rate (per '000)	14.3	13.3	
Death rate (per '000)	7.0	7.1	
No. of households ('000)	20.2	20.7	21.5
Total exports (US$ million)			
Total imports (US$ million)			
Tourism receipts (US$ million)			
Tourist spending (US$ million)			

Average household size 1995 (persons)	2.43				
Urban population 1995 (%)	62.5				
Age analysis (%) (1991)	*0-14* 20.1		*15-64* 66.1		*65+* 13.8
Population by sex (%)					
Life expectancy (years)					
Infant mortality (deaths per '000 live births)					
Adult literacy (%)					

Angola

Area (km²)   1,246,700

Currency   New kwanza (Kw = 100 lwei)

Location   Angola lies on the western (Atlantic) coast of southern Africa. It is bounded in the south by Namibia, in the east and north by Zaire, and in the east by Zambia. The capital is Luanda.

Head of State   President José Eduardo dos Santos

Head of Government   Fernando Franca van Dunem (June 1996)

Ruling Party   People's Movement for the Liberation of Angola - Worker's Party (MPLA-PA).

Political Structure   The period since 1990 has been repeatedly marred by outbreaks of conflict which blunted the hopes that the long years of civil war might be over. Although the country's first free elections were held successfully in October 1992, the refusal of the UNITA rebels to accept the outcome suggested that a renewed period of chaos could be in store. Indeed, the civil war did restart in 1993-1994, leading to a temporary evacuation of foreign workers. A peace treaty was signed with the rebels in late 1994 and plans for a power-sharing agreement were put into action. In August 1995, Jonas Savimbi, leader of the UNITA rebels, declared that the war was officially over. Progress has nevertheless been slow and the UN still maintains over 7,000 troops in the country. At present, Angola's political system revolves around an executive President who is answerable to an elected National People's Assembly. In practice, the president can rule by decree. In June 1996, he dismissed his prime minister, Marcolino Moco, the whole cabinet and the governor of the central bank. The new government is led by Fernando Franca van Dunem, president of the national assembly and a close friend of the President.

Last Elections   Elections were held in October 1992, in which the government of the ruling MPLA-PA faced competition for the first time from opposition parties. The MPLA-PA received more than 60% of the national vote - though much less in many rural areas. The UNITA rebels, who won the remaining 40% with the backing of many opposition parties, denounced the result as a sham and tried to reopen the war although their international sponsors were no longer willing to provide them with logistical support.

Political Risk   The government shunts backwards and forwards as reformers in the World Bank and the IMF push for change and former socialists warn of the danger of street riots. Meanwhile, negotiations between the MPLA and Jonas Savimbi's UNITA grind on. The rebels are reluctant to disarm and have been slow to move their troops into UN-controlled camps as previously agreed. The risks to foreign investors and local businesses remains high. However, the main threat probably comes from the MPLA's gross mismanagement of the economy which, along with the civil war, has created vast poverty in a country which should otherwise would be rich by African standards, owing to its abundant oil reserves. If the economic deterioration continues, the MPLA risks playing into UNITA's hands as it prepares a new future as a political opposition movement.

International Disputes   Unless the MPLA takes drastic measures, it will remain cut off from structural adjustment support from the IMF, ruling out a rescheduling of its massive official debts. The $1 billion in aid which has been promised by donors to rebuild the economy can also be compromised.

Economy   Angola's economic performance in 1995 was the worst on record, strengthening the calls for market reforms. Inflation hit 3,700% and a fifth of the population was dependent on aid for survival. A government think tank is now working on a new reform package for approval by the MPLA. Although artificially low prices have kept the urban population relatively happy, they have penalised businesses and stifled initiatives. Foreign debts have piled up as money is recklessly printed to cover growing budget deficits. Angola badly needs the $1 billion which donors have promised to rebuild its war-torn economy. Whether its gets the money or not depends on two factors: peace and a credible package of economic reforms.

Main Industries   In addition to its oil reserves, Angola has vast amounts of precious metals and diamonds. The authorities, however, have lost control over many of these resource-rich areas in the aftermath of the civil war. Oil production remains the only staple activity, accounting for as much as 90% of exports. National and foreign-owned producers have been reporting new finds virtually every year, and Angola's output of around 300,000 barrels a day makes it the second largest producer in sub-Saharan Africa after Nigeria. Agriculture employs more than 70% of the workforce on less than 2% of the land. But with sporadic water supplies, yearly outbreaks of cholera and much of the country off-limits to farmers, agricultural output has plummeted and malnutrition is widespread. Nevertheless, bananas, coffee, palm products and timber are grown for export. Domestic crops centre on maize, cassava and potatoes.

Energy   Virtually all of Angola's needs are domestically supplied. Less than 1% of the total is accounted for by electricity, and most of this is generated from hydro-electric resources, with a limited amount of thermal power in use.

	1993	1994	1995
Inflation (% change)	1,840.0	5,964.7	3,700.0
Exchange rate (per US$)	6,708.39	506,879.00	519,308.00
Interest rate			
GDP (% real growth)	2.0	2.0	
GDP (Billion units of national currency)	470.9	29,131.6	1,129,142.4
GDP (US$ million)	7,848.8	8,241.3	
GDP per capita (US$)	763.5	772.4	
Consumption (Billion units of national currency)	263,700.0	16,312,430.0	
Consumption (US$ million)	3,931.2	4,619.0	
Consumption per capita (US$)	382.4	432.9	
Population, mid-year ('000)	10,280.0	10,670.0	10,674.1
Birth rate (per '000)	47.1	45.4	
Death rate (per '000)	19.2	19.5	
No. of households ('000)	2,472.0	2,405.0	2,435.9
Total exports (US$ million)	3,020.0	3,424.4	3,691.0
Total imports (US$ million)	1,600.0	1,441.2	1,805.0
Tourism receipts (US$ million)	20.0	22.0	23.0
Tourist spending (US$ million)	91.8	101.1	

Average household size 1995 (persons)	4.21				
Urban population 1995 (%)	32.2				
Age analysis (%) (1990)	*0-14*	46.5	*15-64*	49.5	*65+* 4.0
Population by sex (%) (1990)	*Male*	48.6	*Female*	51.4	
Life expectancy (years) (1990-95)	*Male*	44.9	*Female*	48.1	
Infant mortality (deaths per '000 live births) (1993)	124.2				
Adult literacy (%) (1990)	41.7				

TRADING PARTNERS

Major export destinations 1995 (% share)		Major import sources 1995 (% share)	
USA	65.9	Portugal	22.6
Germany	7.2	USA	16.9
China	4.4	France	9.9
Spain	3.7	Russia	5.3

Anguilla

Area (km²) 91

Currency East Caribbean dollar (EC$ = 100 cents)

Location Anguilla is located at the northern limit of the Leeward Islands group, north of St Kitts and to the east of the British Virgin Islands and Puerto Rico. The island is built on coral and is entirely low-lying. The climate is equable, with occasional threat from hurricanes. The capital is The Valley.

Head of State HM Queen Elizabeth II

Head of Government Hubert Hughes (March 1994)

Ruling Party Anguilla United Party (AUP) and Anguilla Democratic Party (ADP) form a coalition.

Political Structure As a Dependent Territory of the United Kingdom, ultimate sovereignty rests with the British monarch, although in practice the Chief Minister governs. Until 1980, Anguilla was technically a part of St Christopher (St Kitts)/Nevis/Anguilla, but this proved to be an unhappy union and the Anguillans repudiated the St Kitts administration. The 1982 Constitution came into operation in May 1990.

Last Elections General elections were held in 1994 when the ruling Anguilla National Alliance, the Anguilla Democratic Party and the Anguilla United Party each won two of the seven seats - the remaining seat going to an independent. The AUP and ADP thereupon formed a coalition government.

Political Risk Despite its relatively low level of spending power, Anguilla is generally regarded as politically safe. However, the vulnerability of the climate to droughts and/or hurricanes has highlighted some potential for poverty-related unrest in the recent past.

Economy The country's fast-growing domestic industries have done little to limit dependence on remittances from Anguillans employed in other countries, or on grants from the British Government. However, its range of activity is sufficiently broad to provide a reasonable degree of protection from a slump in any particular sector.

Main Industries Anguilla's burgeoning tourist industry has all but eclipsed the traditional activities of farming and fishing. Hotel construction has largely financed the accompanying development of infrastructure although day excursions from St Maarten remain the backbone of the industry. Agriculture, not normally a highly productive sector, has benefited in recent years from relatively good rainfall. The farming sector is characterised by smallholdings with bananas, yams, pineapples and coconuts being major export crops. Anguilla's important financial services sector is probably the fastest-growing part of the economy. The sector once had a poor reputation in international financial circles but a host of new laws have been enacted to strengthen operations and expand the range of services offered.

Energy The bulk of Anguilla's energy derives from oil, most of which is imported from Venezuela. Otherwise, it uses firewood and some geothermal resources.

	1993	1994	1995
Inflation (% change)	4.0	3.0	3.0
Exchange rate (per US$)	2.70	2.70	2.70
Interest rate			
GDP (% real growth)	2.5	-3.9	-3.7
GDP (Million units of national currency)	153.8	152.2	151.0
GDP (US$ million)	57.0	56.4	55.9
GDP per capita (US$)	6,329.2	5,640.6	5,594.9
Consumption (Million units of national currency)	104.3	103.4	106.5
Consumption (US$ million)	38.6	38.3	39.5
Consumption per capita (US$)	4,292.2	3,832.0	3,947.0
Population, mid-year ('000)	9.0	10.0	10.0
Birth rate (per '000)	18.4	17.2	16.9
Death rate (per '000)	6.4	6.7	
No. of households ('000)	1.6	1.6	1.6
Total exports (US$ million)			
Total imports (US$ million)			
Tourism receipts (US$ million)	43.0	43.2	
Tourist spending (US$ million)	1.0	1.0	1.0

Average household size 1995 (persons)	5.94				
Urban population 1994					
Age analysis (%) (1992)	*0-14*	30.5	*15-64*	62.0	*65+* 7.4
Population by sex (%) (1992)	*Male*	50.0	*Female*	50.0	
Life expectancy (years)					
Infant mortality (deaths per '000 live births)					
Adult literacy (%)					

Antigua

Area (km²)   442

Currency   East Caribbean dollar (EC$ = 100 cents)

Location   Antigua, along with Barbuda (25 miles to Antigua's north) forms part of the Leeward Islands in the Eastern Caribbean. Also included in the Leewards is the uninhabited islet of Redonda (25 miles south-west of Antigua). The capital is St John's.

Head of State   HM Queen Elizabeth II

Head of Government   Rt Hon Lester Bird

Ruling Party   Antigua Labour Party (ALP)

Political Structure   As Antigua is a member of the British Commonwealth, the British monarch is the titular head of state. In practice, the Prime Minister appoints the British Governor (currently Sir Wilfred Ebenezer Jacobs). Legislative authority is vested in the 17-member parliament and a 17-member Senate (Upper House) which is appointed by the Governor-General.

Last Elections   The 1994 elections to the 17-member House of Representatives resulted in another win for the ALP, which has held power since 1976. The ALP claimed 11 seats (down from 15 in the previous administration) while the opposition United National Democratic Party raised its representation from one seat to five. The remaining seat went to the Barbuda People's Movement.

Political Risk   Despite its fairly high standard of living, Antigua and Barbuda have been plagued by periodic unrest since the late 1980s. The main source of difficulties has been allegations that the former Prime Minister, Vere C Bird, was involved in corrupt practices. A British government report also suggested links with Colombian drug dealers and gun-running. The street demonstrations which followed threatened to destabilise the entire region. Meanwhile, economic reforms introduced to cut budget deficits have proven to be deeply unpopular. Despite all this opposition, Vere C Bird's nephew, Lester Bird, was appointed in March 1994 to succeed him.

Economy   Antigua's generally booming economy relies heavily on tourism and public officials would like to encourage more diversification. The island's image as a tourist destination is also hampered by complaints of high prices and corruption. Income tax was abolished in 1994 and special measures have been introduced to attract foreign capital and to bolster Antigua's offshore financial services.

Main Industries   Tourism accounts for nearly 70% of GDP and is the driving force for development of the country's infrastructure. Farming, which suffers from recurrent droughts and soil erosion, generates no more than 7% of GDP in a typical year. Sugar, maize, fruit and vegetables are grown for domestic consumption, and bananas and coconuts for export. The country also has considerable mineral resources, including barytes, limestone and clay, but these remain under-developed, partly for environmental reasons. The financial services sector is small but has the potential to expand rapidly.

Energy   Nearly all of Antigua's energy needs are met by imports of oil from Trinidad and Tobago, which in turn derives them from Venezuela. There are, however, some hopes of developing geothermal energy.

	1993	1994	1995
Inflation (% change)	1.9	4.0	3.0
Exchange rate (per US$)	2.70	2.70	2.70
Interest rate (% per annum)	13.0	12.5	12.0
GDP (% real growth)	2.7	-2.0	3.0
GDP (Million units of national currency)	1,045.7	1,065.3	1,130.2
GDP (US$ million)	387.3	394.8	418.3
GDP per capita (US$)	6,454.9	6,580.1	6,971.5
Consumption (Million units of national currency)	888.1	901.0	929.3
Consumption (US$ million)	328.9	333.9	343.9
Consumption per capita (US$)	5,482.1	5,565.2	5,732.2
Population, mid-year ('000)	60.0	60.0	60.0
Birth rate (per '000)	25.2	24.3	
Death rate (per '000)	8.5		
No. of households ('000)	17.8	17.7	18.1
Total exports (US$ million)	54.3	60.0	
Total imports (US$ million)	170.6	150.0	
Tourism receipts (US$ million)	372.0	387.3	
Tourist spending (US$ million)	21.2	22.0	22.0

Average household size 1995 (persons)	3.22				
Urban population 1995 (%)	35.8				
Age analysis (%) (1991)	*0-14* 38.0		*15-64* 57.0		*65+* 5.0
Population by sex (%)					
Life expectancy (years) (1958-61)	*Male* 60.5		*Female* 64.3		
Infant mortality (deaths per '000 live births)					
Adult literacy (%)					

Argentina

Area (km²)   2,777,815

Currency   Peso argentino (P = 100 centavos = 10,000 australes)

Location   Argentina is the second largest state in South America and occupies most of the continent south of the Tropic of Capricorn and east of the Andes. With its only coastline facing the Atlantic, Argentina's terrain varies from the vast prairies of the north to the mountains of the east and the sub-Antarctic south. The capital is Buenos Aires.

Head of State   President Carlos Menem

Head of Government   President Carlos Menem

Ruling Party   Justicialist Party

Political Structure   A new constitution was introduced in August 1994 which effectively cemented the country's departure from the military system that ran the country in the 1960s and 1970s. The practical purpose of the new constitution, however, was to allow President Carlos Menem to run for a third term of office, which he won in 1995. Argentina comprises a Federal District, 23 provinces and the National Territory of Tierra del Fuego, all of which enjoy varying degrees of autonomy. The executive President is elected every six years, answering to a 257-seat Chamber of Deputies and a 72-seat Senate.

Last Elections   After two rounds of elections in 1995, Menem's government will be the first in two decades to enjoy a majority in both houses of Congress. His Justicialist Party now holds 132 seats of 257 in the Chamber and 38 of 72 in the Senate. In the presidential elections held in May 1995, Menem was re-appointed with 49.8% of the vote.

Political Risk   Argentina has settled successfully into democratic patterns of politics after the chaos and repression of the military era. An encouraging result of that transformation is the government's trouble-free negotiations to reschedule its foreign debts and the country's new-found ability to attract foreign capital. Yet the economy remains vulnerable to short-term crises such as the one which followed the Mexican crisis in early 1995. Menem, himself, will face more difficulties in dealing with Congress even though his party has a comfortable majority. The constitutional changes that allowed him to seek a second four-year term have also reduced his ability to govern by decree as he had in the past.

International Disputes   Relations with the United Kingdom are much improved since the Falklands war helped to bring about the overthrow of the country's military government in 1982. Argentina has also settled its 150-year-old dispute with Chile over three islands in the far south (Picton, Lennox and Nueva). Arbitration decided in October 1994 that the so-called Laguna del Desierto belonged to Argentina.

Economy   Argentina's GDP declined by about 2.5% in 1995. The result was partly due to the hesitance of foreign investors in the aftermath of the Mexican crisis. Other contributing factors were a credit crunch and a record high unemployment, both of which made consumers extremely cautious. Wages, too, were falling as private companies trimmed pay packages or demanded longer working hours for the same pay. During the past four years, the jobless rate tripled as inefficient businesses were weeded out. Now, it is once again beginning to subside. Economists predict that growth will be modest in 1996 - around 2%. Exports are rising by around 30% per year but account for only 7.5% of GDP which is not a large enough share to spur economic growth.

Main Industries   Argentina's traditional major resource has been its agricultural sector, especially its wheat crops and its cattle raising, which together provide over 80% of the country's exports. Maize, oats, barley, rye and a range of soft and citrus fruits are also grown for export. Spin-offs from agriculture, such as fruit canning, meat packing and leather processing, account for a sizeable portion of the country's industrial activity. In addition, the manufacturing sector includes a sophisticated range of engineering products, along with large-scale production of automobiles, textiles, clothing and plastics. The composition of both the manufacturing and retailing sector has changed dramatically since the economy was opened up to foreign investment. Small-scale enterprises have been replaced with much larger operations that can sell at lower prices and maintain higher quality. Huge reserves of coal, lead, zinc, tungsten, iron ore, sulphur, mica and salt are the backbone of the mining industry, although the country's silver and gold mining is in decline. There are considerable quantities of beryllium, manganese and other metals, but these are under-exploited. Finally, the country's oil and gas fields, located in various places throughout the country, supply a refinery at San Lorenzo.

Energy   The bulk of Argentina's energy requirements are supplied domestically, with oil and gas accounting for 95% of primary production. Hydro-electric sources generate a third of the country's electricity. Argentina also has a number of nuclear power stations which are being privatised. In 1995, the government began licensing of oil prospecting activities off the coast of the Falklands/Malvinas islands.

	1993	1994	1995
Inflation (% change)	10.6	4.2	3.4
Exchange rate (per US$)	1.00	1.00	1.00
Interest rate (% per annum)	6.0	10.1	19.5
GDP (% real growth)	2.1	4.9	-2.5
GDP (Million units of national currency)	257,570.0	281,645.0	306,024.7
GDP (US$ million)	257,827.8	281,504.2	306,055.3
GDP per capita (US$)	7,657.5	8,235.9	8,848.1
Consumption (Million units of national currency)	212,889.0	245,163.1	277,437.0
Consumption (US$ million)	213,102.1	245,040.6	277,464.7
Consumption per capita (US$)	6,329.1	7,169.1	8,021.5
Population, mid-year ('000)	33,670.0	34,180.0	34,590.0
Birth rate (per '000)	19.8	18.6	18.1
Death rate (per '000)	7.9	8.8	9.0
No. of households ('000)	12,280.0	12,429.0	12,577.0
Total exports (US$ million)	13,118.0	15,659.0	20,967.0
Total imports (US$ million)	16,784.0	21,527.0	20,123.0
Tourism receipts (US$ million)	3,614.0	3,969.3	4,275.0
Tourist spending (US$ million)	2,445.0	2,724.0	2,900.0

Average household size 1995 (persons)	2.61				
Urban population 1996 (%)	88.1				
Age analysis (%) (1994)	*0-14* 29.0		*15-64* 61.5		*65+* 9.5
Population by sex (%) (1993)	*Male* 49.5		*Female* 50.5		
Life expectancy (years) (1990)	*Male* 67.3		*Female* 74.0		
Infant mortality (deaths per '000 live births) (1993)	23.1				
Adult literacy (%) (1995)	95.9				

TRADING PARTNERS

Major export destinations 1995 (% share)		Major import sources 1995 (% share)	
Brazil	24.9	Brazil	20.8
USA	8.0	USA	20.3
Chile	6.4	Germany	6.7
Netherlands	5.6	Netherlands	6.5

Armenia

Area (km²)   29,800

Currency   Dram (= 100 luma)

Location   Geographically, the Republic of Armenia occupies the south-western sector of the landmass known as Transcaucasia, and borders Turkey and Iran in the south; politically, it spans the gulf between the former Soviet Union and the Islamic states of the Middle East. Armenia was formed as a protective haven for members of the Armenian church from all parts of the region. The capital is Yerevan.

Head of State   President Levon Ter-Petrosyan (1992)

Head of Government   Hrand Bagratian (1993)

Ruling Party   Armenian Pan-National Movement

Political Structure   Armenia declared its unilateral independence from the Soviet Union in August 1990, a decision confirmed by a referendum the following month when 94% voted in favour. Under the new structure, which was finalised in December 1991, Armenia's executive President is elected by popular vote and is answerable to a 185-seat Supreme Soviet (Parliament), with 21 ministries. President Levon Ter-Petrosyan was confirmed in office in October 1991, when he obtained 83% of the vote.

Last Elections   Elections in June 1995 returned Ter-Petrosyan and his government to power. The Organisation of Security and Cooperation in Europe, which monitored the elections, warily declared the poll to be "free but not fair".

Political Risk   Armenia's ethnic ties with Nagorny-Karabakh and Nakhichevan, two predominantly Armenian enclaves within Azerbaijan, has created a number of serious problems for both countries. Armenian activists in both regions have run an armed campaign for secession of the two enclaves. The intensity of the fighting has now receded but could abruptly resume. One strange benefit of the unrest is that most people blame their continuing poverty on the upheavals rather than on the difficulty of converting from communism to capitalism. In April 1996, Armenia entered into a Transcaucasus-EU Pact that also includes Georgia and Azerbaijan and is intended to help stabilise this explosive region. The Pact offers trade concessions and access to certain EU loans in return for democratic and economic reforms.

International Disputes   Armenia has a serious dispute with neighbouring Azerbaijan over the sovereignty of Nagorny-Karabakh. It has also encountered opposition from Turkey, where ethnic Armenian militants still demand the creation of their own Armenian state. In 1992, Turkish troops crossed the border to defend non-Armenian communities in Nakhichevan. Armenia has not revived any territorial claims in respect of the Turkish Armenian population, yet the fact remains that most of its population were moved to the area as a result of the massacres which the Islamic Turkish authorities inflicted on their peoples in 1914-1915, and some tensions remain.

Economy   Although terribly poor, Armenia has proved to be a model of economic self-discipline. Its budget has been drastically slashed since independence and inflation has been brought to a halt. The same applies to foreign debt which has been reduced to comfortable levels. Meanwhile, industrial production is rising rapidly, albeit from negligible levels. With these achievements, Armenia has strong support from the IMF and in 1995 announced that it planned to sell off the 10 largest state-owned enterprises. The country also enjoys access to a rich and vigorous diaspora which has willingly provided capital, earning it the title of "Israel in the Caucasus".

Main Industries   Armenia's fertile valleys mean that the economy relies heavily on agriculture, with crops of grain, sugar beet, potatoes and other vegetables, as well as grapes and other fruit. Cattle, sheep and pigs are the main forms of livestock. Industry is restricted to basic manufactures but remains severely disrupted by shortages of power and political instability. Much of the country's existing industrial capacity is woefully obsolete but is slowly being modernised.

Energy   Armenia has been starved of energy as its Muslim neighbours, Azerbaijan and Turkey, exerted pressure during the long-running dispute over the enclave of Nagorny-Karabakh. The situation has now improved, although the country's only nuclear power station has been closed since an earthquake in 1988.

	1993	1994	1995
Inflation (% change)	287.8	100.0	26.7
Exchange rate (per US$)	193.20	300.00	400.00
Interest rate			
GDP (% real growth)	-15.0	5.0	7.0
GDP			
GDP (US$ million)	4,766.2	4,009.5	4,522.7
GDP per capita (US$)	1,277.8	1,129.4	1,202.8
Consumption			
Consumption (US$ million)	3,589.0	3,019.2	3,475.0
Consumption per capita (US$)	962.2	850.5	924.2
Population, mid-year ('000)	3,730.0	3,550.0	3,760.0
Birth rate (per '000)	15.8	14.2	
Death rate (per '000)	7.4	6.8	
No. of households ('000)	803.6	761.6	784.6
Total exports (US$ million)	11.0	14.4	
Total imports (US$ million)	179.4	232.0	
Tourism receipts (US$ million)			
Tourist spending (US$ million)			

Average household size 1995 (persons)	4.43				
Urban population 1995 (%)	68.7				
Age analysis (%) (1991)	*0-14* 46.6		*15-64* 49.1		*65+* 4.3
Population by sex (%) (1989)	*Male* 49.0		*Female* 51.0		
Life expectancy (years) (1990)	*Male* 67.9		*Female* 73.4		
Infant mortality (deaths per '000 live births) (1993)	17.7				
Adult literacy (%) (1989)	98.8				

TRADING PARTNERS

Major export destinations 1995 (% share)		Major import sources 1995 (% share)	
Russia	47.2	Russia	56.8
Belgium/Luxembourg	23.6	USA	19.5
Canada	16.1	Germany	6.3
Germany	6.5	Belgium/Luxembourg	4.5

Aruba

Area (km²) 193

Currency Aruban guilder

Location Aruba is located in the Leeward Islands chain within the Caribbean Sea, about 70 km west of Curaçao, the capital island of the Netherlands Antilles and no more than 30 km north of the Venezuelan coast. The country enjoys a warm tropical climate, with relatively little susceptibility to hurricanes. The capital is Oranjestad.

Head of State HM Queen Beatrix (Netherlands)

Head of Government Hendrik Eman

Ruling Party The Aruban People's Party (Movimiento Electoral di Pueblo) forms a coalition with the Aruban Liberal Organisation (OLA).

Political Structure Aruba is an overseas territory of the Netherlands. It was formerly part of the Netherlands Antilles but became a separate political entity in January 1986 before achieving full independence in 1996.

Last Elections Elections to the 21-member Staten held in July 1994 led to an upset for the ruling Movimiento Electoral di Pueblo and the Accion Democratico Nacional, which won only a total of 9 seats, compared with 10 for the Arubaanse Volkspartij (AVP) and 2 for the OLS. The AVP and OLA went on to form a coalition.

Political Risk Aruba has one of the highest per capita incomes in the Caribbean region, thanks mainly to its oil activities. However, the island's delicate balance of political power remains a source of some concern. Local tensions have subsided as oil prices on world markets have improved.

International Disputes Relations with the Netherlands Antilles have been strained since Aruba became a separate entity within the Dutch empire. The Netherlands Antilles once derived considerable revenues from Aruba's tourism activity and its economy has suffered as a result of Aruba's new political status.

Economy Aruba's economy has had a difficult launch from the security of its once close relationship with the Netherlands. Having been forced to concentrate on tourism as its main line of development, Aruba requires major investment if this industry is to succeed in the competitive Caribbean environment. Meanwhile, the scope for developing the financial services sector has been reduced by bilateral tax evasion agreements involving the United States.

Main Industries The bulk of Aruba's income is derived from tourism, with large numbers of visitors from the Netherlands, the USA, Venezuela, Canada and other Caribbean countries. The climate is warm and dry, although there are no fresh water supplies and every litre has to be imported. The island's foreign-owned oil transhipment terminal, which once produced as much as a third of Aruba's total revenues, has been closed for over ten years. The government has been unable to secure a contract with regional suppliers of crude oil. Closure of the oil terminal also resulted in the loss of many ship-repairing facilities which provided another non-tourist source of income. With no significant areas of cultivable land (the terrain is mainly sandy and dry), the government is searching for other sources of income and employment; financial services are regarded as one possible alternative.

Energy Most of Aruba's energy requirements derive from the oil and gas industry with the bulk of supplies coming from other islands in the Netherlands Antilles group.

	1993	1994	1995
Inflation (% change)	5.2	6.3	3.4
Exchange rate (per US$)	1.79	1.79	1.79
Interest rate (% per annum)	10.6	10.6	10.6
GDP (% real growth)	3.0	-1.2	1.0
GDP (Million units of national currency)	1,140.6	1,197.6	1,250.7
GDP (US$ million)	637.2	669.5	698.2
GDP per capita (US$)	9,103.0	9,564.3	9,834.5
Consumption (Million units of national currency)	756.3	802.0	842.2
Consumption (US$ million)	422.5	448.3	470.2
Consumption per capita (US$)	6,035.9	6,404.9	6,622.7
Population, mid-year ('000)	70.0	70.0	71.0
Birth rate (per '000)	16.3	15.0	14.8
Death rate (per '000)	6.2	6.1	6.0
No. of households ('000)	15.6	16.1	16.5
Total exports (US$ million)	1,154.4	1,296.8	
Total imports (US$ million)	1,546.5	1,607.3	
Tourism receipts (US$ million)	464.0	468.4	515.8
Tourist spending (US$ million)	57.6	65.1	72.6

Average household size 1995 (persons)	4.13				
Urban population 1994 (%)	69.5				
Age analysis (%) (1981)	*0-14* 25.4		*15-64* 68.0		*65+* 6.6
Population by sex (%) (1981)	*Male* 48.6		*Female* 51.4		
Life expectancy (years) (1972-78)	*Male* 68.3		*Female* 74.4		
Infant mortality (deaths per '000 live births)					
Adult literacy (%)					

Australia

Area (km²)   7,682,300

Currency   Australian dollar (A$ = 100 cents)

Location   Some 3,680 km from its eastern tip to its western extreme, Australia is the world's second largest island. The country lies about 1,000 km from New Zealand, and about 500 km south of Indonesia. Thus its climate ranges from the sub-tropical in the north to the significantly colder regions of the south. The capital is Canberra.

Head of State   HM Queen Elizabeth II

Head of Government   John Howard (1996)

Ruling Party   Australian Liberal Party

Political Structure   Australia is a federation of six states and two territories (Northern Territory and Capital Territory of Canberra), each of which exercises considerable autonomy over its own affairs. The country's central affairs are run by a Cabinet which answers to a 148-member House of Representatives, elected for a term of three years, and an elected 76-member Senate with 12 seats drawn from the various parliaments of the states and territories. The question of Australia's status in the Commonwealth was a key issue when the Labor Party was in power. The new prime minister is a monarchist, although he has promised to set up a constitutional convention in 1997.

Last Elections   The Liberal Party was returned to power in March 1996 with a sufficient majority to rule in their own right, without support from the rural-based National Party with whom they had contested the election.

Political Risk   The Labor Party kept the country relatively strike-free during its reign. Trade unions say that the party's defeat will end their restraint. The new prime minister attaches much more importance to human rights than did the previous government and this stance could also be a source of some animosity.

International Disputes   Australia is in dispute with Papua New Guinea over certain unresolved matters concerning its extraction of gold and other minerals from Bougainville. It is also contesting a compensation claim by Nauru, in respect of allegations that it stripped that country of its phosphate reserves without making provision for any secondary economic activity there. If the government strengthens its stance on human rights, relations with Indonesia will be threatened owing to the latter's policies in East Timor.

Economy   The Australian economy enjoyed a mild recovery in late 1995 and early 1996. GDP was growing at around 5% at the beginning of 1996 and inflation, after shooting above 5% in late 1995, has eased again. The main difficulty continues to be the current-account deficit, which, at 4.5% of GDP, is one of the biggest among the industrialised countries. Unemployment also remains stubbornly high (8.7% in the first quarter of 1996) and the new government will be expected to act quickly or lose public support. Labour market reform will be a particular area of focus for the prime minister. Another will be a renewed effort to cut back on government regulations, especially in the transport industry (mainly road, ports and container handling) where Australia lags far behind in productivity.

Main Industries   Australia's large agricultural sector specialises in wheat and sheep rearing. Together, these two activities account for more than half of the country's export revenues. Other important cash crops are tropical and sub-tropical fruits such as bananas and pineapples. With vast amounts of natural resources, the country is a major producer of coal, bauxite, copper, iron ore, manganese, nickel, lead, uranium, limestone and gemstones; the health of the domestic economy is particular sensitive to movements in the world prices of these commodities. Development of the oil and gas industry has also been proceeding at a rapid pace in recent years. Manufacturing has moved away from the processing of agricultural and mineral raw materials but is subject to a maze of regulations, despite a long campaign to liberalise markets. The country nevertheless boasts a wide range of sophisticated engineering activities and is a large producer of motor vehicles for the domestic market.

Energy   Two-thirds of Australia's energy requirements are met with domestic supplies of coal (also a major export commodity). The remainder is largely derived from oil, some of which is domestically produced.

	1993	1994	1995
Inflation (% change)	1.8	1.9	4.6
Exchange rate (per US$)	1.47	1.37	1.35
Interest rate (% per annum)	10.5	11.0	15.0
GDP (% real growth)	3.4	4.5	0.4
GDP (Million units of national currency)	415,740.0	442,570.0	464,810.0
GDP (US$ million)	282,739.4	323,705.4	344,380.2
GDP per capita (US$)	16,013.4	18,146.5	19,079.2
Consumption (Million units of national currency)	263,433.0	272,588.0	282,946.0
Consumption (US$ million)	179,157.4	199,376.8	209,636.2
Consumption per capita (US$)	10,146.9	11,176.8	11,614.2
Population, mid-year ('000)	17,656.4	17,838.4	18,050.0
Birth rate (per '000)	14.7	14.5	14.2
Death rate (per '000)	6.9	7.1	6.9
No. of households ('000)	6,482.6	6,634.8	6,767.9
Total exports (US$ million)	42,723.0	47,538.0	53,067.0
Total imports (US$ million)	45,577.0	53,425.0	61,286.0
Tourism receipts (US$ million)	4,655.0	5,957.5	6,875.0
Tourist spending (US$ million)	4,100.0	4,731.2	5,362.4

Average household size 1995 (persons)	2.55				
Urban population 1995 (%)	85.0				
Age analysis (%) (1995)	*0-14* 22.1		*15-64* 67.5		*65+* 10.4
Population by sex (%) (1995)	*Male* 49.8		*Female* 50.2		
Life expectancy (years) (1990)	*Male* 73.9		*Female* 80.1		
Infant mortality (deaths per '000 live births) (1994)	5.9				
Adult literacy (%) (1995)	99.0				

TRADING PARTNERS

Major export destinations 1995 (% share)		Major import sources 1995 (% share)	
Japan	23.9	USA	21.1
South Korea	8.6	Japan	15.8
New Zealand	6.8	Germany	6.9
USA	6.5	United Kingdom	5.8

Austria

Area (km²)   83,855

Currency   Schilling (Sch = 100 groschen)

Location   Austria occupies a strategic position in the centre of Western Europe, bordering on Germany and the Czech and Slovak republics in the north, Italy and Slovenia in the south, and Switzerland in the west. Its position has contributed greatly to its role as a trade centre for dealings with East and Central Europe. The climate is temperate, but becomes very cold in winter because of the high altitude. The capital is Vienna.

Head of State   President Thomas Klestil (July 1992)

Head of Government   Franz Vranitzky (1986)

Ruling Party   Sozialdemokratische Partei Österreichs (SPÖ) leads a coalition with the centre-right Österreichische Volkspartei (ÖVP).

Political Structure   The Republic of Austria was formed only in 1955 following the end of the post-war administration by the Western allies. It consists of nine provinces which have little autonomy. The country has a non-executive President who is elected every six years by popular vote, and a bicameral Federal Assembly with a 183-member Nationalrat and a 63-member Bundesrat, or Upper House. Both bodies are elected for four years at a time. Austria became a full member of the EU in January 1995.

Last Elections   Austria's "Grand Coalition" nearly broke down in 1995, forcing a general election in November of that year. The ruling SPÖ made some gains in that election and the coalition with the ÖVP was restored. The country's right-wing Freedom Party (FPÖ) maintained its minority position in the Assembly while the Grüne Alternative lost several seats.

Political Risk   With its high standard of living, its stable political structure and its recent entry into the EU, Austria is a market with little political risk. Its central location within Europe and its vigorous trading links with the emerging markets of Eastern Europe mean that the probability of the current recession deepening is very low. However, Austria's post-war tradition of distributing jobs and favours among the two ruling parties will gradually be scrapped.

International Disputes   Occasional disagreements arise with the Italian authorities over the sovereignty of Trentino-Alto-Adige, a predominantly German-speaking part of Italy occupied by German and Austrian forces in the 1940s. Austria's insistence on levying a road tax on motor transport moving through its western provinces has caused a heated debate within the EU.

Economy   Austria's industries have historically been handicapped by the heavy overmanning which derived, in large part, from their ownership by the state. The country's large industrial concerns are now being privatised and a considerable contraction of the surplus workforce is likely. Austria's public deficit has soared in recent years as a result of generous pension programmes and other subsidies. The new government has taken several unpopular steps to reduce spending and bring the deficit in line with the EU's Maastricht requirements.

Main Industries   Austria's largest single industry is tourism, with foreign currency earnings from 15-20 million visitors every year contributing as much as 30% of the country's economy. The sector also employs a large proportion of the workforce. Tourism receipts dropped in 1995, however, owing to the high value of the schilling and the growth of competition from other destinations. Manufacturing, including sophisticated light and heavy engineering, is also vital to the economy, with producers of machine tools and automobile components being especially competitive in international markets. Farming, on the other hand, is declining in importance. Although the country has an ample rainfall and an equable summer climate, its production of fruit, wheat, potatoes and sugar beets is mainly intended to meet domestic needs. On the other hand, its wine, dairy products and pork products reach a wide international market.

Energy   Austria's electricity supply comes mainly from hydro-electricity, which is also one of its major exports. It does, however, still rely heavily on oil and gas (some obtained from the former Soviet Union) for its domestic and industrial heating.

	1993	1994	1995
Inflation (% change)	3.6	3.0	2.3
Exchange rate (per US$)	11.63	11.42	10.08
Interest rate (% per annum)	7.0	5.1	4.6
GDP (% real growth)	-0.6	-10.4	-0.5
GDP (Billion units of national currency)	2,117.8	1,954.9	1,990.6
GDP (US$ million)	182,098.0	171,152.2	197,468.4
GDP per capita (US$)	22,790.7	21,314.1	24,469.4
Consumption (Billion units of national currency)	1,168.3	1,234.8	1,264.4
Consumption (US$ million)	100,455.7	108,107.2	125,429.0
Consumption per capita (US$)	12,572.7	13,462.9	15,542.6
Population, mid-year ('000)	7,990.0	8,030.0	8,070.0
Birth rate (per '000)	11.8	11.5	11.0
Death rate (per '000)	10.3	10.1	10.0
No. of households ('000)	3,179.0	3,243.8	3,276.0
Total exports (US$ million)	40,174.0	45,215.0	
Total imports (US$ million)	48,578.0	55,343.0	
Tourism receipts (US$ million)	13,566.0	13,125.0	12,500.0
Tourist spending (US$ million)	8,180.0	8,914.3	8,987.0

Average household size 1995 (persons)	2.35				
Urban population 1995 (%)	55.5				
Age analysis (%) (1995)	*0-14* 17.4		*15-64* 67.2		*65+* 15.4
Population by sex (%) (1995)	*Male* 47.2		*Female* 52.8		
Life expectancy (years) (1994)	*Male* 73.3		*Female* 79.7		
Infant mortality (deaths per '000 live births) (1994)	6.1				
Adult literacy (%) (1995)	98.0				

TRADING PARTNERS

Major export destinations 1995 (% share)		Major import sources 1995 (% share)	
Germany	23.7	Germany	44.4
Italy	9.2	Italy	9.0
Switzerland	6.9	France	5.5
France	4.5	Switzerland	4.7

Azerbaijan

Area (km²)   86,600

Currency   Manat (M = 100 gopik). The rouble is still in use, but is gradually being phased out

Location   The Republic of Azerbaijan lies in the eastern Transcaucasian region, bordering the Caspian Sea from Grozny to Baku. It includes the autonomous provinces of Nagorny-Karabakh (mainly Armenian in character) and Nakhichevan, which was obtained from Iran recently. The capital is Baku.

Head of State   President Geidar Aliyev (June 1993)

Head of Government   Fuad Kuliyev (October 1994)

Ruling Party   Azerbaijani Popular Front/Khalqu Jibhasi

Political Structure   Azerbaijan was one of the last states to declare its independence from the Soviet Union. The move came in August 1991 and was later confirmed by a 99.6% vote in a referendum. Azerbaijan did, however, remain within the Commonwealth of Independent States. The country has an executive Presidency appointed by a 360-member Supreme Soviet which is in turn elected by popular vote. Aliyev crushed an attempted coup in March 1995 and extended a state of emergency imposed after a previous coup attempt in 1994. A full, multi-party system has yet to be created. In practice, Azerbaijan aligns itself more closely with Russia than do other countries in this volatile region.

Last Elections   The last full elections to the 360-member Azerbaijani Supreme Soviet took place in September/October 1990 when the ruling Communist Party (CP) won a convincing victory with more than 260 seats. Yet the opposition parties had been allowed to put up only 218 candidates against 921 for the CP. In the June 1992 elections to the Presidency, a 76% turnout returned Abulfez Elbichey with 59% of the vote. Elbichey was overthrown in June 1993 by a military-backed administration led by Col. Surat Guseinov, who thereupon installed the former communist, Geidar Aliyev, as President.

Political Risk   Political dissent in Azerbaijan is vigorous but is also severely punished. President Elbichey, the former leader of the Azerbaijani Popular Front, was abruptly removed from office in 1993 after angering Mr Aliyev with his anti-Russian policies. Aliyev, who has been steadily rebuilding ties to Moscow, is simultaneously trying to attract Turkish and Western investment. Violence and rebellion in the ethnically Armenian enclave of Nagorny-Karabakh and the Autonomous Region of Nakhichevan can always re-emerge, but has subsided for the time being. In April 1996, Azerbaijan entered into a Transcaucasus-EU Pact that also includes Armenia and Georgia and is intended to help stabilise this explosive region. The Pact offers trade concessions and access to certain EU loans in return for democratic and economic reforms.

International Disputes   Apart from the growing political dissent at home, Azerbaijan is locked in almost continuous dispute with Armenia over the issue of Nagorny-Karabakh and Nakhichevan, where political violence has erupted over Armenian demands for greater autonomy. Many thousands have been killed, including perhaps 15,000 Azeri troops. Over a million refugees have been created as a result of the insurrection. Several ceasefires have been negotiated but have failed to hold. Despite all these tensions, the country has launched a military co-operation pact with neighbouring Turkey.

Economy   Azerbaijan's president says he wants to build a "new Kuwait" on the shore of the Caspian Sea. It would help greatly if the country could just reverse its downward spiral; GDP fell by around 10% in 1995 after dropping by 22% in the previous year. Inflation is under control and the government has at last given its approval for a programme of privatisation. The country clearly has enough crude oil resources to improve its standard of living dramatically. But to put these resources to good use, it needs a peaceful, and lasting, solution to the problems in Nagorny-Karabakh.

Main Industries   Apart from electricity generation, which is based on the country's rich mineral deposits, Azerbaijan has a well-established steel and cement industry. However, production has been badly damaged since 1993 by the near-cessation of raw material supplies from other parts of the former Soviet Union. Some western management and investment is coming into the country as a part of various deals where state-owned plants are to be run by western interests. Much of Azerbaijan's aluminium industry is now operated in this manner. Agriculture is centred on the production of various crops (grain, cotton, tea, fruit and vegetables) and the rearing of livestock. Wine is also produced in many areas.

Energy   Azerbaijan is believed to have at least 70 billion barrels of oil and substantial deposits of natural gas. These resources are proving highly attractive for foreign investors from Turkey, Western Europe and Russia. After lengthy negotiations with Moscow, it has been agreed that two "early-oil" pipelines will carry oil from Azerbaijan's Caspian fields. One will go through southern Russia while the other goes through Georgia. If all proceeds according to schedule, the country should be producing 700,000 barrels of oil per day within 15 years. This would be worth about $4.2 billion a year at today's prices.

	1993	1994	1995
Inflation (% change)	287.8		
Exchange rate (per US$)	1.75	193.20	4,395.00
Interest rate			
GDP (% real growth)	-23.0	-21.0	-10.0
GDP (Million units of national currency)	6,325,198.4	4,933,654.8	4,089,999.9
GDP (US$ million)	23,426.7	25,536.5	23,075.2
GDP per capita (US$)	3,174.3	3,418.5	3,076.7
Consumption (Million units of national currency)	4,216,799.0	3,319,079.4	2,889,123.4
Consumption (US$ million)	15,617.8	17,179.5	16,300.0
Consumption per capita (US$)	2,116.2	2,299.8	2,173.3
Population, mid-year ('000)	7,380.0	7,470.0	7,500.0
Birth rate (per '000)	25.9	23.0	
Death rate (per '000)		6.6	
No. of households ('000)	1,462.6	1,467.9	1,512.7
Total exports (US$ million)	70.7	101.6	
Total imports (US$ million)	199.0	220.0	
Tourism receipts (US$ million)			
Tourist spending (US$ million)			

Average household size 1995 (persons)	4.83		
Urban population 1995 (%)	7.0		
Age analysis (%) (1991)	*0-14* 48.6	*15-64* 47.1	*65+* 4.3
Population by sex (%) (1989)	*Male* 48.8	*Female* 51.2	
Life expectancy (years) (1989)	*Male* 66.6	*Female* 74.2	
Infant mortality (deaths per '000 live births)			
Adult literacy (%) (1989)	97.3		

TRADING PARTNERS

Major export destinations 1995 (% share)		Major import sources 1995 (% share)	
Iran	43.6	Turkmenistan	29.9
Russia	13.0	Ukraine	13.2
Ukraine	11.6	Iran	10.2
Turkmenistan	3.4	Russia	8.6

Bahamas

Area (km²)   13,865

Currency   Bahamian dollar (B$ = 100 cents)

Location   The Bahamas are made up of some 700 islands in the Atlantic Ocean, of which 30 are inhabited. They extend from just off the coast of Florida (USA) to within a short distance of Cuba and Haiti. The capital is Nassau.

Head of State   HM Queen Elizabeth II

Head of Government   Hubert Ingraham

Ruling Party   Free National Movement

Political Structure   The Bahamas are an independent member of the British Commonwealth with a British-appointed Governor-General who exercises only nominal powers. The Prime Minister and his Cabinet are answerable to a 49-member House of Assembly (Lower House of Parliament) and to a 16-member Senate. Elections to the House of Assembly are normally held every five years while members of the Senate are appointed.

Last Elections   General elections were held in August 1992 when Lynden Pindling and his Progressive Liberal Party (PLP) were defeated after four terms in office. The Free National Movement (FNM) achieved a clear victory, taking 33 of the 49 seats in the House of Assembly. Hubert Ingraham of the FNM went on to form a new government.

Political Risk   Ingraham's landslide victory for the FNM marks the culmination of a rising discontent with the discredited administration of Sir Lynden Pindling, in which a worsening economic situation was exacerbated by allegations of corruption. In recent years, much official attention has focused on the rising rate of violent crime.

International Disputes   Relations with Haiti have been repeatedly strained owing to the large number of Haitian refugees that arrived in the Bahamas during 1993-1995. The threat of illegal Haitian refugees has lessened now that conditions in their country have improved.

Economy   The economy of the Bahamas has begun to recover from the recession which prompted the change in government in 1992. The resumption of growth owes much to the stronger US economy which has brought a return of high-spending visitors. The financial sector is also performing well and the island's 400 offshore banks now control over $300 billion in banking deposits. The Bahamas continues to maintain its status as a tax haven, with no corporate, personal income, capital gains, withholding, inheritance or estate taxes. Banking secrecy is preserved as there are no tax information exchange agreements with other countries.

Main Industries   Two-thirds of the country's income has traditionally derived from tourism, a sector which also finances the development of most of the Bahamas' infrastructure, produces the bulk of the government's revenue and generates half of all foreign exchange. The majority of visitors come from the USA or Canada but the island's tourist agency is increasingly targeting Europeans. An equally important source of income is the island's financial services sector, which benefits from an almost total absence of taxation. Tight banking secrecy laws have recently been diluted as a result of US pressure, but the banking sector continues to attract considerable foreign capital nevertheless. Farming caters mainly to the domestic market. Limestone and salt are mined for export, and there are pharmaceuticals and chemicals manufacturing plants in the capital of Freeport. Oil transhipment and bunkering operations are conducted in the harbour.

Energy   Most of the country's energy needs are met by imports of oil and gas, or by natural materials such as firewood. All electricity generation is derived from thermal plants.

	1993	1994	1995
Inflation (% change)	2.7	1.4	2.0
Exchange rate (per US$)	1.00	1.00	1.00
Interest rate (% per annum)	7.5	6.9	6.8
GDP (% real growth)	-1.7	0.0	1.5
GDP (Million units of national currency)	2,460.9	2,495.4	2,583.5
GDP (US$ million)	2,460.9	2,495.4	2,583.5
GDP per capita (US$)	9,114.4	9,242.2	9,533.2
Consumption (Million units of national currency)	2,054.3	2,072.8	2,122.1
Consumption (US$ million)	2,054.3	2,072.8	2,122.1
Consumption per capita (US$)	7,608.5	7,677.0	7,830.6
Population, mid-year ('000)	270.0	270.0	271.0
Birth rate (per '000)	19.4	18.9	
Death rate (per '000)	4.9	5.4	
No. of households ('000)	52.9	53.6	55.7
Total exports (US$ million)	498.9	764.0	
Total imports (US$ million)	1,372.6	1,770.8	
Tourism receipts (US$ million)	1,304.0	1,332.4	1,415.0
Tourist spending (US$ million)	195.0	199.2	203.9

Average household size 1995 (persons)	4.79				
Urban population 1996 (%)	86.5				
Age analysis (%) (1992)	*0-14* 32.2		*15-64* 63.1		*65+* 4.7
Population by sex (%) (1992)	*Male* 48.8		*Female* 51.2		
Life expectancy (years) (1985)	*Male* 68.2		*Female* 74.5		
Infant mortality (deaths per '000 live births) (1992)	24.0				
Adult literacy (%)					

TRADING PARTNERS

Major export destinations 1995 (% share)		Major import sources 1995 (% share)	
USA	21.9	USA	32.1
Spain	14.3	Denmark	10.5
Greece	9.5	Iran	9.6
Norway	8.4	Spain	7.0

Bahrain

Area (km²)   661

Currency   Bahraini dinar (BD = 1000 fils)

Location   Bahrain is made up of a group of islands located in the midst of the Gulf, about 24 km off the eastern coast of Saudi Arabia. The main urban centre is on Bahrain island, but the country's airport is located on the island of Muharraq. The capital is Manama.

Head of State   HH Shaikh Isa bin Sulman Al Khalifa

Head of Government   HE Shaikh Khalifa bin Sulman Al Khalifa

Ruling Party   There are no political parties in Bahrain.

Political Structure   Bahrain is an absolute monarchy in which traditional consultative procedures, involving senior figures in the tribal hierarchy, are preferred to a formal parliamentary system. In addition, a 30-member Consultative Council was established and met for the first time in 1993. The Council, which has only limited powers, is headed by the Transport Minister Ibrahim Mohammed Humaidan, and charged with handling certain political matters. Sunni families rule the country, although a majority of the population are Shiites who feel politically and economically disenfranchised.

Last Elections   Theoretically, Bahrain's 1973 Constitution provides for a 30-member National Assembly elected by popular mandate. However, there have been no elections in Bahrain since the Assembly was forcibly dissolved in 1975, allegedly for interfering with the system of government. The possibility of restoring a multi-party system remains under discussion but is unlikely, given the rising degree of violence and political turmoil in the country.

Political Risk   Bahrain has long been an area of political calm but that began to change in 1995 and 1996. Street protests and sabotage have surged across the island state. The government responded by releasing from jail its most prominent protestor and a former member of Parliament, Sheikh Abdel Amir Jamri. The Sheikh was released on the understanding that he would counsel restraint among his followers. His efforts failed, however, and when opposition rallies started drawing crowds of up to 50,000, he was again arrested in January 1996. Foreigners are now being singled out for attacks and bombings. Alarmed at the threat to its economy, the government has largely abandoned talk of dialogue, and the Defence Ministry has threatened to impose martial law. These events assume an international significance since more than 40% of the world's exported oil is shipped from the Gulf and Bahrain is the administrative headquarters for the US Navy's Fifth Fleet.

International Disputes   The whole territory of Bahrain is technically claimed by Iran, although that claim has not been formally stated since 1979. The government of Bahrain asserts that Iran is tacitly supporting and encouraging the internal disturbances, though the Iranians vehemently deny this. Qatar lays claim to the Hawar Islands, which are situated only about two kilometres from the Qatari coast but are governed by Bahrain. The issue here concerns exploration rights for offshore gas and oil. The matter was referred to the International Court of Justice in July 1994 and should eventually be resolved peaceably.

Economy   Bahrain's economy has been broadening in scope since the early 1980s, when the original decision was taken to move away from the country's heavy dependence on oil activities. In the process, the government has issued an open appeal for foreign investment, a trend which is rarely seen in the Arab Middle East. That policy has not been effective and its failure is partly responsible for the unrest which exists today. Originally, the Sunni rulers used their abundant oil revenues to modernise the economy and create a generous welfare state. But a combination of falling oil prices and fast population growth has forced them to rein in these benefits. Unemployment, which is concentrated among the rural Shiites, was estimated to up to 30% in mid-1996.

Main Industries   Bahrain's principal activity revolves, inevitably, around oil production from its own fields and from the processing of other countries' oil at its Sipra refinery. However, it is actively developing a heavy industrial base which includes metal smelting and metal products manufacturing. Agriculture is of marginal importance, although there are fishing industries and pearl culture. Of more interest has been the country's banking and financial services industry, which has periodically aroused the indignation of its strongest supporter, Saudi Arabia. However, Bahrain's attempt to attract international banks with tax-haven facilities appears likely to continue.

Energy   Virtually all of Bahrain's energy requirements, including the prodigious costs of running its desalination plants, are met from indigenous supplies of petroleum.

	1993	1994	1995
Inflation (% change)	2.5	8.0	
Exchange rate (per US$)	0.38	0.38	0.38
Interest rate (% per annum)	11.0	10.8	
GDP (% real growth)	4.0	-3.2	
GDP (Million units of national currency)	1,747.6	1,826.2	1,908.3
GDP (US$ million)	4,598.9	4,805.8	5,021.9
GDP per capita (US$)	8,516.6	8,581.8	8,511.8
Consumption (Million units of national currency)	582.0	635.6	669.7
Consumption (US$ million)	1,531.6	1,672.6	1,762.2
Consumption per capita (US$)	2,836.3	2,986.8	2,986.8
Population, mid-year ('000)	540.0	560.0	590.0
Birth rate (per '000)	30.2	24.7	
Death rate (per '000)	4.0	3.0	
No. of households ('000)	136.3	142.0	152.6
Total exports (US$ million)	3,710.0	3,454.0	3,930.0
Total imports (US$ million)	3,858.0	3,737.0	3,501.0
Tourism receipts (US$ million)			
Tourist spending (US$ million)	152.0	164.5	173.3

Average household size 1995 (persons)	3.75				
Urban population 1995 (%)	90.3				
Age analysis (%) (1991)	*0-14* 31.7		*15-64* 66.1		*65+* 2.2
Population by sex (%) (1991)	*Male* 57.9		*Female* 42.1		
Life expectancy (years) (1986-91)	*Male* 66.8		*Female* 69.4		
Infant mortality (deaths per '000 live births) (1994)	18.0				
Adult literacy (%) (1991)	84.1				

TRADING PARTNERS

Major export destinations 1995 (% share)		Major import sources 1995 (% share)	
India	17.2	Saudi Arabia	46.6
Japan	9.6	USA	7.2
South Korea	5.4	United Kingdom	6.9
Saudi Arabia	4.4	Germany	4.4

Bangladesh

Area (km²) 144,000

Currency Taka (= 100 poisha)

Location Bangladesh is a low-lying and densely populated territory lying in the Bay of Bengal between India and Myanmar. The country occupies most of the delta of the river Ganges, and has a tropical and humid climate. The capital is Dhaka.

Head of State President Abdurrahman Biswas (1991)

Head of Government Sheikh Hasina Wazed

Ruling Party Awami League leads a coalition with the Jatiya Dal.

Political Structure Bangladesh is an independent member of the Commonwealth, with an executive President. Mohammed Ershad, who seized power in 1982, declared himself President for life but was deposed in 1990 after allegations of corruption, and a system of election by popular mandate was brought in. Legislative authority rests in the 330-seat Jatiya Sangsad (Parliament), 300 of whose members are elected. It is worth noting that Bangladeshi politics are highly susceptible to party switching, and that strong volatility results.

Last Elections The legitimacy of the general elections in February 1996 was strongly questioned when the government was returned on an extremely low ballot (probably no more than 15%) amidst allegations of vote-rigging. Prior to the election, the opposition Awami League had campaigned in the streets demanding that a neutral interim government be temporarily installed to oversee the ballot. The eventual result was a second nationwide ballot held in June 1996 under the watchful eyes of a neutral caretaker administration. Although neither of the main parties won a majority, Sheikh Hasina Wazed of the Awami League was likely to emerge as the new prime minister with the support of the Jatiya Dal, the party which finished third in the latest poll.

Political Risk Many observers expected the army to step in when the results of the February 1996 election came under suspicion. Such a scenario has been played out repeatedly in the years since Bangladesh attained independence in 1971. Yet in this instance the army refrained. The country's extreme poverty nevertheless remains a potential source of conflict which often takes the form of local insurrection. Such problems arose in the spring of 1995, when political activists launched an anti-government protest campaign, and similar disruptions occurred after the February 1996 ballot.

International Disputes Bangladesh is in conflict with India over the ownership of a island which was formed in the Hariabhanga Delta by a cyclone and tidal wave in 1970. It has also faced hostility from Myanmar, over its acceptance of thousands of Myanmar refugees, but a repatriation agreement between the two countries was signed in 1992. Meanwhile, relations with France have been soured by that country's sheltering of the dissident writer Taslima Nasreem, who fled Bangladesh after threats to her life.

Economy Although it is still one of the dozen poorest countries in the world, Bangladesh has prospered in recent years. By deregulating trade and industry, the government has enabled business to push growth to nearly 5% per annum in recent years. This achievement stands in marked contrast to the earlier record when the country barely maintained average earnings at the subsistence level. Meanwhile, the Government has stuck by an unpopular round of austerity measures, including major tax increases and deep cuts in public spending.

Main Industries Bangladesh's single biggest activity is the production of raw jute, for which it is the world's largest supplier. The country is also a significant grower of tea, rice, cotton and sugar cane. Fishing is an important source of protein. The majority of the country's industries revolve around the processing of these raw materials but manufacturing activity also includes petroleum refining, cement manufacture and pharmaceuticals. The clothing industry has grown from almost nothing to a business employing 1 million people and accounting for more than 60% of the country's exports. There are some oil and gas resources, but in general the country's flat landscape confirms the expectation that there are few other minerals to be found.

Energy Bangladesh's extremely modest energy needs are mainly satisfied from natural gas deposits from within its own river delta. Thermal plants supply all but about 12% of its electricity requirements, the remainder being obtained from hydro-electric schemes.

	1993	1994	1995
Inflation (% change)	3.0	5.3	1.0
Exchange rate (per US$)	39.57	40.21	39.92
Interest rate (% per annum)	15.0	14.4	14.0
GDP (% real growth)	0.6	3.2	4.5
GDP (Million units of national currency)	947,900.0	1,030,360.0	1,119,993.4
GDP (US$ million)	23,955.0	25,624.5	28,055.9
GDP per capita (US$)	207.9	217.5	233.2
Consumption (Million units of national currency)	584,336.6	638,313.3	653,745.5
Consumption (US$ million)	14,767.2	15,874.5	16,376.4
Consumption per capita (US$)	128.2	134.8	136.1
Population, mid-year ('000)	115,200.0	117,790.0	120,311.0
Birth rate (per '000)	39.5	35.0	
Death rate (per '000)	15.0	13.7	
No. of households ('000)	20,612.9	21,161.5	22,236.7
Total exports (US$ million)	2,272.0	2,661.0	3,174.0
Total imports (US$ million)	4,001.0	4,701.0	6,496.0
Tourism receipts (US$ million)	15.0	16.3	
Tourist spending (US$ million)	153.0	166.1	171.4

Average household size 1995 (persons)	5.29		
Urban population 1995 (%)	18.3		
Age analysis (%) (1990)	*0-14* 43.8	*15-64* 46.3	*65+* 10.0
Population by sex (%) (1990)	*Male* 51.6	*Female* 48.4	
Life expectancy (years) (1990)	*Male* 52.1	*Female* 51.5	
Infant mortality (deaths per '000 live births) (1993)	107.8		
Adult literacy (%) (1990)	35.3		

TRADING PARTNERS

Major export destinations 1995 (% share)		Major import sources 1995 (% share)	
USA	34.5	China	9.8
Germany	8.7	South Korea	9.3
United Kingdom	8.6	India	9.1
Italy	6.4	Hong Kong	8.5

Barbados

Area (km²) 430

Currency Barbados dollar (BD$ = 100 cents)

Location Barbados, the most easterly of the Caribbean islands, is some 30 km long and 20 km wide. With its pleasant climate (subject to occasional storms in the autumn months), it has proved popular as a tourist venue. The capital is Bridgetown.

Head of State HM Queen Elizabeth II

Head of Government Hon. Owen Arthur (September 1994)

Ruling Party Barbados Labour Party

Political Structure Barbados, an independent member of the Commonwealth, has a 28-seat House of Assembly whose members are elected by universal suffrage for a term of five years, and a 21-member Senate. The sovereign, Queen Elizabeth II, is represented by a Governor-General, who appoints the Prime Minister on the advice of Parliament.

Last Elections General elections to the House of Assembly were held in September 1994, when the Barbados Labour Party (BLP) of Owen Arthur defeated the Democratic Labour Party (DLP) of L. Erskine Sandiford, which had ruled since 1984. The BLP won 19 of the seats in the House of Assembly, against only nine for the outgoing DLP. The National Democratic Party, a DLP splinter group, failed to win any seats.

Political Risk Owen Arthur's victory reflects a long-term deterioration in support for his predecessor, Erskine Sandiford, as well as a high degree of factional infighting within the DLP itself since the death of its charismatic leader Errol Barrow. Tempers rise during economic downturns - which are usually the result of a slump in tourism revenues. Nevertheless, Barbados remains a low political risk.

Economy Unemployment (currently over 20%) is a major drag on economic growth. The island also depends heavily on expatriate remittances which decline whenever the US economy is in recession. The rate of growth, which was negligible for several years, rose to about 1.5% in 1994. Assistance from the IMF and World Bank should help to improve the economy's performance in the future. The government has now introduced a value-added tax which will also help it to fund spending on development projects and infrastructure.

Main Industries Barbados relies very heavily on its tourist industry to provide both employment and foreign exchange. Tourism suffered in 1993-1994 owing to a decline in numbers of visitors from the United States and Europe but has recovered in the period since then. Most industrial production centres on the processing of raw materials such as sugar cane or crude oil. However, the sector also includes rum distillers, chemicals, electronic goods, clothing and various assembly processes that are operated in collaboration with US firms.

Energy Barbados depends on imports of oil for most its energy needs but also trades in this commodity. Electricity is supplied exclusively by thermal power stations, although the exploitation of potential geothermal sources is currently under consideration.

	1993	1994	1995
Inflation (% change)	1.1	0.1	1.9
Exchange rate (per US$)	2.01	2.01	2.01
Interest rate (% per annum)	8.9	9.1	10.0
GDP (% real growth)	0.2	1.5	1.5
GDP (Million units of national currency)	3,301.0	3,477.0	3,662.4
GDP (US$ million)	1,642.3	1,729.9	1,822.1
GDP per capita (US$)	6,316.5	6,730.9	7,116.7
Consumption (Million units of national currency)	2,019.0	2,072.5	2,103.9
Consumption (US$ million)	1,004.5	1,031.1	1,046.7
Consumption per capita (US$)	3,863.4	4,012.0	4,088.3
Population, mid-year ('000)	260.0	257.0	256.0
Birth rate (per '000)	16.4	15.6	13.1
Death rate (per '000)	8.6	8.4	9.4
No. of households ('000)	53.6	53.3	54.5
Total exports (US$ million)	179.0	185.0	235.0
Total imports (US$ million)	574.0	611.0	763.0
Tourism receipts (US$ million)	502.0	522.8	
Tourist spending (US$ million)	44.5	46.3	47.0

Average household size 1995 (persons)	4.58		
Urban population 1995 (%)	47.4		
Age analysis (%) (1992)	*0-14* 25.1	*15-64* 63.6	*65+* 11.4
Population by sex (%) (1992)	*Male* 47.8	*Female* 52.2	
Life expectancy (years) (1985-90)	*Male* 71.9	*Female* 76.9	
Infant mortality (deaths per '000 live births) (1992)	9.1		
Adult literacy (%) (1970)	99.3		

TRADING PARTNERS

Major export destinations 1995 (% share)		Major import sources 1995 (% share)	
USA	22.4	USA	30.0
United Kingdom	18.7	United Kingdom	27.7
Trinidad and Tobago	11.4	Trinidad and Tobago	14.0
Jamaica	7.4	Japan	4.7

Belarus

Area (km²)   207,595

Currency   Ruble

Location   Belarus (Byelorussia, or White Russia), lies in the far west of the former Soviet Union. It borders on Poland in the west, Lithuania and Latvia in the north and Ukraine in the south. The country is a large and not always well-drained plain that is served by several major rivers, including the Pripyat, which forms the upper reaches of the Dnepr. The capital is Minsk.

Head of State   President Aleksandr Lukaschenko (July 1994)

Head of Government   Mikhas Chigir (July 1994)

Ruling Party   Belarus Social Democratic Party leads a coalition.

Political Structure   Belarus declared its independence from the old USSR in August 1990. The republic has a non-executive President who is directly elected by universal suffrage for a term of five years. The 1994 Constitution created a 260-member Parliament that is responsible for all legislative affairs. Since independence, the public has favoured closer ties with Russia and in 1996 Belarus signed two integration agreements with Moscow. The first is modelled on the previous Commonwealth of Independent States and includes Kazakhstan and Kyrgyzstan but the second is a much deeper integration accord which binds Belarus to Russia. Under the latest treaty, the two countries would stay independent but Lukaschenko does not shy away from calling for an outright confederation.

Last Elections   Lukaschenko's reformist administration received a majority of the votes cast in the presidential elections of 1994. Legislative elections held in March and May 1995 failed to produce a workable result because of a rule that all elected deputies needed at least 50% of the votes in their various constituencies and that a minimum turnout of 50% was necessary. As a result, only 102 of the 260 seats were actually filled, most of them won by communists.

Political Risk   Belarus is returning to Soviet-era authoritarian practices. The president is strongly committed to a command economy. He expects Russia's industrial and manufacturing giants to revive the commercial activities that gave his country the highest living standards in the former Soviet Union. That strategy is probably out of date, since a number of these concerns have been privatised and unwilling to turn the clock back. Many observers predict that the latest treaty signed with Moscow will flounder once the Russian authorities begin to calculate the costs of absorbing their impoverished neighbour.

Economy   Belarus' economy is predominantly agricultural and many of its industries depend mainly on imports for their raw materials and intermediate supplies. For example, 90% of the republic's raw materials are imported from Russia, a situation which has given rise to some difficulties in recent years. Inflation and unemployment are other serious problems which go unchecked. In March 1996, the government passed a new budget with a fiscal deficit of 6% which will be impossible to finance without a large jump in inflation. The 1996 treaty with Russia promises no improvement. It envisages that a common monetary and fiscal policy will be in place by the end of 1997, when negotiations on a common currency would begin. Belarus and Russia would each contribute 3% of their annual budgets to a single fund to finance new capital and military projects.

Main Industries   Belarus' main industries are engineering, machine tools, agricultural equipment, chemicals, motor vehicles and some consumer durables such as watches, televisions and radios. Forestry and agriculture, notably potatoes, grain, peat and cattle, are also important.

Energy   Belarus has no significant energy sources of its own, except for peat, and is almost wholly reliant on imports. It buys cheap energy from Russia which has slowly been raising subsidised gas export prices.

	1993	1994	1995
Inflation (% change)	1,500.0	131.2	
Exchange rate (per US$)	5,710.00	15,076.00	
Interest rate			
GDP (% real growth)	-12.0	-20.0	-12.0
GDP (Billion units of national currency)	33,407.6		
GDP (US$ million)	10,360.0	10,350.0	9,108.0
GDP per capita (US$)	1,000.0	1,000.0	880.4
Consumption			
Consumption (US$ million)	4,972.0	4,927.0	4,435.0
Consumption per capita (US$)	479.9	476.0	428.7
Population, mid-year ('000)	10,360.0	10,350.0	10,345.0
Birth rate (per '000)		10.7	
Death rate (per '000)	11.5	12.5	
No. of households ('000)	3,037.1	3,049.3	3,135.7
Total exports (US$ million)	682.6	1,072.4	
Total imports (US$ million)	1,277.8	1,839.6	
Tourism receipts (US$ million)			
Tourist spending (US$ million)			

Average household size 1995 (persons)	3.22		
Urban population 1995 (%)	71.2		
Age analysis (%) (1995)	*0-14* 23.1	*15-64* 66.5	*65+* 10.4
Population by sex (%) (1995)	*Male* 46.8	*Female* 53.2	
Life expectancy (years) (1991)	*Male* 66.3	*Female* 75.6	
Infant mortality (deaths per '000 live births) (1992)	12.4		
Adult literacy (%) (1989)	97.9		

TRADING PARTNERS

Major export destinations 1995 (% share)		Major import sources 1995 (% share)	
Russia	63.4	Russia	69.8
Germany	10.9	Germany	11.6
Poland	4.9	Lithuania	4.6
Lithuania	4.5	Poland	2.8

Belgium

Area (km²) 30,520

Currency Belgian franc (BF = 100 centimes)

Location Belgium lies on the north-western coast of continental Europe, facing the North Sea some distance north of the English Channel. The land is largely flat and low-lying, although there are some mineral-bearing hills to the east. Belgium's excellent road and rail communications make it an obvious choice for the administrative centre of the European Union. The climate is moderate with mild winters. The capital is Brussels.

Head of State HM King Albert II (1993)

Head of Government Jean-Luc deHaene (1992)

Ruling Party Christian Democratic Party leads a broad-based coalition with the Socialist Party.

Political Structure The early 1990s have brought changes in the Belgian system which have not been widely recognised outside the country. The country's political system has been amended to reflect ethnic divisions between Dutch-speaking Flanders and French-speaking Wallonia, each of which has its own parliament. Brussels, which is 80% French-speaking, also has its own assembly. Most political parties exist as separate French and Dutch-speaking divisions. Belgium is a constitutional monarchy in which the monarch has often been required to mediate and to propose governments. There is a 160-seat Chamber of Representatives, normally elected for four years, and a 184-member Senate.

Last Elections General elections were held in May 1995, when both the traditional parties once again lost ground to the far-right Flemish Vlaams Blok and the environmentalist Ecolo. The two Christian Democrat parties secured only 49 of the 160 seats in the Chamber of Representatives, while the two socialist parties won 41 seats and the two liberal parties won 49 seats. Ecolo and Agalev, the two main "green" parties, won 12 seats, and various regional groups took the remaining seats.

Political Risk Belgium's centre-left coalition has repeatedly vowed that the country will be among the first to meet the Maastricht criteria and adopt the Euro. To achieve that goal, the government has had to impose a series of very harsh austerity measures - some of them in force for over three years. The result (apart from recession) is growing signs of unrest. Sporadic strikes, protests over education cuts, failed businesses and disputes between French and Flemish speakers are evidence that the country's integrationist ambitions are taking a heavy toll on the economy. Dissatisfaction with deHaene's policies and the EU in general will mount without some quick improvement in the economy's performance.

International Disputes In a sense, Belgium's entire history has been one continuous dispute. Intense rivalries between Dutch and French speakers have periodically broken out into inter-communal violence, although both France and the Netherlands have been careful not to get involved.

Economy Belgium's GDP shrank during 1995 but since then the economy has shown signs of stabilising. Rates of unemployment are uncomfortably high (at least 14.5% in March 1996) and any hopes for a significant improvement in the near future are dim. Analysts calculate that the economy would have to grow by around 2.2% a year in order to reduce the number of jobless. This rate is far above the most optimistic forecasts for 1996. Aside from the reductions in spending and tight fiscal policy needed to achieve the Maastricht criteria, the country has been hurt by the strength of the Belgian franc. Exports, which represent about two-thirds of all production, are crucial. Unfortunately, Belgium competes directly with Italy in important areas such as textiles, metal-working and furniture and has lost export markets as result of the lira's devaluation.

Main Industries Belgium's industrial heartland lies in the south and east of the country, where a predominantly French-speaking population once operated a massive coal mining and steel manufacturing industry. These industries have been steadily contracting since the cemented1980s, leaving behind large pockets of unemployment in the surrounding regions. Farming has proved to be much more reliable as a source of income, with potatoes, sugar beet, wheat, barley, dairy cattle and pig production all being profitable. A large proportion of the country's industry and its exports of manufactures are focused on raw materials and processed goods and this fact may be working to Belgium's disadvantage during the present European recession. These types of industries perform well around the peak of an economic cycle but demand drops off early in a slowdown as downstream industries reduce stocks.

Energy Belgium's consumption of nuclear energy is among the highest in Europe, accounting for almost a tenth of all primary use. This is about the same as solid fuels, in which the country once specialised. Crude oil still accounts for almost half of the total energy consumption.

	1993	1994	1995
Inflation (% change)	2.8	2.4	1.5
Exchange rate (per US$)	34.60	33.46	29.48
Interest rate (% per annum)	11.8	9.4	8.4
GDP (% real growth)	-0.2	2.2	-0.5
GDP (Billion units of national currency)	7,285.0	7,621.0	7,697.0
GDP (US$ million)	210,549.1	227,764.5	261,092.3
GDP per capita (US$)	20,887.8	22,595.7	25,541.4
Consumption (Billion units of national currency)	4,514.3	4,722.2	4,932.1
Consumption (US$ million)	130,471.1	141,129.7	167,303.3
Consumption per capita (US$)	12,943.6	14,001.0	16,366.5
Population, mid-year ('000)	10,080.0	10,080.0	10,222.3
Birth rate (per '000)	12.1	11.7	11.6
Death rate (per '000)	10.6	10.4	10.2
No. of households ('000)	3,724.3	3,739.4	3,754.0
Total exports (US$ million)	121,400.0	95,120.0	
Total imports (US$ million)	123,232.0	124,660.0	
Tourism receipts (US$ million)	4,071.0	5,182.6	5,250.0
Tourist spending (US$ million)	6,363.0	6,914.4	8,196.7

Average household size 1995 (persons)	2.56				
Urban population 1995 (%)	97.0				
Age analysis (%) (1992)	*0-14* 18.1		*15-64* 66.7		*65+* 15.1
Population by sex (%) (1995)	*Male* 49.2		*Female* 50.8		
Life expectancy (years) (1993)	*Male* 73.0		*Female* 79.8		
Infant mortality (deaths per '000 live births) (1993)	8.0				
Adult literacy (%) (1983)	98.0				

TRADING PARTNERS

Major export destinations 1995 (% share)		Major import sources 1995 (% share)	
Germany	20.7	Germany	22.6
France	17.4	France	15.8
Netherlands	10.5	Netherlands	13.1
United Kingdom	8.4	USA	8.6

Belize

Area (km²) 22,965

Currency Belize dollar (BZ$ = 100 cents)

Location Belize lies on the Caribbean coast of Central America, bounded in the north by Mexico and in the south and west by Guatemala. The coastal areas are mainly swamp, although inland they rise to meet the Maya mountain range. The country has a sub-tropical climate and is subject to hurricanes in the autumn months. The capital is Belmopan.

Head of State HM Queen Elizabeth II

Head of Government Manuel Esquivel (June 1993)

Ruling Party United Democratic Party

Political Structure Belize, an independent member of the Commonwealth since 1981, has a bicameral National Assembly. The country's 28-member House of Representatives is elected by popular vote for a five-year term, while its eight-member Senate is appointed by the Governor-General. In 1991, Belize opened formal diplomatic relations with Guatemala, which had long maintained a claim on the whole territory of Belize. The possibility of political union with Dominica, St Lucia and St Vincent and the Grenadines has also been discussed.

Last Elections Snap elections to the House of Representatives were called in June 1993 by the incumbent Prime Minister, George Price. The outcome was an unexpected defeat for Price and his People's United Party (PUP) at the hands of the United Democratic Party, which obtained 16 seats compared with the PUP's 12. Manuel Esquivel, leader of the UDP, subsequently replaced Price as Prime Minister.

Political Risk The delicate political balance in the country is some cause for concern. In practice, much is likely to depend on the health of the country's economy - particularly, its success in exporting agricultural products to the EU.

International Disputes Doubts about Belize's future linger following a renewed claim by the new Guatemala government to the sovereignty of the entire territory, which is still regarded in Guatemala's 1945 Constitution as its 23rd department. Guatemala, however, is unlikely to press hard on this matter since it could alienate some international donors.

Economy Belize remains one of the poorer countries in the Caribbean region, offering only a limited prospects as a consumer market. Government spending is over budget, and efforts to trim it back exert serious pressures on the economy. Policy-makers hope (perhaps optimistically) that warmer relations with the USA will bring additional aid.

Main Industries Belize depends heavily on its agricultural sector which employs over 40% of the workforce. Maize, rice, root vegetables, sugar beet and fruit are the major products, while bananas, citrus fruits and sugar cane are grown for export. Fishery products, especially lobsters and conches, are sold in the USA. Industry is generally being held back by a shortage of imported inputs, although the gradual development of a tourist industry is creating new opportunities. There is no railway system, a factor which has also slowed development.

Energy Belize derives almost all its energy requirements from imports of oil and natural gas, a process which has become easier in recent years as tensions with Guatemala have eased and with the completion of its own deep-water quays at Belize City. All of the country's electricity is derived from thermal power plants. Oil companies continue to search for offshore oil and gas. Since the 1960s, 13 wells have been drilled in and around the former British colony, all without success. In April 1996, a new consortium announced plans to spend $6 million on another exploratory offshore well.

	1993	1994	1995
Inflation (% change)	1.4	2.6	2.9
Exchange rate (per US$)	2.00	2.00	2.00
Interest rate (% per annum)	14.4	14.8	15.7
GDP (% real growth)	7.6	2.6	2.0
GDP (Million units of national currency)	1,049.2	1,104.6	1,159.4
GDP (US$ million)	524.6	552.3	579.7
GDP per capita (US$)	36,506.6	37,368.1	36,947.1
Consumption (Million units of national currency)	653.6	700.2	753.4
Consumption (US$ million)	326.8	350.1	376.7
Consumption per capita (US$)	22,741.8	23,687.4	24,007.3
Population, mid-year ('000)	210.0	210.0	215.4
Birth rate (per '000)	24.9	22.0	
Death rate (per '000)	4.3	4.1	
No. of households ('000)	74.5	74.9	78.1
Total exports (US$ million)	119.0	128.0	139.0
Total imports (US$ million)	281.0	260.0	258.0
Tourism receipts (US$ million)	73.0	75.6	
Tourist spending (US$ million)	21.0	21.7	23.3

Average household size 1995 (persons)	2.66				
Urban population 1995 (%)	46.8				
Age analysis (%) (1990)	*0-14* 36.4		*15-64* 58.9		*65+* 4.7
Population by sex (%) (1990)	*Male* 5.8		*Female* 94.2		
Life expectancy (years) (1991)	*Male* 70.0		*Female* 74.1		
Infant mortality (deaths per '000 live births) (1993)	22.1				
Adult literacy (%) (1970)	91.2				

Benin

Area (km²) 112,620

Currency CFA franc (= 100 centimes)

Location Benin, one of the poorest countries in Africa, is a small state located on the West African coastline with the Gulf of Guinea to the south. The country is bounded by Togo in the west, Burkina Faso and Niger in the north and Nigeria in the east. The capital is Porto Novo.

Head of State President Mathieu Kérékou (1996)

Head of Government Mathieu Kérékou (1996)

Ruling Party A multi-party coalition seems likely to be formed.

Political Structure Benin's transition to multi-party democracy began in 1991 when the first elections were held under the terms of the 1990 Constitution. In practice, all power rests with the President who is elected by universal suffrage for a five-year term, and answers to the 83-seat National Assembly (itself elected for a four-year term). The president organises a multi-party coalition, although splits and defections are commonplace in Benin politics.

Last Elections Elections to the country's National Assembly were held in March 1995, when some 31 parties competed for 83 seats. The results - produced after a delay of nearly two months - showed that opposition parties had obtained 49 of the 83 seats. The Union pour le Triomphe du Renouveau Démocratique, which had hitherto ruled the country, won only 19 seats - an improvement, admittedly, on the 12 seats it had won in the 1991 elections. Much confusion resulted from the elections to the presidential office which took place in 1996. Mathieu Kérékou, the dictator thrown out through the ballot box in 1991, appears to have been brought back by voters disillusioned with the previous president, Nicéphore Soglo. Final results were still unknown at the time of publication and will depend on Kérékou's ability to form a multi-party coalition.

Political Risk The minority character of the Government and the country's limited political maturity is a constant source of uncertainty about the country's stability. Recurrent charges of corruption have been levelled against the government since the 1990 constitutional reform was implemented.

Economy Benin's severe poverty is in part the result of its inhospitable climate and in part the result of decades of political mismanagement. Since the economic reforms of the early 1990s, however, the prospects for improvement have been growing. Financial support from the IMF and international donors (especially France) have helped to bring the country back from economic bankruptcy. Improvements in the world prices of cocoa and other commodities exported by Benin led to a sharp increase in GDP in 1995.

Main Industries Benin's economy is almost exclusively dominated by its agricultural sector which produces cocoa, coffee, cotton, palm oil and groundnuts. The parched soil will not normally support conventional fruit or vegetable crops. Much of the population subsists on maize, sorghum or wheat. There are deposits of gold, chrome and iron, although these are of only limited size. Oil has been extracted since the early 1980s, but again the scale of the deposits is not large. Benin has no tourist industry and the industrial sector serves mainly the domestic markets.

Energy Benin derives virtually all of its almost negligible energy requirements from imported oil and gas resources. It has no hydro-electric plants to produce electricity at present.

	1993	1994	1995
Inflation (% change)	0.4	38.5	14.5
Exchange rate (per US$)	283.16	555.20	498.70
Interest rate (% per annum)	17.5		
GDP (% real growth)	2.0	1.5	9.1
GDP (Million units of national currency)	601,700.0	845,600.0	1,056,600.0
GDP (US$ million)	2,124.9	1,523.1	2,118.7
GDP per capita (US$)	407.1	285.2	381.1
Consumption (Million units of national currency)	492,919.0	701,848.0	855,846.0
Consumption (US$ milllon)	1,740.8	1,264.1	1,716.2
Consumption per capita (US$)	333.5	236.7	308.7
Population, mid-year ('000)	5,220.0	5,340.0	5,560.0
Birth rate (per '000)	48.7	47.7	
Death rate (per '000)	17.8	14.4	
No. of households ('000)	1,225.7	1,260.1	1,338.1
Total exports (US$ million)	181.0	163.0	102.6
Total imports (US$ million)	614.0	493.0	697.3
Tourism receipts (US$ million)	38.0	41.1	
Tourist spending (US$ million)	13.0	14.1	16.0

Average household size 1995 (persons)	4.03		
Urban population 1995 (%)	31.3		
Age analysis (%) (1987)	*0-14* 46.6	*15-64* 51.0	*65+* 2.5
Population by sex (%) (1992)	*Male* 48.7	*Female* 51.3	
Life expectancy (years) (1990-95)	*Male* 45.9	*Female* 49.8	
Infant mortality (deaths per '000 live births) (1993)	85.8		
Adult literacy (%) (1990)	23.4		

TRADING PARTNERS

Major export destinations 1995 (% share)		Major import sources 1995 (% share)	
Morocco	36.9	France	20.1
Portugal	9.2	Thailand	12.6
Spain	5.3	United Kingdom	8.9
Italy	5.3	Hong Kong	8.8

Bermuda

Area (km²)   54

Currency   Bermudan dollar (BD$ = 100 cents)

Location   Bermuda comprises a group of some 150 small islands, of which 20 are inhabited. The group lies in the Western Atlantic, over 900 km off the coast of South Carolina. The climate is variable, with a susceptibility to hurricanes during the autumn. The capital is Hamilton.

Head of State   HM Queen Elizabeth II

Head of Government   David Saul (1995)

Ruling Party   United Bermuda Party

Political Structure   Bermuda, a British Dependent Territory, has a 40-member House of Assembly which exercises legislative authority and is elected by universal suffrage for a term of five years. There is also an 11-member Senate whose members are nominated by the Governor. The Governor also appoints the Prime Minister, on the basis of advice from the House of Assembly, and the Premier then appoints his own Cabinet. There has been intense discussion about the possibility of declaring independence from the UK, but in August 1995 the government lost a referendum on the subject. Prime Minister Sir John Swan thereupon resigned and was replaced by David Saul.

Last Elections   General elections were held in October 1993 to the House of Assembly, in which the United Bermuda Party won its eighth successive victory, with 22 of the 40 seats. The Progressive Labour Party, which supports total independence from the UK, raised its electoral share from 15 seats to 16, while the National Liberal Party and the Independent Environmentalist Party each won one seat.

Political Risk   With a high standard of living, Bermuda represents one of the richest and most stable Caribbean markets. The issue of independence was defeated in 1995 but is likely to be resumed at a later date. The country's heavy dependence on tourism implies some degree of economic risk which occasionally has political repercussions. Hotels are classified as an "essential industry", meaning that the government can impose its decisions by force of law.

Economy   Bermuda's economy is among the most affluent in the Atlantic/Caribbean nexus, thanks mainly to the large number of offshore investment funds based on the islands. Nevertheless, the country's close dependence on the twin pillars of tourism and financial services renders it vulnerable.

Main Industries   Bermuda's principal activity is tourism, which accounts for the largest single proportion of all employment and attracts 8-10 visitors for every resident in a typical year. The Government has agreed guidelines for a relaunch of the tourism industry. There is very little domestic food production, although some fish are exported. Manufacturing tends to centre on perfumes, flowers and pharmaceuticals. Of growing importance in recent years has been the offshore financial services industry, which is attracted to Bermuda by a series of tax concessions and by tight rules on banking secrecy. Sophisticated telecommunications are another reason for the exponential growth of this sector. A third is the country's relative proximity (900 kilometres) to the coast of the United States. New laws have recently been passed to strengthen confidence in the country's offshore banking services.

Energy   Like most of its counterparts in the Atlantic, Bermuda is entirely dependent on imports of oil and gas for its energy needs; it is, however, considering experimenting with geothermal power.

	1993	1994	1995
Inflation (% change)	4.0	3.0	3.3
Exchange rate (per US$)	1.00	1.00	1.00
Interest rate			
GDP (% real growth)	1.3	-4.0	-1.4
GDP (Million units of national currency)	1,949.0	1,929.5	1,966.9
GDP (US$ million)	1,949.0	1,929.5	1,966.9
GDP per capita (US$)	32,483.3	32,158.3	31,724.2
Consumption (Million units of national currency)	1,379.8	1,379.7	1,407.0
Consumption (US$ million)	1,379.8	1,379.7	1,407.0
Consumption per capita (US$)	22,996.7	22,995.0	22,693.5
Population, mid-year ('000)	60.0	60.0	62.0
Birth rate (per '000)	16.2	15.1	
Death rate (per '000)	7.9	7.3	
No. of households ('000)	12.6	13.1	13.8
Total exports (US$ million)	42.0	38.0	
Total imports (US$ million)	400.0	400.0	
Tourism receipts (US$ million)	505.0	491.8	
Tourist spending (US$ million)	139.0	135.4	138.1

Average household size 1995 (persons)	4.35				
Urban population 1995 (%)	100.0				
Age analysis (%) (1990)	*0-14* 19.9		*15-64* 70.7		*65+* 9.4
Population by sex (%) (1990)	*Male* 48.8		*Female* 51.2		
Life expectancy (years) (1980)	*Male* 68.8		*Female* 76.3		
Infant mortality (deaths per '000 live births) (1992)	7.0				
Adult literacy (%) (1970)	98.4				

Bhutan

Area (km²)   46,620

Currency   Ngultrum (Ng = 100 chetrum)

Location   Bhutan is a small and sparsely populated state located in the Himalayan mountain range, between India and Tibet, which is part of China. The mountainous character of the landscape precludes all possibility of intensive agriculture, forcing much of the workforce to seek employment abroad. The capital is Thimphu.

Head of State   HM King Jigme Singye Wangchuk

Head of Government   HM King Jigme Singye Wangchuk

Ruling Party   There are no legal political parties in Bhutan.

Political Structure   The Kingdom of Bhutan is a hereditary limited monarchy in which the King shares power with the Council of Ministers, the Tshogdu (National Assembly) and the chief priest of the Buddhist religion in Bhutan (Je Khempo). The 150-member Tshogdu includes 105 elected representatives and 45 appointed members. It has the power to vote the King out of office and is required to pass a vote of confidence in him every three years. The King favours a gradual democratisation of the political process and has threatened to abdicate if nothing substantial is agreed.

Last Elections   There are no general elections in Bhutan. The 105 elective delegates to the Tshogdu are elected in their various constituencies when the need arises and are not allowed to represent political groups.

Political Risk   With one of the lowest per capita incomes in the world, and with one of the most impenetrable political systems, Bhutan has little real attraction for Western businesses.

International Disputes   Bhutan's relations with neighbouring Nepal have been seriously strained by the latter's accusations of human rights offences against 100,000 ethnic Nepalese residing in Bhutan, of which about 85,000 are refugees. Meanwhile, the army has occasionally crossed the border into India in pursuit of pro-democracy activists. Talks intended to relieve tensions were initiated in 1995.

Economy   The government has an ambitious privatisation plan which promises to get rid of the rigid five-year plan system now discredited in most other parts of the region. Meanwhile, there has been a strong emphasis on building new roads and other communications links to improve the country's international standing.

Main Industries   Bhutan's economy is almost entirely dominated by agriculture, which employs 90% of the workforce. The country is self-sufficient in foodstuffs despite its sometimes inhospitable climate. Its main export crops are cardamom and fruit, most of which are destined for India. Other crops include wheat, rice, barley, vegetables and potatoes. Bhutan has very little industry, although there is now a cement factory, a distillery and some chemical plants. The country has a mining industry which exports coal to India and a growing tourist trade.

Energy   Bhutan's coal industries provide the greater part of the Kingdom's modest energy needs. Yet the vast majority of its electricity is generated by hydro-electric dams rather than by thermal power stations.

	1993	1994	1995
Inflation (% change)	11.2	7.0	1.5
Exchange rate (per US$)	30.49	31.37	31.82
Interest rate (% per annum)	17.0	16.6	
GDP (% real growth)	-9.0	5.2	-1.9
GDP (Million units of national currency)	7,120.9	8,012.5	7,973.1
GDP (US$ million)	233.5	255.4	253.7
GDP per capita (US$)	146.0	158.6	155.6
Consumption (Million units of national currency)	4,054.7	4,406.9	4,305.5
Consumption (US$ million)	133.0	140.5	135.3
Consumption per capita (US$)	83.1	87.3	83.0
Population, mid-year ('000)	1,600.0	1,610.0	1,630.5
Birth rate (per '000)	39.6	39.3	
Death rate (per '000)	15.7	15.3	
No. of households ('000)	335.9	341.8	356.1
Total exports (US$ million)	66.0	70.0	
Total imports (US$ million)	52.0	53.0	
Tourism receipts (US$ million)	3.0	3.8	
Tourist spending (US$ million)			

Average household size 1995 (persons)	4.47		
Urban population 1995 (%)	6.4		
Age analysis (%)			
Population by sex (%)			
Life expectancy (years) (1990)	*Male* 48.6	*Female* 47.1	
Infant mortality (deaths per '000 live births) (1993)	124.0		
Adult literacy (%) (1990)	38.4		

Bolivia

Area (km^2)   1,098,575

Currency   Boliviano (= 100 centavos)

Location   Bolivia, a landlocked republic located in central South America, is bordered by Brazil in the north and east, by Argentina and Paraguay in the south, and by Chile and Peru in the west. Its mountainous terrain, though well stocked with minerals, makes for poor farming. There are, however, some 20,000 km of navigable rivers. The capital is Sucre.

Head of State   President Gonzalo Sánchez de Lozada

Head of Government   President Gonzalo Sánchez de Lozada

Ruling Party   A national coalition of the Movimiento Nacionalista Revolucionario (MNR) and the Movimiento Bolivia Libre (MBL). The Union Civica Solidaridad (UCS) left the coalition in September 1994.

Political Structure   Bolivia has an executive President who is elected every four years by universal suffrage, together with the 130-member Chamber of Deputies and the 27-member Senate. Each of the country's nine departments has its own administration and prefect who is appointed by the President. Bolivia's political past has been exceptionally turbulent, with over 180 coups in the years between independence in 1825 and 1980. Major constitutional reforms have been discussed in recent years.

Last Elections   Congressional elections were held in June 1993, when the ruling MNR obtained 52 seats in the Lower House and 17 in the Senate, compared with 35 seats and eight seats for its coalition partner, the Acuerdo Patriótica (AP). The UCS obtained 20 Lower and one Upper house seat, and the MBL won seven Lower but no Upper house seats. At the same time Sánchez de Lozada was elected President.

Political Risk   The major political issue in Bolivia at present is the Government's attempt to eradicate coca farming - often the only profitable resource for poor peasants and the source of up to a fifth of the country's foreign exchange earnings. The authorities were forced into a U-turn in 1994 when they decriminalised the consumption, but not the distribution, of coca. In October 1995 the US threatened to block all foreign aid if the targets for reducing the area devoted to coca were not met. Farmers, however, remain unenthusiastic about switching to other crops which are less profitable and more difficult to grow. Meanwhile, a wave of strikes by trade unions opposing privatisation and a string of corruption cases involving government officials have undermined confidence in the administration.

International Disputes   Bolivia has made some progress in resolving its dispute with Peru over that country's annexation of the Tarapacá region which represents Bolivia's main outlet to the Pacific. But the country is still in bitter dispute with Chile over a comparable issue dating from 1884, when Chile seized the Bolivian port of Antofagasta and left the country landlocked. A Bolivian proposal for the return of the city was made in 1987; its rejection by Chile led to the closure of mutual diplomatic relations.

Economy   Bolivia's economy remains stricken by crisis and uncertainty, despite its many natural resources. This is partly because of political mismanagement over the last four decades, but also partly due to the failure of farmers and others to co-operate effectively with one another. With no tourist industry of any size, and with a poor external image, it is especially dependent on international aid. The country's bold new programme for privatisation and capitalisation have yet to deliver an improvement in economic performance.

Main Industries   Bolivia's abundant mineral resources are the largest single contributor to GDP. The country is one of the world's largest producers of tin and has deposits of copper, lead, silver, zinc, antimony, wolfram and gold in considerable quantity. The abundance of natural resources has attracted interest from investors in many countries, although recent profits have been only modest. Agriculture is poorly developed and output seldom exceeds subsistence level for most farmers. Although they produce rice, barley, oats, wheat, sugar cane and other products, coca and cocaine are the dominant crops. The major export crops (aside from cocaine) are rubber, cotton and herbs.

Energy   Bolivia meets all of its own energy requirements, thanks in part to its oil reserves and in part to the hydro-electric power generated in the mountains. It exports natural gas to its neighbours.

	1993	1994	1995
Inflation (% change)	8.5	7.9	10.2
Exchange rate (per US$)	4.27	4.62	4.81
Interest rate (% per annum)	53.9	55.6	51.0
GDP (% real growth)	4.0	4.2	3.7
GDP (Million units of national currency)	25,637.0	29,104.0	33,470.0
GDP (US$ million)	6,004.0	6,299.6	6,958.4
GDP per capita (US$)	849.2	870.1	939.1
Consumption (Million units of national currency)	20,490.2	23,531.7	27,376.5
Consumption (US$ million)	4,798.6	5,093.4	5,691.6
Consumption per capita (US$)	678.7	703.5	768.1
Population, mid-year ('000)	7,070.0	7,240.0	7,410.0
Birth rate (per '000)	31.0	32.2	
Death rate (per '000)	10.6	10.6	
No. of households ('000)	1,662.2	1,711.9	1,803.4
Total exports (US$ million)	728.0	1,032.0	1,101.0
Total imports (US$ million)	1,206.0	1,209.0	1,424.0
Tourism receipts (US$ million)	115.0	120.8	
Tourist spending (US$ million)	151.0	158.6	177.2

Average household size 1995 (persons)	4.02				
Urban population 1995 (%)	60.8				
Age analysis (%) (1991)	*0-14* 36.3		*15-64* 60.2		*65+* 3.5
Population by sex (%) (1992)	*Male* 49.3		*Female* 50.7		
Life expectancy (years) (1990-95)	*Male* 57.7		*Female* 61.0		
Infant mortality (deaths per '000 live births)					
Adult literacy (%) (1992)	80.1				

TRADING PARTNERS

Major export destinations 1995 (% share)		Major import sources 1995 (% share)	
USA	23.7	USA	16.9
Peru	13.5	Argentina	16.2
France	7.9	Brazil	15.1
Colombia	6.7	Chile	10.5

© Euromonitor 1996

Bosnia-Herzegovina

Area (km²) 51,129

Currency Dinar

Location Bosnia-Herzegovina lies in the centre of the former territory of Yugoslavia, with its eastern borders alongside Serbia and the western edge against Croatia. The mountainous interior gives way to a stretch of coastline in the south-west running down to the city of Dubrovnik. The capital is Sarajevo.

Head of State President Alija Izetbegovic

Head of Government Hasan Muratovic (1996)

Ruling Party Party of Democratic Action (SDA) leads a multi-party coalition.

Political Structure Although an uneasy peace has come to Bosnia, the situation remains terribly complicated and civil war could quickly return. One of the dominating political forces in the country is the SDA, a Muslim nationalist party led by Bosnia's president, Alija Izetbegovic. The party controls much of the army, the civil service and public enterprises. Muslims who do not belong to the SDA, let alone non-Muslims, find it hard to get decent jobs. Opposition is led by Haris Siladzic, who resigned as head of government in 1995 but is still one of the country's vice presidents. The Izetbegovic political wing argues that multicultural idealism proved to be of little value over the past four years and that a fierce nationalism is needed to fend off the country's neighbours. Siladzic's supporters counter that multiculturalism - the idea that Serbs, Muslims and Croats must live together - is needed to keep the West's support. The nationalist view is currently dominate but if Bosnia is to hold together the more liberal view must prevail.

Last Elections The elections of December 1990 for the 240-seat bicameral Assembly resulted in a win for the two major nationalist parties. Since then, the results have been rendered largely irrelevant by the outbreak of hostilities and the splintering of any remnant of political consensus.

Political Risk Bosnia-Herzegovina is clearly an unacceptable political and economic risk at present. NATO's Implementation Force (Ifor) will probably withdraw in early 1997 and many observers fear that some sort of war could follow.

International Disputes The Muslim-Croat federation constructed out of the Dayton agreement is extremely shaky. This was supposed to create eight cantons plus the city of Sarajevo but by cemented1996 only one canton actually existed. Much will depend on Croatia's tactics in 1996. The Americans have a great deal of influence over the governments of Bosnia and Croatia, and some over Serbia. If the USA remains committed to peace, all three governments will be reluctant to renege on the Dayton agreement. Such a decision would risk international sanctions and the loss of international aid.

Economy The World Bank estimates that it will require nearly $5 billion over three years to repair the ravages of war and revive Bosnia's shattered economy - not counting the cost of resettling the country's 2.7 million refugees. The Bosnian government's own estimate is much higher, at $43 billion. In March 1996, the country's Moslem and Croat leaders agreed to shore up their fragile federation by creating a customs union. The agreement provides for a single state budget and a unitary banking system.

Main Industries Bosnia-Herzegovina's economy relies almost exclusively on agriculture. Its industrial capabilities would be limited even in peacetime. The area does not have an extensive tourist industry.

	1993	1994	1995
Inflation (% change)			
Exchange rate (per US$)			
Interest rate			
GDP (% real growth)	-15.0	-23.5	
GDP (Million units of national currency)	510,000.0	390,000.0	
GDP (US$ million)	2,147.4	1,721.0	
GDP per capita (US$)	484.7	385.9	
Consumption (Million units of national currency)	340,000.0	260,000.0	
Consumption (US$ million)	1,431.6	1,147.3	
Consumption per capita (US$)	323.2	257.2	
Population, mid-year ('000)	4,430.0	4,460.0	4,480.0
Birth rate (per '000)	8.0	13.3	
Death rate (per '000)	33.0	33.0	
No. of households ('000)	650.9	613.8	613.0
Total exports (US$ million)			
Total imports (US$ million)			
Tourism receipts (US$ million)			
Tourist spending (US$ million)			

Average household size 1995 (persons)	6.90		
Urban population 1995 (%)	49.0		
Age analysis (%)			
Population by sex (%)			
Life expectancy (years) (1991)	*Male* 69.7	*Female* 75.2	
Infant mortality (deaths per '000 live births)			
Adult literacy (%)			

TRADING PARTNERS

Major export destinations 1995 (% share)		Major import sources 1995 (% share)	
Italy	31.0	Croatia	43.7
Germany	25.3	Russia	21.3
Croatia	14.8	Germany	8.9
Slovenia	7.5	Italy	7.1

Botswana

Area (km²) 575,000

Currency   Pula (P = 100 thebe)

Location   Botswana is a landlocked territory in central southern Africa. It is bounded by South Africa in the south and east, by Zimbabwe in the north-east, and by Namibia in the west and north. There is also a short northern border with Zambia. The country has a varied climate, ranging from the swamplands of the Okavango and Limpopo to the deserts of the Kgalagadi. The capital is Gaborone.

Head of State   President Sir Ketumile (Quett) Masire

Head of Government   President Sir Ketumile (Quett) Masire

Ruling Party   Botswana Democratic Party

Political Structure   Botswana is an independent member of the Commonwealth in which an executive President is elected by universal suffrage for a term of five years. Legislative power is vested in the National Assembly, which has 34 members elected in the normal way, as well as four specially elected members and two seats which are held ex officio. Draft legislation is considered by the 15-member House of Chiefs, wherever it pertains to constitutional or chieftaincy matters.

Last Elections   Legislative elections were held in October 1994, when the ruling Botswana Democratic Party (BDP) was returned to power with a significantly reduced majority. Most of the remaining seats went to the Botswana National Front (BNF), a group which draws its support from the urban working class. The voting age was reduced from 21 to 18 years in April 1995.

Political Risk   The current administration faces frequent criticism as it has effectively lost its reputation for running one of the most stable African economies. The two main political parties have been dogged by splits, divisions and allegations of corruption. In particular, the ruling BDP has come under pressure after a series of political scandals involving land sales. Finally, there is a major problem with AIDS, which the government readily acknowledges has the power to devastate the economy.

International Disputes   There have been some tensions with Namibia over the construction of a new military base near Gaborone, and over the sovereignty of the tiny island of Kasikili on the Lobe river. The latter issue was referred to the International Court of Justice in 1995.

Economy   The bright prospects of Botswana's mining sector offer hopes of a major expansion in the consumer economy during the next few years. This assessment, however, depends heavily on the development of world prices for key commodities. A weak diamond market during the first half of the 1990s had serious repercussions for the economy, leading to a four-fold increase in the budget deficit in 1993/1994. The relationship with South Africa will be of crucial importance in future years.

Main Industries   Botswana's economy relies to a large extent on its agricultural sector, especially cattle herding which accounts for over 85% of total farming production. Otherwise, the land is generally too dry to permit much arable crop production. Although farming provides a modest and largely subsistence level of income for most of the population, the more important source of income lies in the minerals sector. Botswana has large but only partially explored deposits of diamonds and coal. Even so, it is already among the world's largest diamond producers. Manufacturing is only small-scale and caters mainly to local needs.

Energy   Botswana's coal resources, together with natural fuels such as brushwood, account for most of its needs. A sizeable proportion of its electricity is of hydro-electric origin, although some of this is imported.

	1993	1994	1995
Inflation (% change)	14.3	10.5	10.5
Exchange rate (per US$)	2.42	2.68	2.76
Interest rate (% per annum)	14.9	13.9	14.2
GDP (% real growth)	6.6	10.1	8.3
GDP (Million units of national currency)	8,491.4	10,328.3	12,364.3
GDP (US$ million)	3,508.8	3,853.8	4,479.8
GDP per capita (US$)	2,436.7	2,657.8	3,068.4
Consumption (Million units of national currency)	2,047.0	2,339.1	2,630.7
Consumption (US$ million)	845.9	872.8	953.2
Consumption per capita (US$)	587.4	601.9	652.8
Population, mid-year ('000)	1,440.0	1,450.0	1,460.0
Birth rate (per '000)	42.5	42.2	
Death rate (per '000)	6.6	6.4	
No. of households ('000)	343.2	357.5	380.9
Total exports (US$ million)	1,780.0	1,845.0	
Total imports (US$ million)	1,771.0	1,638.0	1,676.0
Tourism receipts (US$ million)			
Tourist spending (US$ million)	30.0	29.7	32.4

Average household size 1995 (persons)	3.85				
Urban population 1995 (%)	28.1				
Age analysis (%) (1991)	*0-14* 42.8	*15-64* 50.6	*65+* 6.7
Population by sex (%) (1991)	*Male* 47.8	*Female* 52.2	
Life expectancy (years) (1985-90)	*Male* 55.5	*Female* 61.5	
Infant mortality (deaths per '000 live births) (1993)	43.0		
Adult literacy (%) (1990)	73.7		

Brazil

Area (km²)   8,511,965

Currency   Real (= 100 centavos)

Location   Brazil, the largest country in South America, occupies some two-thirds of the continent's entire Atlantic coast and has a wide range of climatic conditions, from the humid equatorial states of the north to the cooler and drier south. Much of the country is made up of dense tropical forest and jungle, and apart from the capital, Brasília, there are no settlements of any size in the interior of the country. The capital is Brasilia.

Head of State   President Fernando Henrique Cardoso (inaugurated January 1995)

Head of Government   President Fernando Henrique Cardoso

Ruling Party   Brazilian Social Democratic Party leads a four-party coalition.

Political Structure   Brazil has an executive President who is elected by popular mandate for a term of four years and is answerable to a bicameral National Congress. Whereas the Senate's 72 members are elected for eight years, with one-third or two-thirds coming up for re-election every four years, the Chamber of Deputies is elected by universal suffrage every four years. The size of the Chamber may vary, but is usually around 490. Recent presidential history has been stormy. In December 1992 the incumbent President Collor de Mello was forced to resign after being impeached on charges of corruption and drugs activity. He was succeeded by the relatively open-handed Itamar Franco (December 1992) who proved unable to stabilise the economy. Fernando Henrique Cardoso, who as Finance Minister had engineered a dramatic fall in inflation and a more stable currency, took over in October 1994.

Last Elections   In the presidential elections of October 1994, Fernando Henrique Cardoso won easily with 54% of the vote. His nearest rival was Luis Ignacio Lula da Silva, a former trade unionist, with 28% of the vote. The congressional elections held at the same time gave the Main Cardoso Aliance 182 seats in the House of Deputies and 33 seats in the Senate. The Brazilian Democratic Movement (PMDB), which generally supports Cardoso, gained 107 seats in the House and 23 in the Senate. These figures mean very little, however, since no fewer than 18 different political parties are represented in Congress and they operate without any real form of party discipline. Indeed, the conflict between the president and the two chambers has meant that not a single democratically elected president has completed his term of office since 1926. Cardoso, like all his predecessors, is finding it very difficult to work with such a chaotic congress.

Political Risk   The current president has a strong mandate for change in economic policy and political culture but the party system encourages corruption, deal-making and shifting alliances. Fiscal reforms and improvements in the social security system are needed to stabilise Brazil's economy. However, they will be extremely difficult to implement in the current political environment. An overvalued currency and the gradual opening of the economy to international markets adds to the uncertainties which plague business. Meanwhile, economic reforms are proving to be highly painful for private citizens, especially in rural communities. Urban violence is also on the rise, reaching epidemic proportions in some of the larger cities.

International Disputes   Brazil has a long-standing disagreement with Argentina over the use of waterways for power generation but has moderated its objections now that both countries are members of Mercosur. In the north, Brazil's relations with Guyana and Suriname have been strained by guerrilla activity. The Brazilians, however, have used their influence to mediate local disputes between the two countries.

Economy   The government has managed a sharp fall in rates of inflation which has provided a much-needed boost to consumer spending. Brazil is a founding member of the Mercosur customs union and this has injected new life into its export sector. Both foreign investment and exports are rising rapidly and Brazil expects to be the main beneficiary of the new trade association. The government has also had considerable success with its privatisation plans, raising nearly $9 billion between 1991 and 1995, with another $2 billion of sell-offs scheduled for 1996 and 1997.

Main Industries   Brazil's massive mineral deposits, especially in the Minas Gerais region, account for the largest single source of foreign exchange. Bauxite, iron ore, manganese, chrome, lead, zinc, tungsten and nickel are the major metals being mined. There are also gemstones and the search continues for oil deposits. Agriculture, though favoured by a humid and warm climate, has underperformed. Coffee and oranges are nevertheless two of the country's most profitable exports and are strongly promoted by the government. Many farmers earn only subsistence incomes. The country boasts a well diversified and sophisticated manufacturing sector. Its energy and telecommunications industries (which are in the process of privatisation) are among the biggest in the developing world. Consumer electronics, computers and software, as well as a wide range of heavy industries producing everything from steel to automobiles and planes, are prominent in the country.

Energy   Brazil gets more than half its energy requirements from oil and gas, much of it imported. The bulk of its electricity is obtained domestically from hydro-electric plants. Privatisation of the country's electricity distribution network and electricity-generating assets is planned for 1996/1997.

	1993	1994	1995
Inflation (% change)	2,148.4	2,668.5	84.4
Exchange rate (per US$)	.03	0.64	0.92
Interest rate (% per annum)	5,757.0	13,533.0	29.8
GDP (% real growth)	5.0	7.0	3.0
GDP (Billion units of national currency)	14,039,000.0	355,567.0	
GDP (US$ million)	473,000.0	510,000.0	550,000.0
GDP per capita (US$)	3,121.4	3,317.3	3,529.7
Consumption (Billion units of national currency)	6,625,161.4		
Consumption (US$ million)	223,214.0	329,043.0	485,140.3
Consumption per capita (US$)	1,473.0	2,140.3	3,113.5
Population, mid-year ('000)	151,534.0	153,740.0	155,820.0
Birth rate (per '000)	24.7	22.9	21.7
Death rate (per '000)	7.9	6.9	7.9
No. of households ('000)	36,905.0	37,564.7	38,434.0
Total exports (US$ million)	38,597.0	43,558.0	46,506.0
Total imports (US$ million)	27,740.0	35,997.0	53,783.0
Tourism receipts (US$ million)	1,449.0	1,352.0	1,425.0
Tourist spending (US$ million)	1,842.0	1,947.2	2,870.9

Average household size 1995 (persons)	3.89		
Urban population 1995 (%)	78.3		
Age analysis (%) (1994)	*0-14* 32.8	*15-64* 62.1	*65+* 5.1
Population by sex (%) (1994)	*Male* 49.9	*Female* 50.1	
Life expectancy (years) (1995)	*Male* 63.8	*Female* 70.4	
Infant mortality (deaths per '000 live births) (1995)	44.6		
Adult literacy (%) (1994)	82.1		

TRADING PARTNERS

Major export destinations 1995 (% share)		Major import sources 1995 (% share)	
USA	18.5	USA	22.9
Argentina	8.1	Argentina	10.7
Japan	7.8	Germany	10.2
Germany	6.9	Italy	6.7

British Virgin Islands

Area (km²) 153

Currency US dollar (US$ = 100 cents)

Location The British Virgin Islands lie in the Eastern Caribbean, to the east of Puerto Rico and north-east of St Kitts and Nevis. Only about 16 of the 60-plus islands administered by Britain (as distinct from those run by the United States) are inhabited. All except the coral island of Anegada are hilly or mountainous. The capital is Road Town.

Head of State HM Queen Elizabeth II

Head of Government Hon. H. Lavity Stoutt

Ruling Party Virgin Islands Party

Political Structure The British Virgin Islands, a United Kingdom Crown Colony, are governed to a large extent by the local assembly (Legislative Council), despite the presence of a Governor appointed by the Crown who formally presides over an Executive Council. At present, the Legislative Council has nine elected members as well as the Speaker and the Attorney General, but its elected membership is to be increased to 13 under a complex electoral reform currently nearing completion.

Last Elections In the general elections of November 1990, the ruling Virgin Islands Party obtained six seats against three for the United Party of Conrad Maduro.

Political Risk With a high standard of living and a successful up-market tourist industry, the British Virgin Islands offer an attractive target for British or foreign exporters. The extensive tax haven facilities on offer in the islands are complemented by a high level of political security.

Economy Fees from the incorporation of international business companies account for nearly half the islands' total income. Most other income is generated from financial services and tourism.

Main Industries The islands' small number of expensive resorts are complemented by a growing number of others aimed at the mass market. Traditionally, this sector accounted for the bulk of islands' income, but that situation has now changed as the financial sector has become larger and more sophisticated. The islands are now home to over 140,000 international business companies and the number is growing steadily. New laws have now been introduced to construct a full-service offshore jurisdiction. Agriculture is a minor activity in comparison with these more lucrative operations. There is some cultivation of fruit and vegetables and fish are exported. Industry centres on the processing of agricultural products, especially rum manufacturing, although there is a stone quarry and a paint factory.

	1993	1994	1995
Inflation (% change)	4.0	3.0	3.0
Exchange rate (per US$)	1.00	1.00	1.00
Interest rate			
GDP (% real growth)	1.6	-4.4	-1.4
GDP (Million units of national currency)	167.4	165.0	167.6
GDP (US$ million)	167.4	165.0	167.6
GDP per capita (US$)	9,300.0	8,684.2	8,355.3
Consumption (Million units of national currency)	102.9	102.4	105.0
Consumption (US$ million)	102.9	102.4	105.0
Consumption per capita (US$)	5,716.7	5,389.5	5,235.2
Population, mid-year ('000)	18.0	19.0	20.1
Birth rate (per '000)	23.3	20.3	
Death rate (per '000)	6.6	6.1	
No. of households ('000)	4.3	4.3	4.5
Total exports (US$ million)			
Total imports (US$ million)			
Tourism receipts (US$ million)	122.0	122.0	
Tourist spending (US$ million)	35.0	35.0	35.9

Average household size 1995 (persons)	4.20				
Urban population 1994					
Age analysis (%) (1988)	*0-14* 29.0		*15-64* 64.5		*65+* 6.5
Population by sex (%) (1988)	*Male* 49.2		*Female* 50.8		
Life expectancy (years)					
Infant mortality (deaths per '000 live births)					
Adult literacy (%) (1970)	98.3				

Brunei

Area (km²)   5,765

Currency   Brunei dollar (S = 100 sen)

Location   The Sultanate of Brunei lies on the north-western coast of the island of Borneo and is surrounded on all sides by Malaysian territory. The country has a humid and tropical climate. The capital is Bandar Seri Begawan.

Head of State   HM Sultan Sir Muda Hassanal Bolkiah Mu'izzadin Waddaulah

Head of Government   HM Sultan Sir Muda Hassanal Bolkiah Mu'izzadin Waddaulah

Ruling Party   There are no legal political parties.

Political Structure   Brunei achieved full independence from the United Kingdom in 1984 and is ruled by an executive monarch, the Sultan, in whose hands all legal powers are vested. The Sultan is assisted by a Council of Ministers, a Religious Council and a Privy Council. However, part of the Constitution has been revoked since 1962, when massive protests developed, and a state of emergency was declared which has yet to be revoked. The Sultan disbanded the Legislative Council in 1984 and now rules by decree.

Last Elections   There are no elections in Brunei.

Political Risk   The considerable wealth of Brunei makes it a valuable potential target for foreign exporters of high-value goods, yet the small size of the country combined with its unusually autocratic style of government means that its markets are sometimes difficult to penetrate. The economy is unusually vulnerable to swings in the world prices of oil and natural gas on which it largely depends. However, Brunei is a member of the Association of South-East Asian Nations (ASEAN) and has recently demonstrated more interest in other schemes for regional and inter-regional co-operation.

International Disputes   The whole territory of Brunei is subject to an old claim by Malaysia which has remained dormant for some time. Brunei is also one of several countries making a claim for the sovereignty of the Spratly Islands.

Economy   Brunei's economy is one of the most affluent in the Far East. Its planned diversification away from oil could reinforce this fortunate position in the longer run. The country's membership in the ASEAN group should also help to offset its historical policy of isolation and encourage the development of non-oil industries.

Main Industries   Brunei's income is almost entirely derived from its oil and gas resources which account for around 70% of annual revenues in a typical year. The country is also attempting to attract foreign investors to expand its manufacturing sector. Agriculture is largely limited to yams, bananas and cassava, mainly for the domestic market, but there are also considerable stocks of hardwoods which are exported. There are plans to develop a financial centre, based on the country's policy of low taxation and banking secrecy.

Energy   Brunei's energy needs are almost exclusively met from the oil and (more importantly) the natural gas resources around its coastline. It has no electricity generating capacity which does not rely on burning fossil fuels.

	1993	1994	1995
Inflation (% change)	15.0	-7.1	2.0
Exchange rate (per US$)	1.60	1.50	1.40
Interest rate			
GDP (% real growth)	1.2	1.8	1.5
GDP (Million units of national currency)	16,422.1	15,542.9	16,091.6
GDP (US$ million)	10,263.8	10,361.9	11,494.0
GDP per capita (US$)	36,656.5	37,006.9	40,260.2
Consumption (Million units of national currency)	10,888.9	10,409.0	10,884.2
Consumption (US$ million)	6,805.6	6,939.3	7,774.4
Consumption per capita (US$)	24,305.6	24,783.3	27,231.7
Population, mid-year ('000)	280.0	280.0	285.5
Birth rate (per '000)	22.9	26.2	
Death rate (per '000)	3.7	3.7	
No. of households ('000)	58.4	58.7	61.0
Total exports (US$ million)			
Total imports (US$ million)			
Tourism receipts (US$ million)	33.9	35.7	
Tourist spending (US$ million)			

Average household size 1995 (persons)	4.53		
Urban population 1995 (%)	57.8		
Age analysis (%) (1992)	*0-14* 34.5	*15-64* 63.0	*65+* 2.7
Population by sex (%) (1992)	*Male* 52.9	*Female* 48.4	
Life expectancy (years) (1990)	*Male* 74.4	*Female* 74.4	
Infant mortality (deaths per '000 live births) (1992)	9.6		
Adult literacy (%) (1981)	77.8		

TRADING PARTNERS

Major export destinations 1995 (% share)		Major import sources 1995 (% share)	
Japan	57.4	United Kingdom	15.7
Singapore	10.1	Malaysia	11.2
Thailand	9.2	USA	8.0
United Kingdom	9.1	Japan	5.2

Bulgaria

Area (km²)   110,910

Currency   Lev (= 100 stotinki)

Location   With its southern borders meeting Turkey, Greece, Macedonia and Serbia, and its northern border meeting Romania, Bulgaria has been exposed to a wide range of cultures. The climate is equable, with low rainfall especially along the popular Black Sea coast. The capital is Sofia.

Head of State   President Zhelyu Zhelev (1990)

Head of Government   Zhan Videnov (January 1995)

Ruling Party   A "government of experts" appointed after the December 1994 elections was replaced in January 1995 by a coalition of the Bulgarian Socialist Party (BSP) and the Peasant's Party (BZNS).

Political Structure   The victory of the BSP, heir to the former communist party, disappointed many western observers. Bulgaria's strongly anti-communist president has recently chastised the government for its Stalinist methods but some members of the administration offer reasons for hope. In a country where the middle class, the institutions of democratic government and the law are weak, the result is a government at the mercy of powerful domestic and foreign interest groups. Meanwhile, the opposition Union of Demographic Forces (UDF) is struggling to restore its credibility after its incompetent first experience of power. Videnov hopes to emulate the Polish example and bring the presidency into socialist hands. With the next general election still three years away, political attention is already focusing on what should be a bruising campaign.

Last Elections   General elections were held in December 1994, when the incumbent Bulgarian Socialist Party (the renamed Bulgarian Communist Party) won an absolute majority, reversing the defeat it had suffered in the 1991 poll. In the presidential elections of January 1992, President Zhelyu Zhelev was reappointed with 53% of the vote. He was defeated, however, in the June 1996 primary to determine his party's presidential candidate in the autumn election.

Political Risk   Bulgaria's apparent unwillingness to make a clean break with its communist past leaves its political future in some doubt. Russia's influence in the wider Balkan region is also certain to grow as its economic strength and self-confidence return. The Russian military has threatened to deploy in Bulgaria if NATO were to expand into Poland. Bulgaria is certain to become more important as a transit point for energy in the future, with both the East and West manoeuvring for influence.

International Disputes   Bulgaria today is drastically smaller than its historical predecessor which controlled practically the whole area from Germany down to the Greek and Turkish Mediterranean. Greece and the former Yugoslav republic of Macedonia are at pains to refute Bulgaria's claim that Macedonia, a Slavic-speaking region, was historically a Bulgarian state. The issue has seldom acquired more than cultural importance and full-scale territorial claims have not been made since the 1960s.

Economy   Because Bulgaria's economy was the most closely integrated of all Soviet satellites, it suffered worst from the collapse of the Soviet trade regime. Fortunately, real GDP rose by 2.5% in 1995, the first economic good news in years for Bulgaria. Markets in OECD countries now account for 50% of total trade, although heavy dependence on Russian oil and gas mean that 40% of imports are still from the east. The government, however, has been slow to introduce the types of structural reforms that a thriving capitalist economy requires. Big increases in domestic and foreign investment and a modern banking system are urgently needed if Bulgaria is to sustain its current rate of economic progress.

Main Industries   Bulgaria's changing economic structure has brought a number of new industries to the fore, including engineering and chemicals. The bulk of the work force is still dependent on farming and the country's all-important food processing industries. The sector produces a wide range of cereal crops, as well as fruit, vegetables and wine for export. Bulgaria has several important mineral deposits such as iron, coal and limestone, but these have yet to be developed. There is a possibility of oil prospecting in the Black Sea. Tourism holds much promise as an earner of income and foreign exchange if it is developed and promoted (especially sites along the Black Sea coast). So far, however, it has been neglected and mismanaged by tourist authorities. The energy sector is being developed and will soon be making a much bigger contribution to the economy. Bulgaria is a crucial part of Russia's ambitious plans to supply gas to western and southern Europe. Over $500 million of investment is planned to create the Bulgarian infrastructure for transhipment of gas supplies.

Energy   Solid fuels account for over half of all Bulgaria's energy requirements, with oil and natural gas imports from Russia making up most of the remainder. The country's commitment to close down its potentially dangerous Kozlodui nuclear power station (which presently supplies about a third of all electricity) will sharply increase gas consumption by the year 2000.

	1993	1994	1995
Inflation (% change)	64.9	49.3	32.9
Exchange rate (per US$)	31.00	56.87	67.17
Interest rate (% per annum)	63.1	93.9	39.8
GDP (% real growth)	-2.0	1.0	2.5
GDP (Billion units of national currency)	298.9	548.0	746.5
GDP (US$ million)	9,643.0	9,636.3	11,113.9
GDP per capita (US$)	1,138.6	1,141.7	1,336.3
Consumption (Billion units of national currency)	218.7	295.6	355.0
Consumption (US$ million)	7,053.9	5,197.8	5,284.4
Consumption per capita (US$)	832.9	615.9	635.4
Population, mid-year ('000)	8,469.0	8,440.0	8,316.7
Birth rate (per '000)	10.0	9.4	
Death rate (per '000)	12.9	13.2	
No. of households ('000)	3,011.0	3,015.0	3,019.0
Total exports (US$ million)			
Total imports (US$ million)			
Tourism receipts (US$ million)	307.0	230.2	
Tourist spending (US$ million)	257.0	192.7	195.9

Average household size 1995 (persons)	2.66				
Urban population 1995 (%)	70.7				
Age analysis (%) (1995)	*0-14* 21.2		*15-64* 66.4		*65+* 12.4
Population by sex (%) (1995)	*Male* 49.5		*Female* 50.5		
Life expectancy (years) (1994)	*Male* 67.3		*Female* 74.8		
Infant mortality (deaths per '000 live births) (1994)	16.3				
Adult literacy (%) (1992)	97.9				

TRADING PARTNERS

Major export destinations 1995 (% share)		Major import sources 1995 (% share)	
Germany	13.9	Ukraine	15.2
Italy	12.8	Germany	15.1
Russia	9.1	Russia	10.8
Turkey	7.4	Greece	8.5

Burkina Faso

Area (km²)   274,122

Currency   CFA franc (= 100 centimes)

Location   Burkina Faso, the former Upper Volta, is a landlocked state in north-west Africa, which is bounded in the north and west by Mali, in the east by Niger, and in the south by Côte d'Ivoire, Ghana, Benin and Togo. The country's especially arid climate and hard soil makes farming difficult. The capital is Ouagadougou.

Head of State   President Blaise Compaoré (1991)

Head of Government   Roch Christian Kaboré (March 1994)

Ruling Party   Organisation for Popular Democracy - Labour Movement (OPT-MT)

Political Structure   Burkina Faso, which was known until 1984 as Upper Volta, has an executive President who is elected by universal suffrage for a seven-year term. A 107-member National Assembly, also elected by universal suffrage, was established in 1992. From 1980 until the multi-party elections of 1992, the country was ruled first directly by the President and then by a transitional government. The first President, Thomas Sankara, was killed in a 1987 revolt which eventually brought the more moderate Blaise Compaoré to power.

Last Elections   Legislative elections were held in May 1992, when the OPT-MT of President Blaise Compaoré won 78 of the 107 seats. The National Convention of Progressive Patriots-Social Democratic Party (CNPP-PSD) won eight seats, the African Democratic Assembly six, and the African Independent Party three. Four other parties each won one seat, and four results were undeclared. The voter turnout was below 29%,and the election was marred by allegations of ballot-rigging.

Political Risk   The restoration of multi-party democracy to Burkina Faso has not quelled the demand for improvements in the electoral system. Nor has it removed the possibility of continued social unrest. Poverty is widespread, meaning that any deterioration in the economy can give rise to severe social problems and political unrest.

International Disputes   Burkina Faso's relations with Benin have been damaged in recent years by the ongoing hostilities within both countries.

Economy   Burkina Faso's economy performed surprisingly well in 1995 thanks to an improvement in world commodity prices. French experts estimate that GDP grew by 5.5-6% in the past year. The turnaround, which follows several years of negligible growth, should lift many inhabitants above the subsistence level for the first time in a decade. The country is also a major recipient of international aid from the World Bank, the IMF and the French government.

Main Industries   Burkina Faso's agricultural sector relies heavily on animal husbandry as a source of income. Much of the country's land is too dry to permit a significant amount of farming. Manufacturing is limited to simple, small-scale establishments engaged in agro-processing activities for the local market. The country has some mineral deposits which are being actively mined. These include gold, copper, bauxite, manganese and graphite.

Energy   The bulk of Burkina's very modest fuel requirements is met by natural resources such as brushwood. In the absence of coal deposits, oil remains the main source of thermally-generated energy.

	1993	1994	1995
Inflation (% change)	0.6	25.2	7.4
Exchange rate (per US$)	283.16	555.20	498.70
Interest rate (% per annum)	17.5		
GDP (% real growth)	2.4	1.3	5.8
GDP (Billion units of national currency)	843.2	1,468.5	1,667.9
GDP (US$ million)	2,977.8	2,645.0	3,344.4
GDP per capita (US$)	307.6	259.8	327.9
Consumption (Billion units of national currency)	355.7	625.8	718.0
Consumption (US$ million)	1,256.2	1,127.2	1,439.8
Consumption per capita (US$)	129.8	110.7	141.2
Population, mid-year ('000)	9,680.0	10,180.0	10,200.0
Birth rate (per '000)	46.8	48.4	
Death rate (per '000)	18.2	18.2	
No. of households ('000)	2,174.5	2,232.7	2,323.5
Total exports (US$ million)	283.0	678.4	
Total imports (US$ million)	650.0	578.0	
Tourism receipts (US$ million)	8.0	7.1	
Tourist spending (US$ million)	35.0	30.9	

Average household size 1995 (persons)	4.33				
Urban population 1995 (%)	27.2				
Age analysis (%) (1985)	*0-14* 48.3		*15-64* 47.6		*65+* 4.1
Population by sex (%) (1985)	*Male* 48.1		*Female* 51.9		
Life expectancy (years) (1990-95)	*Male* 45.8		*Female* 49.1		
Infant mortality (deaths per '000 live births) (1993)	129.9				
Adult literacy (%) (1990)	18.2				

TRADING PARTNERS

Major export destinations 1995 (% share)		Major import sources 1995 (% share)	
France	13.3	Côte d'Ivoire	24.5
Italy	11.0	France	19.0
Côte d'Ivoire	10.3	Togo	3.3
Malaysia	3.9	Japan	2.9

Burundi

Area (km²)   27,835

Currency   Burundi franc (= 100 centimes)

Location   The tiny landlocked republic of Burundi is located to the north-east of Tanzania, with Rwanda to the north and Zaire to the west. It lies along the rivers which feed into Lake Tanganyika further south. The climate is tropical, although there is an ample supply of water available from the rivers. The capital is Bujumbura.

Head of State   Sylvestre Ntibantunganya (October 1994)

Head of Government   Antoine Nduwayo (March 1995)

Ruling Party   Front pour la Démocratie en Burundi leads a power-sharing government for a four-year transitional period.

Political Structure   Burundi's Hutu president and its Tutsi prime minister remain pitted against one another just as resolutely as the country's two tribes. Like neighbouring Rwanda, Burundi has been chronically subverted by fierce rivalries between these two groups ever since the assassination of its first Hutu president, Melchior Ndadaye, in late 1993. Cyprien Ntaryamira was appointed to succeed him in January 1994, but he too was murdered, together with the Rwandan president, in April 1994. Sylvestre Ntibantunganya, who thereupon succeeded him as acting President, was confirmed in this role in October 1994, and in March 1995 he went on to form his first civilian government.

Last Elections   The first multi-party elections since 1970 were held in June 1993, when the Front pour la Démocratie en Burundi (then led by the subsequently murdered Melchior Ndadaye) won 65 of the 81 seats in Parliament, compared with 16 for the incumbent Union pour le Progrès National of Pierre Buyoya. In presidential elections held on the same day, Ndadaye ousted Buyoya with 65% of the vote in which 97% of the electorate participated. The presidential elections of September 1994 confirmed Ntibantunganya's position as head of state.

Political Risk   The government, which is a mixture of Hutu and Tutsi politicians, remains feeble, isolated and paralysed. The only real power in the country is the army, which is little more than a Tutsi militia. The military is happy to leave a powerless government in charge, but would not allow a UN peacekeeping force inside the country.

International Disputes   Rwanda and Zaire are host to some 50,000 Burundi refugees, who claim to have been driven abroad by racial persecution. Relations with both countries have fallen to a new low after mutual allegations about the mistreatment of minorities.

Economy   Burundi's modest economy and geographical inaccessibility combine to make it improbable that the country will see a major expansion of its limited industrial base in the 1990s. Moreover, the likelihood of large international aid awards has receded with the recent political problems in the country. GDP shrank by 8.5% in 1993, by around 12% in 1994 and a similar amount in 1995.

Main Industries   Burundi's economy is a rudimentary one, with more than 80% of the population dependent on agriculture - generally on a subsistence basis. The major cash crop is coffee, which accounts for 70% of all export revenues, but cotton and tea are also sold on the international markets. There has been some prospecting for minerals, and major deposits of zinc have been located. However, their difficult location makes them uneconomic to extract.

Energy   The greater part of Burundi's very modest energy needs is met by solid fuels such as coal, or by natural fuels such as brushwood. Hydro-electric power accounts for virtually all of its limited electricity consumption, however.

	1993	1994	1995
Inflation (% change)	9.7	14.8	19.3
Exchange rate (per US$)	242.78	252.66	245.70
Interest rate			
GDP (% real growth)	-8.5	-12.0	-11.0
GDP (Million units of national currency)	250,686.0	269,584.0	286,236.2
GDP (US$ million)	1,032.6	1,067.0	1,165.0
GDP per capita (US$)	173.2	174.1	184.6
Consumption (Million units of national currency)	218,822.0	236,175.0	251,676.9
Consumption (US$ million)	901.3	934.8	1,024.3
Consumption per capita (US$)	151.2	152.5	162.3
Population, mid-year ('000)	5,960.0	6,130.0	6,310.0
Birth rate (per '000)	45.6	44.0	
Death rate (per '000)	15.9	14.9	
No. of households ('000)	995.0	1,028.9	1,089.1
Total exports (US$ million)	68.0	108.0	
Total imports (US$ million)	204.0	224.0	234.0
Tourism receipts (US$ million)	3.0	2.9	
Tourist spending (US$ million)	20.0	19.2	

Average household size 1995 (persons)	5.66		
Urban population 1995 (%)	7.5		
Age analysis (%) (1991)	*0-14* 46.0	*15-64* 50.0	*65+* 4.0
Population by sex (%) (1991)	*Male* 48.6	*Female* 51.4	
Life expectancy (years) (1990-95)	*Male* 48.4	*Female* 51.9	
Infant mortality (deaths per '000 live births) (1993)	102.0		
Adult literacy (%) (1990)	50.0		

TRADING PARTNERS

Major export destinations 1995 (% share)		Major import sources 1995 (% share)	
Germany	23.7	Belgium/Luxembourg	14.1
Belgium/Luxembourg	21.7	Germany	7.5
USA	9.9	Japan	7.5
France	7.5	France	7.2

Cambodia

Area (km²)   181,000

Currency   Riel (R = 100 sen)

Location   Cambodia, the former Kampuchea, is located at the centre of the Indochinese peninsula with Vietnam to the south and east, Laos to the north and Thailand to the north-west. Its access to the sea is through a 300-kilometre stretch of land adjoining the Gulf of Thailand. Most of the country is near-impenetrable jungle. The climate is tropical and extremely humid. The capital is Phnom-Penh.

Head of State   King Norodom Sihanouk

Head of Government   Prince Norodom Ranariddh. Hun Sen, the leader of a rival party, occupies the position of second prime minister

Ruling Party   Prince Ranariddh's royalist United National Front party, known as Funcinpec, narrowly won the 1993 election, but in an unusual power-sharing arrangement, Hun Sen's Cambodian People's Party was accepted as a partner in the government.

Political Structure   The State of Cambodia resumed its traditional title in 1990, having been known since the late 1970s as Kampuchea or Democratic Kampuchea. The country suffered appallingly during the forced collectivist reforms imposed by the Khmer Rouge of Pol Pot in the 1970s. Vietnamese troops invaded the country in 1978 and installed a pro-Vietnamese regime, sparking a civil war with the Khmer Rouge. That war ended in 1990 with a UN-sponsored compromise which effectively left the Khmer Rouge as a junior partner in the administration of Prince Norodom Sihanouk. Khmer Rouge representatives later withdrew from effective government and the military embarked on an intensive and only partially successful campaign (in collaboration with UN troops) to rid the country of its former Khmer Rouge soldiers. Today, approximately 5,000 of these fighters remain in the jungles.

Last Elections   The first multi-party elections to the 120-member Assembly since 1973 were held in May 1993, when the United National Front won 58 seats, the Cambodian People's Party 51, the Buddhist Liberal Democrats 10 and the National Liberation Movement one seat. The turnout was 90%. In September 1993 the country had received its first Constituent Assembly and provisional Constitution, promising a multi-party system and a limited monarchy.

Political Risk   The withdrawal of the Khmer Rouge from politics and its subsequent defeat on the battlefield have been beneficial factors in the development of the economy as a whole. However, Hun Sen was a Khmer Rouge commander until 1979 and the tension between him and Prince Ranariddh is great. The Khmer Rouge itself is still capable of winning battles, although its soldiers are closer to being bandits than rebels. Meanwhile, King Sihanouk has announced that he is dying, that his son will be his successor and that the royalist party will probably collapse. The real struggle in Cambodia today is not against the Khmer Rouge but over the legacy of the nearly $3 billion effort by the UN to put in place a free and democratic government.

International Disputes   The severe political trials faced by Cambodia during the last 100 years have left their mark on the country's relations with Thailand and Vietnam. Thailand, which played host to the Khmer Rouge rebels during their decade-long struggle to regain control, still engages in occasional cross-border fire over alleged drug-running practices and complains when Cambodian troops enter its territory during "hot pursuit" operations against the Khmers. Vietnam has renounced its occupation of Cambodia, which continued from 1978 to 1990, but relations have yet to be normalised.

Economy   Cambodia's economic future remains precarious as its delicate political balance of left and ultra-left politicians attempt to convince the international community of their good intent. The economy's growth prospects are constrained by the government's continued reliance on five-year plans as a means of guiding development. The country's best chance to achieve some measurable improvement in living standards is that one of the energy consortiums exploring off its coast will find oil and/or gas. Preliminary wells have already demonstrated the existence of hydrocarbons but it is still uncertain that these are available in commercial quantities.

Main Industries   Cambodia's gradual industrialisation process still leaves agriculture as the major sector of the economy. Rice, maize, palm sugar, pepper and timber are all harvested, although all but the timber are mainly for domestic consumption. Rubber is also exported nowadays. The industrial structure is now being rebuilt after the ravages of the Khmer Rouge in the 1970s and early 1980s and a capitalist approach is being gently encouraged. The country's regulations governing foreign investment have recently been liberalised.

Energy   Most of Cambodia's extremely modest energy requirements are met either from coal or natural fuels such as firewood. Its electricity production, however, is almost 40% derived from hydro-electric power plants.

	1993	1994	1995
Inflation (% change)		4.1	3.0
Exchange rate (per US$)	3,508.32	2,591.35	2,378.50
Interest rate			
GDP (% real growth)			
GDP (Billion units of national currency)	33,000.0		
GDP (US$ million)	9,406.2		
GDP per capita (US$)	1,010.3		
Consumption (Billion units of national currency)	14,795.8		
Consumption (US$ million)	4,217.3		
Consumption per capita (US$)	453.0		
Population, mid-year ('000)	9,310.0	9,570.0	9,837.7
Birth rate (per '000)	43.5	45.1	
Death rate (per '000)	14.3	13.8	
No. of households ('000)	2,056.0	2,110.6	2,225.1
Total exports (US$ million)			
Total imports (US$ million)			
Tourism receipts (US$ million)	48.0	47.5	
Tourist spending (US$ million)	4.0	4.0	

Average household size 1995 (persons)	4.31		
Urban population 1995 (%)	20.7		
Age analysis (%) (1992)	*0-14* 46.9	*15-64* 47.7	*65+* 5.4
Population by sex (%) (1992)	*Male* 46.3	*Female* 53.7	
Life expectancy (years) (1990)	*Male* 47.0	*Female* 49.9	
Infant mortality (deaths per '000 live births) (1993)	115.7		
Adult literacy (%) (1990)	35.2		

Cameroon

Area (km²) 465,500

Currency CFA franc (= 100 centimes)

Location Cameroon lies on the West African Atlantic coast facing south-westwards into the Gulf of Guinea. With Nigeria to the west, Gabon, Equatorial Guinea and Congo to the south, and the Central African Republic and Chad to the east and north-east, it has a tropical but dry climate. The capital is Yaoundé.

Head of State President Paul Biya (1982)

Head of Government Simon Achidi Achu (1992)

Ruling Party The Cameroon Democratic Movement leads a coalition of three governing parties.

Political Structure Cameroon was a one-party socialist state from 1964 (when all but the ruling party were banned) until 1992. Under the 1990 Constitution, the executive President and the 180-member National Assembly are elected for a five-year term by popular mandate. An attempt was made in December 1994 to set up a constitutional consultative committee, but it quickly collapsed.

Last Elections The country's first multi-party elections since 1964 were held in March 1992, when the ruling Cameroon People's Party won 88 of the 180 seats. The National Union for Democracy and Progress won 68 seats, the Union of the Peoples of Cameroon won 18 and the Movement for the Defence of the Republic captured six seats in the far north of the country. Voter turnout was officially quoted at 60%, but in the west it fell as low as 10%. The presidential elections which followed in October 1992 were regarded as fraudulent. President Biya has gradually acquired wide powers to rule by decree.

Political Risk The return of multi-party parliamentary democracy has been widely welcomed but the international community has become increasingly concerned that there has been no progress on human rights or the reform the existing constitution. Social unrest is frequent and the division between the country's English and French-speaking population is an uneasy one. Donor countries are reluctant to provide aid to a government regarded as corrupt.

International Disputes Cameroon has an ongoing dispute with Nigeria over the oil-rich Bakassi peninsula, where there have been border clashes. Nigeria claims that French troops have been involved but the Chirac government has denied this. Nigerian troops have occupied Diamond Island and Djabane, both important oil-producing regions. Cameroon has become the 52nd member of the Commonwealth. The government believes the move will give it more international respectability.

Economy Although one of the poorer economies in Africa, Cameroon's oil production gives it some degree of security. Agricultural reforms have been initiated but donors are still dubious about the government's political intentions. Prospective investors may be reassured by the decision to join the Commonwealth. A 50% devaluation in the CFA franc occurred in 1994 and has caused a severe escalation of the country's external debts.

Main Industries Cameroon's dominant agricultural sector consists almost exclusively of smallholdings but the government hopes to develop larger-scale agro-industrial complexes which will boost productivity. Cocoa, coffee, bananas, groundnuts, rubber and palm products are grown for export. The country's industrial development centres on bauxite at present, with a large aluminium smelter at Edéa. There is also an oil refinery which processes part of Cameroon's 7-8 million tonnes of crude oil production in a typical year.

Energy Oil and natural gas, largely domestically produced, account for all but a tiny fraction of the country's energy requirements. More than 98% of Cameroon's electricity needs are supplied by hydro-electric power stations.

	1993	1994	1995
Inflation (% change)	-3.2	35.1	13.9
Exchange rate (per US$)	283.16	555.20	498.70
Interest rate (% per annum)	17.5	17.5	16.0
GDP (% real growth)	4.0	-19.7	-7.9
GDP (Million units of national currency)	3,171,000.0	3,439,000.0	3,609,046.2
GDP (US$ million)	11,198.6	6,194.2	7,236.9
GDP per capita (US$)	894.5	481.3	544.9
Consumption (Million units of national currency)	3,219,931.5	4,558,933.0	6,246,030.8
Consumption (US$ million)	11,371.4	8,211.3	12,524.6
Consumption per capita (US$)	908.3	638.0	943.1
Population, mid-year ('000)	12,520.0	12,870.0	13,280.0
Birth rate (per '000)	40.7	40.5	
Death rate (per '000)	15.4	12.2	
No. of households ('000)	3,269.6	3,370.0	3,566.3
Total exports (US$ million)	1,883.0	1,360.0	
Total imports (US$ million)	1,102.0	728.0	
Tourism receipts (US$ million)	47.0	38.8	
Tourist spending (US$ million)	225.0	185.7	283.2

Average household size 1995 (persons)	3.63				
Urban population 1995 (%)	44.9				
Age analysis (%) (1986)	*0-14* 45.2		*15-64* 51.1		*65+* 3.7
Population by sex (%) (1986)	*Male* 49.9		*Female* 50.1		
Life expectancy (years) (1990-95)	*Male* 54.5		*Female* 57.5		
Infant mortality (deaths per '000 live births) (1993)	63.0				
Adult literacy (%) (1990)	54.1				

TRADING PARTNERS

Major export destinations 1995 (% share)		Major import sources 1995 (% share)	
France	18.7	France	39.4
Italy	13.8	Belgium/Luxembourg	6.0
Spain	13.2	Senegal	5.7
Senegal	10.2	Germany	5.3

Canada

Area (km²)   9,922,385

Currency   Canadian dollar (C$ = 100 cents)

Location   Extending some 3,000 miles from the Pacific Ocean in the west to the Arctic Atlantic in the east, Canada occupies virtually the entire northern half of the North American continent. The capital is Ottawa.

Head of State   HM Queen Elizabeth II

Head of Government   Jean Chrétien

Ruling Party   Liberal Party

Political Structure   The Dominion of Canada comprises a federation of 12 provinces and territories, each of which exercises considerable political autonomy over its own affairs. The Northwest Territories are to be divided so as to create an Indian territory, to be known as Nunavut. Québec, which is French-speaking, narrowly rejected a referendum on secession from the Federation in 1995. The House of Commons in Ottawa has 295 members and the Senate (Upper House) 107. A Governor-General represents the monarch.

Last Elections   The elections of October 1993 brought a spectacular defeat for the Progressive Conservative Party which had ruled the country since 1984. The Conservatives retained only two seats in the Commons after a disastrous campaign. The Liberal Party, which had previously held 82 seats, increased its representation to 178 and went on to form the new government. Meanwhile, the secessionist Bloc Québecois with 54 seats, and the Reform Party with 52 became the official opposition. The left-wing New Democratic Party retained only eight of its 44 seats. There were two independents.

Political Risk   Relations with the United States have generally been strengthened by implementation of the North American Free Trade Agreement (NAFTA), which came into effect in January 1994. Fears that Québec would soon become a separate country were widespread after the province's narrow rejection of independence in 1995. Now, Québec's premier, Lucien Bouchard, has dampened his rhetoric (possibly after he realised the economic costs of such a move) and has announced that there will be no new referendum before the next provincial election in September 1999. The government's negotiations with its indigenous people could eventually be even more dramatic than its problems with Québec. A total of 47 native land claims must be settled. These cover almost all of the province of British Columbia (950,000 square kilometres).

International Disputes   Canada has no significant territorial disputes. Relations with the EU have been strained by disputes over fishing rights around Iceland and off the coast of Ireland. A further dispute with France over fisheries and oil exploration around St Pierre and Miquelon was settled in December 1994. A major dispute over the fishing rights of Spanish vessels within the waters of Newfoundland broke out in 1995.

Economy   High levels of spending in previous years coincided with a contraction in mineral and raw material prices and left Canada with a serious overspending problem. The Government has sought to remedy the situation with tight fiscal policies and higher taxes. The moribund export sector is now showing signs of growth thanks mainly to impetus provided by NAFTA. Social and political tensions have been raised by the high level of unemployment experienced during the 1990s. The government will also probably have to come up with very large amounts of cash to settle the many land claims of its native populations.

Main Industries   Canada is the world's largest producer of zinc and uranium and has substantial reserves of nickel, potash, cobalt, silver and gold. Although Canada has a growing range of manufacturing industries, most activity centres on the processing of raw materials - principally timber, fish and mineral products. The smaller number of large companies supplying finished products such as motor vehicles and electronics have a strong market not only at home but in the United States. Fishing and agriculture still comprise a third of GDP, with wheat and barley being the predominant agricultural exports.

Energy   Canada has substantial natural gas resources and is one of the world's biggest producers with an annual output in excess of 90 million tonnes of oil equivalent a year. Domestic oil reserves, however, will suffice for only 10 years' production at present rates. Some 60% of all electricity is generated by hydro-electric sources.

	1993	1994	1995
Inflation (% change)	1.8	0.3	2.0
Exchange rate (per US$)	1.29	1.37	1.37
Interest rate (% per annum)	5.9	6.9	8.9
GDP (% real growth)	1.6	3.9	2.1
GDP (Million units of national currency)	711,658.0	741,510.0	770,429.0
GDP (US$ million)	551,672.9	541,248.2	562,356.9
GDP per capita (US$)	19,062.6	18,504.2	18,992.1
Consumption (Million units of national currency)	437,298.5	455,186.6	474,183.4
Consumption (US$ million)	338,991.1	332,253.0	346,119.3
Consumption per capita (US$)	11,713.6	11,359.1	11,689.3
Population, mid-year ('000)	28,940.0	29,250.0	29,610.0
Birth rate (per '000)	14.0	14.1	14.1
Death rate (per '000)	7.2	7.4	7.3
No. of households ('000)	10,247.0	10,524.0	10,808.0
Total exports (US$ million)	145,178.0	165,376.0	192,197.0
Total imports (US$ million)	139,035.0	155,072.0	168,426.0
Tourism receipts (US$ million)	5,897.0	6,309.8	7,048.0
Tourist spending (US$ million)	12,931.0	9,940.1	9,565.7

Average household size 1995 (persons)	2.64				
Urban population 1995 (%)	76.7				
Age analysis (%) (1995)	*0-14* 20.2		*15-64* 67.9		*65+* 11.9
Population by sex (%) (1995)	*Male* 49.1		*Female* 50.9		
Life expectancy (years) (1995)	*Male* 74.9		*Female* 81.0		
Infant mortality (deaths per '000 live births) (1994)	6.2				
Adult literacy (%) (1986)	96.6				

TRADING PARTNERS

Major export destinations 1995 (% share)		Major import sources 1995 (% share)	
USA	79.9	USA	66.1
Japan	4.6	Japan	5.6
United Kingdom	1.4	United Kingdom	2.4
China	1.2	Mexico	2.3

Cape Verde

Area (km²)   4,035

Currency   Escudo (Esc = 100 centavos)

Location   Cape Verde, one of the smallest African states, consists of two groups of islands (known as the Windward and Leeward Islands) off the Atlantic coast of West Africa, some 500 km west of Senegal. The capital is Praia.

Head of State   President António Mascarenhas Monteiro (1991)

Head of Government   M. Carlos Veiga

Ruling Party   Movimento para Democracia

Political Structure   The Republic of Cape Verde became independent from Portugal in 1985 and quickly established itself as a one-party state with a socialist orientation. An attempt was made to reforge a previous political alliance with Guinea-Bissau, but this idea was dropped after political changes in the latter country. Under the 1990 Constitution the country has an executive President, elected by popular mandate for a five-year term, who answers to a 79-member National Assembly, also elected for five years.

Last Elections   The country's first multi-party elections were held in 1991, when the Movimento para Democracia (MPD) obtained some 65% of the votes and assumed a 56-seat majority in the 79-member National Assembly. The main opposition party is the Partido Africano da Independência de Cabo Verde which had ruled until the elections. The first free presidential elections followed soon afterwards when candidate António Monteiro, the MPD's candidate, won a convincing victory.

Political Risk   As in so many other African countries, the resumption of multi-party politics has opened up the potential for foreign assistance. Cape Verde, however, is both an extremely poor and politically immature country. Rumours of coup attempts are frequent and the stability of the government is shaky.

Economy   The country's political difficulties are mirrored to a considerable extent by the economic problems it faces. As much as 80% of the country's GDP comes from abroad, half of it in the form of remittances by expatriate workers and the remainder being aid from bilateral donors. These funds are effectively the main source of consumer purchasing power.

Main Industries   Recurrent and severe droughts have gradually decimated Cape Verde's agricultural sector. Today, only the farms in the country's irrigated valleys are reliable producers of basic foodstuffs. Their main crops include maize, sugar cane and groundnuts, although coffee and bananas are grown for export. There is also an important fishing industry which provides a range of products for export. Cape Verde has very little domestic industry of any importance, the main activities revolving around the processing of agricultural raw materials (flour milling, rum manufacture, fish processing) and ship repair. The mining industry centres on the extraction of pozzuolana, a volcanic rock, and the production of sea salt which is obtained by an evaporation process.

Energy   Cape Verde is entirely dependent on imported energy supplies, mainly in the form of oil and natural gas. All electricity is produced by thermal power stations.

	1993	1994	1995
Inflation (% change)	10.5	2.4	8.3
Exchange rate (per US$)	80.43	81.89	82.70
Interest rate (% per annum)	10.0	10.7	12.0
GDP (% real growth)	10.3	3.1	6.7
GDP (Million units of national currency)	29,617.4	31,268.4	36,132.5
GDP (US$ million)	368.2	381.8	436.9
GDP per capita (US$)	995.2	1,005.0	1,118.4
Consumption (Million units of national currency)	17,866.5	19,194.7	22,571.3
Consumption (US$ million)	222.1	234.4	272.9
Consumption per capita (US$)	600.4	616.9	698.7
Population, mid-year ('000)	370.0	380.0	390.7
Birth rate (per '000)	41.2	46.2	
Death rate (per '000)	8.0	7.9	
No. of households ('000)	87.0	89.8	94.9
Total exports (US$ million)	6.0	8.0	
Total imports (US$ million)	188.9	220.0	
Tourism receipts (US$ million)			
Tourist spending (US$ million)	20.0	20.9	24.3

Average household size 1995 (persons)	4.02				
Urban population 1995 (%)	54.3				
Age analysis (%) (1990)	*0-14* 45.0		*15-64* 49.2		*65+* 5.8
Population by sex (%) (1990)	*Male* 47.3		*Female* 52.7		
Life expectancy (years) (1990)	*Male* 63.5		*Female* 71.3		
Infant mortality (deaths per '000 live births)					
Adult literacy (%) (1990)	62.9				

Cayman Islands

Area (km²)   259

Currency   Cayman Islands dollar (CI$ = 100 cents)

Location   The Cayman Islands lie in the Caribbean, about 230 km south of Cuba and 300 km north-west of Jamaica. The climate is consistently warm, with only light rainfall. The capital is George Town.

Head of State   HM Queen Elizabeth II

Head of Government   Governor Michael Gore

Ruling Party   There are no formal political parties in the Cayman Islands, though some exist in practice. A "National Team" governs.

Political Structure   The Cayman Islands, which were a dependency of Jamaica until 1962, have been a United Kingdom Dependent Territory ever since. There has been no serious move to replace the system created by the 1972 Constitution, which awards all executive power to the Governor and the eight-member Executive Council (of which four members are elected by the Legislative Assembly, with the Governor and the other three ex officio members). The Legislative Assembly has 18 members, of whom 3 are officials and the other 15 are elected by universal suffrage for a term of five years. A move introduced in 1987 granted resident Cayman Islanders certain electoral privileges over immigrants.

Last Elections   Elections to the Legislative Assembly were last held in November 1992, when all the candidates presented themselves as independents. However, 12 of the 15 elected members belonged to the Progressive Democratic Party, the first legal party.

Political Risk   The Islands' status as a dependent territory and their relatively high level of per capita income yield a stable economic and political system.

Economy   The dependency's liberal taxation and financial regulation policies have won it both popularity and notoriety over the years. Affluence is high, thanks to the considerable revenues from import duties and other fee incomes, but the Cayman Islands' economic reliance on financial services means that the economy could suffer as a result of drastic shifts in the regulatory environments of their offshore competitors. The currency is often stronger than the US dollar, a factor which periodically impacts on the tourism sector.

Main Industries   Tourism is the fastest-growing source of income in the Caymans, with a wide range of facilities on offer. Revenues from this sector are the main source of funding for the country's infrastructure development. Tourism accounts for almost half of all foreign exchange earnings and employs a third of the workforce. Even more important is the financial services industry (now growing by as much as 25% a year). International offshore funds have been attracted by a complete absence of income tax or other corporate taxes, and the islands have more than 550 banks - one for every 38 people in the country - and 24,000 registered companies, or virtually one per resident. The industry's international reputation has been further enhanced by legal treaties which have been signed with both the US and the UK to discourage money laundering and related financial crime.

Energy   All of the country's energy requirements are imported, with oil predominating. All electricity generation derives from thermal stations.

	1993	1994	1995
Inflation (% change)	9.0	-2.3	2.0
Exchange rate (per US$)	0.85	0.83	0.83
Interest rate			
GDP (% real growth)	3.5	2.9	3.2
GDP (Million units of national currency)	820.8	825.3	868.7
GDP (US$ million)	963.4	997.2	1,049.0
GDP per capita (US$)	33,220.0	33,240.7	34,965.1
Consumption (Million units of national currency)	382.4	388.3	412.7
Consumption (US$ million)	448.9	469.2	498.4
Consumption per capita (US$)	15,478.4	15,639.6	16,611.9
Population, mid-year ('000)	29.0	30.0	30.0
Birth rate (per '000)	18.1	17.0	
Death rate (per '000)	4.2	4.8	
No. of households ('000)	6.0	6.2	6.5
Total exports (US$ million)			
Total imports (US$ million)			
Tourism receipts (US$ million)	252.0	255.9	
Tourist spending (US$ million)			

Average household size 1995 (persons)	4.60				
Urban population 1995 (%)	100.0				
Age analysis (%) (1991)	*0-14* 21.5		*15-64* 61.3		*65+* 17.2
Population by sex (%) (1991)	*Male* 48.2		*Female* 51.8		
Life expectancy (years)					
Infant mortality (deaths per '000 live births) (1991)	14.0				
Adult literacy (%) (1970)	97.5				

Central African Republic

Area (km²)   624,975

Currency   CFA franc (= 100 centimes)

Location   The Central African Republic is located, as its name suggests, in the geographic centre of the continent. It borders on Congo and Zaire in the south, Chad in the north, Sudan in the east and Cameroon in the west. Although there are important watercourses in the east of the country, much of the rest is semi-desert, and climatic conditions are dry tropical. The capital is Bangui.

Head of State   President Ange-Félix Patasse (1993)

Head of Government   Gabriel Koyambonnou (April 1995)

Ruling Party   Central African People's Liberation Party leads a four-party coalition.

Political Structure   Talks to restore multi-party democracy were held in 1993 and 1994 following the collapse of the "Grand National Debate" during 1992. Current plans for the constitution envisage that the President would be only semi-executive for a six-year term, with most of the power being vested in the Prime Minister. For the time being, however, the President has the authority to rule by decree over the National Assembly, which is itself elected for a five-year term.

Last Elections   The country's first multi-party elections were held in 1992, but were immediately cancelled after charges of voting irregularities. A limited poll followed in August and September 1993, when the Central African People's Liberation Party of Ange-Félix Patasse was elected - though without an absolute majority. At the same time Patasse was elected President, with 52% of the votes in the second round of balloting. Since then, fresh elections have been repeatedly promised, and repeatedly postponed.

Political Risk   Despite renewed attempts to restore political stability, the CAR is plagued by recurrent violence and political disagreements. The political, legal and economic issues which divide the country's leaders are unlikely to be resolved in the near future. The situation worsened in 1996 when the country's military mutinied and began looting and releasing prisoners; President Patasse was forced to take refuge with the French army stationed in the country. The latest crisis stems from corruption which has become commonplace since the CAR gained independence from France in 1965.

Economy   The CAR has massive foreign debts which it is unable to service at present. Agricultural productivity is low and few profitable manufacturing enterprises are to be found in the country. Much of this malaise can be attributed to mismanagement and political unrest. The economy depends heavily on foreign aid, mainly from France.

Main Industries   Efforts to establish a stronger non-agricultural base have made little headway. The CAR's economy depends heavily on farming and is dominated by small landholders, most of which produce for subsistence purposes. Cattle herding is the major activity, although cotton and coffee are more important as sources of export revenues. Mining is the other major economic activity, with diamonds, gold, uranium, copper and manganese being extracted in the west of the country. In the late 1980s the mineral sector provided half of GDP but its share has declined sharply in the 1990s.

	1993	1994	1995
Inflation (% change)	-2.9	24.6	41.6
Exchange rate (per US$)	283.16	555.20	498.70
Interest rate (% per annum)	17.5	17.5	16.0
GDP (% real growth)	2.0	7.5	-2.0
GDP (Million units of national currency)	351,103.9	574,077.8	796,636.3
GDP (US$ million)	1,239.9	1,034.0	1,597.4
GDP per capita (US$)	392.4	320.1	485.5
Consumption (Million units of national currency)	197,519.5	314,076.1	423,851.8
Consumption (US$ million)	697.6	565.7	849.9
Consumption per capita (US$)	220.7	175.1	258.3
Population, mid-year ('000)	3,160.0	3,230.0	3,290.0
Birth rate (per '000)	45.6	42.3	
Death rate (per '000)	16.6	18.8	
No. of households ('000)	585.5	595.0	618.2
Total exports (US$ million)	110.0	150.0	187.0
Total imports (US$ million)	126.0	142.0	189.0
Tourism receipts (US$ million)			
Tourist spending (US$ million)	4.0	3.4	5.1

Average household size 1995 (persons)	5.16				
Urban population 1995 (%)	39.3				
Age analysis (%) (1988)	*0-14* 45.0		*15-64* 49.2		*65+* 5.8
Population by sex (%) (1988)	*Male* 48.5		*Female* 51.5		
Life expectancy (years) (1990-95)	*Male* 46.9		*Female* 51.9		
Infant mortality (deaths per '000 live births) (1993)	101.7				
Adult literacy (%) (1990)	37.7				

TRADING PARTNERS

Major export destinations 1995 (% share)		Major import sources 1995 (% share)	
Belgium/Luxembourg	55.6	France	16.9
Spain	8.8	Japan	10.8
France	7.8	Cameroon	5.3
Italy	7.4	Italy	3.4

Chad

Area (km²) 1,284,000

Currency CFA franc (= 100 centimes)

Location Chad, one of the largest and most sparsely populated countries in Africa, is located in central North Africa. Libya is to the north, Sudan to the east, and Niger and Cameroon to the west. The Central African Republic borders on the country's more fertile southern regions. The climate is dry tropical, with little rainfall. The capital is N'Djaména.

Head of State President Idriss Déby (1991)

Head of Government Koibla Djimasta (April 1995)

Ruling Party Patriotic Salvation Movement, a non-party coalition which includes the only four legal parties.

Political Structure Severe and violent conflict became commonplace in Chad throughout the first half of the 1990s. Major disputes include an open rebellion against President Déby and at least two abortive coup attempts in recent years. Chad is only now beginning to emerge from decades of wars, some of them internal and others waged against neighbouring countries.

Last Elections There have been no multi-party elections in Chad in recent years. Opposition parties such as the Rally for Democracy and Progress, the Union for Democracy and the Republic, or the Chadian Union for Democracy and Progress, have only been permitted since 1993. Elections would not have been possible in any case, given the constant and escalating level of violence.

Political Risk The most serious internal security worries were partially addressed in 1994 when a general ceasefire was negotiated between the major warring factions. However, this modest success has not dispelled fears that Chad has yet to regain sufficiently full control of its economy. The active involvement of the French authorities is a positive factor in pushing the country towards a peaceful resolution to its many conflicts.

International Disputes Chad has blamed Nigeria openly for allowing rebel forces to group within its borders in order to launch attacks on Chadian armed forces. Chad's relations with Nigeria are in any case strained by a disagreement about various islands in Lake Chad and the two countries came to armed conflict over the issue in 1983. Chad also maintains a claim against Libya for the return of the Aozou Strip, a border area some 300 kilometres wide across the entire 1,200 km border between the two countries. Libya was awarded rights to this area, which it formally annexed in 1973, in a disputed post-war agreement. In 1994, the International Court of Justice found in Chad's favour on the issue and Libya withdrew its troops.

Economy The country is continually battling against a dry and frequently drought-ridden climate and the prospects for a major consumer upturn remain slim. However, Chad has generally managed to avoid the worst privations being experienced by its neighbours in recent years. if the country's internal political situation should stabilise, its attraction to foreign investors will be greatly enhanced. Otherwise, Chad remains heavily dependent on France.

Main Industries Agriculture is by far the most important economic activity, employing 90% of the workforce and providing more than 80% of GDP in a typical year. Cotton, the major export crop, is grown in the south of the country, while cattle herding, the other main source of foreign revenues, is conducted in the central regions. Variety is provided by an oilfield at Kanem, and by the mining of salt around Lake Chad. Industrial development is at an extremely low level.

Energy Chad's own oilfield provides a large proportion of its oil and gas requirements, although some has to be imported. The low level of industrialisation limits the demand for energy and natural fuels such as brushwood are probably still the most important source of fuel.

	1993	1994	1995
Inflation (% change)	-7.1	40.4	26.7
Exchange rate (per US$)	283.16	555.20	498.70
Interest rate (% per annum)	17.5	17.0	16.0
GDP (% real growth)	-10.4		1.0
GDP (Million units of national currency)	339,000.0	475,956.0	609,066.6
GDP (US$ million)	1,197.2	857.3	1,221.3
GDP per capita (US$)	196.3	138.0	192.4
Consumption (Million units of national currency)	132,882.2	222,776.3	219,428.0
Consumption (US$ million)	469.3	401.3	440.0
Consumption per capita (US$)	77.0	64.6	69.3
Population, mid-year ('000)	6,098.0	6,210.0	6,347.3
Birth rate (per '000)	43.7	42.1	
Death rate (per '000)	20.5	20.6	
No. of households ('000)	1,179.3	1,207.0	1,266.9
Total exports (US$ million)	132.0	156.0	
Total imports (US$ million)	201.0	185.0	
Tourism receipts (US$ million)	23.0	18.2	
Tourist spending (US$ million)	12.0	9.5	10.4

Average household size 1995 (persons)	4.89				
Urban population 1995 (%)	21.4				
Age analysis (%) (1978)	*0-14* 37.4		*15-64* 59.9		*65+* 2.6
Population by sex (%) (1978)	*Male* 51.5		*Female* 48.5		
Life expectancy (years) (1990-95)	*Male* 45.9		*Female* 49.1		
Infant mortality (deaths per '000 live births) (1993)	122.0				
Adult literacy (%) (1990)	29.8				

Chile

Area (km²) 751,625

Currency Chilean peso (P = 100 centavos)

Location Although never more than about 200 km in depth, Chile occupies the greater part of South America's Pacific coastline, with Argentina to its east over the Andes mountains and Peru and Bolivia to the north. In the south its Tierra del Fuego regions are sub-Antarctic in character. The extraordinary range of climatic conditions which result is one of the most striking features of the country. The capital is Santiago.

Head of State President Eduardo Frei Ruiz-Tagle (March 1994)

Head of Government President Eduardo Frei Ruiz-Tagle

Ruling Party Christian Democratic Party leads a broad-based coalition of Parties for Democracy.

Political Structure Chile was a parliamentary democracy before power was seized in 1973 in a coup which established Gen. Augusto Pinochet as President, ruling largely by decree. In 1989, constitutional reforms led to elections in which an executive President would be elected for a four-year term. Pinochet was promptly voted out of office, being succeeded first by Patricio Aylwin and then by Eduardo Frei. There is a 47-member Senate and a 120-member Chamber of Deputies, elected for four years.

Last Elections Presidential elections held in December 1993 resulted in a landslide win for the Christian Democrat candidate Eduardo Frei Ruiz-Tagle, who was contesting the seat vacated by Patricio Aylwin. Congressional elections held at the same time failed to confirm the dominance of the right-wing alliance around the Christian Democrats, which fell short of a working majority in either the Lower or the Upper House of Parliament, though it remained in office.

Political Risk Vestiges of the old regime still exist. General Pinochet hangs on a head of the army. Eight unelected "institutional" senators hold the balance of power in the Senate, two of them appointed by Pinochet. Overall, however, the return to democracy has been smooth and the leadership of the government impressive. Unfortunately for Chile, its hopes of joining the North American Free Trade Association (NAFTA) were dashed in 1996 when the Clinton administration refused to submit the proposal to Congress for political reasons.

International Disputes Chile has an ongoing disagreement with Bolivia about that country's call for the restoration of its access to the Pacific Ocean. Relations with Argentina have occasionally been strained over the issue of watercourse developments. However, Chile has now settled its 150-year-old dispute with Argentina over three islands in the far south (Picton, Lennox and Nueva).

Economy Chile has an economy that is difficult to find fault with. Inflation remains in single digits and falling. The government consistently runs a healthy budget surplus and has ample foreign reserves. Exports have grown by more than 20% for several years and the unemployment rate, at under 6%, is one of the lowest in Latin America. Economic success has brought problems of its own, however. Chile desperately needs better infrastructure if it is to persuade private investors to come up with some of the $10 billion in additional capital that will be required between 1995 and the year 2000. The country also needs new export markets which partly explains its desire to join Mercosur now that its application to NAFTA has been derailed.

Main Industries Chile's agricultural sector depends on livestock rearing in the plateaux and extensive crop farming in the central region - including fruit, vegetables, sugar beet, grapes and citrus products as well as ample cereal crops. There are large timber areas in the centre and south of the country, and the warm Pacific waters provide scope for a large and active fishing industry. Copper remains the country's largest export but there are also huge deposits of iron ore, nitrates, molybdenum, mercury and manganese. Manufacturing has flourished as the private sector has taken hold. The country's small and medium-sized firms have rapidly won new foreign markets, with processed fruits and vegetables and fine wines becoming important foreign-exchange earners. Major investments are being made in roadways and other infrastructure facilities.

Energy Although Chile has its own oil and gas wells, they can meet less than a third of its total energy requirements and most of the remainder has to be imported. About half of the country's electricity is generated by hydro-electric power stations: there is doubtless room for an expansion.

	1993	1994	1995
Inflation (% change)	12.7	11.4	8.2
Exchange rate (per US$)	404.35	420.08	396.57
Interest rate (% per annum)	24.3	20.3	18.2
GDP (% real growth)	6.4	4.5	12.6
GDP (Million units of national currency)	18,453,500.0	21,917,900.0	26,702,100.0
GDP (US$ million)	45,637.4	52,175.5	67,332.6
GDP per capita (US$)	3,314.3	3,729.5	4,741.7
Consumption (Million units of national currency)	11,707,300.0	13,905,190.0	16,940,389.5
Consumption (US$ million)	28,953.4	33,101.3	42,717.3
Consumption per capita (US$)	2,102.6	2,366.1	3,008.3
Population, mid-year ('000)	13,770.0	13,990.0	14,200.0
Birth rate (per '000)	21.8	20.6	
Death rate (per '000)	6.7	5.5	
No. of households ('000)	3,081.1	3,128.0	3,260.7
Total exports (US$ million)	9,199.0	11,604.0	16,039.0
Total imports (US$ million)	11,125.0	11,825.0	15,914.0
Tourism receipts (US$ million)	824.0	833.3	900.0
Tourist spending (US$ million)	568.0	650.8	839.9

Average household size 1995 (persons)	4.25				
Urban population 1995 (%)	83.9				
Age analysis (%) (1994)	*0-14*	30.6	*15-64*	63.1	*65+* 6.3
Population by sex (%) (1994)	*Male*	49.4	*Female*	50.6	
Life expectancy (years) (1990-95)	*Male*	68.5	*Female*	75.6	
Infant mortality (deaths per '000 live births) (1993)	13.1				
Adult literacy (%) (1990)	93.4				

TRADING PARTNERS

Major export destinations 1995 (% share)		Major import sources 1995 (% share)	
Japan	19.2	USA	24.2
USA	13.2	Argentina	9.2
Germany	6.4	Brazil	7.3
South Korea	5.5	Japan	6.4

China

Area (km²) 9,597,000

Currency Renminbi/Yuan (RMB/Y = 100 fen)

Location Occupying the entire 5,000-kilometre spread from the Sea of Japan and the East China Sea in the east to the Afghan border in the west, China has one of the longest international boundaries in the world and the largest population. In the north and north-west, its border is shared with Mongolia, Russia, Tajikistan, Kyrgyzstan and Kazakhstan. In the west, it meets Afghanistan and Pakistan, while India, Nepal, Bhutan, Myanmar, Laos and Vietnam lie to the south. The capital is Beijing.

Head of State President Jiang Zemin (1993)

Head of Government Li Peng

Ruling Party Chinese Communist Party

Political Structure China's 1992 Constitution vests all legislative authority in the 3,000-member National People's Congress, which is elected every five years. However, because the Congress meets only once a year, the Communist Party undertakes most political decisions. Recent developments in China reveal little evidence that the country's commitment to pluralism is keeping pace with the changes in its economy. As an enfeebled Deng Xiaoping fades from the scene, the country's new leaders engage in a game of transition politics. The latest session of the Central Committee in late 1995 approved appointments to the Central Military Commission that bolstered President Jiang Zemin. Deng's health is so precarious that he is beyond influencing developments. However, as long as he remains, China's new generation of leaders will be somewhat constrained.

Last Elections In the five-yearly National People's Congress elections, the vast majority of the elected delegates are from the Chinese Communist Party.

Political Risk Prospects for a smooth transition after the inevitable eventual death of Deng have improved in the past year but do not preclude a power struggle at some time in the near future. The Communist Party has a legacy of unresolved issues that can not be dealt with while he lives. Not least of these is a serious accounting of the Tiananmen massacre in 1989, which would include an assessment of Deng's own role.

International Disputes China reacts strongly whenever it perceives that its sovereignty is infringed. Its ongoing battle with Taiwan has heated up after the latter's efforts to gain international recognition and the Taiwanese elections in 1996. These tensions led to a considerable deterioration in ties with the USA. Other issues which mar US-Chinese relations include human rights, American objections to China's membership in the World Trade Organisation, China's sales of nuclear facilities to Pakistan and trading relations between the two countries. The country's strained relations with Vietnam have been improving but could deteriorate again now that Vietnam has signed a contract with Conoco to explore for oil north of the disputed Spratly Islands. China strongly warned the Vietnamese not to proceed with their plans for exploration in April 1996. Problems in Tibet, the Chinese province where Beijing is often accused of maltreating dissidents, have eased, although the Dalai Lama has been unable to conclude successful talks in Beijing with Chinese rulers.

Economy The state statistical office estimates that GDP grew by an impressive 9.7% in 1995 and the government expects growth in 1996 to exceed the target of 8%. Meanwhile, retail price increases have been running between 10% and 20% since 1994 and analysts doubt Beijing's ability to hold the rate of increase to single digits. China is becoming a significant force in international trade and could be the world's fourth largest trading nation by the end of the decade (after the USA, Germany, and Japan). Membership in the WTO will be essential if the country achieves this status. To appease US critics of the country's trade regime, China announced drastic reductions in its tariff schedules in 1996. This is a move that large agricultural exporters, including the USA, Canada and Australia, have demanded. Beijing is proceeding cautiously, however, because it does not wish to harm the interests of peasant farmers.

Main Industries The vast majority of China's population still relies on collectivised agriculture for its livelihood. Rice is the main food crop, although other cereals are grown in the north. Most of the country's cash crops (tea, sugar, cotton and fibre crops) are grown in the south and west of the country. Farm production is rising but can not keep pace with demand as China's population grows and becomes more affluent. The most rapid changes in the economy are occurring in industry where the creation of free economic zones, especially in the east and south-east of the country, has encouraged a massive expansion. Meanwhile, the government is struggling to rid itself of some of the state-owned manufacturers. Progress is slow (in part for ideological reasons) and around 60% of fixed assets in the industrial sector are still owned by the state. China has massive underdeveloped mineral resources. Coal, iron ore and tin are among the more important, but there are also significant oil deposits in the South China Sea and in the northern provinces.

Energy With the development of its (rather low quality) crude oil in the South China Sea, the country appears capable of achieving a substantial degree of self-sufficiency in the 1990s. Meanwhile, coal and natural fuels such as firewood will continue to provide up to 80% of all fuel needs.

	1993	1994	1995
Inflation (% change)	14.6	24.2	16.9
Exchange rate (per US$)	5.76	8.62	8.36
Interest rate (% per annum)	10.6	11.0	7.9
GDP (% real growth)	13.1	5.0	9.7
GDP (Billion units of national currency)	3,451.5	4,500.6	5,773.3
GDP (US$ million)	599,220.5	522,109.0	690,586.1
GDP per capita (US$)	500.9	407.6	533.5
Consumption (Billion units of national currency)	1,568.3	2,070.1	2,688.2
Consumption (US$ million)	272,265.6	240,150.8	321,556.6
Consumption per capita (US$)	227.6	187.5	248.4
Population, mid-year ('000)	1,196,400.0	1,280,800.0	1,294,400.0
Birth rate (per '000)	17.8	17.7	
Death rate (per '000)	6.5	6.5	
No. of households ('000)	220,460.0	304,711.0	357,063.8
Total exports (US$ million)	90,970.0	121,047.0	148,797.0
Total imports (US$ million)	103,088.0	115,681.0	129,113.0
Tourism receipts (US$ million)	4,683.0	7,323.0	14,000.0
Tourist spending (US$ million)	2,797.0	3,036.0	4,065.1

Average household size 1995 (persons)	3.99				
Urban population 1995 (%)	30.3				
Age analysis (%) (1994)	*0-14* 26.8		*15-64* 67.0		*65+* 6.2
Population by sex (%) (1994)	*Male* 51.1		*Female* 48.9		
Life expectancy (years) (1995)	*Male* 69.4		*Female* 73.0		
Infant mortality (deaths per '000 live births) (1995)	27.0				
Adult literacy (%) (1990)	77.8				

TRADING PARTNERS

Major export destinations 1995 (% share)		Major import sources 1995 (% share)	
Hong Kong	25.5	Japan	21.9
Japan	18.6	USA	12.2
USA	16.9	Hong Kong	6.8
Germany	3.8	Germany	5.6

Colombia

Area (km²)   1,138,915

Currency   Colombian peso ($ = 100 centavos)

Location   Colombia, one of the most deceptively affluent states in South America, forms the geographical link between Central and South America. Meeting the Isthmus of Panama in the west, it is bordered on the south and east by Ecuador, Peru, Venezuela and Brazil, and has coastlines on both the Caribbean and the Pacific. Its climate is warm and temperate in the coastal strip, but arid in the inland plateaux. The capital is Bogotá.

Head of State   President Ernesto Samper Pizano (August 1994)

Head of Government   President Ernesto Samper Pizano (August 1994)

Ruling Party   Liberal Party

Political Structure   Colombia has an executive President who answers to a 102-member Senate and a House of Representatives with 161 elected members. Constitutional reform has been under way for many years, but in practice the issue has been repeatedly overshadowed by concerns about the eradication of the gangs who operate the drug trade.

Last Elections   Parliamentary elections were held in March 1994, in which the ruling Liberal Party gained an overwhelming majority of the vote, with opposition groups such as the former guerrilla group M-19 obtaining only around 5%. But disruption of the polls was severe and as much as 70% of the electorate abstained. Earlier, the municipal elections of March 1992 had produced a severe setback for the Liberals, showing instead a clear level of support for opponents of the Government's soft line on drug traffickers. Presidential elections in mid-1994 resulted in a victory for the Liberal Party's Ernesto Samper over the conservative Andrés Pastrani. Only two years later, Samper was facing serious charges of accepting $6 million for his presidential campaign from the drug lords.

Political Risk   Fears that Colombia will become a narco-democracy remain paramount. There has been a shift in power, however. The Cali "bosses" still influence the gangs' operations from jail but their organisation has been weakened. Bogota's drug enforcers claim that they now have the upper hand, although some new generation of under-lords could soon come into power. Meanwhile, President Samper fights for his political life against charges that his administration has been corrupted by drug money. Colombia is paying a price whether Samper wins or loses. He has already moved away from his country's fiscal conservatism into a "blatant" campaign to buy public support.

International Disputes   In March 1996 Colombia was "decertified" by the Clinton administration in the USA as not doing enough to control drug production and drug trade. Colombia also has strained relations with Venezuela, after Colombian allegations that the Venezuela government has been assisting Colombian rebels and drug runners. In March 1995 some 5,000 Venezuelan troops massed in the border area, leading to a stand-off involving another 6,000 Colombian troops.

Economy   With a tradition of democracy and free enterprise, Colombians are proud of the openness of their country. Beneath the surface, however, lies strong oligarchic roots. Industry is dominated by a handful of firms that are tightly linked through a web of cross-holdings and conglomerates. Thus the boundaries between business and politics are becoming blurred. As a result, many of the government's economic reforms have actually worsened the country's distribution of income and wealth. Growth of GDP exceeded 5% in 1995 for the third straight year and officials predict a similar result in 1996. But even if this forecast is met, poverty is likely to worsen. Economic reforms have attracted foreign companies which have cost many workers their jobs. Meanwhile, the country's strict labour laws have been relaxed, making it possible for employers to hire and fire at will. These moves were needed, but no social net exists to help the newly unemployed find new jobs. Moreover, the government is in danger of losing control over the country to the drug lords. Colombia will continue to offer moderately good returns for those investors willing to take the risks. However, with more stable and less violent economies in neighbouring countries, the risk-adverse investor will not have to look far to find alternatives.

Main Industries   In the agricultural sector, sugar, bananas, cotton and meat are growing in importance as the international coffee market has become more unstable. Colombia has vast and still under-exploited reserves of minerals. Besides coal and oil, both of which are exported in substantial quantities, Colombia's mineral reserves include deposits of gold, silver, copper, iron ore, platinum, bauxite, gypsum, limestone, phosphates, sulphur and uranium. Most of the country's involves metal fabrication and the processing of raw materials. Textiles, leather goods and paper products are some of Colombia's larger industries.

Energy   Colombia has substantial quantities of both oil and coal, and together these make up virtually all of its energy requirements. The start of oil production from Cusiana in 1995 should boost the country's export potential and there are major plans to expand oil production and exploration with foreign investment. Over 80% of the country's electricity is provided by hydro-electric power.

	1993	1994	1995
Inflation (% change)	22.6	23.8	21.0
Exchange rate (per US$)	863.06	844.84	911.37
Interest rate (% per annum)	35.8	40.5	42.7
GDP (% real growth)	5.3	5.3	5.3
GDP (Million units of national currency)	41,931,600.0	54,636,665.0	69,614,214.0
GDP (US$ million)	48,584.8	64,671.0	76,384.1
GDP per capita (US$)	1,431.1	1,873.4	2,176.2
Consumption (Million units of national currency)	28,293,760.0	36,809,614.6	46,827,704.5
Consumption (US$ million)	32,783.1	43,569.9	51,381.7
Consumption per capita (US$)	965.6	1,262.2	1,463.9
Population, mid-year ('000)	33,950.0	34,520.0	35,100.0
Birth rate (per '000)	18.1	22.6	
Death rate (per '000)	6.1	6.2	
No. of households ('000)	7,948.6	8,112.6	8,482.0
Total exports (US$ million)	8,399.0	9,764.0	2,311.0
Total imports (US$ million)	9,832.0	11,883.0	13,853.0
Tourism receipts (US$ million)	737.3	793.7	850.0
Tourist spending (US$ million)	754.6	1,002.7	1,182.5

Average household size 1995 (persons)	4.04				
Urban population 1995 (%)	72.7				
Age analysis (%) (1992)	*0-14* 34.4		*15-64* 61.3		*65+* 4.3
Population by sex (%) (1992)	*Male* 49.6		*Female* 50.4		
Life expectancy (years) (1990-95)	*Male* 66.4		*Female* 72.3		
Infant mortality (deaths per '000 live births) (1993)	37.0				
Adult literacy (%) (1990)	86.7				

TRADING PARTNERS

Major export destinations 1995 (% share)		Major import sources 1995 (% share)	
USA	36.3	USA	37.9
Germany	8.3	Japan	9.9
Venezuela	5.9	Venezuela	8.1
Belgium/Luxembourg	3.2	Germany	5.1

Comoros

Area (km²)   1,860

Currency   Comoros franc (= 100 centimes)

Location   The Comoros are an archipelago of islands in the Indian Ocean, situated between Mozambique and the island of Madagascar. They retain both French and Islamic cultural traditions - with the latter becoming more important in recent years. The climate is tropical and many islands are heavily forested. The capital is Moroni.

Head of State   President Mohammed Djohar (December 1993)

Head of Government   Caabi el Yachroutou Mohamed (April 1995)

Ruling Party   A coalition of former opposition groups is in power.

Political Structure   Comoros held its first multi-party elected body with a new constitution in November 1992. The new plan provided for a system with a President elected for a five-year term, renewable once only, and a 15-member Senate consisting of five representatives from each island. Legislative power is exercised by a 42-member Federal Assembly elected for a four-year term.

Last Elections   Legislative elections were held in December 1993, when the President's supporters won 24 of the 42 seats in the Federal Assembly. These results confirmed those of an earlier poll in November 1992, when voting was disrupted by violence and opposition parties boycotted the election. By 1994, the situation had deteriorated to the point where the opposition parties were invited to form a coalition.

Political Risk   Political strains, driven in part by the desire for further reforms in the constitutional system, culminated in a military coup in October 1995 which was led by a French soldier of fortune, Robert Denard. The disruption lasted only six days and was ended when President Chirac dispatched a small French invasion force.

Economy   The country remains highly dependent on its trade relationship with France, and its lack of self-sufficiency in food products is the source of some concern. In years when the economy performs poorly, French aid will account for as much as 40% of GDP.

Main Industries   The Comoros economy depends almost entirely on the agricultural sector, and particularly on the vanilla crop. This commodity, together with copra and cloves, generates the bulk of the country's foreign exchange revenues. The Comoros also has a large extent of natural forest which offers substantial scope for timber exporting. Agriculture employs over 80% of the workforce, although some are engaged only in subsistence farming of cassava, sweet potatoes, rice and bananas. The soil is of poor quality and farmers suffer from poor weather conditions. The industrial sector is largely limited to the processing of essential oils, especially from ylang-ylang, but there are also a few factories making soft drinks, plastics and timber products.

Energy   All of the country's fuel requirements, apart from brushwood and similar fuels, are imported. A hydro-electric dam is currently under construction, however, and this should provide some degree of self-sufficiency in electricity.

	1993	1994	1995
Inflation (% change)	5.0	37.6	15.8
Exchange rate (per US$)	283.16	416.40	498.70
Interest rate			
GDP (% real growth)	1.1	5.0	3.1
GDP (Million units of national currency)	79,288.6	133,080.0	158,823.0
GDP (US$ million)	280.0	319.6	318.5
GDP per capita (US$)	459.0	507.3	493.8
Consumption (Million units of national currency)	45,557.9	65,623.7	67,213.5
Consumption (US$ million)	160.9	157.6	134.8
Consumption per capita (US$)	263.8	250.2	209.0
Population, mid-year ('000)	610.0	630.0	645.0
Birth rate (per '000)	47.8	46.5	
Death rate (per '000)	13.9	11.0	
No. of households ('000)	106.5	106.5	108.1
Total exports (US$ million)			
Total imports (US$ million)			
Tourism receipts (US$ million)	9.2	9.5	
Tourist spending (US$ million)			

Average household size 1995 (persons)	5.62				
Urban population 1995 (%)	30.7				
Age analysis (%) (1980)	*0-14* 47.2	*15-64* 48.5	*65+* 4.3
Population by sex (%) (1980)	*Male* 49.9	*Female* 50.1	
Life expectancy (years) (1990-95)	*Male* 55.5	*Female* 56.5	
Infant mortality (deaths per '000 live births) (1993)	88.9		
Adult literacy (%) (1980)	47.9		

Congo

Area (km²)   342,000

Currency   CFA franc (= 100 centimes)

Location   Congo is a long triangle of land, dominated by tropical forest, which follows the Congo River south from Cameroon and the Central African Republic, between Gabon and Zaire, to meet the sea just north of Angola. The climate is hot and humid. The capital is Brazzaville.

Head of State   President Pascal Lissouba (August 1992)

Head of Government   Gen. Jacques-Joachim Yhombi-Opango (June 1993)

Ruling Party   Pan-African Union for Social Democracy (UPADS) leads a coalition with the Union for Democracy and Republic (UDR) and others.

Political Structure   The traditional dominance of the Congolese Labour Party came to an abrupt end in July 1992, with the country's first multi-party elections in many decades. The new system, which replaces the old collectivist system, provides for an executive President elected for a term of five years. Legislative authority is vested in a 125-member National Assembly (Lower House of Parliament) and a 60-member Senate (Upper House).

Last Elections   Elections to the National Assembly were held in May and June 1993, when the coalition government of President Pascal Lissouba won 69 of the 125 seats in the Assembly and all of the 11 constituencies (UPADS seven, UDR four). Despite the decisive win, there were calls for new elections and these took place in many districts during October 1993. By-elections in May 1995 confirmed that the government was in difficulty when five of the seven seats went to opposition parties.

Political Risk   The situation has eased since 1993 when a wave of political unrest undermined much of the confidence in the democratically elected government. However, occasions of violence have recurred, even after most of the armed guerrillas had been incorporated into the army. The government's refusal to cut its bloated civil service or to reduce state corporation payrolls has bought it some degree of security, but its reluctance has also cost it support among international donors. Should it bow to international appeals to introduce the desired reforms, the level of domestic unrest can be expected to rise sharply.

International Disputes   Relations with France, the Congo's major source of international aid, are occasionally strained owning to the slow pace of economic reform.

Economy   At present the country's economy is still run on the lines of a five-year plan system, with most strategic decisions being taken by the Government. The Congo is potentially rich, but has mortgaged its oil revenues until 2012 and has refused to introduce many of the reforms which the IMF and international aid donors want. The country's internal finances are extremely precarious while the volume of its external debt has risen substantially during the past two years.

Main Industries   The Congo produces up to eight million tonnes of oil a year, together with substantial amounts of lead, zinc and gold. The mineral and energy sector undoubtedly has scope for further development, but its prospects will not be realised as long as the internal situation remains uncertain. Agriculture is poorly developed with less than 1% of the land area under cultivation - most of it in the Niari alluvial valley. However, the Government still hopes to achieve full self-sufficiency by the year 2000. Most farming involves the cultivation of subsistence crops such as cassava, yams, groundnuts and manioc. Coffee, cocoa, sugar and tobacco are grown for export and returns from these crops have rose significantly in 1995. Manufacturing typically accounts for less than 5% of GDP and tends to centre on the processing of raw materials for the domestic market. There are substantial timber resources in the country but little is suitable for commercial exploitation.

Energy   Congo produces an exportable surplus of crude oil which generates as much as 90% of its foreign exchange earnings. It also has considerable hydro-electric potential and the sector supplies virtually all of its electricity needs.

	1993	1994	1995
Inflation (% change)	2.0		
Exchange rate (per US$)	283.16	555.20	498.70
Interest rate (% per annum)	17.5	17.5	16.0
GDP (% real growth)	-8.7	4.0	4.0
GDP (Billion units of national currency)	676.0	1,417.3	1,345.5
GDP (US$ million)	2,387.3	2,552.8	2,698.0
GDP per capita (US$)	978.4	1,013.0	1,045.7
Consumption (Billion units of national currency)	459.0	962.3	913.5
Consumption (US$ million)	1,621.0	1,733.2	1,831.8
Consumption per capita (US$)	664.3	687.8	710.0
Population, mid-year ('000)	2,440.0	2,520.0	2,580.0
Birth rate (per '000)	45.6	40.3	
Death rate (per '000)	14.9	16.5	
No. of households ('000)	389.4	403.0	426.0
Total exports (US$ million)	1,069.0		
Total imports (US$ million)	582.0		
Tourism receipts (US$ million)	2.0	2.1	
Tourist spending (US$ million)	81.0	85.4	90.3

Average household size 1995 (persons)	5.94				
Urban population 1995 (%)	58.8				
Age analysis (%) (1985)	*0-14* 44.7		*15-64* 50.4		*65+* 5.0
Population by sex (%) (1985)	*Male* 48.5		*Female* 51.5		
Life expectancy (years) (1990-95)	*Male* 48.9		*Female* 53.8		
Infant mortality (deaths per '000 live births) (1993)	83.6				
Adult literacy (%) (1990)	56.6				

TRADING PARTNERS

Major export destinations 1995 (% share)		Major import sources 1995 (% share)	
Belgium/Luxembourg	26.1	Netherlands	28.7
Italy	17.3	France	28.2
USA	14.8	Italy	12.5
Netherlands	9.6	USA	5.4

Costa Rica

Area (km²) 50,900

Currency Colón (= 100 céntimos)

Location Costa Rica meets the Isthmus of Panama at its northern extreme. Nicaragua lies to the north. The country has coasts facing both the Caribbean and the Pacific. However, its coastal lowlands are too humid for intensive development while its upland plains have a pleasant climate. The capital is San José.

Head of State President José Maria Figueres (February 1994)

Head of Government President José Maria Figueres (February 1994)

Ruling Party Partido de Liberación Nacional (February 1994)

Political Structure Costa Rica has an executive President elected by universal suffrage for a term of four years and answerable to the 57-member Legislative Assembly, also elected for four years. The President is assisted by two Vice-Presidents and appoints the Cabinet personally. A Labour Council was formed in 1991 to address the growing demands of trade unions for a reform of the labour and social market.

Last Elections In the Legislative Assembly elections of February 1994, the ruling Partido Unidad Social Cristiana won only 25 of the 57 seats and was overthrown by the Partido de Liberación Nacional (PLN), which had lost power in the 1990 elections. Four seats were won by smaller parties and by independents. In the presidential elections on the same day, José Maria Figueres was returned with 49.6% of the vote, compared with 47.5% for the outgoing President Rafael Angel Calderón Fournier.

Political Risk Public discontent with the Government's economic record raises the possibility of a swing back to the left-wing administration of the PLN. Such an outcome would probably lead to a scaling-down of the current austerity programmes and a discontinuation of plans to privatise many state-owned enterprises. That outcome would be a setback but, otherwise, the level of political risk remains reasonably slight.

Economy Fears of political instability have subsided in recent years as rates of economic growth have improved. Costa Rica has a generally high relative standard of living and plays a central role in the politics of the region. In June 1995 the country entered into a free trade agreement with Mexico, which should lead to an improvement in market access for all of North America.

Main Industries Costa Rica's economy relies largely on its agriculture, with coffee, bananas, sugar, cut flowers and cattle being exported. Cocoa, rice, maize, cassava, ginger, melons, pineapples and flowers are also grown for domestic consumption. The country became embroiled in a bitter row with the EU over the latter's regulations governing banana imports, but that issue was at least temporarily resolved in mid-1995. There is a sizeable tourist industry which can be expected to grow during the latter part of the 1990s. The industrial sector is fairly well diversified and developed, with pharmaceuticals, chemicals (including fertilisers), textiles, clothing, vehicles, and electrical and electronic goods being manufactured.

Energy Costa Rica relies on imports, mainly of oil and gas, to cover most of its energy needs. It does, however, have a substantial hydro-electric capacity which provides most of its electricity.

	1993	1994	1995
Inflation (% change)	9.8	13.5	23.2
Exchange rate (per US$)	142.17	157.07	178.88
Interest rate (% per annum)	30.0	33.0	36.7
GDP (% real growth)	5.6	8.5	7.0
GDP (Million units of national currency)	1,068,542.0	1,315,722.0	1,735,140.4
GDP (US$ million)	7,515.9	8,376.7	9,700.0
GDP per capita (US$)	2,505.3	2,728.6	3,087.7
Consumption (Million units of national currency)	648,463.0	781,887.0	1,009,719.5
Consumption (US$ million)	4,561.2	4,978.0	5,644.7
Consumption per capita (US$)	1,520.4	1,621.5	1,796.8
Population, mid-year ('000)	3,000.0	3,070.0	3,141.5
Birth rate (per '000)	26.8	26.2	
Death rate (per '000)	3.9	3.5	
No. of households ('000)	687.7	707.3	744.5
Total exports (US$ million)	2,049.0	2,215.0	2,577.0
Total imports (US$ million)	2,885.0	3,025.0	3,252.0
Tourism receipts (US$ million)	577.0	626.0	718.0
Tourist spending (US$ million)	262.0	284.6	322.7

Average household size 1995 (persons)	4.12				
Urban population 1995 (%)	49.7				
Age analysis (%) (1992)	*0-14* 36.6		*15-64* 58.9		*65+* 4.5
Population by sex (%) (1992)	*Male* 50.0		*Female* 50.0		
Life expectancy (years) (1990-95)	*Male* 72.9		*Female* 77.6		
Infant mortality (deaths per '000 live births) (1992)	13.8				
Adult literacy (%) (1990)	92.8				

TRADING PARTNERS

Major export destinations 1995 (% share)		Major import sources 1995 (% share)	
USA	71.7	USA	57.8
Germany	12.6	Mexico	4.3
Canada	4.7	Guatemala	3.6
United Kingdom	4.4	Colombia	3.5

Côte d'Ivoire

Area (km²) 322,465

Currency CFA franc (= 100 centimes)

Location Côte d'Ivoire is located on the Atlantic coast of West Africa, with a short coastal stretch facing southward into the Gulf of Guinea. Inland, the country broadens out considerably to meet Guinea, Burkina Faso and Mali in the north, Ghana in the east and Liberia in the west. The climate is tropical and humid, but a rich soil means that agriculture is strong. The seat of government is Abidjan.

Head of State President Henri Konan Bédié (December 1993)

Head of Government Daniel Kablan Duncan

Ruling Party Parti Démocratique de la Côte d'Ivoire (PDCI) leads a five-party Presidential Group coalition.

Political Structure Côte d'Ivoire, the former Ivory Coast, became fully independent from France in 1960. The executive President exercises a large degree of power and is elected for five years by universal suffrage. Legislative authority is vested in the 175-member National Assembly, which is also elected for five years. Mindful of any challenge to his authority, President Bédié pushed through a new law in 1994 which requires that presidential candidates must have two Ivorian parents. Significantly, his main rival for the post does not meet this requirement.

Last Elections The country's second multi-party elections, held in October 1995, were accompanied by violence and charges of fraud but returned the president to office. Elections to the National Assembly in December 1995 were more peaceful and gave the ruling PDCI 147 of 175 seats.

Political Risk The internal political situation has been steadily deteriorating since the beginning of the 1990s. The 1995 elections marked the bloodiest period in the country since it obtained independence from France in 1960. Several opposition politicians are popular among Ivorian voters but their political parties are fragmented and have little chance against Bédié's heavy-handedness. There is little danger of a general uprising against the PDCI which has been in power for 30 years. Nevertheless, Côte d'Ivoire's democratic traditions leave much to be desired.

International Disputes Relations with Liberia are occasionally strained as a result of border disputes.

Economy The country's continuing dependence on volatile commodity markets poses a recurrent problem. The boom in the world prices of cotton, cocoa and tropical woods have spurred a recovery. GDP grew by more than 6% in 1995, reversing several years of decline and recession. Meanwhile, the government has cut import tariffs, introduced tax breaks and lower bureaucratic hurdles to lure investors and privatised several state enterprises. Much of the economic turnaround is also attributed to the 50% devaluation of the French-backed Central African franc which was forced through by the IMF and the World Bank in 1994. A huge new oil find could boost growth even further with optimists predicting that the annual rate of increase in GDP will reach double figures by 1998.

Main Industries Côte d'Ivoire's economy is still largely dependent on agriculture, with cocoa and coffee being grown for export together with cotton, timber and palm oil. The country's aggressive development of cocoa plantations was partly responsible for a slump in world prices at the beginning of this decade and plans to double the acreage devoted to the trees by the year 2000 have been scaled back. Industry remains poorly developed, largely because of the ineffectiveness of previous attempts to attract foreign capital. The government has had more success in the past two years and industries engaged in the processing of agricultural raw materials have been expanding. These include: textiles, matting, carpets, footwear and leather goods. Ambitious plans to develop steel and cement plants are also under way. The country has few mineral deposits, although exploration is under way and there are opportunities to expand the small-scale gold and diamond mining which currently goes on.

Energy Côte d'Ivoire has not been self-sufficient in crude oil in recent years. The existing field, which once yielded seven million barrels a year, is in decline. The country's new oil find is expected to reverse this situation. Hydro-electric power generates 40% of the current needs and two new dams are under construction.

	1993	1994	1995
Inflation (% change)	2.2	26.1	14.2
Exchange rate (per US$)	283.16	555.20	498.70
Interest rate (% per annum)	17.5	17.5	16.0
GDP (% real growth)	-3.4	-0.5	6.2
GDP (Million units of national currency)	2,972,880.6	3,135,914.1	3,803,249.2
GDP (US$ million)	10,498.9	5,648.3	7,626.3
GDP per capita (US$)	796.6	412.3	535.9
Consumption (Million units of national currency)	2,249,068.1	2,372,407.5	2,877,265.3
Consumption (US$ million)	7,942.7	4,273.1	5,769.5
Consumption per capita (US$)	602.6	311.9	405.4
Population, mid-year ('000)	13,180.0	13,700.0	14,230.0
Birth rate (per '000)	47.9	46.5	47.6
Death rate (per '000)	11.9	11.1	
No. of households ('000)	2,734.9	2,857.0	3,052.2
Total exports (US$ million)	2,840.0	3,384.0	
Total imports (US$ million)	4,900.0	2,044.0	
Tourism receipts (US$ million)	64.0	67.2	
Tourist spending (US$ million)	199.0	209.1	

Average household size 1995 (persons)	4.56				
Urban population 1995 (%)	43.6				
Age analysis (%) (1988)	*0-14* 47.2		*15-64* 50.6		*65+* 2.2
Population by sex (%) (1988)	*Male* 51.1		*Female* 48.9		
Life expectancy (years) (1990-95)	*Male* 49.7		*Female* 52.4		
Infant mortality (deaths per '000 live births) (1993)	91.7				
Adult literacy (%) (1990)	53.8				

TRADING PARTNERS

Major export destinations 1995 (% share)		Major import sources 1995 (% share)	
France	18.7	France	53.6
Germany	8.3	Nigeria	30.0
Italy	8.0	USA	9.4
USA	4.2	Italy	6.0

Croatia

Area (km²) 56,538

Currency Kuna (introduced May 1994)

Location Croatia lies in the north of the old Yugoslavia, with its western edge straddling the Adriatic coast and sharing an eastern border with Hungary. To the north is Slovenia, with Bosnia and Serbia to the south. The coastal strip and islands soon give way to mountains but, in the east, the hills are replaced by a flat plain. The capital is Zagreb.

Head of State President Franjo Tudjman

Head of Government Zlateko Matesa

Ruling Party Croatian Democratic Union

Political Structure Croatia's political system is dominated by an executive President who appoints a Prime Minister and Cabinet. Legislative authority is vested in a 136-seat Chamber of Deputies and a 63-seat Chamber of Districts.

Last Elections In the general elections held in November 1995, Franjo Tudjman's ruling Democratic Union emerged as the largest party with 45% of the vote and over 70 of the 127 seats in parliament. However, Tudjman's party fell short of the two-thirds parliamentary majority needed to make the constitutional changes that would increase the president's powers.

Political Risk The chances that Croatia will become entangled in a new Bosnian civil war are receding, although the possibility of local violence remains high. The country's improved outlook results largely from the fact that President Tudjman got virtually everything he wanted in 1995, whether on the battlefield or at the negotiating table. His army reconquered Western Slavonia and Krajina. Meanwhile, at Dayton he won agreement that Eastern Slavonia - the one sliver of Croatia that is still held by Serbs, and borders on Serbia - will revert to Croat control in two years. When that happens, President Tudjman will have regained control of all Croatia. Tudjman's commitment to democracy nevertheless remains questionable.

International Disputes Relations with Serbia are difficult. However, Croatia has achieved all of its wartime aims and now wants to avoid any disputes that might jeopardise its efforts to join the international community. Serbia has strongly objected to Croatia's efforts to renegotiate its share of the former Yugoslavia's international debt.

Economy Croatia has a broadly-developed economy by the standards of the former Yugoslavia, with a developed industrial base and extensive tourist attractions, especially along the coastal region. The latter will require considerable investment to repair war damage and to bring them up to Western European standards. Croatia is nearing an agreement with western banks which calls for it to accept 28.5% of the former Yugoslavia's foreign debt. Such an agreement would allow the country to borrow in European markets and would be a prerequisite for obtaining a debt rating which is adequate to attract lenders.

Main Industries Capacity in Croatia's principal industries (engineering, food processing, beverages) has been less severely restricted by the civil war than has industry in other regions of the former Yugoslavia. Roads and factories are being rapidly rebuilt and a concerted effort is being made to re-establish the tourist industry.

Energy Much of the country's power-generating capacity was destroyed during the war and must now be rebuilt. The reabsorption of Krajina, the former Serbian enclave, into Croatia will help to resolve the country's energy problems since that region is a net exporter of country's hydro-electric power.

	1993	1994	1995
Inflation (% change)	1,486.3	107.2	4.1
Exchange rate (per US$)		5.70	5.84
Interest rate (% per annum)	23.0	22.9	20.2
GDP (% real growth)	-3.0	1.0	2.0
GDP (Million units of national currency)	52,436.5	109,734.9	116,518.7
GDP (US$ million)	19,348.0	19,251.7	19,951.8
GDP per capita (US$)	4,299.6	4,278.2	4,363.9
Consumption			
Consumption (US$ million)			
Consumption per capita (US$)			
Population, mid-year ('000)	4,500.0	4,500.0	4,572.0
Birth rate (per '000)	11.2	10.2	
Death rate (per '000)	10.8	10.5	
No. of households ('000)	833.3	785.7	789.5
Total exports (US$ million)	3,913.0	4,259.0	4,633.0
Total imports (US$ million)	4,667.0	5,231.0	7,582.0
Tourism receipts (US$ million)			
Tourist spending (US$ million)			

Average household size 1995 (persons)	5.44		
Urban population 1995 (%)	64.4		
Age analysis (%)			
Population by sex (%) (1981)	*Male* 48.4	*Female* 51.6	
Life expectancy (years) (1991)	*Male* 66.8	*Female* 74.8	
Infant mortality (deaths per '000 live births) (1992)	11.6		
Adult literacy (%) (1991)	96.7		

TRADING PARTNERS

Major export destinations 1995 (% share)		Major import sources 1995 (% share)	
Italy	23.4	Italy	21.1
Germany	21.4	Germany	20.3
Slovenia	11.7	Slovenia	8.7
Bosnia-Herzegovina	6.9	Austria	6.7

Cuba

Area (km²)   114,525

Currency   Cuban peso (P = 100 centavos). A new, partially convertible peso was introduced in 1995

Location   The Republic of Cuba is an archipelago which includes Cuba, the largest island in the Caribbean. Extending more than 800 km from east to west, the country lies just 145 km south of the Florida coast. Its proximity has drawn the ire of successive US administrations - on account of both its communist ideology and the thousands of refugees who seek sanctuary in the USA. The capital is Havana.

Head of State   President Fidel Castro Ruz (1976)

Head of Government   President Fidel Castro Ruz

Ruling Party   Partido Comunista de Cuba

Political Structure   Constitutional changes in 1992 have not altered Cuba's official commitment to a communist society. Indeed, Castro's powers have now been enhanced so as to allow him to declare a state of emergency at any time.

Last Elections   The first direct elections to the National Assembly of Popular Power (Parliament), previously appointed by the country's 14 provincial assemblies, took place in March 1993, when all 589 official candidates for the 589 seats were successful. The claimed turnout was 99.6%.

Political Risk   Weakened by the withdrawal of aid from the former Soviet Union, Cuba is changing but at a glacial pace. Much of the country remains in economic and physical ruin, compounded by a 34-year US trade embargo. Yet the revolution is not necessarily bound to crumble. Castro's communist party retains a strong hold over the hearts and minds of the Cuban people. Polls conducted by American newspapers show that a majority believe the benefits of the revolution, such as universal health care and education, outweigh its indifference to human rights and free enterprise. Nevertheless, it is clear that Castroism can not survive the death of its founder, now nearly 70 years old. Fidel's brother, Raul, has been designated as his successor. But Raul is reclusive, unpopular and will have no influence after Fidel. Opponents wait in Miami but they are not the nucleus for political opposition. One possible focus for future political opposition could be the Catholic church which is already involved in providing food, medicine and housing.

International Disputes   Castro has been trying to cultivate better relationships with the USA for several years but his efforts were dashed in early 1996 when Cuba shot down two unarmed light aircraft that were working for the Cuban resistance in Miami. In response, a harsh new law was passed by the US congress to tighten the existing embargo. Fortunately for Cuba, many aspects of the law relate to the treatment of investments in Cuba by third parties and are probably not enforceable.

Economy   Cubans agree that their wholesale acceptance of the Soviet economic model was a mistake but they have no alternative philosophy to replace it. The government believes that Eastern Europe has proceeded too fast with reforms and therefore proceeds very cautiously, accepting some ideas and rejecting others. In 1994, Cuba slashed its budget deficit by nearly 75%, mainly by increasing duties on cigarettes, alcohol and petrol and by halving subsidies to loss-making enterprises. More cuts in subsidies in 1996 should further reduce the deficit. Private farmers' markets are now permitted, Cubans are allowed to hold dollars, foreign investment is sought (albeit cautiously) and some state enterprises are being broken up. Observers both inside and outside Cuba now agree that the economy grew by 2.5% in 1995.

Main Industries   Cuba's economy is still highly dependent on its sugar crop, which is sold not only in its raw and semi-refined form but also as rum and other spirits. Recent harvests, however, have gone from bad to worse, mainly owing to a lack of cash. The sugar harvest in 1990 was a record 8.1 million tonnes but by 1995 the figure had fallen to 3.3 million tonnes, the lowest for 50 years. The country is also well known for its exports of citrus fruit, cigars and other tobacco products. The tobacco industry has suffered severely in recent years, but international demand for Cuban cigars is presently strong and there is a shortage in world markets. The manufacturing sector is starved of cash with many state-owned firms operating at only 20% of capacity (but fully staffed). Private retail stores are not allowed, so many retailers are 1-2 person operations that simply move from place to place to avoid the police. The tourist sector continues to make some progress despite the US embargo. Arrivals and revenues rose in both 1994 and 1995 and a small increase is forecast for 1996.

Energy   Cuba relies on imports of oil for most of its energy needs and virtually all of its electricity is supplied by thermal rather than hydro-electric sources. There have been chronic energy shortages since 1993 when Russia halted deliveries of crude oil. Meanwhile, 11 oil prospecting blocks have been sold to foreign buyers.

	1993	1994	1995
Inflation (% change)	8.0	34.2	
Exchange rate (per US$)	0.70	1.00	1.00
Interest rate			
GDP (% real growth)	-14.9	0.7	2.5
GDP (Million units of national currency)	28,665.3	38,739.7	40,502.0
GDP (US$ million)	40,950.4	38,739.7	40,502.0
GDP per capita (US$)	3,756.9	3,534.6	3,664.8
Consumption (Million units of national currency)	23,841.7	32,220.9	33,686.7
Consumption (US$ million)	34,059.6	32,220.9	33,686.7
Consumption per capita (US$)	3,124.7	2,939.9	3,048.1
Population, mid-year ('000)	10,900.0	10,960.0	11,051.6
Birth rate (per '000)	14.0	16.6	
Death rate (per '000)	7.2	6.5	
No. of households ('000)	2,639.8	2,671.2	2,769.6
Total exports (US$ million)			
Total imports (US$ million)			
Tourism receipts (US$ million)	720.0	687.1	
Tourist spending (US$ million)			

Average household size 1995 (persons)	3.90				
Urban population 1995 (%)	76.0				
Age analysis (%) (1991)	*0-14* 22.6		*15-64* 68.6		*65+* 8.8
Population by sex (%) (1991)	*Male* 50.3		*Female* 49.7		
Life expectancy (years) (1985-90)	*Male* 72.7		*Female* 76.3		
Infant mortality (deaths per '000 live births) (1992)	10.2				
Adult literacy (%) (1990)	94.0				

Cyprus

Area (km^2) 9,250

Currency Cyprus pound (C£ = 100 cents)

Location Cyprus is located in the eastern Mediterranean, barely 150 km south of Turkey and much closer to Syria than to Greece, whose descendants represent by far the largest sector of the population. The climate is warm and dry. The capital is Nicosia.

Head of State President Glafcos Clerides (Northern Cyprus: Rauf Denktash)

Head of Government President Glafcos Clerides (Northern Cyprus: Hakki Atun)

Ruling Party Democratic Rally leads a coalition with the Democratic Party. In Northern Cyprus, the Democratic Party and the Republican Turkish Party form a coalition.

Political Structure For international purposes, Cyprus is represented by the south of the island, where a Greek majority elects an executive President and a 56-seat House of Representatives. A further 20 unoccupied seats are reserved for Turkish Cypriots. The so-called "Turkish Republic of Northern Cyprus", which was declared after the Turkish invasion of 1974, has an executive President and 50-seat Parliament. The two sides have been talking under UN auspices about proposals for a federal union, in which the 38% of the island controlled by Turkish Cypriots should shrink to 28%. In 1995 the council of Nicosia voted to change the capital's name from Nicosia to its Greek nomenclature, Lefkosia.

Last Elections Elections to the House of Representatives took place in May 1996. The centre-right Democratic Rally held on to power, although AKEL, the Communist Party, increased its share of the vote. The results were a boost for President Glafcos Clerides, who was expected to stand for re-election in 1998. Clerides narrowly defeated ex-President Georgios Vassiliou in presidential elections in February 1993, but both Vassiliou and his wife were elected to parliament in the latest round of elections, running under the banner of the Free Democrats, a party which he founded. Elections were held in the Turkish sector in December 1993, when Hakki Atun was reappointed as Prime Minister. Denktash was re-elected President of Northern Cyprus in April 1995.

Political Risk The political climate in Cyprus has been relatively calm for several years, but ethnic divisions run extremely deep and may prove more intractable than expected. The fate of divided Nicosia and the return of the Greek-owned properties in Northern Cyprus which were expropriated by Turkey after the 1974 war will be crucial. However, the prospect of guerrilla action in the south has diminished, and its economy appears healthy. The UN would like to withdraw its peace-keeping forces which have been on the island for over 20 years, but fears that fighting could then recur have prevented this move.

International Disputes Virtually the entire history of Cyprus revolves around the ongoing territorial dispute between Greece and Turkey which culminated in the Turkish invasion of 1974. About 80% of the country's residents are of Greek descent, but the island was in Turkish control from the late Middle Ages until 1914 when it was annexed by Britain. During the 1950s, Greek activists promoted political union with Greece and stepped up their pressure after independence in 1960. Turkish Cypriots boycotted the Cypriot Parliament and a stand-off developed which still continues. In 1974, military activists launched a Greek-backed coup against the Cyprus Government and installed a hard-line pro-union administration in Nicosia. Turkey responded by invading the north of the island and declared a "Turkish Republic of Northern Cyprus", unrecognised by any country except Turkey.

Economy Cyprus's economy, although basically stable, relies very heavily on imports to meet its raw material needs. Revenues from tourism are usually sufficient to cover the import bill but in years when the number of international visitors drops, the island may run a large current-account deficit. The failure so far of the "proximity talks" to reach a settlement has also depressed investment. With an extensive network of double taxation treaties, the island has also emerged as an important offshore financial centre. More than 20,000 companies are now registered in Cyprus, which is also home to some 30 offshore banks.

Main Industries Cyprus has a mixed economy, with a surprising number of manufacturing industries that are mainly geared to serve the domestic market. Manufacturing is more developed in the Greek portion of the island than in Turkish areas. On the whole, however, Cyprus depends on agriculture and tourism for the bulk of its income and employment. Farm exports include citrus fruits, figs, dates and of course wine. Cereal crops such as wheat, barley and potatoes are also grown. It seems likely that agriculture provides nearly all the foreign resources coming into the north of the country. In the Greek sector, tourism is an equally important economic force. The island's pleasant climate and its particular affinity with the British (who have had troops stationed there for many decades) have made it a popular holiday destination.

Energy Crude oil, all of which has to be imported, is the primary source of energy in Cyprus. All electricity is produced by thermal plants.

	1993	**1994**	**1995**
Inflation (% change)	4.9	4.7	2.6
Exchange rate (per US$)	0.50	0.49	0.45
Interest rate (% per annum)	9.0	8.8	8.5
GDP (% real growth)	2.1	9.1	2.2
GDP (Million units of national currency)	3,223.5	3,680.9	3,860.0
GDP (US$ million)	6,447.0	7,512.0	8,577.8
GDP per capita (US$)	8,954.2	10,290.5	11,540.9
Consumption (Million units of national currency)	2,894.2	3,239.2	3,329.3
Consumption (US$ million)	5,788.4	6,610.6	7,398.4
Consumption per capita (US$)	8,039.4	9,055.6	9,954.1
Population, mid-year ('000)	720.0	730.0	743.3
Birth rate (per '000)	16.8	14.3	
Death rate (per '000)	7.7	6.8	
No. of households ('000)	233.0	238.4	249.7
Total exports (US$ million)	867.0	967.0	1,229.0
Total imports (US$ million)	2,590.0	3,018.0	3,694.0
Tourism receipts (US$ million)	1,396.0	1,457.1	
Tourist spending (US$ million)	133.0	138.8	155.3

Average household size 1995 (persons)	2.91				
Urban population 1995 (%)	54.1				
Age analysis (%) (1995)	*0-14*	25.3	*15-64*	64.5	*65+* 10.3
Population by sex (%) (1995)	*Male*	49.3	*Female*	50.7	
Life expectancy (years) (1991)	*Male*	73.9	*Female*	78.4	
Infant mortality (deaths per '000 live births) (1992)	8.7				
Adult literacy (%) (1987)	94.0				

TRADING PARTNERS

Major export destinations 1995 (% share)		Major import sources 1995 (% share)	
United Kingdom	15.7	USA	12.3
Russia	13.6	United Kingdom	11.7
Bulgaria	8.4	Italy	9.6
Greece	6.5	Germany	8.3

Czech Republic

Area (km²)   78,864

Currency   Koruna (Kcs = 100 heller)

Location   The Czech Republic formed part of a federation with Slovakia until January 1993, when the two parted. The country is located in central Europe, south-east of Germany, with Poland to the north, Austria to the south and Slovakia to the west. The climate is temperate with harsh winters. The capital is Prague.

Head of State   President Vaclav Havel (1993)

Head of Government   Vaclav Klaus (1992)

Ruling Party   Civic Democratic Party (ODS), in alliance with the Christian Democratic Union (KDU-CSL) and the Civic Democratic Alliance (ODA), leads a coalition followig the inconclusive 1996 election results.

Political Structure   Until the end of 1992 Czechoslovakia was a federation of two ethnically distinct states, the Czech and Slovak republics, which had been forged in 1919. From 1993, however, they declared their independence. The governing coalition is led by Vaclav Klaus' Civic Democratic Party in co-operation with the Christian Democratic Party and two other junior coalition members. The arrangement is sometimes an uneasy one as opinions differ on fundamental issues such as the role of the Catholic church, questions of regional government and the possible role of a second parliamentary chamber.

Last Elections   Sixteen parties competed in the June 1996 elections to the 200-member parliament. Vaclav Klaus's three-party centre-right coalition won 99 seats, which was 13 fewer than in the previous parliament. The opposition Social Democrats (CSSD) took 61 seats (24 previously), the far-left Communists won 22 (35 previously) and the far-right Republicans received 18 (14 previously). President Havel turned to Vaclav Klaus to form a new government. This political deadlock nevertheless promises a great deal of uncertainty in a country renowned for its relative predictability.

Political Risk   By the standards of Eastern Europe, the Czech Republic presents few political risks. With a high standard of living, a skilled workforce and a vigorous commitment to capitalism, prospects remain good. International endorsement of the country's policies was made explicit when the Czechs became the 26th member of the OECD in November 1995. The country expects to become a member of the EU by the end of the century.

Economy   The private sector's share of GDP is the highest in all of Eastern Europe at around 70% in 1996. The country has already reached the standards typical of advanced industrial economies in terms of its systems of trade and foreign exchange. GDP grew by about 4% in 1995 and is forecast to rise by over 5% in 1996. Meanwhile, inflation has fallen to well below 10%. However, the ability of the economy to compete abroad is being severely tested and will be tried further unless a period of post-privatisation restructuring picks up speed.

Main Industries   Engineering industries were a centrepiece of the Czech economy before the communist takeover and are flourishing once again now that a free market has returned. Heavy and precision manufacturing are two of the most competitive and rapidly growing sectors of the economy. Oil refining and car production are other industries which have benefited greatly from foreign investment. Agricultural productivity is also high by Eastern European standards. The country has an ample exportable surplus of meat and is self-sufficient in wheat, barley, vegetables, potatoes and fruit. There are extensive forests offering substantial scope for timber development.

Energy   The Czech Republic is self-sufficient in coal and lignite, which together account for around two-thirds of all total energy requirements. The country imports all its oil and gas supplies while about 27% of its electricity comes from nuclear power stations (mainly of the Soviet type).

	1993	1994	1995
Inflation (% change)	20.8	10.1	9.1
Exchange rate (per US$)	29.15	28.79	26.56
Interest rate (% per annum)	14.1	13.1	12.8
GDP (% real growth)	-5.9	2.6	4.0
GDP (Million units of national currency)	910,600.0	1,037,500.0	1,212,000.0
GDP (US$ million)	31,238.4	36,036.8	45,632.5
GDP per capita (US$)	3,023.9	3,486.5	4,410.2
Consumption (Million units of national currency)	580,357.0	637,950.0	726,844.0
Consumption (US$ million)	19,909.3	22,158.7	27,366.1
Consumption per capita (US$)	1,927.2	2,143.8	2,644.8
Population, mid-year ('000)	10,330.6	10,336.2	10,347.2
Birth rate (per '000)	11.7	10.3	9.3
Death rate (per '000)	11.4	11.4	11.4
No. of households ('000)	3,540.0	3,463.0	3,395.0
Total exports (US$ million)	13,205.0	14,252.0	21,613.0
Total imports (US$ million)	13,341.0	15,636.0	26,527.0
Tourism receipts (US$ million)	1,558.0	1,996.1	2,497.0
Tourist spending (US$ million)	525.0	606.5	700.5

Average household size 1995 (persons)	2.84				
Urban population 1995 (%)	65.4				
Age analysis (%) (1995)	*0-14* 24.1		*15-64* 64.2		*65+* 11.7
Population by sex (%) (1995)	*Male* 48.9		*Female* 51.1		
Life expectancy (years) (1993)	*Male* 69.3		*Female* 76.4		
Infant mortality (deaths per '000 live births) (1994)	7.9				
Adult literacy (%)					

TRADING PARTNERS

Major export destinations 1995 (% share)		Major import sources 1995 (% share)	
Germany	39.7	Germany	39.7
Slovakia	21.0	Slovakia	14.7
Austria	5.9	Russia	8.8
Italy	4.5	Italy	6.3

Denmark

Area (km²) 43,075

Currency Danish kroner (DKr = 100 ore)

Location Denmark is an archipelago of low-lying islands which control the straits between the Baltic Sea and the North Sea. Bordering on Germany to the south, but identifying more closely with Sweden (which is no more than 50 km across the Oresund strait), it is building a road and rail link to reach Stockholm via Malmö. The country also includes the Faroe Islands in the North Sea and Greenland, which lies in the North Atlantic off the coast of Canada. The capital is Copenhagen.

Head of State HM Queen Margrethe II

Head of Government Poul Nyrup Rasmussen (1993)

Ruling Party Social Democratic Party leads a six-party coalition with the Radical Liberals and Centre Democrats.

Political Structure The Kingdom of Denmark is a constitutional monarchy in which executive authority lies with a Prime Minister who answers to a 179-member unicameral Parliament, the Folketing. The Folketing in turn is elected by universal adult suffrage for a term of four years. In a referendum in April 1992, Danish voters rejected the ratification of the EU's Maastricht Treaty on political and economic union; but a year later they voted to accept an amended version which gave them more autonomy. Greenland, for its part, is steadily distancing itself from Denmark over the issue of EU membership.

Last Elections The Folketing elections of September 1994 produced a shock for the Social Democratic/Liberal coalition which had ruled the country since the 1990 polls. Although the ruling Social Democrats retained 62 of their 69 seats, and their coalition partners, the Radical Liberals, won eight seats instead of 7 in 1990, the Christian People's Party, which had also been part of the coalition, lost all four of its seats in the Folketing. Meanwhile, the centre-right grouping of the Conservatives won 35 seats, the Liberals 22, the Progress Party 16, the Centre Democrats nine and the Christian People's Party four. The opposition on the other hand, won 55 seats, the Socialist People's Party 24, and the Radical Liberals 10. Elections to the Greenland assembly were held in March 1995, when the nationalist Siumut enlarged its majority.

Political Risk Denmark faces no serious risk of any anti-democratic political change which might worry investors. Indeed, the commitment to multi-party voting, schisms and all, is what helps to keep the Folketing unstable and the Government powerless to act. More serious is the currency risk caused by excessive external debts.

International Disputes Denmark's overseas territory of Greenland is engaged in a territorial dispute with Norway concerning the ownership of shipping rights in the region. The two sides are continuing talks aimed at resolving the problem, however.

Economy Denmark's well-publicised scepticism about the EU reflects its longer-standing ties with the Scandinavian bloc. The new road links with Sweden are considered particularly symbolic of this relationship.

Main Industries Denmark's agricultural sector remains the backbone of the economy, with thousands of mainly small farms supplying pigmeat products, dairy goods and cereals such as wheat and barley. Farming is so intensive, however, that it has recurrently threatened serious environmental consequences in Denmark's low-lying and often marshy landscape. Farmers are bound by special legislation requiring safe storage and treatment of wastes. Danish industry has been developing particularly rapidly in recent years, with engineering, food processing, pharmaceuticals and brewing among the major activities. Biotechnology is gaining in importance, and there is a large shipbuilding industry.

Energy Denmark has natural gas resources in the North Sea, and currently exports about a third of its production. Otherwise it relies on imported fuels, especially coal. Only 0.1% of its electricity comes from nuclear power stations.

	1993	1994	1995
Inflation (% change)	1.3	2.0	2.1
Exchange rate (per US$)	6.48	6.36	5.60
Interest rate (% per annum)	10.5	8.3	7.9
GDP (% real growth)	1.3	4.5	4.0
GDP (Billion units of national currency)	873.2	929.0	958.0
GDP (US$ million)	134,753.1	146,069.2	171,071.4
GDP per capita (US$)	25,964.0	28,090.2	32,709.6
Consumption (Billion units of national currency)	451.4	490.4	528.0
Consumption (US$ million)	69,660.5	77,106.9	94,285.7
Consumption per capita (US$)	13,422.1	14,828.3	18,027.9
Population, mid-year ('000)	5,190.0	5,200.0	5,230.0
Birth rate (per '000)	13.0	13.4	13.1
Death rate (per '000)	12.1	11.8	11.1
No. of households ('000)	2,285.9	2,298.6	2,312.0
Total exports (US$ million)	37,168.0	41,417.0	48,973.0
Total imports (US$ million)	30,542.0	34,878.0	43,161.0
Tourism receipts (US$ million)	3,052.0	3,175.4	3,350.0
Tourist spending (US$ million)	3,214.0	3,529.3	4,315.6

Average household size 1995 (persons)	2.15				
Urban population 1995 (%)	85.2				
Age analysis (%) (1995)	*0-14* 16.7		*15-64* 67.7		*65+* 15.6
Population by sex (%) (1995)	*Male* 49.4		*Female* 50.6		
Life expectancy (years) (1995)	*Male* 73.0		*Female* 79.0		
Infant mortality (deaths per '000 live births) (1993)	5.7				
Adult literacy (%) (1981)	99.0				

TRADING PARTNERS

Major export destinations 1995 (% share)		Major import sources 1995 (% share)	
Germany	15.8	Germany	24.5
Sweden	8.7	Sweden	9.4
United Kingdom	5.8	United Kingdom	7.6
Norway	4.5	Netherlands	6.3

Djibouti

Area (km²) 23,000

Currency Djibouti franc (= 100 centimes)

Location The Republic of Djibouti is a tiny country on the north-east African approach from the Indian Ocean to the Red Sea (the so-called Horn of Africa). It is bounded in the north, west and south-west by Eritrea and Ethiopia, and in the south-east by Somalia. Across the Gulf of Aden it faces the Republic of Yemen. The capital is Djibouti.

Head of State President Hassan Gouled Aptidon (1977)

Head of Government Barkat Gourad Hamadou

Ruling Party Rassemblement Populaire pour le Progrès (RPP)

Political Structure Djibouti, which became independent from France in 1977, has been ruled continuously since then by President Hassan Gouled Aptidon. He was re-elected in April 1987, for a term of six years, and was not technically entitled to stand for a third term of office when his term expired in 1993. Nevertheless, he was returned to power in that year. The President answers to a 65-member Chamber of Deputies, which serves a five-year term of office.

Last Elections The first multi-party congressional election was held in December 1992, when the RPP won 78% of the vote and took all 65 seats in the Chamber of Deputies. Presidential elections followed in May 1993, when President Hassan obtained 60.8% of the vote against 22% for Mohammed Djaba Elabe.

Political Risk A formal end to the country's devastating civil war came in June 1994 after seven years of fighting. During that time a sizeable portion of the country's population (up to 15,000 people) had fled to Ethiopia. Conversely, there has been an influx of refugees from the wars in neighbouring Ethiopia and Somalia. Repeated charges of torture and other human rights abuses were levelled against the rebels during the civil war.

International Disputes Relations with Somalia and Ethiopia have been strained in recent years as a result of the ongoing political tensions in all these countries.

Economy Djibouti would clearly have enough economic problems to tackle without the crises in neighbouring Ethiopia and Somalia. Under present conditions, the country is forced to rely heavily on foreign assistance, mainly from France.

Main Industries Much of Djibouti's income derives mainly from its excellent port facilities and its strategic position in the approaches to the Red Sea. The agricultural sector remains underdeveloped and the country's harsh, dry climate militates against any substantial expansion at present. With nearly half its population subsisting through nomadic cattle herding, 95% of all food requirements are imported. Industry, on the other hand, is better developed, though it represents no more than 15% of GDP. Djibouti has a substantial construction sector which feeds a large cement industry. Smaller industries which are being encouraged include water bottling, tanning, paint processing and meat processing. There are some mineral deposits, mainly copper, gypsum and sulphur, but these are not mined commercially. More important has been the discovery of an offshore gas field.

Energy Djibouti's recent gas finds ought to produce an exportable surplus in the near future. Otherwise, it remains dependent on imports for oil and other fuels with which to run its power stations.

	1993	1994	1995
Inflation (% change)	10.0	5.0	8.3
Exchange rate (per US$)	177.72	177.72	175.20
Interest rate			
GDP (% real growth)	-3.3	0.2	1.5
GDP (Million units of national currency)	50,016.5	52,640.7	57,865.0
GDP (US$ million)	281.4	296.2	330.3
GDP per capita (US$)	502.6	519.7	566.3
Consumption (Million units of national currency)	33,171.7	34,912.0	38,376.7
Consumption (US$ million)	186.7	196.4	219.0
Consumption per capita (US$)	333.3	344.7	375.6
Population, mid-year ('000)	560.0	570.0	583.2
Birth rate (per '000)	38.1	42.9	
Death rate (per '000)	18.7	15.8	
No. of households ('000)	108.6	111.1	116.7
Total exports (US$ million)	55.0	70.0	
Total Imports (US$ million)	300.0	400.0	
Tourism receipts (US$ million)	13.0	13.6	
Tourist spending (US$ million)	7.0	7.3	8.1

Average household size 1995 (persons)	4.87		
Urban population 1995 (%)	82.8		
Age analysis (%)			
Population by sex (%)			
Life expectancy (years) (1990-95)	*Male* 46.7	*Female* 50.0	
Infant mortality (deaths per '000 live births) (1993)	114.9		
Adult literacy (%)			

Dominica

Area (km²) 751

Currency East Caribbean dollar (EC$ = 100 cents)

Location Dominica forms part of the Lesser Antilles, in the Windward Islands group, lying between Guadeloupe and Martinique. Its volcanic soil is very fertile and its climate is generally equable, although subject to hurricanes. The capital is Roseau.

Head of State President Crispin Sorhaindo (October 1993)

Head of Government Edison James (June 1995)

Ruling Party Dominica United Workers' Party (DUWP)

Political Structure Dominica, an independent republic within the Commonwealth, is formally ruled by an executive President, who in practice hands most of his legislative authority to the Prime Minister and her Cabinet. There is a unicameral House of Assembly, whose 30 members include nine appointed members, but whose other members are elected by universal suffrage for a five-year term. The House then elects the President, for a maximum of two five-year terms. Dominica is considering political union with Grenada, St Lucia and St Vincent and the Grenadines.

Last Elections Elections were held in May 1995 to the House of Assembly, when the ruling Dominica Freedom Party was narrowly defeated by the Dominica United Workers' Party, with 10 seats to the DUWP's 11. The DUWP then went on to form a government.

Political Risk The deterioration of the Government's political position has caused some concern in recent years, with growing protests about trade union rights and restrictions on the freedom of expression. Even the presence of an effective democratic system has proved insufficient to stem a rising tide of political violence.The capital, Roseau, has been under a state of emergency for more than a year.

Economy Despite an abundance of natural advantages, Dominica's economy remains among the weakest in the Caribbean, and at present there are few indications of an imminent upturn. Remittances from expatriate labour are a major source of income. Moreover, the economy depends to a large extent on the EU's policy governing banana imports, a factor over which the country has little real control.

Main Industries Dominica's fertile volcanic soil provides ample opportunity for the development of an excellent agricultural industry. Bananas, limes, copra and bay oil are produced for export while meat production and fishing are conducted principally for the domestic population. There is extensive forest cover providing scope for timber extraction. Industries tend on the whole to centre on the processing of agricultural raw materials: rum manufacture is a major activity. There are also fruit canning plants, tobacco processing sheds and plants making soap and other light products. Tourism, although growing fast, is less intensively developed than in many other Caribbean states. The problem is due partly to the poor provision of roads, airports and other infrastructure facilities, and partly to the fact that nearly all beaches comprise black volcanic sand.

Energy Dominica imports all of its fuel requirements, with oil and gas predominating. Just over half of its electricity derives from hydro-electric schemes, with thermal stations providing the rest.

	1993	1994	1995
Inflation (% change)	1.6	1.6	
Exchange rate (per US$)	2.70	2.70	2.70
Interest rate (% per annum)	10.0	9.6	10.3
GDP (% real growth)	0.4	2.3	1.3
GDP (Million units of national currency)	537.8	558.7	566.1
GDP (US$ million)	199.2	206.9	209.7
GDP per capita (US$)	2,845.5	2,956.1	2,995.3
Consumption (Million units of national currency)	383.2	370.6	382.8
Consumption (US$ million)	141.9	137.3	141.8
Consumption per capita (US$)	2,027.5	1,960.8	2,025.4
Population, mid-year ('000)	70.0	70.0	70.0
Birth rate (per '000)	20.2	20.5	20.7
Death rate (per '000)	5.0	5.1	
No. of households ('000)	16.1	16.2	16.3
Total exports (US$ million)	48.3	60.0	
Total imports (US$ million)	98.8	150.0	
Tourism receipts (US$ million)	29.0	29.6	
Tourist spending (US$ million)	5.0	5.1	5.3

Average household size 1995 (persons)	4.11				
Urban population 1994					
Age analysis (%) (1989)	*0-14* 35.0	*15-64* 56.6	*65+* 8.3		
Population by sex (%) (1989)	*Male* 46.3	*Female* 53.7			
Life expectancy (years) (1958-62)	*Male* 57.0	*Female* 59.2			
Infant mortality (deaths per '000 live births)					
Adult literacy (%) (1970)	94.1				

Dominican Republic

Area (km²) 48,440

Currency Dominican Republic peso (RD$ = 100 centavos)

Location The Dominican Republic lies in the Greater Antilles, north of Venezuela. It occupies the eastern half of the island of Hispaniola, with the state of Haiti in the west. The climate is equable, although often humid at sea level and the soil is adequate agriculture. The capital is Santo Domingo.

Head of State President Leonel Fernandez (1996)

Head of Government President Leonel Fernandez (1996)

Ruling Party Liberation Party

Political Structure The Dominican Republic is ruled by an executive President who is elected for a four-year term by universal suffrage. The president answers to a 120-member Chamber of Deputies and a 30-member Senate - all elected similarly for four-year terms. The country consists of 26 provinces, each of which is run by an appointed governor, and the Distrito Nacional around the capital Santo Domingo.

Last Elections Leonel Fernandez was to be installed as President in August 1996 following two rounds of polling. A centrist, Fernandez leads the Liberation Party and received 51.3% of the vote in the second round. The result was a setback for the Partido Reformista Social Cristiano (PRSC) which had dominated the political scene for most of the preceding 30 years. The Liberation Party has few representatives in the legislature and the incoming president's policies will have to be approved by PRSC lawmakers.

Political Risk The changes that are expected to follow the installation of Balaguer's successor should be more a matter of style than substance. The progressive deregulation of the economy, which started with a clearly reluctant Balaguer under pressure from foreign donors and creditors, will be continued. An expanding economy has contributed to a calmer political atmosphere in the country. The previous administration succeeded in implementing a severe austerity programme. Its relative successes in curbing inflation and reducing foreign debt will make it easier for the new administration to turn its attention to improvements in living conditions.

International Disputes The Dominican Republic's occasional disputes with Haiti have receded into the background with the change of government in the latter country.

Economy The country's central bank estimates that GDP grew by 4.8% in 1995. Private economists argue that the figure is a gross overestimation. Whatever the case, growth in the industrial sector is being driven by expansion in communications, transport and construction. Income from tourism was mainly responsible for covering an import deficit of around $2 billion. The country has managed to attract foreign investment from Asia and the United States, thanks largely to the creation of free trade zones, and this has helped to create employment while assisting in the diversification of the manufacturing sector.

Main Industries The agricultural sector specialises in producing coffee, tobacco and cocoa for export, and bananas, maize, rice and molasses for the home market. Production of sugar, once the pillar of the economy, has contracted in recent years because of problems encountered by the heavily-indebted state-owned producer. Agriculture employs around half of the workforce. Major industries in the manufacturing sector include the production of cement, beer, glass products, plastics, paints and paper as well as activities such as the processing and canning of fruit and the manufacture of groundnut oil. There are significant deposits of gold, silver and ferro-nickel, although all are in decline. Bauxite is also present, its extraction being something of an on-off affair according to the marginal state of the world metals markets.

Energy Although small deposits of crude oil have been located at Chaco Largo, the Dominican Republic remains dependent on oil imports for most of its energy needs and all of its electricity generating requirements. The economy has suffered for years from an inadequate electricity supply, mainly because the state-owned industry has not been able to keep pace with increasing demand.

	1993	1994	1995
Inflation (% change)	5.2	8.3	12.5
Exchange rate (per US$)	12.68	13.16	13.75
Interest rate			
GDP (% real growth)	2.1	4.3	4.7
GDP (Million units of national currency)	120,572.0	136,206.0	160,456.0
GDP (US$ million)	9,508.8	10,350.0	11,669.5
GDP per capita (US$)	1,247.9	1,332.0	1,475.3
Consumption (Million units of national currency)	91,684.0	99,544.0	112,705.9
Consumption (US$ million)	7,230.6	7,564.1	8,196.8
Consumption per capita (US$)	948.9	973.5	1,036.3
Population, mid-year ('000)	7,620.0	7,770.0	7,910.0
Birth rate (per '000)	27.7	24.9	
Death rate (per '000)		1.3	
No. of households ('000)	1,517.9	1,565.4	1,645.6
Total exports (US$ million)	611.0	633.0	765.0
Total imports (US$ million)	2,436.0	2,626.0	2,976.0
Tourism receipts (US$ million)	1,234.0	1,147.8	1,250.0
Tourist spending (US$ million)	118.0	125.5	136.0

Average household size 1995 (persons)	4.72				
Urban population 1995 (%)	64.6				
Age analysis (%) (1980)	*0-14* 47.6		*15-64* 49.3		*65+* 3.1
Population by sex (%) (1991)	*Male* 50.1		*Female* 49.9		
Life expectancy (years) (1990-95)	*Male* 67.6		*Female* 71.7		
Infant mortality (deaths per '000 live births) (1993)	42.0				
Adult literacy (%) (1990)	83.3				

TRADING PARTNERS

Major export destinations 1995 (% share)		Major import sources 1995 (% share)	
USA	46.9	USA	50.7
Germany	13.1	Mexico	8.6
Belgium/Luxembourg	6.1	Venezuela	8.3
Spain	6.0	Japan	5.0

Ecuador

Area (km²)   263,950

Currency   Sucre (S = 100 centavos)

Location   Ecuador lies on the western (Pacific) coast of South America, where it is bordered in the north and east by Colombia and in the south and east by Peru. The republic also includes the territory covered by the Galapagos Islands, about 1,000 km off the coast. The country has some of the highest mountains in South America, peaking at over 6,000 metres, and is extensively forested - although the coastal regions are often damp and humid. The capital is Quito.

Head of State   A new president will replace Sixto Durán Ballén in July 1996

Head of Government   A new president will replace Sixto Durán Ballén in July 1996

Ruling Party   Social Christian Party (PSC) is expected to continue to lead a multi-party coalition of the right.

Political Structure   Ecuador has an executive President who is chosen by universal suffrage for a single, non-renewable four-year term. He appoints his own Cabinet and reports to a 77-member Congress. Twelve members are elected by national ballot for a four-year term while the remainder are appointed by regional assemblies for a two-year term. The 20 provinces enjoy a substantial degree of political autonomy.

Last Elections   Nine presidential candidates competed in the first round of elections held in May 1996. A runoff was scheduled in July 1996 but Jaime Nebot of the Social Christian Party is expected to gain the largest congressional block and succeed Sixto Durán Ballén to the presidency. The main opposition is the Roldosista Party led by Abdala Bucaram who has urban support but attracts too much criticism to become president.

Political Risk   The position is complicated by severe fragmentation between the dozens of political parties. In 1995, centre-left parties realigned to form a new majority in Congress. The Social Christians may now be the biggest party in the new Congress, but with no overall majority. Their candidate for the August 1996 election, Jaime Nebot, is very popular with the public. Many doubt that Congress will go ahead with economic reforms before the next elections and Nebot, if elected, promises to scrap the existing reform proposals.

International Disputes   Ecuador has a serious political conflict with Peru, which disputes its claim to some 325,000 square kilometres of land in the north of the country. The densely forested land, lying between the Marañón and Amazon rivers, was awarded to Peru in the 1942 Protocol of Rio de Janeiro after a period of war. Its importance lies in its oil reserves, which are all-important to Peru. Open war broke out once again between the two countries in 1994/95 over the issue, although they reopened their borders in September 1995 amid renewed attempts to find a settlement.

Economy   Ecuador's economy was badly hurt by last year's war with Peru. The total costs of that conflict are unknown but estimates of the direct cost are widely assumed to be about $340 million, or 2% of GDP. The country needs much more capital investment but its programme of economic reforms have yet to impress international lenders such as the IMF. The government has managed to bring inflation down and to maintain modest rates of growth. Nevertheless, about half the workforce is unemployed or under-employed. The economy has responded better than expected to the government's reduction in trade barriers and its export sector performs well.

Main Industries   Oil development and oil processing remain the most important sectors of the Ecuadorian economy. Despite attempts to diversify, the commodity still provides over 70% of all foreign exchange revenues and the country has reserves estimated at one billion barrels. Agriculture employs nearly 50% of the workforce. Farm productivity is low, despite the country's favourable climate and good soil quality. Bananas are Ecuador's single most important export product after oil. Other major export crops are sugar, maize, soya, rice, cocoa and coffee. Timber is extracted for export. Fishing is the third main export earner with tuna, sardines and shrimps predominating. Industry centres on the processing of agricultural raw materials: fish canning, rum manufacture and palm oil milling.

Energy   Ecuador has a vast exportable surplus of oil and natural gas and has been expanding its exploration activities, by opening up around 3.2 million hectares to foreign companies in the Amazon region. Environmental groups have responded with protests about the damage this will do to the Amazon basin. Meanwhile, over 80% of the country's electricity needs are still being met by hydro-electric power stations rather than by oil. The country gets 60% of its power from one big hydroelectric scheme, which is silting up and is at risk from drought. The power shortages which result pose serious problems for the country's economy.

	1993	1994	1995
Inflation (% change)	45.0	27.3	22.9
Exchange rate (per US$)	1,919.10	2,196.70	2,514.80
Interest rate (% per annum)	47.8	44.0	55.7
GDP (% real growth)	1.7	3.4	3.5
GDP (Million units of national currency)	27,451,000.0	36,368,000.0	46,260,641.5
GDP (US$ million)	14,304.1	16,555.7	18,395.4
GDP per capita (US$)	1,302.7	1,475.6	1,605.2
Consumption (Million units of national currency)	19,375,000.0	26,816,000.0	35,635,041.3
Consumption (US$ million)	10,095.9	12,207.4	14,170.1
Consumption per capita (US$)	919.5	1,088.0	1,236.5
Population, mid-year ('000)	10,980.0	11,220.0	11,460.0
Birth rate (per '000)	21.8	21.8	
Death rate (per '000)	4.8	4.8	
No. of households ('000)	2,339.0	2,468.2	2,626.3
Total exports (US$ million)	2,904.0	3,820.0	4,307.0
Total imports (US$ million)	2,562.0	3,690.0	4,193.0
Tourism receipts (US$ million)	230.0	232.0	244.9
Tourist spending (US$ million)	190.0	218.5	220.4

Average household size 1995 (persons)	4.32		
Urban population 1995 (%)	58.4		
Age analysis (%) (1994)	*0-14* 36.9	*15-64* 58.8	*65+* 4.3
Population by sex (%) (1994)	*Male* 50.3	*Female* 49.7	
Life expectancy (years) (1994)	*Male* 63.5	*Female* 67.5	
Infant mortality (deaths per '000 live births) (1993)	35.3		
Adult literacy (%) (1990)	87.3		

TRADING PARTNERS

Major export destinations 1995 (% share)		Major import sources 1995 (% share)	
USA	47.7	USA	40.1
Germany	7.5	Japan	10.0
South Korea	7.3	Colombia	9.5
Chile	4.4	Germany	5.9

Egypt

Area (km²)   997,739

Currency   Egyptian pound (£E = 100 piastres)

Location   The Arab Republic of Egypt is situated at the extreme eastern end of North Africa's Mediterranean coast. Bordering on Israel to the north and east, with Sudan to the south and Libya to the west, it is in fact more closely linked with Saudi Arabia, with which it shares the strategically important Red Sea. Egypt is the keeper of the Suez Canal, one of its main sources of income. There is agriculture around the Nile delta; elsewhere the terrain is mostly desert. The capital is Cairo.

Head of State   President Muhammad Hosni Mubarak (1981)

Head of Government   Kamel Ganzouri (1996)

Ruling Party   National Democratic Party

Political Structure   The period since 1990 has been marked by a succession of insurgencies associated with Islamic militancy. Coup plots and even regular assassination attempts have been uncovered. This has presented the Egyptian government with a political problem, forcing President Mubarak to call for a national debate in 1994 on possible changes in the country's political direction. Egypt's 1972 Constitution provides for an executive President who answers to a unicameral People's Assembly with 454 members, 10 of whom he appoints personally. The People's Assembly, which is elected by universal suffrage for a term of five years, then elects the President for a six-year term. There is also a 210-member Consultative Council (Majlis as-Shoura) which includes 140 elected members and 70 appointed by the President.

Last Elections   The National Democratic Party won a sweeping victory in the last general elections to the People's Assembly, in November-December 1990, with 348 of the 444 elected seats. Independent candidates won 83 seats. However, the validity of the election was compromised by the boycott imposed by the three largest opposition parties. Only about 30% of the electorate voted. President Mubarak, who personally appointed another 10 delegates to the Assembly, was himself re-elected in October 1993.

Political Risk   The rise of Islamic fundamentalism continues to be a serious threat which has the potential to disrupt key industries and discourage foreign investors. Optimists believe that terrorist activities have peaked and, indeed, they appear to have subsided in 1996. Most of the violence is currently confined to villages in the Nile Valley or occasional, high-profile attacks abroad such as the attempted assassination of Mubarak in Ethiopia in June 1995. Nevertheless, over 12,000 suspected militants were still in jail in 1996 and some analysts argue that Cairo is merely postponing its problems to a later date. Cairo's easy relations with Saudi Arabia and the Western world would still offer valuable safeguards if the level of violence should escalate once again.

International Disputes   The resurgence of militant Islam has opened up some of Egypt's old wounds. Relations with Sudan and Iran are strained and Egypt has accused both countries of fomenting religious discontent. The country has only recently regained much of the good will it had lost among its Arab neighbours as a result of signing the 1979 Camp David agreement. Relations with other Arab countries have improved because of Egypt's backing for the Afghan Mujaheddin, support for Saudi Arabia in the Gulf War of 1991 and the strong stand it has taken against Colonel Qaddafi of Libya.

Economy   Kamel Ganzouri was appointed prime minister in 1996 with a mandate to rejuvenate the sagging economy and renew the impetus of economic reform. The previous administration of Mohamed Sidki is credited with bringing inflation down to its lowest level in 40 years (4.9% in 1995) and sharply reducing the budget deficit. Disappointments stem from the failure to embark on a programme of privatisation, deregulation or removal of trade barriers. The result is that unemployment is at least 20% and economic growth is only around 2.2% per year. Poverty is also rampant since at least a quarter of the country's 60 million inhabitant live on less than $35 a month.

Main Industries   Egypt's agricultural sector is concentrated in the Nile delta which is the most fertile part of the country. Cotton is a major cash crop and a big earner of foreign exchange. This is especially true now that the private sector, rather than a government-appointed marketing board, has authority for marketing and selling cotton. Egypt is also self-sufficient in the production of maize, wheat, rice and sugar cane, thanks in part to an ambitious irrigation programme which has extended the cultivable area. Tourism represents a small but growing sector of the country's foreign trade. More important still is the Suez Canal, which provides up to a third of Egypt's revenues. Oil and gas development produce most of the rest and support a growing oil refining industry. Other important industries include: textiles, clothing, machine tools, electrical goods and chemical products.

Energy   Egypt has a large exportable surplus of hydrocarbons as well as massive hydro-electric resources from the Aswan and High Dams.

	1993	1994	1995
Inflation (% change)	12.1	8.2	4.9
Exchange rate (per US$)	3.37	3.39	3.40
Interest rate (% per annum)	18.3	16.5	
GDP (% real growth)	5.0	2.8	2.2
GDP (Million units of national currency)	157,300.0	175,000.0	205,000.0
GDP (US$ million)	46,676.6	51,622.4	60,294.1
GDP per capita (US$)	826.3	885.0	1,018.0
Consumption (Million units of national currency)	115,000.0	130,500.0	143,950.0
Consumption (US$ million)	34,124.6	38,495.6	42,338.2
Consumption per capita (US$)	604.1	660.0	714.8
Population, mid-year ('000)	56,490.0	58,330.0	59,230.0
Birth rate (per '000)	34.6	29.7	
Death rate (per '000)	9.1	7.2	
No. of households ('000)	13,476.4	13,984.9	14,396.7
Total exports (US$ million)	2,244.0	3,463.0	
Total imports (US$ million)	8,184.0	10,185.0	
Tourism receipts (US$ million)	1,332.0	1,351.6	
Tourist spending (US$ million)	1,048.0	1,063.4	1,169.5

Average household size 1995 (persons)	3.96				
Urban population 1995 (%)	44.8				
Age analysis (%) (1990)	*0-14*	46.8	*15-64*	51.1	*65+* 2.2
Population by sex (%) (1990)	*Male*	49.7	*Female*	50.3	
Life expectancy (years) (1985-90)	*Male*	57.8	*Female*	60.3	
Infant mortality (deaths per '000 live births) (1992)	36.2				
Adult literacy (%) (1990)	48.4				

TRADING PARTNERS

Major export destinations 1995 (% share)		Major import sources 1995 (% share)	
USA	18.8	Italy	16 6
Germany	9.3	USA	9.7
France	7.9	Greece	8.9
Italy	7.5	United Kingdom	6.6

El Salvador

Area (km²)   21,395

Currency   Salvadorean colón (C = 100 centavos)

Location   El Salvador is a long coastal strip, never more than 80 km in width, which extends for some 250 km along the Pacific coast of Central America, with Guatemala to the north and west and Honduras to the east and north-east. Its favourable climate and important position have helped to make it one of the most densely populated areas of the developing world. The terrain is mainly mountainous, with several extinct volcanoes. The capital is San Salvador.

Head of State   President Armando Calderon Sol (March 1994)

Head of Government   President Armando Calderon Sol

Ruling Party   Alianza Republicana Nacionalista (ARENA)

Political Structure   The executive President is elected by universal suffrage for a term of five years, and answers to a unicameral Legislative Assembly whose membership was expanded from 60 to 84 seats in March 1991.

Last Elections   The first presidential elections since the end of the civil war were held in March 1994, when the ruling ARENA parties failed to obtain the absolute majority they needed to avoid a second round of voting. They did, however, managed to hold on to power. Meanwhile, elections were held to the 84-seat Legislative Assembly, when ARENA won 39 seats, the Farabundo Marti National Liberation Front (a former guerrilla movement) won 21 and the Partido Democrático Cristiano took 18 seats. The Partido de Conciliación Nacional won four seats and the Christian Democrats only one seat. The next election is scheduled for March 1997.

Political Risk   El Salvador's political credibility in the international community was damaged by its poor record on human rights. Four years of peace after the country's long civil war is bringing improvements, however. After righting some of the wrongs which occurred in the war, the government has begun to turn its attention to repairing and modernising the economy. The degree of risk falls as this process continues.

International Disputes   The violent political disputes which wrecked the country during the civil war have subsided, leaving no international disagreements behind. A change in the policy of the United States with regard to El Salvador has helped to defuse tensions.

Economy   El Salvador's economy has improved dramatically over the past four years. High growth and moderate inflation have been achieved along with balance-of-payments stability and reduced foreign debt. Now the Government has embarked on a reform programme that includes privatising the country's inefficient large companies. In 1995, President Calderon Sol appointed a commissioner for privatisation to accelerate the process. His remit is to promote deregulation and competition and to privatise pensions, electricity distribution, San Salvador's airport and the state telecoms company.

Main Industries   The agricultural sector dominates in the El Salvadorian economy. Plots are small and relatively inefficient, however, and productivity is low. Most farming is for subsistence but cash crops include sugar, cotton and especially coffee. Products grown for the domestic market include maize, rice, sesame and fruit. Industrial development has been proceeding rapidly since peace was restored. Leading industries include: textiles, clothing, furniture and other wood products, cement, fabricated steel and consumer household goods.

Energy   El Salvador relies on imports for its entire supply of petroleum and petroleum products, having little of its own refining capacity. It is, however, almost self-sufficient in electricity, thanks largely to its considerable hydro-electric generating capacity.

	1993	1994	1995
Inflation (% change)	18.6	10.6	10.0
Exchange rate (per US$)	8.67	8.75	8.76
Interest rate (% per annum)	19.4	19.0	19.1
GDP (% real growth)	2.2	2.0	12.7
GDP (Million units of national currency)	66,239.0	67,766.1	84,011.0
GDP (US$ million)	7,640.0	7,744.7	9,590.3
GDP per capita (US$)	1,384.1	1,373.2	1,678.7
Consumption (Million units of national currency)	52,782.0	54,213.0	67,475.5
Consumption (US$ million)	6,087.9	6,195.8	7,702.7
Consumption per capita (US$)	1,102.9	1,098.5	1,348.3
Population, mid-year ('000)	5,520.0	5,640.0	5,713.1
Birth rate (per '000)	32.3	32.8	
Death rate (per '000)	7.1	6.6	
No. of households ('000)	1,236.9	1,245.1	1,290.8
Total exports (US$ million)	732.0	844.0	998.0
Total imports (US$ million)	1,912.0	2,249.0	2,853.0
Tourism receipts (US$ million)	121.0	124.3	
Tourist spending (US$ million)	61.0	62.7	77.9

Average household size 1995 (persons)	4.30		
Urban population 1995 (%)	45.1		
Age analysis (%) (1991)	*0-14* 36.1	*15-64* 58.2	*65+* 5.8
Population by sex (%) (1992)	*Male* 48.0	*Female* 52.0	
Life expectancy (years) (1985-90)	*Male* 58.0	*Female* 66.5	
Infant mortality (deaths per '000 live births) (1992)	19.2		
Adult literacy (%) (1990)	73.0		

TRADING PARTNERS

Major export destinations 1995 (% share)		Major import sources 1995 (% share)	
USA	72.7	USA	41.7
Germany	24.1	Guatemala	9.6
Guatemala	15.5	Japan	5.5
Costa Rica	11.2	Venezuela	5.2

Equatorial Guinea

Area (km²)   28,050

Currency   CFA franc (= 100 centimes)

Location   Equatorial Guinea comprises the mainland territory of Río Muni, located on the West African Atlantic coast between Cameroon and Gabon, and also the islands of Bioko, Pagalu and the Corisco group. The region has a warm, dry climate and has suffered from drought and environmental mismanagement in recent years. The capital is Malabo.

Head of State   President Teodoro Obiang Nguema Mbasogo (1979)

Head of Government   Capt. Silvestre Siale Bileka

Ruling Party   Partido Democrático de Guinea Ecuatorial (PDGE)

Political Structure   Although officially a multi-party state, Equatorial Guinea's policitical scene is completely dominated by the PDGE. Four other political parties exist, but any serious opposition to the president is not tolerated. The 80-member parliament enjoys only lukewarm support among the people.

Last Elections   The first multi-party elections were held in November 1993, when the PDGE won 68 of the 80 seats. That poll, however, was criticised as unrepresentative by both domestic and foreign observers, and it was estimated that only about 20% of the population voted. The latest election on 25 February 1996 returned the president to power but did nothing to impress the international community after intimidation and violence persuaded the other contesting parties to pull out.

Political Risk   Equatorial Guinea's low standing in the international political community has continued to decline because of events during the last election which included the arrest of opposition leaders and official charges of witchcraft being levied against the US ambassador. As one of the poorest countries in Africa, Equatorial Guinea can be only be described as a difficult and risky market.

Economy   Equatorial Guinea's dependence on foreign aid is already substantial and likely to grow without better economic management or some other source of income. Prospects for the domestic market will therefore centre on the availability of bilateral or multilateral aid programmes. Meanwhile, the devaluation of the CFA franc in 1994 has increased the cost of imports and led to a rise in external debts.

Main Industries   Equatorial Guinea's sparse landscape offers little scope for intensive agriculture. Cocoa and coffee are its only real exports and can be grown in only a small area of the country. Elsewhere, cassava, sweet potatoes, palm oil and bananas are produced as subsistence crops. Gradually, agricultural output has declined and the country has become a comparatively large importer of food. With a meagre resource base, the only other exports are timber (mainly from the Río Muni area) and a small amount of alluvial gold. The country has virtually no industry and carries out little or no processing of these resources.

Energy   Oil and gas deposits have been located offshore. Walter International, a small US company, began operation in 1991 and its modest success has attracted the attention of others. In October 1995 Mobil announced plans to begin production of 40,000 barrels per day from one field by the end of 1996. Analysts predict that Mobil's figure could quadruple within two years. Such an outcome would make Equatorial Guinea a wealthy state but better governance would be essential if its people are to reap any of the benefits.

	1993	1994	1995
Inflation (% change)	4.0	10.0	
Exchange rate (per US$)	283.16	555.20	498.70
Interest rate (% per annum)	17.5	17.5	16.0
GDP (% real growth)	6.6	6.5	4.0
GDP (Million units of national currency)	53,100.0	61,877.8	64,352.9
GDP (US$ million)	187.5	111.5	129.0
GDP per capita (US$)	494.8	287.3	324.2
Consumption (Million units of national currency)	29,850.5	35,576.9	37,842.3
Consumption (US$ million)	105.4	64.1	75.9
Consumption per capita (US$)	278.2	165.2	190.6
Population, mid-year ('000)	379.0	388.0	398.1
Birth rate (per '000)	43.5	40.7	
Death rate (per '000)	20.7	18.2	
No. of households ('000)	89.7	92.3	97.3
Total exports (US$ million)	62.0		
Total imports (US$ million)	60.0	100.0	
Tourism receipts (US$ million)			
Tourist spending (US$ million)			

Average household size 1995 (persons)	3.99				
Urban population 1995 (%)	42.2				
Age analysis (%) (1990)	*0-14* 42.6		*15-64* 53.4		*65+* 4.0
Population by sex (%) (1993)	*Male* 49.3		*Female* 50.7		
Life expectancy (years) (1990-95)	*Male* 46.4		*Female* 49.6		
Infant mortality (deaths per '000 live births) (1993)	16.6				
Adult literacy (%) (1983)	62.0				

Eritrea

Area (km²) 93,679

Currency Birr (= 100 cents)

Location Eritrea, a large and predominantly mountainous area of the old Ethiopian republic, became independent in May 1993. The state lies in north-east Africa along the Red Sea coast, facing Saudi Arabia and the Republic of Yemen across the water. In the west it borders on Djibouti, in the south on Kenya, in the east on Sudan and in the south-west on Somalia. The country has a warm and desert climate and is prone to periodic drought. The capital is Asmara.

Head of State President Issaias Afewerki (May 1993)

Head of Government President Issaias Afewerki

Ruling Party People's Front for Democracy and Justice (PFDJ, formerly the Eritrean People's Liberation Front - EPLF)

Political Structure Eritrea has an executive President and a unicameral 150-member National Assembly which consists of 75 Central Committee members of the ruling PFDJ, together with 75 others, of whom at least 11 must be women. The National Assembly elects the President directly. Executive Power is vested in a 24-member State Council chaired by the President.

Last Elections The country's first elections since independence from Ethiopia took place in July 1994, when the EPRF won 284 of the 303 declared results. Full multi-party elections are due to be held by 1997.

Political Risk International acceptance of the new Eritrean state has been very rapid, but there are still major problems. As much as 20% of the population was displaced during the independence war with Ethiopia, and the country still has around 500,000 refugees scattered throughout Sudan.

International Disputes Eritrea's independence came at the end of a ten-year battle with Ethiopia. The war caused severe disruptions which resulted in major dislocations of population in that part of Africa. Diplomatic relations with Sudan were severed in December 1994, after mutual allegations of security and border infringements. Eritrean opposition is now based in Sudan and President Issaias has promised to provide arms to Sudan's own dissidents in the southern part of that country. In 1996, Eritrea came close to war with Yemen over the Dahlak Islands in the Red Sea but peace talks have now been opened to resolve the dispute.

Economy Eritrea's territory contains much of the good arable land in the former Ethiopia, though like Ethiopia, it has faced recurrent droughts in recent years. The United Nations has sponsored a US$262 million aid programme for restoring the economy, but it is thought unlikely that the country can achieve self-sufficiency in foodstuffs until well after 2000.

Main Industries Agriculture is minimal and there is virtually no industry. The country has some mineral reserves, mainly copper, potash, gold and platinum, but these have not yet been exploited seriously.

Energy At present, wood and brushwood are among the major fuels. Eritrea does, however, have substantial hydro-electric power generating capacity.

	1993	1994	1995
Inflation (% change)	7.4	6.7	9.4
Exchange rate (per US$)	5.00	5.42	5.21
Interest rate			
GDP (% real growth)			
GDP			
GDP (US$ million)			
GDP per capita (US$)			
Consumption			
Consumption (US$ million)			
Consumption per capita (US$)			
Population, mid-year ('000)	3,345.0	3,274.4	3,295.0
Birth rate (per '000)	43.0	36.7	
Death rate (per '000)	15.2		
No. of households ('000)			
Total exports (US$ million)			
Total imports (US$ million)			
Tourism receipts (US$ million)			
Tourist spending (US$ million)			
Average household size 1995 (persons)			
Urban population 1995 (%)	17.2		
Age analysis (%)			
Population by sex (%)			
Life expectancy (years)			
Infant mortality (deaths per '000 live births) (1993)	105.2		
Adult literacy (%)			

Estonia

Area (km²) 45,226

Currency Kroon (linked to German Mark)

Location Estonia, the smallest of the three Baltic republics, faces Finland across the Gulf of Finland, with Latvia to the south and Russia dominating its entire eastern frontier. Like Latvia, its land is mainly low-lying and marshy, and its territory includes some 800 islands in the Baltic. The capital is Tallinn.

Head of State President Lennart Meri (1992)

Head of Government Tiit Vahi (March 1995)

Ruling Party Coalition Party and Rural Union bloc lead a coalition with the Centre Party.

Political Structure Estonia was one of the first Soviet states to declare its formal secession from the USSR, in the summer of 1991. It was recognised in September 1991. The Riigikogu (Parliament, or Supreme Council) has 101 members and appoints the President directly. However, a referendum held in June 1992 endorsed a new constitution allowing for the first new President to be directly elected, with subsequent Presidents being appointed by the Parliament.

Last Elections Elections to the new 101-member Parliament were held in March 1995, when the ruling right-wing Fatherland Group (Isamaa) suffered big losses. A less staunchly pro-market group led by the Coalition Party and the Rural Union took 41 seats and formed a coalition with the Centre Party which won 16 seats. The government-led Fatherland Group and its allies finished far behind with only 8 seats, while another 19 seats were awarded to the Estonian Reform Party. The Moderates bloc won 6 seats, the Our Home is Estonia bloc won 6, and the "Right-Wingers" (the Republican People's Party) won 5 seats.

Political Risk With its linguistic, cultural and physical proximity to a supportive Finland and a firm sense of national identity, Estonia is proving to be one of the most resilient of the former Soviet states. Discontent among the elderly and rural Estonians, and frustration with an arrogant ruling style, has eroded support for market reforms but successive governments have shown no signs of swerving from the path. Estonia has applied for membership in the EU and NATO and is supported by its Scandinavian neighbours.

International Disputes The revival of nationalist sentiment in neighbouring Russia has aroused fears in Estonia, which have been reflected in an unexpectedly fierce counter-attack against Russian interests. The withdrawal of the Russian military has been completed but this has not prevented an ongoing disagreement about various pieces of land which Russia had previously annexed from Estonia.

Economy Estonia was one of the most prosperous Soviet republics and has successfully attracted a large number of joint ventures with Western companies. Meanwhile, aggressive pro-market administrators have drastically transformed the economy. Agriculture accounted for 20% of GDP in 1991 but for only 7% in 1996. The economy has responded strongly, growing by 4% in 1995, and with even larger gains being forecast for subsequent years. A controversial privatisation programme is scheduled to be completed in 1996 after transferring 74% of large state-owned enterprises to private hands. Rapid growth is bringing large increases in imports, with the current-account deficit rising to $220 million in 1995. High rates of inflation and an underdeveloped financial sector are other weaknesses.

Main Industries Estonia has substantial deposits of minerals (including phosphates, and oil-shale) as well as extensive forest resources which provide the basis for timber and paper industries. There are well-established engineering, machine-building and textile industries, along with important consumer goods and food-processing industries. Agriculture is based mainly on livestock rearing, although dairy farming is also important.

Energy Estonia's deposits of oil-shale, used in power stations to generate electricity, provide the basis for exports of power. Since independence, however, the country has suffered fuel shortages which have been prompted by disputes over large price increases imposed by Russia.

	1993	1994	1995
Inflation (% change)	89.8	47.7	28.9
Exchange rate (per US$)	13.22	12.80	11.50
Interest rate (% per annum)	27.3	23.1	16.0
GDP (% real growth)	-15.5	-6.6	4.0
GDP (Million units of national currency)	21,918.0	30,227.6	40,521.9
GDP (US$ million)	1,657.9	2,361.5	3,523.6
GDP per capita (US$)	1,092.9	1,574.4	2,372.8
Consumption (Million units of national currency)	12,591.3	17,455.9	19,514.0
Consumption (US$ million)	952.4	1,363.7	1,696.9
Consumption per capita (US$)	627.8	909.2	1,142.7
Population, mid-year ('000)	1,517.0	1,500.0	1,485.0
Birth rate (per '000)	10.0	9.5	8.8
Death rate (per '000)	14.0	14.8	13.8
No. of households ('000)	419.0	415.0	413.0
Total exports (US$ million)	805.0	1,299.0	
Total imports (US$ million)	896.0	1,660.0	
Tourism receipts (US$ million)	51.0	60.1	
Tourist spending (US$ million)	26.0	30.7	38.2

Average household size 1995 (persons)	3.43				
Urban population 1995 (%)	70.0				
Age analysis (%) (1995)	*0-14* 20.7		*15-64* 66.2		*65+* 13.1
Population by sex (%) (1995)	*Male* 46.6		*Female* 53.4		
Life expectancy (years) (1993)	*Male* 62.4		*Female* 73.8		
Infant mortality (deaths per '000 live births) (1994)	14.5				
Adult literacy (%) (1989)	99.7				

TRADING PARTNERS

Major export destinations 1995 (% share)		Major import sources 1995 (% share)	
Russia	19.5	Finland	34.6
Finland	19.2	Russia	17.1
Sweden	12.2	Sweden	11.2
Germany	5.2	Germany	7.8

Ethiopia

Area (km²)   1,023,050

Currency   Birr (= 100 cents)

Location   Ethiopia is a large and predominantly mountainous state lying in north-east Africa along the Red Sea coast, and facing Saudi Arabia and the Republic of Yemen across the water. In the west it borders on Djibouti, in the south on Kenya, in the east on Sudan and in the south-west on Somalia. The country has a warm and desert climate and is prone to periodic drought. The capital is Addis Ababa.

Head of State   President Meles Zenawi (1991)

Head of Government   Tamirat Layne (1991)

Ruling Party   Ethiopian People's Revolutionary Democratic Front (EPRF) leads a broad-based coalition.

Political Structure   Ethiopia has an executive President and an 87-member Council of Representatives designed to operate in the interim period, while the socialist one-party state which ruled it for many years is dismantled. During the 1980s the country's political and economic life was devastated by the civil war between the government and the Eritrean People's Revolutionary Democratic Front. Eritrea was been recognised as independent by the international community since early 1993. A new constitution declared in December 1994 established a federal government and divided the country into nine states, each of which retains the right to secede if it wishes.

Last Elections   June 1994 brought the first elections to the 547-member Constituent Assembly since the overthrow of President Mengistu Haile Mariam. The ruling EPRF obtained 484 seats, with most of the remainder going to minority groups. New elections to the newly created regional councils, and again to the national parliament (now expanded to 548 seats) were held in May 1995. Although the ruling EPRF obtained most of the votes, this was largely due to a mass boycott of the polls by most opposition parties. Consequently, the position of the EPRF is somewhat uncertain.

Political Risk   The settlement of the Eritrea question opens up the potential for a major expansion of activities in this huge country. Yet the extreme poverty of the population, together with the difficulties of transforming a planned economy with very limited resources will require many years to accomplish. The difficulties encountered in establishing an election process do not bode well. Meanwhile, there is the persistent threat of famine.

International Disputes   Ethiopia's main dispute has been with the northern region of Eritrea, where secessionist rebels finally succeeded in their aim of establishing full independence for the region, leaving the country without a northern sea corridor. Ethiopia is also at odds with Somalia over the Ogaden region, the vast triangular desert area which comprises the whole south-east of the country. Somalia claims sovereignty over the area, maintaining that it is merely a Somali-inhabited region under foreign occupation by Ethiopia. The Arab League backs Somalia against the Ethiopian claim.

Economy   In a good year Ethiopia's economy provides an adequate degree of self-sufficiency, but there have been few good years in the last decade. Recurrent droughts, such as the one experienced in 1993 and 1994, and the disruption of war have rendered the whole country very largely dependent on foreign aid. In April 1995 the government secured an economic co-operation agreement with Eritrea.

Main Industries   Ethiopia's agricultural sector employs some 85% of the workforce and produces 50% of GDP in a typical year. The harsh and arid landscape which characterises much of the country is suitable only for cattle herding, but in the river valleys farmers grow wheat, coffee (the main cash crop), maize and barley. The whole country is subject to periodic severe droughts, however, and multilateral aid is frequently required to ensure adequate food supplies. Manufacturing is mainly on a local scale and caters to the domestic market. There are mineral reserves, mainly copper, potash, gold and platinum, but these have not yet been exploited seriously - the result in part of the crippling civil war.

Energy   Ethiopia has hopes of locating oil in the Ogaden region, but this is small comfort since it may eventually lose the region to Somalia. At present, wood and brushwood are among the major fuels. Ethiopia does, however, have substantial hydro-electric power generating capacity.

	1993	1994	1995
Inflation (% change)	3.5	7.6	10.7
Exchange rate (per US$)	5.00	5.95	5.72
Interest rate (% per annum)	14.0	14.3	15.1
GDP (% real growth)	14.0	-2.2	1.7
GDP (Million units of national currency)	26,035.0	27,397.0	30,856.0
GDP (US$ million)	5,207.0	4,604.5	5,394.4
GDP per capita (US$)	97.8	83.8	95.2
Consumption (Million units of national currency)	22,307.0	23,645.0	26,824.3
Consumption (US$ million)	4,461.4	3,973.9	4,689.6
Consumption per capita (US$)	83.8	72.3	82.7
Population, mid-year ('000)	53,240.0	54,940.0	56,680.0
Birth rate (per '000)	48.5	45.0	
Death rate (per '000)	22.4	18.3	
No. of households ('000)	10,823.4	11,224.9	11,911.1
Total exports (US$ million)	199.0	372.0	
Total imports (US$ million)	787.0	1,033.0	
Tourism receipts (US$ million)			
Tourist spending (US$ million)			

Average household size 1995 (persons)	4.65				
Urban population 1995 (%)	13.4				
Age analysis (%) (1989)	*0-14* 48.8		*15-64* 48.1		*65+* 3.0
Population by sex (%) (1992)	*Male* 50.2		*Female* 49.8		
Life expectancy (years) (1990-95)	*Male* 45.9		*Female* 49.1		
Infant mortality (deaths per '000 live births) (1993)	119.2				
Adult literacy (%) (1984)	24.3				

TRADING PARTNERS

Major export destinations 1995 (% share)		Major import sources 1995 (% share)	
Germany	35.6	Italy	15.8
Japan	13.2	USA	12.2
Italy	11.4	Germany	9.6
USA	8.7	Japan	8.2

Fiji

Area (km²)   18,330

Currency   Fiji dollar (F$ = 100 cents)

Location   Fiji lies in the South Pacific, about 1,600 km north of New Zealand and north-east of Tonga. The country comprises 332 islands and some 500 atolls and reefs, of which about 100 are inhabited. The terrain is mainly low-lying, although there are large volcanic ranges on most of the larger islands. The climate is warm and tropical, with some risk of cyclones. The capital is Suva.

Head of State   President Ratu Sir Kamisese Mara (December 1993)

Head of Government   Maj.-Gen. Sitiveni Rabuka

Ruling Party   Soqosoqo ni Vakavulewa ni Taukei (Fijian Political Party) leads a coalition with the Fijian Nationalist Party.

Political Structure   Fiji left the Commonwealth in 1987 after two successive coups in which ethnic Fijians asserted their precedence over the ethnic Chinese and Indians who were effectively running the country at the time. The new Constitution, approved in July 1990, reserves an automatic majority of 37 in the 70-member House of Representatives (Lower House of Parliament) for ethnic Fijians - compared to 27 seats for Indians and six for other races. The Melanesian community has its own Assembly, the 56-member Council of Chiefs.

Last Elections   A general election held in February 1994 confirmed the dominant position of the coup leader Maj.-Gen. Sitiveni Rabuka, whose Soqosoqo ni Vakavulewa ni Taukei (SVT) party won 31 of the 37 Fijian seats in the 70-member House of Representatives. The General Voters' Party, a more moderate party advocating the same policies as the FPP, won another four of the seats reserved for Chinese, Europeans and others, and the Fijian Association, a splinter group of SVT dissidents, won a disappointing five seats.

Political Risk   The general elections held during the 1990s clearly confirm the dominance and cohesion of the Fijian ethnic group in the period since the 1987 coups. Yet the considerable disagreements between the various ethnic subgroups make it clear that the potential for conflict still exists, even within the FPP itself. The Prime Minister has shown many times that he is prepared to use force to retain order.

International Disputes   Fiji's major dispute with the UK, and the reason for its removal from the Commonwealth in 1987, was the military coup which reflected the racial tensions between its various ethnic groups. Otherwise the country has no outstanding disputes in progress. In 1993 it resumed a military alliance with New Zealand, indicating that its political rehabilitation was well advanced.

Economy   Fiji's relations with much of the international community suffered in the aftermath of the racially motivated coup which took place in the 1980s. As a result, the country still receives only modest international help. Its domestic economy is reasonably strong, however, and its central role at the hub of the Pacific Islands communications network has inevitably ensured that it remains a country to be courted by its neighbours.

Main Industries   Fiji's economy relies mainly on its agricultural sector, which employs well over half of the workforce. Sugar cane, coconuts and copra are the three main export crops while potatoes, rice, vegetables and root crops are grown for domestic consumption alongside the usual tropical fruits. Agricultural production has periodically been ravaged by cyclones (as in 1993) and by occasional earthquakes. There is a sizeable timber industry and an important fishing industry. Manufacturing tends to be small scale and primarily concerned with the processing of agricultural raw materials. Much more important is tourism, which is the country's second biggest foreign currency earner.

Energy   Fiji relies on imported oil and gas for most of the energy needs which it cannot cover with indigenous sources such as brushwood or timber. There may be scope for geothermal power in the future. Meanwhile, three-quarters of the country's electricity is produced by hydro-electric plants.

	1993	1994	1995
Inflation (% change)	5.2	0.6	2.2
Exchange rate (per US$)	1.54	1.46	1.41
Interest rate (% per annum)	11.7	11.3	11.1
GDP (% real growth)	2.0	3.3	5.6
GDP (Million units of national currency)	2,540.0	2,640.0	2,850.0
GDP (US$ million)	1,649.4	1,808.2	2,021.3
GDP per capita (US$)	2,142.0	2,348.3	2,591.4
Consumption (Million units of national currency)	1,688.8	1,725.4	1,830.9
Consumption (US$ million)	1,096.6	1,181.8	1,298.5
Consumption per capita (US$)	1,424.2	1,534.8	1,664.8
Population, mid-year ('000)	770.0	770.0	780.0
Birth rate (per '000)	24.8	24.7	
Death rate (per '000)	5.0	5.4	
No. of households ('000)	132.5	136.6	143.7
Total exports (US$ million)	405.0	509.0	607.0
Total imports (US$ million)	634.0	724.0	864.0
Tourism receipts (US$ million)	236.0	252.0	
Tourist spending (US$ million)	39.0	41.6	45.7

Average household size 1995 (persons)	5.35				
Urban population 1995 (%)	40.7				
Age analysis (%) (1986)	*0-14*	38.2	*15-64*	58.5	*65+* 3.3
Population by sex (%) (1986)	*Male*	50.7	*Female*	49.3	
Life expectancy (years) (1990)	*Male*	62.8	*Female*	67.1	
Infant mortality (deaths per '000 live births) (1992)	25.0				
Adult literacy (%) (1986)	87.2				

TRADING PARTNERS

Major export destinations 1995 (% share)		Major import sources 1995 (% share)	
Australia	23.5	Australia	42.0
United Kingdom	16.2	New Zealand	18.0
USA	12.9	Singapore	7.8
Japan	9.4	Japan	6.6

Finland

Area (km²) 337,030

Currency Markka (= 100 penniä)

Location Finland, lying on the Baltic coast with its western border bridging Sweden and Norway, and with its entire eastern flank meeting the countries of the former Soviet Union, was ideally placed to develop a role as an entrepôt for East-West trade in the 1970s and 1980s. Most of the territory is forested, with the main habitation centres to the south. The climate ranges from sub-Arctic in the north to temperate in the south. The capital is Helsinki.

Head of State Martti Ahtisaari (February 1994)

Head of Government Paavo Lipponen (April 1995)

Ruling Party Social Democratic Party leads a coalition with the National Coalition Party, the Left Wing Alliance, the Greens and the Swedish People's Party. The Finnish Christian Union withdrew from the coalition in June 1994.

Political Structure Finland has a semi-executive President who exercises extensive political powers even though the main executive functions are vested in the Prime Minister. Elected by universal suffrage for a six-year term, the President may appoint any Prime Minister and Cabinet who can secure the approval of the 200-member Eduskunta (Parliament). The Eduskunta is itself elected for a four-year term. In January 1995 Finland became a full member of the European Union.

Last Elections Elections to the Eduskunta were held in March 1995, when the Social Democrats regained much of the ground they had lost in the 1991 elections, obtaining 63 of the 200 seats against 44 for the Centre Party which had soundly defeated it in 1991. The National Coalition Party won 39 seats, the Left-Wing Alliance won 22 seats, and the Swedish People's Party held its representation at 12 seats. The Greens won 9 seats, the Finnish Christian League won 7, the Young Finns won 2, and the Finnish Rural Party saw its representation plummet from seven seats to one, while the Ecological Party also won one seat.

Political Risk Finland presents no appreciable political risks at present. A larger number of Finns now endorse their country's entry into the EU than initially, when the country voted to join. Probably the most difficult issues for Finland lie in the EU's evolution of a common foreign and security policy, because the country is holding to its neutral stance. Helsinki has not joined the Western European Union, the EU's fledgling defence arm. It keeps a wary eye fixed on Moscow and is nervous of Russia's opposition to NATO expansion.

International Disputes Finland and Sweden disagree over the ownership of a group of islands in the Gulf of Bothnia, which Finland, the current owner, calls Ahvenanmaa and Sweden calls the Aaland Islands. The issue, which dates back to 1809, will not harm bilateral relations, however.

Economy Finland's economy has recorded some of the highest growth rates in Western Europe in the past two years while having the lowest rate of inflation. This represents a remarkable turnaround; in 1993 the Finns emerged from the deepest recession of any industrialised country since World War Two. Simultaneously, the country's strenuous efforts to slash public spending are bearing fruit, rehabilitating Finland's reputation with financial markets and allowing it to claim, credibly, that it will meet the Maastricht criteria for economic and monetary union. The one weak spot in Finland's recent performance is an unemployment rate of 17%, the second highest in Europe after Spain.

Main Industries Finland's major industry is forestry which supplies a large paper and timber products sector. The country also has a well-developed glass and ceramics industry. It produces a variety of household goods and other consumer items and has an extremely important heavy goods industry producing ships, cement, steel products and machine tools.

Energy For hydrocarbons, Finland relies totally on imports of oil and gas, which it once obtained from the Soviet Union. Plans for a substantial expansion of Finnish gas drilling projects in Russia have been frequently discussed, in an effort to secure new supplies. Nuclear energy accounts for about a sixth of the country's total energy needs.

	1993	1994	1995
Inflation (% change)	2.1	1.1	1.0
Exchange rate (per US$)	5.71	5.22	4.37
Interest rate (% per annum)	10.0	7.9	7.8
GDP (% real growth)	-1.4	4.8	7.0
GDP (Billion units of national currency)	480.5	509.1	550.1
GDP (US$ million)	84,145.4	97,521.1	125,871.9
GDP per capita (US$)	16,609.8	19,165.7	24,632.5
Consumption (Billion units of national currency)	258.7	268.0	277.9
Consumption (US$ million)	45,298.8	51,343.3	63,582.8
Consumption per capita (US$)	8,941.7	10,090.5	12,442.8
Population, mid-year ('000)	5,066.0	5,088.3	5,110.0
Birth rate (per '000)	12.8	12.9	12.4
Death rate (per '000)	10.1	9.4	9.7
No. of households ('000)	2,094.0	2,118.0	2,142.0
Total exports (US$ million)	23,446.0	29,658.0	
Total imports (US$ million)	18,032.0	23,214.0	
Tourism receipts (US$ million)	1,239.0	1,435.6	1,450.0
Tourist spending (US$ million)	1,617.0	1,903.5	2,357.3

Average household size 1995 (persons)	2.28				
Urban population 1995 (%)	63.2				
Age analysis (%) (1995)	*0-14* 19.0		*15-64* 66.7		*65+* 14.3
Population by sex (%) (1995)	*Male* 48.7		*Female* 51.3		
Life expectancy (years) (1993-94)	*Male* 72.1		*Female* 79.5		
Infant mortality (deaths per '000 live births) (1993)	4.4				
Adult literacy (%) (1982)	99.0				

TRADING PARTNERS

Major export destinations 1995 (% share)		Major import sources 1995 (% share)	
Germany	11.6	Germany	17.1
Sweden	8.7	Russia	10.4
United Kingdom	8.7	Sweden	10.2
USA	5.9	United Kingdom	8.5

France

Area (km²) 543,965

Currency French franc (FF = 100 centimes)

Location France, the largest country in Western Europe, also lies at the heart of the continent. It meets Spain and Andorra in the south, across the Pyrenees and Italy in the south-east. Switzerland and Germany lie to the east and Belgium and Luxembourg in the north. Its role as a communications channel for the United Kingdom will prove central in the 1990s. The terrain is extremely varied, and its climate ranges from temperate and wet in the north to Mediterranean in the south. The capital is Paris.

Head of State President Jacques Chirac (1995)

Head of Government Alain Juppé (May 1995)

Ruling Party Rassemblement pour la République leads a right-wing coalition with the Union pour la Démocratie Française.

Political Structure France has a semi-executive Presidency in which the head of state, elected by universal suffrage for a seven-year term, appoints a Prime Minister in accordance with the bicameral Parliament. The 577-seat National Assembly is elected every five years, and one third of the Senate's 321 members come up for re-election every three years, for a nine-year term. France has an unusually centralised decision-making process for a country of its size - even those concerning the four overseas departments (Guadeloupe, Martinique, French Guiana and Réunion).

Last Elections The last full legislative elections took place in March 1993 and resulted in a resounding defeat for the ruling Parti Socialiste, which won only 70 of the 577 National Assembly seats, compared with 213 for the Union pour la Démocratie Française, 247 for the Gaullist Rassemblement pour la République, and 23 for the Parti Communiste. Consequently, President Mitterrand was reluctantly obliged to enter a "cohabitation" arrangement with a right-wing coalition government led by Edouard Balladur. Presidential elections in 1995 brought a comfortable win for Jacques Chirac, a former Prime Minister and leader of the Union pour la Démocratie Française.

Political Risk The shift away from the former socialist coalition indicates a hardening of social attitudes, caused by economic austerity, with the main manifestation being the rise in hostility to immigrants. Such suspicions have been heightened by the string of racially-motivated attacks on immigrants in southern France since 1992, and in the subsequent wave of Muslim-inspired attacks, both in Paris and on French citizens in North Africa. The government's efforts to reduce spending in order to meet the Maastricht criteria have prompted strikes and unrest from France's powerful trade unions.

International Disputes Although France has relinquished control over most of its former dependencies, its continued sovereignty over external departments and dependencies such as New Caledonia has aroused periodic discontent among separatist and nationalist factions there. France's unilateral decision to resume nuclear testing in the South Pacific seriously damaged its international standing. The country's decision to return to NATO after a 30-year absence represents a significant step in its gradual rapprochement with the Atlantic alliance.

Economy The strikes and labour unrest which occurred in 1995 and 1996 have hurt the economy's performance. The latest estimates indicate that GDP grew by 2.2% in 1995. Meanwhile, government forecasts for growth in 1996 have been scaled back from the 2.8% predicted in the 1996 budget to 1.3%. Consumer spending remains steady and most economists believe that the country will be able to avoid a recession. Slower growth, however, will make it harder for the government to meet its Maastricht-related goal of reducing the public deficit's share in GDP and reforming the fiscal system.

Main Industries France's economy features a developed industrial manufacturing base which includes not only high-technology goods (vehicles, aircraft, computer equipment, etc) but also a number of very large companies making basic goods. The industrial structure is unusual for an industrialised country, in that the state still controls a large proportion of the heavy strategic goods industries as well as institutions such as banks and communications companies. The government stresses its plans for a major privatisation programme but progress lags far behind that in neighbouring countries. The agricultural sector continues to be an important part of the French economy. Farms are unusually small by European standards, and even though the soil quality is usually excellent, they remain inefficient and require massive financial support. France grows soft fruits, cereals, maize, root vegetables, sugar beet and sunflowers, and is famed for its wine production. The completion of the Channel Tunnel has substantially enhanced the country's ability to export to the United Kingdom.

Energy France, along with Belgium, is one of Europe's largest consumer of nuclear energy, obtaining nearly 75% of its total electricity needs from its nuclear reactors. It has some small deposits of oil and gas, but remains dependent on imports for most of its needs.

	1993	1994	1995
Inflation (% change)	2.1	1.7	1.8
Exchange rate (per US$)	5.66	5.55	4.99
Interest rate (% per annum)	8.9	7.9	8.1
GDP (% real growth)	-1.4	2.5	2.2
GDP (Billion units of national currency)	7,083.0	7,380.0	7,678.1
GDP (US$ million)	1,251,413.4	1,329,729.7	1,538,701.9
GDP per capita (US$)	21,703.3	22,964.7	26,515.6
Consumption (Billion units of national currency)	4,300.2	4,433.9	4,583.8
Consumption (US$ million)	759,749.6	798,900.9	918,594.4
Consumption per capita (US$)	13,176.4	13,797.2	15,829.6
Population, mid-year ('000)	57,660.0	57,903.3	58,030.0
Birth rate (per '000)	12.3	12.3	13.0
Death rate (per '000)	9.2	9.3	9.1
No. of households ('000)	22,307.0	22,549.4	22,793.0
Total exports (US$ million)	209,349.0	235,905.0	286,480.0
Total imports (US$ million)	201,838.0	230,188.0	274,566.0
Tourism receipts (US$ million)	23,410.0	25,630.4	
Tourist spending (US$ million)	12,805.0	13,747.5	15,807.2

Average household size 1995 (persons)	2.44				
Urban population 1995 (%)	72.8				
Age analysis (%) (1995)	*0-14* 19.4		*15-64* 66.0		*65+* 14.6
Population by sex (%) (1995)	*Male* 48.4		*Female* 51.6		
Life expectancy (years) (1994)	*Male* 73.6		*Female* 81.8		
Infant mortality (deaths per '000 live births) (1992)	6.8				
Adult literacy (%) (1984)	99.0				

TRADING PARTNERS

Major export destinations 1995 (% share)		Major import sources 1995 (% share)	
Germany	17.5	Germany	18.3
Italy	9.5	Italy	9.6
United Kingdom	9.2	Belgium/Luxembourg	8.7
Spain	7.3	United Kingdom	7.6

French Guiana

Area (km²)   91,000

Currency   French franc (FF = 100 centimes)

Location   Located on the north-eastern Atlantic coast of South America, between Suriname in the west and Brazil in the east and south, French Guiana is a predominantly forested region with a number of large rivers flowing down from a high sierra in the south. The climate is humid and tropical. The capital is Cayenne.

Head of State   President Jacques Chirac (France)

Head of Government   Elie Castor

Ruling Party   Parti Socialiste Guyanais

Political Structure   French Guiana is an external department of France and is therefore governed to a considerable degree from Paris. The country sends deputies to the French Assemblée Nationale, and is represented at the European Union. Since being accorded regional status in 1974, however, it elects its own 31-member Regional Council for a term of six years, with responsibility for economic and social planning. Other executive power rests in a 16-member General Council.

Last Elections   The last full elections were to the French Assemblée Nationale in 1993, in which the Rassemblement pour la République returned one delegate and the left wing returned one "dissident" member.

Political Risk   French Guiana has one of the lowest per capita incomes in the Caribbean region and has suffered from decades of neglect. Sporadic unrest has been reported among the indigenous population, reflecting dissatisfaction with the state of rule from Paris.

International Disputes   Part of French Guiana's south-western corner is claimed by Suriname, which alleges that a poor interpretation of a bilateral French-British agreement in the nineteenth century wrongly awarded the land between the Itany and Marouini (subsidiaries of the Litany and Maroni rivers) to the French. The land is, however, deeply impenetrable and has little mineral significance; however, there is some hydro-electric potential.

Economy   French Guiana's economy remains one of the most neglected in South America, with serious economic and indeed social problems. Its dependence on Paris has not always proved to its advantage, and it has proved difficult to attract foreign investors. At present, therefore, France is likely to continue to be its principal economic mainstay.

Main Industries   French Guiana relies almost exclusively on its agricultural sector to employ and feed the population, and yet only 0.1% of the land surface is actually cultivated - most of the remainder being jungle. Export crops are limited to sugar and similar products. Most of the population is engaged in subsistence farming of rice, maize and bananas. There are, however, a small number of cattle farms. Timber, the most obvious natural asset, is at present only marginally exploited because of a lack of infrastructure facilities. There is also a growing fishing fleet, which may offer more opportunity for diversifying the export economy away from sugar and timber. Industry tends to be restricted to the small area around the European Space Agency's launch site at Kourou - which alone generates a fifth of GDP. The mining sector produces a modest quantity of gold.

Energy   The Petit Saut hydro-electric scheme was completed in 1993, despite strong protests from the environmental lobby. The project is expected to fulfil all the country's electricity needs. Otherwise, the country relies almost entirely on imports for all fuel supplies except natural resources such as brushwood and timber.

	1993	1994	1995
Inflation (% change)	2.2	3.0	1.5
Exchange rate (per US$)	5.66	5.55	4.99
Interest rate			
GDP (% real growth)	2.0	1.9	2.0
GDP (Million units of national currency)	3,206.9	3,363.3	3,480.3
GDP (US$ million)	566.6	606.0	697.5
GDP per capita (US$)	4,197.0	4,488.9	4,810.1
Consumption (Million units of national currency)	2,127.5	2,231.3	2,309.0
Consumption (US$ million)	375.9	402.0	462.7
Consumption per capita (US$)	2,784.3	2,978.0	3,191.2
Population, mid-year ('000)	135.0	135.0	145.0
Birth rate (per '000)	27.7	25.8	
Death rate (per '000)	4.9	4.7	
No. of households ('000)	24.1	24.3	25.9
Total exports (US$ million)	79.0	82.0	
Total imports (US$ million)	810.0	830.0	
Tourism receipts (US$ million)			
Tourist spending (US$ million)			

Average household size 1995 (persons)	5.29				
Urban population 1995 (%)	76.5				
Age analysis (%) (1982)	*0-14* 32.6		*15-64* 62.6		*65+* 4.8
Population by sex (%) (1990)	*Male* 52.1		*Female* 47.9		
Life expectancy (years)					
Infant mortality (deaths per '000 live births) (1992)	22.0				
Adult literacy (%) (1982)	83.0				

French Polynesia

Area (km²) 3,940

Currency Franc CFP (= 100 centimes)

Location French Polynesia consists of five separate groups of islands in the South Pacific. Included are Tahiti and Moorea, the remaining Society Islands, the Leeward Islands, the Tuamotu Islands, the Gambier Islands and the Marquesa Islands. With most of the territory composed of coral reefs, the land seldom rises far above sea level. The capital is Papeete.

Head of State President Jacques Chirac (France)

Head of Government Gaston Flosse (1991)

Ruling Party Tahoeraa Huiraatira/Rassemblement pour la République leads a coalition with Pupu Here Ai'a Te Nunaa Ia Ora.

Political Structure French Polynesia is one of the four French Overseas Territories, which do not enjoy full département status but are regarded as an integral part of France. As such, most important decisions are taken in France rather than locally. The 41-member Territorial Assembly is elected by universal suffrage for a term of four or sometimes five years, and it elects its own representatives to the National Assembly in Paris. Executive power is wielded locally by the President of the Territorial Government, who approximates to a Prime Minister.

Last Elections In the legislative elections of March 1991, the Tahoeraa Huiraatira of Gaston Flosse won 18 of the 41 parliamentary seats and formed a coalition with the small Ai'a Api. After violent protests over economic reforms Ai'a Api left the Government, whereupon Flosse joined up with the Ai'a Te Nunaa La Ora, giving him 23 seats in all. The incumbent Government of Alexandre Lentieff, Te Tiamara, secured only 14 seats, while the hard-line independence party Tavini Huiraatira held four.

Political Risk French Polynesia has seen little of the ethnic resentment which has been common in New Caledonia in recent years, and at present the ethnic issue is dormant. The islands have occasionally experienced significant and sometimes violent protests over tax increases but these have had limited political significance.

International Disputes A revival of long-standing tensions with the government of France over that country's practice of using Mururoa and Fangataufa atolls for nuclear weapons testing reemerged in 1995. When France resumed its testing, the island of Tahiti erupted in violent protests.

Economy Although the economy remains centred on tourism and exports, the Government is trying to promote the domestic economy with a range of incentives to improve the infrastructure and make the country more self-sufficient.

Main Industries French Polynesia's economy is heavily based on tourism, which provides a fifth of GDP although the sector employs no more than a small proportion of the population. The country is particularly popular with French, German and American visitors; less so with New Zealanders, who have an outstanding disagreement with the French Government. Agriculture remains underdeveloped, accounting for no more than 4% of GDP although the Government is seeking to expand the sector. Copra, vanilla and fruit are grown for the export market, and pineapples, bananas, mangoes, pawpaws and cereals for the home market. Timber is grown for export. The country's industries consist mainly of fruit canning, soap making with coconut oil, and brewing. There are phosphate reserves, but these have not been mined since the 1930s.

Energy The country relies on imports for the greater part of its energy needs, except for timber and fuelwood.

	1993	1994	1995
Inflation (% change)	10.0	5.0	5.5
Exchange rate (per US$)	106.66	97.41	90.96
Interest rate			
GDP (% real growth)	-3.3	-3.1	-2.0
GDP (Million units of national currency)	66,711.6	67,893.9	70,195.5
GDP (US$ million)	625.5	697.0	771.7
GDP per capita (US$)	2,978.4	3,319.0	3,629.5
Consumption (Million units of national currency)	44,234.1	45,018.0	46,544.1
Consumption (US$ million)	414.7	462.1	511.7
Consumption per capita (US$)	1,974.9	2,200.7	2,406.6
Population, mid-year ('000)	210.0	210.0	212.6
Birth rate (per '000)	24.6	22.2	
Death rate (per '000)	5.1	4.5	
No. of households ('000)	34.9	35.1	36.3
Total exports (US$ million)			
Total imports (US$ million)			
Tourism receipts (US$ million)	182.0	205.9	
Tourist spending (US$ million)			

Average household size 1995 (persons)	5.69		
Urban population 1995 (%)	56.4		
Age analysis (%) (1988)	*0-14* 35.9	*15-64* 60.9	*65+* 3.1
Population by sex (%) (1988)	*Male* 52.1	*Female* 47.9	
Life expectancy (years) (1990-95)	*Male* 67.2	*Female* 72.8	
Infant mortality (deaths per '000 live births) (1992)	12.7		
Adult literacy (%)			

Gabon

Area (km²) 2,667,665

Currency CFA franc (= 100 centimes)

Location The Gabonese Republic straddles the equator on the Atlantic coast of Africa between Equatorial Guinea and Cameroon in the north and Congo in the south and south-east. It has a warm and occasionally humid equatorial climate. The capital is Libreville.

Head of State President El Hadj Omar Bongo (1967)

Head of Government Paulin Obame-Nguema (October 1994)

Ruling Party Parti Démocratique Gabonais

Political Structure Gabon, which achieved independence from France in 1960, was run as a single-party socialist system from 1968 until March 1991, when a new multi-party Constitution came into force. The country has an executive President who is elected by universal suffrage for a seven-year term. He answers to a 120-member National Assembly (Parliament) which is elected every five years.

Last Elections At the general election of March 1991 the Parti Démocratique Gabonais won 66 seats in the 120-member National Assembly. Bongo was re-elected as President in 1993, but the announcement was greeted with serious rioting and his main presidential rival, Mda Abessole, immediately announced the formation of a rival government, called the "High Council of Resistance".

Political Risk Gabon's transition from a single-party to a multi-party state has been less easy than many observers had first assumed. Political opposition is fierce and there is every likelihood that the growing hostility to President Bongo will result in his forced removal at some point.

International Disputes There have been some protests about the repatriation of illegal immigrants, some 70,000 of whom had been returned to neighbouring countries by April 1995.

Economy Gabon's economy, although potentially wealthy and reasonably diversified, remains handicapped by massive past overspending. Austerity plans have become a necessary element of the country's economic life for most of the last ten years. Some relief was obtained in 1995 when world prices for coffee and cocoa rose sharply and led to an improvement in GDP. The world prices for these commodities are rather volatile, however, making Gabon's chances for sustained growth unlikely.

Main Industries Gabon relies almost exclusively on its oil industries, which provide more than 80% of its export earnings in a typical year and 45% of GDP. There is also mineral activity involving manganese and uranium. The latter supplies a tenth of France's enormous needs. Agriculture, by comparison, produces no more than 4% of GDP and less than 1% of the total land area is under cultivation. Cocoa, coffee, rubber, sugar cane and coffee are grown for export, while cassava, maize, groundnuts and vegetables are produced for the domestic market. Since 75% of the country is forested, opportunities for timber sales always exist. Industrial development is very limited, with manufacturing supplying no more than 5% of GDP. Apart from chemicals, petroleum refining and textiles, almost all activities centre on the processing of agricultural raw materials.

Energy Gabon is entirely self-sufficient in oil and gas, and extensive onshore exploration is in progress to find more supplies.

	1993	1994	1995
Inflation (% change)	-8.9	36.2	22.8
Exchange rate (per US$)	283.16	555.20	498.70
Interest rate (% per annum)	17.5	17.5	16.0
GDP (% real growth)	6.8	-1.0	1.0
GDP (Million units of national currency)	1,733,730.3	2,337,727.3	2,899,436.4
GDP (US$ million)	6,122.8	4,210.6	5,814.0
GDP per capita (US$)	4,917.9	3,289.5	4,489.6
Consumption (Million units of national currency)	882,388.4	1,324,986.0	1,830,080.6
Consumption (US$ million)	3,116.2	2,386.5	3,669.7
Consumption per capita (US$)	2,503.0	1,864.5	2,833.7
Population, mid-year ('000)	1,245.0	1,280.0	1,295.0
Birth rate (per '000)	42.2	38.5	
Death rate (per '000)	17.2	13.9	
No. of households ('000)	171.2	175.6	180.3
Total exports (US$ million)	2,295.0	2,318.0	
Total imports (US$ million)	845.0	738.0	
Tourism receipts (US$ million)	5.0	5.3	
Tourist spending (US$ million)	132.0	140.4	215.9

Average household size 1995 (persons)	6.93
Urban population 1995 (%)	50.0
Age analysis (%)	
Population by sex (%)	
Life expectancy (years) (1990-95)	*Male* 57.9 *Female* 55.2
Infant mortality (deaths per '000 live births) (1993)	94.0
Adult literacy (%) (1990)	60.7

TRADING PARTNERS

Major export destinations 1995 (% share)		Major import sources 1995 (% share)	
USA	56.4	France	38.3
France	11.9	Côte d'Ivoire	13.6
Japan	4.9	USA	6.1
China	4.3	Netherlands	5.6

Gambia

Area (km²)   10,690

Currency   Dalasi (D = 100 butut)

Location   The state of The Gambia takes the form of a narrow strip bordering the banks of the River Gambia on the Atlantic coast of West Africa, It has a short coastline but is otherwise surrounded by the republic of Senegal. The climate is generally hot and extremely dry, although there is rain in the spring. The capital is Banjul.

Head of State   Captain Yahya Jameh (July 1994)

Head of Government   Captain Yahya Jameh (July 1994)

Ruling Party   All parties are currently banned.

Political Structure   The Gambia has been independent since 1965 became a republic in 1970. The constitution provides for an executive President who is elected for a five-year term by universal suffrage, along with a 50-member unicameral legislative assembly, the House of Representatives. In 1994, the constitution was suspended when President Alhaji Sir Dawda Kairaba Jawara was deposed in a bloodless coup led by Captain Yahya Jameh. The international community responded by suspending aid (which accounted for over 20% of GDP in 1993) and declaring Gambia unsafe for tourists which had been the other mainstay of the economy. Nevertheless, Yahya Jameh continues to rule with an iron hand.

Last Elections   Elections for the 36 House of Representatives seats were held in April 1992, when the People's Progressive Party (PPP) obtained 25, the National Convention Party six, and the Gambia People's Party two; independents took the remaining seats. The presidential elections of April 1992 showed a 58.4% share of the vote for the PPP's Alhaiji Sir Dawda Jawara, who began his fifth term before being deposed. Captain Jameh first announced that democracy would be restored in December 1998 but under pressure from the international community he has now agreed to hold elections by July 1996 and to return the Gambia to civilian rule.

Political Risk   It is uncertain that Jameh will adhere to his latest version of an electoral schedule. No voter registration has begun, free political activity by parties or individuals is still banned and all opponents of the current regime are dealt with harshly. Meanwhile, Jameh and his cohorts engage in exotic projects such as the construction of a $1 million copy of the Arc de Triomphe on the main street of the capital, Banjul, to commemorate their 1994 coup.

Economy   The Gambia's economy is deteriorating rapidly now that foreign aid is frozen and tourism is in decline. The effects of these constraints are compounded by drought and political disruption.

Main Industries   Tourism, which was once a key component of GDP, has fallen by 60% since 1994. Agriculture now accounts for nearly half of the country's GDP and employs over 80% of the workforce. Groundnuts are the main export crop, providing half of all export earnings. Rice, maize, millet, cassava and sorghum are grown for the home market, not always in adequate quantities. The agricultural sector has been badly hit by poor weather and other disruption, and Gambia normally needs to import a large proportion of its meat and live animals. Industry remains underdeveloped despite government efforts to encourage expansion and diversification. Most major activities centre on the processing of raw materials such as groundnuts. Attempts to attract foreign capital have met with little response, given the political situation in the country today. There are known deposits of kaolin and rutile, but little extraction at present.

Energy   All energy requirements except for fuelwood are currently imported. All the country's electricity is generated by thermal power stations, although hydro-electric resources are to be developed at a considerable speed.

	1993	1994	1995
Inflation (% change)	6.5	1.7	7.0
Exchange rate (per US$)	9.13	9.58	9.66
Interest rate (% per annum)	26.1	25.0	25.0
GDP (% real growth)	8.8	12.7	6.0
GDP (Million units of national currency)	2,518.5	2,886.3	3,273.6
GDP (US$ million)	275.8	301.3	338.9
GDP per capita (US$)	267.8	279.0	310.9
Consumption (Million units of national currency)	2,631.8	2,952.3	3,277.6
Consumption (US$ million)	288.3	308.2	339.3
Consumption per capita (US$)	279.9	285.3	311.3
Population, mid-year ('000)	1,030.0	1,080.0	1,090.0
Birth rate (per '000)	43.7	46 4	
Death rate (per '000)	22.7	18.9	
No. of households ('000)	189.2	193.9	205.2
Total exports (US$ million)	52.0	32.0	
Total imports (US$ million)	243.0	209.0	
Tourism receipts (US$ million)	26.0	27.0	
Tourist spending (US$ million)	13.1	13.6	15.0

Average household size 1995 (persons)	5.29				
Urban population 1995 (%)	25.5				
Age analysis (%) (1983)	*0-14* 43.8		*15-64* 52.5		*65+* 3.7
Population by sex (%) (1993)	*Male* 50.2		*Female* 49.8		
Life expectancy (years) (1990-95)	*Male* 43.4		*Female* 46.6		
Infant mortality (deaths per '000 live births) (1993)	132.0				
Adult literacy (%) (1990)	27.2				

TRADING PARTNERS

Major export destinations 1995 (% share)		Major import sources 1995 (% share)	
Japan	30 4	China	20.9
Senegal	10.8	Hong Kong	11.1
Hong Kong	10.1	United Kingdom	8.1
France	9.7	Netherlands	6.9

Georgia

Area (km²)   70,000

Currency   Coupon

Location   Georgia is one of the smallest but most influential states to have emerged from the former USSR. Located on the Black Sea, it borders on Turkey in the south, Armenia in the east and the Russian Federation in the north. Its mainly mountainous terrain includes the Greater Caucasus in the north and the Lesser Caucasus in the south, with a plain in between, divided by a further ridge. The climate is temperate to warm. The capital is Tblisi.

Head of State   President Eduard Shevardnadze (1993)

Head of Government   Otar Patsatsia (August 1993)

Ruling Party   Round Table/Free Georgia hold a majority bloc in the Supreme Soviet.

Political Structure   Georgia's independent stance was perhaps most precisely typified by the fact that it was the last of the former Soviet states, apart from the Baltic states, to join the Confederation of Independent States; its decision was taken only in October 1993. Although Georgia has an executive Prime Minister, the role of the President has been somewhat more important in recent years, particularly in view of the very serious deterioration in the political and internal security climates since the brutal repressions of the late 1980s by the former communist authorities. However, the long-standing rebellion in Abkhazia came to a satisfactory conclusion in November 1994, when the region adopted its own constitution - describing itself, illegally, as a sovereign state. In September 1995, Shevardnadze launched a severe crackdown on political opponents, with dozens being arrested after a failed assassination attempt in which the President was injured by a car bomb.

Last Elections   Full elections to the Supreme Soviet were held in November 1995 when the Round Table coalition won a resounding victory with over 70% of the vote in a big turnout. The result assures the pro-western, pro-market Shevardnadze another five years in office. Not all Georgians warm to him but almost everyone acknowledges his efficiency and international clout. Despite the violence that occasionally rocks Georgian politics, his grip on power is strengthened by the victory at the polls.

Political Risk   The fierce factional infighting between the various ethnic groups appears to have subsided. Yet the ceasefire signed with the Abkhaz rebels in mid-1994 came only after some 30,000 deaths and has left much bitterness. In April 1996, Georgia entered into a Transcaucasus-EU Pact that also includes Armenia and Azerbaijan and is meant to help stabilise this explosive region. The Pact offers trade concessions and access to certain EU loans in return for democratic and economic reforms. Such tangible progress, in conjunction with the country's improved economic prospects, make Georgia one of the most attractive of the Caucasian economies.

International Disputes   The severe clashes of the period since 1990 have resulted not merely from political differences, but also from resistance among the South Ossetians to the abolition of their autonomous province in 1990.

Economy   Georgia's economy depends heavily on mineral deposits and agricultural resources. Much of this was wasted after years of political unrest, although a great deal of the technology and equipment would not have been viable today in any case. The Government has initiated a programme of economic reform and is proceeding with the sell-off of several state-run enterprises. Foreign investment is rising, and as it does, the economy looks much healthier. Strong support from the IMF is also helping to rejuvenate the economy.

Main Industries   Agriculture makes up an important part of the economy, thanks to the mild climate which allows the cultivation of a wide range of crops, including tea, tobacco, citrus fruits and flowers. The country has deposits of manganese and coal, and a number of oil refineries are in operation in Batumi. Industry is very capital-intensive and based mainly on mineral resources. Metallurgy, construction materials and machine building are other important manufacturing operations.

Energy   Georgia's power generation revolves around its deposits of oil and coal, as well as a number of hydroelectric installations. In the past, its dependence on imported oil supplies has caused political problems with its neighbours. The closure of its oil pipelines from Central Asia in 1994 led to a major crisis at home. Construction of a new pipeline from the Caspian is underway and another, even bigger one is planned. Once these are completed, the country's energy situation will be vastly improved.

	1993	1994	1995
Inflation (% change)			
Exchange rate (per US$)	12,280.00	1,073,327.00	
Interest rate			
GDP (% real growth)	-39.0	-35.0	-5.0
GDP (Million units of national currency)	14,750.0		
GDP (US$ million)			
GDP per capita (US$)			
Consumption			
Consumption (US$ million)			
Consumption per capita (US$)			
Population, mid-year ('000)	5,450.0	5,450.0	5,460.0
Birth rate (per '000)	16.9	16.1	
Death rate (per '000)	8.5	8.7	
No. of households ('000)	1,240.9	1,249.4	1,288.0
Total exports (US$ million)			
Total imports (US$ million)			
Tourism receipts (US$ million)			
Tourist spending (US$ million)			

Average household size 1995 (persons)	4.14				
Urban population 1995 (%)	58.5				
Age analysis (%) (1995)	*0-14* 24.8	*15-64* 66.4	*65+* 8.8
Population by sex (%) (1995)	*Male* 47.7	*Female* 52.3	
Life expectancy (years) (1989)	*Male* 68.1	*Female* 75.7	
Infant mortality (deaths per '000 live births)			
Adult literacy (%) (1989)	99.0		

TRADING PARTNERS

Major export destinations 1995 (% share)		Major import sources 1995 (% share)	
Russia	47.4	USA	19.1
Greece	10.2	Russia	13.4
USA	9.3	Azerbaijan	8.8
Italy	6.6	Romania	8.5

Germany

Area (km²) 356,840

Currency Deutsche Mark (DM = 100 pfennig)

Location Germany occupies a central position in Western Europe with strong cultural and economic ties with the countries of Eastern Europe as bordering on no less than six EU and EFTA countries. The country's terrain ranges from the marshes of the Danish border in the north to the Bavarian Alps in the south. The five eastern Länder of the German Federal Republic, together with the eastern sector of Berlin, formed the German Democratic Republic until unification in 1990. They include a wide range of land types, ranging from the flat Baltic wetlands of the north to the uplands of Thüringen and the mountainous Czech border to the south and east, as well as large tracts of agricultural plains, especially in the areas west of Berlin, and on the Polish border. The capital is Berlin.

Head of State Roman Herzog (May 1994)

Head of Government Helmut Kohl (1982)

Ruling Party Christian Democrats (CDU), in coalition with the Christian Social Union (in Bavaria) and the Free Democrats (FDP).

Political Structure The Federal Republic of Germany comprises 16 states (Länder), of which 11 formerly belonged to West Germany and five to the East. Germany has an extensively devolved political structure. At federal level the non-executive President appoints a Chancellor to lead his Government, in accordance with a 672-member Bundestag (Parliament) elected for four years. The Bundesrat (Upper House) is indirectly elected. The Länder each have their own Parliament and Premier.

Last Elections New Bundestag elections were held in October 1994, in which the ruling CDU/FDP centre-right coalition was returned to power with a reduced majority. The CDU/CSU won 294 seats in the Bundestag (down from 319 in 1990), while the FDP won 47 (79 in 1990), the SPD 252 (compared to 239) and the PDS, the successors to the former East German Communists, 30 seats, up from 17 in 1990. The environmentalist Green Party re-entered parliament with 49 seats, having failed to meet the 5% entry requirement in the 1990 elections. Roman Herzog replaced Richard von Weizsäcker as President following the presidential elections held in May 1994. Provincial elections held in March 1996 gave Kohl's coalition a new lease on office when his coalition partner, the FDP, showed surprising strength. The result assures Kohl of at least two more years in office.

International Disputes Germany has no outstanding territorial issues with any of its immediate neighbours, and has abandoned its former claims for the restoration of the East German lands lost to Poland and the Soviet Union after the Second World War. With the reunification of the two countries, all outstanding disputes came to an end.

Economy Kohl's recent political successes mean he will face increased pressure to do something about Germany's daunting economic problems. Record-high unemployment - 4.3 million jobless in 1996 - is the most serious problem facing politicians. Their answer, a programme known as the "Alliance for Jobs", has so far failed to garner support from industry. Although inflation remains modest (about 1.8% in 1995), more wage restraint is needed, especially after the 1995-1996 wage round which pushed pay up by nearly 5% a year. The deterioration of the German economy is reflected in its growth of GDP which rose by only 1.9% in 1995 after a gain of 2.9% the previous year. An even lower rate of growth is forecast for 1996 (1.5%). In the longer run, Germany's politicians will have to find some way to alter that peculiar mix of capitalism, welfarism and consensus that sets the country apart. Those decisions will be politically sensitive ones - especially if they antagonise the trade unions or the country's many family-run firms.

Main Industries Manufacturing contributes a larger share of national income than in almost any other European state. Motor vehicles, precision engineering, brewing, chemicals, pharmaceuticals and heavy metal products are particular strengths. Other industries such as steel are still large but encountering intense international competition and slowly contracting. Agriculture accounts for only a small proportion of GDP. Farms are small (although larger in the East), and crops include wheat, barley, potatoes, apples and grapes for wine-making. In the East, most rural communities have been severely affected by the discontinuation of the collectivised system of farming and the closure of many communist-run factories.

Energy Germany has vast reserves of coal and lignite. However, high extraction costs mean that it has to endure substantial subsidies in order to keep the affected workforces engaged. Arduous restrictions imposed by environmental concerns add to those costs. Germany remains dependent on imports for all oil supplies, although there are some gas resources in the North Sea. The East German coal mining industry was finally privatised in 1994. The region's Russian-built nuclear power plants have been the source of much controversy recently between those who demand their closure and those who maintain that Germany cannot manage without them.

	1993	1994	1995
Inflation (% change)	4.1	3.0	1.8
Exchange rate (per US$)	1.65	1.62	1.43
Interest rate (% per annum)	12.9	11.5	9.5
GDP (% real growth)	-1.1	2.9	1.9
GDP (Billion units of national currency)	2,854.0	2,978.0	3,040.5
GDP (US$ million)	1,729,697.0	1,838,271.6	2,126,223.8
GDP per capita (US$)	21,305.1	22,580.6	25,947.3
Consumption (Billion units of national currency)	1,834.4	1,902.4	1,969.1
Consumption (US$ million)	1,111,763.6	1,174,302.5	1,377,026.6
Consumption per capita (US$)	13,693.9	14,424.6	16,804.5
Population, mid-year ('000)	81,187.0	81,409.5	81,944.0
Birth rate (per '000)	9.8	9.5	9.3
Death rate (per '000)	11.1	10.8	10.6
No. of households ('000)	34,760.0	34,953.4	35,140.0
Total exports (US$ million)	380,154.0	427,179.0	509,421.0
Total imports (US$ million)	348,631.0	381,659.0	445,660.0
Tourism receipts (US$ million)	10,509.0	11,308.3	
Tourist spending (US$ million)	37,514.0	40,367.2	47,335.9

Average household size 1995 (persons)	2.21				
Urban population 1995 (%)	86.6				
Age analysis (%) (1995)	*0-14* 16.3		*15-64* 68.4		*65+* 15.3
Population by sex (%) (1995)	*Male* 48.6		*Female* 51.4		
Life expectancy (years) (1994)	*Male* 73.3		*Female* 79.6		
Infant mortality (deaths per '000 live births) (1992)	6.2				
Adult literacy (%) (1985)	99.0				

TRADING PARTNERS

Major export destinations 1995 (% share)		Major import sources 1995 (% share)	
France	10.9	France	11.5
Italy	8.5	United Kingdom	8.0
Netherlands	6.9	USA	7.5
USA	6.9	Italy	7.5

Ghana

Area (km²) 238,305

Currency Cedi (C = 100 pesawas)

Location Ghana, the former Gold Coast, lies on the Atlantic coast of West Africa, facing southward in the Gulf of Guinea. Côte d'Ivoire lies to the east, Burkina Faso to the north and Togo to the east. The climate is warm and tropical and occasionally humid. The capital is Accra.

Head of State Flt.-Lt (retd) Jerry Rawlings

Head of Government Kow Nkensen Arkaah (Vice-President)

Ruling Party National Democratic Congress (NDC)

Political Structure Ghana has an executive President who governs through an essentially benevolent military administration. The current administration seized power in a military coup in 1981, following a prolonged period of instability but has recently held elections (see below). Political dissent has been allowed for some time under the freedom of association laws. The Fourth Republic was pronounced in January 1993, following the 1992 elections, with Rawlings as President for life. Most of the Cabinet have military backgrounds. In principle, however, the Constitution provides for a 200-member House of Parliament, and for a 25-member Council of State whose members are personally appointed.

Last Elections Parliamentary elections were held in December 1992, when the National Democratic Congress won an overwhelming majority, largely as a result of a boycott by the four major opposition parties. Presidential elections took place in November 1992, when Flt-Lt Rawlings obtained 58% of the vote.

Political Risk Despite the apparently uncompromising attitude of Flt.-Lt Rawlings toward the question of devolving political power away from the NDC - at least, until recently - he has in fact achieved widespread respect for implementing tough economic policies and has largely restored Ghana's good relations with its foreign partners. The country's positive image was marred in early 1994 by serious clashes in northern Ghana, in which some 1,000 people were reported to have been killed after protesting about the allocation of land rights. However, the state of emergency was repealed in August 1994. The early progress of the Fourth Republic will provide valuable pointers as to the government's long-term stability.

International Disputes Ghana and Togo dispute the sovereignty over the northern reaches of the Volta River in the east of the country and the southern coastal area around Lomé. The two areas, part of the former German Togoland, were awarded to Ghana in 1919 but the issue remains unresolved despite UN mediation. Tension with the EU has grown after Ghana (on advice from the World Bank) invested and turned over large tracts of land to produce bananas. The EU takes 40% of world production and operates a complex quota system. Ghana, as a new producer, is excluded.

Economy The success of the Government in turning round the country's overspent and often corrupt economy has been reflected in a growing interest from abroad in Ghanaian projects. The country's widely based economy remains a further safeguard against future downturns. Ghana's Export Council has received millions of dollars to develop non-traditional exports. Although competitive, several of the bigger projects such as the country's banana-producing project on the Volta River Estates are near bankruptcy because they lack access to major markets.

Main Industries Ghana derives half its GDP and most of its foreign exchange revenues from agriculture. Cocoa is grown for export, as well as bananas, kola nuts, limes, coffee and copra. Domestic crops, which tend to be grown on small plantations and smallholdings, include cassava, plantains, rice, maize, sorghum, millet and yams. Fishing is important, and there are vast potential reserves of timber. Mining, principally of gold, is the next most important sector of the economy, accounting for around 15% of exports. There are also industrial-quality diamonds and huge bauxite reserves, although exploitation of these remains at a low level. Industry has failed to prosper in recent decades, contributing no more than 10% of GDP. Most activities centre on raw materials of some sort, although there are some large metal-working plants. The sector has suffered from shortfalls in investment.

Energy Ghana has an exportable surplus of petroleum, thanks to its onshore field at Saltpond and its offshore Tano area. A refinery at Tano ensures the adequacy of supplies of downstream products. The country's first nuclear reactor was commissioned in early 1995.

	1993	1994	1995
Inflation (% change)	25.0	24.9	59.5
Exchange rate (per US$)	649.06	956.71	1,190.10
Interest rate			
GDP (% real growth)	5.7	4.0	3.0
GDP (Billion units of national currency)	3,932.9	5,108.7	8,392.8
GDP (US$ million)	6,059.4	5,339.8	7,052.2
GDP per capita (US$)	368.4	315.2	406.5
Consumption (Billion units of national currency)	3,424.8	4,540.0	7,611.6
Consumption (US$ million)	5,276.6	4,745.4	6,395.8
Consumption per capita (US$)	320.8	280.1	368.6
Population, mid-year ('000)	16,450.0	16,940.0	17,350.0
Birth rate (per '000)	41.7	44.1	
Death rate (per '000)	11.7	11.8	
No. of households ('000)	2,765.9	2,855.1	3,019.3
Total exports (US$ million)			
Total imports (US$ million)			
Tourism receipts (US$ million)	206.0	210.8	
Tourist spending (US$ million)	15.3	15.6	17.5

Average household size 1995 (persons)	5.64		
Urban population 1995 (%)	36.3		
Age analysis (%) (1991)	*0-14* 45.4	*15-64* 51.8	*65+* 2.8
Population by sex (%)			
Life expectancy (years) (1990-95)	*Male* 54.2	*Female* 57.8	
Infant mortality (deaths per '000 live births) (1993)	81.1		
Adult literacy (%) (1990)	60.3		

TRADING PARTNERS

Major export destinations 1995 (% share)		Major import sources 1995 (% share)	
United Kingdom	15.0	United Kingdom	16.7
Germany	12.6	Nigeria	15.8
USA	11.5	Germany	7.1
Togo	8.2	USA	6.4

Gibraltar

Area (km²) 6

Currency Gibraltar pound (G£ = 100 pence)

Location Located on the southern tip of Spain, Gibraltar faces the coast of North Africa across a narrow strip of water which controls the western access to the Mediterranean Sea. Hence the immense strategic importance attached over the centuries to its ownership, both as a defensive position and as a centre for the transhipment of sea cargoes. The capital is Gibraltar.

Head of State HM Queen Elizabeth II

Head of Government Peter Caruana (1996)

Ruling Party Gibraltar Social Democratic Party (GSD)

Political Structure Gibraltar, a British dependent territory, is technically ruled from London, although in practice most of its decisions are taken not by the UK-appointed Governor but by the locally elected Chief Minister and his Cabinet. They are answerable to a House of Assembly (Parliament) comprising 15 elected members, an independent Speaker, the Attorney-General and the Financial and Development Secretary.

Last Elections Elections in May 1996 gave a majority of the 15 elected seats in the House of Assembly to Peter Caruana and his GSD. The turnout among the country's 18,000 voters was very high. The result should mean a significant change in relations with Spain after eight years of leadership by Joe Bossano and his Gibraltar Socialist Labour Party (GSLP).

Political Risk Gibraltar remains the subject of a territorial dispute between Britain and Spain. The previous administration of Bossano and the GSLP had insisted on an independent line which caused problems with both London and Madrid but the GSD takes a more conciliatory line. Gibraltar's odd status, half in and half out of the EU, and its blatant failure to implement a series of EU directives intended to curb money laundering, are the current source of difficulties. In response, Britain has threatened to impose direct rule from London. Gibraltar lost its significance as an Atlantic gateway when Spain joined NATO in 1982 and its bargaining power is now much reduced.

International Disputes The entire territory is claimed by Spain, which has been advancing its demands in recent years for the return of Gibraltar from British sovereignty. Problems have arisen over plans to build a new airport, which Spain claims would necessarily infringe on its own air space, repeated charges of money laundering, crime and smuggling of tobacco, which deprives the Spanish of tax revenue. Caruana wants to establish warmer relations with Spain and his election should lead to reduced tensions with Madrid.

Economy The territory's considerable dependence on the United Kingdom has been one of the major characteristics of the last few decades; yet its attractive and strategic location has enabled it to develop its role as a tourist resort to the maximum. Living standards are higher than in Spain.

Main Industries Gibraltar's economy relies very heavily on tourism, which contributes up to half of all economic activity in one form or another. Despite the ongoing disputes between Spain and the UK, Spanish visitors often arrive for shopping or for short breaks. Other visitors may be motivated more by reasons to do with tax evasion than duty-free shopping. Gibraltar's port and transhipment activities continue to make an important contribution to the economy. The colony's proximity to the North African coast is only one reason for the 3,000-4,000 merchant vessels which dock every year. Local authorities hope to develop an off-shore tax haven and centre for financial-services. But Britain's insistence on banking controls even stricter than those imposed by the EU would probably prevent this development.

Energy Gibraltar depends completely on imports for all its fuel needs - some being bought in from Spain. All the limited amount of domestic electricity generation is produced by thermal stations.

	1993	1994	1995
Inflation (% change)	6.5	5.0	3.8
Exchange rate (per US$)	0.68	0.64	0.61
Interest rate			
GDP (% real growth)	1.9	7.5	4.7
GDP (Million units of national currency)	118.7	134.0	145.6
GDP (US$ million)	173.4	209.7	240.6
GDP per capita (US$)	5,778.7	6,989.0	8,021.5
Consumption (Million units of national currency)	89.7	101.2	109.9
Consumption (US$ million)	131.0	158.3	181.6
Consumption per capita (US$)	4,366.9	5,278.3	6,054.3
Population, mid-year ('000)	30.0	30.0	30.0
Birth rate (per '000)	17.0	15.4	
Death rate (per '000)	9.8	8.9	
No. of households ('000)	7.3	7.1	7.2
Total exports (US$ million)			
Total imports (US$ million)			
Tourism receipts (US$ million)	80.0	101.7	
Tourist spending (US$ million)			

Average household size 1995 (persons)	4.01				
Urban population 1995 (%)	100.0				
Age analysis (%) (1981)	*0-14* 23.8	*15-64* 66.1	*65+* 10.5		
Population by sex (%) (1995)	*Male* 53.0	*Female* 47.0			
Life expectancy (years)					
Infant mortality (deaths per '000 live births)					
Adult literacy (%) (1985)	98.0				

Greece

Area (km²) 131,985

Currency Drachma (= 100 leptae)

Location Greece comprises the mainland and the archipelago which lies in the Mediterranean between the Adriatic and the Aegean and also includes the larger islands of Corfu and Crete, some distance to the south-east. The country is largely mountainous but there are lowlands in the east along the Bulgarian and Turkish borders. The close proximity with Turkey and the large numbers of Greek islands (some within 20 km of the Turkish coast) have caused occasional conflict between the two states. The capital is Athens.

Head of State President Kostas Stephanopoulos (March 1995)

Head of Government Costas Simitis (1996)

Ruling Party Pan-Hellenic Socialist Movement (PASOK)

Political Structure Greece's modern political system was installed in 1975 following a national referendum. The country has a non-executive president who is elected by parliament for a five-year term. The president's main function is to guarantee its political system and supervise its proper functioning. The President appoints his own Cabinet, and is answerable to a 300-member Assembly (Parliament) which is itself elected for a five-year term. After assuming office in January 1996, the current president swore in a new reformist government and appointed the strongly pro-EU Theodoros Pangalos as foreign minister.

Last Elections The prime minister assumed office in a special election held in January 1996. He replaced Andreas Papandreou, the 76-year-old founder of PASOK who had dominated Greek politics for 15 years and was forced to resign for reasons of ill health. The new leader of PASOK will be decided in elections to be held later in 1996. The prime minister does not have to be the party leader, but if Simitis were to be defeated in the up-coming elections, this would be seen as a vote of no confidence and could wreck his prime ministership.

Political Risk The deterioration of the domestic economy since the boom years of the early 1980s has obliged the Government to implement a stiff austerity policy which periodically arouses public protests. Simitis lacks the authority of his predecessor and will have difficulty maintaining these policies and pushing through a proposed civil-service reform. He has more appeal among the voters, however, large numbers of whom disapproved of Papandreou's foreign policy decisions - for example, his 1994 embargo of Macedonia damaged Greece's international standing - and his insistence on leaving patronage in the hands of close friends.

International Disputes Although Greece has no major outstanding territorial disputes with any of its neighbours, tensions have been raised on a number of fronts in recent years. The country came close to armed conflict with Turkey over a tiny island in the Aegean in late 1995 and the Turkish occupation of Northern Cyprus continues to be a political problem. Greece still refuses to participate in any NATO exercise where Turkey is represented, but its membership in the West European Union can be regarded as encouraging sign. The independence of Macedonia has been opposed by Greece but this policy looked likely to be scrapped following Papandreou's resignation.

Economy Until recently, Greece's economy has been largely state-run but the new administration is a zealous supporter of gradual privatisation as well as austerity and monetary rigour. Inflation is slowing and the public deficit has been reduced while the rate of growth is edging upward. However, unemployment remains high and Greek industry still has the lowest levels of productivity in the EU. Soft Euro-loans account for 6% of the country's GDP but, so far, the country has apparently failed to make good use of this massive amount of money.

Main Industries Agriculture is still the mainstay of the economy, employing a quarter of the population and producing up to a third of GDP. The country's main crops are: tree fruits, vegetables, olives, tobacco, sugar, rice and some wheat. Goats and sheep are raised in the mountainous areas. Manufacturing has made great progress since the country's accession to the EU, although many of the larger enterprises are still state-owned and overmanned. Textiles, cement, steel, chemicals and fertilisers predominate. The country's shipowners control the world's largest commercial fleet (16% of global cargo-carrying capacity). With downward pressure on freight rates, the industry is likely to contract. Greece's tourist industry is well-known.

Energy Greece's small oil deposits are far from adequate to cover its fuel needs; large quantities of both oil and gas have to be imported. Its lignite resources are used for electricity generation.

	1993	1994	1995
Inflation (% change)	14.4	10.9	9.3
Exchange rate (per US$)	229.25	242.60	231.60
Interest rate (% per annum)	28.6	27.4	23.0
GDP (% real growth)	-1.4	15.1	9.3
GDP (Billion units of national currency)	16,760.4	21,396.3	25,553.0
GDP (US$ million)	73,109.7	88,195.8	110,332.5
GDP per capita (US$)	7,063.7	8,459.2	10,566.2
Consumption (Billion units of national currency)	12,664.4	14,192.7	14,219.6
Consumption (US$ million)	55,242.7	58,502.5	61,397.2
Consumption per capita (US$)	5,337.5	5,611.2	5,879.8
Population, mid-year ('000)	10,350.0	10,426.0	10,442.0
Birth rate (per '000)	10.0	9.9	0.8
Death rate (per '000)	9.4	9.3	9.3
No. of households ('000)	3,607.0	3,621.0	3,635.0
Total exports (US$ million)	8,435.0	9,384.0	
Total imports (US$ million)	22,011.0	21,466.0	
Tourism receipts (US$ million)	3,293.0	3,687.8	
Tourist spending (US$ million)	1,003.0	1,123.3	1,178.9

Average household size 1995 (persons)	2.74				
Urban population 1995 (%)	65.2				
Age analysis (%) (1995)	*0-14* 16.7		*15-64* 68.5		*65+* 14.8
Population by sex (%) (1995)	*Male* 48.4		*Female* 51.6		
Life expectancy (years) (1994)	*Male* 74.9		*Female* 79.9		
Infant mortality (deaths per '000 live births) (1994)	8.3				
Adult literacy (%) (1991)	95.2				

TRADING PARTNERS

Major export destinations 1995 (% share)		Major import sources 1995 (% share)	
Germany	20.2	Italy	17.2
Italy	14.5	Germany	15.5
United Kingdom	6.0	France	9.0
France	5.9	Netherlands	6.1

Grenada

Area (km²)   345

Currency   East Caribbean dollar (EC$ = 100 cents)

Location   The island of Grenada lies at the southernmost tip of the archipelago known as the Windward Islands, in the Eastern Caribbean, about 140 km north of Trinidad and Tobago and 170 km north-west of Barbados. The territory includes some of the Grenadines islets. The climate is equable, although increasingly subject to hurricanes. The capital is St George's.

Head of State   HM Queen Elizabeth II

Head of Government   Keith Mitchell (May 1995)

Ruling Party   New National Party

Political Structure   As an independent member of the Commonwealth, Grenada is essentially self-governing, with the British Crown being represented by a Governor-General. The Prime Minister is answerable to a 15-member Parliament elected by popular mandate for a term of five years. There is also a 13-member Senate, appointed by the Governor-General.

Last Elections   The general elections of June 1995 produced a major upset for the ruling National Democratic Congress, which won only seven of the 15 seats in the House of Representatives. The New National Party won eight seats and formed a government.

Political Risk   The political climate deteriorated sharply in 1993 and early 1994 when economic and social divisions wrecked the country. Disagreements over economic policy have led to splits in the ruling coalition which has governed since the American invasion of 1983 put an end to the regime of the former Prime Minister Maurice Bishop. So far, it has been only the weakness of the opposition which has prevented a serious worsening of the situation. Grenada nevertheless continues to be active in seeking harmony in the Caribbean and generally favours some form of integration with St Vincent, St Lucia and Dominica.

International Disputes   Grenada's external economy relies largely on its agriculture sector, which produces two-thirds of its foreign currency revenues but only 15% of GDP. Nutmeg, mace, cocoa, bananas and other products are raised for export, while cereals and fruit are destined mainly for the home market. Industry revolves around the processing of food products, such as honey, rum and lime juice derivatives. Timber products and furniture are also manufactured. Tourism is by far the important sector of the economy, accounting for 70% of GDP and attracting visitors from the UK and the USA. This is only a small-scale operation, with total arrivals numbering only 20,000-30,000 a year, but the numbers are now growing rapidly.

Main Industries   Grenada's economy is suffering to some extent from the legacy of its very large debts built up in the past. Unemployment is high, and the country relies heavily both on workers' remittances from abroad and on grant aid from the UK. Unfortunately, trade unions have mounted a massive and relatively successful campaign to block the country's much-needed economic reforms, adopted in accordance with instructions from the International Monetary Fund.

	1993	1994	1995
Inflation (% change)	2.8	2.6	3.0
Exchange rate (per US$)	2.70	2.70	2.70
Interest rate (% per annum)	10.5	10.5	10.5
GDP (% real growth)	4.5	1.3	2.9
GDP (Million units of national currency)	676.0	702.5	744.5
GDP (US$ million)	250.4	260.2	275.7
GDP per capita (US$)	2,781.9	2,890.9	3,063.8
Consumption (Million units of national currency)	433.7	445.4	466.5
Consumption (US$ million)	160.6	165.0	172.8
Consumption per capita (US$)	1,784.8	1,832.9	1,919.7
Population, mid-year ('000)	90.0	90.0	90.0
Birth rate (per '000)	39.0	30.3	
Death rate (per '000)		6.2	
No. of households ('000)	17.0	16.7	16.8
Total exports (US$ million)	22.0	24.0	
Total imports (US$ million)	109.5	125.0	
Tourism receipts (US$ million)	42.0	44.8	
Tourist spending (US$ million)			

Average household size 1995 (persons)	5.11				
Urban population 1990 (%)	8.0				
Age analysis (%) (1981)	*0-14* 38.6		*15-64* 54.1		*65+* 7.3
Population by sex (%) (1981)	*Male* 48.1		*Female* 51.9		
Life expectancy (years) (1959-61)	*Male* 60.1		*Female* 65.6		
Infant mortality (deaths per '000 live births) (1992)	15.0				
Adult literacy (%) (1970)	97.8				

Guadeloupe

Area (km²) 1,780

Currency French franc (= 100 centimes)

Location The French overseas department of Guadeloupe is the northernmost territory of the Windward Islands group of the Caribbean and comprises the two islands of Grande-Terre and Basse-Terre, together with Marie-Galante, La Désirade and Iles des Saintes, and the St Martin and St Barthélemy group, which lie within the Leeward group. The climate is tropical/Caribbean, with some tendency toward hurricanes in the autumn months. The capital is Basse Terre.

Head of State Jacques Chirac (France)

Head of Government Dominique Larifla (President of the General Council)

Ruling Party Fédération Guadeloupéenne du Rassemblement pour la République

Political Structure As a part of the French Antilles, Guadeloupe is an external department of France and is governed to a considerable degree from Paris. The country sends deputies to the French Assemblée Nationale, and is represented at the EU. Since being accorded regional status in 1974, however, Guadeloupe elects its own 41-member Regional Council for a term of six years, with responsibility for economic and social planning. Other executive power rests in a 42-member General Council.

Last Elections The last full elections were to the French Assemblée Nationale in 1993, when the Rassemblement pour la République returned two delegates, the Communists one and the Socialists one. The March 1992 elections to the Regional Council had also produced a win for the RPR, but the results were subsequently been annulled because of irregularities. The succeeding elections in January 1993 produced another win for the RPR, with 22 of the 41 seats in the Regional Council. The Parti Socialiste won four seats, the Parti Progressiste Démocratique Guadeloupéenne won four, the (dissident left-wing) FRUI-G party won three, the Union Populaire pour la Libération de Guadeloupe won three, and the Parti Communiste Guadeloupéen won two.

Political Risk Guadeloupe has only a relatively low level of per capita spending power, but is regarded nevertheless as a reliable base for business activity.

Economy Guadeloupe's perennial trade deficit is only partially covered by its tourism revenues, and for the most part the country is forced to rely on remittances from France.

Main Industries Guadeloupe's agricultural sector, although the largest part of the economy, is still unable to ensure self-sufficiency. A large proportion of the country's food is imported from France. Bananas and sugar cane are grown for export, and maize, tree fruits and yams for the domestic market. Guadeloupe is developing its timber trade. Although the industrial sector employs 15% of the workforce, it provides only 12% of GDP. Activities revolve almost exclusively around the processing of agricultural materials: rum, food processing, timber products etc. There is an industrial freeport at Jarry, and a fair-sized ship repair business. Tourism is being developed, with France as the main target area at present.

Energy The country's fuel needs are met exclusively with imports, the only viable local resource being fuelwood and brushwood. All electricity is generated by thermal stations.

	1993	1994	1995
Inflation (% change)	4.0	6.0	1.5
Exchange rate (per US$)	5.66	5.55	4.99
Interest rate			
GDP (% real growth)	-3.1	-1.1	
GDP (Million units of national currency)	2,974.5	3,119.6	3,166.4
GDP (US$ million)	525.5	562.1	634.5
GDP per capita (US$)	1,281.8	1,338.3	1,493.1
Consumption (Million units of national currency)	1,971.8	2,068.0	2,099.0
Consumption (US$ million)	348.4	372.6	420.6
Consumption per capita (US$)	849.7	887.2	989.8
Population, mid-year ('000)	410.0	420.0	425.0
Birth rate (per '000)	25.7	17.7	
Death rate (per '000)	6.0	5.9	
No. of households ('000)	86.4	86.8	89.9
Total exports (US$ million)	130.0	140.0	
Total imports (US$ million)	1,700.0	1,800.0	
Tourism receipts (US$ million)	370.0	401.5	
Tourist spending (US$ million)			

Average household size 1995 (persons)	4.60				
Urban population 1995 (%)	99.4				
Age analysis (%) (1992)	*0-14* 26.4		*15-64* 64.8		*65+* 8.8
Population by sex (%) (1992)	*Male* 48.4		*Female* 51.6		
Life expectancy (years) (1985-90)	*Male* 70.1		*Female* 77.1		
Infant mortality (deaths per '000 live births) (1992)	10.3				
Adult literacy (%) (1982)	90.0				

Guam

Area (km²)   450

Currency   US dollar (US$ = 100 cents)

Location   Guam is the largest island in the Mariana group, lying 5,300 km west of Honolulu and 2,170 km south of Japan. The climate is characterised by hot wet weather from June to November, but is cooler and drier in the winter months. The capital is Agaña.

Head of State   President Bill Clinton (USA)

Head of Government   Joseph F. Ada (Governor) (1987)

Ruling Party   Democratic Party

Political Structure   Guam's status as a US unincorporated territory is currently under review in the light of the general US withdrawal from the Pacific region. A referendum in 1982 produced a majority in favour of commonwealth status, but since then opinion has shifted back toward the status quo. The Guam authorities are particularly anxious to acquire a right of veto over the extraterritorial application of US law. The Governor is elected every four years and the 21-member Legislature for two years. Guam also elects one non-voting delegate to the US Congress in Washington.

Last Elections   Elections to the Guam Legislature are held every two years, and the election system mirrors that in the United States. In the November 1992 elections the Democrats won 14 of the 21 seats while the Republicans won 7. In the same month Joseph F. Ada was re-elected to the Governorship.

Political Risk   The moderation of pro-commonwealth sentiment runs to some extent counter to the wishes of the US itself, which is reducing its military commitment steadily. Potential for secessionist dissent exists only among the indigenous Chamorros, who currently comprise 45% of the population but who will become more important as US personnel leave the military bases. A serious deterioration in the local economy would exacerbate the situation. The island is occasionally subject to severe earthquakes, with the last major one occurring in 1993.

Economy   Guam's economy remains basically dependent on the United States, despite the tourism inflows from Japan and other parts of the region. The Government is attempting to encourage foreign investment with a range of incentives aimed at widening the economic base.

Main Industries   Guam's most prominent and profitable activities have traditionally centred on servicing the US troop presence, which once provided most of the employment on the island but which clearly cannot be expected to last indefinitely. Otherwise, tourism is the main activity, with substantial revenues especially from the Japanese who comprise 70% of all visitors. Agriculture is only of modest significance, with most farms being run on a part-time basis. The country is a producer of cassava, bananas, coconuts, sugar cane, fruit, vegetables, sweet potatoes and breadfruit. Fishing is important, and there are a wide variety of animals kept for meat. Industry, on the other hand, is very modest in scale, employing less than 4% of the workforce although it offers a wide spread of activities: cement production, food processing, textiles and clothing, oil processing and even watch manufacture.

Energy   Guam imports all of its fuel needs, although it has an ample supply of petroleum products on tap as a result of its own oil processing activities.

	1993	1994	1995
Inflation (% change)	2.7	3.0	2.8
Exchange rate (per US$)	1.00	1.00	1.00
Interest rate			
GDP (% real growth)	-2.1	-1.9	-1.1
GDP (Million units of national currency)	1,000.6	1,010.6	1,027.0
GDP (US$ million)	1,000.6	1,010.6	1,027.0
GDP per capita (US$)	7,147.1	6,737.3	6,846.5
Consumption (Million units of national currency)	663.5	670.2	681.1
Consumption (US$ million)	663.5	670.2	681.1
Consumption per capita (US$)	4,739.3	4,468.0	4,540.8
Population, mid-year ('000)	140.0	150.0	150.0
Birth rate (per '000)	24.6	25.7	
Death rate (per '000)	4.3	3.9	
No. of households ('000)	24.2	24.3	24.4
Total exports (US$ million)			
Total imports (US$ million)			
Tourism receipts (US$ million)	950.0	973.9	
Tourist spending (US$ million)			

Average household size 1995 (persons)	5.86				
Urban population 1995 (%)	38.2				
Age analysis (%) (1990)	*0-14* 31.7		*15-64* 64.4		*65+* 3.9
Population by sex (%) (1990)	*Male* 53.3		*Female* 46.7		
Life expectancy (years) (1990)	*Male* 72.1		*Female* 72.1		
Infant mortality (deaths per '000 live births) (1992)	9.8				
Adult literacy (%) (1990)	99.0				

Guatemala

Area (km²) 108,890

Currency Quetzal (Q$ = 100 centavos)

Location Guatemala lies directly across the Central American isthmus to the south of Mexico. It has a short coastline on the Caribbean Sea and a much longer one on the Pacific Ocean. The southern part of the country is mountainous, while the northern areas, bounded by Mexico and Belize, are relatively flat. The climate is generally humid and much of the country is forested. Earthquakes are frequent, as a result of the volcanic activity in the country. The capital is Guatemala City.

Head of State President Alvaro Arzu

Head of Government President Alvaro Arzu

Ruling Party National Advancement Party

Political Structure Guatemala is a republic with an executive President who is elected by popular mandate for a five-year term - although this term is to be reduced to four years under constitutional changes agreed in the referendum of January 1994. Of the 94 members in the unicameral National Congress (hitherto 116), about three-quarters are directly elected and the remainder appointed according to a system of proportional representation.

Last Elections In general elections held in January 1996, the pro-business candidate, Alvaro Arzu, defeated a populist rival who was supported by the former dictator General Efrain Rios Montt. The turnout was only 37%, however, and the margin of victory was tiny.

Political Risk Guatemala's army and the main rebel groups announced a truce in March 1996 after 35 years of fighting. In May 1996, the government signed a social reform agreement with the guerrillas which most observers regard as a significant breakthrough in improving relations between the two groups.

International Disputes Guatemala's relations with Mexico have been strained as a result of its alleged involvement in the Chaiapas rebellion of 1994. President Arzu's predecessor also seemed likely to revive the old territorial claim on Belize, which was a British dependent territory until the 1970s. However, the current administration has shown little interest in this issue. If the claim were to be revived, diplomatic relations with the UK would be jeopardised, to say nothing of those with Belize.

Economy Guatemala's economy appears broadly based and potentially sturdy. The only factor holding it back is the political uncertainty which continues to pervade the country. Allegations of human rights abuses, as long as they last, will do little to remedy this situation. GDP nevertheless grew by about 4% in 1994 and preliminary figures for 1995 suggest that the pace has been maintained.

Main Industries Agriculture is still the mainstay of the economy, employing 55% of the workforce even though it produces no more than a quarter of GDP. Coffee, sugar cane, bananas and cotton are the main cash crops, with maize, rice, wheat, fruit and vegetables grown for domestic consumption. Guatemala has an underdeveloped fishing industry. The industrial sector is moderately developed, contributing about 15% of GDP. Traditional activities have centred on agricultural products, but textiles, paper, pharmaceuticals, chemicals, plastics and electronics are now being manufactured. Mineral activity is mainly small-scale, but includes iron, lead, antimony, zinc, silver, cadmium and tungsten. Of more interest is the oil and gas potential resulting from recent finds; yet investment from abroad has been slow, deterred in part by the government's long-running battle with rebel groups.

Energy Guatemala's indigenous oil resources are insufficient at present to cover the country's requirements, and supplies are imported from Venezuela. Over 90% of the country's electricity is generated by hydro-electric schemes.

	1993	1994	1995
Inflation (% change)	11.8	10.9	18.6
Exchange rate (per US$)	5.64	5.25	5.83
Interest rate (% per annum)	24.7	22.9	
GDP (% real growth)	3.0	5.4	4.2
GDP (Million units of national currency)	63,733.0	74,491.0	92,053.4
GDP (US$ million)	11,300.2	14,188.8	15,789.6
GDP per capita (US$)	1,126.6	1,374.9	1,486.8
Consumption (Million units of national currency)	53,926.0	67,859.3	90,285.3
Consumption (US$ million)	9,561.3	12,925.6	15,486.3
Consumption per capita (US$)	953.3	1,252.5	1,458.2
Population, mid-year ('000)	10,030.0	10,320.0	10,620.0
Birth rate (per '000)	36.9	35.4	
Death rate (per '000)	7.5	8.6	
No. of households ('000)	2,012.6	2,081.3	2,202.9
Total exports (US$ million)	1,340.0	1,522.0	
Total imports (US$ million)	2,599.0	2,604.0	
Tourism receipts (US$ million)	265.0	353.1	
Tourist spending (US$ million)	116.0	154.6	185.2

Average household size 1995 (persons)	4.71				
Urban population 1995 (%)	41.5				
Age analysis (%) (1990)	*0-14* 45.4		*15-64* 51.4		*65+* 3.2
Population by sex (%) (1990)	*Male* 50.5		*Female* 49.5		
Life expectancy (years) (1985-90)	*Male* 59.7		*Female* 64.4		
Infant mortality (deaths per '000 live births)					
Adult literacy (%) (1990)	55.1				

TRADING PARTNERS

Major export destinations 1995 (% share)		Major import sources 1995 (% share)	
USA	50.8	USA	49.4
El Salvador	8.2	Mexico	5.1
Germany	4.9	El Salvador	4.8
Costa Rica	3.6	Venezuela	4.1

Guinea

Area (km²) 245,855

Currency Franc guinéen (= 100 centimes)

Location Guinea lies on the Atlantic coast of West Africa with Senegal and Guinea-Bissau to the north, Mali and Côte d'Ivoire to the east, and Liberia and Sierra Leone to the south. The climate is dry, despite the presence of the sources of major African rivers such as the Senegal, the Niger and the Gambia. The capital is Conakry.

Head of State President Maj.-Gen. Lansana Conté (1984)

Head of Government President Maj.-Gen. Lansana Conté

Ruling Party Although parties are no longer banned, no one party holds power.

Political Structure Guinea's 1982 Constitution was placed in suspense upon the military takeover of 1984 which brought the present Administration to power, but a new draft was approved by a national referendum in December 1990. At present the country is run by the Transitional Committee for National Recovery, whose membership has been cut from 36 members to 15, and a full two-party system is scheduled for the future.

Last Elections The first multi-party elections took place in December 1993, when President Conté was confirmed in office. Further elections to the legislature took place in June 1995, when the ruling coalition was returned to office.

Political Risk The re-election of President Conté in December 1993 triggered a wave of violent protests. Much of the organised opposition to the regime is co-ordinated from abroad, in the continuing absence of measures guaranteeing freedom of speech. Foreign investment and international relations have suffered accordingly. The army mutinied in February 1996. President Conté subsequently dismissed his minister of defence and assumed direct control over the military.

International Disputes Given the political turmoil in many of its neighbour states, especially in the south, it is unsurprising that Guinea has been repeatedly drawn into repeated confrontations with its neighbours.

Economy Guinea's mineral wealth is thrown into sharp relief by the poverty of its population. A lack of basic infrastructure facilities (especially roads) is a serious handicap to development. External lenders are now restoring loan facilities to the country, and a full-scale drive is under way to secure new project finance, especially in the field of mining.

Main Industries Over 80% of Guinea's population depends on subsistence farming for its livelihood. Agriculture, however, is a much smaller contributor to national income than mineral extraction. Only 3% of the land is cultivated with bananas, groundnuts, oil palm, cotton, pineapples and coffee grown for export. Cassava, rice and maize are the staples for the domestic market. Manufacturing provides as much as a quarter of GDP, but is almost exclusively geared to serve the domestic market. The only large-scale manufacturing installation is a bauxite smelting plant. Mining provides another quarter of GDP and practically all the country's export revenues. Guinea has vast bauxite reserves, significant diamond stocks and some gold.

Energy Although the country is actively searching for offshore petroleum resources, its only indigenous energy source is its considerable hydro-electric potential.

	1993	1994	1995
Inflation (% change)	20.0	8.0	4.0
Exchange rate (per US$)	955.50	961.60	1,000.50
Interest rate (% per annum)	24.5	22.0	21.5
GDP (% real growth)	4.8	-3.2	0.8
GDP (Million units of national currency)	2,074,710.1	2,168,408.0	2,272,895.1
GDP (US$ million)	2,171.3	2,255.0	2,271.8
GDP per capita (US$)	344.3	347.4	339.5
Consumption (Million units of national currency)	693,918.0	725,256.6	760,203.8
Consumption (US$ million)	726.2	754.2	759.8
Consumption per capita (US$)	115.2	116.2	113.6
Population, mid-year ('000)	6,306.0	6,491.1	6,690.8
Birth rate (per '000)	50.6	44.1	
Death rate (per '000)	20.3	19.2	
No. of households ('000)	1,107.9	1,146.1	1,214.3
Total exports (US$ million)	590.0	668.0	
Total imports (US$ million)	582.7	760.8	
Tourism receipts (US$ million)	6.0	6.1	
Tourist spending (US$ million)	28.0	28.7	28.9

Average household size 1995 (persons)	5.38		
Urban population 1995 (%)	29.6		
Age analysis (%) (1991)	*0-14* 46.7	*15-64* 50.7	*65+* 2.6
Population by sex (%)			
Life expectancy (years) (1990-95)	*Male* 44.0	*Female* 45.0	
Infant mortality (deaths per '000 live births) (1993)	134.2		
Adult literacy (%) (1990)	24.0		

TRADING PARTNERS

Major export destinations 1995 (% share)		Major import sources 1995 (% share)	
Belgium/Luxembourg	28.6	France	19.6
USA	14.7	Côte d'Ivoire	16.8
Spain	10.1	USA	9.2
Ireland	9.4	Belgium/Luxembourg	7.4

Guinea-Bissau

Area (km²)   36,125

Currency   Guinea peso (= 100 centavos)

Location   Guinea-Bissau, the former Portuguese Guinea, is a small triangle of land lying on the Atlantic coast of West Africa, between Senegal to the north and Guinea to the south and east. Until the nineteenth century, it shared a political union with Cape Verde. Attempts to revive that union were hurriedly dropped in the mid-1980s after a coup attempt. The country is low-lying, yet suffers from recurrent drought. The capital is Bissau.

Head of State   President Joao Bernando Vieira

Head of Government   Manuel Saturnino da Costa (October 1994)

Ruling Party   Partido Africano da Independência da Guiné e Cabo Verde (PAIGC)

Political Structure   The democratic system was restored in 1994 with the elections which brought the Vieira Administration to power. This poll was the first real test of President Vieira's power since the execution of his Vice-President in 1986, and his apparently easy win afforded some reassurance in the face of considerable doubts about his political record. The Assembly appoints a 15-member Council of State (Cabinet), which governs the country.

Last Elections   The first multi-party elections to the 100-member National Assembly were held in July and August 1994, when the PAIGC gained 64 seats on a turnout of less than 50%. President Vieira, who took power in the 1980 coup, was re-elected unopposed for a further five-year term at the same time.

Political Risk   Guinea-Bissau must inevitably be considered a high risk area in view of its restrictive security policies, its foreign exchange controls and the degree of political suppression which is practised. Occasional demonstrations and a coup attempt in 1993 underline the degree of political and social unrest which normally prevails in the country.

Economy   Recurrent political crisis has prevented economic reform and undermined international confidence in the country. Guinea-Bissau has applied, unsuccessfully, to join the CFA franc zone, the inference being that its currency is not sufficiently stable at present. However, the country has received financial assistance from the World Bank to aid in restructuring its economy.

Main Industries   Agriculture employs over 80% of the population and accounts for the bulk of the country's meagre income. About 8% of the land area is cultivated, and subsistence farming predominates - with intermittent and frequently serious drought. Cashews and groundnuts are grown for export, together with tobacco, sugar and palm kernels. The domestic population relies on cassava, millet, sorghum and maize. There are few industries of any size, and it is estimated that they only contribute about 5% of GDP between them. Apart from a small car assembly plant, most activity centres on agricultural produce. Guinea-Bissau has bauxite resources, but it is uneconomic at present to exploit them.

Energy   Guinea-Bissau depends entirely on imported oil at present, but there are moves to develop the country's hydro-electric potential.

	1993	1994	1995
Inflation (% change)	48.1	15.2	34.3
Exchange rate (per US$)	10,082.00	12,892.00	16,065.00
Interest rate (% per annum)	63.6	36.3	
GDP (% real growth)	6.5	-1.4	1.5
GDP (Billion units of national currency)	2,365.7	2,685.8	3,661.1
GDP (US$ million)	234.6	208.3	227.9
GDP per capita (US$)	228.3	199.2	213.3
Consumption (Billion units of national currency)	2,246.5	2,551.0	3,478.1
Consumption (US$ million)	222.8	197.9	216.5
Consumption per capita (US$)	216.8	189.2	202.6
Population, mid-year ('000)	1,028.0	1,045.9	1,068.6
Birth rate (per '000)	42.7	40.8	
Death rate (per '000)	21.3	22.3	
No. of households ('000)	189.4	193.7	203.1
Total exports (US$ million)	16.0	32.0	
Total imports (US$ million)	62.0	63.0	
Tourism receipts (US$ million)			
Tourist spending (US$ million)			

Average household size 1995 (persons)	5.13		
Urban population 1995 (%)	22.2		
Age analysis (%) (1989)	*0-14* 43.3	*15-64* 53.7	*65+* 3.1
Population by sex (%) (1989)	*Male* 48.4	*Female* 51.6	
Life expectancy (years) (1990-95)	*Male* 41.9	*Female* 45.1	
Infant mortality (deaths per '000 live births) (1993)	140.0		
Adult literacy (%) (1990)	36.5		

TRADING PARTNERS

Major export destinations 1995 (% share)		Major import sources 1995 (% share)	
Thailand	29.9	Spain	45.8
Portugal	29.4	India	26.0
Netherlands	4.6	Italy	13.7
Senegal	3.2	Thailand	6.1

Guyana

Area (km²)   214,970

Currency   Guyana dollar (G$ = 100 cents)

Location   Guyana, the former British Guiana, lies on the north-eastern coast of South America, its coast facing north-east into the Atlantic. It is bordered in the west by Venezuela, in the east by Suriname (the former Dutch Guiana), and in the far south by Brazil. The terrain is heavily forested, and the climate is humid and sub-tropical. The capital is Georgetown.

Head of State   Cheddi Jagan (October 1992)

Head of Government   Sam Hinds

Ruling Party   The People's Progressive Party-Civic

Political Structure   Guyana, an independent member of the Commonwealth, has a semi-executive President who in fact exercises considerable powers. He also leads a 65-member National Assembly of 53 members elected for a five-year term and 12 regional deputies. The country was for many years so firmly identified with the policies of the former ruling People's National Congress (PNC) that it amounted to a single-party state, but by 1991 the rising tensions surrounding the former President, Desmond Hoyte, had become so severe that he was forced to declare a state of emergency, in an ultimately unsuccessful attempt to quieten his opponents. He was removed from power shortly afterwards.

Last Elections   The last full election was held in October 1992, when Desmond Hoyte's PNC lost its strong parliamentary majority to the People's Progressive Party-Civic (PPP). Supporters of the PPP are predominantly Indian in origin, whereas Afro-Caribbeans tend to support the PNC. Local elections in August 1994 yielded stronger support for the PPP.

Political Risk   Election of the Jagan administration was encouraging to many foreign investors who were concerned at the conduct of President Hoyte. However, the results alienated other Caribbean countries that supported Hoyte's Afro-Caribbean administration in preference to Jagan's largely Asian party. Concern has also surrounded a threat by the country's 40,000 bush Indians that they would forcibly resist any attempt to extend forestry operations into the jungle regions which still make up most of the country.

International Disputes   Like French Guiana, Guyana faces a claim from Suriname for the return of a triangle of jungle land deep in the interior of the country. The so-called New River Triangle dispute arose because of an erroneous assumption as to which of two tributaries of the Corantijn River was the longer. The area in question has little economic significance, although some strategic importance.

Economy   The Guyanese economy remains in deep crisis after many years of overspending. Fortunately, foreign investment has begun to increase as the pseudo-one-party policies of the Hoyte regime have been gradually dismantled. The Government has ambitious plans for an industrial restructuring.

Main Industries   Guyana's economy depends heavily on the world market for bauxite. Processing of bauxite, diamonds and gold are the major industrial activities as well. Farming, although it accounts for over a quarter of the country's GDP, is mainly for subsistence purposes. Cash crops, which include sugar, coconuts and rice, are only grown near the coast since the inland terrain is too elevated and hostile. Domestic markets consume mainly cereals, fruit and vegetables. Guyana is also self-sufficient in meat and fish.

Energy   Like French Guiana, Guyana hopes to bolster its domestic production of energy with a massive hydro-electricity project. Otherwise, it remains heavily dependent on imported oil supplies, despite some promising oil finds on its own territory.

	1993	1994	1995
Inflation (% change)	15.0	7.3	
Exchange rate (per US$)	126.70	138.30	142.90
Interest rate (% per annum)	19.4	18.4	19.2
GDP (% real growth)	6.2	17.8	2.5
GDP (Million units of national currency)	59,124.0	74,715.0	76,582.9
GDP (US$ million)	466.6	540.2	535.9
GDP per capita (US$)	571.9	657.2	649.6
Consumption (Million units of national currency)	29,134.0	34,141.8	32,452.8
Consumption (US$ million)	229.9	246.9	227.1
Consumption per capita (US$)	281.8	300.3	275.3
Population, mid-year ('000)	816.0	822.0	825.0
Birth rate (per '000)	22.8	20.0	
Death rate (per '000)		7.4	
No. of households ('000)	170.0	172.1	178.1
Total exports (US$ million)	423.0	439.0	467.0
Total imports (US$ million)	484.0		
Tourism receipts (US$ million)	36.0	38.9	
Tourist spending (US$ million)			

Average household size 1995 (persons)	4.54				
Urban population 1995 (%)	36.2				
Age analysis (%) (1980)	*0-14* 40.8		*15-64* 55.3		*65+* 3.9
Population by sex (%) (1980)	*Male* 49.5		*Female* 50.5		
Life expectancy (years) (1990-95)	*Male* 62.4		*Female* 68.0		
Infant mortality (deaths per '000 live births)					
Adult literacy (%) (1990)	96.4				

TRADING PARTNERS

Major export destinations 1995 (% share)		Major import sources 1995 (% share)	
Canada	34.2	USA	26.3
USA	24.7	Italy	17.8
United Kingdom	19.5	Trinidad and Tobago	12.9
Germany	8.0	Netherlands Antilles	12.4

Haiti

Area (km²)   27,750

Currency   Gourde (G = 100 centimes)

Location   Haiti shares the large Caribbean island of Hispaniola with the Dominican Republic, occupying the western half. At its western extreme the country is no more than 80 km from Cuba and 160 km from Jamaica. The terrain is largely mountainous with fertile valleys. The climate is tropical and generally constant in character. The capital is Port-au-Prince.

Head of State   Rene Preval (1996)

Head of Government   Smarck Michel

Ruling Party   Front Nationale pour le Changement et la Démocratie en Haiti

Political Structure   September 1994 brought a resolution of a political dispute dating back to the overthrow of the newly-elected president Jean-Bertrand Aristide in 1991. With the assistance of a US invasion force, Aristide was returned to power and the military rulers - the military president Emile Jonassaint and his chief of staff Raoul Cedras - left the country.

Last Elections   When Rene Preval took over from Jean-Bertrand Aristide following the presidential elections in December 1995, this marked the first peaceful handover by one elected president to another in 192 years of Haitian independence. The turnout was a meagre 25% of the electorate owing to fears of violence, a dull campaign and the fact that Haitians have been asked to vote four times since June 1995.

Political Risk   Foreign donors were frustrated by Aristide's refusal to push ahead with privatisation and suspended around $100 million in aid. If President Preval goes ahead with the privatisation programme, he will anger many in the leftist Lavalas coalition that brought him to power. A US decision to withhold an additional $45 million in economic aid during 1996 has put more pressure on Preval. Critics in Washington claim that the Haitians have not investigated more than 25 killings which are believed to be politically motivated. Haiti, on the other hand, argues that its small and untrained police force is doing everything it can.

International Disputes   Haiti's problems with its Caribbean neighbours subsided once the pre-Aristide regime was removed from power. Meanwhile, poor Haitians are becoming increasingly critical of the new government because it has not brought them jobs. In the first quarter of 1996, American Coast Guard vessels reported a sharp rise in the numbers of refugees that were apprehended and returned to the island.

Economy   In 1995 the International Monetary Fund released new loans for Haiti in recognition of the progress it had made under Aristide. But the economy remains at an extremely low ebb after the failure of successive governments to rectify the structural weaknesses bequeathed by their dictatorial and generally corrupt predecessors, and the currency was devalued by around 40% in August 1994. The United States may be expected to inject considerable sums of capital into the economy, but the country will still need further help.

Main Industries   Haiti's economy relies overwhelmingly on the agricultural sector, which employs 70% of the workforce even though it contributes no more than about 35% of GDP. Coffee is grown for export, together with sugar and mangoes; yet most people rely on the subsistence farming of maize, sorghum, rice, beans and fruit. The sector is handicapped by poor irrigation and recurrent droughts. Industry contributes about 15% of GDP in a typical year, and is mainly found in the area around Port-au-Prince. Food processing and other activities involving raw materials predominate, but there is some manufacturing of other low-cost goods. Haiti has deposits of copper, silver, bauxite, gold, marble, lignite and asphalt, but only bauxite has ever been mined, and this too is shut down at present.

Energy   Haiti has no natural fuels except for lignite, and relies on imports for all its requirements.

	1993	1994	1995
Inflation (% change)	22.6	42.6	25.5
Exchange rate (per US$)	12.89	12.95	19.02
Interest rate			
GDP (% real growth)	-6.7	-6.2	-3.5
GDP (Million units of national currency)	41,738.0	55,828.2	67,612.2
GDP (US$ million)	3,238.0	4,311.1	3,554.8
GDP per capita (US$)	469.3	612.4	495.1
Consumption (Million units of national currency)	15,047.0	18,967.0	21,646.9
Consumption (US$ million)	1,167.3	1,464.6	1,138.1
Consumption per capita (US$)	169.2	208.0	158.5
Population, mid-year ('000)	6,900.0	7,040.0	7,180.0
Birth rate (per '000)	35.3	39.7	
Death rate (per '000)	11.9	12.1	
No. of households ('000)	1,301.6	1,334.7	1,400.7
Total exports (US$ million)	80.0	82.0	153.0
Total imports (US$ million)	355.0	252.0	697.0
Tourism receipts (US$ million)	46.0	60.9	
Tourist spending (US$ million)	35.9	47.5	36.9

Average household size 1995 (persons)	5.01				
Urban population 1995 (%)	31.6				
Age analysis (%) (1988)	*0-14* 39.2		*15-64* 54.9		*65+* 5.9
Population by sex (%) (1988)	*Male* 48.5		*Female* 51.5		
Life expectancy (years) (1990-95)	*Male* 55.0		*Female* 58.3		
Infant mortality (deaths per '000 live births) (1993)	86.2				
Adult literacy (%) (1990)	53.0				

TRADING PARTNERS

Major export destinations 1995 (% share)		Major import sources 1995 (% share)	
USA	75.7	USA	65.0
France	6.4	Netherlands Antilles	7.5
Germany	4.7	Japan	4.4
Italy	4.4	France	3.4

Honduras

Area (km²)   112,085

Currency   Lempira (L = 100 centavos)

Location   Honduras occupies a central position in the Central American isthmus, located between Guatemala in the west and Nicaragua in the east, with El Salvador on its southern border. Consequently, its Caribbean coastline is significantly longer than its Pacific frontage, which is less than 80 km in total. The country has a largely mountainous character, and three-quarters of the land is covered by forest. The climate is tropical and generally humid. The capital is Tegucigalpa.

Head of State   President Carlos Roberto Reina Idiaquez (December 1993)

Head of Government   President Carlos Roberto Reina Idiaquez (December 1993)

Ruling Party   Liberal Party of Honduras (PLH)

Political Structure   Honduras has an executive President who is directly elected by popular mandate for a four-year term. He and his Cabinet are answerable to a 128-member National Assembly. The country's first indigenous municipality was created in mid-1994, following a wave of political protests among Indian populations.

Last Elections   Elections were held in November 1993 to the National Assembly, when the centre-right wing PLH defeated the right-wing National Party of Honduras, with 52% of the vote against 41%. President Carlos Roberto Reina was elected in December of that year.

Political Risk   The unpopular but ultimately successful austerity measures introduced by the Government in recent years have gained the approval of the country's external creditors but they have seriously affected the middle and lower income classes. However, the present government (unlike many other Latin American countries with similar experiences) is gaining some credibility with the population because it is trying to bring justice many of those who in the military who repeatedly violated human rights during the 1980s and early 1990s. Courts are investigating the victims' cases and the new commander-in-chief of the armed forces has vowed that his units will obey the country's laws. Several individuals in the previous Callejas government have been jailed and charged with corruption.

Economy   The present government inherited an economic mess from its predecessor. It has brought the fiscal deficit under control, begun to sort out the foreign debt and loosen the army's grip on state-owned companies. The rate of growth has also picked up, averaging about 4% in 1995, after a contraction in the previous year. Efforts to reduce inflation have met with less success. Prices rose by almost 30% in 1995, although the government only granted a 9% pay increase and this brought it into conflict with trade unions.

Main Industries   The tourist sector is growing surprisingly rapidly. However, agriculture is still the single largest sector of the economy, accounting for nearly a quarter of total GDP and up to 65% of export revenues. Bananas and coffee are cultivated for export, together with cotton, tobacco and meat (mainly frozen). New crops are being encouraged; these include cocoa, melons and citrus fruits. Most of the population relies on maize, rice, sorghum and beans. The fishing industry is small but increasing in importance. Industry consists mainly of small-scale establishments involved in food processing or the manufacture of furniture, textiles and clothing. There is a limited amount of mining for gold, silver, zinc and lead.

Energy   Honduras is able to produce as much as 75% of its own energy requirements, thanks to offshore oil resources. The country has a substantial export surplus in electricity, due mainly to its extensive hydro-electric facilities.

	1993	1994	1995
Inflation (% change)	10.7	21.7	29.5
Exchange rate (per US$)	7.26	9.40	9.35
Interest rate (% per annum)	22.1	24.7	27.0
GDP (% real growth)	8.7	-0.5	4.0
GDP (Million units of national currency)	22,444.0	28,715.0	37,350.0
GDP (US$ million)	3,091.5	3,054.8	3,994.7
GDP per capita (US$)	553.0	529.4	671.4
Consumption (Million units of national currency)	14,670.0	18,231.5	23,035.0
Consumption (US$ million)	2,020.7	1,939.5	2,463.6
Consumption per capita (US$)	361.5	336.1	414.1
Population, mid-year ('000)	5,590.0	5,770.0	5,950.0
Birth rate (per '000)	37.1	35.0	
Death rate (per '000)	6.1	6.2	
No. of households ('000)	1,062.6	1,101.4	1,168.1
Total exports (US$ million)	814.0	843.0	1,061.0
Total imports (US$ million)	1,130.0	1,056.0	1,219.0
Tourism receipts (US$ million)	32.0	29.7	
Tourist spending (US$ million)	39.0	36.1	45.9

Average household size 1995 (persons)	4.98				
Urban population 1995 (%)	43.9				
Age analysis (%) (1992)	*0-14* 42.8		*15-64* 51.2		*65+* 5.9
Population by sex (%) (1992)	*Male* 48.9		*Female* 51.1		
Life expectancy (years) (1990-95)	*Male* 65.4		*Female* 70.1		
Infant mortality (deaths per '000 live births) (1993)	43.0				
Adult literacy (%) (1990)	73.1				

TRADING PARTNERS

Major export destinations 1995 (% share)		Major import sources 1995 (% share)	
USA	65.0	USA	60.5
Germany	7.7	Guatemala	4.7
Japan	6.3	Japan	3.8
Spain	3.0	Mexico	2.3

Hong Kong

Area (km²)   1,062

Currency   Hong Kong dollar (HK$ = 100 cents)

Location   Hong Kong occupies an important strategic position at the mouth of the Pearl River where it conducts an active trading business to, and on behalf of, the People's Republic of China. Besides the city itself, the territory includes the Kowloon island area and the so-called New Territories, which are mainly residential. Hong Kong has a mild climate, but summers and early autumns are very wet. The capital is Victoria.

Head of State   HM Queen Elizabeth II

Head of Government   HE Christopher Patten (Governor)

Ruling Party   Liberal parties, including the United Democrats of Hong Kong, hold a working majority in the Legislative Council.

Political Structure   Hong Kong, which is currently a Crown Colony, will be turned over to China in July 1997. In March 1996, the Preparatory Committee which overseas the transition on behalf of China decided to abolish Hong Kong's democratically elected Legislative Council (Legco) and to replace it with an appointed "provisional" legislature. Hong Kong's civil servants will also be required to cooperate with the new provisional body.

Last Elections   The first full elections to the Legislative Council were held in September 1991, when the United Democrats of Hong Kong won a sweeping victory with 12 of the 18 directly elected seats. Other allied democratic parties took an additional three seats, and the remaining three were won by independents. None of the four candidates backed by China won a seat in that election. Moreover, in the direct elections to the district councils in September 1994, both the United Democrats and "pro-democracy" independent candidates made further gains. These democratic gains may be short-lived, however. Hong Kong businessmen who dominate the Preparatory Committee that will guide China's takeover and choose the post-1997 provisional legislature are gradually easing themselves out of the British camp and into the Chinese one.

Political Risk   Hong Kong's handover to China in 1997 is beginning to have an impact on patterns of investment and capital movements. That effect may be only short term but the sources of foreign capital inflows will almost certainly change as the Chinese diaspora funnel even more of their capital back into the country via Hong Kong while the share of funds coming from western economies is reduced.

International Disputes   Political disputes over the degree of political autonomy to be granted to a Chinese-governed Hong Kong have been vigorous but the British have lost the argument. Chinese-based businessmen in Hong Kong clearly expect to benefit, though local surveys of young people indicate that over two-fifths of those between 15 and 24 years want to emigrate before the 1997 takeover.

Economy   As 1997 draws near, Hong Kong's relationship with China is becoming one of symbiosis. The colony's businessmen employ around 3 million in Guangdong province alone. Over 60% of China's trade passes through Hong Kong's ports and about $20 billion of the country's hard currency reserves are held in the city-state. This division of labour will be accentuated in the future; Hong Kong will become the capital for finance, trade and services for southern China. Such rapid integration has its costs. As the prices of land and labour in Hong Kong soar, multinationals are reconsidering their decision to locate regional offices in the city-state. Several have gone to the mainland itself, while others have moved elsewhere in Asia. Meanwhile, the colony is losing 60,000 middle-class professionals each year. Unless the trend is reversed, Hong Kong's high-value services will be syphoned off to other Asian hubs.

Main Industries   Hong Kong's industrial sector ranges from heavy chemical and steel manufacturing to high-technology and electronic goods. There is a massive range of small-scale enterprises making toys, precision goods and clothing. Equally important is Hong Kong's vast entrepôt trade activity, mainly with China and with South East Asia; the mainland is keen to learn from the colony's trading skills after 1997. Finally, Hong Kong's expertise in financial services is well known. It has the second largest stock market in the Far East with futures, money market activities and other derivatives being particularly well developed.

Energy   Lacking any resources of its own, Hong Kong is entirely dependent on imports for all its fuel needs. Electricity and coal are imported from China, and oil from South East Asia. Hong Kong has benefited from the opening of a Chinese nuclear power station in Shenzhen, but the development has aroused environmental fears in the Colony.

	1993	**1994**	**1995**
Inflation (% change)	8.7	8.6	9.2
Exchange rate (per US$)	7.74	7.73	7.74
Interest rate (% per annum)	7.5	7.0	5.7
GDP (% real growth)	6.5	4.3	0.1
GDP (Million units of national currency)	897,595.0	1,016,600.0	1,111,400.0
GDP (US$ million)	115,968.3	131,513.6	143,591.7
GDP per capita (US$)	19,589.2	21,696.9	23,198.1
Consumption (Million units of national currency)	515,312.0	600,080.0	653,700.0
Consumption (US$ million)	66,577.8	77,630.0	84,457.4
Consumption per capita (US$)	11,246.2	12,807.3	13,644.6
Population, mid-year ('000)	5,920.0	6,061.4	6,189.8
Birth rate (per '000)	11.9	11.8	11.0
Death rate (per '000)	5.2	5.0	5.0
No. of households ('000)	1,676.7	1,740.0	1,797.0
Total exports (US$ million)	135,248.0	151,395.0	173,754.0
Total imports (US$ million)	138,658.0	161,777.0	192,774.0
Tourism receipts (US$ million)	7,562.0	8,318.1	9,075.0
Tourist spending (US$ million)			

Average household size 1995 (persons)	3.31		
Urban population 1996 (%)	95.0		
Age analysis (%) (1995)	*0-14* 19.0	*15-64* 71.5	*65+* 9.5
Population by sex (%) (1995)	*Male* 50.8	*Female* 49.2	
Life expectancy (years) (1995)	*Male* 76.0	*Female* 81.0	
Infant mortality (deaths per '000 live births) (1995)	5.0		
Adult literacy (%) (1971)	77.3		

TRADING PARTNERS

Major export destinations 1995 (% share)		Major import sources 1995 (% share)	
China	33.3	China	36.1
USA	22.1	Japan	15.0
Japan	5.9	USA	7.7
Germany	4.2	Singapore	5.2

Hungary

Area (km²) 93,030

Currency Forint (= 100 fillér)

Location Hungary, one of the first Eastern European countries to depart from the communist ethic, has long-standing historical ties with Austria to the west, which have been renewed in recent years. Bordering on Serbia, Croatia and Slovenia to the south, Romania and Ukraine to the east and the Slovak Republic to the north, it is an important gateway between Western Europe and the developing East. Its terrain is mixed, with large agricultural areas but with mountains along the border with Romania. The capital is Budapest.

Head of State Arpad Goncz (re-elected June 1995)

Head of Government Gyula Horn

Ruling Party The Hungarian Socialist Party leads a coalition with the Alliance of Free Democrats.

Political Structure Hungary's political structure has been radically reshaped since the revision of the ruling Hungarian Socialist Workers' Party in 1987-89 and its eclipse in the first multi-party elections of 1990. The country has a non-executive President and a Prime Minister who is accountable to a unicameral National Assembly elected by popular mandate for a term of five years. The National Assembly elects the President. Since April 1995, the country's Romany element has had its own 53-seat Parliament.

Last Elections Elections to the unicameral National Assembly were held in May 1994, when the Hungarian Socialist Party (the former communist party) won a convincing victory with 209 of the 386 seats. The liberal SZDSZ won 52 seats and the liberal FIDESZ 20; the conservative KDNP won 22; the centre-right populist Magyar Demokrata Fórum (Hungarian Democratic Forum) won 37 (compared with the 165 it had held); the FKGP 26; and independents won the remaining 20 seats.

Political Risk Hungary's Government, relying as it does on the support of minority parties, has always been vulnerable to political upsets. The country's bloated welfare state is proving to be a more difficult problem to resolve. Disputes over the pace of reform have already led to the resignation of several ministers. The government has little time to move ahead with changes in the welfare system. Soon, all political parties will turn their attention to the next round of elections in 1998.

International Disputes Few people or governments care so passionately about minority rights as the Hungarians. Their concerns date back to the inter-war period when the Treaty of Trianon transferred Transylvania to Romania. The loss of a large ethnic Hungarian population still causes resentment today. The current government is working to secure bilateral "basic treaties" which guarantee and codify the rights of minorities. However, the Hungarians know that they must proceed carefully in these negotiations. If relations with their neighbours were to deteriorate seriously, Hungary's chances of joining the EU would be jeopardised.

Economy Hungary's GDP grew by 1.5% in 1995, down from 3% in 1994. The advances were led by exports which rose by 15-16% in real terms while imports remained close to 1994 levels. Privatisation helped to bring in a record $5 billion in foreign investment in 1995 - equivalent to around 12% of GDP. Most of this will be used to pay off some of Hungary's $32 billion in gross foreign debt which is the highest per capita debt in the former eastern block. All this was good enough for Hungary to enter the OECD in 1996 - an important step in Hungarian eyes - towards membership in the EU.

Main Industries The Hungarians say they plan to complete their privatisation programme by the end of 1997 when 80-85% of the economy will be in private hands. The government has already sold stakes in most of the country's electricity and gas utilities, the national telecommunications company and some banks. Apart from engineering and heavy industries, Hungary has an established electronics sector, a growing automobile and automobile components industry and strong companies in chemicals, pharmaceuticals and heavy goods. The agricultural sector, which has undergone enormous structural changes, now enjoys levels of productivity that are higher than in most other Eastern European countries. One of the economy's weaker areas is banking and finance, despite government efforts to boost the sector with bank bailouts of $3 billion over the past four years.

Energy Hungary has indigenous coal resources, but relies for gas and most of its oil supplies on the former Soviet Union. However, its geographical position and easy access from the West make it easy for the country to organise alternative supplies if that should ever be necessary.

	1993	1994	1995
Inflation (% change)	22.5	18.9	28.2
Exchange rate (per US$)	91.93	105.16	123.73
Interest rate (% per annum)	25.4	27.4	32.6
GDP (% real growth)	-4.1	3.4	1.5
GDP (Billion units of national currency)	3,537.8	4,350.9	5,661.5
GDP (US$ million)	38,483.6	41,374.1	45,757.1
GDP per capita (US$)	3,738.5	4,032.6	4,477.2
Consumption (Billion units of national currency)	2,110.7	2,427.0	2,623.4
Consumption (US$ million)	22,959.7	23,079.1	21,202.8
Consumption per capita (US$)	2,230.4	2,249.4	2,074.6
Population, mid-year ('000)	10,294.0	10,260.0	10,220.0
Birth rate (per '000)	11.4	11.3	11.0
Death rate (per '000)	14.6	14.0	14.0
No. of households ('000)	3,910.0	3,955.0	3,979.0
Total exports (US$ million)	8,918.0	10,733.0	12,540.0
Total imports (US$ million)	12,597.0	14,438.0	15,073.0
Tourism receipts (US$ million)	1,181.0	1,427.0	1,575.0
Tourist spending (US$ million)	750.0	806.0	740.5

Average household size 1995 (persons)	2.46				
Urban population 1995 (%)	64.7				
Age analysis (%) (1995)	*0-14* 21.1		*15-64* 65.8		*65+* 13.1
Population by sex (%) (1995)	*Male* 47.9		*Female* 52.1		
Life expectancy (years) (1994)	*Male* 64.8		*Female* 74.2		
Infant mortality (deaths per '000 live births) (1995)	11.0				
Adult literacy (%) (1983)	98.0				

TRADING PARTNERS

Major export destinations 1995 (% share)		Major import sources 1995 (% share)	
Germany	30.1	Germany	26.0
Austria	8.6	Austria	10.0
Italy	8.3	Russia	8.8
Russia	6.1	Italy	7.4

Iceland

Area (km²)   102,820

Currency   Icelandic króna (= 100 aurar)

Location   Located in the North Atlantic, Iceland is a large volcanic island and enjoys generally clear summers. Recurrent volcanic eruptions in the 13th-17th centuries almost depopulated the island, but they have not been serious in recent times. Rich fishing grounds and the harnessing of geothermal energy are important to the economy. The capital is Reykjavik.

Head of State   Olafur Ragnar Grimsson (June 1996)

Head of Government   David Oddsson

Ruling Party   Sjalfstaedisflokkurin (Independence Party-IP) leads a coalition with Framsoknarflokkurin (Progressive Party).

Political Structure   Iceland's President exercises somewhat more than merely a ceremonial role, being deeply involved in both domestic and international affairs. However, the day-to-day running of the country is left to the Prime Minister and the Cabinet, who are appointed by the 63-member Althing (Parliament). The Althing is a unicameral assembly. Although elected in one body by universal mandate, it designates one-third of its members after the election as an Upper House. The Althing sits for a term of four years, as does the President.

Last Elections   General elections to the Althing were held in April 1995, when the IP scored a convincing victory, with 25 of the 63 seats, compared with 15 for the Framsoknarflokkurin (Progressive Party), 7 for the Social Democrats, 9 for the Althydubandalag (People's Alliance), and three for the Samtök um Kvennalista (Women's Alliance). The IP then went on to form a coalition with the Progressive Party. In the presidential elections of June 1996, the left-wing candidate, Olafur Ragnar Grimsson, succeeded Mrs Vigdis Finnbogadottir, who had held office for 16 years.

Political Risk   The last five years have seen a perceptible reversal of the anti-European trend which was dominant during most of the 1980s. The depletion of fish stocks is forcing some restructuring of the economy while recurrent inflationary pressures are a perennial problem for the government. The lack of any political instability during a period of severe hardship has nevertheless been remarkable.

International Disputes   Recurrent disputes break out between Iceland and its neighbours over fishery rights, and especially over its alleged infringement of EU fisheries. Norway, in particular, is claiming a disputed area around the Svalbard islands where it claims a unilateral 200-mile fishing limit.

Economy   Iceland's economy remains vulnerable to the single-product character of its activities, and tensions with the EU over fishing rights have done little to assuage fears about the country's growth prospects. Yet the massive inflation rates of previous years have now been brought under control, thanks to vigorous austerity programmes. Despite some misgivings about its ties to Europe, Iceland joined the extended Economic Area of the European Union in 1994.

Main Industries   Despite a massive push to diversify in recent decades, Iceland's economy still relies heavily on fishing. Sheep are reared in large numbers, but otherwise agricultural activity tends to be restrained by the poor weather conditions. Most industry is located around Reykjavik and other major towns, but is fragmented and suffers badly from poor transport connections, including an almost total lack of road or rail links in many areas. A surplus of geothermal energy has fostered the growth of large, energy-intensive activities such as aluminium smelting and steel manufacture. On the other hand, most consumer goods are imported.

Energy   Iceland has vast geothermal potential in its volcanic rock structure, of which only a small part is currently exploited. With sufficient capital investment, it could easily become a major exporter of electricity by the late 1990s.

	1993	1994	1995
Inflation (% change)	4.1	1.6	1.7
Exchange rate (per US$)	67.60	69.94	64.89
Interest rate (% per annum)	14.1	10.6	11.6
GDP (% real growth)	-0.8	3.7	3.6
GDP (Million units of national currency)	410,982.0	433,000.0	456,200.0
GDP (US$ million)	6,079.6	6,191.0	7,030.4
GDP per capita (US$)	23,116.4	23,274.5	26,232.7
Consumption (Million units of national currency)	248,952.0	257,461.0	266,262.2
Consumption (US$ million)	3,682.7	3,681.2	4,103.3
Consumption per capita (US$)	14,002.7	13,839.0	15,310.8
Population, mid-year ('000)	263.0	266.0	268.0
Birth rate (per '000)	14.0	16.3	
Death rate (per '000)	6.8	6.5	
No. of households ('000)	107.4	109.1	113.3
Total exports (US$ million)	1,399.0	1,623.0	
Total imports (US$ million)	1,349.0	1,472.0	1,756.0
Tourism receipts (US$ million)	132.0	134.9	
Tourist spending (US$ million)	264.0	269.8	300.7

Average household size 1995 (persons)	2.32				
Urban population 1995 (%)	91.6				
Age analysis (%) (1995)	*0-14* 25.0		*15-64* 63.5		*65+* 11.5
Population by sex (%) (1994)	*Male* 50.3		*Female* 49.7		
Life expectancy (years) (1995)	*Male* 76.3		*Female* 81.3		
Infant mortality (deaths per '000 live births) (1994)	3.2				
Adult literacy (%) (1984)	100.0				

TRADING PARTNERS

Major export destinations 1995 (% share)		Major import sources 1995 (% share)	
United Kingdom	19.5	Germany	11.4
Japan	15.1	Norway	10.3
Germany	14.4	United Kingdom	10.1
USA	11.8	USA	9.2

India

Area (km²) 3,166,830

Currency Indian rupee (Rs = 100 paise)

Location India, the world's second most populous country, occupies the central northern coast of the Indian Ocean, where it is bounded in the west by Pakistan, in the north by Tibet (a region of China), Bhutan and Nepal, and in the east by Myanmar and Bangladesh. Spanning the equator, its climate is tropical and occasionally prone to violent storms. The capital is New Delhi.

Head of State President Shankar Dayal Sharma (July 1992)

Head of Government H D Gowda

Ruling Party United Front leads a coalition which includes the Congress I Party.

Political Structure India is essentially a federation of 25 states and seven union territories, spanning extremes of terrain and climate, and encompassing a very large number of ethnic groups. Ethnic and religious clashes characterise national politics at every level. The President holds all executive power, and appoints the Prime Minister and his Cabinet on the basis of election results to the Lok Sabha (Parliament). The Lok Sabha has 545 seats while the Rajya Sabha (Council of States) has 245 members.

Last Elections Elections in the various states take place at regular intervals, and often produce sharply differing results from those at national level. The country's eleventh national elections, which were held in May 1996, produced an upset when the Hindu nationalist Bharatiya Janata Party (BJP) became the biggest party in the Lok Sabha with 189 seats. The United Front took 180 seats, the Congress Party and its allies claimed another 136 seats, and smaller parties won the remainder. Lacking a majority, the BJP coaltion lasted only two weeks and was replaced by the United Front coalition, which has the support of the Congress Party and a disparate group of regional and low-caste parties.

Political Risk Ethnic and religious disagreements continue to create a disconcerting backdrop to governmental attempts to forge national unity, or to implement a national strategy. Religious assassins have killed two of the last three Prime Ministers. Yet the country remains intact and its economy functions well. Coastal areas are markedly more stable and more prosperous than those in the north and east. The possibility of clashes with Pakistan is a recurrent danger. Meanwhile, the government feels confident enough to propose elections in the disputed state of Jammu and Kashmir in 1996 - the first in eight years. In the past, more than 20,000 people have died in the state fighting against Indian rule.

International Disputes India is in grave dispute with Pakistan over the latter's claims to part of the northern state of Kashmir, and despite repeated attempts at mediation the two countries remain in a state of some tension over the region. Relations with Nepal, with Bhutan and with China are also frequently soured by China's two claims in Arunachal Pradesh (in the far east) and in the far north - although a growing tolerance is creeping in. Sri Lankan militants have repeatedly called on India's Government to support them in their guerrilla activities for an independent Tamil state, and India did indeed become involved in the mid-1980s, although only as a peacekeeper. In 1994 the state of relations with the United States was deteriorating, after US accusations of human rights abuses in Punjab.

Economy India's economy grew by over 5% in 1994 and 1995 and the government expects a rate of more than 6% in 1996. Policy makers intend to hold inflation down to 6-8% (compared with 11.5% in 1994) by imposing a much tighter budget in the current fiscal year. Nevertheless, some analysts have doubts about the government's ability to cut the fiscal deficit while others argue that the recent round of cuts in tariffs and excise duties is not sufficient to keep the reform process on track. In other fields, the government's progress is not disputed. Exports are growing rapidly, improvements in the current account have swelled foreign exchange reserves to nearly $20 billion and the stock of foreign debt fell in 1995 by $270 million.

Main Industries India's agricultural sector still accounts for the bulk of GDP and employment, although most regions struggle to achieve self-sufficiency. Major export crops are cotton, jute, sugar cane and tea; otherwise, most people rely on rice, wheat (not usually maize), pulses and vegetables. Livestock are raised in most areas, despite religious objections to both beef and pork consumption in different areas. Industry is highly diversified and sufficiently developed to offer a high degree of self-sufficiency. Many of the largest are state-owned, but the government is making headway in selling these off to the private sector. Steel making, the manufacture of heavy machinery and equipment and of precision engineering products (which includes vehicle manufacture and machine tools) loom large in the industrial sector. Other rapidly growing industries include computer hardware and software and banking and finance. Textiles and clothing, food and leather goods manufacturers are smaller industries but account for a larger portion of export revenues.

Energy India has vast offshore oil and gas reserves which are now being tapped to provide an exportable surplus. However, domestically-mined coal is still the basic fuel in use.

	1993	1994	1995
Inflation (% change)	6.4	10.2	10.2
Exchange rate (per US$)	30.49	31.37	32.40
Interest rate (% per annum)	16.3	15.0	13.0
GDP (% real growth)	5.5	7.1	5.3
GDP (Million units of national currency)	8,010,300.0	9,456,200.0	10,973,031.2
GDP (US$ million)	262,718.9	301,440.9	338,673.8
GDP per capita (US$)	297.2	328.2	362.9
Consumption (Million units of national currency)	4,795,900.0	5,170,709.0	5,479,894.2
Consumption (US$ million)	157,294.2	164,829.7	169,132.5
Consumption per capita (US$)	178.0	179.4	181.2
Population, mid-year ('000)	883,910.0	918,570.0	933,170.0
Birth rate (per '000)	28.4	28.5	
Death rate (per '000)	10.3	10.3	
No. of households ('000)	178,517.6	182,496.0	190,864.1
Total exports (US$ million)	21,553.0	25,075.0	30,539.0
Total imports (US$ million)	22,761.0	26,846.0	34,399.0
Tourism receipts (US$ million)	1,568.0	1,752.0	
Tourist spending (US$ million)	567.0	661.0	678.3

Average household size 1995 (persons)	4.78				
Urban population 1995 (%)	26.8				
Age analysis (%) (1991)	*0-14* 36.0		*15-64* 59.9		*65+* 4.1
Population by sex (%) (1991)	*Male* 51.8		*Female* 48.2		
Life expectancy (years) (1993)	*Male* 60.4		*Female* 61.2		
Infant mortality (deaths per '000 live births) (1992)	88.0				
Adult literacy (%) (1990)	48.2				

TRADING PARTNERS

Major export destinations 1995 (% share)		Major import sources 1995 (% share)	
USA	18.3	USA	10.9
Japan	8.5	Germany	9.0
Germany	7.4	Japan	8.3
United Kingdom	6.6	United Kingdom	8.3

Indonesia

Area (km²) 1,919,445

Currency Rupiah (Rp = 100 sen)

Location Indonesia, the largest Muslim state in the world, is also one of the world's most geographically dispersed nations. Essentially, it comprises a group of archipelagos which sweep from the larger islands of Sumatra and Java (in the west), through Sulawesi (in the centre) and Timor (in the south) to the territory of Irian Jaya (Western New Guinea), the western half of the island whose eastern part is Papua New Guinea. To this is added the territory of Kalimtan and the Molucca Islands. The capital is Jakarta.

Head of State President Suharto

Head of Government President Suharto

Ruling Party Sekretariat Bersana Golongan (Golkar)

Political Structure Indonesia's ethnically diverse population is dominated by Javanese factions around President Suharto who exercises almost absolute power through the ruling Golkar coalition, which has strong army backing. The President is elected for a five-year term by the 1,000-member People's Consultative Assembly. Half the assemble is elected by universal franchise with the remainder appointed by the President, often from the armed forces.

Last Elections The ruling Golkar group was returned to power in the general elections of June 1992, with a slightly reduced majority in the 400-seat House of Representatives. Golkar won 299 seats and came first in all 27 provinces. The two legal opposition parties, the (Islamic) United Development Party and the (populist) Democratic Party of Indonesia, won 61 and 40 seats respectively. In March 1993 President Suharto was re-elected, unopposed.

Political Risk Approaching the age of 75, President Suharto is growing remote from his people. The death of his wife in 1996 robbed him of his closest advisor and could hasten his departure from office. Minor rebellions have long been simmering in East Timor (a territory taken over by Indonesia in the 1970s) and in the jungles of Irian Jaya and northern Sumatra. Now, riots, strikes and protests are occurring in less distant parts and more frequently. To some extent, the discontent is masked by growing prosperity but the new wealth is not evenly spread.

International Disputes Indonesia's domination of East Timor has been a constant source of international criticism which is renewed with each report of human rights violations in that country. Relations with Papua New Guinea are strained by the periodic rush of refugees fleeing from local fighting in Aceh Province. Indonesia also faces claims from Malaysia for the return of two islands, Sipadan and Ligitan, where Jakarta wants to develop tourist facilities. Finally, Indonesia is one of the many claimants for the sovereignty of the Spratly Islands in the South China Sea, where oil deposits are thought to have been located.

Economy Indonesia's growth has been steady throughout the 1990s, ranging between 6 and 7.75%. This consistency masks the country's huge problem with its foreign debt. The government claimed that foreign debt at the end of 1995 stood at around $88 billion, although private economists believe it exceeds $100 billion. This sum would be equivalent to $550 per person in a country where per capita income is just $750. Government officials must also deregulate the economy and disburse state revenues more efficiently if Indonesia is to attract more foreign investment. Some improvements in the investment environment are urgent since Indonesia faces increasingly intense competition for foreign capital from China, India and Vietnam.

Main Industries Agriculture accounts for the largest portion of total economic activity, though it matters less to the country's trade balance. Over 70% of the population are engaged in the sector, producing copra, rubber, kapok, spices and coffee for the export market and rice, fruit and vegetables for the domestic market. There is also a huge forestry industry dealing mainly in hardwoods. The heart of the manufacturing sector is the country's big conglomerates. Long known as "crony capitalists" because they receive so many government favours, these big firms are gradually becoming more dependent on market forces. The top 300 of these companies account for half of Indonesia's GDP and the most are owned by non-ethnic Indonesians (mainly Chinese). Minerals are especially important for the country's export performance. Indonesia is the world's third largest tin producer and has reserves of petroleum, coal, nickel, bauxite, phosphates, manganese, gold and silver. Crude oil alone contributes 80% of all foreign exchange revenues.

Energy The country has large supplies of oil and gas and is a member of the Organisation of Petroleum Exporting Countries (OPEC). Its energy policies, however, are usually determined in Jakarta and are relatively independent of OPEC. Because oil production is falling and domestic energy consumption is rising, Indonesia expects to become a net importer of oil in the next decade. It will need to develop new export-oriented industries to replace the lost foreign exchange earnings from oil.

	1993	1994	1995
Inflation (% change)	9.7	8.5	9.4
Exchange rate (per US$)	2,087.10	2,160.80	2,244.20
Interest rate (% per annum)	20.2	17.5	16.5
GDP (% real growth)	7.0	6.0	8.1
GDP (Billion units of national currency)	329,776.0	379,212.0	383,051.0
GDP (US$ million)	158,006.8	175,496.1	170,684.9
GDP per capita (US$)	842.3	920.4	881.0
Consumption (Billion units of national currency)	183,500.0	194,200.0	180,540.2
Consumption (US$ million)	87,921.0	89,874.1	80,447.5
Consumption per capita (US$)	468.7	471.3	415.2
Population, mid-year ('000)	187,600.0	190,680.0	193,750.0
Birth rate (per '000)	24.7	24.5	
Death rate (per '000)	11.6	11.5	
No. of households ('000)	40,730.6	41,320.0	43,064.8
Total exports (US$ million)	36,823.0	40,054.0	45,417.0
Total imports (US$ million)	28,328.0	31,985.0	40,918.0
Tourism receipts (US$ million)	2,955.0	3,129.0	
Tourist spending (US$ million)			

Average household size 1995 (persons)	4.38				
Urban population 1995 (%)	35.4				
Age analysis (%) (1990)	*0-14* 36.0		*15-64* 59.8		*65+* 4.1
Population by sex (%) (1990)	*Male* 50.5		*Female* 49.5		
Life expectancy (years) (1992)	*Male* 58.2		*Female* 61.9		
Infant mortality (deaths per '000 live births) (1993)	58.1				
Adult literacy (%) (1995)	84.0				

TRADING PARTNERS

Major export destinations 1995 (% share)		Major import sources 1995 (% share)	
Japan	42.2	Japan	29.0
USA	23.9	USA	9.5
South Korea	9.8	South Korea	8.5
Germany	5.7	Germany	7.8

Iran

Area (km²) 1,648,000

Currency Iranian rial (R = 100 dinars)

Location Iran, the largest non-Arab country in the Middle East, occupies the land mass between the Caucasus in the north (Turkey, Azerbaijan and Turkmenistan), the Afghan and Pakistani borders to the east and south-east, and Iraq to the west. It lies on the east coast of the Persian (Arabian) Gulf, facing Saudi Arabia, Bahrain and the United Arab Emirates. Iran has sizeable oil resources beneath its largely desert terrain. The capital is Tehran.

Head of State President Ali Akhbar Rafsanjani (1989)

Head of Government President Ali Akhbar Rafsanjani

Ruling Party There are no officially recognised political parties.

Political Structure Modern Iran has its foundations in the Islamic revolution of 1979/1980, when the religious supporters of Ayatollah Ruhollah Khomeini overcame and ousted Shah Reza Pahlavi. The last legal political party, the Islamic Republican Party, was disbanded in 1987, at which point religion became the main political criterion. Under the present system, political power rests loosely in the clerical and religious hierarchy, which exercises its authority mainly through the 76-member Assembly of Experts.

Last Elections The last elections took place in March and April 1996 when Iranians voted for a new 270-seat Majlis (Parliament). Hard-line followers of the late Ayatollah Khomeini, known as the Association of Combatant Clergymen, took only 102 seats and lost their majority in the Majlis. The results represent a minor victory for Rafsanjani and his technocrats. Their two-month-old party, which is known as the Servants of the Constitution, will take 90 seats in the new parliament. Although it can not initiate laws, the Majlis can block the president's policies and its speaker has considerable influence. The new parliament will also serve as a springboard for the presidential election in 1997, when Rafsanjani, having served two successive terms, must step down.

Political Risk Iran's mullahs remained firmly entrenched in the government but there are divisions within the leadership. Some believe that the incompetence of Iran's political leaders has hurt the country. Open debate and criticism of top government officials has also become more common. Many observers expect that technocrats will eventually displace the mullahs and assume control over most government functions. Even if they do, it will be a slow process. Although the religious authorities know that political reform is a very popular cause, they are likely to remain in power for some time.

International Disputes Iran's disputes with Iraq reflect not only the ethnic disputes between Arabs and Iranians, but also differences between the militant adherents of Iran's predominantly Shia religion and the orthodox Sunni Islam practised in most other areas of the Middle East. Although the two countries reached a settlement in 1990 under which both retreated to their 1975 borders, no peace treaty has yet been signed. Israel has accused Iran of providing financial and logistical support to the Hamas in their efforts to undermine the Israel-Palestine peace treaty. Iran also lays claim, in principle, to the entire territory of Bahrain, although it has not asserted its territorial rights since 1979. However, it does have a live claim to three strategic islands located in the Straits of Hormuz which belong to the United Arab Emirates. The USA supports the UAE in this dispute and the two countries launched joint naval exercises in the area in 1996. Representatives of the EU have told Iran that it must publicly reject support of terrorism before relations can improve.

Economy Iran has gradually begun to move away from some of the more extreme economic views that it embraced in the 1980s. In general, economics rather than ideology is starting to take Iran's attempt to develop trade with Central Asia, its pursuit of some $6 billion of foreign investment for its oil and gas industry and its expected bid to join the World Trade Organisation. The powerful bazaaris continue to monopolise the economy but their hold is gradually being eroded.

Main Industries Iran depends heavily on the oil industry, although its economy is more diversified than that of most its neighbours. The country's oilfields, all of which are nationalised, have been worked by the National Iranian Oil Company since 1979 when foreign companies were removed. European oil companies now want to resume these contacts but the US government opposes these moves and has unsuccessfully tried to initiate an embargo of the country. Iran is currently producing about three million barrels of oil per day, a sixth of the entire total for the OPEC countries, and has several petrochemicals and plastics installations. The development of non-oil exports is hindered by the bazaaris - the powerful monopolistic traders who offer vital support to the Islamic regime. Agriculture generates a fifth of GDP and is concentrated in the fertile valleys of the north and west. Wheat, barley, rice, cotton and sugar beet are grown for mainly domestic consumption; there are also timber resources in the north and west.

Energy Iran is entirely self-sufficient in oil and gas, which generates over 95% of its total fuel requirements. Nevertheless, a sixth of its electricity comes from hydro-electric sources.

	1993	1994	1995
Inflation (% change)	21.2	31.5	49.6
Exchange rate (per US$)	1,267.77	1,748.75	2,498.63
Interest rate			
GDP (% real growth)			
GDP (Billion units of national currency)	93,610.0	129,777.0	
GDP (US$ million)	778,680.0	682,977.8	730,000.0
GDP per capita (US$)	13,313.0	11,424.9	11,932.4
Consumption (Billion units of national currency)	613,362.3	742,080.3	
Consumption (US$ million)	483,812.0	424,349.0	
Consumption per capita (US$)	8,271.7	7,098.5	
Population, mid-year ('000)	58,490.0	59,780.0	61,178.1
Birth rate (per '000)	34.8	42.4	
Death rate (per '000)		7.8	
No. of households ('000)	11,072.6	11,373.4	11,966.1
Total exports (US$ million)	21,884.0	196,616.0	
Total imports (US$ million)	1,748.8	12,424.0	
Tourism receipts (US$ million)	39.0	34.0	
Tourist spending (US$ million)			

Average household size 1995 (persons)	4.99		
Urban population 1995 (%)	59.0		
Age analysis (%) (1986)	*0-14* 45.5	*15-64* 51.5	*65+* 3.1
Population by sex (%) (1986)	*Male* 51.1	*Female* 48.9	
Life expectancy (years) (1990)	*Male* 65.8	*Female* 66.7	
Infant mortality (deaths per '000 live births) (1992)	53.0		
Adult literacy (%) (1991)	65.7		

TRADING PARTNERS

Major export destinations 1995 (% share)		Major import sources 1995 (% share)	
Japan	13.6	Germany	13.0
Italy	7.4	United Arab Emirates	9.1
France	6.2	Japan	6.1
Greece	4.1	Argentina	5.3

Iraq

Area (km²)   438,445

Currency   Iraqi dinar (ID = 100 fils)

Location   Iraq, situated across the Persian (Arabian) Gulf from Iran, is much less of a desert state, being watered by the Tigris and Euphrates rivers. The country borders on Saudi Arabia and Kuwait in the south, on Syria and Jordan in the west, and on Turkey in the north. It has substantial oil resources. The capital is Baghdad.

Head of State   President Saddam Hussein (1979)

Head of Government   None

Ruling Party   Arab Ba'ath Socialist Party

Political Structure   The overthrow of the monarchy in 1958 led to the creation of a republic which has been dominated since the late 1970s by Saddam Hussein. Hussein, who has been chief of the armed forces for most of this time, was also Prime Minister from 1979 to March 1991. The President is elected by the Revolutionary Command Council (RCC) from among its members, and appoints the Cabinet. The RCC shares legislative powers with the 250-member National Assembly, which is elected by universal suffrage for a term of five years.

Last Elections   A national referendum to affirm Hussein as president for seven more years took place in October 1995. The Kurdish minority held their own (officially unrecognised) elections to the (equally unrecognised) 105-member Iraqi Kurdistan National Assembly in May 1992, when the Kurdistan Democratic Party and the Patriotic Union of Kurdistan each obtained 50 seats. The remaining five seats were reserved for Christian Assyrians.

Political Risk   The international embargo on trade with Iraq has some holes that European companies have slipped through. Its effects, however, have devastated the domestic consumer market. Sanctions allow food and medicine to be imported. But without oil sales, there is no money to pay for them. Over 4 million people are thought to be at severe nutritional risk. Political opposition among the population remains at best muted, and the most serious instances of political opposition in the Kurdish areas of northern Iraq were met with brutal force by government forces in 1994 and 1995. There have been several unofficial reports of coup attempts against Saddam. Yet the anti-Saddam forces outside the country remain disorganised and ineffective.

International Disputes   Like Qaddafi, Saddam has become one of the world's international pariahs and will never be able to rehabilitate his reputation. Although Iraq's attack on Kuwait resulted from a long-standing territorial claim against that country, its action has isolated it from other Arab states. Iraq also has a border dispute with Saudi Arabia over an ill-defined treaty, which has been shelved by the creation of a 300-kilometre diamond-shaped neutral zone where neither is allowed to be active. Meanwhile, the ending of the war with Iran in 1990 has yet to be sealed with the signature of a bilateral peace treaty.

Economy   The international isolation of the economy in the aftermath of the Gulf War has seriously reduced standards of living. Iraq used to import almost three-quarters of its food, but prices now put imports out of the reach of most. The monthly cost of basic foodstuffs on the open market for a family of five is the nominal equivalent of $26 - a monthly salary for a professional. Most Iraqis - about 70% of the population - are forced to survive on government rations, which supply only half of minimum calorific requirements. The UN estimates that nearly 30% of children under five are severely malnourished and that the infant mortality rate in this once prosperous country has risen to match that of impoverished Sudan.

Main Industries   Despite repeated attempts to have the UN's decision reversed, Iraq has yet to negotiate the lifting of the international embargo on exports of oil. The country is still allowed to produce for domestic consumption and is thought to be exporting some oil surreptitiously. The oil industry was nationalised in 1972 and contributes 98% of all export revenues in a typical year. Agriculture is well developed in Iraq, and although rainfall patterns are crucial, it can often produce two harvests a year. The sector suffers, however, from a lack of structural investment, and the soil is declining in quality.

Energy   Iraq is fully self-sufficient in oil, gas and electricity. But the UN sanctions mean in effect that it can only produce about one million barrels per day, against a total capacity of 3.8 million barrels per day.

	1993	1994	1995
Inflation (% change)	10.0	-0.8	2.0
Exchange rate (per US$)	0.31	0.31	0.56
Interest rate			
GDP (% real growth)	-9.8	-8.6	
GDP (Million units of national currency)	16,895.1	15,314.8	25,591.7
GDP (US$ million)	53,960.7	49,402.6	45,456.0
GDP per capita (US$)	2,774.3	2,484.1	2,231.8
Consumption (Million units of national currency)	11,984.3	10,863.3	18,153.0
Consumption (US$ million)	38,276.3	35,042.9	32,243.4
Consumption per capita (US$)	1,967.9	1,762.0	1,583.1
Population, mid-year ('000)	19,450.0	19,887.8	20,367.3
Birth rate (per '000)	26.7	34.1	
Death rate (per '000)	6.7	7.3	
No. of households ('000)	3,605.1	3,704.7	3,900.0
Total exports (US$ million)			
Total imports (US$ million)			
Tourism receipts (US$ million)			
Tourist spending (US$ million)			

Average household size 1995 (persons)	5.10				
Urban population 1995 (%)	74.6				
Age analysis (%) (1988)	*0-14* 44.5		*15-64* 52.1		*65+* 3.4
Population by sex (%) (1988)	*Male* 51.4		*Female* 48.6		
Life expectancy (years) (1990)	*Male* 77.4		*Female* 78.2		
Infant mortality (deaths per '000 live births) (1993)	73.0				
Adult literacy (%) (1990)	59.7				

Ireland

Area (km²) 68,895

Currency Punt (I£ = 100 pence)

Location The Republic of Ireland (Eire) comprises the greater part of an island off the west coast of Great Britain, the remaining northern part of the island forming part of the United Kingdom. With little mountainous terrain but considerable areas of hills and down, Ireland's wet though pleasantly mild climate contributes to good agricultural conditions. The capital is Dublin.

Head of State President Mary Robinson (1990)

Head of Government John Bruton (December 1994)

Ruling Party Fine Gael leads a coalition with Labour and the Democratic Left.

Political Structure Ireland's President is elected for a seven-year term by universal suffrage, but most executive powers are exercised by a Prime Minister and Cabinet appointed from among the National Parliament (Oireachtas). The House of Representatives (Dail Eireann), or Lower House, has 166 members elected by universal suffrage for five years, and the Senate (Seanad Eireann), or Upper House, has 60.

Last Elections A general election was held in November 1992, when the Labour Party made sweeping gains at the expense of Fianna Fáil and Fine Gael. The final distribution of seats in the Dail was Fianna Fáil 68, Fine Gael 45, Labour Party 33, Progressive Democrats 10 and Democratic Left 4. However, the coalition led by Fianna Fáil collapsed in November 1994 after the Labour Party withdrew, and a Fine Gael-led coalition came into office shortly afterwards. President Mary Robinson, the country's first female President, was elected in November 1990.

Political Risk Ireland's Emergency Powers Act - a law designed to prevent terrorism - was repealed in 1994. The decision reflects an overall improvement in the country's situation and has made investors feel more secure about their commitment to the country. In fact, the rapprochement with the UK over Northern Ireland has made a major contribution to the successful functioning of Ireland's political system. The country has a strong commitment to the EU, but it still faces the prospect that the US and Japanese investors that have provided the main impetus for industrial expansion in earlier years will begin to look elsewhere as the EU becomes more tightly integrated.

International Disputes Ireland maintains a constitutional claim to the territory of Northern Ireland - an issue which has given rise to three decades of violent terrorist activity against the authorities in Britain and in Northern Ireland and has polarised public opinion among both the predominantly Protestant population of those territories and the predominantly Roman Catholic population of Ireland itself. Conditions improved significantly in 1995 but new terrorist attacks in the UK during 1996 have complicated the situation.

Economy Ireland's economy began to recover from recession in 1994-95 with reported rates of growth which were some of the highest in the OECD. One result was an improvement in the country's crippling unemployment problem. Nevertheless, the jobless rate (13% in 1995) is still the second highest in the EU after Spain. The recent improvement in the economy has also served to stem the flow of net migration, a trend which has caused Ireland to lose many of its young and more skilled workers in the past. One reason for Ireland's recovery is the impressive performance of its export sector. Another is the subsidies it receives from the as a relatively poor member, Ireland gets structural funds worth more than 2% of its GDP. A third boost to the economy is the government's practice of giving grants and low corporate-tax rates to foreign-owned firms specialising in computers, pharmaceuticals and financial services. The biggest worry is public finance. With the economy growing so fast, spending on roads and other infrastructure must rise and is producing a deficit. Health and education are other areas which require additional cash.

Main Industries Ireland's economy has traditionally relied to a substantial extent on farming, but in recent years the industrial base has developed rapidly due mainly to a concerted policy of government sponsorship, which includes the creation of free trade zones. Industry now contributes about 35% of GDP, compared to just under 10% from agriculture. The country has a comparatively skilled work force and relies heavily on the service sector to generate most of its income and employment. Services presently account for around 55% of GDP and employ some 58% of the workforce.

Energy Ireland has large reserves of coal and peat, but its primary requirement is for imports of oil and gas. Some deposits have been located in the Irish Sea.

	1993	1994	1995
Inflation (% change)	1.4	2.3	2.5
Exchange rate (per US$)	0.68	0.67	0.62
Interest rate (% per annum)	9.9	6.1	6.6
GDP (% real growth)	4.0	5.3	2.0
GDP (Million units of national currency)	32,290.0	34,783.4	36,350.0
GDP (US$ million)	47,276.7	52,102.2	58,281.2
GDP per capita (US$)	13,242.8	14,553.7	16,279.7
Consumption (Million units of national currency)	18,065.0	18,736.0	19,377.0
Consumption (US$ million)	26,449.5	28,064.7	31,067.8
Consumption per capita (US$)	7,408.8	7,839.3	8,678.2
Population, mid-year ('000)	3,570.0	3,580.0	3,580.0
Birth rate (per '000)	14.0	13.4	14.3
Death rate (per '000)	8.6	8.6	8.6
No. of households ('000)	867.0	865.3	865.0
Total exports (US$ million)	28,611.0	34,370.0	
Total imports (US$ million)	21,386.0	25,508.0	
Tourism receipts (US$ million)	1,639.0	1,829.4	
Tourist spending (US$ million)	1,256.0	1,401.9	1,551.9

Average household size 1995 (persons)	3.93				
Urban population 1995 (%)	57.5				
Age analysis (%) (1995)	*0-14*	26.8	*15-64*	61.8	*65+* 11.4
Population by sex (%) (1995)	*Male*	49.7	*Female*	50.3	
Life expectancy (years) (1993)	*Male*	72.3	*Female*	77.9	
Infant mortality (deaths per '000 live births) (1993)	6.0				
Adult literacy (%) (1984)	99.0				

TRADING PARTNERS

Major export destinations 1995 (% share)		Major import sources 1995 (% share)	
United Kingdom	26.1	United Kingdom	36.7
Germany	14.1	USA	16.7
France	9.1	Germany	7.2
USA	8.4	Japan	5.5

Israel

Area (km²) 20,770

Currency New shekel (NIS = 100 agorot)

Location Israel, which occupies the lower third of the eastern Mediterranean coastline, was formed in 1948 as a thin strip of mainly Jordanian and Palestinian-owned land. But its territory was extended in the Six Day War of 1967 to include territories seized from Jordan on the West Bank of the Jordan River, as well as some Syrian and Egyptian land. The country has a typically Middle Eastern climate, with warm summers. The capital is Jerusalem.

Head of State President Ezer Weizmann (May 1993)

Head of Government Benjamin Netanyahu (May 1996)

Ruling Party Likud Party leads a right-wing alliance.

Political Structure The territory of Israel was created in 1948 to provide a homeland for displaced Jews. Carved out of mainly Palestinian-owned land, it was effectively extended after the 1967 war to the West Bank territory, including East Jerusalem (formerly in Jordan). A seven-year campaign of Palestinian disruption and non-co-operation was partially resolved in 1994 with Israeli recognition of Palestinian autonomy in the West Bank and the creation of a Palestinian parliament. Israel also withdrew from the Gaza Strip in 1994, after occupying it since 1967. Israel has an non-executive President and a Parliament (Knesset) which consists of 120 members. In 1996, a change in election procedures was introduced which allows voters to cast two ballots, one for the prime minister and the other for a party. Until now, people only voted for one of thirty-odd parties which then haggled over the prime minister. The change is meant to reduce the negotiating power of the small parties.

Last Elections Elections to the 120-member Knesset (Lower House of Parliament) took place in May 1996 following the assassination of Itzhak Rabin. The result was a narrow win for Benjamin Netanyahu and the Likud Party over Shimon Peres' Labour Party. Overall, both the Likud and Labour Parties have a reduced number of seats in the new Knesset while a number of smaller parties, such as the Tsomet, Moledet and Tehit, have all boosted their representation. Presidential elections were held in March 1993, when Ezer Weizmann was elected by a large majority.

Political Risk An unwritten agreement brokered by the Americans in 1993 confined Israel's war with Hizbullah to military targets in Israel's occupation zone in southern Lebanon. That agreement broke down prior to the elections in 1996 when Israel attacked Beirut, sealed its port and forced thousands to flee villages in southern Lebanon. Israel's relations with Syria are the reason for this small war. The Syrians control Hizbullah and the Israelis hope to force Damascus to reopen peace negotiations which have remained dormant for the time being. This strategy, however, was formulated when the Labour Party was in power and may be altered now that the Likud Party leads the country. The business community in Israel is also uneasy about the change in leadership, fearing that the new administration's hard-line approach will jeopardise its new-found access to markets in surrounding countries.

International Disputes Israel's agreement to Palestinian control over the West Bank, along with peace agreements with Egypt and Jordan, had fuelled hopes of a wider peace throughout the western world. These hopes were thrown into doubt after Israel's move against Lebanon in April 1996. This was, the first time Israel had invaded its northern neighbour since 1982. Israel hopes to isolate Syria which continues to resist peace negotiations by punishing its Hizbullah representatives in Lebanon. The recent Israel-Turkey security pacts and the stationing of a US air squadron in Jordan are all part of this plan. Military force is now intended to persuade the Syrians to rein in Hizbullah and enter into new peace negotiations. The risk, however, is that it could create even stronger ties between Syria and the Lebanese people.

Economy The Israeli economy is actually growing at a satisfactory rate and should attract more foreign investors if the peace momentum can be sustained. However, the country's perennial trade deficit and its soaring inflation have created pressures which have worsened since the arrival of thousands of refugees from Eastern Europe in the early 1990s. Despite its general commitment to free trade and free enterprise, Israel's economy actually retains many of the collectivist hallmarks of its Government's historical predecessors, in its nationalised industries and its comprehensive social care systems - excluding the West Bank.

Main Industries Israel's agricultural sector is highly productive, thanks in a large part to the country's mild climate and fertile soil. Wheat, oranges, strawberries, cut flowers, avocados, millet and sorghum are the main crops, although the country produces a very wide variety of fruits. The area under cultivation includes a substantial part of the occupied West Bank. The country also boasts a wide range of industrial activities which include many advanced and sophisticated firms involved in the production of military products, electronics, aerospace and computer software. It is also a major clothing and textiles manufacturer. Although Israel has no significant mineral resources, diamond cutting and polishing are major export activities.

Energy Israel depends on imports for all basic fuels. It has no hydro-electric capacity.

	1993	1994	1995
Inflation (% change)	10.9	12.3	10.0
Exchange rate (per US$)	2.83	3.01	3.01
Interest rate (% per annum)	16.4	17.4	20.2
GDP (% real growth)	3.2	7.1	3.5
GDP (Million units of national currency)	184,078.0	221,456.0	252,127.7
GDP (US$ million)	65,042.9	73,546.5	83,743.9
GDP per capita (US$)	12,365.6	13,670.4	14,812.7
Consumption (Million units of national currency)	116,317.0	141,959.0	163,957.1
Consumption (US$ million)	41,100.0	47,145.2	54,458.1
Consumption per capita (US$)	7,813.7	8,763.1	9,632.6
Population, mid-year ('000)	5,260.0	5,380.0	5,653.5
Birth rate (per '000)	21.4	21.2	
Death rate (per '000)	6.3	6.4	
No. of households ('000)	1,354.7	1,362.0	1,438.3
Total exports (US$ million)	14,826.0	16,881.0	19,028.0
Total imports (US$ million)	22,623.0	25,237.0	29,632.0
Tourism receipts (US$ million)	2,110.0	2,294.2	
Tourist spending (US$ million)	2,313.0	2,514.9	2,905.0

Average household size 1995 (persons)	3.75		
Urban population 1995 (%)	90.6		
Age analysis (%) (1992)	*0-14* 31.1	*15-64* 59.6	*65+* 9.2
Population by sex (%)			
Life expectancy (years) (1991)	*Male* 75.1	*Female* 78.5	
Infant mortality (deaths per '000 live births) (1991)	9.2		
Adult literacy (%) (1992)	94.9		

TRADING PARTNERS

Major export destinations 1995 (% share)		Major import sources 1995 (% share)	
USA	30.4	USA	19.5
Japan	6.8	Belgium/Luxembourg	11.1
United Kingdom	5.7	Germany	10.5
Germany	5.6	Italy	8.4

Italy

Area (km²)   301,245

Currency   Lira (= 100 centesimi)

Location   Located in the centre of southern Europe, Italy is a long strip of land, seldom exceeding 200 km in width, which extends south-eastward for some 1,000 km into the Mediterranean. In the north, where it meets with France, Switzerland, Austria and Slovenia, the territory broadens out to include the industrial cities of Milan, Turin and Genoa; in the south it divides into two peninsulas, the lower of which almost connects with the island of Sicily. The capital is Rome.

Head of State   President Oscar Luigi Scalfaro (1992)

Head of Government   Romano Prodi (1996)

Ruling Party   A multi-party coalition led by the Olive Tree and the Democratic Party of the Left (former communist party)

Political Structure   Italy has been a republic since 1946, when it abolished the monarchy and initiated the present system, whereby a President, elected by Parliament for a seven-year term, exercises only semi-executive functions. In practice, however, the country's repeated political crises demand almost constant political involvement by the president. The 630-member Chamber of Deputies (Lower House) is elected for five years by universal suffrage, as are all but seven of the 315-member Senate. Italy's political system has been continually plagued by mounting evidence of political corruption and graft. The types of reforms that are necessary to ensure stable governments and working parliamentary majorities have eluded the country's leaders throughout the 1990s.

Last Elections   The general elections held in April 1996 yielded a victory for the centre-left Olive Tree coalition. The group gained control of the Senate, claiming 157 of the 315 seats, and came close to doing the same in the Chamber of Deputies where it won 284 of 630 seats. Although the results are not an overwhelming triumph for the centre-left, they amount to a rejection for Silvio Berlusconi's right wing Freedom Alliance which had been pressing for new elections. The Northern League, which defected from the Berlusconi government in 1994 and ran on its own this time, fared better. The League is now the largest party in the area north of the river Po, which is one of the richest bits of Europe. This election, the third in four years, was the first where voters were offered a clear choice between the centre-left and the centre-right.

Political Risk   Italy's politics are characterised by extreme splintering of political opinion, and all governments are finely balanced coalitions. In recent years the campaign of the security forces against organised crime has led to a series of charges against senior political figures. The delicate political balance, and its consequent need for compromise at all times, has prevented the government from addressing important matters of electoral reform or the severe inefficiencies in the state sector which controls most major industries. Recent governments have proven equally ineffective in confronting organised crime which exerts a heavy influence on local politics, especially in the south of the country.

International Disputes   Italy has no active and outstanding territorial disputes, having never accepted the claims made by some Austrian groups in respect of the German-speaking South Tyrolean regions in Trentino. However, it does demand compensation from Slovenia for the dispossession of Italian citizens during the post-war era.

Economy   Italy's considerable dependence on the state sector remains a source of some concern within the EU, but most observers expect the new government to press ahead with aggressive plans for privatisation. Success in this endeavour would help to reduce the country's massive public debt which has slowed the rate of growth throughout the 1990s. Finally, political stability should allow the lira to return to the European exchange rate system. Reforms of the civil service and pension programme have been delayed by the political paralysis and must be tackled by the new government.

Main Industries   Italy's well-diversified economy includes a large and well-developed industrial sector producing sophisticated engineering, electronics, chemicals, steel products and above all food products. Many of the heavier industries are state-owned and a number are making large losses. However, Italy also has a great many small and medium-sized companies that are highly competitive, flexible and profitable. The bulk of these smaller firms are located in the north of the country. Agriculture is well diversified, producing soft fruits and vegetables (especially tomatoes, courgettes and similar water-dependent products) as well as wheat, olives and citrus products for export. The most fertile areas are in the north; but in the south, the population depends almost exclusively on agriculture. Italy has no indigenous minerals, although its metal processing plants are important. It does, however, have a very large services sector.

Energy   Italy has some oil resources in the area around Sicily, but otherwise it relies on supplies from Algeria and Libya for most of its oil and gas. Solid fuels account for less than 10% of all needs and hydro-electricity less than 4%.

	1993	1994	1995
Inflation (% change)	4.5	4.0	5.3
Exchange rate (per US$)	1,573.70	1,612.40	1,628.60
Interest rate (% per annum)	13.9	11.2	13.9
GDP (% real growth)	-1.0	1.2	-2.1
GDP ('000 million units of national currency)	1,559.4	1,641.0	1,691.9
GDP (US$ million)	990,913.1	1,017,737.5	1,038,867.7
GDP per capita (US$)	17,363.1	17,794.8	18,125.3
Consumption ('000 million units of national currency)	961.6	1,030.3	1,089.0
Consumption (US$ million)	611,030.7	638,982.9	668,654.7
Consumption per capita (US$)	10,706.7	11,172.4	11,666.1
Population, mid-year ('000)	57,070.0	57,193.0	57,316.0
Birth rate (per '000)	9.4	9.3	9.3
Death rate (per '000)	9.5	9.5	9.6
No. of households ('000)	21,472.0	22,234.1	22,260.0
Total exports (US$ million)	169,153.0	189,805.0	
Total imports (US$ million)	148,273.0	167,685.0	
Tourism receipts (US$ million)	20,521.0	21,341.8	
Tourist spending (US$ million)	13,053.0	13,575.1	14,205.5

Average household size 1995 (persons)	2.44				
Urban population 1995 (%)	66.6				
Age analysis (%) (1995)	*0-14* 15.1		*15-64* 69.0		*65+* 15.9
Population by sex (%) (1995)	*Male* 48.4		*Female* 51.6		
Life expectancy (years) (1994)	*Male* 74.7		*Female* 81.2		
Infant mortality (deaths per '000 live births) (1992)	8.3				
Adult literacy (%) (1990)	97.1				

TRADING PARTNERS

Major export destinations 1995 (% share)		Major import sources 1995 (% share)	
Germany	18.9	Germany	15.2
France	13.0	France	13.8
USA	7.4	United Kingdom	5.8
United Kingdom	6.2	Netherlands	5.4

Jamaica

Area (km²) 11,425

Currency Jamaican dollar (J$ = 100 cents)

Location Jamaica is centrally located in the western Caribbean, lying some 145 km south of Cuba and 160 km south-west of Haiti. The country has a pleasant climate, although subject to hurricanes and heavy rains in the October-November period. The capital is Kingston.

Head of State HM Queen Elizabeth II

Head of Government Rt Hon. Percival Patterson (March 1989)

Ruling Party People's National Party (PNP)

Political Structure Jamaica, an independent member of the Commonwealth, is ruled by a Prime Minister and Cabinet who are drawn from a 60-member House of Representatives (Lower House), elected by universal suffrage for a five-year term. The Governor-General, who represents the Crown, has only formal functions. There is a 21-member Senate (Upper House), whose functions are mainly advisory. The constituency character of the electoral system means that parliamentary representation is often out of proportion to the levels of actual electoral support.

Last Elections General elections to the House of Representatives were held in March 1993, when the People's National Party of Percival Patterson won a landslide victory, obtaining 54 of the 60 parliamentary seats, while the Jamaican Labour Party won only six seats. However, the PNP did less well in urban centres than in the country as a whole.

Political Risk Jamaica has a history of acrimonious relations with its international lenders. The situation culminated in 1996 when the country ceased to be a borrowing member of the IMF. Government officials claimed a victory but with foreign reserves covering only three months of imports it may be a pyrrhic one. IMF agreements in recent years have become synonymous with deterioration of the economy and the end of the relationship in no way indicates that the wayward economy is settling down. The value of the currency sank by nearly 20% in the second half of 1995 and if any serious economic shocks should now occur the government can not turn to international lenders for help.

Economy Jamaica's economy has made substantial progress since the 1980s when a combination of protectionism, extravagant public spending and falling commodity prices plunged the economy into a recession. The structure of the island's economy continues to be a problem, however. Many industries have considerable excess capacity and are making losses or recording only marginal profits. Businesses claim that the high interest rates - a government tool for damping demand and reducing pressure on the exchange rate - are driving them out of business. The country has extremely high levels of unemployment and a currency which is constantly under pressure in international markets. Rates of growth remain low (just under 1% in 1994 and 1995) and will not improve until Jamaica's structural and macroeconomic problems have been addressed.

Main Industries Jamaica's most important industry is tourism. American and Canadian visitors are the main source of revenues but the industry has also been targeting the European market. The number of international visitors has been steadily growing at a time when many other Caribbean destinations have seen the tourist revenues slump. A sizeable portion of the tourist sector is state-owned but this has not discouraged a strong surge in foreign investment. Agriculture contributes only 5-10% of GDP, but employs a quarter of the workforce. Sugar cane, coffee, pineapples and bananas are grown for export, while rice, maize and vegetables are produced for domestic consumption. The tropical climate makes for rapid growth, but vulnerability to hurricanes is a problem. The industrial base is fairly well diversified with food processing, textiles, clothing and timber and wood products being especially important. The island also has a major petrochemicals plant, and export-free zones have been established to encourage further diversification.

Energy Jamaica imports almost all of its energy requirements, although it obtains Venezuelan and Mexican supplies at favourable prices.

	1993	1994	1995
Inflation (% change)	22.1	35.1	19.9
Exchange rate (per US$)	24.95	31.93	33.19
Interest rate (% per annum)	43.7	49.5	43.6
GDP (% real growth)	9.9	1.6	0.9
GDP (Million units of national currency)	95,785.0	131,497.9	159,085.0
GDP (US$ million)	3,839.1	4,118.3	4,793.2
GDP per capita (US$)	1,593.0	1,647.3	1,894.5
Consumption (Million units of national currency)	57,979.0	79,554.8	96,194.7
Consumption (US$ million)	2,323.8	2,491.5	2,898.3
Consumption per capita (US$)	964.2	996.6	1,145.6
Population, mid-year ('000)	2,410.0	2,500.0	2,530.0
Birth rate (per '000)	26.1	23.7	21.2
Death rate (per '000)	4.9	5.4	
No. of households ('000)	480.5	500.9	521.3
Total exports (US$ million)	1,069.0	1,192.0	1,099.0
Total imports (US$ million)	2,097.0	2,164.0	2,709.3
Tourism receipts (US$ million)	942.0	988.7	
Tourist spending (US$ million)	64.0	67.2	78.2

Average household size 1995 (persons)	4.61		
Urban population 1995 (%)	53.7		
Age analysis (%) (1990)	*0-14* 39.7	*15-64* 53.4	*65+* 6.9
Population by sex (%) (1990)	*Male* 49.0	*Female* 51.0	
Life expectancy (years) (1990-95)	*Male* 71.4	*Female* 75.8	
Infant mortality (deaths per '000 live births) (1992)	17.0		
Adult literacy (%) (1990)	98.4		

TRADING PARTNERS

Major export destinations 1995 (% share)		Major import sources 1995 (% share)	
USA	43.3	USA	54.6
United Kingdom	12.7	Mexico	5.4
Canada	8.6	Japan	4.8
Norway	7.6	United Kingdom	4.4

Japan

Area (km²) 369,700

Currency Yen (= 100 sen)

Location Located (at its nearest point) 150 km east of the Korean peninsula and about 1,500 km north-east of the Chinese mainland, Japan is situated in the northern Pacific Ocean with the Sea of Japan to its east. The country mainly comprises four volcanic islands - Hokkaido, Honshu, Shikoku and Kyushu, of which Honshu is the largest. There are also a considerable number of smaller islands. The climate is temperate, with mild winters. The capital is Tokyo.

Head of State HM Emperor Akihito (1989)

Head of Government Ryutaro Hashimoto (1995)

Ruling Party Liberal Democratic Party coalition

Political Structure Japan is a constitutional monarchy in which the Emperor Akihito plays only a ceremonial role. All political power is vested in a Diet (Parliament), which includes a 512-member House of Representatives elected by universal suffrage for a term of four years, and a 252-member Senate that serves a six-year term of office with half of its members coming up for election every three years.

Last Elections The general elections of July 1993 produced a defeat for the Liberal Democratic Party (LDP), which had held an absolute majority since 1955. Allegations of corruption involving senior LDP figures led voters to turn to breakaway parties, including the Japan New Party of Morihiro Hosokawa, the New Harbinger Party of Asahiko Mihara, and the New Born Party of Tsutomo Hata. A series of coalition governments, some of them excluding the LDP, followed over the next two and a half years. In 1995, Tomiichi Murayama brought the prime minister's office back to the LDP but resigned in January 1996 for reasons of incompetence. He was replaced by Ryutaro Hashimoto who is admired for his detailed grasp of policy and his spirited defiance of American trade negotiators.

Political Risk In power for almost half a century, Hashimoto's LDP is now being strongly challenged by Ichiro Ozawa's New Frontier Party. Issues such as electoral reform, political corruption, trade relations and tax reform have been ignored for years but are likely to determine who the winner of the next elections will be. Japan is gradually moving away from its long-standing tradition of bureaucratic control over virtually every aspect of the economy. The eventual result is still unclear but it will almost certainly represent a welcome change in the country's economic landscape.

International Disputes Japan had an important territorial dispute with the former Soviet Union, concerning the ownership of the four southern Kurile islands which were seized by the USSR after the Second World War. Meanwhile, Japan has been attempting to address its record of barbarism in Korea, Malaysia and mainland China during the 1930s and 1940s. A formal apology for war crimes and related atrocities was issued by Japan in 1995, the 50th anniversary of the ending of the Second World War. Unrest and anti-American sentiment on Okinawa has led to a renegotiation of the agreement on US forces on the island. Several bases will be closed over the next 5-7 years.

Economy After several years of stagnation, Japan's economy is beginning to pick up again. Growth in the last quarter of 1995 was strong and economists are predicting an increase of about 3% in 1996. The initial impetus for this recovery is coming from government spending and corporate investment but the restructuring that many companies have gone through should help to sustain the pace of growth in the future. Industrial production, corporate profits and construction are all showing big improvements and should ensure that growth remains healthy for the next couple of years.

Main Industries Japan's economy relies to an unusual extent on its manufacturing industries, which account for more than half of the country's GDP. Japan is known for its sophisticated high-technology products and its motor industries, both of which have traditionally focused on export markets. Steel, shipbuilding, chemicals and consumer electronics are other important industries. Agriculture is the main activity in most non-urban areas and farms are generally small and fairly inefficient. Rice, wheat, fruit and vegetables are grown for the domestic market, and fishing is an important industry. Japan imposes high tariffs on imports of many food products. The financial services industry is legendary for its size if not its sophistication.

Energy Japan's total reliance on imports for its oil supplies has been a major problem in the past. The country's energy sector is surrounding by a thicket of regulations which not only protects its firms but keeps prices high. Japanese consumers pay about 40% more per kilowatt-hour than do Germans, and the price differential with the USA is even greater. Some of these regulations will be dismantled in 1996, making energy slightly cheaper and energy suppliers slightly less profitable.

	1993	1994	1995
Inflation (% change)	1.3	0.7	-0.1
Exchange rate (per US$)	111.20	102.21	94.02
Interest rate (% per annum)	4.4	4.1	3.5
GDP (% real growth)	-0.2	-0.6	2.0
GDP (Billion units of national currency)	468,769.0	469,240.0	478,497.0
GDP (US$ million)	4,215,548.6	4,590,940.2	5,089,310.8
GDP per capita (US$)	33,813.7	36,739.3	40,597.9
Consumption (Billion units of national currency)	267,125.0	277,800.0	288,475.0
Consumption (US$ million)	2,402,203.2	2,717,933.7	3,068,230.2
Consumption per capita (US$)	19,268.5	21,750.4	24,475.5
Population, mid-year ('000)	124,670.0	124,960.0	125,359.0
Birth rate (per '000)	9.5	10.1	10.0
Death rate (per '000)	7.0	7.0	7.0
No. of households ('000)	40,552.5	40,549.0	40,547.5
Total exports (US$ million)	362,244.0	397,005.0	443,125.0
Total imports (US$ million)	241,624.0	275,235.0	335,975.0
Tourism receipts (US$ million)	3,557.0	3,922.7	4,238.4
Tourist spending (US$ million)	26,860.0	29,621.7	31,383.4

Average household size 1995 (persons)	2.94				
Urban population 1995 (%)	77.6				
Age analysis (%) (1992)	*0-14* 17.3		*15-64* 69.7		*65+* 13.0
Population by sex (%) (1992)	*Male* 49.1		*Female* 50.9		
Life expectancy (years) (1995)	*Male* 76.8		*Female* 82.9		
Infant mortality (deaths per '000 live births) (1995)	4.3				
Adult literacy (%) (1995)	98.5				

TRADING PARTNERS

Major export destinations 1995 (% share)		Major import sources 1995 (% share)	
USA	27.9	USA	22.5
South Korea	7.1	China	10.4
Hong Kong	6.3	South Korea	5.0
Singapore	5.1	Australia	4.4

Jordan

Area (km²) 90,650

Currency Jordanian dinar (JD = 1,000 fils)

Location The Hashemite Kingdom of Jordan lies just to the east of Israel, at the eastern end of the Mediterranean, and would have been landlocked by the creation of Israel in 1948 if it did not have access to a narrow channel running into the Red Sea. Jordan is bounded in the north by Syria, in the south by Saudi Arabia, and in the east by Iraq. It lost much of its West Bank territory to Israel after the 1967 war. The capital is Amman.

Head of State King Hussein ibn Talal

Head of Government Abdul Salam Majali (1993)

Ruling Party The Parliamentary Arab-Islamic Coalition Front, a coalition of Islamic groups and nationalists.

Political Structure Jordan is a constitutional monarchy in which the King plays an especially active role. The country has an 80-member House of Representatives, reduced substantially from the 142 delegates in the former assembly; but in practice the country was effectively ruled by the armed forces for many years. Indeed, it was only in April 1992 that the last of the martial law provisions imposed in the aftermath of the 1967 war with Israel were removed - most of them having remained in force until July 1991. Political parties were legalised in July 1992. Israel withdrew from the West Bank and the Gaza Strip in May 1994 and Jordan was expected to play a role in advising the new administration.

Last Elections The first multi-party elections to the House of Representatives were held in November 1993, when parties aligned with the Muslim Brotherhood won 16 of the 80 seats, with a further 14 seats going to related Islamic groups.

Political Risk Jordan's image as one of the more stable political risks in the Middle East was dented in 1995 by the assassination attempt on King Hussein. The country's peace accord with Israel is bringing economic benefits in terms of additional tourism and economic assistance from the EU but many Jordanians are uncomfortable with the speed of the political shift. They are also he is now firmly aligned with the USA against his one-time ally, and wants to pull together the quarrelling strands of the Iraqi opposition.

International Disputes Jordan's international status was greatly enhanced by King Hussein's close relationship with Israel's former prime minister, Yitzhak Rabin, and the peace accord the two leaders negotiated. That move is a major source of domestic dissatisfaction in Jordan but has relieved international pressure on the king.

Economy Jordan's economy has experienced a dramatic recovery since 1992, despite the loss of substantial Iraqi business. Growth of GDP was nearly 6% in 1995 and the government predicts a better performance in 1996. Much of the economy remains rooted in collectivism, but policy makers are actively trying to encourage development of the private sector. Unemployment, which presently averages near 20%, remains a serious problem. Hopefully, some of these people may eventually be absorbed in the tourist sector. With each visitor spending about $500, tourism added nearly 1% to Jordan's GDP in 1995 and should provide a much bigger injection in 1969.

Main Industries Jordan's economy relies mainly on farming, with smallholders producing wheat, barley, olives, lentils, tobacco, fruit and vegetables. A persistent shortage of water and a lack of irrigation facilities means that yields are small and productivity is low. Typically, the country is able to meet only a quarter of its food needs. The manufacturing sector is well diversified with production of cement, steel, glass, paints, plastics, fertilisers, food products and pharmaceuticals being prominent. Almost all manufacturing firms are small in size and few are capable of competing in overseas markets. Petroleum products are the main revenue earner in this sector. A recent development following the peace accord with Israel is the rapid growth of tourism. Over 100,000 international visitors (many of them Israelis) were recorded in 1995 and about 300,000 are expected in 1996.

Energy Jordan has an indigenous oil deposit at Azraq, and gas deposits have been found at Al Risba in the north-east. Otherwise, its only resource is oil shale at Laijun which could be used for electricity generation.

	1993	1994	1995
Inflation (% change)	4.7	3.5	2.4
Exchange rate (per US$)	0.69	0.70	0.70
Interest rate (% per annum)	9.0	9.0	9.0
GDP (% real growth)	6.5	4.3	5.8
GDP (Million units of national currency)	3,883.0	4,190.6	4,620.8
GDP (US$ million)	5,604.8	5,953.4	6,587.0
GDP per capita (US$)	1,134.6	1,144.9	1,206.4
Consumption (Million units of national currency)	2,985.0	3,237.7	3,588.1
Consumption (US$ million)	4,308.6	4,599.7	5,114.9
Consumption per capita (US$)	872.2	884.5	936.8
Population, mid-year ('000)	4,940.0	5,200.0	5,460.0
Birth rate (per '000)	38.8	27.0	
Death rate (per '000)	5.5	2.4	
No. of households ('000)	1,016.9	1,055.9	1,131.3
Total exports (US$ million)	1,232.0	1,424.0	1,769.0
Total imports (US$ million)	3,539.0	3,382.0	3,698.0
Tourism receipts (US$ million)	563.0	598.1	
Tourist spending (US$ million)	365.0	367.2	368.0

Average household size 1995 (persons)	4.59				
Urban population 1995 (%)	71.5				
Age analysis (%) (1989)	*0-14* 48.1	*15-64* 49.3	*65+* 2.6		
Population by sex (%) (1989)	*Male* 52.3	*Female* 47.7			
Life expectancy (years) (1990-95)	*Male* 66.2	*Female* 69.8			
Infant mortality (deaths per '000 live births) (1993)	36.0				
Adult literacy (%) (1991)	83.2				

TRADING PARTNERS

Major export destinations 1995 (% share)		Major import sources 1995 (% share)	
India	11.7	USA	9.5
Saudi Arabia	9.6	Germany	8.4
Syria	3.8	Italy	7.3
Indonesia	3.7	France	6.1

Kazakhstan

Area (km²)   2,717,300

Currency   Tenge

Location   Until it achieved independence in 1991, Kazakhstan was one of the largest states in the old USSR. Lying directly to the south of Russia, it extends some 2,500 km from the Caspian Sea in the west to the Chinese/Mongolian border in the east, and borders on the almost dried out Aral Sea and Lake Balkash. The land is mainly of steppe type, or of desert, and is richly endowed with minerals. The capital is Alma Ata.

Head of State   President Nursultan Nazarbayev (1991)

Head of Government   Akezhan Kazhageldin (Interim Prime Minister, October 1994)

Ruling Party   Congress of People's Unity of Kazakhstan is the largest party.

Political Structure   Kazakhstan declared its independence only in October 1990, having tried in vain to campaign for the vanishing Soviet Union, and it remains controlled by the Socialist Party of Kazakhstan, the renamed Communist Party. The constitution introduced in 1993 provides for a Supreme Soviet consisting of 360 members elected by universal suffrage and an executive President is similarly elected. In 1994 the government decided that the capital would be moved to Akmola and in 1996 the country entered into an integration agreement with Russia, Belarus and Kyrgyzstan. The goals of this agreement differ very little from those of the larger Commonwealth of Independent States, the loose alliance that succeeded the Soviet Union.

Last Elections   The electoral system is in crisis. Following the March 1994 elections to the Supreme Soviet, the first since the pre-independence days of March 1990, it was reported that candidates loyal to the President had won two-thirds of the 177 seats. But the election was condemned by EU observers over alleged voting irregularities. In March 1995 the results were annulled without new elections being called. At the same time President Nazarbayev requested and obtained an extension of his presidential mandate, enabling him to rule virtually by decree. The electorate approved a new constitution in September 1995 which made his removal from power almost impossible.

Political Risk   Kazakhstan, despite its considerable economic potential, remains problematic because of its unwillingness to renounce the collectivist principles of the communist era. However, the authorities have instituted a number of free economic zones and made a start with pro-capitalist economic reforms which may take some years to develop. Kazakhstan's central location and relatively homogeneous population structure will add to its importance in years to come. The country enjoys good relations with the United States and with many Western investor nations. In April 1996, the country signed a political-military treaty with Russia, China, Kyrgyzstan and Tajikistan designed to reduce tensions among the five countries.

Economy   GDP has fallen by nearly 50% between 1992 and 1995. Analysts now predict that the worst of the recession is over but the country's living standards are terribly low. Despite its historical role as one of the breadbaskets of the former Soviet Union, Kazakhstan's agricultural sector remains underdeveloped and poorly organised. The government attempted to privatise all farms by 1995, but the move has only partially succeeded. In January 1994 the country entered into an economic union with Kyrgyzstan and Uzbekistan.

Main Industries   Though the economic base is still meagre, the growth of the industrial sector has been striking. Industrial production rose from 20% of GDP in 1990 to 44% by 1994. Kazakhstan possesses enormous mineral, and especially, energy resources. It has an important primary extracting and mining industry which constitutes the basis of the country's exports. In contrast, there is very little production of consumer goods, nor a modern machine building sector. The country's infrastructure is very rundown and most enterprises suffer from acute shortages of capital.

Energy   Kazakhstan was one of the largest energy producers in the former Soviet Union, and it has tried to move rapidly to open up its oil and gas exploration activities to foreign investors. By 1994, companies from Italy, the United Kingdom and the USA were drilling. Russia was also reported to be keen to get involved.

	1993	1994	1995
Inflation (% change)	450.0	66.1	
Exchange rate (per US$)	1,095.00	2,000.00	
Interest rate (% per annum)	65.0		
GDP (% real growth)	-12.9	-25.1	-18.5
GDP			
GDP (US$ million)	29,700.0	20,000.0	16,350.0
GDP per capita (US$)	1,758.4	1,174.4	985.5
Consumption			
Consumption (US$ million)	22,900.0	15,300.0	12,625.0
Consumption per capita (US$)	1,355.8	898.4	761.0
Population, mid-year ('000)	16,890.0	17,030.0	16,590.0
Birth rate (per '000)	18.7	19.4	
Death rate (per '000)	9.3		
No. of households ('000)	3,162.8	3,189.1	3,243.6
Total exports (US$ million)			
Total imports (US$ million)			
Tourism receipts (US$ million)			
Tourist spending (US$ million)			

Average household size 1995 (persons)	4.86				
Urban population 1995 (%)	59.7				
Age analysis (%) (1992)	*0-14* 45.6	*15-64* 51.1	*65+* 3.3
Population by sex (%) (1989)	*Male* 48.4	*Female* 51.6	
Life expectancy (years) (1990)	*Male* 63.8	*Female* 73.1	
Infant mortality (deaths per '000 live births) (1992)	26.3		
Adult literacy (%) (1989)	97.5		

TRADING PARTNERS

Major export destinations 1995 (% share)		Major import sources 1995 (% share)	
Russia	70.5	Russia	71.7
China	5.1	Germany	7.9
Poland	3.3	Lithuania	2.2
Italy	3.0	Turkey	1.7

Kenya

Area (km²)   582,645

Currency   Kenya shilling (Ksh = 100 cents)

Location   Kenya lies on the Indian Ocean coast of central East Africa, where it is bounded in the north by Eritrea, Ethiopia, Sudan and Somalia, in the west by Uganda and in the south by Tanzania. Although subject to occasional drought, the country has an equable climate and numerous major watercourses. The capital is Nairobi.

Head of State   President Daniel arap Moi

Head of Government   President Daniel arap Moi

Ruling Party   Kenya African National Union (KANU)

Political Structure   Kenya has an executive Presidency whose incumbent since independence, President Moi, has exerted an almost unchallenged level of influence over the country's affairs. There is a multi-party system in operation, in which opposition figures are elected to Parliament in the normal way. The President, however, has used his extensive personal powers since the late 1980s to imprison and to suspend many opponents. Criticism of the regime - both within the international community and from opponents within the country - has become increasingly harsh.

Last Elections   Presidential elections took place in January 1993, at which President Moi won 1.8 million votes, ahead of three opponents. Legislative elections at the same time gave Moi's KANU party 95 seats in the 188-seat parliament, compared with 31 for all opposition parties. Since the elections were held, the opposition has regrouped into a new party led by Richard Leakey and known as the Safina Party.

Political Risk   International donors express serious doubts about the government's commitment to privatisation and civil service reform. They are also highly critical of the frequent extrabudgetary outlays for favourite projects which make a mockery of the financial system. Meanwhile, the repression of political opposition has steadily worsened, with the government seeking power to decide which parties are allowed to stand in elections and tightening its control over radio, television and the press. The new political opposition reorganised into a new party in 1995 but had to wait eight months before receiving permission to organise branches and recruit members.

International Disputes   Kenya's border with Somalia is disputed but the issue has been dormant for more than a decade. The government of Sudan accuses Kenya of supporting the rebels fighting in the south of that country.

Economy   Kenya's economy grew by 3% in 1994 and nearly 5% in 1995. Those results are commendable, given the year-long stalemate over international aid. Both the IMF and the World Bank are refusing to disperse hundreds of mullions of dollars as a result of international dissatisfaction with President's Moi's reform proposals and his suppression of political and ethnic opposition. In the long run these delays will mean a bigger budget deficit, higher government borrowing and a surge in inflation.

Main Industries   Kenya's agricultural sector is still the cornerstone of the economy, despite the recent rise of tourism. Over 80% of the workforce is engaged in the fields, producing coffee, tea, cotton, sugar, tobacco and pyrethrum for export; domestic crops include maize, sorghum, cassava and beans, and there are substantial livestock herds. Yet the entire sector is vulnerable to drought. Tourism is increasing in importance but progress is uneven. Recent political uncertainties, together with the poor management of the country's game reserves and the growth of crime, have combined to depress the growth of tourism. Manufacturing provides up to 15% of GDP in a typical year, and has attracted significant foreign investment. Beside the normal food processing activities, Kenya has a significant engineering industry and manufactures textiles, glass and construction materials.

Energy   Kenya imports 75% of its domestic energy needs, although efforts are under way to develop domestic resources. Major hydro-electric investments have been planned but some are being delayed by the international community's refusal to release aid money.

	1993	1994	1995
Inflation (% change)	45.8	29.0	0.8
Exchange rate (per US$)	58.00	56.05	51.40
Interest rate (% per annum)	22.0	13.0	14.0
GDP (% real growth)	-8.0	3.0	4.8
GDP (Million units of national currency)	320,086.0	389,868.0	411,850.3
GDP (US$ million)	5,518.7	6,955.7	8,012.7
GDP per capita (US$)	196.3	237.5	262.5
Consumption (Million units of national currency)	212,980.0	274,518.1	306,883.9
Consumption (US$ million)	3,672.1	4,897.7	5,970.5
Consumption per capita (US$)	130.6	167.2	195.6
Population, mid-year ('000)	28,110.0	29,290.0	30,520.0
Birth rate (per '000)	46.5	42.4	
Death rate (per '000)	11.7	11.7	
No. of households ('000)	5,573.6	5,836.4	6,252.0
Total exports (US$ million)	1,336.0	1,609.0	1,722.0
Total imports (US$ million)	1,711.0	2,156.0	2,700.0
Tourism receipts (US$ million)	413.0	519.3	
Tourist spending (US$ million)	48.0	60.4	73.6

Average household size 1995 (persons)	4.64				
Urban population 1995 (%)	27.7				
Age analysis (%) (1985)	*0-14* 51.3		*15-64* 46.6		*65+* 2.1
Population by sex (%) (1985)	*Male* 49.8		*Female* 50.2		
Life expectancy (years) (1990-95)	*Male* 54.2		*Female* 57.3		
Infant mortality (deaths per '000 live births) (1993)	69.3				
Adult literacy (%) (1990)	69.0				

TRADING PARTNERS

Major export destinations 1995 (% share)		Major import sources 1995 (% share)	
United Kingdom	12.6	United Kingdom	13.3
Germany	9.0	Japan	9.4
Uganda	8.2	United Arab Emirates	9.1
Tanzania	6.6	Germany	6.3

Kiribati

Area (km²)   684

Currency   Australian dollar (A$ = 100 cents)

Location   Kiribati, the former Gilbert Islands, is a group of 33 islands and atolls in the south-west central Pacific, of which the largest is Banaba, the former Ocean Island. The climate is warm and equable, but the terrain is extremely flat, seldom rising more than four metres above sea level. The capital is Bairiki.

Head of State   President Teburoro Tito (October 1994)

Head of Government   President Teburoro Tito (October 1994)

Ruling Party   Maneaban Te Mauri (MTM) Party

Political Structure   Kiribati (pronounced Kiribass) is an independent republic within the Commonwealth, whose executive President (Beretitenti) is popularly elected from among the members of the House of Assembly (Maneaba). The House, a unicameral parliament, has 41 members of whom two are appointed representatives of the Banaban community. The others are all elected by universal suffrage for a period of up to four years - although the President may dissolve Parliament at any time and order fresh elections.

Last Elections   Elections to the 39 elected seats in the House of Assembly were held in July 1994, when the ruling National Progressive Party won only 7 seats and therefore lost its majority to the Maneaban Te Mauri (MTM) Party. Presidential elections were held in September 1994, in which Tito took over from Teatao Teannaki.

Political Risk   Kiribati's legislative system has been come under scrutiny following recent allegations of electoral fraud. The country has made some headway in tackling its large trade deficits but it remains extremely vulnerable to any fall in the world market prices for its main exports.

Economy   With its domestic economy stagnating, Kiribati's economy is likely to remain heavily dependent on aid from the United Kingdom and New Zealand, and on investment from Australia. An approach has been made by Japan to use Christmas Island as a launch site for space projects.

Main Industries   Kiribati's small-scale economy relies heavily on its agricultural sector, which produces copra and fish for world markets. Pawpaw, bananas, breadfruit, root crops and maize are grown for the domestic market. Most farms are smallholdings and suffer from low productivity. The situation is made more difficult because the soil quality is deteriorating and there is little investment to reverse the trend. Industry remains largely limited to the processing of agricultural raw materials such as food products, textiles, clothing and furniture. The country's phosphate reserves are no longer mined, although there are still known deposits of copper, platinum and manganese which have yet to be exploited commercially.

Energy   Kiribati's limited energy needs are met in part by domestic resources such as fuelwood and brushwood. Otherwise, all requirements have to be imported.

	1993	1994	1995
Inflation (% change)	0.9	3.0	2.0
Exchange rate (per US$)	1.48	1.29	1.35
Interest rate			
GDP (% real growth)	-2.0	-2.0	-1.0
GDP (Million units of national currency)	43.6	44.0	44.4
GDP (US$ million)	29.5	34.1	32.9
GDP per capita (US$)	369.0	426.6	401.1
Consumption (Million units of national currency)	28.9	29.2	29.5
Consumption (US$ million)	19.6	22.6	21.9
Consumption per capita (US$)	244.6	283.1	266.5
Population, mid-year ('000)	80.0	80.0	82.0
Birth rate (per '000)	27.7	31.6	
Death rate (per '000)	7.9	8.3	
No. of households ('000)	12.8	13.4	14.1
Total exports (US$ million)			
Total imports (US$ million)			
Tourism receipts (US$ million)	1.0	1.1	
Tourist spending (US$ million)			

Average household size 1995 (persons)	5.51				
Urban population 1995 (%)	35.7				
Age analysis (%) (1978)	*0-14* 41.1		*15-64* 55.2		*65+* 3.7
Population by sex (%) (1978)	*Male* 49.3		*Female* 50.7		
Life expectancy (years) (1990)	*Male* 53.1		*Female* 53.1		
Infant mortality (deaths per '000 live births) (1991)	56.0				
Adult literacy (%)					

Kuwait

Area (km²) 24,280

Currency Kuwaiti dinar (= 10 dirhams)

Location The tiny state of Kuwait includes a mainland area and several small islands. It lies at a strategically important point on the northern extreme of the Persian (Arabian) Gulf which allows it to serve as a transhipment point for oil supplies from Saudi Arabia (and formerly Iraq). Lacking any fresh river water or other natural supplies, it is obliged to manufacture its own through massive desalination plants. The greater part of the population lives in Kuwait City. The capital is Kuwait City.

Head of State HH Shaikh Jabir Al Ahmad As Sabah

Head of Government HH Shaikh Saad Al Abdullah

Ruling Party There are no political parties in Kuwait.

Political Structure Kuwait became an independent state in 1961, having been a British protectorate since 1899. The Amir exercises almost complete political control. In 1986, he dissolved the National Assembly (Parliament), and ruled by decree for some years thereafter. Growing pressure for political reform was overtaken by the Iraqi invasion of August 1990 and the ensuing Gulf War. In April 1991, following the liberation by allied forces, the Amir appointed an interim government and announced elections. In November 1994 Iraq formally recognised the independence of Kuwait, thus apparently renouncing any territorial claim over the state.

Last Elections The first elections to the 50-seat National Assembly were held in October 1992, when Islamic candidates obtained about 18 seats, with another 12 seats going to liberal opposition figures. Candidates for the Government won 30 seats and were expected to dominate the new Assembly.

Political Risk The elections held in October 1992 were criticised by some but still helped the royal family to establish some democratic credentials after a decade of retreat from these principles. Kuwait maintains close ties with Saudi Arabia as well as with several powerful western nations and this, too, gives it security. Though modern and westernised in many ways, the country is equally backward in others. Women have no vote and there are persistent allegations of human rights abuses, especially against the large immigrant population which performs most of the manual labour in the country.

International Disputes Under extreme pressure from the UN, Iraq has renounced its territorial claims on Kuwait but few doubt that these would be reasserted if the implicit threat of western military power were withdrawn. Kuwait's mutual boundary with Saudi Arabia has never been adequately defined to the two countries' mutual satisfaction, although there is no serious hostility over the issue. Consequently, an area some 150 kilometres square was designated in 1922 as a neutral zone. In practice, the two countries have found it better to exploit the region's oil resources jointly and to share the resulting oil. This arrangement proved an economic lifeline to Kuwait in 1991, after its own oil wells had been blown up by retreating Iraqi forces.

Economy The country's economic reconstruction after the chaos inflicted by Iraq was generally considered to be complete by 1994, following massive investment, both by the Kuwaiti government and by Saudi Arabia. The construction industry has been a major beneficiary. Unemployment still exists, although the government has now forced many of the non-nationals who held jobs before the war to leave the country. Palestinian immigrants who supported Iraq during the war were the main target of this move.

Main Industries The reconstruction of Kuwait following the Iraqi invasion provided unique opportunities for foreign investors and contractors as the country rapidly rebuilt its infrastructure and oil industry. The economy is dominated to an unusual extent by the oil sector which provides well over 80% of national revenues. Kuwait's oilfield sharing arrangements with Saudi Arabia are a crucial feature, as are its oil port and shipping facilities. It also has large oil refining and processing facilities and has invested in a range of light industries, including glass, textiles, paper, furniture and mineral and construction materials. Agriculture has virtually no role to play in the economy and virtually all foods are imported. The country has extensive overseas investments that are concentrated in downstream industries which use its crude oil. These include chemicals and petrol distribution.

Energy Kuwait is fully self-sufficient in all forms of energy.

	1993	1994	1995
Inflation (% change)	0.4	0.3	4.3
Exchange rate (per US$)	0.30	0.30	0.30
Interest rate (% per annum)	7.9		
GDP (% real growth)	17.6	0.8	2.5
GDP (Million units of national currency)	7,134.0	7,214.0	7,712.3
GDP (US$ million)	23,875.5	24,046.7	25,828.2
GDP per capita (US$)	16,353.1	14,843.6	15,283.0
Consumption (Million units of national currency)	2,537.0	2,594.0	2,804.0
Consumption (US$ million)	8,490.6	8,646.7	9,390.6
Consumption per capita (US$)	5,815.5	5,337.4	5,556.6
Population, mid-year ('000)	1,460.0	1,620.0	1,690.0
Birth rate (per '000)	25.6	24.0	
Death rate (per '000)	2.4	2.1	
No. of households ('000)	183.0	205.0	226.1
Total exports (US$ million)	10,248.0	11,614.0	13,036.0
Total imports (US$ million)	7,036.0	6,697.0	7,139.0
Tourism receipts (US$ million)	83.0	77.3	
Tourist spending (US$ million)	1,888.0	1,758.8	1,910.1

Average household size 1995 (persons)	7.10				
Urban population 1995 (%)	97.0				
Age analysis (%) (1990)	*0-14*	36.6	*15-64*	62.2	*65+* 1.2
Population by sex (%) (1990)	*Male*	56.5	*Female*	43.5	
Life expectancy (years) (1990-95)	*Male*	73.3	*Female*	77.2	
Infant mortality (deaths per '000 live births) (1993)	12.3				
Adult literacy (%) (1990)	77.1				

TRADING PARTNERS

Major export destinations 1995 (% share)		Major import sources 1995 (% share)	
USA	34.3	USA	21.8
Japan	19.3	United Kingdom	11.8
Singapore	8.1	Japan	9.6
Netherlands	7.9	Germany	6.0

Kyrgyzstan

Area (km²) 198,500

Currency Som (= 200 roubles)

Location Kyrgyzstan (Khirghizstan) is a mountainous region lying in the northern part of Soviet Central Asia, and borders on China, from which it is separated by the Pamir-Altai mountain range. Most of the population live in the plains, where cattle-raising is a major activity, but there are extensive mineral deposits. The capital is Bishkek.

Head of State President Askar Akayev

Head of Government Apas Jumagulov (resigned September 1994)

Ruling Party Democratic Movement of Kyrgyzstan

Political Structure Like Kazakhstan, Kyrgyzstan initially tried to maintain the Soviet political system and declared independence only in December 1990. The country has an executive President who is elected by universal suffrage for a maximum of two five-year terms, and who leads a Cabinet of Ministers. The Supreme Soviet has 350 directly elected members. A new constitution was adopted in May 1993, in which early ambitions to implement an Islamic state were dropped. In 1996, the country entered into an integration agreement with Russia, Belarus and Kazakhstan. The goals of this new agreement differ little from those of the larger Commonwealth of Independent States which was the loose alliance that succeeded the Soviet Union.

Last Elections Askar Akayev was returned to power in February 1995, despite harsh criticism concerning the weak policies of his government. His plans for reform had previously received solid support in a 1994 referendum which produced a 96% majority in his favour. In September 1994 the president had dissolved parliament and ruled by decree until the 1995 elections.

Political Risk The political risks in the still immature state of Kyrgyzstan are outweighed, for many investors, by the enormous potential in its mineral resources, which are being opened up almost without limitation to foreigners. The process of land reform is progressing well and has helped to relieve tensions. In April 1996, Kyrgyzstan signed a political-military treaty with Russia, China, Tajikistan and Kazakhstan intended to enhance mutual trust in the region.

Economy The economy grew slightly in 1995 after contracting by more than 30% during the two previous years. Nevertheless, GDP in 1995 was still only about 48% of its 1989 level. The country continues to rely heavily on the markets in other countries of the former Soviet Union, with over 70% of its total trade (both imports and exports) still depending on this group. A modest programme of privatisation has been announced, but energy and minerals are excluded from the sell-off.

Main Industries At the end of the 1980s agriculture accounted for about 35% of GDP and provided employment for 40% of the population. The second largest sector was industry, which contributed around 30% of GDP and generated employment for some 20% of the population. Both sectors have suffered badly after the demise of the Soviet Union. Agriculture centres on the production of grain and livestock. Light industry includes production of silk, woollen and cotton textiles, clothing and food processing. Exploration and mining is the major source of foreign exchange as Kyrgyzstan is rich in various types of mineral resources and is one of the largest producers of mercury and antimony for which there is high demand in world markets.

Energy The energy sector is to receive a high priority in the development process in order to reduce the amount of imported energy and to provide for a more rational use of energy resources. New hydroelectric power plants are being constructed and several of the older coal mine are being rehabilitated. Meanwhile, the government is calling for new bids for the exploration of oil and gas deposits.

	1993	1994	1995
Inflation (% change)	600.0	178.3	
Exchange rate (per US$)	11.30		
Interest rate			
GDP (% real growth)	-16.4	-25.0	0.6
GDP			
GDP (US$ million)	1,133.9	850.4	855.5
GDP per capita (US$)	250.3	184.9	183.2
Consumption			
Consumption (US$ million)	678.0	508.0	510.5
Consumption per capita (US$)	149.7	110.4	109.3
Population, mid-year ('000)	4,530.0	4,600.0	4,670.0
Birth rate (per '000)	30.8	24.6	
Death rate (per '000)		8.3	
No. of households ('000)	843.4	860.7	899.1
Total exports (US$ million)	520.0	135.6	
Total Imports (US$ million)	150.0	157.2	
Tourism receipts (US$ million)			
Tourist spending (US$ million)			

Average household size 1995 (persons)	4.93		
Urban population 1995 (%)	38.9		
Age analysis (%) (1991, est)	*0-14* 44.6	*15-64* 51.1	*65+* 4.3
Population by sex (%) (1989)	*Male* 48.8	*Female* 51.2	
Life expectancy (years) (1991)	*Male* 64.6	*Female* 72.7	
Infant mortality (deaths per '000 live births) (1992)	31.6		
Adult literacy (%) (1989)	97.0		

TRADING PARTNERS

Major export destinations 1995 (% share)		Major import sources 1995 (% share)	
China	40.0	China	28.8
Russia	32.7	Russia	28.1
Germany	7.9	Germany	7.8
USA	4.3	USA	6.6

Laos

Area (km²)   236,725

Currency   Kip (= 100 at)

Location   Laos runs from north-east to south-west through the northernmost part of the central Indochina peninsula. The country borders on China and Myanmar in the north, on Thailand in the west, and on Cambodia in the south. In the east, Vietnam follows its entire length in such a way as to shut it off from the South China Sea. The country has a tropical and generally humid climate. The capital is Vientiane.

Head of State   President Nouhak Phoumsavanh

Head of Government   Gen. Khamtay Siphandone (1991)

Ruling Party   Lao People's Revolutionary Party (LPRP)

Political Structure   The Lao Constitution, approved in August 1991, provides in principle for the creation of a National Assembly to be elected by universal suffrage and to serve for five years. The Assembly elects the executive President, who also serves for five years.

Last Elections   The last full elections to the new National Assembly took place in December 1992, following the death of President Phomvihane, in which 154 LPRP-approved candidates contested the 85 seats. Nouhak Phoumsavanh was elected President by the Supreme People's Assembly in November 1992, itself made up of LPRP members.

Political Risk   Laos has frequently been cited as a promising market for foreign goods, especially in the light of the foreign aid being despatched to the country. Yet some degree of caution is advised, at least until such time as its political system has completed the transition to a multi-party democracy with full voting rights. Progress toward the latter has been disappointingly slow. Meanwhile, developers grumble that the ruling party is stuck in the Stalinist past and has no clear idea of how to promote the country's economic development.

International Disputes   Relations with neighbouring Thailand have been repeatedly strained by the high level of border activity involving Thai and Cambodian militias. In the past, Laos' exports of electricity to Thailand accounted for around 75% of the country's hard-currency earnings, and the government has worked hard to restore good relations.

Economy   Subsistence agriculture is presently the country's main source of income and employment, but that was not always the case. In the past, the Laotian economy earned most of its revenues from energy exports and hopes to reclaim these revenues in the future. At the sixth national congress in March 1996 Laotian leaders gave their qualified endorsement to more than 60 development projects which recognised the country's vast potential as a producer of hydro-electric power. Laos has signed a new agreement with Thailand to export 1,500 million megawatts of electricity a year by the 2000 and Vietnam is seeking an agreement to import 2,000 million megawatts by 2010. Altogether, more than 40 other energy-related projects are under government consideration. Growing opposition from environmentalists and villagers who have had to be relocated could slow these developments. The scale of these hydro-power plants is huge and spending is spurring a boom in investment and consumer spending.

Main Industries   Agriculture employs over 80% of the workforce and accounts for well over 70% of GDP. Major crops include rice, maize, sweet potatoes, cassava, fruit and vegetables, some of which are grown in elaborately irrigated plantations. Exports of electricity have slumped badly owing to problems at the country's larger hydro-electric dams and tensions with buyers in neighbouring markets. Exports of timber (mainly teak) are presently the country's leading earner of foreign exchange. The bulk of the country's industry is small-scale and is limited to coastal and urban regions. Tin and coal are currently mined, and there is some oil extraction potential.

Energy   Laos provides a small proportion of its own oil needs and uses domestically mined coal. By March 1996 the country had signed over 20 agreements for hydro-electric plants to produce more than 7,000 million megawatts. All this will be carried out by independent power producers.

	1993	1994	1995
Inflation (% change)	6.3	6.7	19.6
Exchange rate (per US$)	721.74	720.54	795.20
Interest rate (% per annum)	25.3	24.0	25.7
GDP (% real growth)	7.1	9.1	5.4
GDP (Million units of national currency)	951,000.0	1,107,000.0	1,395,000.0
GDP (US$ million)	1,317.6	1,536.3	1,754.3
GDP per capita (US$)	286.4	324.1	359.5
Consumption (Million units of national currency)	561,338.5	569,669.2	625,864.2
Consumption (US$ million)	777.8	790.6	787.1
Consumption per capita (US$)	169.1	166.8	161.3
Population, mid-year ('000)	4,600.0	4,740.0	4,880.0
Birth rate (per '000)	45.2	43.2	
Death rate (per '000)	15.2	14.7	
No. of households ('000)	804.7	831.5	879.9
Total exports (US$ million)	241.0	300.0	348.0
Total imports (US$ million)	432.0	564.0	587.0
Tourism receipts (US$ million)			
Tourist spending (US$ million)			

Average household size 1995 (persons)	5.27		
Urban population 1995 (%)	21.7		
Age analysis (%) (1991, est)	*0-14* 43.6	*15-64* 53.4	*65+* 3.0
Population by sex (%)			
Life expectancy (years) (1990)	*Male* 47.0	*Female* 50.0	
Infant mortality (deaths per '000 live births) (1993)	97.0		
Adult literacy (%) (1985)	83.9		

Latvia

Area (km²)   64,589

Currency   Lat

Location   Latvia, the second smallest of the three Baltic republics, lies between Lithuania in the south and Estonia in the north, with Russia dominating its eastern border, and with the Baltic Sea and the Gulf of Finland extending to the west. The land is mainly flat and low-lying, although chains of hills run through it. The capital is Riga.

Head of State   President Guntis Ulmanis (July 1993)

Head of Government   Andris Skele (April 1996)

Ruling Party   A centre-right wing coalition governs the country.

Political Structure   Latvia's independence was officially recognised in September 1991, some six months after its original declaration. The country has a semi-executive President, who is the de facto Chairman of the Supreme Council (Augstaka Padome, or Parliament). Full elections to the Council have been postponed, pending the passage of controversial new laws on human rights, which effectively prevent all persons not having Latvian citizenship from voting.

Last Elections   Latvia's strongly pro-western reformist president, Guntis Ulmanis, was re-elected to a second term by parliament in June 1996. The country's second general election since the restoration of sovereignty was held in October 1995. The results produced no clear winners. The Latvian Way, which was the dominant party in the previous coalition, received just less than 15% of the vote - abou half its share in the 1993 election, Another 30% was equally divided between the Movement for Latvia, which is led by a German citizen who speaks little Latvian, and the Saimnieks (roughly translated as "Master in Your Own Home") who are mainly ex-communist functionaries. Following complicated negotiations, a compromise candidate, Andris Skele, was chosen as the new prime minister.

Political Risk   The large Russian minority that came to Latvia after 1945 remains a source of constant tension. The question of rights and citizenship will continue to provoke the ire of Russian nationalists and raise doubts in the west about the country's commitment to Brussels-style democracy. Latvia's clear sense of national identity is a positive factor in many ways but could stand in the way of co-operation with other states. In October 1995, Latvia formally applied for membership in the EU.

International Disputes   The country's only serious dispute, with Russia, ended in 1995 when Russia agreed to withdraw its 10,000 remaining troops from the region. However, Latvia's 1.3 million Russian-speaking inhabitants continues to create tensions. Most have still not qualified as citizens and are unable to vote.

Economy   The Latvian economy contracted between 1990 and 1993 but by 1995 the recession may have ended. Consumers were especially hurt by the collapse of about a third of the country's 67 banks (including the largest one) in late 1995. Despite low inflation (by ex-Soviet standards), low unemployment and a slight improvement in growth performance, pensioners and the poor have seen a big drop in their living standards. About half of the country's foreign trade is now oriented to the west but that figure needs to rise. Foreign investment, although not flooding in, is helping to boost the economy. The relatively slow pace of privatisation hinders growth while the black economy is estimated to be over 30% of the official economy.

Main Industries   Latvia has a well established manufacturing base, accounting for around 60% of GNP. Most of these firms are in heavy industries such as chemicals and petrochemicals, metal-working and machine-building. Agriculture contributes around one-fifth of GNP and is centred on the cultivation of crops such as potatoes, cereals and fodder crops, along with dairy farming.

Energy   Latvia is dependent on imported fuels for its energy requirements and has suffered from severe shortages of essential fuels since independence.

	1993	1994	1995
Inflation (% change)	108.8	36.6	30.0
Exchange rate (per US$)	0.60	0.55	0.53
Interest rate (% per annum)	86.4	55.9	34.6
GDP (% real growth)	-14.9	1.9	-11.1
GDP (Million units of national currency)	1,467.0	2,042.6	2,360.7
GDP (US$ million)	2,465.5	3,727.4	4,471.9
GDP per capita (US$)	953.4	1,461.7	1,781.6
Consumption (Million units of national currency)	140,309.0	196,320.0	241,273.0
Consumption (US$ million)	235,813.4	358,248.2	457,043.0
Consumption per capita (US$)	91,188.5	140,489.5	182,088.8
Population, mid-year ('000)	2,586.0	2,550.0	2,510.0
Birth rate (per '000)	10.3	9.5	8.5
Death rate (per '000)	15.2	16.4	15.9
No. of households ('000)	623.0	617.0	625.3
Total exports (US$ million)	963.0	962.0	1,283.0
Total imports (US$ million)	872.0	1,251.0	1,916.0
Tourism receipts (US$ million)			
Tourist spending (US$ million)			

Average household size 1995 (persons)	3.81				
Urban population 1995 (%)	69.1				
Age analysis (%) (1995)	*0-14* 20.7		*15-64* 65.9		*65+* 13.4
Population by sex (%) (1995)	*Male* 46.3		*Female* 53.7		
Life expectancy (years) (1994)	*Male* 60.7		*Female* 72.9		
Infant mortality (deaths per '000 live births) (1994)	15.5				
Adult literacy (%) (1989)	99.5				

TRADING PARTNERS

Major export destinations 1995 (% share)		Major import sources 1995 (% share)	
Russia	24.9	Russia	20.4
Germany	13.9	Germany	14.7
Sweden	9.5	Sweden	7.6
United Kingdom	9.2	Lithuania	5.2

Lebanon

Area (km²)   10,400

Currency   Lebanese pound (£L = 100 piastres)

Location   Lebanon is a narrow (100 km wide) strip of land running from north to south for about 220 km along the eastern coastline of the Mediterranean. In the south it is bordered by Israel and in the north and east by Syria. The country has a temperate Mediterranean climate with warm summers but occasionally cool winters, especially in the hills. There is fertile agricultural land. The capital is Beirut.

Head of State   President Elias Hrawi (1989)

Head of Government   Rafiq al-Hariri

Ruling Party   Parti Socialiste Progressiste leads a coalition.

Political Structure   The electoral system has been only recently restored, having been effectively shelved since 1979. In the interim, the National Assembly was kept going by continually voting to extend its term of office. The current Assembly has 128 seats with the largest factions being Maronite Christians (34 sets), Sunni Moslems (27), Shia Muslims (27) and Greek Orthodox Christians(14). Lebanon's multi-member constituencies - with different seats reserved for different sects - encourages gerrymandering and shifting alliances. The Sunnis probably wield the most influence because the prime minister is a member of that group and claims considerable power. Voters can pick as many candidates as there are seats, but the chosen candidates can not all come from the same sect. The idea is to promote mixing and moderate candidates, but in practice the approach the approach is a cumbersome one.

Last Elections   The parliamentary elections in 1992 were the first in 20 years and produced a strong vote for the Parti Socialiste Progressiste. The Islamic militant organisation, Hizbullah, participated for the first time and also fared well. However, the results were questionable owing to a boycott by the Maronite Christians and the half-hearted participation of the Phalangist Party. Fresh elections are expected in 1996, when Rafiq Hariri plans to enter parliament for the first time, and the Christians are under instruction to take part.

Political Risk   The southern portion of Lebanon remains occupied by around 1,000 Israeli soldiers and some 2,500 members of the Israeli-controlled "South Lebanon Army". Other parts of Lebanon are patrolled by 40,000 Syrian soldiers and the Beqaa valley is home to around 500 full-time Hizbullah fighters and an unknown number of Iranian revolutionary guards. Not surprisingly, Lebanon places great hopes on regional peace as a way to regain some of its sovereignty. But whatever happens, the country will still have to work closely with Syria. It has signed numerous treaties with its powerful neighbour and has agreements covering almost every aspect of cross-border activity.

International Disputes   Lebanon hopes that if peace comes Israel will withdraw its troops. Should that happen, there would be no reason for the UN presence and no excuse for the Syrian one. The South Lebanon Army could also be disbanded. The difficulty with this scenario is that the Israelis will want guarantees that there will be no threats to their borders - and they have more confidence in Syria's ability to control the Hizbullah than Lebanon's. Syria's troops may therefore be in the country for some time to come.

Economy   Lebanon's economy shrank by two-thirds during the war but its rapid recovery has taken many observers by surprise. GDP has grown by about 7% per year since 1992. It will have to maintain or improve on that performance for at least 10 more years to regain the position it enjoyed prior to the war. The total cost of repairing damage to the country's roads, ports, power plants, schools and hospitals is estimated to be in excess of $15 billion. Some of this capital will be raised through contracts known as "build, operate and transfer" (BOT), a device often used by cash-strapped governments. The country's public finances, its trade deficit and high level of unemployment (about 20%) look depressing but could be turned around quickly with efficient financial arrangements and capital inflows from the millions of overseas Lebanese.

Main Industries   Lebanon's shattered urban economy does not affect the situation in the rest of the country, where the intensely fertile soil favours the agricultural sector. Wheat, barley, maize, fruit, potatoes, tobacco and olives are major crops, and output is ample to meet the country's needs. Industry has been surprisingly successful considering the extent of the disruption inflicted by the civil war. Lebanon's manufacturers tend to concentrate around the coastal urban areas, and include textiles, cement, chemicals, petroleum refining and light industries making goods for the domestic consumer market. Petroleum refining and financial services were two of the mainstays of the Lebanese economy which suffered badly in the war. It may be some time before Beirut regains its position as the key financial centre in the Middle East but the funds to rebuild the refining industry will not be hard to raise.

Energy   Lebanon is self-sufficient in hydrocarbons and has a number of electricity generating stations, 90% of which are thermal with the remainder hydro-electric. Most of the sector was quickly restored or survived the war intact.

	1993	**1994**	**1995**
Inflation (% change)	15.7	6.8	5.0
Exchange rate (per US$)	1,741.40	1,680.10	1,623.10
Interest rate (% per annum)	28.5	23.9	24.5
GDP (% real growth)	10.0	8.5	7.0
GDP (Million units of national currency)	7,529,471.8	8,725,001.3	9,802,539.0
GDP (US$ million)	4,323.8	5,193.1	6,039.4
GDP per capita (US$)	1,538.7	1,784.6	2,006.4
Consumption (Million units of national currency)	5,865,458.5	7,130,887.2	8,405,378.1
Consumption (US$ million)	3,368.2	4,244.3	5,178.6
Consumption per capita (US$)	1,198.7	1,458.5	1,720.5
Population, mid-year ('000)	2,810.0	2,910.0	3,010.0
Birth rate (per '000)	26.9	27.9	
Death rate (per '000)	7.1	6.6	
No. of households ('000)	610.7	637.7	664.7
Total exports (US$ million)			
Total imports (US$ million)			
Tourism receipts (US$ million)			
Tourist spending (US$ million)			

Average household size 1995 (persons)	4.30				
Urban population 1995 (%)	87.2				
Age analysis (%) (1991, est)	*0-14* 36.0		*15-64* 59.0		*65+* 5.0
Population by sex (%) (1970)	*Male* 50.8		*Female* 49.2		
Life expectancy (years) (1990-95)	*Male* 66.6		*Female* 70.5		
Infant mortality (deaths per '000 live births) (1993)	34.0				
Adult literacy (%) (1995)	92.4				

TRADING PARTNERS

Major export destinations 1995 (% share)		Major import sources 1995 (% share)	
Switzerland	12.3	Italy	14.7
China	12.1	France	9.8
Brazil	7.6	USA	9.4
Saudi Arabia	6.6	Syria	7.7

Lesotho

Area (km²) 30,345

Currency Loti (= 100 lisente)

Location Lesotho is a small mountainous territory lying in southern Africa, where it is surrounded on all sides by the Republic of South Africa. Although a third of its land is classified as lowland, the remainder is all above 2,000 metres and rises to more than 3,500 metres. The capital is Maseru.

Head of State HM Mohato Moshoeshoe II (restored to power 1994; killed in 1996)

Head of Government Ntsu Mokhehle (August 1994)

Ruling Party Basotho Congress Party (1992)

Political Structure The chaotic nature of Lesotho's recent political history reflects a bitter power struggle which has been going on for many years. King Moshoeshoe was first deposed in 1990 in a bloodless coup. The new leader of the ruling Military Council, Justin Lekhanya, was himself deposed in a bloodless coup by Col Elias Tutsoane Ramaema. Then, in August 1994, the new King Letsie III proclaimed a royal coup against his own parliament, in a move to cement his hold on power. Parliament responded by forcing Letsie III to abdicate in favour of Moshoeshoe who was subsequently killed in a car accident in 1996. Negotiations to determine the new head of state are underway.

Last Elections The first multi-party elections in recent years were held in March 1993, when the Basotho Congress Party (BCP) won about five times as many votes as the Basotho National Party of the deposed leader Justin Lekhanya.

Political Risk Now, as in the past, events move so rapidly in Lesotho that it is sometimes difficult to be precise about issues of political stability. At the root of all political intrigue is the status of the reservoirs which serve South Africa, and whose preservation and management are of such overwhelming importance. A serious wave of political kidnappings have recently underlined the fragility of the situation.

International Disputes The entire validity of Lesotho's borders with South Africa remains in dispute, with Lesotho claiming that a tribal agreement signed in 1869 was unjust.

Economy The generally depressed state of the economy reflects the low level of confidence in the regime and the serious climatic conditions which have prevailed in recent years. The relationship with South Africa will remain a largely determining factor in future years.

Main Industries Lesotho's economy depends almost entirely on its agricultural sector, which employs most of the population and contributes about 20% of GDP. Almost all farming is for subsistence purposes. Maize, sorghum and beans dominate though livestock herding is also important. However, droughts and persistent mismanagement have reduced yields in recent years. textiles, clothing, food products and pharmaceuticals are traded for fuel imports and other goods. Lesotho's diamond mining activities have now been closed down after many years of decline, although there is still some freelancing. The country has deposits of peat, iron ore, uranium and lead.

Energy Apart from firewood, Lesotho depends on imports for all its fuel resources. Completion of the Highlands Water Scheme should give the country enough hydro-electric power to become a substantial exporter of electricity.

	1993	1994	1995
Inflation (% change)	13.1	8.2	8.4
Exchange rate (per US$)	3.26	3.54	3.63
Interest rate (% per annum)	16.5		
GDP (% real growth)	-7.6	9.6	1.3
GDP (Million units of national currency)	2,331.4	2,763.8	3,034.9
GDP (US$ million)	715.2	780.7	836.1
GDP per capita (US$)	368.6	390.4	407.8
Consumption (Million units of national currency)	2,799.7	3,133.8	3,249.2
Consumption (US$ million)	858.8	885.3	895.1
Consumption per capita (US$)	442.7	442.6	436.6
Population, mid-year ('000)	1,940.0	2,000.0	2,050.0
Birth rate (per '000)	39.9	34.0	
Death rate (per '000)	10.0	9.2	
No. of households ('000)	325.0	335.0	353.6
Total exports (US$ million)	90.0	130.0	
Total imports (US$ million)	750.0	670.0	
Tourism receipts (US$ million)	17.0	17.3	
Tourist spending (US$ million)	7.0	7.1	7.2

Average household size 1995 (persons)	5.51				
Urban population 1995 (%)	23.1				
Age analysis (%) (1991, est)	*0-14* 43.1		*15-64* 53.2		*65+* 3.7
Population by sex (%) (1987)	*Male* 48.2		*Female* 51.9		
Life expectancy (years) (1990-95)	*Male* 58.0		*Female* 63.0		
Infant mortality (deaths per '000 live births) (1993)	79.0				
Adult literacy (%) (1995)	71.3				

Liberia

Area (km²)   111,370

Currency   Liberian dollar (L$ = 100 cents)

Location   Located on the Atlantic coast of West Africa, Liberia lies between Sierra Leone in the north-west, Guinea in the north-east, and Côte d'Ivoire in the south-east. The country has a mixed landscape, rising from the coastal plains to the upper plateaux further inland. The climate is tropical, and is often humid. The capital is Monrovia.

Head of State   David Kpormakr (chairman of the Council of State)

Ruling Party   None. A six-member Council of State with a revolving presidency was established in 1995. The Council, which includes the three main warlords, was committed to elections once the warring factions have been disarmed. However, a civil war rages in the country at present.

Political Structure   Liberia's political system disappeared during the first half of the 1990s. The first peace treaty signed in 1993 failed to hold and a second one was concluded in August 1995. All six of the main warring factions are party to this latest treaty. The most important of the groups the Liberian Peace Council headed by George Boley, the Ulimo faction led by Alhaji Kromah and Charles Taylor's National Patriotic Front.

Last Elections   Elections were originally scheduled to take place in December 1995 but were postponed after continual breaches of the peace treaty. The latest treaty, negotiated by the Nigerians in 1995, called for an election in August 1996 but this will no longer be possible because of the civil war.

Political Risk   Liberia continues to be one of the most unstable states in West Africa, and should be regarded with considerable caution - all the more so since the government system itself seems to be in dispute. The latest round of violence began in January 1996 when Ulimo-J, a breakaway faction of Ulimo itself, opened up a new front. Fighting between Ulimo-J and the West African peacekeeping force has continued since then. This has delayed the elaborate plan for demobilising the rival militias, as well as plans for the August election.

International Disputes   The bitter internal feuding between Liberia's warring factions has seriously destabilised the governments of surrounding countries, to the point where they have accused and occasionally exchanged fire with Liberia. Sierra Leone and Guinea have both been particularly badly affected.

Economy   The severe damage inflicted by the civil war of the late 1980s and early 1990s continues to limit the country's growth prospects. Liberia has no hope of attracting any foreign investment and most of its meagre wealth has been destroyed in the fighting. International aid may be the only way to get the country back on its feet but that can only begin once the war is settled.

Main Industries   Liberia's main industrial activity is the mining of iron ore, and to a lesser extent, diamonds and gold. These three minerals contribute two-thirds of export revenues although they account for only 5% of all employment. For most people, farming is still the most important activity. Employing nearly 80% of the workforce, the sector produces rubber, coffee, cocoa and timber for export. A majority of the population live on a subsistence basis, growing cassava, rice and various root vegetables. A growing fishing industry is developing. Manufacturing is at a very rudimentary stage, with mainly small companies producing textiles, food products, timber goods, chemicals and cement. Liberia has a free enterprise zone intended for the tax-free export processing of various goods, and it derives very considerable revenues from its use as a flag of convenience in international shipping.

Energy   Liberia relies on imports for all its petroleum needs, although exploration is under way for domestic resources, and its general lack of hydro-electric capacity means that oil is still the most popular means of generating electricity.

	1993	1994	1995
Inflation (% change)			
Exchange rate (per US$)	1.00	1.00	1.00
Interest rate (% per annum)	16.0	14.5	
GDP (% real growth)	4.2	1.1	0.5
GDP (Million units of national currency)	2,275.7	2,300.8	2,312.3
GDP (US$ million)	2,275.7	2,300.8	2,312.3
GDP per capita (US$)	862.0	852.1	837.8
Consumption (Million units of national currency)	743.8	775.9	804.6
Consumption (US$ million)	743.8	775.9	804.6
Consumption per capita (US$)	281.7	287.4	291.5
Population, mid-year ('000)	2,640.0	2,700.0	2,760.0
Birth rate (per '000)	47.3	43.5	
Death rate (per '000)	14.2	15.6	
No. of households ('000)	487.3	500.9	514.5
Total exports (US$ million)	470.0	419.6	
Total imports (US$ million)	3,000.0	3,900.0	
Tourism receipts (US$ million)			
Tourist spending (US$ million)			

Average household size 1995 (persons)	5.10				
Urban population 1995 (%)	45.0				
Age analysis (%) (1984)	*0-14* 43.2		*15-64* 52.7		*65+* 4.1
Population by sex (%) (1984)	*Male* 50.6		*Female* 49.4		
Life expectancy (years) (1990-95)	*Male* 54.0		*Female* 57.0		
Infant mortality (deaths per '000 live births) (1993)	125.9				
Adult literacy (%) (1995)	38.3				

TRADING PARTNERS

Major export destinations 1995 (% share)		Major import sources 1995 (% share)	
Belgium/Luxembourg	61.8	Japan	28.6
Greece	7.2	South Korea	22.2
Singapore	6.4	Italy	18.8
Malaysia	2.8	Singapore	5.2

© Euromonitor 1996

Libya

Area (km²) 1,759,540

Currency Libyan dinar (LD = 100 dirhams)

Location The Arab Jamahiriya of Libya occupies the centre of the North African Mediterranean coast, lying between Algeria and Tunisia in the west, Egypt and Sudan in the east and Niger and Chad in the south. The interior of the country consists almost entirely of rocky and sandy deserts. The south is part of the Sahara desert, peopled mainly by nomads. On the coast, however, the terrain becomes much milder and greener. Temperatures are generally Saharan. The capital is Tripoli.

Head of State President Col Muammar al-Qaddafi

Head of Government Maj.-Gen. Majid al-Qa'ud (Secretary of the General People's Congress)

Ruling Party Technically, there are no parties, with the Arab Socialist Union the sole authorised political group.

Political Structure Strictly speaking, Col Qaddafi has no formal post and no title except "Leader of the Revolution and Supreme Commander of the Armed Forces". In practice, he is effectively the country's President. Power is nominally vested in the Libyan people, acting through some 1,500 "basic people's congresses" at local level, and influencing the activities of the national General People's Congress (GPC) and its Secretariat. The GPC meets for about one week every year. In 1994 the country took a step toward Islamic rule, when Sharia law was introduced throughout the country and the clergy were empowered to issue decrees for the first time.

Last Elections There have been no multi-party elections in recent years.

Political Risk Given the extreme degree of Libya's isolation from much of the Arab world, and the deliberate isolation by the Western world, trade and investment in Libya remain fraught with difficulties. There are no reasons to suppose that Col Qaddafi's position is in any danger, however. His people enjoy a fairly high standard of living, thanks largely to oil revenues. Indeed, he stands in more danger from rivals abroad, in Chad, in Egypt or possibly in Sudan. The new laws of 1994 ban the consumption and possession of alcohol, which are subject to extreme penalties.

International Disputes Libya's strategic alliances over the years have left it with a curious mix of relationships. Libya has had to return to Chad a piece of land known as the Aozou Strip - a mineral-rich border area some 300 kilometres wide across the whole 1,200 km border. Although Libya was originally awarded the land after the second World War, Chad maintained its protests - especially after 1987, when Libya moved troops into the border zone. In February 1994 the International Court of Justice found in Chad's favour, and the area returned to Chadian possession. The country's relations with the West are dogged by Libya's refusal to hand over the three persons suspected of planting the bomb which destroyed a US-owned airliner over Lockerbie in Scotland; trade sanctions still apply. More recently, the USA has accused Libya of building a plant to produce chemical weapons. The Libyans reject this view and even some US allies are sceptical. Qaddafi has angered several Arab countries by expelling thousands of foreign workers (mainly Palestinians) who have spilled over into Egypt and Tunisia.

Economy Libya's economy has been able to endure the strains of political isolation with surprising ease, thanks largely to the importance of its oil industries. Occasional drops in export revenues due to oil price weaknesses have sometimes forced the government to make major cutbacks in public spending. Meanwhile, the Government has announced a limited privatisation programme.

Main Industries Libya's economy relies almost exclusively on the oil sector, which generates 45% of GDP and well over 90% of export earnings. The country's proven reserves, which approach 25 billion barrels, consist mainly of high-quality light crude. There are also extensive natural gas reserves in evidence. All production is owned and controlled by the state. Agriculture produces a mere 2% of GDP, though it employs 15-20% of the workforce. Cultivated land is limited to the coastal areas and a few oases. The government, however, has plans for a massive "man-made river" to provide irrigation. Barley, wheat, oats, dates, potatoes, tomatoes and fruit are grown. Industry is moderately developed, with a wide range of activities providing a high degree of self-sufficiency. There is a shortage of sophisticated engineering, however. Nearly all industry is owned by the state.

Energy Libya has an ample export surplus of oil and gas, and work is progressing on two vast new hydro-electric plants. A nuclear power plant at Sirte is also under construction.

	1993	1994	1995
Inflation (% change)	6.0	7.9	
Exchange rate (per US$)	0.33	0.36	0.36
Interest rate (% per annum)	7.0		
GDP (% real growth)	-2.8	-2.1	0.8
GDP (Million units of national currency)	10,478.9	10,872.0	10,959.0
GDP (US$ million)	31,754.2	30,200.0	30,441.6
GDP per capita (US$)	6,756.2	6,163.3	5,959.8
Consumption (Million units of national currency)	5,329.2	5,638.9	5,796.9
Consumption (US$ million)	16,149.1	15,663.6	16,102.4
Consumption per capita (US$)	3,436.0	3,196.7	3,152.5
Population, mid-year ('000)	4,700.0	4,900.0	5,107.8
Birth rate (per '000)	43.9	45.3	
Death rate (per '000)	10.3	8.1	
No. of households ('000)	910.0	953.4	999.0
Total exports (US$ million)	9,000.0	8,008.0	
Total imports (US$ million)	4,761.0	4,964.0	
Tourism receipts (US$ million)	5.0	4.7	
Tourist spending (US$ million)	148.4	139.2	143.1

Average household size 1995 (persons)	4.86		
Urban population 1995 (%)	86.0		
Age analysis (%) (1984)	*0-14* 49.7	*15-64* 38.7	*65+* 11.6
Population by sex (%) (1984)	*Male* 51.1	*Female* 48.9	
Life expectancy (years) (1990-95)	*Male* 61.6	*Female* 65.0	
Infant mortality (deaths per '000 live births) (1993)	68.3		
Adult literacy (%) (1995)	63.8		

TRADING PARTNERS

Major export destinations 1995 (% share)		Major import sources 1995 (% share)	
Italy	39.6	Italy	20.8
Germany	16.5	Germany	13.9
Spain	12.2	United Kingdom	8.2
Turkey	3.8	Japan	4.3

Liechtenstein

Area (km²)   160

Currency   Swiss franc (SFr = 100 rappen)

Location   Liechtenstein lies in Alpine territory to the east of Switzerland, bordering on the Austrian province of Vorarlberg. Thanks in part to excellent communications, the country's prominence is mainly to due to its activities as a tax haven and banking centre. It is represented abroad by the Swiss authorities. The capital is Vaduz.

Head of State   Prince Hans-Adam II

Head of Government   Mario Frick (1994)

Ruling Party   Vaterländische Union (VU-Patriotic Party) and Fortschrittliche Bürgerpartei (FBP-Progressive Citizens' Party).

Political Structure   Liechtenstein is a constitutional monarchy in which executive power is exercised by the Prime Minister rather than the Grand Duke. In practice, a firm duopoly exists between the VU and FBP, which share the cabinet posts. The Landtag (Parliament) is elected by popular mandate for a five-year term and has 25 members. Only a few of the residents are eligible to vote, since the great majority of the population comprises foreign nationals. Prince Hans-Adam persuaded the conservative legislators to join the European Economic Area in 1993, taking the country one step ahead of Switzerland, with which it is linked in an economic union. In 1995, he proposed a constitutional amendment giving Parliament the right to dissolve the monarchy if it wishes. In 1996, he suggested a referendum on incorporating Liechtenstein into Austria or Switzerland which he believes would be a better solution than a republic.

Last Elections   An inconclusive election to the 25-seat Landtag was held in February 1993, when the VU obtained 12 seats with 44% of the vote in a 90% turnout, and the FBP 11 seats. The Freie Wählerliste (Free Voters' List), which had failed to win any seats in 1989, won two seats on 10% of the vote. By the end of the summer, however, it was apparent that the new system was not working, and new elections were held in October, in which the VU was able to extend its majority and thus achieve a workable government. Women were allowed to vote for the first time in 1989 but moves to lower the voting age from 20 to 18 were rejected in a national referendum in June 1992. The next elections will be held in 1997.

Political Risk   With its legendary political stability, Liechtenstein is regarded as one of the most stable and affluent societies in Europe. Its ability to attract foreign capital is founded historically on its strong banking secrecy laws, but these are coming under attack both from the European Union and from Switzerland itself, where much of its wealth originates. A major dilution of these laws would leave its economy vulnerable.

Economy   Liechtenstein's special position within Europe has been challenged by the advent of the Single European Market and the compromises being forced upon its larger neighbour Switzerland in the area of banking secrecy. Yet there is a strong likelihood that its advantages to the world of international financial services will remain for the foreseeable future. Unemployment, at 1.3%, is among the lowest in Europe.

Main Industries   Liechtenstein's principal activity is still the provision of financial services, which contribute more than half of all GDP. Industry is limited in scale but of a specialist nature. A sophisticated light engineering industry has expertise in machine tools, artificial limbs (especially false teeth) and semiconductor technology. Also included in the industrial sector are textile manufacturers and companies making domestic water heating equipment. Farming is important despite the relative lack of available land, with cattle, fruit and vegetables being grown mainly on small plots of land.

Energy   Liechtenstein relies on its neighbours for virtually all its fuel requirements, including electricity.

	1993	1994	1995
Inflation (% change)	2.2	-1.0	0.4
Exchange rate (per US$)	1.52	1.31	1.18
Interest rate			
GDP (% real growth)	1.2	-5.9	0.7
GDP (Million units of national currency)	1,592.1	1,481.6	1,497.9
GDP (US$ million)	1,047.4	1,131.0	1,269.4
GDP per capita (US$)	34,914.5	37,699.7	41,621.0
Consumption (Million units of national currency)	750.0	697.9	705.5
Consumption (US$ million)	493.4	532.7	597.9
Consumption per capita (US$)	16,447.4	17,758.3	19,604.1
Population, mid-year ('000)	30.0	30.0	30.5
Birth rate (per '000)	12.4	13.1	12.9
Death rate (per '000)	6.0	6.6	6.5
No. of households ('000)	11.4	11.7	11.9
Total exports (US$ million)	1,650.0	1,800.0	
Total imports (US$ million)	1,450.0	1,500.0	
Tourism receipts (US$ million)			
Tourist spending (US$ million)			

Average household size 1995 (persons)	2.43				
Urban population 1995 (%)	21.4				
Age analysis (%) (1990)	*0-14*	19.6	*15-64*	69.9	*65+* 11.2
Population by sex (%)					
Life expectancy (years) (1980-84)	*Male*	66.0	*Female*	72.9	
Infant mortality (deaths per '000 live births)					
Adult literacy (%) (1985)	100.0				

Lithuania

Area (km²)   65,300

Currency   Litas

Location   Lithuania, the most southerly of the three Baltic republics, lies on the Baltic coast with Latvia to its north, Poland to the south, and Belarus to the east. There is also a small Russian enclave on the Baltic coast, around Zelenogradsk. The region, which is ethnically distinct, is largely swampland and lakes, with forestry being the most important natural resource. The capital is Vilnius.

Head of State   President Algirdas Brazauskas (1993)

Head of Government   Adolfas Slezevicius (March 1993)

Ruling Party   Democratic Labour Party

Political Structure   Lithuania was the first of the former Soviet states to declare unilateral independence from the USSR. Under the October 1993 Constitution the country has an executive President who chairs the 141-seat Seimas (formerly Auksiausiogi Taryba, or Supreme Council). The Council, for its part, is elected by popular mandate for a term of four years. Lithuania has applied for membership in the EU and hopes to join NATO.

Last Elections   At the parliamentary elections held in November 1993, the Democratic Labour Party (formerly the Communist Party) came to power, winning 72 seats in the 141-member Seimas while the nationalist Sajudis won 36 seats. The last presidential elections were held in February 1993 when Algirdas Brazauskas won a 60% majority.

Political Risk   The enthusiasm and sense of identity which drove Lithuania to independence have given way to a new mood of realism as the country struggles with its transition to a market economy. Government officials have belatedly realised that they face a rapidly mounting financial crisis. Foreign debt shot up from $8 million in 1994 to $388 million a year later, mostly to cover energy imports. The deterioration stems from several mistakes, but the most serious has probably been the government's reluctance to free prices. Meanwhile, many blame politicians for discouraging foreign investors, citing parliament's refusal to allow foreigners to own land.

International Disputes   Lithuania has resolutely dismissed Russian objections to its cultural identity, and identifies itself more closely with Poland. The country, however, is particularly vulnerable to Russian pressure because it provides the only land link to the heavily militarised Russian enclave of Kaliningrad, which would be the first line of defence against an expanded NATO.

Economy   Like the other Baltic States the Lithuanian Government embarked on a programme of economic reforms in the early 1990s. A radical restructuring of industry, coupled with the collapse of traditional export markets, led to a 23% fall in GDP and an even larger contraction of industrial output in 1993. Since then, the economy has stabilised and GDP grew by more than 3% in 1995. Privatisation was a key element in the reform programme and has accelerated the reorientation of trade from Eastern to Western Europe. Shortages of fuel and raw materials continue to create occasional bottlenecks and slow the pace of growth.

Main Industries   Lithuania is less industrialised than the other Baltic States. Important manufacturing industries are machine-building and metal-working which concentrate on the production of agricultural machinery, food processing equipment, shipbuilding and maintenance equipment. Before independence, the bulk of this machinery was sold to other republics of the USSR but many firms now have no viable market. The agricultural sector accounts for 12% of GDP with meat, dairy and fish products being major exports.

Energy   Lithuania is almost totally dependent on imports for its energy requirements and has periodically been forced to introduce energy rationing, along with big increases in the prices of electricity and petrol for consumers. Russia is the main source of the country's oil and gas supplies.

	1993	1994	1995
Inflation (% change)	410.2	72.2	39.7
Exchange rate (per US$)	3.90	4.00	4.00
Interest rate (% per annum)	91.9	62.3	27.1
GDP (% real growth)	-23.0	-11.2	3.1
GDP (Million units of national currency)	11,107.9	16,981.0	24,457.9
GDP (US$ million)	2,848.2	4,245.3	6,114.5
GDP per capita (US$)	763.6	1,141.2	1,648.1
Consumption (Million units of national currency)	131,796.0	96,750.0	125,780.0
Consumption (US$ million)	33,793.8	24,187.5	31,445.0
Consumption per capita (US$)	9,060.0	6,502.0	8,475.7
Population, mid-year ('000)	3,730.0	3,720.0	3,710.0
Birth rate (per '000)	12.5	11.5	11.1
Death rate (per '000)	12.3	12.5	12.2
No. of households ('000)	1,013.0	1,009.0	1,007.0
Total exports (US$ million)	2,025.0	2,029.0	2,698.0
Total imports (US$ million)	2,279.0	2,353.0	3,010.0
Tourism receipts (US$ million)			
Tourist spending (US$ million)			

Average household size 1995 (persons)	3.50				
Urban population 1995 (%)	72.1				
Age analysis (%) (1995)	*0-14* 22.3		*15-64* 66.3		*65+* 11.4
Population by sex (%) (1995)	*Male* 47.3		*Female* 52.7		
Life expectancy (years) (1992)	*Male* 64.9		*Female* 76.0		
Infant mortality (deaths per '000 live births) (1994)	14.1				
Adult literacy (%) (1989)	98.4				

TRADING PARTNERS

Major export destinations 1995 (% share)		Major import sources 1995 (% share)	
Germany	13.6	Russia	30.3
Russia	12.8	Germany	14.3
Belarus	9.7	Ukraine	7.0
Ukraine	9.1	Belarus	5.3

Luxembourg

Area (km²)   2,585

Currency   Luxembourg franc, at par with Belgian franc (LUF = 100 centimes)

Location   The Duchy of Luxembourg is situated in north-western Europe, on the coalfields which extend from Lille in northern France through Belgium and into the Ruhr valley. With Germany to its east, Belgium to the north-west and France to the south, its excellent communications have helped to make it one of the most important trade and transport centres in the EU. Its climate is temperate, with generally mild winters. The capital is Luxembourg-Ville.

Head of State   Grand Duke Jean

Head of Government   Jean-Claude Juncker (January 1995)

Ruling Party   Christian Social Party in coalition with Socialist Workers' Party.

Political Structure   As a constitutional monarchy, Luxembourg vests all legislative authority in the unicameral Chamber of Deputies and in the Cabinet. For the last decade the country has been ruled by a broad coalition of right and left, allowing a substantial degree of continuity and stability. In 1989 the Chamber of Deputies was reduced in size from 64 seats to 60 in order to accommodate a shrinkage in the electorate. The Chamber is elected by popular mandate for a term of five years.

Last Elections   Elections to the Chamber of Deputies were held in June 1994, when the Christian Social Party won 21 of 60 seats, compared with 17 for the Socialist Workers' Party and 12 for the Democrats (Parti démocratique). The environmentalist Di Grëng Alternativ gained four seats, and the Comité d'Action 5/6, a party campaigning on the single issue of pensions, won five. Jacques Santer, who had become premier in 1984, left the post in January 1995 to become President of the European Commission, and was replaced by Jean-Claude Juncker.

Political Risk   Luxembourg is regarded as one of the most secure countries in Europe, thanks not only to its political stability but also to its powerful attraction as an offshore banking centre. The transition from its former dependence on steel and coal is now complete. High living standards combined with a central location in the EU reinforce this position. It would, however, be vulnerable to any EU legislation which adversely affected its financial markets.

Economy   Luxembourg's conversion from heavy goods producer to financial services provider has been entirely successful, owing in part to its advantageous location between Belgium, France and Germany. The country has a customs union with Belgium, and their currencies are mutually acceptable. Even so, economic growth is modest owing to the economy's extensive integration with other European countries which are currently in recession.

Main Industries   Luxembourg's industrial sector, which once specialised in heavy industries such as steel and coal processing, underwent a drastic restructuring in favour of lighter industries. The restructuring was mainly the result of pressure applied by the EU in order to close down surplus capacity. Nowadays, light engineering, food products and high technology are at least as important as the country's more capital-intensive industries. The country sought, with considerable success, to establish its financial services. Luxembourg is particularly strong in bond trading and has virtually cornered the market in several types of investment funds favoured by Western Europeans. The total funds under management exceeded $340 billion in 1995 and total deposits with Luxembourg banks was a staggering $517 billion. Farming is adequate to provide a substantial degree of self-sufficiency in food products, mainly wheat, potatoes and other vegetables.

Energy   Luxembourg has large remaining coal stocks, but in practice it relies on oil and gas imports from abroad for a large proportion of its needs.

	1993	1994	1995
Inflation (% change)	3.6	2.2	1.9
Exchange rate (per US$)	34.60	33.46	29.48
Interest rate (% per annum)	7.7	6.6	6.5
GDP (% real growth)	1.0	-0.6	-0.3
GDP (Billion units of national currency)	354.9	360.7	366.7
GDP (US$ million)	10,258.1	10,781.2	12,437.2
GDP per capita (US$)	25,774.1	26,892.6	30,861.7
Consumption (Billion units of national currency)	194.3	199.2	204.1
Consumption (US$ million)	5,615.0	5,952.5	6,923.9
Consumption per capita (US$)	14,108.1	14,847.9	17,180.8
Population, mid-year ('000)	398.0	400.9	403.0
Birth rate (per '000)	13.4	13.0	12.7
Death rate (per '000)	9.8	9.4	9.5
No. of households ('000)	137.0	137.9	138.0
Total exports (US$ million)	6,358.4	6,500.0	
Total imports (US$ million)	8,092.5	8,500.0	
Tourism receipts (US$ million)			
Tourist spending (US$ million)			

Average household size 1995 (persons)	2.77				
Urban population 1995 (%)	89.1				
Age analysis (%) (1995)	*0-14* 17.5		*15-64* 68.3		*65+* 14.2
Population by sex (%) (1995)	*Male* 49.4		*Female* 50.6		
Life expectancy (years) (1994)	*Male* 72.6		*Female* 79.1		
Infant mortality (deaths per '000 live births) (1993)	6.0				
Adult literacy (%) (1982)	100.0				

Macau

Area (km²) 16

Currency Pataca (Pt = 100 avos)

Location Macau (Macao) is a tiny territory at the mouth of the Pearl River in southern China, and is adjacent to Hong Kong, with which it has a ferry link. Consisting almost entirely of a port and two small islands, Taipa and Coloane, the entire country is only about 16 square km in size. Like Hong Kong, it was built to service Portugal's trade with China in the nineteenth century. Macau has a pleasant, warm climate. The capital is Macau.

Head of State President Jorge Sampio (Portugal) (1996)

Head of Government Gen. Vasco Rocha Vieira

Ruling Party There are no political parties in Macau.

Political Structure Macau, currently described as a Special Territory of Portugal, will return to Chinese rule in 1999, when it becomes the Chinese Special Administrative Region (SAR) of Macau. The constitution gives the Governor full executive power except in the field of foreign affairs, which are determined by Portugal. He presides over a 23-member Legislative Assembly which includes eight directly elected members, seven government appointees and eight nominated by businesses. A Basic Law has been agreed with China for the period after the handover in 1999. The legal arrangements for the transfer are similar to those agreed for Hong Kong. Yet there is little of the acrimony that is apparent in the latter case.

Last Elections Elections to the Legislative Assembly were held in October 1988, when independent "liberals" were appointed to three of the eight directly elected seats.

Political Risk Like Hong Kong, Macau has received assurances that China intends to let it keep its capitalist structure indefinitely. Preparations for the handover are certainly proceeding much more smoothly in Macau. A portion of its legislature has been chosen through universal suffrage since 1976 and China has voiced no objections, despite its criticism of Hong Kong's partial democratisation. The better relations stem in part from history. Portugal administers Macau on China's sufferance and Lisbon has twice offered it back - during the cultural revolution and again after the Portuguese revolution in 1994.

International Disputes Macau's disputes with China are all but over. Portugal has now agreed that the country should revert to Chinese rule in 1999 when its lease expires, whereupon it will become a special administrative area of China.

Economy Macau's economy is visibility coming under the sway of China. Mainland interests have a 50% stake in building the new airport. The state-owned Bank of China and its affiliates have nearly two-fifths of Macau's banking deposits. Easy money policies in China fuelled a property craze in 1992, when private investments from the mainland rose by 40%. By 1996 there were some 30% more homes than there were households in Macau. The neighbouring economic zone of Zhuhai has a workforce six times the size of Macau's on a sixth of the pay. Macau hopes to become the service hub for the southern part of the Pearl River Delta but its economic future remains uncertain.

Main Industries Macau's principal industry is tourism, which attracts visitors from all over the world to its gambling centres. Gambling taxes provide 60% of all government revenues. There are, however, a number of manufacturing companies making textiles and high-technology goods. More important, perhaps, are the considerable revenues from foreign trade, especially with Hong Kong and China. A huge land reclamation project, funded with mainland money, will leave Macau with twice as much acreage at the end of the century as at the beginning.

Energy Macau depends entirely on imports for all forms of energy.

	1993	1994	1995
Inflation (% change)	7.5	6.3	6.4
Exchange rate (per US$)	8.00	7.99	8.00
Interest rate			
GDP (% real growth)	5.0	4.0	2.0
GDP (Million units of national currency)	37,985.4	41,993.6	45,574.8
GDP (US$ million)	4,748.2	5,255.8	5,696.9
GDP per capita (US$)	12,174.8	13,139.4	13,894.8
Consumption (Million units of national currency)	16,959.8	17,694.5	18,123.0
Consumption (US$ milllon)	2,120.0	2,214.6	2,265.4
Consumption per capita (US$)	5,435.8	5,536.5	5,525.3
Population, mid-year ('000)	390.0	400.0	410.0
Birth rate (per '000)	15.3	15.2	
Death rate (per '000)	4.0	3.3	
No. of households ('000)	117.1	122.2	127.3
Total exports (US$ million)	1,950.0	1,866.0	
Total imports (US$ million)	21,000.0	2,126.2	
Tourism receipts (US$ million)	2,500.0	2,553.1	
Tourist spending (US$ million)	71.0	72.5	74.2

Average household size 1995 (persons)	3.06				
Urban population 1995 (%)	98.8				
Age analysis (%) (1992)	*0-14* 24.4		*15-64* 69.1		*65+* 6.6
Population by sex (%) (1991)	*Male* 48.7		*Female* 51.3		
Life expectancy (years) (1988)	*Male* 75.0		*Female* 80.3		
Infant mortality (deaths per '000 live births) (1992)	7.3				
Adult literacy (%) (1970)	79.4				

Macedonia

Area (km²)   25,713

Currency   Denar

Location   Macedonia covers 25,713 square km in the far south of the old Yugoslavia and borders Bulgaria in the east, Albania in the west and Greece to the south. It is characterised by mainly mountainous scenery with a river valley running north to south through its centre. The capital is Skopje.

Head of State   President Kiro Gligorov

Head of Government   Branko Crvenkovski

Ruling Party   Social Democratic Party of Macedonia

Political Structure   Macedonia is the most recent European nation to receive full recognition by the EU and the UN. Its acceptance was held up by Greece's refusal to recognise its name, on the grounds that Greece already laid claim to a region named Macedonia on the northern Aegean coast - a small part of the very large Macedonian territory which had existed in the Middle Ages. However, acceptance followed in 1993 after the state agreed to be known as the Former Yugoslav Republic of Macedonia. The country has a non-executive President and an elected Cabinet which answers to a unicameral Parliament.

Last Elections   Legislative elections were held in October and November 1994. The result was a coalition government between President Gligorov's party of free-market Liberals, known as the Alliance of Macedonia, and the Social Democrats (ex-communists). The coalition collapsed in February 1996 and the Social Democrats are now in charge.

Political Risk   Macedonia's popular president, Gligorov, was nearly killed by a car-bomb in October 1995. He has now recovered and resumed office but the coalition he fashioned fell apart in the meantime. Gligorov has led his new country through an extremely difficult period but he is 78 years old and still enfeebled from the assassination attempt. He is still the chief guarantor of his country's political stability but the country can not continue to rely on an ageing political father-figure. Relations with Greece have been severely strained in recent years but are now improving, thanks in part to a change in leadership in Greece.

International Disputes   Greece's unilateral trade ban on the disputed territory has now been lifted. Concessions to the country's ethnic Albanians have helped to relieve tensions with that country.

Economy   The economy is starting to pick up. Inflation fell from 57% in 1994 to 9% in 1995. A privatisation plan lets managers acquire control of their companies and pay the bills out of future profits. Unemployment is exceptionally high (45%) though most workers now have jobs in the private sector. More foreign aid is coming into the country and Macedonia's chances of getting cheap loans are improving.

Main Industries   Industries in Macedonia include brewing, flour milling, tobacco, textiles, carpets and cement. Most of the country is agrarian; its population depends mainly on farming with some mineral extraction.

Energy   There are shortages of virtually all fuels. Electricity supply problems have sometimes led to a declaration of a state of emergency.

	1993	1994	1995
Inflation (% change)	581.0	57.0	9.0
Exchange rate (per US$)			
Interest rate			
GDP (% real growth)	-8.0	-4.0	-4.0
GDP			
GDP (US$ million)	1,676.9	1,610.0	1,538.0
GDP per capita (US$)	791.0	752.3	712.0
Consumption			
Consumption (US$ million)			
Consumption per capita (US$)			
Population, mid-year ('000)	2,120.0	2,140.0	2,160.0
Birth rate (per '000)	13.4	13.2	13.2
Death rate (per '000)	10.0	10.1	10.2
No. of households ('000)			
Total exports (US$ million)	489.8	644.0	
Total imports (US$ million)			
Tourism receipts (US$ million)			
Tourist spending (US$ million)			

Average household size 1995 (persons)			
Urban population 1995 (%)	59.9		
Age analysis (%)			
Population by sex (%) (1991)	*Male* 50.5	*Female* 49.5	
Life expectancy (years) (1991)	*Male* 71.5	*Female* 75.9	
Infant mortality (deaths per '000 live births)			
Adult literacy (%)			

TRADING PARTNERS

Major export destinations 1995 (% share)		Major import sources 1995 (% share)	
Germany	31.0	Germany	24.2
Italy	19.6	Italy	21.2
Russia	8.9	Slovenia	16.7
Slovenia	8.4	Austria	5.2

Madagascar

Area (km²) 594,180

Currency Franc malgache (franc MG = 100 centimes)

Location The island of Madagascar lies in the Indian Ocean, about 500 km off the coast of Mozambique. It is the fourth largest island in the world, measuring some 2,000 km from north to south. The country has a mountainous elevation, with substantial lowland areas, and enjoys a warm and moderate climate. The capital is Antananarivo.

Head of State President Albert Zafy (1993)

Head of Government Richard Adriamanjato (1995)

Ruling Party Comité des Forces Vives, an alliance of the National Union for Democracy and Development and the Rasalama Active Forces Cartel.

Political Structure Madagascar, which was known until 1975 as the Malagasy Republic, became independent from France in 1960. The President is elected by universal suffrage for a seven-year term but, traditionally, it has been the Prime Minister who directs the country through a 138-member National Assembly. However, in 1995 President Zafy won a referendum which gives him - and not parliament - the right to appoint the prime minister. A new Constitution, known as the Third Republic, was introduced in 1992, allowing for multi-party democracy. A senate, appointed by an electoral college, is provided for in the Constitution but has yet to be appointed.

Last Elections The National People's Assembly was last elected in June 1993, when the Comité des Forces Vives won 48 of the 138 seats, compared with 10 for the GRAD party, 10 seats for the Famima Party of the outgoing President Didier Ratsiraka, and four seats for the Fihaonana Party of the then Prime Minister Guy Razanamasy (who was replaced in August 1993 by Francisque Ravony). The Leader Party obtained eight seats. Effectively, this left the new President Zafy controlling 74 of the 138 seats.

Political Risk The president's bizarre scheme to raise capital by what he referred to as "parallel financing" drew criticism from the international community and international lending institutions. The objective was ostensibly to attract private financing for development projects but suspicion is widespread that the scheme is actually permitting the laundering of drug money. Funds have poured into the country but little have reached the people. The IMF threatened to suspend its aid if parallel financing was not abandoned. When the prime minister, Francisque Ravony, sided with the IMF, he was removed following a referendum giving the president (and not parliament) the authority to appoint the holder of this office.

International Disputes Madagascar has a claim against France for the return of various largely uninhabited islands, which are currently administered as part of the Réunion territory. The United Nations has endorsed Madagascar's claim for the islands.

Economy By mid-1995 there was a rising tide of discontent about the government's handling of the economy. Consumers are being squeezed by an austerity programme which was imposed in an effort to end the overspending and reduce the country's high level of external debt. Despite these efforts, Madagascar has about $5 billion in unserviced debt and a dismal credit-rating record. Even worse, malnutrition is rampant and the country's per capita income has plummeted to about $230.

Main Industries Madagascar's economy relies very heavily on agriculture, which employs 80% of the workforce, mainly in a subsistence capacity. Most of the farming is in the drier, western half of the island where rice, maize, bananas and sweet potatoes are grown for the domestic market. Forestry is important, though conservationists are pressing for restraint. Industrial development is limited and dominated by small-scale activities such as food processing, soap making, textile manufacture and brewing. There are, however, plants making cement and fertilisers. Madagascar has large resources of chrome, gold, graphite, uranium, iron ore and nickel, but at present only chrome and graphite are being exploited. There are a number of companies mining precious and semi-precious stones.

Energy Madagascar has located offshore oil deposits of up to 200 million barrels, but these are unlikely to be enough for self-sufficiency. At present, all supplies are imported. There are hydro-electric resources which generate some 60% of the country's electricity requirements.

	1993	1994	1995
Inflation (% change)	10.0	38.9	49.1
Exchange rate (per US$)	1,913.80	3,067.30	4,006.20
Interest rate			
GDP (% real growth)	5.3	1.9	3.6
GDP (Billion units of national currency)	6,450.9	9,131.1	14,105.0
GDP (US$ million)	3,370.7	2,976.9	3,520.8
GDP per capita (US$)	243.4	208.2	238.3
Consumption (Billion units of national currency)	5,798.0	8,245.0	12,795.3
Consumption (US$ million)	3,029.6	2,688.0	3,193.9
Consumption per capita (US$)	218.7	188.0	216.2
Population, mid-year ('000)	13,850.0	14,300.0	14,775.0
Birth rate (per '000)	44.6	45.2	
Death rate (per '000)	14.9	13.4	
No. of households ('000)	2,438.9	2,526.8	2,723.0
Total exports (US$ million)	454.6	485.3	
Total imports (US$ million)	546.0	875.0	
Tourism receipts (US$ million)	41.0	58.3	
Tourist spending (US$ million)	42.3	60.1	71.4

Average household size 1995 (persons)	5.15				
Urban population 1995 (%)	27.1				
Age analysis (%) (1991, est)	*0-14* 45.1		*15-64* 51.9		*65+* 3.0
Population by sex (%) (1993)	*Male* 49.5		*Female* 50.5		
Life expectancy (years) (1990-95)	*Male* 61.6		*Female* 65.0		
Infant mortality (deaths per '000 live births) (1993)	93.0				
Adult literacy (%) (1995)	80.2				

TRADING PARTNERS

Major export destinations 1995 (% share)		Major import sources 1995 (% share)	
France	65.0	France	47.5
USA	13.4	Japan	6.4
Germany	13.2	Germany	5.9
Italy	8.3	USA	3.7

Malawi

Area (km²) 94,080

Currency Kwacha (K = 100 tambala)

Location Malawi is a long, landlocked triangular strip of country lying in central South-East Africa, where it is bounded in the south by Mozambique, in the north by Tanzania, and in the west by Zambia. The territory is fertile and permeated with large rivers and has a pleasant sub-tropical climate. The capital is Lilongwe.

Head of State President Baktili Muluzu (May 1994)

Head of Government Baktili Muluzu

Ruling Party The United Democratic Party (UDP) dominates a coalition.

Political Structure Malawi has an executive President who appoints his own Cabinet. Theoretically, all legislative power is vested in the National Assembly with 177 elected officials. A Senate is also provided for in the Constitution, but it is disbarred from taking office until May 1999.

Last Elections Elections held in May 1994 produced a hung government for the United Democratic Party of Baktili Muluzu, which won only 84 of the 177 elected seats. The Congress Party of former President Hastings Kamuzu Banda won 52 seats. Other seats went mainly to independents and smaller parties. Thereupon Banda stood down as President in favour of Muluzu. The UDP's ability to rule has been increasingly challenged as opposition parties become better organised.

Political Risk The removal of President Banda marked the end of a period of popular opposition to his increasingly autocratic rule. Banda, along with several colleagues, was subsequently charged with the murder of a rival politician during the 1980s. Many critics fear that the current government is following the practices of its predecessor by devoting too much of its energies to attacks on opponents rather than on the development of a coherent set of economic policies to promote stronger growth.

International Disputes Malawi has reached agreement with neighbouring Tanzania on a land corridor allowing it access to the Indian Ocean, which should enhance the country's prosperity. It has a dispute with Tanzania, however, over the ownership of territorial water rights in Lake Malawi (called Lake Nyasa by Tanzania) where their borders meet. Malawi has also been accused of harbouring refugees from neighbouring Mozambique, despite a repatriation agreement negotiated in late 1993.

Economy Malawi's economy remains constrained by political and economic uncertainties at present, and by the tensions along its borders. It does, however, have considerable scope for expansion. Foreign exchange controls were lifted in 1994 and overseas investors have responded positively. Recurrent droughts have the growth of domestic incomes.

Main Industries Agriculture contributes around 40% of GDP in a typical year and employs over 85% of the workforce. Export crops such as tobacco, tea or sugar account for over 75% of export revenues and have traditionally been produced by larger farms. Smallholders, who normally produce maize and groundnuts for subsistence purposes, are being encouraged to expand into cash crops. Manufacturing covers a fairly wide range of consumer products, including food processing, pharmaceuticals, cement and tobacco products. Tourism is being developed. Malawi has large reserves of coal, some of which are extracted, and there are known deposits of uranium, phosphates, bauxite, graphite and asbestos.

Energy Half of the country's fuel requirements are met with domestic coal mining. Otherwise, the country depends on imports of oil. The vast majority of Malawi's electricity is generated by hydro-electric stations.

	1993	1994	1995
Inflation (% change)	19.7	34.7	25.0
Exchange rate (per US$)	4.40	8.74	15.32
Interest rate (% per annum)	29.5	31.0	
GDP (% real growth)	13.0	-6.3	-2.1
GDP (Million units of national currency)	8,881.6	11,209.3	13,720.2
GDP (US$ million)	2,018.5	1,282.5	895.6
GDP per capita (US$)	221.1	135.6	91.5
Consumption (Million units of national currency)	7,236.0	8,924.7	10,675.4
Consumption (US$ million)	1,644.5	1,021.1	696.8
Consumption per capita (US$)	180.1	107.9	71.2
Population, mid-year ('000)	9,130.0	9,460.0	9,790.0
Birth rate (per '000)	55.0	50.4	
Death rate (per '000)	21.7	23.2	
No. of households ('000)	1,653.3	1,647.0	1,651.0
Total exports (US$ million)	320.0	325.0	
Total imports (US$ million)	546.0	491.0	
Tourism receipts (US$ million)	16.5	18.1	
Tourist spending (US$ million)	3.0	3.3	2.3

Average household size 1995 (persons)	5.63		
Urban population 1995 (%)	13.5		
Age analysis (%) (1991)	*0-14* 48.3	*15-64* 49.2	*65+* 2.5
Population by sex (%) (1991)	*Male* 48.8	*Female* 51.2	
Life expectancy (years) (1992-95)	*Male* 43.5	*Female* 46.8	
Infant mortality (deaths per '000 live births)			
Adult literacy (%) (1995)	56.4		

TRADING PARTNERS

Major export destinations 1995 (% share)		Major import sources 1995 (% share)	
South Africa	42.3	South Africa	44.1
Germany	4.9	Germany	5.0
United Kingdom	4.3	United Kingdom	4.5
USA	3.7	Austria	3.7

Malaysia

Area (km²)   332,965

Currency   Malaysian dollar/Ringgit (= 100 cents)

Location   Malaysia, one of the largest countries in the Asia-Pacific group, comprises the 11 states of Peninsular Malaysia, where the bulk of the population live, as well as the predominantly forested areas of Sabah and Sarawak, across the South China Sea on the northern coast of Borneo. Its climate is tropical and often humid. The capital is Kuala Lumpur.

Head of State   HM Sultan Ja'afar ibni Abdul Rahman (1994)

Head of Government   Datuk Seri Dr Mahathir Mohamed

Ruling Party   The Barisan Nasional (National Front) coalition, dominated by the United Malays National Organisation (UMNO).

Political Structure   Malaysia is a constitutional monarchy in which, unusually, the monarch (Yang di-Pertuan Agong) is elected every five years from among the tribal elders of peninsular Malaysia. The influence of the monarchy is limited, however, by new measures introduced in 1994. All effective power is actually exercised by the Prime Minister and his Cabinet, who report to a bicameral legislature. The House of Representatives (Dewan Rakyat, or Lower House) has 180 members elected for five years, while the 70-member Senate (Dewan Negara) is appointed by the monarch. There are numerous regional assemblies. Constitutional amendments in 1993 reduced the legal immunity of the nine Malay rulers, and in practice all but two of the regional Assemblies are controlled by the National Front coalition. A new federal capital, to be called Putrajaya, is now being built near Kuala Lumpur, and is due for completion in 2008.

Last Elections   The May 1995 elections to the House of Representatives produced a landslide victory for the ruling UMNO coalition. Opposition groups were combined in the Angkatan Perpaduan Ummah coalition, but as in 1990 they failed to make a significant impact.

Political Risk   Mahathir's position has substantially improved since the publication of the revised policy which discriminates less openly against the country's Indians and Chinese in favour of the Malay majority. Nevertheless, his Government has had to take tough and sometimes controversial action against dissidents and employs an active press censorship department. Illegal immigration has become so widespread in Malaysia that it is now described as a threat to national security. Mainly from Indonesia and the Philippines, foreigners account for an eighth of the work force and at least 500,000 are illegal.

International Disputes   Malaysia resolutely rejects a claim by the Philippines for the sovereignty of the entire territory of Sabah, its easternmost province. The issue led to a serious breakdown in bilateral relations in the 1960s. Despite continuous negotiations since 1969, the issue remains live. Malaysia is also pressing Indonesia for the return of two islands, Sipadan and Ligitan. It is one of many claimants for the sovereignty of the Spratly Islands in the South China Seas, where oil prospecting has been in progress.

Economy   Malaysia's GDP has been expanding at an impressive pace (typically 8-9% per year) since the late 1980s. Foreign investment has been pouring in, the government is spending huge amounts on a host of construction projects and home-grown conglomerates have become a force throughout the region. These developments are welcome but they are taking a toll. The country simply does not have enough workers (particularly skilled ones). As a result, inflation is on the rise, imports are increasingly outstripping exports and a few foreign companies have begun to relocate to cheaper markets. Policy makers concede that the country must increase its exports to staunch a growing balance-of-payments deficit and are attempting to restrain domestic consumption. Yet the government insists that its ultimate objective - to turn Malaysia into a fully developed country by 2020 - will be achieved. Private economists admit that the country's economic performance is one of the best in Asia. However, they also argue that new kinds of labour-saving investment must be encouraged. Without this shift, Malaysia's impressive growth performance will soon be jeopardised.

Main Industries   Malaysia's agricultural sector is an important foreign-exchange earner with exports of rubber (of which it produces 40% of world requirements), palm oil, cocoa, coconuts, peppers, sugar cane and tea. It derives a considerable portion of its foreign revenues from its extensive timber industry, although operations have aroused deep concern among conservationists. The country's mineral resources also make an important contribution to the economy. Malaysia is the world's largest tin producer and has ample deposits of gold, coal and other minerals. The state-owned oilfields contain up to four billion barrels of oil and supply all domestic requirements. The manufacturing sector is rapidly growing, with the traditional raw materials processing industries giving way to engineering, automobile production, electronic components and consumer electronics.

Energy   Malaysia is self-sufficient in all fuels. Thanks largely to the abundance of hydrocarbons, hydro-electricity provides no more than a third of all electricity.

	1993	1994	1995
Inflation (% change)	3.5	3.7	5.3
Exchange rate (per US$)	2.57	2.62	2.51
Interest rate (% per annum)	9.1	7.6	7.6
GDP (% real growth)	8.7	9.6	8.1
GDP (Million units of national currency)	163,039.0	185,344.0	210,975.8
GDP (US$ million)	82,193.0	92,857.0	84,054.1
GDP per capita (US$)	4,312.3	4,725.5	4,268.9
Consumption (Million units of national currency)	82,193.0	92,857.0	105,041.6
Consumption (US$ million)	31,981.7	35,441.6	41,849.3
Consumption per capita (US$)	1,677.9	1,803.6	2,125.4
Population, mid-year ('000)	19,060.0	19,650.0	19,690.0
Birth rate (per '000)	28.6	26.8	
Death rate (per '000)	4.5	4.6	
No. of households ('000)	3,850.9	3,897.0	4,028.0
Total exports (US$ million)	47,122.0	58,756.0	74,045.0
Total imports (US$ million)	45,657.0	59,581.0	76,612.0
Tourism receipts (US$ million)	1,876.0	2,099.2	
Tourist spending (US$ million)	1,960.0	2,193.2	2,589.7

Average household size 1995 (persons)	4.64				
Urban population 1995 (%)	53.7				
Age analysis (%) (1992)	*0-14* 36.4		*15-64* 59.7		*65+* 3.9
Population by sex (%) (1992)	*Male* 50.4		*Female* 49.6		
Life expectancy (years) (1993)	*Male* 69.1		*Female* 73.8		
Infant mortality (deaths per '000 live births) (1993)	13.0				
Adult literacy (%) (1995)	83.5				

TRADING PARTNERS

Major export destinations 1995 (% share)		Major import sources 1995 (% share)	
USA	21.6	Japan	27.8
Singapore	17.3	USA	16.3
Japan	13.1	Singapore	10.6
Hong Kong	5.4	Germany	4.7

Maldives

Area (km²)   298

Currency   Rufiyaa (Rf = 100 laris)

Location   The Maldives are a group of 1,190 coral islands lying in the central Indian Ocean, some 675 km south-west of Sri Lanka and extending for almost 1,000 km from one extreme to the other. Only about 200 of the islands are inhabited and none extends more than 2.5 metres above sea level. The capital is Malé.

Head of State   President Maumoon Abdul Gayoom (1978)

Head of Government   President Maumoon Abdul Gayoom

Ruling Party   There are no political parties in the Maldives.

Political Structure   The Republic of Maldives is an independent member of the Commonwealth in which all executive functions are vested in the President and his Cabinet. The President is elected for a five-year term of office. He reports to a 48-member Citizens' Assembly (Majlis) and appoints eight members of that group. The remainder are elected by universal adult suffrage for a term of five years.

Last Elections   Elections to the Majlis were held in October 1994, when all candidates were obliged to campaign on independent tickets in the absence of political parties. The President was re-elected unopposed in October 1993.

Political Risk   Allegations of corruption and nepotism among the President's family have periodically re-emerged over the past several years. A full-scale coup attempt was launched against Gayoom in 1988, although it was foiled by a contingent of Indian paratroopers called in from India. More recently, there have been calls for a fully elected Majlis, but these have been energetically suppressed by the Government.

International Disputes   The Maldives has become an outspoken supporter of international moves to curb global warming. Fears of a rise in global sea levels have given rise to the very real possibility that a sizeable proportion of the landmass could become submerged in the next 30 years.

Economy   The Maldives has a diversified and potentially prosperous economy, but still requires additional funds if it is to raise its infrastructure facilities to a level which would facilitate a major expansion of the tourist industry.

Main Industries   The islands rely to a substantial degree on the tourist industry, with 85% of all visitors coming from Western Europe. Yet farming and fisheries are still the main activity for most of the population, providing about a third of GDP. Fishing alone contributes a fifth of all exports, with tuna and salted fish predominating. Industry is only barely developed, and rarely contributes more than 6-7% of GDP. Activity centres on the processing of agricultural raw materials and there is a sizeable garments industry. Construction is almost as important and stands to benefit from the growth in tourism activity. Otherwise shipping and ship repairing are the largest areas of the economy.

	1993	1994	1995
Inflation (% change)	20.2	11.0	4.6
Exchange rate (per US$)	10.96	11.59	11.78
Interest rate (% per annum)	7.8		
GDP (% real growth)	-4.0	-1.3	
GDP (Million units of national currency)	1,391.0	1,524.1	1,594.2
GDP (US$ million)	126.9	131.5	135.3
GDP per capita (US$)	528.8	526.0	520.5
Consumption (Million units of national currency)	816.7	894.4	935.1
Consumption (US$ million)	74.5	77.2	79.4
Consumption per capita (US$)	310.5	308.7	305.3
Population, mid-year ('000)	240.0	250.0	260.0
Birth rate (per '000)	39.6	43.6	
Death rate (per '000)	6.3	6.2	
No. of households ('000)	40.9	42.9	44.7
Total exports (US$ million)	35.0	46.0	52.0
Total imports (US$ million)	185.0	222.0	260.0
Tourism receipts (US$ million)	146.0	147.4	
Tourist spending (US$ million)	29.0	29.3	30.1

Average household size 1995 (persons)	5.53				
Urban population 1995 (%)	26.8				
Age analysis (%) (1990)	*0-14* 46.9		*15-64* 50.1		*65+* 2.7
Population by sex (%) (1990)	*Male* 51.3		*Female* 48.7		
Life expectancy (years) (1990)	*Male* 55.3		*Female* 55.3		
Infant mortality (deaths per '000 live births)					
Adult literacy (%) (1995)	93.2				

Mali

Area (km²)   1,240,140

Currency   CFA franc (= 100 centimes)

Location   Mali, the former French colony of Soudan, lies in the geographic centre of North-West Africa, an area of almost unbroken desert except for the marshlands of the upper Niger and the slightly more hospitable Niger valley further down towards the capital Bamako. With Algeria to the north, Mauritania and Senegal to the west, Burkina Faso and Niger to the east and Côte d'Ivoire and Guinea to the south, its only access to the sea is through Senegal, Guinea or The Gambia. The capital is Bamako.

Head of State   President Alpha Oumar Konaré (June 1992)

Head of Government   Ibrahim Boubakar Keita (February 1994)

Ruling Party   Alliance for Democracy in Mali (ADEMA) leads a three-party coalition.

Political Structure   Mali's political system has been generally confused since the March 1991 overthrow of President Moussa Traoré, who came to power in the 1968 coup. The 25-member Transition Committee for the Salvation of the People which succeeded him was later withdrawn and was replaced in 1992 by an elected Parliament. Traoré was sentenced to death for murder in February 1993.

Last Elections   Alpha Oumar Konaré was elected President in April 1992, after winning 69% of the second-ballot votes in a national election. His party had earlier won the March 1992 elections to the national Parliament, with 76 of the 116 elected seats. The National Committee for Democratic Initiative won nine seats, the Sudanese Union-African Democratic Rally eight, the Popular Movement for the Development of the Republic of West Africa six, and various other 17 seats. 13 seats were reserved for representatives of Malian expatriates. Yet most of the major opposition parties had boycotted the poll, raising doubts as to its validity.

Political Risk   A prolonged drought and a series of domestic disturbances in Mali have created particular problems for the Government in recent years. By 1995, the government's control over the country was becoming shaky. Periodic rebellions by the nomadic Tuareg tribesmen have eased since 1992, when a ceasefire was agreed to make way for ongoing talks, but a renewed government offensive was launched in November 1994. Meanwhile, there have been serious disturbances among students.

International Disputes   Despite its poverty and its inability to defend itself adequately without French assistance, Mali has found itself repeatedly drawn into the conflicts of its neighbours.

Economy   Mali's parched climate and its geographical isolation from the rest of the world have combined to present major obstacles to its economic development. An improvement in world commodity prices brought some relief in 1995 but the country still relies heavily on external assistance, especially from France. Meanwhile, a 50% devaluation of the CFA franc has made it more difficult for the government to service its foreign debt.

Main Industries   The agricultural sector is by far the largest area of the economy, employing over 80% of the workforce in some capacity - albeit generally in a subsistence capacity - and contributing around a quarter of GDP. Cotton, groundnuts, wheat, sorghum and fruit and vegetables are grown for export, while rice, millet, sorghum, maize and groundnuts are the staples for the domestic population. There is a substantial amount of cattle herding in the dry zones. Minerals are an important source of foreign currency, with uranium, salt, gold and phosphates being mined. There are known deposits of bauxite, iron, manganese and tin, but these are only marginally exploited. Industry remains limited to the fulfilment of local needs, and centres on the processing of agricultural raw materials.

Energy   Mali relies on imports for the greater part of its modest energy requirements. It does, however, have enough electricity to meet its own needs, with Bamako being fed by a hydro-electric system.

	1993	1994	1995
Inflation (% change)	-0.3	6.2	3.5
Exchange rate (per US$)	283.16	555.20	498.70
Interest rate (% per annum)	17.5	17.5	16.0
GDP (% real growth)	3.3	-0.2	0.5
GDP (Million units of national currency)	709,500.0	973,700.0	1,012,818.4
GDP (US$ million)	2,505.7	1,753.8	2,030.9
GDP per capita (US$)	247.2	167.9	192.3
Consumption (Million units of national currency)	433,069.1	449,650.5	353,856.0
Consumption (US$ million)	1,529.4	809.9	709.6
Consumption per capita (US$)	150.9	77.5	67.2
Population, mid-year ('000)	10,135.0	10,448.4	10,560.0
Birth rate (per '000)	50.3	51.8	
Death rate (per '000)	21.8	20.6	
No. of households ('000)	1,828.5	1,894.4	1,987.0
Total exports (US$ million)	169.6	265.8	
Total imports (US$ million)	600.0	970.8	
Tourism receipts (US$ million)	11.0	11.5	
Tourist spending (US$ million)	61.0	63.6	55.7

Average household size 1995 (persons)	5.05				
Urban population 1995 (%)	27.0				
Age analysis (%) (1987)	*0-14* 45.9		*15-64* 50.3		*65+* 3.8
Population by sex (%) (1987)	*Male* 48.9		*Female* 51.1		
Life expectancy (years) (1987)	*Male* 55.2		*Female* 58.7		
Infant mortality (deaths per '000 live births)					
Adult literacy (%) (1995)	31.0				

TRADING PARTNERS

Major export destinations 1995 (% share)		Major import sources 1995 (% share)	
Belgium/Luxembourg	32.2	Côte d'Ivoire	26.3
Italy	20.2	France	17.2
Spain	8.6	Senegal	4.1
France	8.6	Hong Kong	2.6

Malta

Area (km²)   316

Currency   Maltese lira (LM = 100 cents)

Location   Malta lies in the southern half of the central Mediterranean, some 100 km south of Sicily. Its close proximity to North Africa (Algeria, Tunisia and Libya) has left its mark on the country's character, as has its traditional activity in the world of shipping. The climate is warm and generally dry. The capital is Valletta.

Head of State   President Ugo Mifsud Bonici (April 1994)

Head of Government   Edward Fenech-Adami

Ruling Party   Partit Nazzjonalista (Nationalist Party)

Political Structure   Malta, an independent member of the Commonwealth, has a House of Representatives whose 65 members are elected for a five-year term by universal suffrage. It in turn appoints the President for five years, and he then appoints the Prime Minister and his Cabinet. Between 1987 and 1989 an additional four "bonus" seats were allocated to the ruling Nationalist Party, intended to help it through a period of severe political deadlock.

Last Elections   Elections to the House of Representatives were held in February 1992, when the the opposition Malta Democratic Party won the remaining 31 seats on 46.5% of the vote, while the Democratic Alternative won 1.7% of the vote but no seats. The turnout was unusually high, at 96%. In April 1994, Ugo Mifsud Bonici was appointed on the expiry of President Vincent Tabone's term of office.

Political Risk   Malta presents no significant risks from a political point of view, having demonstrated a commitment to working democracy over a number of years. Negotiations on Malta's membership in the EU should start by the spring of 1998 and could be concluded within months. This would mean that Malta should be a full member by the year 2000.

Economy   The Maltese economy is flourishing. Output in 1995 grew by more than 6% in real terms and the rate of inflation is expected to fall again this year. The state of government finances looks equally impressive with public debt at 36% of GDP - far lower than in any EU country except for Luxembourg. These achievements make a strong case for Malta's entry into the EU and member states agreed at the Cannes summit in 1995 that negotiations on membership would begin following the EU's 1996 inter-governmental conference.

Main Industries   Malta's successful economy derives from a strong diversification of its interests. Tourism is the most lucrative sector in terms of foreign revenues, with the great majority of the country's visitors arriving from other parts of Europe, especially Italy and the United Kingdom. Agriculture is also a major export activity, with fruit, vegetables, wheat, grapes and horticultural products (especially cut flowers) produced for the export market. Industry too is fairly well developed, with activities ranging from textiles and food processing to chemicals, plastics, electronic equipment and engineering. The country derives a large part of its revenues from the state-owned Malta Dry Docks, which service a large proportion of the ships in the Mediterranean.

Energy   Malta relies entirely on imports for all fuel requirements.

	1993	1994	1995
Inflation (% change)	4.1	4.1	4.0
Exchange rate (per US$)	0.38	0.38	0.35
Interest rate (% per annum)	8.5	8.5	
GDP (% real growth)	3.5	4.0	6.2
GDP (Million units of national currency)	938.2	1,015.7	1,121.8
GDP (US$ million)	2,468.9	2,672.9	3,205.2
GDP per capita (US$)	6,858.2	7,424.7	8,903.3
Consumption (Million units of national currency)	569.1	616.1	680.5
Consumption (US$ million)	1,497.6	1,621.3	1,944.2
Consumption per capita (US$)	4,160.1	4,503.7	5,400.5
Population, mid-year ('000)	360.0	360.0	360.0
Birth rate (per '000)	14.5	13.6	11.1
Death rate (per '000)	7.9	7.5	6.9
No. of households ('000)	113.0	113.6	114.0
Total exports (US$ million)	1,355.0	1,518.0	1,765.3
Total imports (US$ million)	2,174.0	2,448.0	2,792.0
Tourism receipts (US$ million)	653.0	722.9	
Tourist spending (US$ million)	211.0	233.6	280.1

Average household size 1995 (persons)	3.00				
Urban population 1995 (%)	89.3				
Age analysis (%) (1995)	*0-14* 24.3		*15-64* 64.0		*65+* 11.7
Population by sex (%) (1995)	*Male* 49.1		*Female* 50.9		
Life expectancy (years) (1992)	*Male* 73.0		*Female* 77.8		
Infant mortality (deaths per '000 live births) (1992)	10.3				
Adult literacy (%) (1985)	86.0				

TRADING PARTNERS

Major export destinations 1995 (% share)		Major import sources 1995 (% share)	
Italy	30.4	Italy	35.9
Germany	14.6	United Kingdom	13.8
France	8.8	Germany	10.4
Singapore	8.5	France	7.2

Martinique

Area (km²)   1,079

Currency   French franc (= 100 centimes)

Location   The French overseas département of Martinique is a single island in the Windward Islands group, situated between Dominica in the north and St Lucia in the south. With a benign climate and relatively little hurricane risk, it is a popular tourist resort. The capital is Fort de France.

Head of State   President Jacques Chirac (France)

Head of Government   Emile Maurice

Ruling Party   Union pour la Démocratie Française (RPR-UDF)

Political Structure   As an external department of France, Martinique is governed to a considerable degree from Paris. The country sends deputies to the French Assemblée Nationale and is represented at the EU. Since being accorded regional status in 1974, Martinique elects its own 41-member Regional Council for a term of six years, with responsibility for economic and social planning. Other executive power rests in a 42-member General Council.

Last Elections   The Regional Council elections of 1992 produced a landslide result for the RPR-UDF, which won 16 of the 41 seats compared with nine for the Patriotes Martiniquais, nine for the Parti Progressiste Martiniquais, four for the Parti Communiste Martiniquais, and three for the Nouvelle Génération Socialiste. The last full elections to the French Assemblée Nationale in 1993 returned two delegates for the RPR, one for the Socialists and one for other left-wing groupings.

Political Risk   Secessionist sentiment in Martinique, although not yet sufficient to arouse severe concern, has nevertheless been noticeable in recent years. The island's finely balanced political system has meant that even quite small groupings exert disproportionate influence on the political scene. Recent decisions by the EU to revise the tariffs on banana imports from the Caribbean could damage the local economy, but in the end it seems probable that France will render all assistance which might be required, up to and including a military presence.

Economy   Martinique, like many other French overseas territories, has occasionally felt left out of the mainstream of the decision-making process with regard to its own economy, although it has achieved a better development than most. Tourism appears the most profitable way ahead and the most likely solution to the country's perennial trade deficit.

Main Industries   Martinique's economy depends very heavily on its agricultural sector, which employs the greater part of the workforce although it still does not manage to cover all the country's food requirements - the rest being imported, mainly from France. Bananas and pineapples are taking over from the traditional sugar plantations as export providers, and it is estimated that just over a quarter of the total land area is now cultivated. Fishing is important, with lobsters, crabs and octopus among the major export activities. Industry is only moderately developed, although it employs 15% of the workforce. Martinique manufactures rum, beer, food products, cement and refined sugar. There is also a major ship repair yard and an industrial freeport at Jarry. The tourism sector is the fastest-growing area of the economy at present, with French tourists providing the great majority of the country's annual total of 500,000 visitors.

Energy   Martinique relies on imports for all its energy requirements. There is no hydro-electric capacity, all electricity being supplied by oil-fired generators.

	1993	1994	1995
Inflation (% change)	2.3	3.0	0.8
Exchange rate (per US$)	5.66	5.55	4.99
Interest rate			
GDP (% real growth)	-0.3	1.8	2.5
GDP (Million units of national currency)	12,238.1	12,835.0	13,261.1
GDP (US$ million)	2,162.2	2,312.6	2,657.5
GDP per capita (US$)	5,843.8	6,085.8	6,993.5
Consumption (Million units of national currency)	8,421.6	8,832.4	9,125.7
Consumption (US$ million)	1,487.9	1,591.4	1,828.8
Consumption per capita (US$)	4,021.4	4,188.0	4,812.6
Population, mid-year ('000)	370.0	380.0	380.0
Birth rate (per '000)	15.6	18.0	
Death rate (per '000)	6.1		
No. of households ('000)	81.3	81.7	82.6
Total exports (US$ million)	260.0	280.0	
Total imports (US$ million)	1,490.0	1,400.0	
Tourism receipts (US$ million)	332.0	360.3	
Tourist spending (US$ million)			

Average household size 1995 (persons)	4.37				
Urban population 1995 (%)	93.3				
Age analysis (%) (1990)	*0-14* 23.1		*15-64* 66.8		*65+* 10.1
Population by sex (%) (1992)	*Male* 48.2		*Female* 51.8		
Life expectancy (years) (1990-95)	*Male* 72.9		*Female* 79.4		
Infant mortality (deaths per '000 live births) (1992)	6.2				
Adult literacy (%) (1982)	92.8				

Mauritania

Area (km²)   1,030,700

Currency   Ouguiya (UM = 5 khous)

Location   Mauritania occupies a substantial part of central West Africa, meeting the Atlantic Ocean between Senegal and the disputed territory known as Western Sahara, but extending eastward as far as Mali. It shares a border with Algeria in the north-east. The country is mainly of Saharan type with most of its major settlements located on or near the coast. The capital is Nouakchott.

Head of State   President Col Maaouiya Ould Sidi Mohamed Taya (1984)

Head of Government   Sidi Mohamed Ould Boubakar

Ruling Party   Democratic and Social Republican Party (PRDS) leads a coalition with the opposition Movement of Independent Democrats

Political Structure   Faced with growing pressure from abroad, Mauritania has been steadily democratising its political institutions since 1991. Political parties were legalised for the first time only in July 1991 and the first free elections were held the following spring. Mauritania has a non-executive President; its Prime Minister and Cabinet are answerable to an elected National Assembly, appointed for five years. There is also a Senate, appointed for six years in an indirect election. President Taya came to power in a 1984 coup.

Last Elections   The country's first elections to the National Assembly were held in 1992 when the ruling PRDS won 67 of the 79 elected seats. The Rally for Democracy and National Unity won one seat, the Mauritanian Renewal Party one seat, and various independents 10 seats. However, the poll was boycotted by the leading opposition group, the Union of Democratic Forces, and by five other parties. Only 39% of the electorate voted in the first round of polling, and 33% in the second. Municipal elections held in 1994 confirmed the strength of the PRDS, but in March 1995 the two main parties teamed up to form a national coalition.

Political Risk   Although the country has shown a welcome return to the principles of multi-party democracy in recent years, it is difficult to avoid the impression that this has been achieved under duress rather than being offered voluntarily. The Western Sahara war with Morocco is over and the often severe tensions with neighbouring Senegal appear to have abated but Islamic fundamentalism remains a weighty political force in Mauritania. In the municipal elections of 1990, a fundamentalist list won two-thirds of the seats. Allegations concerning human rights abuses are commonplace. However, the atmosphere was relieved somewhat in October 1994 after an amnesty for about 60 Islamic activists who had been charged with subversion.

International Disputes   Mauritania fought a long war with the Algerian-sponsored Polisario rebels who opposed its move to co-occupy the Western Sahara after Spain had abandoned it in 1976. The country formally relinquished its claim to the southern sector of the Western Sahara in 1979, leaving Algeria and Morocco to fight out the dispute thereafter.

Economy   The country's heavy overseas debts amount to more than twice its GDP and represent a major barrier to growth. Political uncertainties complicate the Government's efforts to foster economic growth.

Main Industries   Mauritania's agricultural sector employs well over 80% of the workforce although it accounts for a mere 12-15% of GDP. Arable or fruit crops are possible only around the Senegal River. Otherwise, cattle herding is the major activity. Fishing is particularly important, with a large fleet producing a substantial proportion of foreign exchange revenues. Mining is the single most important area of the economy, with iron ore reserves providing most foreign exchange. There is also some copper mining, as well as gold and uranium. Industry is mainly intended for the local market and centres on the processing of agricultural raw fish processing, iron smelting, footwear and sugar production.

Energy   Mauritania has no indigenous oil supplies, although prospecting is under way. For most people, fuelwood is the major source of energy. However, a fifth of all electricity is generated through hydro-electric power stations.

	1993	1994	1995
Inflation (% change)	9.3	5.3	
Exchange rate (per US$)	120.81	123.58	128.36
Interest rate (% per annum)	10.0		
GDP (% real growth)	9.7	3.9	6.4
GDP (Million units of national currency)	124,377.8	136,077.6	144,775.4
GDP (US$ million)	1,029.5	1,101.1	1,127.9
GDP per capita (US$)	476.6	498.2	497.8
Consumption (Million units of national currency)	77,802.4	85,121.1	90,562.0
Consumption (US$ million)	644.0	688.8	705.5
Consumption per capita (US$)	298.2	311.7	311.4
Population, mid-year ('000)	2,160.0	2,210.0	2,265.9
Birth rate (per '000)	45.5	45.1	
Death rate (per '000)	20.0	14.4	
No. of households ('000)	525.5	540.4	569.0
Total exports (US$ million)	560.4	548.8	
Total imports (US$ million)	513.1	714.4	
Tourism receipts (US$ million)	14.1	14.9	
Tourist spending (US$ million)	32.0	34.0	34.8

Average household size 1995 (persons)	3.78		
Urban population 1995 (%)	53.8		
Age analysis (%) (1988)	*0-14* 44.1	*15-64* 51.9	*65+* 3.9
Population by sex (%) (1988)	*Male* 49.5	*Female* 50.5	
Life expectancy (years) (1990-95)	*Male* 49.9	*Female* 53.1	
Infant mortality (deaths per '000 live births) (1994)	117.3		
Adult literacy (%) (1995)	37.7		

TRADING PARTNERS

Major export destinations 1995 (% share)		Major import sources 1995 (% share)	
Japan	28.1	France	23.6
Italy	18.2	Spain	8.0
France	12.8	USA	7.4
Spain	10.5	Belgium/Luxembourg	5.7

Mauritius

Area (km²)   1,865

Currency   Mauritian rupee (Rs = 100 cents)

Location   Mauritius comprises a group of islands lying in the Indian Ocean, some 800 km off the eastern coast of Madagascar. It has a mixed population of Asian, European and some African origin. The country has a sub-tropical climate with high humidity throughout the year. The capital is Port Louis.

Head of State   President Cassam Uteem (June 1992)

Head of Government   Aneerood Jugnauth

Ruling Party   Mouvement Socialiste Mauricien (MSM) leads a coalition with the Mouvement Militant Mauricien (MMM), the Organisation du Peuple Rodriguais and the Mouvement des Travaillistes Démocrates.

Political Structure   Mauritius became an independent republic in March 1992, and thereupon left the Commonwealth. A non-executive President is appointed by the Prime Minister. The unicameral Legislative Assembly consists of 62 representatives elected by popular vote for a term of five years while the President appoints a maximum of eight further members. Operation of the political system is hampered by serious personal and political differences which have slowed the country's progress.

Last Elections   The last legislative elections took place in September 1991, when Jugnauth's MSM/MMM coalition won 55 of the 62 directly elected seats in the 70-member Legislative Assembly.

Political Risk   The Government's decision to pursue independence created considerable animosity among the opposition parties. The broadly based coalition nevertheless appears sufficiently secure in power to survive periodic attacks from the opposition. With a moderately high standard of living and thriving export markets, there is little likelihood of any serious political disturbance.

International Disputes   Mauritius seeks the return of Diego Garcia, an island 1,900 kilometres north-east of Mauritius. The tiny island, which forms part of the British Indian Ocean Territory and is home to a large US naval installation, is of strategic importance and the claim is not treated seriously.

Economy   The fairly high standard of living and rapid diversification of the economy should help the country to avoid the worst effects of any economic downturn. Recent economic policies have been aimed at encouraging foreign investment, especially in tourism and attracting financial institutions that specialise in the Indian economy.

Main Industries   Mauritius depends heavily on its tourist industry, which in 1994 attracted some 400,000 visitors and generated Rs 6 billion in income. The industry caters particularly for French, South African and British visitors and has fostered a flourishing construction business. Agriculture remains the mainstay of the economy, with sugar cane, tea and tobacco grown for export. Staples produced for the indigenous population include cereals, fruit and coconut products. There is an important fishing sector. Industry provides only a small proportion of the country's requirements, although it produces molasses and garments for export. There is an industrial freeport where new enterprises involved in industries such as electronics, diamond cutting and plastic products are being established. The island's tax treaty with India has spurred the development of a thriving financial services sector.

Energy   Mauritius relies on imports for all its energy needs, except for a small amount of fuelwood use. All but one-sixth of its electricity derives from thermal power stations.

	1993	1994	1995
Inflation (% change)	10.5	7.3	6.0
Exchange rate (per US$)	17.65	17.96	17.62
Interest rate (% per annum)	16.6	18.9	20.8
GDP (% real growth)	4.1	3.9	3.4
GDP (Million units of national currency)	56,471.0	62,984.0	69,000.0
GDP (US$ million)	3,199.5	3,506.9	3,916.0
GDP per capita (US$)	2,916.6	3,159.4	3,480.3
Consumption (Million units of national currency)	34,973.0	39,496.0	43,811.4
Consumption (US$ million)	1,981.5	2,199.1	2,486.5
Consumption per capita (US$)	1,806.3	1,981.2	2,209.8
Population, mid-year ('000)	1,097.0	1,110.0	1,125.2
Birth rate (per '000)	20.9	19.6	18.3
Death rate (per '000)	6.8	6.4	6.7
No. of households ('000)	207.7	211.9	220.8
Total exports (US$ million)	1,299.0	1,347.0	1,464.0
Total imports (US$ million)	1,715.0	1,930.0	1,878.7
Tourism receipts (US$ million)	301.0	354.8	
Tourist spending (US$ million)	128.0	150.9	170.6

Average household size 1995 (persons)	4.84				
Urban population 1995 (%)	40.6				
Age analysis (%) (1991)	*0-14* 29.6		*15-64* 64.9		*65+* 5.5
Population by sex (%) (1991)	*Male* 49.9		*Female* 50.1		
Life expectancy (years) (1989-91)	*Male* 65.6		*Female* 73.4		
Infant mortality (deaths per '000 live births) (1993)	19.6				
Adult literacy (%) (1995)	82.9				

TRADING PARTNERS

Major export destinations 1995 (% share)		Major import sources 1995 (% share)	
United Kingdom	34.2	France	19.9
France	20.9	South Africa	10.6
USA	15.2	India	7.4
Germany	6.4	Hong Kong	6.9

Mexico

Area (km²)   1,972,545

Currency   Mexican new peso (= 100 centavos)

Location   Mexico, the largest state in Central America and perhaps the most affluent state in Latin America, extends for well over 2,000 km from its northern border with the US down to the boundaries with Guatemala and Belize in the south. It has coastlines on both the Atlantic and the Pacific and embraces a wide range of territorial types. The landscape is partly volcanic and is subject to earthquakes, although in the south it becomes jungle. The capital is Mexico City.

Head of State   President Ernesto Zedillo Ponce de León (December 1994)

Head of Government   President Ernesto Zedillo Ponce de León (December 1994)

Ruling Party   Partido Revolucionario Institucional (PRI)

Political Structure   Mexico, a parliamentary democracy with an executive President, has one of the longest democratic traditions in Latin America. Yet its politics have been dominated so completely by the PRI since 1917 that it is virtually of one-party character. The President is elected for a six-year term by universal suffrage, and the 500-member Federal Chamber of Deputies every three years. There is also a 128-member Senate, half of whom are elected every three years for six years, and numerous regional parliaments which exert considerable powers of autonomy. The system of senate elections is currently undergoing a rolling reform; by 2000, all members will be due for simultaneous election.

Last Elections   Presidential elections were held in August 1994 when Ernesto Zedillo, the candidate for the ruling PRI, won 49% of the vote, against 26% for Diego Fernandez de Cevallos of the Partido Acción Nacional and 17% for Cuauhtemoc Cardenas Solorzano of the Partido de la Revolución Democrática. While a PRI victory had been widely foreseen, the assassination of the main candidate, Luis Donaldo Colosio, in March 1994 cast a shadow over the entire political structure. In the congressional elections of August 1991, the ruling PRI won 320 of the 500 seats in the Chamber of Deputies, including 290 of the 300 seats which were filled on a direct basis - the remainder being elected under proportional representation. The Partido Acción Nacional won 89 seats, while the Partido de la Revolución Democrática saw its vote shrink by 75% and won only 41 seats. The Partido del Frente Cardenista de Reconstrucción Nacional, the Partido de la Revolución Mexicana and the Partido Popular Socialista won 42 seats between them.

Political Risk   The economic crisis of 1995 led to a 50% drop in the value of the Mexican peso and severely undermined foreign confidence in the country's business potential. The Government has been forced to respond with austerity measures which are unpopular and seriously jeopardised the future of the middle class. With US and international assistance, the Mexican peso has steadied, the stock market has bounced back and trade is recovering. Consumer markets in Mexico are still depressed, however, and it will be several years before demand reaches its pre-crash levels. A second threat is the growing influence and wealth of Mexico's drug cartels. With easy access to the American market, experts believe the Mexican drug lords will soon become the most powerful in Latin America. A major political scandal arose in September 1994 when the PRI Secretary-General was assassinated in what appeared to be a drugs-related crime. The brother of ex-President Salinas de Gortari was later charged with his murder.

Economy   An estimated 800,000 jobs have been lost since Mexico's financial crisis plunged the economy into recession. Another 4 million workers (around 10% of the labour force) are employed less than 15 hours per week. The peso's devaluation, coupled with soaring interest rates and a credit freeze, have sharply reduced industrial output and cut incomes. Imports fell by 15% in 1995 with capital goods being hardest hit, reflecting the low levels of investment. Fortunately, exports have been buoyant. The country's trade deficit has turned into a surplus and is an important factor behind the growing confidence expressed in the government's austerity programme. The government is keen to promote foreign direct investment in all sectors of the economy and plans to privatise "everything allowed by the constitution". However, officials must find ways to deal with Mexico's low domestic savings rate, contain the huge costs of the state-run social security system and still create at least 1 million new jobs each year for the country's young work force.

Main Industries   Mexico's expanding economy has a high degree of industrialisation, with traditional activities such as food processing and petroleum products giving way to sophisticated engineering, vehicle manufacture and, increasingly, electronics. There are a large number of companies making consumer durables for the home. Manufactured goods now account for 56% of exports. Oil, however, is probably still the most important area of the external economy, with some 85 billion barrels currently in known reserves and new finds being reported yearly. There are also reserves of uranium, iron ore, gold, silver, copper, zinc and lead. Agriculture is in decline although it still employs 20% of the workforce. Citrus crops, tomatoes, peppers, cotton, coffee and sugar cane are grown wheat, chickpeas, groundnuts, alfalfa and soya are among the domestic crops.

Energy   Mexico is self-sufficient in all its energy needs, including electricity.

	1993	1994	1995
Inflation (% change)	9.8	7.0	35.0
Exchange rate (per US$)	3.12	3.38	6.42
Interest rate (% per annum)	17.4	16.5	43.0
GDP (% real growth)	0.8	3.9	-10.9
GDP (Billion units of national currency)	1,145.4	1,272.8	1,531.1
GDP (US$ million)	367,109.6	376,568.0	238,489.1
GDP per capita (US$)	4,024.9	4,048.7	2,516.2
Consumption (Billion units of national currency)	765.3	860.6	1,118.6
Consumption (US$ million)	245,288.5	254,615.4	174,236.8
Consumption per capita (US$)	2,689.3	2,737.5	1,838.3
Population, mid-year ('000)	91,210.0	93,010.0	94,780.0
Birth rate (per '000)	27.7	26.8	25.9
Death rate (per '000)	4.7	5.0	5.4
No. of households ('000)	18,569.0	19,550.0	19,015.0
Total exports (US$ million)	51,886.0	60,882.0	79,541.5
Total imports (US$ million)	65,366.5	79,345.9	72,453.1
Tourism receipts (US$ million)	6,167.0	6,396.2	
Tourist spending (US$ million)	5,562.0	5,768.7	3,947.6

Average household size 1995 (persons)	4.74		
Urban population 1995 (%)	75.3		
Age analysis (%) (1995)	*0-14* 33.0	*15-64* 62.8	*65+* 4.2
Population by sex (%) (1995)	*Male* 50.1	*Female* 49.9	
Life expectancy (years) (1990-95)	*Male* 67.8	*Female* 73.9	
Infant mortality (deaths per '000 live births) (1993)	17.5		
Adult literacy (%) (1995)	89.6		

TRADING PARTNERS

Major export destinations 1995 (% share)		Major import sources 1995 (% share)	
USA	83.8	USA	74.6
Canada	2.7	Japan	5.0
Japan	1.3	Germany	3.7
Brazil	1.1	Italy	1.1

Moldova

Area (km²) 33,700

Currency Rouble

Location Located in the western part of the former Soviet Union, Moldova is sandwiched between Romania and the Ukraine. It includes a substantial part of the territory to the east of the Pruth river, once known as Bessarabia, and also a predominantly Russian area to the east. The climate is warm and pleasant, and agriculture flourishes. The capital is Kishinev.

Head of State President Mircea Snegur (1991)

Head of Government Andrei Sangheli

Ruling Party Agrarian Democratic Party (ADP)

Political Structure Moldova comprises the bulk of the former Moldavian SSR within the former Soviet Union. It has an executive President and a 380-seat Parliament. The period since independence in August 1991 has been marked by a continuous dispute between the ethnic Russians and Ukrainians who make up over half the population of the Transdniestria province which borders on the Ukraine. Supported by Moscow, rebels in the province started a secessionist war in 1992. However, a referendum held in March 1994 produced a clear majority against any extension of Moldova's relationships with either Romania or Russia, and in 1995 Russia agreed to withdraw all its troops from Transdniestria - a move which was almost unanimously opposed by resident voters.

Last Elections The first full elections under the new Constitution were held in February 1994, when the Agrarian Democratic Party (the largest party) gained 43.2% of the vote, compared with 21.8% for the Socialist Party and the Yedinstvo Unity Movement bloc; 9% for the Peasants and Intellectuals Party; and 7.3% for the Christian Democrats. A loose coalition, the Popular Front of Moldova, was subsequently agreed to form the new administration. Local elections in April 1995 supported the ruling ADP, but they were not observed in Transdnistria where a separate, illegal, poll gave an overwhelming majority to the ruling Patriotic Bloc.

Political Risk In the long term Moldova retains considerable promise, not least because of its fertile soil, good communications and its favourable location and climate. Much will depend on attitudes in Moscow, however. If nationalists or communists gain more influence in Moscow, disputes over control of Transdniestria province will resume.

International Disputes Much of Moldova's rocky relations with its neighbours date back to the 1940s, when the fascist government of Romania was forced to hand over a large part of its most productive land (Bessarabia) to the Soviets. That territory was then attached to a section of land carved out of the Ukraine and renamed the Soviet Republic of Moldova. The Romanian language was downgraded, but remained dominant in daily use. Romania has protested ever since at its loss. With the political changes of the 1990s, Moldova contemplated a renewed liaison, and possibly a full union, with Romania but the current administration rejects this option. Meanwhile, Russian nationalists have demanded a military base in Transdniestria, hard on the western flank of the Ukraine. President Snegur objects, but if the nationalists were ever to gain power in Moscow, the Kremlin may again encourage the Russian community in the province to take matters in their own hands.

Economy The loss of Russian markets, the impact of economic reforms, and a series of droughts and floods resulted in a 30% decline in GDP in 1995. Most of the country's crops were destroyed but analysts expect growth to resume in 1996. Agriculture and forestry account for about two-fifths of GDP in 1995, followed by industry which contributes another 34%. Russia continues to be the country's major foreign market, claiming nearly 50% of all exports (primarily tobacco and tobacco products, fruit juices and machine-made carpets). An ambitious programme of privatisation is now underway. Moldova will also have to reorient its trade to western markets, if it is to attract foreign investment and earn the foreign exchange necessary to modernise its economy.

Main Industries The agricultural sector is all-important in Moldova. Fruit, vegetables, tobacco and grain are the principal crops but there is also significant production of wine. Light industry consists mainly of textiles and consumer goods. In addition, there is a modest chemical industry. The government has instituted a privatisation programme in an effort to aid investment, but progress has been slow to date.

	1993	1994	1995
Inflation (% change)	4,000.0	13.8	
Exchange rate (per US$)	3.64	4.27	4.54
Interest rate			
GDP (% real growth)	-4.9	-19.4	-30.0
GDP			
GDP (US$ million)			
GDP per capita (US$)			
Consumption			
Consumption (US$ million)			
Consumption per capita (US$)			
Population, mid-year ('000)	4,360.0	4,350.0	4,360.0
Birth rate (per '000)	18.9	14.3	
Death rate (per '000)	11.8	12.0	
No. of households ('000)	1,059.8	1,075.9	1,120.0
Total exports (US$ million)			
Total imports (US$ million)			
Tourism receipts (US$ million)			
Tourist spending (US$ million)			

Average household size 1995 (persons)	3.70				
Urban population 1995 (%)	51.7				
Age analysis (%) (1989)	*0-14* 27.9		*15-64* 63.9		*65+* 8.1
Population by sex (%) (1995)	*Male* 47.6		*Female* 52.4		
Life expectancy (years) (1991)	*Male* 65.0		*Female* 71.8		
Infant mortality (deaths per '000 live births) (1994)	22.9				
Adult literacy (%) (1989)	96.4				

TRADING PARTNERS

Major export destinations 1995 (% share)		Major import sources 1995 (% share)	
Russia	61.0	Russia	50.3
Romania	8.1	Germany	14.4
Germany	6.5	Romania	8.6
Bulgaria	5.2	Azerbaijan	3.2

Monaco

Area (km²) 2

Currency French franc (= 100 centimes)

Location Monaco, one of the smallest states in Europe, is a Mediterranean principality which is surrounded on all its land borders by France, although the Italian coastline is within easy reach. The country is entirely urban, having no undeveloped land whatever, apart from parks and gardens. The capital is Monte Carlo.

Head of State HSH Prince Rainier III

Head of Government Paul Dijoud (December 1994)

Ruling Party There are no political parties as such in Monaco.

Political Structure The Principality of Monaco is a hereditary monarchy which has enjoyed French protection since 1861. Legislative power is vested jointly in the Prince and in the 18-member unicameral National Council, which is elected for a five-year term by universal suffrage. Executive power is exercised by the Prince in collaboration with a four-member Council of Government. The judicial code of France applies.

Last Elections The National Council elections of 1993 saw the Liste Campora, an unofficial grouping, obtain 15 of the 18 seats, with the Médecin list obtaining one seat and an independent winning the other. Until then, the National Council had been exclusively composed of members of the Liste Campora's predecessor, the UND. Just over 70% of the 4,500 electorate were reported to have voted in the elections (foreigners having no vote).

Political Risk The Principality's legendary stability, combined with its considerable tourist industry and its favourable climate, have helped to make Monaco one of the most attractive investment destinations in Western Europe. Unlike Liechtenstein, Monaco does not rely significantly on offshore banking services for its income, and it thus has little to fear from changes in EU banking laws. It has, however, been drawn into the EU's system of value added taxes. A campaign is under way to limit the spread of money laundering.

Economy Monaco's special protected status, under the control of France, gives it a high degree of security. Its favourable climate and its low tax rates have ensured the success of its tourism and investment industries.

Main Industries Monaco derives virtually all of its national revenues from tourism and banking. The former appeals particularly to France and Italy and continues to grow in importance with the creation of improved transport links with both countries. The casino at Monte Carlo is still a major source of revenue. Financial services do not benefit from any particular secrecy advantages, (as for example in Liechtenstein), being covered effectively by French law, but the city has proved a popular location for international companies which employ about a sixth of the workforce. Tax rates are low. Agriculture is virtually non-existent, thanks to the wholly built-up nature of the territory. There are, however, a number of manufacturing companies making plastics, electrical goods and electronics, textiles and clothing.

Energy The country depends on imports for all its energy needs.

	1993	1994	1995
Inflation (% change)	2.2	-1.5	
Exchange rate (per US$)	5.66	5.55	4.99
Interest rate			
GDP (% real growth)	2.6	6.5	5.5
GDP (Million units of national currency)	2,373.7	2,489.5	2,626.4
GDP (US$ million)	419.4	448.6	526.3
GDP per capita (US$)	13,979.4	14,952.0	16,978.6
Consumption (Million units of national currency)	2,276.4	2,375.9	2,494.4
Consumption (US$ million)	402.2	428.1	499.9
Consumption per capita (US$)	13,406.4	14,269.7	16,125.4
Population, mid-year ('000)	30.0	30.0	31.0
Birth rate (per '000)	13.3	10.7	
Death rate (per '000)		12.2	
No. of households ('000)	13.0	13.5	14.0
Total exports (US$ million)			
Total imports (US$ million)			
Tourism receipts (US$ million)			
Tourist spending (US$ million)			

Average household size 1995 (persons)	2.10		
Urban population 1995 (%)	100.0		
Age analysis (%) (1982)	*0-14* 12.5	*15-64* 70.3	
Population by sex (%)			
Life expectancy (years) (1992)	*Male* 73.9	*Female* 81.6	
Infant mortality (deaths per '000 live births)			
Adult literacy (%) (1983)	99.0		

Mongolia

Area (km²)   1,565,000

Currency   Tugruk (= 100 möngö)

Location   The Mongolian Republic extends some 1,800 km across the eastern centre of the Asian landmass, running from the Kazakh/Russian border in the west to the start of the Yablonovy mountain range in the east, with Russia always to the north and with China always to the south. The terrain is mountainous, with the south giving way to the Gobi desert. The capital is Ulan Bator.

Head of State   President Punsalmaagiyn Ochirbat (1990)

Head of Government   Puntsagiyn Jasray

Ruling Party   Mongolian People's Revolutionary Party (MPRP)

Political Structure   Mongolia has achieved a significant transition from the single-party communist administration which characterised the country from 1945 to July 1990. Its semi-executive President and its Prime Minister answer to a Parliament comprising a 76-member People's Great Hural (Lower House). The political transformation has been accompanied by radical economic reforms.

Last Elections   Elections to the Great Hural were held in June 1992, when the ruling Mongolian People's Revolutionary Party, only recently converted from its former allegiance to communism, won 70 of the 76 available seats with 57% of the vote. The Mongolian Democratic Party, the Mongolian Party of National Progress and the Mongolian United Party put up an opposing coalition which received 18% of the vote but secured only four seats. The remaining two seats went to the Social Democratic Party and to an independent MPRP member. Presidential elections were held in June 1993, when the incumbent Punsalmaagiyn Ochirbat won 58% of the vote, against 39% for Lodongiyn Tudev.

Political Risk   The return of multi-party parliamentary democracy, together with a commitment to economic reform, have encouraged foreign businesses and investors. Improving trade with China, and the growth of oil prospecting, are other promising trends. Reformers, however, are uneasy that capitalism will create unacceptable inequalities in income. To avoid social unrest, the government continues to subsidise the cost of fuel and utilities. In a country where the average temperature is below freezing seven months each year, big rises in heating costs are unacceptable.

International Disputes   Mongolia has long harboured suspicions that China was planning to annex its territory, and has accused China of ill-treating the Mongol population of Inner Mongolia, a Chinese Autonomous Region. Relations between the two states have stabilised but the Mongolians remain wary. Like Inner Mongolia, many Chinese officials consider what they call "Outer Mongolia" to be part of China. Beijing tolerated Mongolia's servitude to Russia during the communist period mainly on the ground that it was preferable to becoming another Tibet. Now that Russia is no longer the protective brother, Mongolia must keep a watchful eye on its southern neighbour.

Economy   Mongolia's economy suffered when subsidies from the Soviet Union were discontinued. Poverty and unemployment did not exist during that period. Now about 22% of the population live below the poverty line and 9% of the work force have no job. The government hopes that improvements in infrastructure and privatisation will spur growth. Mongolia is the size of Western Europe, but most of the roads outside the capital are just tyre tracks. All small enterprises have been privatised, although a few larger ones are still in government hands. So far, these programmes seem to be having the desired effect. GDP grew by 2.3% in 1994 and increased by another 6.3% in 1995. Meanwhile, investment rose from virtually nothing to $190 million last year.

Main Industries   Mongolia's economy has traditionally centred on agriculture, with a large proportion of the farmers being nomadic cattle herders producing meat, hides and wool. However, various crops are grown in the better-irrigated areas of the north, including fruit, grain, vegetables and animal fodder. Mineral production appears to be the fastest-growing sector of the economy at present, with deposits of copper, molybdenum, gold and other metals being extracted. Foreign investment is now being encouraged. The country's manufacturing base is a rudimentary one, being limited mainly to the processing of agricultural raw materials. However, the open invitation being extended to foreign investment has led to expressions of interest from engineering companies, electrical and electronics goods manufacturers and textile producers.

Energy   Mongolia has substantial coal resources which are now being developed to fund the industrial expansion; otherwise the country depends on imports for its energy needs. Exploration continues for indigenous hydrocarbon resources.

	1993	1994	1995
Inflation (% change)	268.4	87.6	
Exchange rate (per US$)	400.95	412.72	433.14
Interest rate (% per annum)	300.0	233.6	114.9
GDP (% real growth)		2.3	6.3
GDP			
GDP (US$ million)	1,120.0	1,090.0	1,155.0
GDP per capita (US$)	482.8	461.9	480.2
Consumption			
Consumption (US$ million)	788.5	767.4	813.0
Consumption per capita (US$)	339.9	325.2	338.0
Population, mid-year ('000)	2,320.0	2,360.0	2,405.0
Birth rate (per '000)	27.6	33.0	
Death rate (per '000)	7.8	7.0	
No. of households ('000)	474.1	486.7	500.0
Total exports (US$ million)	380.9	324.2	
Total imports (US$ million)	361.5	222.7	
Tourism receipts (US$ million)			
Tourist spending (US$ million)			

Average household size 1995 (persons)	4.57				
Urban population 1995 (%)	60.9				
Age analysis (%) (1991, est)	*0-14* 41.3		*15-64* 55.5		*65+* 3.2
Population by sex (%)					
Life expectancy (years) (1990)	*Male* 60.0		*Female* 62.5		
Infant mortality (deaths per '000 live births) (1993)	59.7				
Adult literacy (%) (1995)	82.9				

Montenegro

Area (km²)   13,812

Currency   Dinar

Location   Montenegro is the smallest of the former Yugoslav regions, with an area of 13,812 square km in the south-west of the old country. Its western border is along the Adriatic and to the south is Albania. A mountainous interior gives way to a thin coastal plain and fertile land around Lake Scutari in the far south. The capital, Titograd, reverted to its former name of Podgorica in 1992. The capital is Podgorica.

Head of State   Momir Bulatovic (1990)

Head of Government   Milo Djukanovic

Ruling Party   Democratic Party of Socialists

Political Structure   Montenegro is one of only two states from the former republic of Yugoslavia to have stayed within the Federation - the other being Serbia. Until 1990, the Federation also included Slovenia, Croatia, Bosnia-Herzegovina and Macedonia. However, the new Yugoslavian system has yet to gain full international recognition.

Last Elections   Legislative elections were held in December 1992 for the Montenegrin Republican Assembly. The Democratic Party of Socialists of Montenegro won the majority of seats with 43% of the vote.

Political Risk   The fragile peace which now exists in Bosnia-Herzegovina only slightly reduces the level of risk associated with Montenegro. The country no longer faces a trade embargo but there is still the possibility that civil war could resume. This danger, along with the country's continued isolation, leaves little hope for optimism in the medium term. The loss of transport links with Greece in the south has effectively sealed the region off from the rest of Europe.

Economy   No reliable statistics have been available for many years on the progress of the Montenegrin economy, which is effectively united with that of Serbia in the new Yugoslavian state. The republic has not suffered to the same extent as Serbia but consumer lifestyles are primitive by the standards of most Eastern European republics.

Main Industries   Agriculture is the only significant type of economic pursuit in the country, with livestock rearing and grain production being the major activities. Tobacco is also produced in the region and there are significant deposits of limestone and other minerals.

	1993	1994	1995
Inflation (% change)	3,000.0		
Exchange rate (per US$)			
Interest rate			
GDP (% real growth)	-5.0		
GDP			
GDP (US$ million)			
GDP per capita (US$)			
Consumption			
Consumption (US$ million)			
Consumption per capita (US$)			
Population, mid-year ('000)	620.1	624.4	626.0
Birth rate (per '000)	13.4	13.2	13.2
Death rate (per '000)	10.0	10.1	10.2
No. of households ('000)	192.6	194.9	198.0
Total exports (US$ million)			
Total imports (US$ million)			
Tourism receipts (US$ million)			
Tourist spending (US$ million)			

Average household size 1995 (persons)	3.00
Urban population 1995 (%)	49.0
Age analysis (%)	
Population by sex (%)	
Life expectancy (years) (1988-89)	*Male* 76.6 *Female* 82.5
Infant mortality (deaths per '000 live births)	
Adult literacy (%) (1990)	92.7

Morocco

Area (km²) 458,730

Currency Moroccan dirham (DH = 100 centimes)

Location Morocco, although far from being the largest country in North West Africa, is probably the most affluent. Its rocky terrain almost meets with Europe across the Strait of Gibraltar, and most of the settlements of any size are located along the Atlantic coast just south-west of Gibraltar. The capital is Rabat.

Head of State HM King Hassan II (1961)

Head of Government Abdellatif Filali (May 1994)

Ruling Party Entente Nationale, a five-party centre-right coalition

Political Structure Morocco is a constitutional monarchy in which legislative authority is vested in a unicameral Chamber of Representatives. At present, two-thirds of the Chamber's 333 members are elected by universal suffrage for a six-year term, while the remainder are chosen by an electoral college. The Prime Minister is appointed accordingly by the monarch. A significant reshaping of the country's regional administrative network took place in 1994 when four new governorates were created. A second parliamentary chamber is soon to be created with all members elected directly. The move would mean new elections and, probably, a change in the prime minister. The King, however, can choose when to hold the poll.

Last Elections The first legislative elections in recent years were held in April 1993, when the ruling coalition of the Union Constitutionnelle, the Rassemblement National des Indépendants and the Mouvement Populaire won 195 seats against 120 for the centre-left Union Socialiste des Forces Populaires and Istiqlal (a fellow member of the Bloc démocratique). Hassan thereupon adopted a non-partisan coalition government in November 1993, which in effect has been a centre-right administration.

Political Risk A political stalemate emerged from the last general elections that has yet to be resolved. The four largest parties, two pro-government and two anti-government, have almost equal representation, and the King is required to reflect this balance of forces in parliament. He has twice approached the opposition to take up government posts and has twice been refused. There is also an easing of political conditions but it does not apply to the more radical religious groups. No Islamist party is allowed to contest elections or challenge the King's position. One of the country's biggest uncertainties is the extent to which extra-parliamentary fundamentalist movements may become a rallying point for protests against the tough economic policies which are in store. With high levels of youth unemployment, the concern is a real one.

International Disputes Morocco has frequently been in conflict with Algeria over the ownership of the Western Sahara, a barren tract of over 1,000 kilometres of coastal territory which Morocco and Mauritania had co-occupied since its abandonment by Spain in 1976. The Algerian-backed Polisario rebels have control of the entire southern area, but have remained in conflict with Morocco. A ceasefire, negotiated in 1991, has been breached countless times. Morocco still has an outstanding claim against Spain for the Spanish exclaves of Ceuta and Melilla, and for three small islands off the coast which still form part of Spain. Spain has rejected talks on the issue. Both a new association agreement and a fishing agreement were concluded with the EU in 1995 but many on both sides remain dissatisfied with the results of the later pact.

Economy The country's highly diversified economy grew strongly in 1994 but a mild recession occurred in 1995. Three years of drought in the last four, a slump in remittances from Moroccan workers abroad and a fall in foreign investment all took their toll. Meanwhile, inflation was rising - though it is still far below the levels of the 1980s. The economy's major threat is unemployment, however. At present trends, the level of unemployment is forecast to reach 27% by the year 2002. With the present rate hovering around 16%, annual growth would have to be at least 7% if sufficient jobs are to be available to prevent a further rise in the number of unemployed. Simultaneously, the government is expected to begin opening up its markets to the EU's exporters as part of its new association agreement.

Main Industries Morocco's mineral sector is the mainstay of the economy, producing phosphates, fluorite, barytes, manganese, cobalt, lead, zinc, copper and antimony. The country is estimated to hold three-quarters of the world's phosphate reserves. Morocco has substantial petroleum processing industries, but so far no oil deposits have been found. Tourism is the second largest earner of foreign exchange, though it accounts for only 7% of GDP and 6% of employment. The sector remains under-developed. Morocco, for example, has 3,800 kilometres of coastline but not one seaside resort. Prices are relatively high and the country has only belatedly realised that it is too upmarket in this competitive industry. Agriculture employs some 40% of the workforce and provides another third of Morocco's exports, with citrus fruits leading the way.

Energy Morocco depends on imports for all its hydrocarbon needs, although its importance as a downstream processor ensures a steady supply of products.

	1993	1994	1995
Inflation (% change)	5.2	5.1	6.1
Exchange rate (per US$)	9.30	9.20	8.50
Interest rate		10.0	
GDP (% real growth)	1.0	2.8	-0.5
GDP (Million units of national currency)	260,923.0	281,908.6	297,609.5
GDP (US$ million)	28,056.2	30,642.2	35,012.9
GDP per capita (US$)	1,076.2	1,152.4	1,291.5
Consumption (Million units of national currency)	159,676.0	177,907.9	193,683.8
Consumption (US$ million)	17,169.5	19,337.8	22,786.3
Consumption per capita (US$)	658.6	727.3	840.5
Population, mid-year ('000)	26,070.0	26,590.0	27,110.0
Birth rate (per '000)	29.1	28.6	
Death rate (per '000)	8.1	8.1	
No. of households ('000)	5,486.3	5,623.7	5,900.0
Total exports (US$ million)	3,991.0	4,013.0	4,584.0
Total imports (US$ million)	6,760.0	7,188.0	8,521.0
Tourism receipts (US$ million)	1,243.0	1,267.0	1,154.0
Tourist spending (US$ million)	245.0	266.3	313.8

Average household size 1995 (persons)	4.37				
Urban population 1995 (%)	48.4				
Age analysis (%) (1990)	*0-14*	36.0	*15-64*	59.2	*65+* 4.8
Population by sex (%) (1990)	*Male*	49.4	*Female*	50.6	
Life expectancy (years) (1990-95)	*Male*	61.6	*Female*	65.0	
Infant mortality (deaths per '000 live births) (1994)	68.3				
Adult literacy (%) (1995)	43.7				

TRADING PARTNERS

Major export destinations 1995 (% share)		Major import sources 1995 (% share)	
France	51.0	Spain	10.0
Germany	12.9	Germany	9.8
Spain	11.8	Italy	8.1
Italy	8.7	USA	6.7

Mozambique

Area (km²)   784,755

Currency   Metical (MT = 100 centavos)

Location   Mozambique extends for as much as 2,500 km along the Indian Ocean coast of East Africa, running from the borders with South Africa and Swaziland in the south to Tanzania in the north. Inland, it borders on Malawi, Zimbabwe and Zambia. Less elevated than other countries in the region, the most fertile areas are in the west, where the Zambezi river is dammed at Cabora Bassa, and on the coast. The climate is tropical but prone to devastating drought. The capital is Maputo.

Head of State   President Joaquim Alberto Chissano (1986)

Head of Government   Pascoal Mocumbi (December 1994)

Ruling Party   Frelimo (Mozambique Liberation Front)

Political Structure   Mozambique's 1990 Constitution marked a significant turn away from the single-party collectivist state which had characterised the country since 1975. The executive President, who had previously served as the de facto chairman of Frelimo, was henceforth to be elected by universal suffrage for a maximum of two five-year terms. Legislative power is vested in the Assembly of the Republic, with 200-250 members who are elected, also by universal suffrage, for a term of five years.

Last Elections   Multi-party elections were held for the first time in October 1994, when 250 members were appointed with an effective 8-seat majority for Chissano's Frelimo group.

Political Risk   Mozambique is still suffering from the damage inflicted on the country's infrastructure (especially transport links) over the last 15 years. Poverty is severe and there is no immediate prospect of the consumer market developing at all rapidly. However, aid is now forthcoming once again from outside sources after the ending of the civil war.

International Disputes   Mozambique's civil war, which raged throughout the 1970s and 1980s, was mainly against the South African-backed Mozambique National Resistance (Renamo) guerrillas, who succeeded in causing massive disruption to the country's infrastructure. Mozambique also demands that neighbouring countries should now return the refugees (numbering more than 1.3 million) who left the country in the 1980s and early 1990s; it has signed agreements with Malawi, Swaziland, Zambia and Zimbabwe to this effect.

Economy   The political reforms of the last five years have been reflected in a reversal of the collectivist trends in the economy and a renewed openness to foreign investment and the profit principle. A five-year plan announced in 1995 included programmes for land reform, price liberalisation, minimum farm prices for producers, and health and education measures. The government ambitiously hopes to increase the growth rate of GDP to 8-9% per annum by 2000. In May 1996, work on the "Maputo Development Corridor" began and should eventually help to boost growth. The road, which will link Mozambique with South Africa, is intended to whisk goods from Johannesburg to Maputo which is the nearest port.

Main Industries   Industrial production has been hampered in the last decade by the internal dislocation of the civil war, but is now starting to pick up, and the Government is encouraging foreign investment. Even so, allegations of poor management and security problems persist. Most manufactured products centre on import substitution, with the majority of plants being based around Beira and Maputo. In fact, Mozambique's economy still depends to a large extent on the agricultural sector, with most farmers living on a subsistence basis. The collectivisation drive of the 1970s and 1980s has now been reversed, and small farmers are being encouraged to develop their own operations. Sugar, cashews, cotton, tea and sisal are grown for export, and there is an important fishing industry.

Energy   Mozambique has coal deposits but so far no oil has been discovered. It does, however, have vast and still only partially developed hydro-electric potential which raises the prospect of an exportable surplus in the next century.

	1993	1994	1995
Inflation (% change)	42.2	57.9	
Exchange rate (per US$)	3,874.24	6,038.59	8,050.70
Interest rate			
GDP (% real growth)	0.0	-3.2	0.1
GDP (Million units of national currency)	5,463,000.0	8,347,960.6	11,030,320.0
GDP (US$ million)	1,410.1	1,382.4	1,370.1
GDP per capita (US$)	90.5	83.2	78.7
Consumption (Million units of national currency)	3,829,000.0	5,774,760.0	7,530,798.8
Consumption (US$ million)	988.3	956.3	935.4
Consumption per capita (US$)	63.4	57.6	53.7
Population, mid-year ('000)	15,580.0	16,610.0	17,420.0
Birth rate (per '000)	44.6	45.0	
Death rate (per '000)	18.5	16.3	
No. of households ('000)	2,721.8	2,916.2	3,131.0
Total exports (US$ million)	132.0	135.0	
Total imports (US$ million)	955.0	731.0	
Tourism receipts (US$ million)			
Tourist spending (US$ million)			

Average household size 1995 (persons)	5.29				
Urban population 1994 (%)	34.3				
Age analysis (%) (1987)	*0-14* 44.3		*15-64* 53.1		*65+* 2.5
Population by sex (%) (1987)	*Male* 48.8		*Female* 51.2		
Life expectancy (years) (1990-95)	*Male* 44.9		*Female* 48.0		
Infant mortality (deaths per '000 live births) (1993)	148.3				
Adult literacy (%) (1995)	40.1				

TRADING PARTNERS

Major export destinations 1995 (% share)		Major import sources 1995 (% share)	
Spain	19.1	Zimbabwe	7.3
Japan	13.6	Saudi Arabia	6.2
India	8.6	USA	4.5
Italy	3.4	United Arab Emirates	3.1

Myanmar

Area (km²)   678,030

Currency   Kyat (= 100 pyas)

Location   Myanmar (Burma) occupies most of the westward-facing coastline of the Indochinese peninsula, extending from the northern Chinese/Laotian border, with Assam (India) and Bangladesh to the west, down to the 600-kilometre-long finger of coastal territory which effectively seals off most of Thailand from the Indian Ocean. The climate is tropical and mainly humid. The capital is Rangoon.

Head of State   President Gen. Than Shwe

Head of Government   President Gen. Than Shwe

Ruling Party   Burmese Socialist Programme Party leads a five-party coalition.

Political Structure   Myanmar, or Burma as it was known until 1988, was run as a one-party socialist state until September 1988, when a military coup overthrew the administration and declared martial law. A 485-member Constituent Assembly was formed in May 1990, but has been repeatedly suspended from meeting. In 1996, a military-run constitutional convention decreed that a newly-elected assembly will choose its president from among three vice-presidents which it elects. All three are to serve five-year terms. The government also reached an agreement in February 1994 on the cessation of hostilities with ethnic insurgents on the Thai border, where the Kachin Independence Organisation had been fighting authorities for more than 30 years.

Last Elections   Multi-party elections to the newly created Constituent Assembly were held in 1990 and contested by some 93 different parties as well as 87 independents. The election produced a crushing defeat for the ruling junta, the State Law and Order Restoration Council, whose own favoured party, the National Unity Party, polled less than 20% of the vote compared with more than 50% for the opposition National League for Democracy (NLD). Shortly afterwards, the junta banned the new Assembly from meeting.

Political Risk   Repeated violations of human rights, associated to some extent with the guerrilla campaigns in Rohingya, continue, although the situation in 1996 is better than in 1995. There are occasional disputes with neighbouring Thailand which is accused of harbouring dissident rebels and infringing upon Myanmar's territory during "hot pursuit" operations against them. Despite its unpopularity, the ruling junta clings to power. To suppress its opponents, the government maintains military spending at levels the economy cannot sustain. Myanmar remains a risky market but its prospects would improve greatly if the effort to suppress political competition were to be scrapped.

International Disputes   The position of Daw San Suu Kyi, the NLD's pro-democracy leader, remains precarious. The fact that she was forbidden from running for the presidency in the 1996 elections has drawn more criticism from the international community.

Economy   Myanmar's government claims that GDP has grown by 8.2% over the past four years. Opposition leaders question that estimate but the economy is clearly improving. Official figures also show that the country has attracted $3 billion in foreign investment. However, only about a third of that has actually been dispersed.

Main Industries   Agriculture accounted for about 63% of GDP in 1995 and provided the main impetus for growth. Farming employs 80% of the workforce. Most of these people work in a subsistence capacity but output in the agricultural co-operatives is rising. Rubber, jute, cotton and tea are grown for export, and maize, millet, beans, sugar cane and wheat for the domestic market. The country has a vast timber export potential which is being exploited now at an ever-faster rate. Myanmar has large but only partially exploited reserves of lead, tin, zinc, silver, wolfram and gemstones. Nearly all industry is nationalised but foreign investors' interest is growing. Tourism is one of the main receipts of foreign investment. A plethora of new hotels, often financed from Singapore and Thailand, is being built in anticipation of a surge of visitors as the country opens up.

Energy   Much of the foreign investment that Myanmar has attracted has gone into the oil and gas sector ($1.2 billion in 1994-1995). Almost all of this was accounted for by one massive project to pipe gas to Thailand. The country's reserves are dwindling, however, and there have been no promising new finds in recent years. Half of all electricity is generated by hydro-electric systems.

	1993	1994	1995
Inflation (% change)	31.8	24.1	25.2
Exchange rate (per US$)	6.16	5.97	5.88
Interest rate			
GDP (% real growth)	5.0	3.7	8.5
GDP (Million units of national currency)	339,084.0	364,170.0	441,588.0
GDP (US$ million)	55,046.1	61,000.0	75,100.0
GDP per capita (US$)	1,276.6	1,388.9	1,668.9
Consumption (Million units of national currency)	301,335.0	309,265.0	334,997.6
Consumption (US$ million)	48,918.0	51,803.2	56,972.4
Consumption per capita (US$)	1,134.5	1,179.5	1,266.1
Population, mid-year ('000)	43,120.0	43,920.0	45,000.0
Birth rate (per '000)	32.5	28.5	
Death rate (per '000)	11.1	9.8	
No. of households ('000)	13,217.3	13,564.9	13,950.0
Total exports (US$ million)	583.0	771.0	846.0
Total imports (US$ million)	390.0	364.0	348.0
Tourism receipts (US$ million)	29.0	31.9	
Tourist spending (US$ million)	2.3	2.5	2.7

Average household size 1995 (persons)	3.06		
Urban population 1995 (%)	26.2		
Age analysis (%) (1987)	*0-14* 37.3	*15-64* 58.8	*65+* 3.9
Population by sex (%) (1987)	*Male* 49.6	*Female* 50.4	
Life expectancy (years) (1990)	*Male* 58.3	*Female* 61.8	
Infant mortality (deaths per '000 live births) (1993)	84.0		
Adult literacy (%) (1995)	83.1		

TRADING PARTNERS

Major export destinations 1995 (% share)		Major import sources 1995 (% share)	
Singapore	22.7	Singapore	1.5
China	16.1	China	1.5
India	15.9	Malaysia	0.6
Japan	10.1	Japan	0.4

Namibia

Area (km²)   824,295

Currency   Namibian dollar (= 100 cents)

Location   Namibia, the former South West Africa, lies on the southern Atlantic coast of the continent, where it is bounded in the south by its former occupying power, South Africa, in the north by Angola and in the east by Botswana. The country's climate is generally dry, although drought is rare. The capital is Windhoek.

Head of State   President Sam Nujoma (1990)

Head of Government   Hage Geingob

Ruling Party   South West Africa People's Organisation (SWAPO)

Political Structure   The Republic of Namibia became fully independent in March 1990, having been effectively annexed by South Africa in 1966 after the United Nations ended that country's right to act as administrator to the territory. Namibia has an executive President who is elected by the Constituent Assembly (Parliament) for a maximum of two five-year terms. The Assembly's 72 members are elected in turn by universal adult suffrage for a term of five years. An Upper House of Parliament was created and held its first session in May 1993.

Last Elections   Elections to the National Assembly were held in December 1994, when SWAPO delegates won 53 of the 72 seats, compared with 41 in 1989, and thus secured a convincing victory. The right-wing Democratic Turnhalle Alliance obtained most of the remaining seats. Sam Nujoma was unanimously elected as President by the Assembly in February 1990, and reappointed in 1995.

Political Risk   The smooth transition of the democratic process in Namibia has encouraged observers who consider it an important potential market for consumer goods. Yet personal consumption levels are still not high and any mismanagement of the economy could have severe economic consequences.

International Disputes   There have been some tensions with Botswana over the construction of a new military base near Gaborone, and over the sovereignty of the tiny island of Kasikili, on the Lobe river. The latter issue was referred to the International Court of Justice in 1995. In 1994, the country reached a settlement on a long-standing dispute with South Africa over the ownership of Walvis Bay (434 square miles), which South Africa formerly claimed as part of its own territory. Under the new agreement South Africa returned the disputed territory unconditionally to Namibian control.

Economy   With its considerable natural resources and its new-found political respectability, Namibia appears to be poised for substantial growth in the 1990s. However, its fragmented communications, especially with Botswana, and its difficult geographical position are hindering factors. Catastrophic droughts in recent years have further damaged the agricultural sector.

Main Industries   Namibia's principal export activity is the extraction of its vast wealth in minerals, particularly diamonds, uranium and tin and lithium. The country has the world's largest open cast uranium mine at Rossing. Other gemstones are present in abundance. Agriculture, however, remains the most important activity for most of the population. Employing 85% of the workforce, it nevertheless produces a mere 6% of GDP. Most farming is done on a subsistence basis, although cattle products are exported. Industry is still small-scale but is growing fast, and the sector centres on the processing of agricultural and mineral raw materials. Most consumer products are currently imported from South Africa.

Energy   Namibia is at present entirely dependent on imports of energy supplies, although prospecting is under way for petroleum and/or natural gas.

	1993	1994	1995
Inflation (% change)	8.5	10.8	11.9
Exchange rate (per US$)	3.27	3.55	3.63
Interest rate (% per annum)	18.0	17.1	18.5
GDP (% real growth)	4.2	10.5	2.3
GDP (Million units of national currency)	8,372.3	10,248.8	11,732.2
GDP (US$ million)	2,560.3	2,887.0	3,232.0
GDP per capita (US$)	1,753.7	1,924.9	2,099.0
Consumption (Million units of national currency)	5,182.0	5,828.0	6,129.4
Consumption (US$ million)	1,584.7	1,641.7	1,688.5
Consumption per capita (US$)	1,085.4	1,094.6	1,096.6
Population, mid-year ('000)	1,460.0	1,499.8	1,539.8
Birth rate (per '000)	41.6	43.4	
Death rate (per '000)	13.2	10.7	
No. of households ('000)	299.7	309.4	322.0
Total exports (US$ million)	1,290.0	1,321.0	
Total imports (US$ million)	1,188.0	1,196.0	
Tourism receipts (US$ million)	91.4	93.5	
Tourist spending (US$ million)	81.3	83.2	85.6

Average household size 1995 (persons)	4.54				
Urban population 1995 (%)	37.4				
Age analysis (%) (1991, est)	*0-14* 45.8		*15-64* 50.9		*65+* 3.3
Population by sex (%) (1991)	*Male* 48.7		*Female* 51.3		
Life expectancy (years) (1990-95)	*Male* 57.5		*Female* 60.0		
Infant mortality (deaths per '000 live births) (1993)	60.0				
Adult literacy (%) (1995)	72.5				

Nauru

Area (km²)   21

Currency   Australian dollar (A$ = 100 cents)

Location   Nauru is a single island, located between Kiribati, the Marshall Islands and the Solomon Islands. Almost circular in shape, it is remarkable for its low-lying terrain and for the virtual exhaustion of viable agricultural land. The climate is warm and dry. The capital is Yaren District.

Head of State   President Bernard Dowiyogo (1989)

Head of Government   President Bernard Dowiyogo

Ruling Party   The Democratic Party of Nauru is the only legal political party.

Political Structure   The Republic of Nauru is an associate member of the Commonwealth, in which the executive President governs with the aid of a Cabinet whose number may not exceed six people. The President is elected for a period of three years from the 18-member unicameral Parliament, which is also elected, by universal suffrage, for a period of three years. Voting is compulsory in all elections.

Last Elections   A general election was held in November 1992, which resulted in the reappointment of Bernard Dowiyogo as President by 10 votes to seven.

Political Risk   Like the Maldives, Nauru has expressed concern at the possibility of being swamped by rising seas in the event that global warming continues to worsen.

International Disputes   The country's longest-running political dispute ended in August 1993, when the Australian Government agreed to pay around A$107 million to Nauru, for the over-exploitation of its only mineral resource, the phosphate (guano) deposits.

Economy   Nauru's economy, based almost entirely on revenue from the extraction of phosphate, remains extremely weak at present, and its dependence on Australia is still growing. It has started to establish itself as an offshore financial centre, but a major financial scandal in 1993 has set the economy back. Nevertheless income per head is among the highest in the world, thanks to phosphate revenue, and the islanders enjoy a high standard of living.

Main Industries   The near-exhaustion of Nauru's only real resource, the phosphate deposits bequeathed by countless generations of passing sea birds, has left the country economically stranded. At present about 1.5 million tonnes of guano phosphate are mined every year, under the auspices of the state-owned Nauru Phosphate Corporation. Agriculture has only very limited possibilities, because of the small amount of cultivable soil - almost exclusively along one coastal strip. Consequently, all production is domestically oriented and a large proportion of the country's food requirements are imported - mainly from Australia.

Energy   All energy requirements are imported at present. There is no scope for hydro-electric development.

	1993	1994	1995
Inflation (% change)	0.9	3.0	4.0
Exchange rate (per US$)	1.48	1.29	1.35
Interest rate			
GDP (% real growth)	0.1	-0.4	2.0
GDP (Million units of national currency)	231.4	237.3	251.7
GDP (US$ million)	156.4	184.0	186.5
GDP per capita (US$)	15,635.1	16,723.0	15,410.3
Consumption (Million units of national currency)	153.4	157.3	166.9
Consumption (US$ million)	103.6	121.9	123.6
Consumption per capita (US$)	10,364.9	11,085.3	10,214.4
Population, mid-year ('000)	10.0	11.0	12.1
Birth rate (per '000)	27.9	28.0	
Death rate (per '000)		5.1	
No. of households ('000)	1.8	1.8	1.9
Total exports (US$ million)			
Total imports (US$ million)			
Tourism receipts (US$ million)			
Tourist spending (US$ million)			

Average household size 1995 (persons)	6.05		
Urban population 1995 (%)	100.0		
Age analysis (%) (1991, est)	*0-14* 35.1	*15-64* 60.8	*65+* 4.1
Population by sex (%)			
Life expectancy (years) (1990)	*Male* 64.3	*Female* 69.2	
Infant mortality (deaths per '000 live births)			
Adult literacy (%)			

Nepal

Area (km²)   141,415

Currency   Nepalese rupee (N Rp = 100 paisa)

Location   Nepal is a 700-kilometre strip of land lying along the summit of the Himalayan mountain range between India and the Tibet Autonomous Region of China. Only a small proportion of the country is less than 2,000 metres above sea level, and the highest peaks approach 9,000 metres. Half the population live in the lowlands, however with three major rivers feeding into the Ganges river basin. The capital is Kathmandu.

Head of State   HM King Birendra Bikram Shah Dev (1972)

Head of Government   Sher Bahadur Deuba (September 1994)

Ruling Party   Nepali Congress Party

Political Structure   The Kingdom of Nepal is a constitutional monarchy in which the King, as the "symbol of Nepalese nationality and the unity of the people of Nepal", has extensive powers. He appoints 10 of the 60 members in the National Council (Rashtriya Sabha) - 15 of the remainder being chosen by an electoral college, and 35 being elected by the House of Representatives (Pratinidhi Sabha). The 205 members of the latter are elected by universal adult suffrage for a five-year term. Political parties were banned from 1960 to 1990. Electoral opinion is subject to deep schisms and to factional feuding.

Last Elections   Elections were held in November 1994, when the narrow absolute majority of the ruling Nepalese Congress Party was overturned by a slender majority for the United Communist Party of Nepal. In September 1996, the communist government fell and was replaced by a centrist coalition led by Sher Bahadur Deuba.

Political Risk   Nepal has made undoubted strides toward democracy in recent years, partly in response to pressure from abroad. Nevertheless, there are periodic instances of strikes and political violence that accentuate security risks.

International Disputes   Nepal's relations with India, where a large proportion of the workforce is engaged, have been occasionally strained. The country also accuses Bhutan of maltreatment of its Nepalese minorities.

Economy   Nepal's difficult political situation has been matched by its economic problems. High rates of unemployment force many men to seek work across the border in India. The government's efforts to streamline its public sector, privatise state-owned enterprises and maintain tight monetary policies are showing results, however. Living standards (especially in Kathmandu) are higher than in many parts of South Asia. In April 1996, international donors agreed on a $993 million aid package for the country which should provide a further boost to the economy.

Main Industries   Nepal's manufacturing economy revolves around the export of carpets, textiles, hides, herbs and other materials. The agricultural sector embraces a variety of activities ranging from rice and grain farming to jute and cattle herding. Productivity in the farming sector is low and declining. Tourism, including mountaineering and hill trekking, is rapidly replacing the agricultural sector as a major economic activity and is currently the country's biggest export revenue earner. Industry is limited in scope and caters only for domestic requirements.

Energy   Nepal relies on imports for most of its energy requirements, apart from timber - which was recently estimated to fulfil as much as three-quarters of total needs. Efforts are under way to develop the hydro-electric generating sector, an area where Nepal has obvious opportunities.

	1993	1994	1995
Inflation (% change)	7.5	8.3	1.8
Exchange rate (per US$)	48.61	49.40	50.54
Interest rate (% per annum)	14.5		
GDP (% real growth)	6.2	7.4	3.0
GDP (Million units of national currency)	171,386.0	199,416.0	209,190.5
GDP (US$ million)	3,525.7	4,036.8	4,139.1
GDP per capita (US$)	169.4	189.2	188.2
Consumption (Million units of national currency)	135,279.0	156,738.0	163,725.2
Consumption (US$ million)	2,782.9	3,172.8	3,239.5
Consumption per capita (US$)	133.7	148.7	147.3
Population, mid-year ('000)	20,810.0	21,337.4	21,988.7
Birth rate (per '000)	39.2	37.6	
Death rate (per '000)	15.3	13.3	
No. of households ('000)	4,603.6	4,743.9	5,015.0
Total exports (US$ million)	390.0	364.0	348.0
Total imports (US$ million)	880.0	1,159.0	1,374.0
Tourism receipts (US$ million)	157.0	204.9	
Tourist spending (US$ million)	93.0	121.4	124.0

Average household size 1995 (persons)	4.17				
Urban population 1995 (%)	13.7				
Age analysis (%) (1986)	*0-14* 42.3	*15-64*	54.7	*65+*	3.0
Population by sex (%) (1991)	*Male* 49.9	*Female*	50.1		
Life expectancy (years) (1990)	*Male* 51.5	*Female*	50.3		
Infant mortality (deaths per '000 live births) (1993)	99.0				
Adult literacy (%) (1995)	27.5				

Netherlands

Area (km²)   41,160

Currency   Netherlands guilder (Fl = 100 cents)

Location   The Netherlands occupies some 250 km of the North Sea coast between Belgium in the south and Germany in the north and east. In reality, its sea frontage is considerably more extensive than this would suggest because of the numerous inlets and tidal internal seas such as the Ijsselmeer and the Wadden Sea. As much as one-third of the land is below water level, having been reclaimed from the sea by an extensive reclamation programme. The capital is Amsterdam.

Head of State   HM Queen Beatrix

Head of Government   Wim Kok (August 1994)

Ruling Party   Partij van de Arbeid (PvdA-Labour Party) leads a coalition with D-66 and the Liberal Party.

Political Structure   The Kingdom of the Netherlands is a constitutional monarchy in which the monarch rules through a Council of Ministers. The bicameral Staten-Generaal (Parliament) comprises a 150-member Lower House (Second Chamber, or Tweede Kamer), whose members are elected by universal suffrage for a four-year term, and a 75-seat First Chamber (Eerste Kamer) which is appointed by the various provincial legislatures for a term of four years. The Netherlands formally rules over the Netherlands Antilles and Aruba, but in practice wide autonomy prevails.

Last Elections   The general elections of May 1994 produced an inconclusive result, with the ruling CDA left holding only 34 of the 150 seats in the Tweede Kamer, against 37 for the socialist PvdA. The Volkspartij voor Vrijheid en Democratie (VVD) won 31 seats, the Democrats 66 obtained 24 and various environmentalist and minority parties won the remaining seats. By August 1994 the Christen Demokratisch Appel (CDA) coalition of ex-Premier Ruud Lubbers was forced to resign, being replaced by a Socialist/Liberal grouping operating on only a narrow electoral margin. Local elections in March 1995 showed clear support for the VVD, which is now bigger than the CDA.

Political Risk   The almost traditional splintering of political views, especially on the left wing, has left the political field open to a practical coalition of centre-right and centre-left parties which has made substantial progress against the undoubted economic and political problems of the moment. The Netherlands is one of the most committed European nations to the principle of European unity and has thrown its weight decisively behind the Maastricht Treaty on political union.

International Disputes   None. The Netherlands, however, has gradually been tightening its immigration laws in an effort to ward off the very large numbers of foreigners entering the country in search of work.

Economy   Rigorous and often painful austerity programmes during the early 1990s led to economic recession, the failure of numerous businesses and comparatively high levels of unemployment. Rates of growth recovered slightly in 1994 and 1995 although the economy's performance still lags behind that of most other EU member states. Inflation, at 1.9% in 1995, is low but the country's debt has steadily edged up each year as growth rates have remained anaemic. Total debt today is almost 80% of GDP, a figure far in excess of the Maastricht criterion of 60%.

Main Industries   The Netherlands' traditional trading activities revolve around its strategic position at the mouth of the River Rhine, and trade, especially in petroleum products, is still of the utmost importance. There are a large number of coastal and international vessels providing cargo services, and an important ship servicing and repair industry exists around Rotterdam. The country's agricultural sector benefits from the low-lying and well-irrigated character of the landscape. Hothouse crops like tomatoes or cut flowers benefit from the use of low-cost gas from the North Sea. The main export crops include greenhouse vegetables, wheat, horticultural goods and vegetables. Industry is reasonably well developed with engineering, vehicle manufacture, electrical and electronic products, chemicals, aerospace and petrochemicals all of international importance.

Energy   The country is fully self-sufficient in natural gas, although some petroleum needs have to be imported. Scope for non-thermal electricity generation is limited to the nuclear option; yet for political reasons this course remains unpopular.

	1993	1994	1995
Inflation (% change)	2.6	2.8	1.9
Exchange rate (per US$)	1.86	1.82	1.61
Interest rate (% per annum)	10.4	8.4	6.9
GDP (% real growth)	-0.7	1.7	1.1
GDP (Billion units of national currency)	573.9	600.0	618.0
GDP (US$ million)	308,548.4	329,670.3	383,850.9
GDP per capita (US$)	20,179.8	21,431.9	24,844.7
Consumption (Billion units of national currency)	350.3	363.4	376.7
Consumption (US$ million)	188,333.3	199,670.3	233,975.2
Consumption per capita (US$)	12,317.4	12,980.6	15,144.0
Population, mid-year ('000)	15,290.0	15,382.2	15,450.0
Birth rate (per '000)	12.8	12.1	12.5
Death rate (per '000)	9.0	8.7	8.4
No. of households ('000)	6,243.0	6,306.6	6,371.0
Total exports (US$ million)	139,127.0	155,554.0	194,498.0
Total imports (US$ million)	124,739.0	139,795.0	174,898.0
Tourism receipts (US$ million)	4,690.0	5,047.6	
Tourist spending (US$ million)	8,974.0	9,658.2	11,317.5

Average household size 1995 (persons)	2.30				
Urban population 1995 (%)	88.9				
Age analysis (%) (1995)	*0-14* 18.2		*15-64* 68.7		*65+* 13.1
Population by sex (%) (1995)	*Male* 49.6		*Female* 50.4		
Life expectancy (years) (1993)	*Male* 74.0		*Female* 80.0		
Infant mortality (deaths per '000 live births) (1993)	6.3				
Adult literacy (%) (1984)	98.0				

TRADING PARTNERS

Major export destinations 1995 (% share)		Major import sources 1995 (% share)	
Germany	22.3	Germany	16.6
Belgium/Luxembourg	9.9	Belgium/Luxembourg	8.4
France	8.7	USA	7.4
USA	3.1	United Kingdom	7.4

Netherlands Antilles

Area (km²) 993

Currency Netherlands Antilles guilder (N Fl = 100 cents)

Location The Netherlands Antilles consists of two groups of islands lying in the Caribbean Sea about 800 km apart. The principal group, which includes the capital Curaçao, lies just 150 km off the coast of Venezuela. Being some 600 km from the nearest other island states (Grenada, to the west), the group has acquired its own character under Dutch domination. Aruba, which once belonged to the group under Dutch sovereignty, negotiated its independence in 1986. The capital is Willemstad.

Head of State HM Queen Beatrix (Netherlands)

Head of Government Miguel Pourier (March 1994)

Ruling Party Antillean Reconstruction Party leads a coalition.

Political Structure The Netherlands Antilles is a Dutch overseas dependency ruled by the Dutch monarch through an appointed governor. In practice, the country enjoys a high degree of political autonomy and is edging toward independence. The country has a unicameral Parliament (Staten) elected by universal suffrage for a four-year term. Aruba, which was part of the group until 1986, became fully independent in 1996. Much attention now focuses on the question of secession by Curaçao, the most affluent island. But Like St Maarten, St Eustatius and Saba, Curaçao has recently voted to remain within the Netherlands Antilles.

Last Elections Elections to the Staten were held in 1994, when the ruling centre-right coalition was overturned by a simple majority for the ARP, which then went on to form a government. Party politics have been unusually volatile in recent years, with changes of allegiance fairly frequent.

Political Risk The Netherlands Antilles depends heavily on earnings from a few commodity exports and is therefore vulnerable to movements in the world prices of these products. Its level of external debt is also especially sensitive to conditions in international commodity markets. Illegal immigration (mainly from the Dominican Republic and from Haiti) is another source of concern. Drug trafficking, especially in Curaçao, has been widely blamed for an upsurge in criminal violence.

International Disputes Aruba's departure from the Netherlands Antilles was initially resisted because of that island's important contribution to tourism. Eventually, opposition lessened as the sentiment in favour of independence grew in the other islands.

Economy The Netherlands Antilles' offshore financial sector currently handles around $60 billion of assets and derives a major portion of its income from these activities. Other important economic activities include tourism and oil refining. The standard of living varies widely between the different islands, however. Economic conditions are also volatile, being influenced by erratic movements in world commodity prices (especially oil) and conditions in international financial markets.

Main Industries The Netherlands Antilles still relies to a large extent on the processing and transhipment of oil, mainly from Venezuela. The oil sector, which is mainly concentrated around Curaçao, contributes as much as 70% of GDP. Farming is limited by the poor soil and the erratic climate; less than 5% of the land area is cultivated for arable purposes. Fruit and vegetables are grown for domestic consumption, and fishing is of only a small-scale character. Industry is small scale as most manufactures are imported. Tourism is the most dynamic sector and probably holds the most potential for the future, with visitors from the Netherlands, the United States and other parts of the Caribbean accounting for the bulk of visitors. The country is working hard to develop its reputation as a centre for offshore financial services.

Energy The country has no indigenous energy resources and depends on imports for all its fuel needs.

	1993	1994	1995
Inflation (% change)	2.1	1.8	1.2
Exchange rate (per US$)	1.79	1.79	1.75
Interest rate (% per annum)	12.6	12.7	12.7
GDP (% real growth)	0.3	0.2	1.1
GDP (Million units of national currency)	3,111.8	3,175.1	3,248.5
GDP (US$ million)	1,738.4	1,773.8	1,856.3
GDP per capita (US$)	9,149.7	8,869.0	8,839.6
Consumption (Million units of national currency)	2,063.4	2,105.3	2,153.9
Consumption (US$ million)	1,152.7	1,176.1	1,230.8
Consumption per capita (US$)	6,067.0	5,880.7	5,861.0
Population, mid-year ('000)	190.0	200.0	210.0
Birth rate (per '000)	18.1	19.7	
Death rate (per '000)	7.0	6.7	
No. of households ('000)	42.5	42.0	42.8
Total exports (US$ million)	1,284.0		
Total imports (US$ million)	1,807.0		
Tourism receipts (US$ million)			
Tourist spending (US$ million)			

Average household size 1995 (persons)	4.66				
Urban population 1995 (%)	69.5				
Age analysis (%) (1989)	*0-14* 26.0		*15-64* 67.1		*65+* 6.9
Population by sex (%) (1992)	*Male* 47.9		*Female* 52.1		
Life expectancy (years) (1992)	*Male* 72.3		*Female* 77.9		
Infant mortality (deaths per '000 live births) (1992)	10.1				
Adult literacy (%) (1981)	93.8				

TRADING PARTNERS

Major export destinations 1995 (% share)		Major import sources 1995 (% share)	
USA	13.3	USA	26.2
Dominican Republic	13.1	Netherlands	9.8
Bahamas	5.4	Italy	7.7
Haiti	5.4	Brazil	5.6

New Caledonia

Area (km²)   19,105

Currency   Franc CFP (= 100 centimes)

Location   New Caledonia, situated in the Western Pacific about 1,500 km east of Australia, is basically a single large island which controls numerous smaller coral reefs and islets. Vanuatu lies directly to the north-east. The capital is Nouméa.

Head of State   President Jacques Chirac (France)

Head of Government   Simon Loueckhote (President of the Territorial Congress)

Ruling Party   Rassemblement pour la Calédonie dans la République (RPR)

Political Structure   New Caledonia is an external department of France and is governed to a considerable degree from Paris. The country sends deputies to the French Assemblée Nationale and is represented at the EU. Since being accorded regional status in 1974, the country elects its own Regional Council for a term of six years, with responsibility for economic and social planning. A referendum was held in 1987 on whether to declare independence, but the vote was boycotted by the Kanak majority which opposed the move.

Last Elections   The last full elections to the French Assemblée Nationale were in 1993 when both seats were won by the RPR. The 1989 elections to the Regional Council produced a hung parliament, with 27 of the 54 seats going to the RPR and 19 to the Front de Libération Nationale Kanake Socialiste.

Political Risk   The rapid rise of ethnic disturbances in New Caledonia, including occasional political violence, has given ample warning that the stability of French rule cannot be regarded as absolute. The 1987 referendum failed only because of the Kanak boycott. The issue is due to go to the vote again in 1998.

International Disputes   The rise of ethnic tensions in the country has led to some separatist sentiment, which has been fuelled by resentment at the allegedly excessive control being exercised by Paris. However, as described above, the 1987 referendum produced a vote in favour of continued allegiance to France.

Economy   At present, New Caledonia's economy is run as an integral part of the French economy, an arrangement which has not always proved satisfactory to the local population. Export earnings rose in 1994 and 1995, but when they are depressed the economy suffers severely and the government demands more aid from France.

Main Industries   New Caledonia's mining operations represent the most important sector of the economy, with nickel and chrome extraction earning well over US$8 million a year. New Caledonia is the world's third largest nickel producer, with over 40% of known world deposits. There are also reserves of iron ore, manganese, cobalt, zinc and lead. Agriculture is depressed at present, not only by a failure of investment but also by the continuing political uncertainty in the country. Export crops include copra and coffee, while sweet potatoes, bananas, pawpaws and vegetables are grown for the domestic market. Cattle raising is an important activity and there are extensive timber removal programmes under way. Industry is varied, ranging from heavy activities like nickel smelting to light industries, textiles and electronics. The tourist industry is also extremely important, though demand from France has been fluctuating recently.

Energy   The country relies on imports for all its basic requirements. It may be a measure of the industrial decline that demand for electricity has been generally falling since the mid-1980s.

	1993	1994	1995
Inflation (% change)	10.0	3.0	0.0
Exchange rate (per US$)	106.66	97.41	97.43
Interest rate			
GDP (% real growth)	3.3	1.7	2.0
GDP (Million units of national currency)	369,596.0	387,116.8	394,924.0
GDP (US$ million)	3,465.2	3,974.1	4,053.4
GDP per capita (US$)	19,251.0	22,078.3	22,519.0
Consumption (Million units of national currency)	189,953.5	198,958.4	202,971.0
Consumption (US$ million)	1,780.9	2,042.5	2,083.2
Consumption per capita (US$)	9,894.0	11,347.1	11,573.6
Population, mid-year ('000)	180.0	180.0	180.0
Birth rate (per '000)	28.8	23.2	
Death rate (per '000)	5.1	5.8	
No. of households ('000)	36.2	36.4	36.9
Total exports (US$ million)	362.8	370.0	
Total imports (US$ million)	900.0	1,000.0	
Tourism receipts (US$ million)	95.0	98.0	
Tourist spending (US$ million)			

Average household size 1995 (persons)	4.63				
Urban population 1995 (%)	62.1				
Age analysis (%) (1989)	*0-14* 32.7		*15-64* 62.9		*65+* 4.4
Population by sex (%) (1989)	*Male* 51.2		*Female* 48.8		
Life expectancy (years) (1989)	*Male* 66.5		*Female* 71.8		
Infant mortality (deaths per '000 live births) (1992)	8.6				
Adult literacy (%) (1976)	91.3				

New Zealand

Area (km²)   265,150

Currency   New Zealand dollar (NZ$ = 100 cents)

Location   The two large islands which make up the greater part of New Zealand are located between the southern Tasman Sea and the South Pacific. They have a total length of almost 1,500 km and extend to a maximum altitude of just over 4,000 metres along the volcanic ridges. The climate is pleasant, though cool in winter. The capital is Wellington.

Head of State   HM Queen Elizabeth II

Head of Government   Jim Bolger (1990)

Ruling Party   New Zealand National Party

Political Structure   New Zealand, an independent member of the Commonwealth, is ruled by the Crown acting through a Governor-General. Executive power is exercised by the Prime Minister, who is appointed by the unicameral House of Representatives (Parliament). The 97 members of the House are elected by universal suffrage for a term of three years. A proportional representation system was introduced in 1995, in preparation for the general elections of November 1996.

Last Elections   General elections were held in November 1993 when the incumbent NZ National Party retained its control of Parliament, winning 68 of the 97 seats with only 49% of the vote. The Labour Party won 28 seats, despite obtaining 35% of the vote, and the left-wing New Labour Party retained its single seat.

Political Risk   New Zealand has resolved an argument with its Maori indigenous peoples over compensation for expropriations of land and property in the past. Immigration, mainly from South Korea, Taiwan and Hong Kong, is an issue of growing significance, however. The country's first racially based political party, the Ethnic Minority Party, was launched in 1996. The move was in response to the new system of proportional representation which gives a greater voice to small parties. It also reflects Asians' growing uneasiness about anti-immigration campaigns in the country which are mainly associated with the conservative and populist group known as the New Zealand First Party. The prime minister's National Party describes the anti-Asian view as xenophobic but the issue is likely to play an important role in the next elections in late 1996.

International Disputes   New Zealand's only serious disputes are with France. One concerns that country's nuclear test programme in the South Pacific. The other relates to France's refusal to hand back two French secret service officers convicted in New Zealand of bombing the Rainbow Warrior, a ship belonging to the environmentalist group Greenpeace. New Zealand differs with Australia on points of defence policy, though the two countries are progressing toward closer economic relationships.

Economy   During 1996 signs of a slowing economy have began to emerge including falling GDP forecasts, a drop in the numbers of people being hired and weaker retail sales. The Reserve Bank, which is required by an act of parliament to keep inflation below 2%, has predicted that the rate would be at its upper limit for the first half of 1996. The size of the current account deficit is a source of more concern and is expected to rise sharply during the year.

Main Industries   New Zealand's diversified economy derives only about 10% of GDP from agriculture - although the sector still generates the greater part of the country's export revenues. Half of the land area is pasture land for sheep and cattle, and half of the remainder is woodland and forest which is used for the extraction of hardwoods. There are nearly 70 million sheep, and apart from the usual arable farming activities (wheat, barley, fruit and vegetables), dairy farming is growing in importance. Industry is twice as important to the domestic economy as agriculture, although it generates relatively little export revenues. Activities range from heavy smelting to light industry, with the production of light engineering and consumer goods being the most prominent. With ample reserves of coal and lignite and a massive offshore gas field, New Zealand should have an exportable surplus of energy supplies. There is also sulphur, iron ore and iron sand, titanium, gold, silver, limestone and dolomite.

Energy   New Zealand has ample energy supplies. However, it relies on imports for its oil supplies while exporting both gas and coal. At least 80% of all electricity comes from hydro-electric installations.

	1993	1994	1995
Inflation (% change)	1.3	1.7	1.9
Exchange rate (per US$)	1.85	1.68	1.52
Interest rate (% per annum)	10.3	9.7	12.2
GDP (% real growth)	4.9	4.0	3.4
GDP (Million units of national currency)	79,630.0	84,230.0	88,758.2
GDP (US$ million)	43,043.2	50,136.9	58,393.6
GDP per capita (US$)	12,476.3	14,365.9	16,495.4
Consumption (Million units of national currency)	46,974.0	48,743.0	52,006.0
Consumption (US$ million)	25,391.4	29,013.7	34,214.5
Consumption per capita (US$)	7,359.8	8,313.4	9,665.1
Population, mid-year ('000)	3,450.0	3,490.0	3,540.0
Birth rate (per '000)	16.9	16.3	16.2
Death rate (per '000)	7.9	7.8	7.8
No. of households ('000)	1,206.1	1,217.0	1,230.0
Total exports (US$ million)	10,537.0	12,181.0	13,736.0
Total imports (US$ million)	9,636.0	11,913.0	13,958.0
Tourism receipts (US$ million)	1,165.0	1,357.6	1,492.0
Tourist spending (US$ million)	1,003.0	1,151.4	1,265.4

Average household size 1995 (persons)	2.73				
Urban population 1995 (%)	86.1				
Age analysis (%) (1994)	*0-14* 23.2	*15-64* 65.1	*65+* 11.7		
Population by sex (%) (1995)	*Male* 49.4	*Female* 50.6			
Life expectancy (years) (1990)	*Male* 72.3	*Female* 78.3			
Infant mortality (deaths per '000 live births) (1994)	7.1				
Adult literacy (%) (1985)	98.5				

TRADING PARTNERS

Major export destinations 1995 (% share)		Major import sources 1995 (% share)	
Australia	20.3	Australia	21.4
Japan	16.2	USA	18.5
USA	9.9	Japan	13.7
United Kingdom	6.1	United Kingdom	5.8

Nicaragua

Area (km²) 148,000

Currency Córdoba oro (gold córdoba) (C = 100 centavos)

Location Nicaragua is the second largest state in Central America, after Mexico. It bridges the section of the Panamanian isthmus which lies between Costa Rica and Honduras and has coastlines on both the Pacific and the Caribbean. The terrain is mountainous to the west, but descends to lowlands in the coastal east. There are two huge inland lakes situated to the north-west and south-east of the capital Managua. The capital is Managua.

Head of State President Violeta Barrios de Chamorro (1990)

Head of Government President Violeta Barrios de Chamorro

Ruling Party Unión Nacional de Opositora formed a coalition in 1994 with the Sandinista National Liberation Front and the Democratic Christian Union.

Political Structure Nicaragua's modern history began in 1979, when the left-wing Frente Sandinista de Liberación Nacional overthrew the Somoza dynasty which had ruled since the 1930s. A bloody guerrilla war and a US blockade followed. The situation improved only slightly after the 1990 elections which brought a centre-right government to power. The 1987 Constitution provides for an executive President, directly elected for a six-year term and a unicameral National Assembly (Parliament), elected by universal suffrage every six years.

Last Elections The legislative elections in 1990 produced a crushing defeat for the ruling Sandinistas, which won only 40% of the vote against 55% for the centre-right Unión Nacional de Opositora.

Political Risk The deterioration in the political structure, including particularly the resumption of armed hostilities between the two rearmed guerrilla groups, suggests strongly that Nicaragua will remain a high risk in political terms for some time to come. There has been some improvement in the north of the country, but the tension between left and right remains great. Complaints about human rights abuses (both past and present) continue.

International Disputes Nicaragua's civil war, which started in 1979 after the Sandinista overthrow of the dictator Somoza, took on an international character in the 1980s when the United States pronounced it an area of strategic importance. Thereafter, large volumes of US military aid were routed to the right-wing Contra rebels attempting to overthrow the Sandinistas. This came most prominently to light during the so-called Irangate scandal of the late 1980s. The situation eased in the 1990s, when the Sandinistas lost a general election to a centre-right government. Fighting flared up again in mid-1993, and although the so-called Recontras agreed to a disarmament plan in 1994 in return for a stake in government, the hand-over of weapons has not been universally observed.

Economy The gradual stabilisation of the political situation appears likely to encourage back some of the many investors who withdrew from the country in previous years. The government claims that the economy is recovering from the deep recession which persisted throughout 1993 and 1994. Inflation has certainly slowed and public officials maintain (with some exaggeration, perhaps) that GDP grew by 4% in 1995 while exports rose by 46%. The benefits of growth are very unevenly spread, however. Unemployment is high and continues to rise. The volume of external debt is another serious problem. The Nicaraguans owe Russia $3.3 billion and are trying to get this sum reduced by 95%. So far, they have made no progress on this issue.

Main Industries Nicaragua relies heavily on its agricultural sector, which employs 45% of the workforce and generates 70% of all exports even though it contributes no more than 25% of GDP. Coffee, cotton and some meat are the main export crops. Wheat, maize, rice, beans and sorghum are grown for the domestic market. Most farmland is in the hands of smallholders and a land distribution programme is under way. Manufacturing provides a further 25% of GDP in a typical year, although production has fluctuated with the changing political situation. Nicaragua has food processing, coffee roasting, textiles, timber and handicrafts, as well as a few heavy industries such as chemicals, cement, metallurgy and petroleum refining. Most large enterprises are still state-owned, although a privatisation programme is being implemented. The country has only limited mineral resources, notably salt, gold, silver, tungsten and lead and zinc.

Energy Apart from fuelwood which still supplies half the country's energy needs, the country relies on imports of petroleum for most of its requirements. Hydro-electric power provides about a third of all electricity, with thermal stations accounting for the rest.

	1993	1994	1995
Inflation (% change)	20.0	8.0	11.0
Exchange rate (per US$)	6.72	7.06	7.51
Interest rate (% per annum)	20.2	20.1	19.9
GDP (% real growth)	4.9	4.6	3.5
GDP (Million units of national currency)	11,015.0	12,445.0	14,427.0
GDP (US$ million)	1,639.1	1,762.7	1,921.0
GDP per capita (US$)	384.8	400.6	423.1
Consumption (Million units of national currency)	9,965.0	11,036.0	12,540.6
Consumption (US$ million)	1,482.9	1,563.2	1,669.8
Consumption per capita (US$)	348.1	355.3	367.8
Population, mid-year ('000)	4,260.0	4,400.0	4,540.0
Birth rate (per '000)	40.4		
Death rate (per '000)	6.8	7.8	
No. of households ('000)	1,206.1	1,217.0	1,238.0
Total exports (US$ million)	267.0	351.0	525.0
Total imports (US$ million)	744.0	875.0	949.0
Tourism receipts (US$ million)	1,165.0	1,337.4	
Tourist spending (US$ million)	1,003.0	1,151.4	1,230.0

Average household size 1995 (persons)	3.48				
Urban population 1995 (%)	62.9				
Age analysis (%) (1991)	*0-14*	47.2	*15-64*	46.8	*65+* 6.0
Population by sex (%) (1991)	*Male*	48.4	*Female*	51.6	
Life expectancy (years) (1990-95)	*Male*	64.8	*Female*	67.7	
Infant mortality (deaths per '000 live births) (1993)	52.1				
Adult literacy (%) (1995)	65.7				

TRADING PARTNERS

Major export destinations 1995 (% share)		Major import sources 1995 (% share)	
USA	43.6	USA	27.5
Germany	10.7	Venezuela	10.5
El Salvador	6.7	Guatemala	8.1
France	4.1	El Salvador	4.9

Niger

Area (km²)   1,186,410

Currency   CFA franc (= 100 centimes)

Location   Niger, occupying much of the centre of North West Africa, is a large and landlocked state which borders on Algeria in the north-west, Libya in the far north, Chad in the east, Nigeria in the south and Benin, Burkina Faso and Mali in the west and south-west. The only cultivable soil in the country lies along the Niger River; elsewhere it is mainly desert or savannah. The capital is Niamey.

Head of State   President Ibrahim Bare Mainassara

Head of Government   President Ibrahim Bare Mainassara

Ruling Party   The Mouvement Nationale pour une Société de Développement (MNSD) led a five-party coalition until removed from power by a military coup in February 1996.

Political Structure   From 1974 until the return of parliamentary democracy in 1993, Niger was run by a military administration. The elections which took place in February 1993 followed a period of serious deterioration in the political climate. Another round of elections occurred in January 1996 after one of the major coalition partners withdrew from the government. A dispute between the previous president, Mahamane Oumane, and the prime minister, Hama Amadou, prompted the military coup which brought Lieutenant-Colonel Ibrahim Bare Mainassara to power in February 1996. Mainassara immediately announced that he had no plans to stay in power and promised to hold new elections.

Last Elections   The elections of January 1996 were necessitated by the withdrawal of the Social Democrats from the coalition led by the MNSD, and produced a sharply reduced majority for the reformed coalition. The military coup which followed the elections was widely condemned by donors and in April 1996 the leaders agreed that new elections would be held in September 1996.

Political Risk   The country remains unstable with a succession of democratic governments being constantly under threat. Unrest and occasional rebellion among the Tuaregs in the north of the country complicate the political situation. The border with Algeria has been closed since 1992, purportedly because of Tuareg attacks, but the general assumption is that the Government was moving to stop the infiltration of Tuareg weapons into the north.

International Disputes   Niger's troubled domestic history has inevitably rubbed off on its relations with its neighbours. The border with Algeria was closed, in an effort to stop the infiltration of weapons to Tuareg rebels in the north. Both the IMF and the EU have suspended financial assistance, pending the resignation of the leaders of the latest military coup and the new elections that have been promised for September 1996.

Economy   Niger's economy remains highly dependent on France for aid. Several years of drought have left the country in a poor condition. Meanwhile the 50% devaluation in the CFA franc, which was announced in March 1994, is likely to cause a severe escalation of the country's external debts.

Main Industries   Niger remains dependent on its meagre agricultural sector for half of its GDP. Employing over 90% of the workforce, the sector produces cotton, hides and leather goods for export, and sorghum, millet, rice and vegetables for the domestic market. Cattle breeding is an important activity, although herds have been hit by drought in recent years. Minerals provide a large part of the country's export earnings but no more than 8% of GDP. Niger has substantial worked deposits of uranium, and some gold, tin, phosphates, coal and molybdenum. A small oilfield was discovered in 1983. Otherwise, progress is minimal. Industry generates about 2% of GDP, mainly producing goods destined for the domestic market. These include processed foods, plastics and construction materials.

Energy   Despite recent oil finds, Niger relies on imports for nearly all its petroleum needs: the only alternatives, apart from coal, are the country's considerable timber resources for fuelwood.

	1993	1994	1995
Inflation (% change)	-1.2	36.0	29.5
Exchange rate (per US$)	283.16	555.20	498.70
Interest rate (% per annum)	17.5	17.5	16.0
GDP (% real growth)	-4.2	-6.6	-1.5
GDP (Million units of national currency)	651,200.0	827,248.0	1,055,216.9
GDP (US$ million)	2,299.8	1,490.0	2,115.9
GDP per capita (US$)	275.1	168.4	230.0
Consumption (Million units of national currency)	465,048.0	620,108.0	830,274.2
Consumption (US$ million)	1,642.4	1,116.9	1,664.9
Consumption per capita (US$)	196.4	126.2	181.0
Population, mid-year ('000)	8,361.0	8,850.0	9,200.0
Birth rate (per '000)	52.5	55.0	
Death rate (per '000)	18.9	21.3	
No. of households ('000)	1,525.3	1,551.3	1,580.0
Total exports (US$ million)	225.0		
Total imports (US$ million)	309.0		
Tourism receipts (US$ million)	16.0	21.8	
Tourist spending (US$ million)	29.0	39.6	59.0

Average household size 1995 (persons)	5.53		
Urban population 1995 (%)	17.0		
Age analysis (%) (1991, est)	*0-14* 47.7	*15-64* 49.8	*65+* 2.5
Population by sex (%)			
Life expectancy (years) (1990-95)	*Male* 44.9	*Female* 48.1	
Infant mortality (deaths per '000 live births) (1993)	124.1		
Adult literacy (%) (1995)	13.6		

TRADING PARTNERS

Major export destinations 1995 (% share)		Major import sources 1995 (% share)	
France	75.1	France	20.3
Côte d'Ivoire	8.0	Côte d'Ivoire	12.6
Canada	4.1	USA	8.5
Nigeria	3.4	Hong Kong	3.7

Nigeria

Area (km²) 923,850

Currency Naira (N = 100 kobo)

Location Nigeria is located on the Atlantic coast of West Africa, where it is bounded in the north by Niger, in the west by Benin, in the east by Chad and on the south-east by Cameroon. It has a generally warm and pleasant tropical climate, although conditions along the 100-kilometre-wide mangrove swamps of the coast are less favourable. The capital is Abuja.

Head of State Gen. Sanni Abacha (1994)

Head of Government Gen. Sanni Abacha

Ruling Party A military-controlled administration has run the country since November 1993.

Political Structure Nigeria, an independent member of the Commonwealth, has been ruled by civilian administrations for only nine of its 35 years of independence. The country's execution of nine supporters of the Ogoni tribe in November 1995 brought trade sanctions, cancellation of some international aid and suspension from the Commonwealth. Nigeria's neighbours, including the Organisation of African Unity, were equally critical. Inside the country, reactions were muted but the situation remains explosive. The Ogonis and other minorities in the oil-producing region have been cut off from the benefits of this resource. At one time 50% of oil revenue was retained locally but the official figure is now down to 3%. Security of land tenure has been abolished and the oil money now goes into the coffers and private pockets of the rich. Regrettably, successive military regimes have turned the one-time federal system into a state of haves and have-nots. These new difficulties only add to the long-standing tribal tensions between the Yoruba, the Hausa and the Fulani.

Last Elections Elections were held in July 1992 to both Houses of the new National Assembly, which started its work in January 1993. In the 91-seat senate (Upper House), the ruling Social Democratic Party (SDP) won 52 seats, the National Republican Convention (NRC) won 37, and two seats were unfilled. In the 593-member House of Representatives, the SDP won 314 seats, the NRC 275, and four seats were unfilled. The SDP is supported mainly by Yoruba voters, and the NRC by Hausas and Fulanis. Only 25% of the electorate voted.

Political Risk If Nigeria's considerable oil wealth has been a major attraction for foreign investors in the past, its dubious political record and its growing reputation for economic crime are equally effective as counter-arguments. Probably half the population of the delta areas lives without adequate roads, water supply or electricity. Their schools are without books and clinics have no drugs. Ken Saro-Wiwa, the Ogoni leader of much of the resistance, expressed the popular anger against these inequalities. He became a threat to the military regime and was subsequently executed.

International Disputes Nigeria still has an ongoing territorial disagreement about various islands in Lake Chad. More recently, Chad has accused Nigeria of harbouring anti-government rebels, and there have been border clashes with Cameroon since the start of 1994, mainly involving the oil-rich Bakassi peninsula. Nigerian troops occupied the Diamond Island and Djabane in January 1994, leading to vigorous protests from Chad.

Economy Nigeria's economy is in recession and social services are collapsing. Inflation in the first quarter of 1996 was around 40%, while statistics on unemployment and violent crime show a sharp rise. The gap between the official and black market exchange rate is widening and the interest rate, at 21%, is about half of the rate of inflation. Extensive government regulation, erratic macroeconomic policies, corruption and an unsavoury international reputation are seriously undermining the Nigerian economy.

Main Industries Nigeria, nominally the most wealthy state in sub-Saharan Africa, owes most of its wealth to its oil production, which provides a fifth of GDP and the great majority of all export revenues. There are also deposits of coal, tin, iron ore, uranium, lead, zinc and gold, not all of which are being exploited. The agricultural sector also makes an important contribution with exports of cocoa, coffee, cotton, palm oil and rubber. The industrial base strongly reflects elements of import substitution, with food products, cigarettes, textiles and steel products being major activities.

Energy Nigeria is self-sufficient in all forms of energy. This has not, however, prevented periodic shortages of all forms of processed fuel. People living in oil-producing regions must often pay more than twice as much for fuel as townspeople because it is transported laboriously by boat back from the refinery.

	1993	1994	1995
Inflation (% change)	57.2	54.4	45.0
Exchange rate (per US$)	22.07	21.94	21.91
Interest rate (% per annum)	31.7	20.5	20.2
GDP (% real growth)	-8.6	-15.6	8.4
GDP (Million units of national currency)	701,473.0	914,334.0	1,436,650.0
GDP (US$ million)	31,784.0	41,674.3	65,570.5
GDP per capita (US$)	302.0	384.2	587.2
Consumption (Million units of national currency)	569,793.0	766,671.0	
Consumption (US$ million)	25,817.5	34,944.0	
Consumption per capita (US$)	245.3	322.2	
Population, mid-year ('000)	105,260.0	108,470.0	111,666.0
Birth rate (per '000)	45.4	43.5	
Death rate (per '000)	15.4	15.4	
No. of households ('000)	20,384.5	20,849.0	21,850.0
Total exports (US$ million)	9,916.0	9,378.0	
Total imports (US$ million)	7,508.0	6,511.0	
Tourism receipts (US$ million)	31.0	30.3	
Tourist spending (US$ million)	234.0	228.4	216.0

Average household size 1995 (persons)	4.86		
Urban population 1995 (%)	39.3		
Age analysis (%) (1986)	*0-14* 30.2	*15-64* 64.5	*65+* 5.3
Population by sex (%) (1991)	*Male* 44.5	*Female* 55.5	
Life expectancy (years) (1990-95)	*Male* 48.8	*Female* 52.0	
Infant mortality (deaths per '000 live births) (1993)	84.2		
Adult literacy (%)			

TRADING PARTNERS

Major export destinations 1995 (% share)		Major import sources 1995 (% share)	
USA	39.2	United Kingdom	13.3
Spain	10.0	USA	11.8
Germany	5.5	Germany	10.1
India	4.0	France	8.2

North Korea

Area (km²)   122,310

Currency   Won (= 100 chon)

Location   North Korea occupies slightly more than half of the Korean peninsula, which lies to the south of the Chinese city of Shenyang. Like South Korea, it has a mixed and often mountainous landscape with extensive tree cover. The climate is temperate and often wet. The capital is Pyongyang.

Head of State   President Kim Jong-Il, though technically the heir to the Presidency, has never been confirmed in office.

Head of Government   Kang Song San

Ruling Party   The Korean Workers' Party is the only legal political party.

Political Structure   The Democratic People's Republic of Korea has been a communist one-party state since 1948. The 1972 Constitution provides for an executive President who is elected by the Supreme People's Assembly, or Parliament. The Assembly's members are elected every four years by universal suffrage, from a single list, but they meet only occasionally. In effect, power is exercised by the Central People's Committee, in which the Korean Workers' Party dominates.

Last Elections   Elections to the Supreme People's Assembly were held in April 1990, when the Korean Workers' Party won all of the 687 seats. Voter turnout was officially reported to have been 99.78%. The autocratic President, Kim Il-Sung, ruled the country from 1949 until his death in July 1994. He was expected to be succeeded by his son Kim Jong-Il, although the move has yet to be confirmed.

Political Risk   Rapprochement with South Korea, the country's traditional rival, is an erratic affair. There have been defections by family members close to Kim Jong-Il but these have been kept secret and little information leaks out of the country. There is considerable evidence that malnutrition and famine are rampant in North Korea. The US government fears that famine might cause a desperate government to indulge in some sort of military stunt. South Korea generally opposes any international food aid, charging that the North is exaggerating the damage to crops done by floods in 1995 and 1996 in order to win sympathy and assistance. North Korea has been tentatively exploring an approach to Japan for aid and/or investment.

International Disputes   In 1994 tensions intensified over North Korea's refusal to ratify international nuclear non-proliferation agreements. After long negotiations and pressure from the USA, the country eventually agreed to allow nuclear inspections. North Korea's relations with South Korea remain sensitive, though it has no outstanding territorial claims on the South. Ties with its southern neighbour have improved somewhat following the withdrawal of aid from the former Soviet Union but government-level contacts between the two countries were suspended in 1994 and have still not been resumed.

Economy   The North Korean economy remains rigidly centralised, and is organised according to five-year plans which are seldom debated. Soviet assistance is no longer available to the country, and in an effort to woo aid donors, the North Koreans have become less secretive. Foreign aid agencies have been invited in and given information to support the North's pleas for help. Emergency food aid is needed as the agricultural sector deteriorates. The rice ration presently given to manual workers has been cut to 300 grams (11 ounces) per day, less than is eaten in the poorest parts of India.

Main Industries   North Korea's economy relies very significantly on the agricultural sector, which employs 45% of the workforce although its contribution to GDP is somewhat smaller. Farming is collectivised and has been largely mechanised, thanks to massive investment. Productivity, however, is very low. Rice, maize, potatoes, millet, sorghum, vegetables, fruit and tobacco are grown for the domestic market. Only silk is exportable, and the considerable timber harvest also goes mainly to the domestic market. All manufacturing is collectivised, and it tends to specialise in heavy industries. Few consumer durables are manufactured in North Korea. The country's generous mineral resources include coal, lignite, clays, phosphates, iron ore, magnesium and tungsten.

Energy   North Korea remains wholly dependent on imports for all but a small proportion of its fuel needs. Coal and a growing amount of hydro-electric power are its only indigenous sources of power at present, apart from fuelwood. The country's plans for a nuclear power system have aroused security fears.

	1993	1994	1995
Inflation (% change)	2.2	-0.2	0.2
Exchange rate (per US$)	2.16	2.15	2.15
Interest rate			
GDP (% real growth)	-0.2	1.9	0.8
GDP (Million units of national currency)	23,050.0	23,487.8	23,711.3
GDP (US$ million)	10,671.3	10,924.6	11,028.5
GDP per capita (US$)	463.0	465.3	460.7
Consumption (Million units of national currency)	3,721.4	3,783.9	3,811.7
Consumption (US$ million)	1,722.9	1,760.0	1,772.9
Consumption per capita (US$)	74.7	75.0	74.1
Population, mid-year ('000)	23,050.0	23,480.0	23,937.2
Birth rate (per '000)	37.6	33.8	
Death rate (per '000)	4.9	5.5	
No. of households ('000)	3,780.4	3,871.4	3,950.0
Total exports (US$ million)			
Total imports (US$ million)			
Tourism receipts (US$ million)			
Tourist spending (US$ million)			

Average household size 1995 (persons)	5.76		
Urban population 1994 (%)	61.3		
Age analysis (%) (1991, est)	*0-14* 38.6	*15-64* 57.3	*65+* 4.1
Population by sex (%)			
Life expectancy (years) (1990)	*Male* 66.2	*Female* 72.7	
Infant mortality (deaths per '000 live births)			
Adult literacy (%)			

Norway

Area (km²)   323,895

Currency   Norwegian krone (= 100 ore)

Location   Norway occupies almost the entire western half of the peninsula which it shares with Sweden, running south-west from the Arctic Circle to meet up with Denmark across the Skagerrak straits which form the entry from the North Sea to the Baltic Sea. With an almost entirely mountainous geography, and with most of its western coastline characterised by deep sea inlets (fjords), most of its population live in the southern coastal lowlands. The capital is Oslo.

Head of State   HM King Harald V (1991)

Head of Government   Gro Harlem Brundtland (1990)

Ruling Party   Det norske Arbeiderparti (Labour Party)

Political Structure   The Kingdom of Norway is a constitutional monarchy with executive power in a Prime Minister and Cabinet, and legislative authority in a unicameral Parliament, the Storting. The Storting's 165 members are elected by universal suffrage for a four-year term. For legislative purposes they divide themselves into an Upper and Lower Chamber (Lagting and Odelsting). Norway became a full member of the European Economic Area in January 1994, but decided against joining the EU in January 1995.

Last Elections   The legislative elections of September 1993 went against the minority left-wing Norske Arbeiderparti (Labour Party), led by Mrs Gro Harlem Brundtland, which had ruled the country since the inconclusive elections of September 1989. The Labour Party actually increased its representation from 63 to 67 seats while its main partner, the Socialist Left (Socialistisk Venstreparti), retained 13 of its 17 seats. This two-party coalition faced stronger opposition from the non-socialist alliance. The non-socialist group was subsequently torn apart by the fierce anti-EU position of the Centre Party Brundtland's government seems stronger than ever.

Political Risk   There is virtually no political risk attached to Norwegian investments and Norwegian markets. The country's "shadow membership" in the EU, by which it seeks to stay as closely informed as possible and to make its voice heard as clearly as possible, ensures that it will become more closely aligned with the rest of Europe as time passes.

International Disputes   The Norwegian dependency of Jan Mayen resolved a long-standing dispute with Greenland (itself a dependency of Denmark) in June 1993, concerning the use of territorial waters in the region of the islands. However, the country is currently locked in dispute with Iceland over the disputed territorial waters around the Svalbard Islands, where Norway claims a 200-km fishing limit, and has similar, though less heated, disagreements with other countries.

Economy   Norway's oil-driven economy is performing impressively and the government has its fiscal affairs well in order. The overall result is that the country could easily meet the Maastricht criteria for economic and monetary union had it voted to join in 1995. Growth slowed slightly in 1995 but still remains above 4%. Inflation, too, has risen but poses no danger to the country's competitive position. Interest rates, which many feared would soar following the negative EU vote, have remained low and unemployment has been falling. In the short run the only potential problem is the cyclical nature of the economy and the danger of overheating. In the longer run petroleum returns are reaching a peak and should start to decline by the end of the century.

Main Industries   Norway's oil industry transformed the economy in the 1970s, brushing aside the timber and agriculture business on which the country depended until then. At present, the oil business provides 20% of GDP and employs a fifth of the workforce either directly or indirectly. Industry comprises 20% of GDP and about 30% of exports in a typical year. The rapid pace of this sector's growth has sometimes created manpower shortages and contributed to inflation. The industrial sector is strongest in engineering, chemicals and timber products as well as oil products. Farming has shrunk in the face of the oil boom and nowadays contributes only 4% of GDP. Farms tend to be small in size, and have required consistent government aid to survive. The country's shipping industry contracted in recent years but the country still operates over a fifth of all the world's gas tankers, cruise fleet and chemical carriers.

Energy   Norway is Western Europe's largest producer of crude oil. It has average daily production of more than 3 million barrels and is expected boost exports of natural gas to between 70 and 80 billion cubic metres by the end of the decade.

	1993	1994	1995
Inflation (% change)	2.3	1.4	2.5
Exchange rate (per US$)	7.09	7.06	6.34
Interest rate (% per annum)	9.2	8.8	8.9
GDP (% real growth)	2.1	4.2	4.0
GDP (Billion units of national currency)	823.3	869.7	925.5
GDP (US$ million)	116,126.9	123,192.6	145,984.2
GDP per capita (US$)	26,931.1	28,407.7	33,482.6
Consumption (Billion units of national currency)	380.5	402.7	429.3
Consumption (US$ million)	53,667.1	57,039.7	67,719.7
Consumption per capita (US$)	12,446.0	13,153.1	15,532.0
Population, mid-year ('000)	4,312.0	4,336.6	4,360.0
Birth rate (per '000)	14.1	13.6	13.8
Death rate (per '000)	11.0	10.1	10.3
No. of households ('000)	1,789.0	1,818.2	1,847.0
Total exports (US$ million)	31,853.0	34,692.0	41,746.0
Total imports (US$ million)	23,956.0	27,308.0	32,702.0
Tourism receipts (US$ million)	1,849.0	1,978.0	
Tourist spending (US$ million)	3,565.0	3,813.6	4,527.7

Average household size 1995 (persons)	2.24				
Urban population 1995 (%)	73.2				
Age analysis (%) (1995)	*0-14* 18.9		*15-64* 65.0		*65+* 16.1
Population by sex (%) (1995)	*Male* 49.5		*Female* 50.5		
Life expectancy (years) (1994)	*Male* 74.9		*Female* 80.6		
Infant mortality (deaths per '000 live births) (1991)	6.2				
Adult literacy (%) (1984)	100.0				

TRADING PARTNERS

Major export destinations 1995 (% share)		Major import sources 1995 (% share)	
United Kingdom	20.0	Sweden	15.4
Germany	12.0	Germany	14.0
Sweden	9.7	United Kingdom	9.8
Netherlands	9.5	Denmark	7.6

Oman

Area (km²)   271,950

Currency   Omani rial (OR = 1000 baiza)

Location   Oman, which lies in the south-eastern extremity of the Arabian peninsula, actually consists of two separate pieces of land. The larger lies on the Arabian Sea, controlling the southern access to the Gulf through the Gulf of Oman; the smaller, but more significant territory, is on the headland which demarcates the boundary between the two related waterways on the tip of the United Arab Emirates territory in the Gulf. The capital is Muscat.

Head of State   Sultan Qaboos Bin-Said (1970)

Head of Government   Sultan Qaboos Bin-Said

Ruling Party   There are no legal political parties in Oman.

Political Structure   The Sultanate of Oman is ruled by decree by the Sultan who deposed his father in the coup of 1970. The Sultan is also Prime Minister and is advised by a Cabinet which he appoints. Since November 1991 there has also been a State Consultative Council whose members are chosen by the Sultan from three candidate lists drawn up by each of the various regions. Although the Council has no powers whatever, its introduction was seen as a move toward greater democratisation. Oman favours tighter co-operation in the Gulf region.

Last Elections   There are no elections in Oman at present, although there has been some discussion on the prospect of non-party polls to be held at some point in the future.

Political Risk   The absolute character of Oman's political leadership and the tight media censorship suggest that a full assessment of the political risk is not practicable at present. The country's efforts to integrate its policies with its Gulf Co-operation Council partners reflect its dependence on the all-important business of oil transhipment. Fortunately, its geographical position on the approaches to the Indian Ocean meant that it was able to remain almost undamaged by the Gulf War of 1991.

Economy   The country's dependence on the oil sector has been reduced to some extent by government action in the 1980s and early 1990s, with encouragement for foreign investment. Like Qatar, Oman is emerging as a significant producer and exporter of liquid natural gas after signing long-term supply contracts with Asian power companies. These call for Oman to supply up to 6 million tonnes a year to South Korea and Thailand. The deals, which are part of a $6 billion gas project, will add 20% to the country's $5 billion of yearly export earnings from its sizeable, but ageing, oilfields.

Main Industries   Oman's economy relies very substantially on the oil sector, which provided 97% of exports in the late 1980s although only about half of the country's GDP. Joint ventures with Western countries have resulted in a number of new projects being explored. The country's strategic position outside the (Persian) Gulf has worked to its advantage in shipping oil from other countries in the past. Agriculture has seen its share of GDP plummet to about 3% as the oil sector has grown. Concentrated exclusively in the northern areas of the country, its main products are alfalfa, dates, bananas, wheat, mangoes and limes together with tomatoes and other water-dependent crops. Fishing is a traditional activity with a long history in Oman. Manufacturing remains limited in scale, partly by the small size of the domestic market and partly by manpower shortages. There are, however, factories producing cement, steel sections, cattle feed plants and a variety of consumer goods. There is also an important mining industry, producing chromate, copper and manganese, and deposits of many more metals have been located.

Energy   Oman is amply self-sufficient in oil and gas and has enough electricity without recourse to hydro-electric schemes.

	1993	1994	1995
Inflation (% change)	7.7	0.1	2.1
Exchange rate (per US$)	0.38	0.38	0.39
Interest rate (% per annum)	8.5	8.6	9.4
GDP (% real growth)	12.4	1.2	5.5
GDP (Million units of national currency)	4,293.9	4,348.8	4,684.6
GDP (US$ million)	11,299.7	11,444.2	12,011.7
GDP per capita (US$)	5,678.3	5,529.7	5,565.5
Consumption (Million units of national currency)	1,791.4	1,856.9	2,047.2
Consumption (US$ million)	4,714.2	4,886.6	5,249.3
Consumption per capita (US$)	2,369.0	2,361.1	2,432.2
Population, mid-year ('000)	1,990.0	2,069.6	2,158.2
Birth rate (per '000)	43.6	40.4	
Death rate (per '000)	4.8	4.8	
No. of households ('000)	516.1	539.4	560.0
Total exports (US$ million)	4,270.0	440.0	
Total imports (US$ million)	4,114.0	3,890.0	
Tourism receipts (US$ million)			
Tourist spending (US$ million)	47.0	47.5	51.0

Average household size 1995 (persons)	3.66				
Urban population 1995 (%)	13.2				
Age analysis (%) (1991, est)	*0-14* 46.5		*15-64* 50.9		*65+* 2.6
Population by sex (%)					
Life expectancy (years) (1990-95)	*Male* 67.7		*Female* 71.8		
Infant mortality (deaths per '000 live births) (1993)	29.7				
Adult literacy (%)					

TRADING PARTNERS

Major export destinations 1995 (% share)		Major import sources 1995 (% share)	
Japan	32.0	United Arab Emirates	21.2
South Korea	14.9	Japan	20.6
Thailand	11.8	United Kingdom	14.9
China	8.3	France	7.8

Pakistan

Area (km²)   803,940

Currency   Pakistani rupee (R = 100 paisa)

Location   Pakistan lies in the north-west corner of the Indian Ocean, where it is bounded in the south and east by India and in the north and west by Afghanistan and Iran. The country is partially low-lying, although its north-western border with Afghanistan is extremely mountainous. The climate is sub-tropical, with heavy rains. The capital is Islamabad.

Head of State   President Farooq Ahmed Khan Legari (November 1993)

Head of Government   Mrs Benazir Bhutto (October 1993)

Ruling Party   Pakistan People's Party

Political Structure   Pakistan, an independent member of the Commonwealth, has an executive President who is elected by universal suffrage and reports to an elected Parliament. In practice, the army is seldom far from the decision-making process, as few presidents have been able to contradict its interest for long. In March 1996 Benazir Bhutto proposed changes in the arrangement for the next general election, due by 1998. She wants to abolish the identity card that registered voters are required to have, arguing that many in rural areas have been disenfranchised because they have no such cards. She also wants to give non-Muslims two votes: one for the seats reserved for minorities and the other for a Muslim candidate. The opposition strongly objects to these proposals because it believes they favour Bhutto's candidacy. Opponents want the election to be held in 1996, not 1998, and to follow the same pattern as the one in 1993.

Last Elections   The last full elections to the National Assembly were held in October 1993, when the Pakistan People's Party (PPP) won 86 of the 207 seats reserved for Muslim organisations, compared with only 45 in 1990. The Islamic Democratic Alliance, which had hitherto ruled with 106 seats, won only 72. The remaining seats were won by independents. Benazir Bhutto of the PPP became Prime Minister after the election. Presidential elections followed in November, when Farooq Ahmed Khan Legari was elected with 274 votes against 168 for the acting president, Wasim Sajjad.

Political Risk   Apart from the long-standing political tensions in the country, there have been periodic clashes in Sind which have been crushed by the army. While the tensions are ethnic in origin, they have been stimulated by political factional fighting in recent years. Nevertheless, the government's methods of control have drawn international criticism for their severity. The opponents of Bhutto's People's Party threaten to boycott the next election if her proposed changes in voting procedures are pushed through. Ominously, this dispute is almost identical with that in Bangladesh (which was once part of Pakistan) in February 1996. The outcome in that country was that the electoral turnout was derisory, and politics moved into the streets.

International Disputes   Pakistan has a long-standing dispute with India about the northern border state of Kashmir, which is ruled by India but claimed by both countries. The Indians have accused Pakistan of fomenting religious and political unrest, and in 1994 there were frequent disturbances in the region. Pakistan has also yet to clarify its position toward the mujaheddin guerrillas who displaced the Afghan Government in 1991. Although it openly supported the guerrillas during the war, it is now concerned over their drug-running activities. Pakistan's nuclear industry is reputed to depend heavily on Chinese technology and this has led to repeated criticisms from the international community aimed at both countries.

Economy   The Pakistani economy grew by 4.7% in the fiscal year 1994-1995. This performance was less than expected and a disappointment to the government and most businesses. Inflation was officially recorded at 13% although many private economists put it closer to 20%. A widening trade deficit has compounded the country's problems and eroded confidence in the government's current five-year plan. Pakistan has negotiated a $600 million standby loan from the IMF to help it cover its foreign exchange shortages and to stabilise the balance of trade and current account. In return, it has agreed with the IMF to reduce the budget deficit, lower its rate of bank borrowing and accelerate the pace of privatisation. The government is under serious pressure to achieve these goals as international lenders and aid donors have left no doubt that they will not tolerate further slippage in the country's reform programme.

Main Industries   Pakistan's agricultural sector accounts employs over 50% of the country's workforce but contributes only about a quarter of total GDP owing to the low levels of productivity in farming. The country is self-sufficient in basic cereals (rice, wheat, maize) and produced a bumper cotton crop in 1995 with exports of over $1 billion. Industry, which is the other major contributor to GDP, is a mixture of traditional, labour-intensive activities and larger, capital-intensive operations. The former includes food processing, textiles, clothing, footwear and leather goods while the latter set of industries is represented by light engineering industry, petrochemicals, steel, industrial chemicals and machine building. Pakistan has enough oil to meet a third of its own requirements, and deposits of coal, limestone, silica, chrome and barytes are worked.

Energy   Pakistan's need for imported energy sources is growing rapidly as its industrialisation proceeds. A fifth of all electricity is provided by hydro-electric power, and nuclear power is in use.

	1993	1994	1995
Inflation (% change)	10.0	12.4	13.0
Exchange rate (per US$)	28.11	30.57	31.60
Interest rate (% per annum)	10.0	9.0	9.0
GDP (% real growth)	1.4	3.8	4.7
GDP (Million units of national currency)	1,341,950.0	1,564,970.0	1,851,531.7
GDP (US$ million)	47,739.2	51,193.0	58,592.8
GDP per capita (US$)	388.8	404.8	449.8
Consumption (Million units of national currency)	968,164.0	1,128,456.0	1,334,368.5
Consumption (US$ million)	34,442.0	36,913.8	42,226.9
Consumption per capita (US$)	280.5	291.9	324.2
Population, mid-year ('000)	122,790.0	126,470.0	130,250.0
Birth rate (per '000)	41.0	42.2	
Death rate (per '000)	11.0	12.4	
No. of households ('000)	18,688.5	19,021.0	19,400.0
Total exports (US$ million)	6,688.0	7,365.0	7,992.0
Total imports (US$ million)	9,500.0	8,889.0	11,461.0
Tourism receipts (US$ million)	155.0	185.0	
Tourist spending (US$ million)	145.0	169.0	193.3

Average household size 1995 (persons)	6.38				
Urban population 1995 (%)	34.7				
Age analysis (%) (1993)	*0-14*	46.9	*15-64*	49.7	*65+* 3.4
Population by sex (%) (1993)	*Male*	51.8	*Female*	48.2	
Life expectancy (years) (1993)	*Male*	59.3	*Female*	60.7	
Infant mortality (deaths per '000 live births) (1991)	101.0				
Adult literacy (%) (1990)	34.8				

TRADING PARTNERS

Major export destinations 1995 (% share)		Major import sources 1995 (% share)	
USA	15.7	Japan	11.5
Hong Kong	7.3	Malaysia	8.2
Japan	6.9	USA	7.5
Germany	6.8	Germany	7.0

Panama

Area (km²)   78,515

Currency   Balboa (B$ = 100 cents)

Location   Panama forms the longest and most slender section of the isthmus which divides Central America from South America, and extends in an S-shape, some 700 km from east to west, between Costa Rica and Colombia. The land is traversed by the Panama Canal, the all-important marine link which connects the Caribbean Sea (and thus the Atlantic Ocean) with the Pacific Ocean. The capital is Panama City.

Head of State   President Ernesto Perez Balladares (June 1994)

Head of Government   President Ernesto Perez Balladares

Ruling Party   Democratic Revolutionary Party leads a coalition.

Political Structure   The 1983 Constitution provides for an executive President who is elected by universal suffrage for a term of five years and a unicameral National Assembly with 71 members who are also elected for five years. Panamanian politics have changed considerably since the removal in 1989 of Gen. Manuel Noriega, who was able to run a sophisticated and corrupt drugs operation because he combined the Presidency with a senior military position. In December 1991 the Assembly approved a constitutional amendment which abolished the national army.

Last Elections   Elections were held in May 1994 to the 71-member National Assembly, resulting in a win for Perez Balladares and his Democratic Revolutionary Party (DRP). The DRP is the party removed from power during the US invasion of 1989.

Political Risk   Panama has effectively granted permanent rights to the US troops who currently keep the peace in the country. The negotiation of a treaty in 1991 allowing the USA access to bank accounts, in exchange for assistance against drug trafficking, adds to the sense of security. Nevertheless, critics of the close relationship with the USA still command considerable political power at local level. There was an unsuccessful coup attempt against President Perez in January 1995.

International Disputes   Panama's strategic importance to Pacific-Atlantic shipping has made it a country of considerable significance to the United States, which has now secured the right to guard its territory with its own armed forces. There are also tensions with Guatemala over Panama's refusal to hand over the fugitive former Guatemalan president Jorge Serrano Elias.

Economy   Panama's economy is still undergoing some amount of a restructuring under the present administration. A programme of fiscal austerity is in operation in an effort to correct the economy's many serious imbalances. However, new US legislation is beginning to erode Panama's scope as a financial centre, a factor which is likely to have a negative effect on growth prospects by the end of the decade. Policy makers are attempting to generate a form of export-led growth by encouraging re-exports from the export processing zone around Panama City and by strengthening the country's international ties. However, their efforts to join the World Trade Organisation have been frustrated by objections from Costa Rica. Growth rates have fallen in recent years, although the government still claims to have achieved a respectful 5% increase in GDP in 1994.

Main Industries   Much of the country's income is generated through the banking sector, which accounts for around 70% of GDP in a typical year. Thanks to tax concessions and other incentives, companies from all over the world have settled in Panama, even though few of them actually trade there. The government's policy of promoting this type of investment has come under attack from local economists who argue that foreign companies are receiving privileges that are not available to local ones. Panama also derives as much as US$1 billion a year from the shipping fees on the Panama Canal and the newly opened Panama Oil Pipeline. Agriculture still contributes about a tenth of GDP and employs a quarter of the workforce. Farm products are significantly more important in terms of exports where they generate two-thirds of the country's visible export revenues. Bananas, sugar cane and coffee are the main agricultural exports. Domestic crops include rice, maize, potatoes, beans and beef. The fishing industry is another major source of foreign exchange revenues as Panama is the world's third biggest shrimp exporter. Manufacturing establishments are mostly small-scale and consist mainly of producers of clothing, footwear, textiles, paper, plastics and electronics products.

Energy   Panama depends almost exclusively on imported oil but has ambitious plans to development its hydro-electric potential which already meets 80% of all electricity needs.

	1993	1994	1995
Inflation (% change)	0.5	1.3	1.0
Exchange rate (per US$)	1.00	1.00	1.00
Interest rate (% per annum)	10.1	10.2	11.1
GDP (% real growth)	8.6	5.0	3.5
GDP (Million units of national currency)	7,102.9	7,420.2	7,756.7
GDP (US$ million)	7,102.9	7,420.2	7,756.7
GDP per capita (US$)	2,807.5	2,876.0	2,949.3
Consumption (Million units of national currency)	3,897.5	3,947.7	4,001.1
Consumption (US$ million)	3,897.5	3,947.7	4,001.1
Consumption per capita (US$)	1,540.5	1,530.1	1,521.3
Population, mid-year ('000)	2,530.0	2,580.0	2,630.0
Birth rate (per '000)	22.8	21.7	
Death rate (per '000)	3.5	3.9	
No. of households ('000)	504.7	513.2	525.0
Total exports (US$ million)	553.0	583.0	596.0
Total imports (US$ million)	2,188.0	2,404.0	2,482.0
Tourism receipts (US$ million)	228.0	231.7	
Tourist spending (US$ million)	129.0	131.1	132.9

Average household size 1995 (persons)	4.76				
Urban population 1995 (%)	53.3				
Age analysis (%) (1992)	*0-14* 34.2		*15-64* 60.9		*65+* 4.9
Population by sex (%) (1993)	*Male* 50.8		*Female* 49.2		
Life expectancy (years) (1990-95)	*Male* 69.8		*Female* 74.7		
Infant mortality (deaths per '000 live births) (1993)	15.0				
Adult literacy (%) (1995)	90.8				

TRADING PARTNERS

Major export destinations 1995 (% share)		Major import sources 1995 (% share)	
USA	21.5	Japan	47.4
Germany	14.2	South Korea	19.9
Japan	3.4	USA	11.2
Costa Rica	3.2	Hong Kong	8.2

Papua New Guinea

Area (km²)   462,840

Currency   Kina (K = 100 toea)

Location   Papua New Guinea, one of the more important island states in the Asia-Pacific region, occupies the eastern half of the old island of New Guinea. It also includes territories in the Solomon Islands group, in the Trobriands, and in the Louisiade Archipelago. The capital is Port Moresby.

Head of State   HM Queen Elizabeth II

Head of Government   Sir Julius Chan (August 1994)

Ruling Party   People's Democratic Movement leads a multi-party coalition.

Political Structure   Papua New Guinea, a member of the British Commonwealth, has a Governor-General who represents the Queen. However, executive power is exercised by a Prime Minister and a National Executive Council, who are appointed by the Governor on the advice of the unicameral National Parliament. The 109 members are elected by universal suffrage for a period of not more than five years. Since 1993, members have been barred from moving any vote of confidence in the Prime Minister until he is at least 18 months into a term of office (see also below). Papua New Guinea receives both military support and economic assistance from Australia.

Last Elections   In the presidential elections of August 1994, Chan won 69 of the parliamentary votes cast against 32 for his rival Bill Skate. Paias Wingti, the incumbent president, did not stand. In the parliamentary elections of June 1992, Pangu Pati had won 22 of the 109 seats, while Wingti's People's Democratic Movement won 15, the People's Action Party 13, the People's Progress Party 10, the Melanesian Alliance nine, the League of National Advancement five, the National Party two and the Melanesian United Front one. There were also 31 independent seats, and one remained unoccupied.

Political Risk   The apparently smooth development of the political system over the past decade conceals a splintered political structure which still presents considerable scope for factional schisms within the ruling party. Meanwhile, the fate of the country's mining potential rests, at least in part, with the Government's success in quelling the industrial disruptions of the recent past. Finally, the country has proved vulnerable in recent years to very powerful earthquakes, the last of which struck in October 1993.

International Disputes   Papua New Guinea has a long-standing argument over the status of Bougainville - part of the archipelago which lies geographically within the Solomon Islands. The gold mines there, which are worked mainly by Australian interests, have raised local standards of living but have resulted in periodic poisoning scares. By 1995 the region's attempts to take itself out of Papua New Guinea had escalated to the status of a war of secession. Bougainville's self-declared autonomy statement was being countered by government attempts to isolate the rebels with a new regional parliament.

Economy   Papua New Guinea's economy is broadly based and has recorded high rates of growth in recent years, albeit from a low base. The country's large foreign debt and service payments restrict its performance. High wage rates for civil servants are a political problem which the Government has been unable to resolve. In 1995, an ambitious programme of privatisation was announced which entailed the sale of the national airline, the post and telecommunications agency, the harbour authorities and the electricity and radio authorities.

Main Industries   Agriculture is the mainstay of the economy, with smallholdings employing more than two-thirds of the workforce and producing a third of GDP. Coconuts, coffee, cocoa, palm oil, rubber, tea and (increasingly) timber are the main export crops, while cassava, bananas, pineapples, sweet potatoes, yams and sago are grown for the domestic market. Industry tends to centre on the processing of agricultural raw materials, with palm oil and coconut oil being particularly important. There are also timber workshops, cement factories, plywood plants and packaging factories. Mining is the most glamorous though not always the most profitable side of the economy. With massive gold and copper deposits being worked in Bougainville, and with active exploration for oil, the sector is of particular interest to Australian companies.

Energy   The country has four huge and potentially oil-filled basins offshore, although their exact content remains uncertain. Meanwhile, it is dependent on thermal energy for three-quarters of its electricity. Despite considerable hydro-electric potential, this energy source has yet to be developed.

	1993	1994	1995
Inflation (% change)	5.0	2.9	17.0
Exchange rate (per US$)	0.98	1.01	1.28
Interest rate (% per annum)	11.3	9.2	11.6
GDP (% real growth)	11.5	3.1	13.4
GDP (Million units of national currency)	4,979.0	5,282.2	7,008.3
GDP (US$ million)	5,080.6	5,229.9	5,475.3
GDP per capita (US$)	1,295.4	1,307.5	1,345.3
Consumption (Million units of national currency)	2,574.0	2,785.8	3,770.6
Consumption (US$ million)	2,626.5	2,758.2	2,945.8
Consumption per capita (US$)	669.7	689.6	723.8
Population, mid-year ('000)	3,922.0	4,000.0	4,070.0
Birth rate (per '000)	33.4	33.5	
Death rate (per '000)	10.7	10.4	
No. of households ('000)	660.5	677.0	692.0
Total exports (US$ million)	2,491.0	2,640.0	2,665.0
Total imports (US$ million)	1,299.0	1,521.0	1,375.0
Tourism receipts (US$ million)	45.0	45.0	45.0
Tourist spending (US$ million)			

Average household size 1995 (persons)	5.59				
Urban population 1995 (%)	16.1				
Age analysis (%) (1990)	*0-14* 40.4		*15-64* 57.2		*65+* 2.5
Population by sex (%) (1990)	*Male* 51.7		*Female* 48.3		
Life expectancy (years) (1990)	*Male* 54.2		*Female* 55.7		
Infant mortality (deaths per '000 live births) (1991)	55.0				
Adult literacy (%) (1995)	72.2				

TRADING PARTNERS

Major export destinations 1995 (% share)		Major import sources 1995 (% share)	
Australia	33.1	Australia	51.5
Japan	24.2	Singapore	13.2
Germany	11.0	Japan	9.3
South Korea	6.9	USA	3.9

Paraguay

Area (km²)   406,750

Currency   Guaraní (G = 100 céntimos)

Location   Paraguay, the geographic centre of South America, is a landlocked state bordered in the north by Bolivia, in the east by Brazil, and in the south and south-west by Argentina. Its terrain is, however, less mountainous than any of these countries. Most of it consists of a marshy plain through which the Paraguay and Pilcomayo rivers flow, interspersed with vast tracts of forest and jungle. The capital is Asunción.

Head of State   Gen. Juan Carlos Wasmosy (1993)

Head of Government   Gen. Juan Carlos Wasmosy (1993)

Ruling Party   Asociación Nacional Republicana - Partido Colorado

Political Structure   The Republic of Paraguay has an executive President who is directly elected by universal suffrage for a five-year term of office. The president answers to a bicameral national Congress comprising a 45-member Senate and an 80-member Chamber of Deputies - both similarly elected for five years. In elections to the Chamber of Deputies, the party which receives the most votes is automatically granted two-thirds of the seats in both Houses.

Last Elections   In the congressional elections held in May 1993 the Colorado Party won 43% of the vote, gaining 40 Lower House seats and 20 Upper House seats. Its main rival was the Partido Liberal Radical Auténtico (Authentic Radicals), which made strong progress to win 32 Lower and 17 Upper House seats. The Encuentro Nacional (National Encounter Party) won eight Upper House and eight Lower House seats. Presidential elections were also held in May 1993, when Wasmosy overtook Domingo Laíno of the Authentic Radicals to win 41% of the vote against 32%. Caballero Vargas of the National Encounter Party obtained 23% of the vote.

Political Risk   Wasmosy is Paraguay's first democratically elected president in 50 years. Unfortunately, his Conservative Colorado party lacks a majority and many in congress relish the novelty of rejecting a president's proposals. Nationalist and statist rivals have stymied much of his reform programme, including privatisation, tariff reductions and tax reform. Meanwhile, the international community is concerned about the mounting influence of the country's drug lords. In April 1996, the President first announced the dismissal of rebellious military strongman, General Lino Oviedo, and then appointed him defence minister after he threatened to launch a military coup. Popular and political pressure later led Wasmosy to reverse himself once again by refusing to appoint Oviedo. By then, the president had lost much credibility, both with voters and international donors.

International Disputes   Paraguay's dispute with Bolivia concerning the area to the north-east of the Paraguay River has been resolved.

Economy   Paraguay's economy is a poor one in comparison with those of its neighbours. Membership in the four-country Mercosur customs union represents an opportunity but threatens many existing industries. The common external tariffs which the agreement has imposed opens the economy to international competition that will gradually eliminate many businesses. Privatisation is being encouraged and will provide a valuable impetus to the creation of a capital market, both channelling under-used local capital into industrial investment and attracting new capital form abroad. Economists, however, estimate that 100,000 state-sector jobs will be lost and opponents of reform have vowed to prevent implementation of the programme.

Main Industries   Paraguay's varied and often inaccessible landscape discourages large-scale exploitation of the mineral sector, which is currently limited to limestone and salt - although ample deposits of copper, iron ore and manganese are known to exist. Instead, the country relies on agriculture for 90% of its exports - mainly soya, cotton, vegetable oils and increasingly timber. Farming is subject to recurrent drought and only 5% of the land area is under cultivation. Industry depends mainly on the processing of raw materials, including textiles and timber products. Cement, steel, and oil refining are other prominent industries.

Energy   Paraguay depends on imports for all of its oil and gas needs, but it is now self-sufficient in electricity due to the inauguration of major new hydro-electric plants on the river Paraná.

	1993	1994	1995
Inflation (% change)	18.5	20.3	21.3
Exchange rate (per US$)	1,744.30	1,911.50	1,961.10
Interest rate (% per annum)	30.8	32.5	
GDP (% real growth)	4.8	3.7	-5.0
GDP (Million units of national currency)	11,991,700.0	14,960,000.0	17,494,200.0
GDP (US$ million)	6,874.8	7,826.3	8,920.6
GDP per capita (US$)	1,504.3	1,665.2	1,846.9
Consumption (Million units of national currency)	9,119,300.0	10,101,693.3	10,489,106.9
Consumption (US$ million)	5,228.1	5,284.7	5,348.6
Consumption per capita (US$)	1,144.0	1,124.4	1,107.4
Population, mid-year ('000)	4,570.0	4,700.0	4,830.0
Birth rate (per '000)	31.3	32.0	
Death rate (per '000)	6.5	4.5	
No. of households ('000)	942.6	974.3	1,020.0
Total exports (US$ million)	725.0	600.0	
Total imports (US$ million)	1,689.0	1,884.0	
Tourism receipts (US$ million)	4,855.0	5,812.1	
Tourist spending (US$ million)	138.0	165.2	167.2

Average household size 1995 (persons)	4.50				
Urban population 1995 (%)	52.7				
Age analysis (%) (1991)	*0-14* 33.0		*15-64* 60.3		*65+* 6.6
Population by sex (%) (1992)	*Male* 50.2		*Female* 49.8		
Life expectancy (years) (1985-90)	*Male* 64.8		*Female* 69.1		
Infant mortality (deaths per '000 live births) (1991)	31.9				
Adult literacy (%) (1995)	92.1				

TRADING PARTNERS

Major export destinations 1995 (% share)		Major import sources 1995 (% share)	
Brazil	43.3	Brazil	26.0
Argentina	5.1	USA	20.2
Netherlands	4.5	Argentina	11.4
Chile	4.3	Hong Kong	9.4

Peru

Area (km²) 1,285,215

Currency New sol (S = 100 céntimos)

Location Peru's 2,000-kilometre Pacific coastline extends from the Ecuadorean border in the north to Chile in the south. Its north-eastern border abuts with Colombia and its eastern frontiers with Brazil and Bolivia. The country includes the northern part of the Andes, although there are also deep jungles in the north-west. The capital is Lima.

Head of State President Alberto Fujimori (1990)

Head of Government Efrain Goldenberg Schreiber (February 1994)

Ruling Party Nuevo Majoridad-Cambio 90, a coalition of independents, was formed in 1990 to back Fujimori.

Political Structure President Alberto Fujimori declared a "presidential coup" in 1992 when he suspended the Constitution, disbanded Parliament and imposed direct rule. In 1993, the President moved back toward parliamentary democracy and a Democratic Constituent Congress approved a new constitution which was subsequently endorsed by a narrow majority in a referendum in October 1993. Under the new Constitution the President will still be elected by universal suffrage for a term of five years and report to the 240-member Congress (120 in the Lower House and 120 in the Upper House) - also elected by universal suffrage for a five-year term. But he will also have the right to veto any military appointment, to override the veto of Congress and to impose the death penalty for terrorism.

Last Elections In the congressional elections of April 1995, the Nuevo Majoridad-Cambio 90 party won a clear majority with 67 of the 120 seats in the Lower House. The Union For Peru won 17 seats, the American Popular Revolutionary Alliance won eight, the Independent Moralising Front won six, Popular Action won five, Renovation and the Popular Christian Party won three each, United Left and Movimiento Obras won two each, and three smaller groups won one seat each. In the presidential elections on the same day, Fujimori won a convincing victory with 64% of the vote, against 21.81% for his nearest rival.

Political Risk Peru was excluded from the international financial system for almost seven years due to its policy of not paying its debts. The government has now restored good relations. Nonetheless, Peru remains among the most indebted Latin American countries. It will continue to hold this dubious distinction even after reaching the expected debt accords with commercial banks and creditor governments later in 1996. The terrorist group known as the "Shining Path" now numbers less than 1,000 guerrillas and appears to be defeated. Other dangers exist, however. The president's cosy accord with the military is under strain as a result of spending curbs which have created bitterness. Fujimori's politics have also created an institutional vacuum leading to an exceptional concentration of power in the presidential office. As a result, Peru's political stability remains fragile.

International Disputes Peru has a dispute with Bolivia, which still seeks to regain access to its Pacific corridor it lost in the 19th century. A more serious division exists with Ecuador, which claims some 325,000 square kilometres of land in the north of the country. The densely forested land between the Marañón and Amazon rivers was awarded to Peru in the 1942 Protocol of Rio de Janeiro. Its importance lies in its oil reserves. Open war broke out in 1994/95 but in September 1995 the two countries reopened their borders amid renewed attempts to find a settlement.

Economy Peru escaped virtually unscathed from the fallout of the Mexican financial crisis, even though its current account deficit came close to matching the scale of that of the larger country. Much of Peru's deficit has been financed by direct investment, including privatisations. Mining sector investments alone are expected to amount to between $6 and 7 billion between now and the end of the century. Meanwhile, the country's programme of economic stabilisation is beginning to bring benefits. Peru's economy has shown the highest growth rates in Latin America over the period 1992-1995 (an average of 8.9%)

Main Industries Peru's impoverished agricultural sector employs 40% of the workforce who survive on subsistence farming. Coca farming, once endemic throughout the region, is being stamped out only with difficulty, and even now it accounts for around 45% of total exports. Cotton, sugar cane, coffee and soya are grown for the export market, and rice, maize, sorghum, potatoes and vegetables for the domestic market. The country has some of the richest fishing grounds in the world but has probably reached its limits both in extraction of anchovy and sardine and in fishmeal processing. Manufacturing contributes about 15% of GDP in a typical year, and construction another 6%. The sector is widely diversified, including rubber, vehicle assembly, engineering, food processing and chemicals. Peru has vast mineral potential, including copper, silver, zinc, gold, iron ore, phosphorus and manganese. New investment is pouring into this sector, with output of copper and gold forecast to double by the end of the century.

Energy Peru is self-sufficient in oil which typically accounts for up half of all energy requirements. The country also has a highly developed hydro-electric power system and a major programme of rural electrification is underway. Nevertheless, Peru faces a severe energy shortage owing to the fact that investment in this sector was nil between 1975 and 1990. National needs will soon outstrip the available generating capacity.

	1993	1994	1995
Inflation (% change)	48.6	23.7	11.1
Exchange rate (per US$)	1,988.30	2,195.00	2,227.50
Interest rate (% per annum)	97.4	53.6	36.6
GDP (% real growth)	7.0	8.6	6.0
GDP (Billion units of national currency)	81,641.0	109,680.0	129,165.7
GDP (US$ million)	41,060.7	49,968.1	57,986.9
GDP per capita (US$)	1,813.7	2,164.1	2,464.4
Consumption (Billion units of national currency)	63,420.0	81,705.0	92,272.4
Consumption (US$ million)	31,896.6	37,223.2	41,424.2
Consumption per capita (US$)	1,408.9	1,612.1	1,760.5
Population, mid-year ('000)	22,639.0	23,090.0	23,530.0
Birth rate (per '000)	29.1	28.7	28.2
Death rate (per '000)	7.8	7.4	7.3
No. of households ('000)	4,755.3	4,838.5	5,057.0
Total exports (US$ million)	3,515.0	4,555.0	5,572.0
Total imports (US$ million)	4,859.0	6,691.0	9,225.0
Tourism receipts (US$ million)	268.0	318.6	
Tourist spending (US$ million)	304.0	361.4	402.2

Average household size 1995 (persons)	4.42				
Urban population 1995 (%)	72.2				
Age analysis (%) (1992)	*0-14* 36.7		*15-64* 59.3		*65+* 3.9
Population by sex (%) (1992)	*Male* 50.3		*Female* 49.7		
Life expectancy (years) (1990-95)	*Male* 62.7		*Female* 66.6		
Infant mortality (deaths per '000 live births) (1994)	71.1				
Adult literacy (%) (1993)	88.7				

TRADING PARTNERS

Major export destinations 1995 (% share)		Major import sources 1995 (% share)	
USA	17.2	USA	38.1
Japan	9.1	Japan	7.2
United Kingdom	7.4	Spain	6.4
Netherlands	5.6	Germany	5.8

Philippines

Area (km²) 300,000

Currency Philippine peso (= 100 centavos)

Location Composed of 11 large islands and some 7,000 smaller islands and atolls, the Philippines lies some 800 km off the coast of Indo-China, north-east of Papua New Guinea and north of Indonesia. The group of islands is some 900 km in length from north to south. The capital is Manila.

Head of State President Fidel Ramos (June 1992)

Head of Government President Fidel Ramos

Ruling Party Lakas ng Edsa-National Union of Christian Democrats (Lakas-NUCD) leads a coalition.

Political Structure The Republic of the Philippines has an executive President who is elected by universal mandate and then appoints a Cabinet. It was not until 1986, however, that the first presidential election was held. Although the incumbent Ferdinand Marcos claimed to have won, he was overthrown by a "People's Power" movement led by Corazon Aquino. In 1992 Gen. Fidel Ramos succeeded Mrs Aquino as President.

Last Elections Elections to the legislature and to local government positions were held in May 1995, when parties supporting President Ramos won an overwhelming majority. In September 1995, however, Ramos declared that he would not be seeking a second term as President when his current term expires in 1998, and he dismissed as "destabilising talk" the idea of amending the constitution to allow this possibility.

Political Risk Periodic violence in the form of terrorist and separatist attacks by Muslim guerrillas have discouraged investment and raised concern about the stability of the regime. The group, known as the Moro National Liberation Front, has been engaged in peace talks with the government since mid-1995 but there has been no progress. President Ramos proposed new initiatives to break the deadlock in April 1996.

International Disputes The Philippines still lays claim to the Malaysian territory of Sabah, one of the most important timber producing areas in South East Asia, which it claims was illegally ceded to the new Malaysian state by Brunei. The dispute has been dormant since the late 1970s, however. The Philippines is one of the many claimants to the territory of the Spratly Islands in the South China Sea, where oil prospecting has been in progress.

Economy The Philippines' economy grew by 5.7% in 1995, but a poor agricultural performance kept the country from achieving its target of 6%. The slowdown nevertheless represented an improvement over 1994 when GNP grew by only 4.4%. Many economists question these figures, however, arguing that growth is understated by a third to a half. The national data fails to incorporate income gains from the black economy which includes remittances from overseas Philippine workers, a sizeable amount of tax evasion and capital repatriation by high income groups. As a result, retail spending, bank deposits and real estate purchases are rising at two-three times the growth of GDP. Whatever the case, the Philippines owes part of its economic gains to a better trade performance and a recovery in manufacturing. Exports rose by almost 30% in 1995 while industrial production expanded by 7% and is expected to grow even faster in 1996.

Main Industries Service industries, which include finance, trade, transportation, communications and storage, have grow rapidly in recent years and now account for about two-fifths of GDP. Farming activities make up another 20% of GDP with the chief crops being rice, maize, tobacco and coconuts. However, agricultural production is vulnerable to the effects of droughts and typhoons and a rice shortage. Mining is another significant sector, with substantial deposits of gold, nickel and other minerals. The Philippines has copper reserves in excess of 3.6 billion tonnes and is the biggest producer in Asia. Manufacturing has become the most dynamic sector with exports of textiles, clothing and electronic products and components growing most rapidly.

Energy About a third of the Philippines' electricity is derived from hydro-electric power, with thermal power accounting for most of the remainder. Exploration is under way for oil and natural gas reserves. At present, however, production of both commodities is modest.

	1993	1994	1995
Inflation (% change)	7.6	9.1	8.1
Exchange rate (per US$)	27.12	26.42	25.70
Interest rate (% per annum)	14.7	15.1	14.7
GDP (% real growth)	1.5	4.4	5.7
GDP (Million units of national currency)	1,475,000.0	1,693,900.0	1,905,300.0
GDP (US$ million)	54,387.9	64,114.3	74,136.2
GDP per capita (US$)	828.5	956.4	1,083.5
Consumption (Million units of national currency)	1,122,500.0	1,237,800.0	1,336,886.3
Consumption (US$ million)	41,390.1	46,850.9	52,018.9
Consumption per capita (US$)	630.5	698.8	760.3
Population, mid-year ('000)	65,650.0	67,040.0	68,420.0
Birth rate (per '000)	30.3	27.3	
Death rate (per '000)	7.2	6.9	
No. of households ('000)	12,373.1	12,493.0	12,750.0
Total exports (US$ million)	11,089.0	13,304.0	17,106.7
Total imports (US$ million)	18,754.0	22,546.0	27,288.0
Tourism receipts (US$ million)	2,250.0	3,110.0	
Tourist spending (US$ million)	130.0	151.8	168.5

Average household size 1995 (persons)	5.10		
Urban population 1995 (%)	54.2		
Age analysis (%) (1992)	*0-14* 37.3	*15-64* 58.5	*65+* 4.2
Population by sex (%) (1992)	*Male* 49.5	*Female* 50.5	
Life expectancy (years) (1992)	*Male* 63.0	*Female* 66.8	
Infant mortality (deaths per '000 live births) (1993)	43.6		
Adult literacy (%) (1990)	94.6		

TRADING PARTNERS

Major export destinations 1995 (% share)		Major import sources 1995 (% share)	
USA	36.0	Japan	22.5
Japan	16.1	USA	18.5
United Kingdom	5.3	Saudi Arabia	6.0
Singapore	5.2	Hong Kong	5.1

Poland

Area (km²) 312,685

Currency Zloty

Location Poland, one of the largest states in eastern central Europe, extends from the 400-kilometre Baltic coast in the north to the Czech and Slovak borders, some 1,200 km to the south, and from Germany in the west to Russia, Lithuania, Belarus and the Ukraine in the east. The country's terrain is of mixed and mainly agricultural quality but is seldom elevated. The capital is Warsaw.

Head of State President Alexander Kwasniewski (1996)

Head of Government Wlodzimierz Cimoszewicz (1996)

Ruling Party The communist Democratic Left Alliance (SLD) leads a coalition with the Polish Peasant Party (PSL).

Political Structure Disillusioned by the fragile unity of the former Solidarity alliance, the Poles replaced Lech Walesa with Alexander Kwasniewski, an adept, ex-communist politician. The younger generation of left-wing politicians are relatively untainted by the Stalinist past and have regrouped behind the leadership of their new president and prime minister. Opinion polls indicate that left-wing parties could be reconfirmed (possibly with a greater majority) at the next elections which should be held in 1997. That prospect is forcing the non-communist opposition to reorganise and seek new alliances with the right-wing Movement for the Rebuilding of Poland (ROP). The new government hopes to become a full member of both the EU and NATO in the near future.

Last Elections The elections in early 1996 produced a defeat for Lech Walesa and his Solidarity alliance. Although a tough fighter, Walesa lost electoral support because of his gaffes, bluster and conspiratorial politics. Leszek Balcerowicz, a former finance minister and father of economic reform, has taken over as leader of the Freedom Union which is the successor to Solidarity. The alliance is sharply divided between a Christian Democratic wing and a free market, liberal wing. Balcerowicz's task is to turn these disparate groups into a free-enterprise, conservative party. On the left, the political scene is equally volatile. The junior coalition partner - the PSL - is strongest in rural areas. It opposes foreign investment and favours protectionism, especially for agricultural products. The SLD is an urban-based party emphasising social security reform, an independent judiciary and closer ties with the West.

Political Risk Poland's political system is still somewhat erratic, and it is too early to say that the democratic mechanism is entirely reliable. Very rapid switches of party allegiance are the order of the day. Western analysts worry that the fragmented non-communist opposition parties will not be able to overcome their personal rivalries and put together an effective opposition that will preserve a genuine multi-party system. Nevertheless, the population has demonstrated a clear commitment to democratic change and the country has led the way in deregulating prices and incomes, privatising state concerns and renegotiating external debts. Many foreign investors regard Poland as the largest and safest consumer market in Eastern Europe. Poland signed a defence co-operation pact with the United States in 1995.

International Disputes Poland has never sought to redress the loss of large tracts of its eastern territories in what is now Russia and the Ukraine, during and after the Second World War. Tensions are periodically stirred by the remarks of right-wing Russian politicians such as Vladimir Zhirinovsky, who favour a partial dismemberment of Poland.

Economy The country's conversion from communism to capitalism actually started back in the late 1970s, but the economic and social costs of the transition have nevertheless been substantial. By 1996, the level of unemployment had begun to fall but it is still more than 14% and higher in rural areas and small towns. The pace of foreign investment is speeding up after successful debt renegotiations in 1994, followed by investment grade credit rating from international agencies in 1995. Investors are attracted by Poland's low-cost base, its large internal market and its potential role as a supplier to eastern markets. Lower taxes and a tight rein on government spending could provide the economy with a good mix of export earnings and domestic investment which should sustain growth. Meanwhile, the privatisation programme should yield another $1 billion in revenues. Copper refining, tobacco companies, brewing and chemicals are the main sell-off targets for 1996.

Main Industries Agriculture is the mainstay of the Polish economy. With a wide range of arable crops, including wheat, root vegetables, potatoes, tomatoes and fruits, the sector provides self-sufficiency in food products and produces an exportable surplus. Big agriculturalists have close ties with manufacturers of alcoholic beverages, canned fruit and vegetable products. Polish industry is rapidly gaining in economic importance and has attained a healthy degree of diversification - ranging from traditional industries such as automobiles, steel and chemicals to more technology-intensive ones like pharmaceuticals and electronics. Industry has benefited from substantial foreign investment as state-owned corporations have been sold off.

Energy Apart from coal, Poland relies on imports of oil and gas for its energy needs. In 1995 the country signed a supply deal with Russia.

	1993	1994	1995
Inflation (% change)	36.9	33.3	26.8
Exchange rate (per US$)	1.81	2.27	2.42
Interest rate (% per annum)	35.3	32.8	26.2
GDP (% real growth)	4.0	1.3	-5.3
GDP (Billion units of national currency)	1,557,800.0	2,103,770.0	2,526,198.6
GDP (US$ million)	86,066.3	92,677.1	104,388.4
GDP per capita (US$)	2,237.9	2,404.7	2,705.1
Consumption (Billion units of national currency)	982,000.0	1,276,000.0	1,498,721.0
Consumption (US$ million)	54,254.1	56,211.5	61,930.6
Consumption per capita (US$)	1,410.7	1,458.5	1,604.8
Population, mid-year ('000)	38,459.0	38,540.0	38,590.0
Birth rate (per '000)	12.8	12.5	11.5
Death rate (per '000)	10.2	10.1	10.0
No. of households ('000)	11,366.0	11,454.0	11,578.0
Total exports (US$ million)	14,143.0	17,042.0	22,320.0
Total imports (US$ million)	18,834.0	21,383.0	27,762.7
Tourism receipts (US$ million)	4,600.0	6,151.0	7,000.0
Tourist spending (US$ million)	181.0	199.8	220.1

Average household size 1995 (persons)	3.17				
Urban population 1995 (%)	61.9				
Age analysis (%) (1995)	*0-14* 23.6		*15-64* 65.7		*65+* 10.7
Population by sex (%) (1995)	*Male* 48.7		*Female* 51.3		
Life expectancy (years) (1994)	*Male* 67.5		*Female* 76.0		
Infant mortality (deaths per '000 live births) (1994)	13.5				
Adult literacy (%) (1995)	99.0				

TRADING PARTNERS

Major export destinations 1995 (% share)		Major import sources 1995 (% share)	
Germany	38.3	Germany	26.6
Netherlands	5.6	Italy	8.6
Russia	5.6	Russia	6.8
Italy	4.9	United Kingdom	5.2

Portugal

Area (km²) 91,630

Currency Portuguese escudo

Location Portugal occupies about half of the Atlantic coast on the Iberian peninsula, and more than three-quarters of the west-facing section, with Spain, its only immediate neighbour, accounting for the rest. The country is broadly rectangular in shape, extending only a maximum of 200 km inland but about 600 km from north to south. The Atlantic archipelagos of the Azores and Madeira also belong to Portugal. The terrain of the mainland country is largely mountainous inland, but there are innumerable fertile valleys lower down. The climate is Mediterranean. The capital is Lisbon.

Head of State Jorge Sampaio (1996)

Head of Government António Guterres (1995)

Ruling Party Partido Socialista Portugues

Political Structure The Republic of Portugal has an executive President who is elected by universal suffrage for a renewable term of five years and appoints the Prime Minister. Legislative authority is vested in the unicameral Assembly of the Republic, whose 230 members are elected by universal suffrage for up to four years at a time. Constitutional reforms enacted in 1982 ended the political powers of the armed forces, on which previous pseudo-dictatorships had relied. Portugal joined the EU in 1986.

Last Elections General elections to the Assembly of the Republic held in October 1995 ended a decade of centre-right leadership under Anibal Cavaco Silva. The winning Socialists came within four seats of a majority and later managed to strike a budget deal with the smaller Popoular party by making concessions on taxes. The current government has no guarantee of lasting out its full four-year term. However, its security was strengthened by the victory of Jorge Sampaio, the Socialist candidate, over Cavaco Silva in the elections for president in January 1996.

Political Risk The ruling Socialist Party faces a severe test in trying to meet the EU's Maastricht criteria. Most economists doubt that Portugal can satisfy the key measure of cutting its annual deficit to 3% of GDP by 1997. They are also sceptical of the country's ability to reduce its public debt below 70% of GDP (the Maastricht target is 60%). Failure to meet these goals will mean that Portugal misses out on the single currency. That outcome could quickly lead to the dismissal of the ruling Socialist Party.

International Disputes Portugal continues to protest to Indonesia about the treatment of the islanders in the former Portuguese territory of East Timor, which it abandoned in 1975. Portugal, like Spain, has been criticised by other EU members about its fishing activities in the North Sea. Its detractors insist that the Portuguese exceed the catch quotas and that their boats have occasionally strayed into other countries' territorial waters.

Economy GDP grew by 2.5% in 1995 and is expected to match that performance in 1996. These rates of growth have not been sufficient to prevent a gentle rise in unemployment which is currently between 6.8 and 7%. Inflation is expected to be between 2.3 and 2.5% in 1996 and should be close to the Maastricht standard which calls for a rate within 1.5 percentage points of the average for the three lowest EU rates. Policy makers are hoping that stronger growth will boost tax collections and help them to meet the Maastricht criteria. The new government's ambitious programme of privatisation is expected to raise about 380 billion escudos in 1996 alone and should make it easier to meet these targets. Officials also intend to boost growth by increasing state investment, which is mostly to go for improvements in transport infrastructure.

Main Industries With generous financial assistance from the EU, Portugal's major industries are laying the basis for solid growth. Diversification has led to the development of industries manufacturing engineering products, transport equipment and electrical machinery. These join Portugal's more traditional manufacturing sectors such as leather and leather products, timber and wood products, textiles and clothing. Agriculture remains the backbone of the economy, with citrus fruits, olives, wines and vegetables being the dominant products. Cork is grown for export, and the country has an important fishery industry. Tourism, the third main source of revenue, has been expanding rapidly, with increasing numbers of Portuguese now taking annual holidays away from home instead of remaining in their home towns as previously. Foreign visitors, especially from France, Germany and the UK, are the major international visitors.

Energy Portugal derives most of its energy needs from imported oil and gas, although it also produces some coal. Hydro-electric potential exists but is only partially developed.

	1993	1994	1995
Inflation (% change)	6.8	4.9	4.1
Exchange rate (per US$)	160.80	165.99	149.97
Interest rate (% per annum)	16.5	15.0	14.9
GDP (% real growth)	-1.0	1.0	2.5
GDP (Billion units of national currency)	12,980.2	13,754.7	14,676.6
GDP (US$ million)	80,722.6	82,864.6	97,863.6
GDP per capita (US$)	8,173.6	8,368.3	9,857.3
Consumption (Billion units of national currency)	8,071.6	8,136.2	8,497.2
Consumption (US$ million)	50,196.5	49,016.2	56,659.3
Consumption per capita (US$)	5,082.7	4,950.0	5,707.0
Population, mid-year ('000)	9,876.0	9,902.2	9,928.0
Birth rate (per '000)	11.5	11.7	11.7
Death rate (per '000)	10.8	9.8	9.6
No. of households ('000)	3,509.0	3,539.7	3,571.0
Total exports (US$ million)	15,429.0	17,899.0	22,628.0
Total imports (US$ million)	24,337.0	26,938.0	32,455.0
Tourism receipts (US$ million)	4,176.0	4,295.9	
Tourist spending (US$ million)	1,846.0	1,899.0	2,195.1

Average household size 1995 (persons)	2.64				
Urban population 1995 (%)	35.6				
Age analysis (%) (1995)	*0-14* 16.7		*15-64* 69.0		*65+* 14.3
Population by sex (%) (1995)	*Male* 47.8		*Female* 52.2		
Life expectancy (years) (1993-94)	*Male* 71.2		*Female* 78.2		
Infant mortality (deaths per '000 live births) (1993)	8.7				
Adult literacy (%) (1990)	85.0				

TRADING PARTNERS

Major export destinations 1995 (% share)		Major import sources 1995 (% share)	
Germany	19.9	Spain	20.6
Spain	14.6	Germany	14.5
France	13.1	France	12.2
United Kingdom	10.0	Italy	9.0

Puerto Rico

Area (km²) 8,960

Currency US dollar (US$ = 100 cents)

Location Puerto Rico is one of the larger islands in the Antilles group, located about 80 km east of Haiti and about 800 km off the coast of Venezuela. With a pleasant Caribbean climate, but with some vulnerability to hurricanes, it has a large population for its size. The capital is San Juan.

Head of State Governor Pedro Rossello (January 1993)

Head of Government Governor Pedro Rossello

Ruling Party Partido Nuevo Progresista (PNP)

Political Structure The Commonwealth of Puerto Rico, an external territory of the United States, has a Resident Commissioner who is elected by universal suffrage for a four-year term, and who has a non-voting seat in the US House of Representatives. Executive authority is vested in an elected Governor and his Cabinet, while legislative power rests with the bicameral Legislative Assembly - which consists of a 27-member Senate and a 53-member House of Representatives, both popularly elected for a four-year term. In recent years, much debate has centred on the question of leaving the US Commonwealth and opting for full independence. Governor Rossello has always favoured such an option; however, two national referenda on the subject have produced majorities against the idea.

Last Elections The legislative elections of November 1992 gave the ruling PNP 20 of the 27 seats in the Senate and 36 of the 53 seats in the House of Representatives. A referendum held in December 1991 came out overwhelmingly for closer integration with the USA, and a subsequent poll in November 1993 confirmed the decision, though by a much smaller margin.

Political Risk The December 1991 referendum in favour of closer integration with the United States has heightened expectations of further political change in the future. Yet many observers feel that Puerto Rico is unlikely to apply for full US statehood, preferring to keep its independence.

Economy As a trust territory of the United States, Puerto Rico has come to rely heavily on its close relationship with its larger neighbour. Yet its development has remained at a low level generally and it depends on migrant labour in the USA for much of its economic well-being. Economic growth has been sluggish for several years but began to pick up in 1995.

Main Industries Puerto Rico's economy is principally dependent on agriculture, with sugar cane, coffee, vegetables, fruit and tobacco being grown for export. There is a substantial fishing industry. Industrial development is progressing rapidly with US assistance, and now includes chemicals, metal products and machinery, motor vehicles and glass and cement. The country is an important entrepôt for petroleum processing and has developed many assembly-type industries which import parts and components from the United States and then re-export the completed products to that country.

Energy The country has no indigenous energy reserves. It relies on imported fuels for most of its requirements. There is some hydro-electric development, though the majority of electricity is derived from thermal stations.

	1993	1994	1995
Inflation (% change)	2.7	3.0	2.5
Exchange rate (per US$)	1.00	1.00	1.00
Interest rate			
GDP (% real growth)	1.0	2.3	3.0
GDP (Million units of national currency)	36,538.4	38,492.2	40,638.1
GDP (US$ million)	36,538.4	38,492.2	40,638.1
GDP per capita (US$)	10,093.5	10,431.5	10,836.8
Consumption (Million units of national currency)	24,233.1	25,528.8	26,951.9
Consumption (US$ million)	24,233.1	25,528.8	26,951.9
Consumption per capita (US$)	6,694.2	6,918.4	7,187.2
Population, mid-year ('000)	3,620.0	3,690.0	3,750.0
Birth rate (per '000)	19.8	17.5	
Death rate (per '000)	7.2	7.9	
No. of households ('000)	597.0	607.0	618.0
Total exports (US$ million)			
Total imports (US$ million)			
Tourism receipts (US$ million)	1,629.0	1,721.6	
Tourist spending (US$ million)	774.0	818.0	863.6

Average household size 1995 (persons)	5.76		
Urban population 1995 (%)	73.4		
Age analysis (%) (1993)	*0-14* 44.8	*15-64* 44.9	*65+* 10.2
Population by sex (%) (1993)	*Male* 49.0	*Female* 51.0	
Life expectancy (years) (1990-92)	*Male* 69.6	*Female* 78.5	
Infant mortality (deaths per '000 live births) (1992)	12.7		
Adult literacy (%) (1980)	89.1		

Qatar

Area (km²)   11,435

Currency   Qatar riyal (QR = 100 dirhams)

Location   Qatar is a small peninsula protruding northward into the Persian (Arabian) Gulf from the north-western extreme of the United Arab Emirates. It also has a very short border with Saudi Arabia. Most of the terrain is sandy and inhospitable and, except for a dwindling number of nomadic tribesmen, virtually all of the population now live in the capital Doha. More important than the industrial and agricultural environment is the vast oil and natural gas reserve which the country controls. The capital is Doha.

Head of State   HH Shaikh Hamad Khalifa al Thani (June 1995)

Head of Government   HH Shaikh Hamad Khalifa al Thani

Ruling Party   There are no political parties in Qatar.

Political Structure   HH Shaikh Hamad Khalifa al Thani assumed power in June 1995, following a palace coup against his father, HH Shaikh Khalifa bin Hamad al Thani, who had ruled since 1972. The coup was prompted by a prolonged period of disagreement between the two men, although it was not clear whether it also related to the growing calls for a democratisation of the country. As before, Qatar is ruled exclusively by the Amir and his immediate family.

Last Elections   There are no elections in Qatar.

Political Risk   The current Amir came to power when he deposed his father while the latter was on a visit to Europe in mid-1995. Supporters of the previous ruler unsuccessfully attempted to reinstate him in February 1996. Despite these events, the country is generally a very stable one and offers little political risk. Qatar's vast offshore gas resources should ensure prosperity for the foreseeable future. Indeed, the only major threats to the current situation would come from external claims on the country's territory or resources. The current ruler has ended press censorship, established ties with Israel and intends to sell gas to Israel.

International Disputes   Qatar has an outstanding claim against Bahrain for the Hawar Islands, which are situated only about two kilometres from the Qatar coast but are governed by Bahrain. The issue of gas and oil exploration rights is of some importance, having prompted an armed conflict in 1986 after Bahrain built an artificial island off one of the shoals. Peace was restored after Saudi Arabian intervention.

Economy   Qatar's economy made enormous strides thanks to the exploitation of its oil and its gas fields. In 1996, it expects to make its first shipments of liquefied natural gas after investments of $6-7 billion. A further $10 billion will be invested in the project by the year 2004. Already rich from daily oil production of 378,000 barrels, Qatar has total proven gas reserves of well over 300,000 billion cubic feet with probable reserves which are more than double that. Only Russia and Iran have greater quantities. Qatar is an active member of the Gulf Co-operation Council.

Main Industries   The country's oil and gas industries are the backbone of the economy, employing the greater part of the active workforce and providing well over 90% of export revenues. Qatar also has a limited industrial sector, concentrating on basic materials such as cement, steel, ammonia, fertiliser and petrochemicals. Farming is generally restricted by a shortage of suitable land, but the Government has ploughed vast resources into irrigation projects aimed at expanding the scope for vegetable cultivation. Fishing is a major industry.

Energy   The 1995 coup is expected to bring forward the date of Qatar's plans to develop its North Gas Field, which had been stalled by the present Amir's father. There are also plans for a pipeline to Dubai. Qatar, of course, meets all of its energy requirements from its own resources, exporting most of the remainder.

	1993	1994	1995
Inflation (% change)	3.0	0.0	
Exchange rate (per US$)	3.64	3.64	3.64
Interest rate (% per annum)	9.5		
GDP (% real growth)	-2.1	11.2	5.0
GDP (Million units of national currency)	26,183.0	29,117.3	30,573.2
GDP (US$ million)	7,193.1	7,999.3	8,399.2
GDP per capita (US$)	12,844.9	13,558.1	13,880.9
Consumption (Million units of national currency)	16,530.5	17,537.3	17,567.0
Consumption (US$ million)	4,541.3	4,817.9	4,826.1
Consumption per capita (US$)	8,109.5	8,166.0	7,975.8
Population, mid-year ('000)	560.0	590.0	605.1
Birth rate (per '000)	19.4	17.8	
Death rate (per '000)	1.6	1.6	
No. of households ('000)	115.5	120.2	127.0
Total exports (US$ million)	2,700.0	3,090.8	
Total imports (US$ million)	1,780.0	1,812.0	
Tourism receipts (US$ million)			
Tourist spending (US$ million)			

Average household size 1995 (persons)	4.53				
Urban population 1995 (%)	91.4				
Age analysis (%) (1986)	*0-14* 27.7		*15-64* 71.2		*65+* 1.0
Population by sex (%) (1986)	*Male* 67.2		*Female* 32.8		
Life expectancy (years) (1990-95)	*Male* 68.8		*Female* 74.2		
Infant mortality (deaths per '000 live births) (1993)	12.8				
Adult literacy (%) (1986)	79.4				

TRADING PARTNERS

Major export destinations 1995 (% share)		Major import sources 1995 (% share)	
Japan	54.7	Germany	14.2
Singapore	7.4	Italy	13.9
Indonesia	5.3	Japan	10.0
Australia	3.5	France	8.5

Réunion

Area (km²)   2,510

Currency   French franc (= 100 centimes)

Location   Réunion, an overseas département of France, is located in the Indian Ocean about 800 km east of the island of Madagascar. The local government also administers a number of other, largely uninhabited islands on behalf of the French authorities. With a warm and pleasant climate, Réunion has a thriving tourist industry. The capital is St Denis.

Head of State   President Jacques Chirac (France)

Head of Government   Pierre Steinmetz (Prefect)

Ruling Party   At national level, the Gaullist Rassemblement pour la République leads a coalition with the Union pour la Démocratie Française. At regional level, the Parti socialiste dominates.

Political Structure   Réunion is an external department of France and is governed to a considerable degree from Paris. The country sends deputies to the French Assemblée Nationale and is represented at the EU. Since being accorded regional status in 1974, Réunion elects its own 45-member Regional Council for a term of six years, with responsibility for economic and social planning. Other executive powers rest in a 44-member General Council.

Last Elections   General Council elections were held in March 1994, when the PS won control from the RPR and the government leader Camille Sudre, of the Free-Dom party, was removed. She was later replaced by Pierre Steinmetz.

Political Risk   The country's relationship with France is sometimes a source of concern, with pro-separatist demonstrations occurring in recent years. Economic problems have prompted demands for more direct action from Paris to deal with unemployment and poverty.

International Disputes   Réunion's administration of several largely uninhabited islands on behalf of France has been challenged by Madagascar which has the endorsement of the United Nations General Assembly for its claim.

Economy   Réunion's economy is heavily dependent on aid from France, which accounts for as much as half of the country's GDP. Expatriate workers are also important to the economy, as domestic unemployment is running at more than 34%.

Main Industries   Over 80% of the country's income derives from sugar cane, which is the only significant crop apart from vegetables grown for domestic consumption. There is an important fishing industry. Industry centres on the processing of agricultural raw materials, in the form of timber, textiles and especially rum manufacturing. There is a small but dynamic tourist industry, catering mainly to visitors from France and Germany.

Energy   Réunion has only a limited amount of domestic energy resources, although there are some natural gas deposits. It produces more than two-thirds of its electricity from hydro-electric sources.

	1993	1994	1995
Inflation (% change)	6.0		
Exchange rate (per US$)	5.95	5.34	4.99
Interest rate			
GDP (% real growth)	-4.0	-2.0	-0.5
GDP (Million units of national currency)	30,945.7	27,772.2	27,633.3
GDP (US$ million)	5,201.0	5,200.8	5,537.7
GDP per capita (US$)	8,255.5	8,126.2	8,384.1
Consumption (Million units of national currency)	20,523.7	18,419.0	18,326.9
Consumption (US$ million)	3,449.4	3,449.3	3,672.7
Consumption per capita (US$)	5,475.2	5,389.5	5,560.5
Population, mid-year ('000)	630.0	640.0	660.5
Dirth rate (per '000)	22.0	26.1	
Death rate (per '000)	5.5	4.9	
No. of households ('000)	107.9	110.8	114.0
Total exports (US$ million)	160.0	160.0	
Total imports (US$ million)	1,910.0	1,700.0	
Tourism receipts (US$ million)			
Tourist spending (US$ million)			

Average household size 1995 (persons)	5.50				
Urban population 1995 (%)	67.8				
Age analysis (%) (1992, est)	*0-14*	31.8	*15-64*	63.0	*65+* 5.2
Population by sex (%) (1990)	*Male*	49.2	*Female*	50.8	
Life expectancy (years) (1990)	*Male*	67.0	*Female*	75.3	
Infant mortality (deaths per '000 live births) (1992)	7.7				
Adult literacy (%) (1982)	78.6				

Romania

Area (km^2)   237,500

Currency   Leu (L = 100 bani)

Location   Romania borders on the Black Sea in the east and the Ukraine and Moldova in the north, with Bulgaria in the south and Hungary and Serbia in the west. The country has hilly and to some extent mountainous areas in the west and the south, and is richly endowed with agricultural land. The capital is Bucharest.

Head of State   President Ion Iliescu (1990)

Head of Government   Nicolai Vacaroiu (1992)

Ruling Party   Social Democracy Party of Romania leads a coalition with the extreme right-wing Romanian National Unity Party and the ultra-nationalist Romania Mare.

Political Structure   Romania's government is dominated by many of the same communists who ran the country under the tyrannical Nicolae Ceausescu. The current president, though non-executive, exercises considerable influence. The government is under growing pressure from international institutions and internal reformers to do more to attract foreign investment and modernise the economy.

Last Elections   President Iliescu was re-elected by a large majority in the September 1992 elections. In parliamentary elections held on the same day the Democratic National Salvation Front emerged as the largest party, though with only 28% of the vote; in July 1993 it renamed itself the Social Democracy Party of Romania.

Political Risk   Public and international dissatisfaction with Romania's left-wing minority government is growing as the economy deteriorates and the slow pace of reforms continues. In early 1996 the government was finally forced to cobble together a new programme for privatisation of the industrial sector to replace the 1991 scheme which was not working. If successful, the 1996 version will sharply reduce the state's control over industry - the one part of the economy where it still enjoys almost total dominance. The collapse of domestic markets for key farm products, foreign exchange scandals and similar fiascos have further undermined confidence in the government.

International Disputes   Russian interest in Moldova has waned, to the relief of the large Romanian contingent in Moldova. Conversely, any possibility of a reunification between Romania and Moldova would arouse deep concern among Moldova's Russian population. Romania's relationship with Hungary has traditionally been poor, as a result of its historical mistreatment of ethnic Hungarians in the north of its territory. Tensions have abated, however, as both countries manoeuvre to join the EU.

Economy   Foreign investors are attracted by the size of the Romanian market - with 23 million inhabitants second in the region only to Poland in terms of size - and by an improved set of macroeconomic indicators. Consumer price inflation fell to around 30% in 1995 and is expected to fall further in 1996. Meanwhile, GDP rose by 4.5% in 1995 and should maintain that pace in 1996. Although exports are rising, there has been an even sharper increase in imports, caused mainly by the need for capital goods to modernise the economy. The trade imbalance is creating a current account deficit which is too large for the economy to finance.

Main Industries   The backbone of the Romanian economy is still the agricultural sector where nearly half the population survives on subsistence farming. Major products include fruit and vegetables, wines and flax which are produced for export. At the start of 1996 about 80% of all agricultural production was in private hands. Analysts hope that this transformation will stimulate investment, generating the much-needed capital to modernise the agricultural sector. Elsewhere in the economy nearly 4,000 state enterprises are to be put up for sale in 1996. These range from heavy industry including huge steel mills, aluminium smelters and oil refineries employing thousands of workers to furniture and clothing factories and street kiosks selling newspapers and fast food. However, many of these enterprises are woefully obsolete and will require major investments if they are to be internationally competitive. Tourism is still fairly limited, except on the Black Sea coast, where several new development projects are under way. Planners are counting on the tourist sector to be one of the main earners of foreign exchange in the future.

Energy   Romania has an important coal industry which supplies all its domestic requirements. It also has limited deposits of petroleum and methane gas, although these are not sufficient to meet its needs in full. Hydro-electric power stations are another important source of energy. Romania's first nuclear power station was under construction in 1994.

	1993	1994	1995
Inflation (% change)	255.2	136.8	32.2
Exchange rate (per US$)	760.05	1,774.37	2,041.30
Interest rate (% per annum)	53.4	66.9	33.0
GDP (% real growth)	1.4	4.9	4.5
GDP (Billion units of national currency)	20,051.0	49,794.8	68,791.0
GDP (US$ million)	26,381.2	28,063.4	33,699.6
GDP per capita (US$)	1,159.4	1,234.6	1,485.9
Consumption (Billion units of national currency)	16,713.0	52,645.0	42,589.0
Consumption (US$ million)	21,989.3	29,669.7	20,863.6
Consumption per capita (US$)	966.4	1,305.3	919.9
Population, mid-year ('000)	22,755.0	22,731.0	22,680.0
Birth rate (per '000)	11.0	11.0	10.0
Death rate (per '000)	11.6	11.6	11.7
No. of households ('000)	7,534.0	7,610.0	7,685.0
Total exports (US$ million)	4,892.0	6,151.0	7,548.0
Total imports (US$ million)	6,522.0	7,109.0	9,424.0
Tourism receipts (US$ million)	1,118.0	1,504.0	
Tourist spending (US$ million)	195.0	279.6	340.0

Average household size 1995 (persons)	2.80				
Urban population 1995 (%)	55.4				
Age analysis (%) (1995)	*0-14* 22.8		*15-64* 67.5		*65+* 9.7
Population by sex (%) (1995)	*Male* 49.1		*Female* 50.9		
Life expectancy (years) (1994)	*Male* 65.9		*Female* 73.3		
Infant mortality (deaths per '000 live births) (1994)	23.9				
Adult literacy (%) (1992)	96.7				

TRADING PARTNERS

Major export destinations 1995 (% share)		Major import sources 1995 (% share)	
Germany	17.8	Germany	16.9
Italy	15.6	Russia	13.7
France	5.6	Italy	13.0
Turkey	4.5	France	5.1

Russia

Area (km²)   17,075,400

Currency   Rouble

Location   Russia, the largest state in Asia, extends nearly 9,000 km from the Finnish border in the west to the Bering Straits in the east, at which point it faces across to the US state of Alaska. The vast terrain ranges from the Arctic wastes of the north to the Caspian Sea in the south, and includes innumerable mountain ranges with vast mineral resources in the Siberian ranges to the east. The capital is Moscow.

Head of State   President Boris Yeltsin (1990)

Head of Government   Victor Chernomyrdin (1992)

Ruling Party   A coalition of hard-line communist and nationalist anti-reformers is in power.

Political Structure   The Russian Republic represents the greater part of the former Soviet Union. The executive President is directly elected by universal suffrage, and answers to a 444-member Supreme Soviet (Parliament) comprising two chambers. There is also a Prime Minister, who is appointed by the President on the Soviet's recommendations, and an extensive network of local councils.

Last Elections   Elections to the lower chamber of the Supreme Soviet in December 1995 produced a shattering result for Yeltsin and the pro-reform groups when the Communist Party won a third of all the seats at stake. Reformers made a comeback in the presidential elections held in June 1996 when Yeltsin took 54% of the popular vote while the communist candidate, Gennadi Zyuganov, received 41%. A contest for power among Yeltsin's supporters was soon launched, however, pitting the retired general, Alexander Lebed, against Viktor Chernomyrdin, the country's prime minister.

Political Risk   The Chechen conflict has already claimed at least 30,000 lives and continues to absorb resources that the country can ill-afford to squander. After more than a year of fighting, the war is beginning to look more and more like Moscow's version of Vietnam. Relations with the USA remain fragile. Potentially serious clashes could emerge over Chechnya, the transport of Caspian Sea oil or Russia's supply of nuclear technology to Iran and Cuba. If any of these issues should become dominant, Russia's access to western capital could quickly be cut off.

International Disputes   Russia' main foreign policy concern is probably to stop, or at least slow, the eastward advance of NATO. The government has offered some compromises such as the admission of ex-communist states to NATO's political wing but not its military structure. Closer to home, Moscow is concerned about the situation in the ex-Soviet republics to the south. Meanwhile, the bloody war in Chechnya continues. Some now fear that it could develop into a protracted, messy fight against deeply entrenched partisan forces. Russia is also engaged in a dispute with Japan over the four Southern Kurile Islands in the Sea of Okhotsk which were seized from Japan at the end of the Second World War, and hopes for an early return to Japanese rule have been blocked by continuing opposition from Moscow.

Economy   Russia took giant steps towards entrenching its nascent market economy in 1995. A tight monetary squeeze cut the monthly rate of inflation from 17.8% in January 1995 to 2.8% in February 1996 - the lowest level since reforms began. The budget deficit was reduced to 2.9% of GDP and, for the first time, was financed entirely through non-inflationary means (external credit and expansion of government debt). The collapse of industrial production finally appeared to bottom out and the value of the rouble was successfully defended. These achievements were won at considerable cost, however. Life expectancy is declining, for example, and the daily calorie intake has fallen by 15% since 1990.

Main Industries   Russia's industrial centres in Moscow and St Petersburg are the most important in the entire former USSR, producing an extensive range of manufactured goods, of which steel, chemicals, engineering products, transport equipment and consumer goods are among the most important. The sector is being privatised, but at considerable cost to the workforce. Agricultural production is almost up to self-sufficiency levels, with the dominant products being potatoes, vegetables, wheat and cattle. There are massive forest resources. Mineral extraction, apart from oil and gas, remains at a high level, with iron ore, copper, aluminium, manganese, salt and precious metals all being produced.

Energy   Russia has traditionally met all energy requirements from its vast resources of coal, oil and gas. However, the need to export as much as possible in order to maximise hard-currency earnings has produced major strains which are compounded by the run-down conditions and obsolete technologies in the energy sector. In 1996, parliament passed a controversial "production-sharing" law which requires that investors cede part of the oil they find to the government in taxes and royalties. The most troubling clause is one which would allow the government to rewrite past agreements, thereby recovering profits from investors who do better than expected. The country's crude oil production is falling and its refineries urgently need modernisation but the change in investment regulations makes foreign companies much more cautious.

	1993	1994	1995
Inflation (% change)	874.6	307.4	197.4
Exchange rate (per US$)	1,200.00	2,205.10	4,555.00
Interest rate			319.5
GDP (% real growth)	-12.0	-15.0	-4.0
GDP			
GDP (US$ million)	685,489.0	712,908.6	684,392.0
GDP per capita (US$)	4,627.0	4,817.9	4,628.6
Consumption			
Consumption (US$ million)	326,292.8	339,344.5	350,500.0
Consumption per capita (US$)	2,202.4	2,293.3	2,370.5
Population, mid-year ('000)	148,150.0	147,970.0	147,860.0
Birth rate (per '000)	9.4	9.5	0.3
Death rate (per '000)	14.5	15.7	14.7
No. of households ('000)	52,120.0	52,100.0	52,107.0
Total exports (US$ million)	44,297.0	66,250.0	79,045.0
Total imports (US$ million)	32,806.0	50,507.0	57,965.0
Tourism receipts (US$ million)			
Tourist spending (US$ million)			

Average household size 1995 (persons)	2.70				
Urban population 1995 (%)	72.9				
Age analysis (%) (1995)	*0-14*	21.5	*15-64*	66.7	*65+* 11.8
Population by sex (%) (1995)	*Male*	46.7	*Female*	53.3	
Life expectancy (years) (1994)	*Male*	58.0	*Female*	71.0	
Infant mortality (deaths per '000 live births) (1994)	18.6				
Adult literacy (%) (1995)	99.0				

TRADING PARTNERS

Major export destinations 1995 (% share)		Major import sources 1995 (% share)	
Ukraine	8.7	Ukraine	11.4
Germany	7.7	Germany	11.3
USA	6.4	Kazakhstan	4.7
Switzerland	4.7	USA	4.6

Rwanda

Area (km²) 26,330

Currency Rwanda franc (RF = 100 centimes)

Location Rwanda, a small state to the west of Tanzania, lies just north of Burundi and is bounded in the west by Zaire and in the north by Uganda. Its position on Lake Kivu has helped to ensure an adequate water supply for irrigation. The capital is Kigali.

Head of State Pasteur Bizimungu (June 1994)

Head of Government Pierre Celestin Rwigema (September 1995)

Ruling Party The Rwandan Patriotic Front leads a broad multi-party coalition

Political Structure The murder in 1994 of President Habyarimana, in what appeared to be an attack launched by groups involved in inter-tribal rivalries, engulfed the country in a wave of mass tribal murders which effectively halved the population. Tribal tensions between the Hutu majority and the Tutsi minority in the south of the country have gradually created a state of anarchy and butchery. The basic problem for Rwanda, and especially for its government, is that a quarter of the country's population is in exile, living in squalid and unsustainable camps in Zaire, Tanzania and Burundi. Mostly Hutus, they are frightened to return, and if they were to go back, they would find their businesses and homes taken over by Tutsis. Under normal circumstances, the country has a non-executive President who appoints the Prime Minister. In practice, however, the murdered President had banned opposition parties in 1991 and ruled by decree since then.

Last Elections Legislative elections were held in December 1988, when all of the 140 candidates for the National Development Council were approved by the ruling MRND. True multi-party elections were originally envisaged for June 1995, but this proved to be impossible.

Political Risk The country's full-scale civil war has forced over 2 million people to flee to neighbouring countries while another 3 million have been displaced at home. Meanwhile, all foreigners were evacuated from the country, and in most cases they have yet to return.

International Disputes Rwanda's relations with Uganda have been badly affected since 1990 when Rwandan rebels belonging to the minority Tutsi tribe launched an invasion from their exile base in Uganda. Relations with Zaire, Uganda and Tanzania are tense because of the large number of Rwandans living in refugee camps in those countries.

Economy Rwanda's economy has been virtually wrecked by the domestic upheaval of recent years which has halved its wage-earning population and destroyed most of what little international goodwill remained. The country desperately needs foreign assistance to get its economy going again. To get that aid, it must create the conditions that will encourage the refugees to return.

Main Industries Rwanda's economy is principally dependent on farming, which supplied over three-quarters of its GDP and export revenues prior to the war. Cash crops include coffee, tea and sugar cane, although vegetables and fruit are also being grown. Industry centres on the processing of agricultural raw materials, such as timber, textiles, beverages and soap. A large portion of the country's existing capacity has been destroyed.

Energy The country has limited indigenous fuel resources and relies heavily on imports. It derives the greater part of its electricity needs from the hydro-electric sector, however.

	1993	1994	1995
Inflation (% change)	12.4	13.4	9.9
Exchange rate (per US$)	144.25	138.38	237.62
Interest rate (% per annum)	15.0		
GDP (% real growth)	-11.7	-8.0	-9.0
GDP (Million units of national currency)	218,754.0	228,332.0	228,352.5
GDP (US$ million)	1,516.5	1,650.0	961.0
GDP per capita (US$)	200.9	212.9	122.4
Consumption (Million units of national currency)	169,696.9	177,127.0	177,143.0
Consumption (US$ million)	1,176.4	1,280.0	745.5
Consumption per capita (US$)	155.8	165.2	95.0
Population, mid-year ('000)	7,550.0	7,750.0	7,850.0
Birth rate (per '000)	49.7	49.2	
Death rate (per '000)	16.6	16.6	
No. of households ('000)	1,346.1	1,357.1	1,370.0
Total exports (US$ million)			
Total imports (US$ million)			
Tourism receipts (US$ million)	2.0	2.2	
Tourist spending (US$ million)	16.6	18.2	10.6

Average household size 1995 (persons)	5.44		
Urban population 1995 (%)	6.1		
Age analysis (%) (1978)	*0-14* 45.6	*15-64* 51.6	*65+* 2.8
Population by sex (%) (1989)	*Male* 48.3	*Female* 51.7	
Life expectancy (years) (1990-95)	*Male* 45.8	*Female* 48.9	
Infant mortality (deaths per '000 live births) (1993)	110.2		
Adult literacy (%) (1995)	60.5		

TRADING PARTNERS

Major export destinations 1995 (% share)		Major import sources 1995 (% share)	
Chile	46.8	Belgium/Luxembourg	15.7
Tanzania	26.8	USA	13.0
Belgium/Luxembourg	14.6	Tanzania	12.4
Netherlands	8.3	Kenya	11.7

Sao Tomé e Príncipe

Area (km²)   964

Currency   Dobra (D = 100 centimes)

Location   Sao Tomé e Príncipe is a federation of two eponymous islands and several islets in the Gulf of Guinea, some 300 km off the Atlantic coast of West Africa. The nearest land point is Libreville in Gabon. The capital is Sao Tomé.

Head of State   President Miguel Trovoada (1995)

Head of Government   Carlos da Graça (October 1995)

Ruling Party   Movimento de Liberaçao de Sao Tomé e Príncipe (MLSTP-PSD)

Political Structure   The Democratic Republic of Sao Tomé e Príncipe was an overseas territory of Portugal until 1975, and quickly became a single-party state run by the socialist Movimento de Liberaçao de Sao Tomé e Príncipe. Multi-party elections became a possibility only in 1990, when a new Constitution was introduced which provided for a semi-executive President who appoints the Prime Minister on the advice of the 55-member legislature. There are plans to award Príncipe a substantial degree of regional autonomy, including the creation of a regional assembly.

Last Elections   The country's second multi-party elections to the 55-member National People's Assembly were held in October 1994, when the ruling Partido de Convergência Democrática lost the majority it had unexpectedly gained in the 1991 elections, winning only 14 of the 55 seats. The MLSTP-PSD, with 27 seats, was returned to power, while the Independent Democratic Action party won 14 seats. Presidential elections in March 1991 produced a landslide for Miguel Trovoada.

Political Risk   The government's cautious pattern of political reform has been welcomed abroad. The country, however, remains poor and vulnerable to swings in the world price of cocoa on which it depends heavily. In August 1995 the government of President Miguel Trovoada was overthrown in a military coup led by Lt Manuel Quintas de Almeida. Only two weeks later, de Almeida handed power back to the President. The Trovoada administration has faced mounting accusations of authoritarianism.

Economy   As Sao Tomé e Príncipe moves away from the one-party system, its economy is being decentralised and deregulated. The poor performance of the export markets has severely hampered the country's development but a mild recovery in cocoa prices is helping to boost the economy.

Main Industries   Agriculture remains the mainstay of the economy, with cocoa providing 75% of GDP. There are some moves toward encouraging alternative crops, however. Industry is limited in scale and is restricted to the coverage of domestic needs: soap, beverages and timber products. Most other products have to be imported.

Energy   The country has little domestic energy resources, and derives the bulk of its needs from imports of oil, gas and coal. It does, however, obtain half of its electricity from hydro-electric sources.

	1993	1994	1995
Inflation (% change)	240.6	80.2	41.7
Exchange rate (per US$)	474.05	949.28	1,444.40
Interest rate			
GDP (% real growth)	0.1	1.6	1.5
GDP (Million units of national currency)	12,230.5	22,402.9	32,227.0
GDP (US$ million)	25.8	23.6	22.3
GDP per capita (US$)	215.0	196.7	185.9
Consumption (Million units of national currency)	4,123.2	8,568.5	13,984.0
Consumption (US$ million)	8.7	9.0	9.7
Consumption per capita (US$)	72.5	75.2	80.7
Population, mid-year ('000)	120.0	120.0	120.0
Birth rate (per '000)	43.0	35.2	
Death rate (per '000)	9.0	8.9	
No. of households ('000)	21.2	21.3	21.4
Total exports (US$ million)	4.7	4.3	
Total imports (US$ million)	31.0	25.0	
Tourism receipts (US$ million)			
Tourist spending (US$ million)			

Average household size 1995 (persons)	5.33				
Urban population 1995 (%)	46.7				
Age analysis (%) (1981)	*0-14* 46.7		*15-64* 48.4		*65+* 4.9
Population by sex (%) (1991)	*Male* 49.4		*Female* 50.6		
Life expectancy (years) (1985)	*Male* 64.3		*Female* 66.8		
Infant mortality (deaths per '000 live births)					
Adult literacy (%) (1981)	57.4				

Saudi Arabia

Area (km²) 2,400,900

Currency Saudi riyal (SR = 20 qursh = 100 halalas)

Location Saudi Arabia, the largest country in the Middle East, occupies the greater part of the Arabian peninsula and borders on both the Persian (Arabian) Gulf and the Red Sea. It faces Iran across the Gulf to the east, and Egypt, Sudan and Ethiopia across the Red Sea to the west. In the south it borders on Yemen and Oman. Its most crucial borders are in the north, where it meets Iraq, Jordan and Kuwait. Saudi Arabia was a major participant in the 1991 Gulf War to drive Iraq back from its invasion of Kuwait. The capital is Riyadh.

Head of State HM King Fahd ibn Abdul Aziz (1982)

Head of Government HM King Fahd ibn Abdul Aziz

Ruling Party There are no political parties in Saudi Arabia.

Political Structure Saudi Arabia is an absolute monarchy in which the majority of senior government posts are filled by members of the royal family. Technically, it has no constitution except for the Koran, reflecting its official role as keeper of the shrines of Makkah and Medina. Saudi Arabia is a Sunni state. Representation takes place primarily through personal petitions to royal figures, but royal audiences are held almost daily. Moves are under way to develop a new constitution, including a 60-member Consultative Council. In 1995, a major Cabinet reshuffle occurred, in what was generally seen as a move to introduce new ideas and more pro-Western attitudes.

Last Elections There are no general elections in Saudi Arabia.

Political Risk Despite the problems which have resulted from falling oil revenues, the royal family remains firmly in control. Sporadic unrest and occasional Muslim-inspired bombings (aimed in part at the US military) have nevertheless occurred and the rulers can expect to face stiffer challenges in the future. In 1995 King Fahd suffered a stroke and handed over power to his half-brother, Crown Prince Abdullah. The King resumed his job as head of state in February 1996 and the official line is that he has fully recovered. Unofficially, he is thought to be still enfeebled, suffering recent memory loss. His reinstatement is believed to signal the reluctance of his powerful full brothers, Prince Sultan, the defence minister, and Prince Nayef, the interior minister, to accept Prince Abdullah's rule.

International Disputes Saudi Arabia's borders have never been fully defined. It has technical border disputes with practically all of its neighbours. In most cases, negotiations have led to agreement on a neutral zone where no oil development is to take place. In the case of Kuwait, Saudi Arabia shares the output of one field with Kuwait, in return for Kuwait's undertaking to export Saudi oil through its port. The dispute with Iraq has been less easy to resolve: a diamond-shaped neutral zone of some 300 km in width was established where no oil activity is permitted. Saudi Arabia takes very seriously its role as the guardian of the Islamic shrines at Makkah and Medina and has often been sharply critical of un-Islamic practices, such as the commercial banking system in Bahrain or the often disruptive activities of Shia pilgrims from Iran. Its relations with Iran are uneasy because the country is suspected of supporting Muslim fundamentalists in Saudi Arabia.

Economy Saudi Arabia's economy grew by about 4.3% in nominal terms in 1995 after growth of only 1.4% in the previous year. These figures would mean that real growth (after taking account of inflation) was negligible in recent years. Government officials attempt to discount recent trends by pointing out that private sector GDP grew by 7.5% in 1995, up from 4% in 1994. Whatever the actual growth figures, Saudi Arabia has a serious problem with its persistent budget deficit. The Gulf war cost the country around $60 billion and immediately followed a collapse in oil prices which had already severely weaken the Saudis' financial position. The 1996 budget proposes to keep a tight lid on government spending, although it does forecast a small increase in the fiscal deficit. Increases in the prices of water, electricity, postal and telephone charges and petroleum products are all in store. However, significant improvements in the country's financial position inevitably depend on movements in world oil prices. In 1995, the average oil sale price rose by 21%, giving the government more manoeuvrability in determining its spending priorities.

Main Industries Production of oil and gas overshadow all other sectors of the economy and account for over 90% of the country's revenues. However, diversification into other industrial sectors is encouraged (and subsidised) with special emphasis on downstream users of petroleum such as bulk and fine chemicals and plastics and other heavy goods including metal processing, textiles, construction materials and some food processing. Although home to one of the world's harshest climates, Saudi Arabia has a large (and heavily subsidised) agricultural sector. It produces some of the world's most expensive wheat and sells the surplus on export markets. Subsidies to wheat farmers were over $1.7 billion in 1993 and were cut to $850 million in 1994. Much more drastic reductions will have to come in the future as these levels of payments can not be sustained.

Energy Saudi Arabia is fully self-sufficient in all energy requirements.

	1993	1994	1995
Inflation (% change)	1.1	0.6	4.9
Exchange rate (per US$)	3.75	3.75	3.75
Interest rate			
GDP (% real growth)	5.6	0.8	0.5
GDP (Million units of national currency)	443,840.0	450,030.0	474,441.9
GDP (US$ million)	118,357.3	120,008.0	126,517.8
GDP per capita (US$)	6,913.4	6,877.2	6,977.0
Consumption (Million units of national currency)	188,158.6	189,600.9	198,647.6
Consumption (US$ million)	50,175.6	50,560.2	52,972.7
Consumption per capita (US$)	2,930.8	2,897.4	2,921.2
Population, mid-year ('000)	17,120.0	17,450.0	18,133.7
Birth rate (per '000)	40.0	35.1	
Death rate (per '000)	4.7	4.5	
No. of households ('000)	2,766.8	2,829.1	2,890.0
Total exports (US$ million)	42,395.0		
Total imports (US$ million)			
Tourism receipts (US$ million)			
Tourist spending (US$ million)			

Average household size 1995 (persons)	5.96				
Urban population 1995 (%)	80.2				
Age analysis (%) (1992,est)	*0-14* 45.3		*15-64* 52.1		*65+* 2.6
Population by sex (%)					
Life expectancy (years) (1990-95)	*Male* 68.4		*Female* 71.4		
Infant mortality (deaths per '000 live births) (1993)	28.9				
Adult literacy (%) (1995)	62.8				

TRADING PARTNERS

Major export destinations 1995 (% share)		Major import sources 1995 (% share)	
Japan	17.6	USA	21.4
USA	14.7	United Kingdom	8.7
South Korea	9.7	Germany	7.8
Singapore	6.9	Japan	7.7

Senegal

Area (km²)   196,720

Currency   CFA franc (= 100 centimes)

Location   Located on the Atlantic coast of West Africa, Senegal is the continent's westernmost point. With Mauritania to the north, Mali to the south-east, and Guinea and Guinea-Bissau to the south, it lies in a deeply depressed and drought-ridden belt with poor soil. Indeed, virtually all the cultivable ground lies along the banks of the River Gambia which is enclosed for most of its useful length by the political enclave of The Gambia. The capital is Dakar.

Head of State   President Abdou Diouf (1981)

Head of Government   Habib Thiam

Ruling Party   Parti socialiste sénégalais (PS) leads a coalition with the Parti démocratique sénégalais.

Political Structure   The Republic of Senegal was proclaimed in September 1960, having seceded from the Federation of Mali, which in turn had left French domination in June 1960. The executive President is also the head of the government and is elected by direct popular vote for a seven-year term. He answers to a 120-member National Assembly, which is elected by universal suffrage for a term of five years.

Last Elections   The May 1993 elections produced a setback for the ruling Parti Socialiste Sénégalais which received only 56.6% of the vote and 84 of the 120 seats in the National Assembly. Meanwhile, 30% and 27 seats went to the Parti Démocratique Sénégalais. Jappoo Liggeyal Senegal won three seats and other minority parties won another six. However, the union of the two main parties in March 1995 brought a better chance of stability. President Diouf, the incumbent President, had been re-elected in February 1993 with 58% of the vote compared with 32% for Abdoulaye Wade.

Political Risk   Economic problems have threatened the country's political system in recent years, but the structure appears to have stood up well to the strain. Improving relations with Mauritania and The Gambia, with which Senegal had a brief political union in the 1980s, have added to the encouraging picture. Relations with Burkina Faso remain troubled, however, and the Government sometimes encounters hostility from rebels in the southern region of Casamance. There are also severe worries about Islamic religious extremists. One such group, the Moustarchidine Oua Moustarchidate, was banned in 1994 after violent incidents in which dozens of people were killed.

International Disputes   Relations with The Gambia are crucial to Senegal. In 1982, after Senegalese troops had helped to put down a rebellion in The Gambia, the two countries formed the so-called federation of Senegambia; but, as in the past, the idea floundered and eventually failed in 1989.

Economy   After several years of stagnation, the performance of Senegal's economy improved in 1995, thanks mainly to stronger demand in commodity markets. The country's finances are in total disarray, however. A 50% devaluation in the CFA franc in 1994 has complicated the country's financial problems and led to a rise in the external debt. Fortunately, Senegal has significant mineral resources, and if world prices continue to be strong, its financial position could improve with proper management. Over three-quarters of the population depend on subsistence farming, but the government has introduced policies to encourage manufacturing operations. A number of austerity budgets have been introduced over the past several years, sometimes causing widespread public hostility.

Main Industries   Senegal's savannah grasslands make it most suitable for cattle herding, mainly by nomadic farmers. However, groundnuts are grown for export. Phosphate mining is also an important export earner, with most products being destined for Europe. There is a limited tourism sector, appealing mainly to French holidaymakers.

Energy   The country has no oil, gas or coal reserves and depends on imports for all requirements that brushwood cannot fulfil. It has no hydro-electric capacity.

	1993	1994	1995
Inflation (% change)	-0.6	32.3	7.9
Exchange rate (per US$)	283.16	555.20	498.70
Interest rate (% per annum)	17.5	17.5	16.0
GDP (% real growth)	1.0	-1.7	2.5
GDP (Million units of national currency)	1,883,049.9	2,447,900.2	2,707,316.4
GDP (US$ million)	6,650.1	4,409.0	5,428.7
GDP per capita (US$)	816.0	544.3	662.0
Consumption (Million units of national currency)	1,014,411.3	1,318,699.8	1,458,449.0
Consumption (US$ million)	3,582.5	2,375.2	2,924.5
Consumption per capita (US$)	439.6	293.2	356.6
Population, mid-year ('000)	8,150.0	8,100.0	8,200.0
Birth rate (per '000)	43.0	43.2	
Death rate (per '000)	16.0	16.0	
No. of households ('000)	1,327.9	1,370.4	1,416.0
Total exports (US$ million)	722.0	700.0	
Total imports (US$ million)	1,105.0	1,322.1	
Tourism receipts (US$ million)	173.0	226.7	
Tourist spending (US$ million)	106.0	138.9	171.0

Average household size 1995 (persons)	5.50		
Urban population 1995 (%)	42.3		
Age analysis (%) (1988)	*0-14* 45.2	*15-64* 51.5	*65+* 3.3
Population by sex (%) (1988)	*Male* 48.8	*Female* 51.2	
Life expectancy (years) (1990-95)	*Male* 48.3	*Female* 50.3	
Infant mortality (deaths per '000 live births) (1993)	68.0		
Adult literacy (%) (1995)	33.1		

TRADING PARTNERS

Major export destinations 1995 (% share)		Major import sources 1995 (% share)	
France	29.8	France	39.2
Italy	12.2	USA	5.8
Mali	7.2	Netherlands	4.3
India	6.0	Italy	4.2

Serbia

Area (km²) 88,361

Currency Dinar

Location Serbia, the largest region in the former Yugoslavia, is the dominant part of what remains of the country. Its northern border is with Hungary and on its eastern side are Romania and Bulgaria. In the centre of the region is Belgrade, the capital and largest town. The region is characterised in geographical terms by mountains and deep river valleys. Serbia includes the autonomous provinces of Kosovo in the south and Vojvodina in the north. The capital is Belgrade.

Head of State Slobodan Milosevic

Head of Government Mirko Marjanovic (February 1994)

Ruling Party Socialist Party of Serbia (SPS)

Political Structure The former state of Yugoslavia included not only the republics of Serbia and Montenegro, which comprise the new Yugoslav state, but also Slovenia, Croatia, Bosnia-Herzegovina and Macedonia. Under the old system, the state was a federation of republics, together with the autonomous Serbian provinces of Kosovo and Vojvodina. The new system has yet to gain international recognition.

Last Elections Legislative elections were held in December 1992 for the 250-seat Serbian Republican Assembly, when the SPS won 101 seats.

Political Risk The political risks associated with Serbia are extremely high. Although a shaky peace now exists, much of Serbia's wealth and income has gone to support their fellow Serbs' war in Bosnia. The UN's trade embargo on the country has been lifted but the economy suffered greatly from this policy as well.

International Disputes Serbia's war with Croatia and Bosnia could resume on a reduced scale if the 1996 peace accord should break down. Relations with Albania are also strained. Albania has accused Serbia of attempting to subvert the ethnic Albanian majority in the latter's Kosovo province. Serbia has a dispute with Slovenia about the latter's tentative agreement to assume responsibility for 18% of the ex-Yugoslavia's debt and has threatened to raise similar objections following the conclusion of Croatia's current negotiations.

Economy The West's embargo of Serbia during the war brought growth to a standstill. The fact that the economy did not collapse or severely contract is a tribute to the Serbs' ingenuity and the effectiveness of the black market. The Serbs desperately need an infusion of capital to restore their economy but inflation, once nearing 100%, has been brought under control.

Main Industries Industrial activities in Serbia are centred largely around Belgrade and include machine tools, electrical equipment, pharmaceuticals, textiles, food-processing and light engineering. Agriculture is important, with fruit, vegetables and tobacco of particular importance.

Energy Serbia has adequate hydro-electric potential, but it is entirely dependent on imports for its oil supplies.

	1993	1994	1995
Inflation (% change)	3,000.0		
Exchange rate (per US$)			
Interest rate			
GDP (% real growth)	-5.0		
GDP			
GDP (US$ million)			
GDP per capita (US$)			
Consumption			
Consumption (US$ million)			
Consumption per capita (US$)			
Population, mid-year ('000)	10,485.0	10,530.0	10,575.2
Birth rate (per '000)	13.4	13.2	13.2
Death rate (per '000)	10.0	10.1	10.2
No. of households ('000)	3,045.0	3,080.0	3,116.0
Total exports (US$ million)	6.9	9.8	
Total imports (US$ million)	66.4	80.8	
Tourism receipts (US$ million)	66.4	80.8	
Tourist spending (US$ million)	23.0		

Average household size 1995 (persons)	3.22		
Urban population 1995 (%)	57.0		
Age analysis (%)			
Population by sex (%)			
Life expectancy (years) (1988-89)	*Male* 70.9	*Female* 76.1	
Infant mortality (deaths per '000 live births)			
Adult literacy (%) (1990)	92.7		

Seychelles

Area (km²) 455

Currency Seychelles rupee (SR = 100 cents)

Location The Seychelles are a group of 115 islands located in the Indian Ocean, to the east of Tanzania and Kenya. Most of the population inhabit the Mahé group of islands, which are of granite and contrast with the low-lying terrain of the other, mainly coral islands. The climate is tropical with the cooler season occurring during the south-east monsoon (late May to September). The capital is Victoria.

Head of State President France Albert René (1977)

Head of Government President France Albert René

Ruling Party Seychelles People's Progressive Front

Political Structure The rule of Sir James Mancham was overthrown in 1977 by a coup led by France Albert René, who thereupon suspended all political parties except for his own Seychelles People's Progressive Front and declared himself President. After fighting off a coup attempt by South African-backed mercenaries in 1981, René went on to institute an executive Presidency in which the President, like all but 11 of the 23-member unicameral National Assembly, is elected for a five-year term, renewable three times. Multi-party politics were readmitted in 1992.

Last Elections A constitutional referendum in 1993 produced a 74% majority in favour of a new multi-party Constitution. The first elections since the 1977 followed shortly afterward. France Albert René's Seychelles People's Progressive Front won 14 of the seats, compared with eight for the opposition Democratic Party and one for the Parti Seselwa. The voter turnout was over 90%.

Political Risk The re-emergence of a multi-party, parliamentary democracy has come about largely because of diplomatic pressure from Britain and France, and its eventual shape remains to be seen. The possibility of local unrest is small, however, given the largely homogeneous domestic population.

International Disputes The Seychelles has no formal disputes with other countries although the international community has been critical of the islands' offshore financial services, arguing that it serves as a haven for money launderers.

Economy Since independence in 1970, per capita output has increased roughly seven-fold. Growth has been spearheaded by tourism, which employs about 30% of the work force and accounts for over 70% of hard-currency earnings. The government encourages private investment to upgrade its tourist industry and make it more competitive in international markets. However, public officials also want to reduce the country's dependence on this sector which was hard-hit during the Gulf War in 1991-1992. Farming, fishing and small-scale manufacturing all receive strong support from the government. Development is hindered by the lack of fresh-water resources.

Main Industries The agricultural sector is small, since only 4% of the Seychelles is arable land. Copra, cinnamon and fish products are the traditional products, but greater emphasis is now being placed on fruit and vegetable crops destined for domestic consumption. Industry is limited to the supply of the country's own needs for basic products: timber products, cement, tobacco and food processing. With over 1.3 million square kilometres of sea area and easy access for cruise liners, tourism is a large money earner. The sector attracted over 120,000 international visitors in 1995 and generated almost 40% of GDP.

Energy The country has only limited fuel resources, apart from brushwood, and relies on imports for most requirements. There is no hydro-electric capacity.

	1993	1994	1995
Inflation (% change)	1.3	1.8	-0.3
Exchange rate (per US$)	5.18	5.06	4.77
Interest rate (% per annum)	14.0		
GDP (% real growth)	-6.5	-3.3	-0.5
GDP (Million units of national currency)	2,419.2	2,381.5	2,362.5
GDP (US$ million)	467.0	470.6	495.3
GDP per capita (US$)	6,671.8	6,723.5	7,075.3
Consumption (Million units of national currency)	1,095.9	1,078.9	1,070.4
Consumption (US$ million)	211.6	213.2	224.4
Consumption per capita (US$)	3,022.3	3,046.0	3,205.7
Population, mid-year ('000)	70.0	70.0	70.0
Birth rate (per '000)	23.9	21.9	21.0
Death rate (per '000)	8.3	8.3	7.0
No. of households ('000)	11.3	11.4	11.5
Total exports (US$ million)	51.0	52.0	
Total imports (US$ million)	238.0	206.0	
Tourism receipts (US$ million)	116.0	120.0	
Tourist spending (US$ million)			

Average household size 1995 (persons)	5.78				
Urban population 1995 (%)	54.5				
Age analysis (%) (1990)	*0-14* 35.0		*15-64* 58.2		*65+* 6.8
Population by sex (%) (1990)	*Male* 49.7		*Female* 50.3		
Life expectancy (years) (1987)	*Male* 65.2		*Female* 74.5		
Infant mortality (deaths per '000 live births) (1993)	13.0				
Adult literacy (%) (1971)	57.7				

Sierra Leone

Area (km²)   72,325

Currency   Leone (Le = 100 cents)

Location   Sierra Leone is located on the Atlantic coast of West Africa, where it is bounded in the north and east by Guinea and in the south by Liberia. The climate is tropical and humid, but affords significant agricultural possibilities. The capital is Freetown.

Head of State   President Ahmad Tejan Kabbah (1996)

Head of Government   Ahmad Tejan Kabbah

Ruling Party   All-People's Congress.

Political Structure   Political parties were banned in Sierra Leone in 1991. Shortly afterward, the National Provisional Ruling Council (NPRC) staged a military coup and the country's House of Representatives was dissolved. Since then the NPRC has been trying to turn itself into a political party. It is opposed by a guerrilla group known as the Revolutionary United Front (RUF) and led by a former army corporal, Foday Sankoh. The RUF is inspired by a populist rejection of government and foreign interference.

Last Elections   After four years of army rule, a civilian, Ahmad Tejan Kabbah, was elected president in March, 1996. The election, which took place in the midst of a civil war, was carried out only because of British insistence and as a condition for the continuation of foreign aid. The UK believed that an election would marginalise the RUF and provided £3 million to pay for it. Voting was preceded by months of political manoeuvring as various politicians tried to gain control over one or more of the presidential candidates. Five of the 13 participating parties won seats in the new 80-member parliament.

Political Risk   Sierra Leone is still wrecked by a civil war. Originally a spin-off from the war in neighbouring Liberia, the unrest is characterised by excessive violence and incoherence carried out by uniformed thugs whose loyalties are unclear. By one set of estimates, the atrocities have driven over a third of the country's 4 million inhabitants from their homes. President Kabbah has promised to make a complete break with the past and to work with the RUF to restore unity and peace. The peaceful transition to civilian rule should ensure a steady flow of foreign assistance.

International Disputes   The country's proximity to the civil war in Liberia is the source of many problems and was a contributory factor in the removal of the old Government during a coup in 1992. The government has received assisted from South African mercenaries while Nigerian troops (who are supposedly peacekeepers) guard Freetown. The RUF insists that all foreign forces must be withdrawn as a precondition for a national conference.

Economy   Clearly, the violence of the last few years has inflicted lasting damage on the economy and drastically diminished the country's prospects. Under more normal circumstances, Sierra Leone's economy has traditionally relied on farming, but the expansion of the mineral sector has created massive new possibilities which are so far largely unrealised. Living standards are very low, except in Freetown itself.

Main Industries   The farming sector, centring on cocoa, coffee, ginger and palm kernels, is still among the biggest contributors to the external economy. Rice, cassava, maize and vegetables are grown for domestic consumption, and there is a sizeable fishing industry. Manufacturing activities are primarily concerned with the processing of raw materials. More important is the mining sector where gold, rutile, bauxite and diamonds are produced for export.

Energy   The country is entirely dependent on imports for most of its requirements, although there is some coal. There are no hydro-electric facilities.

	1993	1994	1995
Inflation (% change)	22.2	24.2	26.0
Exchange rate (per US$)	567.46	586.74	678.92
Interest rate (% per annum)	50.5	27.3	
GDP (% real growth)	7.0	-3.5	-5.0
GDP (Million units of national currency)	396,073.0	474,845.0	568,389.5
GDP (US$ million)	698.0	809.3	837.2
GDP per capita (US$)	162.3	183.5	185.3
Consumption (Million units of national currency)	274,151.0	338,867.0	418,202.1
Consumption (US$ million)	483.1	577.5	616.0
Consumption per capita (US$)	112.4	131.0	136.3
Population, mid-year ('000)	4,300.0	4,409.5	4,518.2
Birth rate (per '000)	49.1	45.1	
Death rate (per '000)	25.1	25.1	
No. of households ('000)	738.3	760.9	790.0
Total exports (US$ million)	118.0	115.0	125.0
Total imports (US$ million)	147.0	151.0	135.0
Tourism receipts (US$ million)	18.0	23.0	
Tourist spending (US$ million)	4.0	5.1	5.4

Average household size 1995 (persons)	5.43				
Urban population 1995 (%)	36.2				
Age analysis (%) (1992, est)	*0-14*	44.5	*15-64*	52.4	*65+* 3.1
Population by sex (%) (1985)	*Male*	49.4	*Female*	50.7	
Life expectancy (years) (1990-95)	*Male*	37.5	*Female*	40.6	
Infant mortality (deaths per '000 live births) (1993)	166.5				
Adult literacy (%) (1995)	31.4				

TRADING PARTNERS

Major export destinations 1995 (% share)		Major import sources 1995 (% share)	
USA	20.4	Côte d'Ivoire	17.4
Spain	11.9	United Kingdom	16.5
United Kingdom	6.8	Belgium/Luxembourg	8.0
Germany	4.2	USA	7.5

Singapore

Area (km²)   616

Currency   Singapore dollar (S$ = 100 cents)

Location   Singapore, although only a tiny and highly urbanised city state on the south-eastern corner of Peninsular Malaysia, owes its extraordinary wealth entirely to its position. Its harbour facilities, oil processing and most recently its highly developed telecommunications systems have given it a central role in the development of the region, despite its relatively isolated position in relation to Japan and China. The capital is Singapore City.

Head of State   President Ong Teng Cheong (August 1993)

Head of Government   Goh Chok Tong (1991)

Ruling Party   People's Action Party (PAP)

Political Structure   The Republic of Singapore, an independent member of the Commonwealth, achieved independence in 1965. Its executive President is elected by the unicameral Parliament for a term of four years; the 81-member Parliament is itself elected every four years, by a complex system of single-member constituencies and by professional constituencies representing professional groups. In January 1991 the Parliament voted to award the President substantially increased powers.

Last Elections   General elections were held prematurely in August 1991, when the PAP saw its support fall from 63% to 61%, while the opposition Singapore Democratic Party (SDP) and Workers' Party (WP) saw their votes increase accordingly. Yet, because of the first-past-the-post electoral system, the PAP carried off 77 of the 81 seats, while the SDP gained three seats and the WP one. In the first democratic presidential elections, held in August 1993, Ong Teng Cheong was appointed with a large majority.

Political Risk   With its very high standards of personal affluence and established political structure, Singapore's only major worry is that its rapidly rising wages may eventually price its industries out of international markets. Electorally, the system is weighted so heavily in favour of the PAP that the poll results tend to obscure any growing dissatisfaction with the party.

International Disputes   Singapore's decision to promote itself as a regional hub for Asian entrepôt trade and as a source of investment capital for Asia has greatly improved its relationship with its neighbours. After many years of tense relations with China, the city-state has emerged as the fifth largest investor in that country and enjoys close ties. Similar processes are underway in several other Asian economies.

Economy   Traditionally one of Asia's fastest-growing economies, Singapore's enviable record is becoming more difficult to sustain as it moves up the economic ladder. GDP still grew by nearly 8% in 1995, although this was lower than the 10% recorded for the previous year. Certainly, there is little danger that future rates of growth will shrink drastically but the government is already planning changes that will transform Singapore into a highly advanced industrial economy. The reason for these concerns is the island economy's labour shortage: labour costs rose by 7.1% in 1995 even though inflation was only 1.7%. Planners' solution is to assist labour-intensive manufacturers to relocate elsewhere in the region, encourage research and high-tech operations at home and serve as the region hub for companies doing business everywhere in Asia.

Main Industries   The island state's development has been rapid, being driven by tourism, a wide range of high-technology manufacturers and big, capital-intensive industries like chemicals, steel, engineering, oil refining as well as a thriving financial services sector. Singapore's growing labour shortage and the steady rise in wage rates has led the government to introduce policies which make it easier for labour-intensive industries such as textiles, clothing and producers of various consumer goods to relocate to more labour-abundant economies. Sponsorship of industrial parks and close bilateral trading relationships with neighbouring countries are used for this purpose. Meanwhile, the government is actively encouraging multinationals to choose Singapore as their operational headquarters for the Asia-Pacific region. Incentives to invest in R&D and the island state's pro-business stance have proven to be important attractions to the multinationals.

Energy   Singapore is wholly dependent on imports for all energy requirements, but it has massive oil refining facilities associated with its ports.

	1993	1994	1995
Inflation (% change)	2.3	3.1	1.7
Exchange rate (per US$)	1.62	1.53	1.42
Interest rate (% per annum)	5.4	5.9	6.4
GDP (% real growth)	10.1	10.6	7.8
GDP (Million units of national currency)	92,348.0	105,313.0	115,457.4
GDP (US$ million)	57,004.9	68,832.0	81,308.0
GDP per capita (US$)	19,862.3	23,492.2	27,193.3
Consumption (Million units of national currency)	38,042.0	39,593.0	39,614.9
Consumption (US$ million)	23,482.7	25,877.8	27,897.8
Consumption per capita (US$)	8,182.1	8,832.0	9,330.4
Population, mid-year ('000)	2,870.0	2,930.0	2,990.0
Birth rate (per '000)	17.6	16.9	16.3
Death rate (per '000)	5.0	4.7	4.8
No. of households ('000)	784.5	797.0	815.0
Total exports (US$ million)	74,012.0	96,826.0	118,265.0
Total imports (US$ million)	85,234.0	102,670.0	124,507.0
Tourism receipts (US$ million)	5,793.0	7,069.3	7,550.0
Tourist spending (US$ million)	3,022.0	3,368.0	3,857.7

Average household size 1995 (persons)	3.49				
Urban population 1996 (%)	100.0				
Age analysis (%) (1992)	*0-14* 23.1		*15-64* 70.6		*65+* 6.3
Population by sex (%) (1992)	*Male* 50.5		*Female* 49.5		
Life expectancy (years) (1995)	*Male* 74.0		*Female* 79.0		
Infant mortality (deaths per '000 live births) (1995)	4.0				
Adult literacy (%) (1995)	92.0				

TRADING PARTNERS

Major export destinations 1995 (% share)		Major import sources 1995 (% share)	
Malaysia	19.2	Japan	21.1
USA	18.2	Malaysia	15.5
Hong Kong	8.6	USA	15.0
Japan	7.8	Thailand	5.2

Slovakia

Area (km²)   49,035

Currency   Koruna (Kcs = 100 heller)

Location   Slovakia, which was linked until January 1993 in a federation with the Czech Republic, is located in central Europe, south-east of Germany and south of Poland, but to the north of Austria and Hungary. The Czech Republic lies to the east. The climate is temperate, with occasionally winters. The capital is Bratislava.

Head of State   President Michal Kovac (1993)

Head of Government   Vladimir Meciar (1994)

Ruling Party   Democratic Union of Slovakia leads a five-party coalition.

Political Structure   From 1919 until the end of 1992 Slovakia was part of a federation with the Czech Republic. At the start of 1993 the two countries began an independent existence.

Last Elections   The controversial Vladimir Meciar was reinstated as Prime Minister during the general elections of October 1994 which gave strong support to his Democratic Union of Slovakia. In so doing he replaced Jozef Moravcik, who had taken over from him in March 1994 after a bout of political infighting. Meciar's return to power was seen as a triumph for the reformist group which had initiated the Republic's original split from the former Czechoslovakia in 1993.

Political Risk   Political infighting between the president and the prime minister has led to the erratic formulation of policy and a loss of confidence in the government. Vacillation about programmes of privatisation, doubts that Meciar's economic policies can deliver the transparent, market-oriented economy required to conform with the EU and blatant discrimination against some minorities are some of the government's major problems. Meciar's desire to replace Michal Kovac and become a president with Gaullist-style executive powers add to the unease voiced by analysts and investors alike.

International Disputes   The country's Hungarian community, which numbers 600,000, has been a recurrent source of tension between Slovakia and Hungary which is accentuated by the latter government's distrust of Meciar. The unease continues despite a treaty of friendship and co-operation which was signed in March 1995. Relations with Germany are also problematic. Curiously, Slovakia insists on referring to the country by its cold-war name (the equivalent of the "German Federal Republic"). The dispute would be unimportant if it were not blocking at least six agreements between Slovakia and its would-be sponsor.

Economy   A cyclical recovery in Slovakia's major industries, coupled with tough monetary controls by the central bank have improved the prospects of Slovakia attaining the "convergence criteria" set by the EU. Inflation in 1995 fell to 10% and is forecast to drop to 8% by 1997. Unemployment, though still too high at around 14%, is falling. Meanwhile, the state budget is marginally in surplus and international investment rating agencies have recently upgraded the country's bonds. Yet discordant voices in the Meciar government raise doubts about Slovakia's will to join the EU. Some talk of a "special relationship" with Russia.

Main Industries   The Slovaks started at an industrial disadvantage. They, not the Czechs, were the main heirs to outdated arms factories from Soviet times. The current government's reluctance to pursue its programme of privatisation vigorously adds to general scepticism about much of the country's industrial base. Volkswagen's decision to double production at its Slovakian plant in 1996 is regarded as one of the most encouraging signs in recent years. The country has a highly skilled and cheap labour force which should attract ample foreign investment if the macroeconomy can be stabilised. The agricultural sector is relatively efficient and produces an exportable surplus of meat, wheat, barley, vegetables, potatoes and fruit. There are extensive forests offering substantial scope for timber development. The tourist sector is also growing and with proper planning could be a major earner of foreign exchange.

Energy   Slovakia is self-sufficient in coal and lignite which, between them, supply up to two-thirds of the country's total energy requirements. Slovakia, however, depends on imports for all its oil and gas supplies. Roughly 27% of all electricity comes from nuclear power stations, mainly of the Soviet type.

	1993	1994	1995
Inflation (% change)	23.2	13.4	10.0
Exchange rate (per US$)	30.67	31.07	29.77
Interest rate (% per annum)	14.4	14.6	15.6
GDP (% real growth)	-12.8	-7.0	6.7
GDP (Billion units of national currency)	369.9	441.3	518.0
GDP (US$ million)	12,060.6	14,203.4	17,400.1
GDP per capita (US$)	2,267.0	2,654.8	3,246.3
Consumption (Billion units of national currency)	260.3	330.6	353.5
Consumption (US$ million)	8,488.7	10,641.8	11,873.3
Consumption per capita (US$)	1,595.6	1,989.1	2,215.2
Population, mid-year ('000)	5,320.0	5,350.0	5,360.0
Birth rate (per '000)		12.4	11.5
Death rate (per '000)			9.8
No. of households ('000)	1,813.0	1,832.0	1,856.0
Total exports (US$ million)	5,451.0	6,587.0	8,019.6
Total imports (US$ million)	6,655.0	6,823.0	10,248.9
Tourism receipts (US$ million)	390.0	460.9	
Tourist spending (US$ million)	262.0	309.6	345.4

Average household size 1995 (persons)	2.74				
Urban population 1995 (%)	58.8				
Age analysis (%) (1995)	*0-14*	24.1	*15-64*	64.2	*65+* 11.7
Population by sex (%) (1995)	*Male*	48.9	*Female*	51.1	
Life expectancy (years) (1993)	*Male*	68.4	*Female*	76.7	
Infant mortality (deaths per '000 live births) (1994)	11.2				
Adult literacy (%)					

TRADING PARTNERS

Major export destinations 1995 (% share)		Major import sources 1995 (% share)	
Czech Republic	37.6	Czech Republic	37.0
Germany	24.4	Germany	21.5
Italy	6.3	Russia	12.8
Austria	5.0	Italy	5.4

Slovenia

Area (km²) 20,254

Currency Tolar (= 100 stotins)

Location Slovenia lies in the far north of the former Yugoslav Federation. It comprises mountains in the west and gentler, flatter land in the east. Three countries border the region - Austria in the north, Italy to the west and Hungary to the east. The capital is Ljubljana.

Head of State Milan Kucan (1992)

Head of Government Janez Drnovsek (1992)

Ruling Party Liberal Democratic Party (LDP) leads a coalition.

Political Structure Slovenia declared its independence in June 1991. The President, who has a mainly ceremonial function, is elected by universal suffrage for a five-year once-renewable period. The bicameral legislature has 130 members - 90 in the National Assembly and 40 in the National Council which is mainly an advisory body. In August 1995 Slovenia gained membership to the Central European Trade Agreement which includes Bulgaria, the Czech Republic, Hungary, Poland and Romania.

Last Elections Parliamentary and presidential elections were held on 6 December 1992. The LDP returned a total of 33 deputies to the National Assembly, while the Slovenian Christian Democrats gained 15 seats, the Associated List 14, the Slovenian National Party 12 and the Slovenian People's Party 10. Milan Kucan gained 64% of the presidential vote.

Political Risk Technically, Slovenia represents only a very slight it has flourishing relations with Austria and with many parts of Eastern Europe. In Western Europe, it enjoys a deserved reputation as a democratic society and rapidly developing capitalist country with good economic prospects.

International Disputes Slovenia's expectation of a trouble-free entry into the EU were shaken by Italy's claims on property and compensation acquired after World War II. Though Rome has withdrawn its objections, nationalistic opponents in Ljubljana have used the incident to raise awareness of the costs involved in joining the EU. Slovenia's agreement with western commercial banks to pay off 18% of the ex-Yugoslavia's $4.3 billion in international debt has been challenged by Serbia. Most bankers think the dispute will only delay agreement.

Economy With a small, open economy and proximity to Germany, industrial northern Italy and central Europe, Slovenia depends heavily on exports. Germany alone accounts for nearly a third of the country's exports and 85% of all commodity exports now go to five countries - Germany, Austria, Croatia, France and Italy. Imports are rising strongly but the combined effect of higher exports and growing tourism has led to an almost embarrassing increase in foreign exchange reserves to over $3 billion. To sustain its export-led growth, Slovenia will have to keep its wage rates under control. Meanwhile, there is a disturbing rise in unemployment to over 9%, and a wave of privatisations over the next few years is expected to add to the roll of job-seekers. Officials hope for a rise in domestic and foreign investment which could smooth the transition to a market economy and help to modernise the country's major industries.

Main Industries With less than 8% of Slovenia's workers in agriculture, the composition of GDP resembles that in western countries to a much greater extent than is true for other parts of Eastern Europe. Farm productivity is high, with large surpluses of maize, wheat, sugar beet and potatoes being produced. Coal, lead, lignite and mercury are mined, while manufacturing industries include cotton fabrics, steel, motor vehicles, numerous consumer products and sports equipment (especially skis). Tourism has deservedly emerged as the most dynamic sector with revenue growth in double digits in every year since 1992. As a crossroads between Eastern and Western Europe, the country is rapidly developing its motorways, ports and rail systems.

Energy Slovenia has some coal, but is otherwise dependent on imports for its fuel needs.

	1993	1994	1995
Inflation (% change)	31.9	19.8	12.6
Exchange rate (per US$)	124.00	117.00	119.34
Interest rate (% per annum)	49.6	39.4	24.8
GDP (% real growth)	1.3	0.8	1.2
GDP (Billion units of national currency)	1,841.3	2,223.3	2,533.5
GDP (US$ million)	14,849.2	19,002.6	21,229.1
GDP per capita (US$)	7,461.9	9,795.1	10,886.7
Consumption			
Consumption (US$ million)			
Consumption per capita (US$)			
Population, mid-year ('000)	1,990.0	1,940.0	1,950.0
Birth rate (per '000)	9.9	9.8	
Death rate (per '000)	10.1	9.7	
No. of households ('000)	509.0	515.0	521.0
Total exports (US$ million)	6,083.0	6,828.0	8,286.0
Total imports (US$ million)	6,529.0	7,304.0	9,452.0
Tourism receipts (US$ million)	734.0	782.3	
Tourist spending (US$ million)	304.0	324.0	

Average household size 1995 (persons)	3.56				
Urban population 1995 (%)	63.6				
Age analysis (%) (1991)	*0-14* 20.6		*15-64* 68.5		*65+* 10.9
Population by sex (%) (1992)	*Male* 48.5		*Female* 51.5		
Life expectancy (years) (1991)	*Male* 69.4		*Female* 77.3		
Infant mortality (deaths per '000 live births) (1993)	6.6				
Adult literacy (%)					

TRADING PARTNERS

Major export destinations 1995 (% share)		Major import sources 1995 (% share)	
Germany	20.6	Italy	22.3
Italy	13.2	Austria	9.6
Croatia	10.8	France	7.8
France	7.7	Croatia	7.7

Solomon Islands

Area (km²)   29,790

Currency   Solomon Island dollar (SI$ = 100 cents)

Location   The Solomon Islands extend some 1,400 km from Bougainville (part of Papua New Guinea) in the north-west to the Santa Cruz islands in the south-east. Although the terrain varies significantly, typical landscapes are mountainous with dense tree cover. The capital is Honiara.

Head of State   HM Queen Elizabeth II

Head of Government   Solomon Mamaloni (November 1994)

Ruling Party   A national coalition of non-National Unity parties.

Political Structure   The Solomon Islands are an independent member of the Commonwealth, in which the Crown is represented by a Governor-General. Legislative authority is vested in the 47-member unicameral Parliament, which is elected by universal adult suffrage for a term of up to four years. The Prime Minister is elected from among the Parliament's members, by secret ballot. Since 1990 the political scene has moved away from party lines and has instead drifted back toward the personal influence of tribal and other figures as the main centres of political opinion.

Last Elections   In the 1993 elections to the National Parliament, the Group for National Unity and Reconciliation won 21 of the 47 seats while the People's Alliance Party won seven seats, the National Action Party five seats, the Labour Party four seats, the United Party four seats and independents six seats.

Political Risk   The political structure is undergoing a period of change in which underlying trends are often obscured by the strengths of individual personalities. Subject to this reservation, the democratic process appears to work reasonably well.

International Disputes   The Solomon Islands are now entering a period of better relations with Papua New Guinea, which contests the ownership of the mineral-rich Bougainville region. Talks are in progress on a resolution of the differences, though it is unlikely that Papua New Guinea will cede them easily.

Economy   The economy performed poorly during the latter half of the 1980s and the early 1990s, owing mainly to the country's relatively remote geographical location and its limited infrastructure. The traditionalist political system also dictated that opportunities for new development would be only slowly taken up, if at all. Growth rates have improved in recent years, thanks to small amounts of foreign investment and a more modern set of macroeconomic policies. At present per capita incomes are close to the levels seen in the Philippines or Indonesia.

Main Industries   The country's economy depends mainly on cash crops such as copra, cocoa and palm oil. Cassava, fruit and vegetables are grown for domestic consumption, and there is an important fishing industry. Occasional damage from cyclones create serious disruptions to the agrarian economy. Tourism is the next most important sector, with visitors from Europe, Australia and the United States. However, authorities are reluctant, for cultural reasons, to see a very rapid expansion of the sector.

Energy   Most of the country's fuel needs are met from firewood or similar sources. All oil has to be imported.

	1993	1994	1995
Inflation (% change)	17.3	13.6	14.4
Exchange rate (per US$)	3.19	3.30	3.27
Interest rate (% per annum)	19.5	15.7	
GDP (% real growth)	-3.0	0.6	-7.9
GDP (Million units of national currency)	500.6	572.1	603.0
GDP (US$ million)	156.9	173.4	184.4
GDP per capita (US$)	442.1	476.2	506.6
Consumption (Million units of national currency)	125.8	143.8	163.9
Consumption (US$ million)	39.4	43.6	50.1
Consumption per capita (US$)	111.1	119.7	137.7
Population, mid-year ('000)	355.0	364.0	364.0
Birth rate (per '000)	40.3	38.9	37.7
Death rate (per '000)	6.8	6.8	6.8
No. of households ('000)	51.8	53.4	55.0
Total exports (US$ million)	94.0	131.4	158.7
Total imports (US$ million)	90.0	149.0	145.8
Tourism receipts (US$ million)	6.0	6.6	
Tourist spending (US$ million)	13.8	15.1	17.4

Average household size 1995 (persons)	6.29				
Urban population 1995 (%)	17.1				
Age analysis (%) (1986)	*0-14* 47.3		*15-64* 49.4		*65+* 3.3
Population by sex (%) (1986)	*Male* 51.9		*Female* 48.1		
Life expectancy (years) (1989)	*Male* 59.7		*Female* 64.9		
Infant mortality (deaths per '000 live births) (1991)	47.0				
Adult literacy (%)					

TRADING PARTNERS

Major export destinations 1995 (% share)		Major import sources 1995 (% share)	
Japan	57.6	Australia	41.3
United Kingdom	8.1	Singapore	12.3
Philippines	5.9	Japan	9.8
USA	3.0	New Zealand	8.0

Somalia

Area (km²) 630,000

Currency Somali shilling (SSh = 100 cents)

Location Somalia occupies the entire eastern tip of the Horn of Africa, with Kenya to its west, Ethiopia to the north-west and Djibouti to the north. Its northern coastline follows the Gulf of Aden, while its eastern coast lies on the Indian Ocean. Somalia's terrain is mixed, with plains toward the Indian Ocean coast but with hills and mountains in the north. Soil quality is poor and a large proportion of the population is nomadic. The capital is Mogadishu.

Head of State Rival claims for president by General Farrah Aideed and Ali Mahdi Muhammad

Head of Government as above

Ruling Party Shifting alliances between various warlords in northern and southern parts of Mogadishu and the surrounding area have completely erased any semblance of a political system.

Political Structure The Republic of Somalia was ruled from 1969 until January 1991 by Maj.-Gen. Siyad Barre, who seized power in a coup and created a socialist state dominated by the Somali Revolutionary Socialist Party. The Constitution remained suspended from 1969 until 1991, when it was reintroduced in its unaltered form. Barre's subsequent removal, and the installation of an interim President, failed to stem the ruinous inter-ethnic feuding and by 1993 the situation had descended into full-scale guerrilla war. Intervention by US and UN troops led to a tentative peace agreement in 1994 which was meant to secure the political rehabilitation of Gen. Farrah Aideed. However, the situation degenerated quickly following the evacuation of UN troops in 1995. No clear leader has emerged from the chaos; meanwhile, the fighting continues.

Last Elections The elections held in April 1996 were of no real significance since the results were immediately disputed and fighting resumed with even greater intensity. The power brokers in this ongoing civil war are General Aideed and businessman-turned-warlord Ali Mahdi Muhammad. Behind the scenes, Ali Hassan Osman, a rich businessman who was once General Aideed's financial backer, negotiates with other warlords in an attempt to isolate his former protégé.

Political Risk The government and social services have completely dissolved as the civil war rages. Multi-clan committees set up to manage key facilities such as the airport and the port have all but collapsed. No real authority exists in the country today.

International Disputes The severe deterioration in Somalia's internal situation in recent years has placed strains on its relationships with neighbouring countries. Formally, the country maintains a claim against Ethiopia for the return of the Ogaden region, the vast triangular desert area which comprises the whole south-east of the country. In reality, no government exists to assert that claim. The Kenyan border is also in doubt but this claim, too, will have to await the restoration of some form of government in Somalia.

Economy Somalia's economy has been wrecked by the civil war. Malnutrition is rising after crops in several areas were hit by floods at the end of 1995. Water supplies are no longer operating in many parts of the country and hospitals have virtually ceased to function.

Main Industries Subsistence farming, mainly of grains, cassava and cattle, is the backbone of the economy, with a very large proportion of the population following a nomadic lifestyle. Food processing, hides, wool and leather products are the main areas of industrial activity.

Energy Somalia has only limited natural fuel resources and relies on imports for most of its needs. There is, however, the possibility of an oil find offshore. The country has no hydro-electric power facilities.

	1993	1994	1995
Inflation (% change)	60.0		
Exchange rate (per US$)	2,626.22	2,618.33	2,583.60
Interest rate			
GDP (% real growth)	-11.0	-10.0	-8.0
GDP (Million units of national currency)	2,524,601.5	2,607,438.0	2,398,843.0
GDP (US$ million)	961.3	995.8	928.5
GDP per capita (US$)	107.4	109.7	101.7
Consumption (Million units of national currency)	1,711,592.7	1,767,753.0	1,626,332.8
Consumption (US$ million)	651.7	675.1	629.5
Consumption per capita (US$)	72.8	74.4	68.9
Population, mid-year ('000)	8,950.0	9,080.0	9,131.7
Birth rate (per '000)	50.2	46.0	
Death rate (per '000)	18.5	18.5	
No. of households ('000)	1,689.7	1,715.1	1,740.5
Total exports (US$ million)	93.6	152.5	
Total imports (US$ million)			
Tourism receipts (US$ million)			
Tourist spending (US$ million)			

Average household size 1995 (persons)	4.98		
Urban population 1995 (%)	25.8		
Age analysis (%) (1992, est)	*0-14* 47.0	*15-64* 50.3	*65+* 2.7
Population by sex (%)			
Life expectancy (years) (1990-95)	*Male* 45.4	*Female* 48.6	
Infant mortality (deaths per '000 live births) (1993)	121.7		
Adult literacy (%) (1995)	24.1		

TRADING PARTNERS

Major export destinations 1995 (% share)		Major import sources 1995 (% share)	
Saudi Arabia	66.3	Kenya	23.0
Italy	13.5	Djibouti	17.3
United Arab Emirates	10.9	Saudi Arabia	5.7
United Kingdom	1.7	USA	3.1

South Africa

Area (km²)   1,184,825

Currency   Rand (R = 100 cents)

Location   South Africa shares borders with Namibia in the north-west, Botswana and Zimbabwe in the north, Mozambique in the north-east and Swaziland in the east. Apart from the sovereign enclaves of Lesotho and Swaziland, it includes various "independent republics" which have no international recognition. The climate is warm and generally dry, but is well suited to agriculture; there are also vast areas of bush and scrub. The capital is Pretoria.

Head of State   President Nelson Mandela (May 1994)

Head of Government   President Nelson Mandela

Ruling Party   The African National Congress (ANC) heads a coalition with the Inkatha Freedom Party. The National Party withdrew from the coalition in May 1996.

Political Structure   The constitutional changes of 1993 and 1994 introduced a full system of universal suffrage for the first time, thus finally ending the apartheid system under which only white electors had the vote. The elections of April 1994 accordingly produced a massive black vote which swept the Xhosa-dominated ANC to power and installed Nelson Mandela as the country's first black President. The "homelands" where black citizens were officially confined under apartheid were effectively disbanded. Under the transitional constitutional arrangements the ANC was required to form a broad coalition with any party which won at least 5% of the vote in the 1994 elections. The executive President is elected by universal suffrage for a five-year term of office. A new constitution was agreed in May 1996, prompting the resignation of the deputy president, F W de Klerk of the National Party. The deputy post is not expected to be filled.

Last Elections   The April 1994 elections to the 400-seat National Assembly resulted in a clear majority for the ANC, which won 252 seats with 63% of the vote. The (predominantly white) National Party (NP) won 82 seats, the Zulu Inkatha movement won another 43 seats and the remainder were divided among four minor parties. Nelson Mandela thereupon became President and accordingly founded a coalition comprising the ANC, NP and Inkatha. In 1996, the NP withdrew from the coalition and began an ambitious reorganisation in order to fortify its opposition to the ruling ANC in time for the 1999 elections.

Political Risk   The country's first full election demonstrated an unexpected degree of co-operation between the rival Xhosa and Zulu groups. However, the possibility of further inter-tribal tensions cannot be ruled out. Inkatha actually withdrew briefly from the governing coalition in 1995 but promptly rejoined. South Africa is now removed from the UN's trade embargo list and signed a trade agreement in March 1995 with the EU.

International Disputes   With South Africa's complete abandonment of its controversial racial policy, the barriers which the international community had erected were dismantled. In 1993, the country ceded the disputed territory of Walvis Bay to Namibia. Co-operation in regional trade is proving harder to develop. Renegotiation of the Southern African Customs Union agreement which links South Africa with six other countries in the region is proving difficult because of disputes between Pretoria and Zimbabwe. Similar disagreements are holding up a finalisation of the trade protocol for the Southern African Development Community. South Africa's insistence on "equitable" development in the region is proving impossible owing to the country's large size in relation to its trading partners.

Economy   GDP grew by 3.5% in 1995, the fastest rate since 1988. Inflation, at 8.7%, was the lowest since 1972 and business confidence is at its most buoyant in more than a decade. Curiously, however, the country's economic policies are coming in for some of the most serious criticism in years. The critics argue that immense economic challenges are not being met. They point out that the economy must grow at an annual rate of at least 6% per year by 2000 if it is to generate the 300,000-500,000 jobs that are needed, as well as to create adequate infrastructure for the entire population. Government officials are making a concerted effort to ensure that the economy's healthy rates of growth have a visible impact in the poorest sections of the country.

Main Industries   Agriculture is an important earner of foreign exchange although the sector accounts for only 5% of GDP. Fruit, cereals, sugar cane, cotton and wines are grown for export. Manufacturing contributes more than a quarter of GDP and is expanding rapidly, with new investment rising by 21% in 1995. New policies to address the role of conglomerates in the economy were introduced in 1996 and are expected to bolster the sector's competitiveness in world markets. After making a modest start in the post-apartheid era, tourism is booming. The country expects over 4.4 million visitors in 1996, with the number of overseas visitors growing by more than 50% a year. South Africa's mining sector offers gold, diamonds, iron ore, copper, manganese, limestone and chrome.

Energy   South Africa has ample supplies of coal and meets some of its oil needs by synthesising coal into an oil substitute. Until 1993, its demand for oil imports had to be met by means of evading the global trade sanctions imposed against it in this area, but these are no longer relevant.

	1993	1994	1995
Inflation (% change)	9.7	9.0	8.7
Exchange rate (per US$)	3.26	3.55	3.63
Interest rate (% per annum)	16.2	15.6	17.9
GDP (% real growth)	1.9	3.6	3.5
GDP (Million units of national currency)	383,071.0	432,753.0	484,621.0
GDP (US$ million)	117,506.4	121,902.3	133,504.4
GDP per capita (US$)	2,965.1	3,014.4	3,237.3
Consumption (Million units of national currency)	230,630.0	256,320.0	282,390.8
Consumption (US$ million)	70,745.4	72,202.8	77,793.6
Consumption per capita (US$)	1,785.1	1,785.4	1,886.4
Population, mid-year ('000)	39,630.0	40,440.0	41,240.0
Birth rate (per '000)	28.1	16.7	
Death rate (per '000)	5.1		
No. of households ('000)	7,897.2	8,037.1	8,190.0
Total exports (US$ million)	24,261.0	24,987.0	27,860.0
Total imports (US$ million)	20,017.0	23,387.0	30,555.0
Tourism receipts (US$ million)	1,190.0	1,227.5	
Tourist spending (US$ million)	1,598.0	1,648.3	1,775.9

Average household size 1995 (persons)	4.78				
Urban population 1995 (%)	50.8				
Age analysis (%) (1991)	*0-14*	34.6	*15-64*	61.1	*65+* 4.3
Population by sex (%) (1994)	*Male*	50.0	*Female*	50.0	
Life expectancy (years) (1990-95)	*Male*	60.0	*Female*	66.0	
Infant mortality (deaths per '000 live births) (1992)	35.1				
Adult literacy (%) (1994)	61.4				

TRADING PARTNERS

Major export destinations 1995 (% share)		Major import sources 1995 (% share)	
Italy	8.4	Germany	15.6
Japan	8.3	United Kingdom	10.9
USA	7.5	USA	10.2
Germany	6.0	Japan	9.2

South Korea

Area (km^2)   98,445

Currency   Won (W = 100 jeon)

Location   The Republic of Korea (South Korea) is located about 500 km off the coast of mainland China, and forms the entire southern half of the Korean peninsula. There are many hundreds of small islands to the south, most of them uninhabited. The territory is mixed in character, with considerable mountainous areas. Consequently, most of the largest settlements are on the southern and eastern coasts, the capital city of Seoul being the notable exception. The capital is Seoul.

Head of State   Kim Young Sam (1992)

Head of Government   Lee Hong Koo (December 1994)

Ruling Party   Democratic Liberal Party (ruling coalition, incorporating two independents)

Political Structure   South Korea has a Prime Minister but in practice real power lies with the executive President. The Constitution grants the National Assembly, whose 299 members are elected by universal suffrage for a four-year term, with most legislative authority. Since the collapse of the Fifth Republic in 1987 following violent protests, the Parliament has been hampered by the small working majority of the ruling party.

Last Elections   Elections to the National Assembly were held in March 1996. The President's Democratic Liberal Party (DLP) won 141 seats, down from the 149 it had controlled in the previous Assembly. The centre-left National Congress for New Politics won 79 seats, followed by the United Liberal Democrats with 48 seats. The voter turnout (64%) was the lowest since the end of the military dictatorship in 1987. The disappointing results could damage the presidential ambitions of the two opposition leaders, Kim Dae-jung and Kim Jong-pil. Presidential elections will be held in 1997 and the incumbent, Kim Young Sam, is constitutionally barred from seeking a second term.

Political Risk   South Korea's reputation for political tranquillity owes much to the Government's firm and sometimes brutal suppression of dissent. The ruling party lost its majority in the 1996 elections to the Assembly but could still achieve parliamentary control by attracting some independents. Nevertheless, the mandate of Kim Young-sam to proceed with economic reforms has been weakened by the outcome.

International Disputes   Tensions between North and South Korea have existed since 1948. The North decided in 1996 to abandon the 1953 armistice agreement that ended the Korean war. The South acknowledges that the North is desperate for food and insists that humanitarian concerns come first in their dealings with their northern neighbour, but politics clearly plays a big role. Contacts have been suspended since the death of the North's leader, Kim Il-Sung, in 1994. South Korea is also working assiduously to improve relations with China and reopened diplomatic relations in 1992. Japan, for its part, is attempting to offer some recompense for the atrocities committed during its annexation of Korea from 1910 to 1945. In 1996, South Korea and Japan opened a dispute over three tiny islands in the sea of Japan which both countries claim.

Economy   South Korea's miraculous progress over the past two decades has been achieved through a combination of generous government support for key industries, a stringent policy of trade protection, cheap capital and favourable exchange rates. Living standards can match those in many industrialised countries. In recognition of its achievements, South Korea will join the Organisation for Economic Co-operation and Development in 1996.

Main Industries   The country's sophisticated manufacturing sector produces all the types of products found in any industrialised country. Major industries include electronics, textiles, motor vehicles, industrial chemicals, steel and shipbuilding as well as food processing, production of consumer goods and wood products. The country's ten largest conglomerates, known as chaebols, account for nearly a quarter of manufacturing output and their share is rising. Such concentration has prompted public resentment of power and led to close links between the chaebols and the military. These considerations make it very difficult for policy makers to lead the economy in the new directions which it must pursue in the next century. Farming is a comparatively minor activity which includes the production of rice, barley, beans and other staple foods, although there is some fruit production. Ginseng and silk are cultivated for export.

Energy   South Korea has a significant coal mining industry but no other hydrocarbon resources of its own. Hydro-electric power accounts for about a tenth of total consumption, but nuclear energy is at least ten times as important.

	1993	1994	1995
Inflation (% change)	4.8	6.3	4.5
Exchange rate (per US$)	802.67	803.45	771.11
Interest rate (% per annum)	8.6	8.5	9.0
GDP (% real growth)	6.3	7.4	10.2
GDP (Billion units of national currency)	267,146.0	305,008.0	351,295.0
GDP (US$ million)	332,821.7	379,622.9	455,570.5
GDP per capita (US$)	7,553.8	8,540.4	10,157.6
Consumption (Billion units of national currency)	143,743.0	164,212.0	189,243.6
Consumption (US$ million)	179,081.1	204,383.6	245,417.2
Consumption per capita (US$)	4,064.5	4,598.1	5,472.0
Population, mid-year ('000)	44,060.0	44,450.0	44,850.0
Birth rate (per '000)	15.1	16.0	
Death rate (per '000)	5.7	5.4	
No. of households ('000)	13,106.4	13,192.0	13,300.0
Total exports (US$ million)	82,236.0	96,013.0	
Total imports (US$ million)	83,800.0	106,696.0	
Tourism receipts (US$ million)	3,510.0	3,920.0	
Tourist spending (US$ million)			

Average household size 1995 (persons)	3.20				
Urban population 1995 (%)	81.0				
Age analysis (%) (1993)	*0-14* 24.4	*15-64* 70.3	*65+* 5.4
Population by sex (%) (1993)	*Male* 50.3	*Female* 49.7	
Life expectancy (years) (1992)	*Male* 67.5	*Female* 73.6	
Infant mortality (deaths per '000 live births) (1993)	10.9		
Adult literacy (%) (1995)	96.3		

TRADING PARTNERS

Major export destinations 1995 (% share)		Major import sources 1995 (% share)	
USA	19.1	Japan	24.5
Japan	13.7	USA	22.5
Hong Kong	8.8	China	5.4
China	7.2	Germany	4.9

Spain

Area (km²) 504,880

Currency Peseta (Pta = 100 céntimos)

Location Spain occupies the greater part of the Iberian peninsula and commands coastal orientations in all four directions; eastward into the Mediterranean, south and west into the Atlantic, and north into the Bay of Biscay. Its only neighbours are Portugal, which it surrounds on both its land borders, and France across the Pyrenees; it is a co-administrator of Andorra. The climate is varied, with mountain ranges and high plateaux and severe heat in the south. The territory of Spain also includes the Balearic islands (in the Mediterranean), the Canary Islands off the Atlantic coast of Morocco, and the Moroccan enclaves of Ceuta and Melilla. The capital is Madrid.

Head of State HM King Juan Carlos I de Borbón y Borbón (1975)

Head of Government Jose Maria Asnar (1996)

Ruling Party People's Party heads a coalition

Political Structure Spain is a constitutional monarchy in which the King plays a relatively modest political role, although he is active in trade promotion. Modern democracy dates from only 1975, when Franco died. The 1978 Constitution created a 350-member Congress of Deputies (Lower House) elected for four years, and an appointed Senate. The administrative regions have been extensively reorganised since the late 1970s to create 17 autonomous regions, including Andalucia, Catalonia and the Basque country.

Last Elections Elections for the Cortes were held in March 1996. The conservative People's Party of Jose Maria Asnar won 156 seats, defeating the ruling Socialist Party of Felipe Gonzales which secured only 141 seats. Asnar's party fell 20 seats short of an outright majority and he was compelled to seek the support of the Catalan nationalists in order to form a government.

Political Risk The last decade has confirmed the political maturity of the Spanish electorate in the post-Franco era, and the commitment to social democratic doctrines which was again underlined in the recent transfer of power. Spain's parliamentary system, however, has developed a peculiarity, with the balance of power vested in political groups that exist only in specific corners of the country. These involve Catalonia and the Basque country, where moderate nationalist forces have supplanted the mainstream Spanish centre-right. On constitutional issues, the Catalans will seek greater concessions for their fiefdom, particularly in such matters as revenue-raising. Asnar, meanwhile, is offering to bargain over taxes. Many Spaniards also remain uneasy about the ruling conservative party's assurances that the new Spanish right has exorcised the ghosts of the authoritarian past. In general, Spain's new government is likely to be weak and any radical reforms will probably be postponed.

International Disputes Spain's only serious dispute is with the UK over the sovereignty of Gibraltar. The Spaniards object to the smuggling of tobacco products which cost their Treasury in lost taxes and charge the leaders in Gibraltar with money laundering and drugs-related profiteering. Spain also objects to plans for a new airport at Gibraltar, which it claims will encroach on its own territory. Spain is in conflict with other EU member states over alleged over-fishing in the North Sea, and in 1995 it became embroiled in a serious dispute with Canada over its activities off the Newfoundland coast. Spain faces a territorial claim from Morocco for the Spanish exclaves of Ceuta and Melilla, and for three small islands off the coast which still form part of Spain.

Economy Government officials have struggled to bring Spain's comparatively high level of inflation (around 4.7%) down to levels acceptable by EU standards. Meanwhile, the country's unemployment is the highest in Western Europe at 23%. More difficulties are in store since Spain meets none of the criteria laid down in the Maastricht treaty. So far, Asnar implausibly insists that Spain can still meet these standards by drastically reducing the budget deficit without undermining its welfare state.

Main Industries Industry is centred in the east (Barcelona) and the north (Bilbao), where a growing range of consumer goods are being added to the heavy, capital-intensive industries which once dominated those regions. Motor vehicles, electronics, steel, chemicals and fertilisers are made, as well as food, wine and tobacco products, leather goods and timber products. Farming is still very important, with a wide variety of crops grown in the lowland areas. Fruits, nuts, olives, tomatoes and peppers are chief export products. The fishing industry is very strong. Tourism is a major foreign exchange earner, contributing up to 15% of GDP - although revenues have been hit in recent years by rival resorts in other countries. The tourist sector is concentrated in coastal areas, especially to the east, and caters largely for British or French visitors - although Spanish consumers are taking more holidays themselves.

Energy Spain has indigenous coal resources and a small quantity of oil, but otherwise no fossil fuels. Imported crude oil still accounts for more than half of its total energy requirements. Nearly 40% of the country's electricity is nuclear, with hydro-electricity providing another 15%.

	1993	1994	1995
Inflation (% change)	4.6	4.7	4.7
Exchange rate (per US$)	127.26	133.96	124.63
Interest rate (% per annum)	12.8	9.0	10.5
GDP (% real growth)	-1.4	1.4	3.0
GDP (Billion units of national currency)	60,904.0	64,673.0	69,722.0
GDP (US$ million)	478,579.3	482,778.4	559,431.9
GDP per capita (US$)	12,245.2	12,318.9	14,274.9
Consumption (Billion units of national currency)	38,511.0	40,854.0	42,686.2
Consumption (US$ million)	302,616.7	304,971.6	342,503.4
Consumption per capita (US$)	7,742.9	7,781.9	8,739.6
Population, mid-year ('000)	39,083.0	39,190.0	39,190.0
Birth rate (per '000)	9.9	11.1	9.1
Death rate (per '000)	8.7	8.8	8.8
No. of households ('000)	14,905.0	14,980.4	15,055.0
Total exports (US$ million)	59,555.0	73,295.0	91,714.0
Total imports (US$ million)	78,626.0	92,510.0	115,056.0
Tourism receipts (US$ million)	19,425.0	19,835.1	
Tourist spending (US$ million)	4,706.0	4,805.3	5,396.7

Average household size 1995 (persons)	2.47				
Urban population 1995 (%)	76.5				
Age analysis (%) (1995)	*0-14*	19.2	*15-64*	67.3	*65+* 13.5
Population by sex (%) (1995)	*Male*	48.7	*Female*	51.3	
Life expectancy (years) (1994)	*Male*	75.3	*Female*	81.0	
Infant mortality (deaths per '000 live births) (1993)	7.6				
Adult literacy (%) (1990)	95.0				

TRADING PARTNERS

Major export destinations 1995 (% share)		Major import sources 1995 (% share)	
France	20.5	France	17.4
Germany	15.4	Germany	15.3
Italy	9.2	United Kingdom	8.8
Portugal	8.3	Italy	8.5

Sri Lanka

Area (km²)   65,610

Currency   Rupee (Rs = 100 cents)

Location   Sri Lanka lies in the Indian Ocean, some 80 km off the southern coast of India. Most of the island is forested, although the soil is ideally suited to agriculture. The climate is humid and tropical. The capital is Colombo.

Head of State   Chandrika Bandaranaika Kumaratunga (November 1994)

Head of Government   Chandrika Bandaranaika Kumaratunga (August 1994)

Ruling Party   Kumaratunga's People's Alliance party forms a coalition with several smaller groups.

Political Structure   The Democratic Socialist Republic of Sri Lanka, which has been independent in its present form since 1978, is a member of the Commonwealth. The country is ruled by an executive President who is elected by universal suffrage for a six-year term. The president appoints a Cabinet in accordance with the 225-seat Parliament - which is itself elected for a five-year term. The country's politics are dominated by ethnic differences; Tamils in the north and east want their own independent republic. A plan for a near-federal government was unveiled by the President in July 1995. Although the plan would have inevitably been watered down before coming law, the February 1996 bombing which killed 80 people makes the prospects for the proposal look dismal. Optimists believe that parliament might still accept some version of the proposal but the government appears to be in no mood to grant further concessions. By mid-1996, President Kumaratunga's coalition had only a one-seat majority in the 225-member assembly and she was having great difficulty in implementing policies.

Last Elections   The last full elections were held in August 1994, when the ruling United National Party lost the majority it had held since 1977 with only 94 of the 225 seats in Parliament, compared with 105 for the People's Alliance of Mrs Chandrika Kumaratunga, 9 for the Independent Tamils, 10 for the Tamil United Liberation Front, and 7 for the Sri Lanka Moslem Congress. At presidential elections in November 1994 Mrs Kumaratunga was also elected President, gaining 62% of the vote to replace Dingiri Banda Wijetunga.

Political Risk   The 1996 Colombo bombing brought further proof that the end of Sri Lanka's hostilities cannot be taken for granted, despite the peace agreement reached in late 1994. The Tamil minority has repeatedly attacked the Sinhala majority who effectively run the country. Widespread strikes among workers on tea, rubber and coconut plantations, a severe drought, electricity shortages and a rising defence budget (estimated to be $670 million in 1996) pose great challenges for the government.

International Disputes   The ethnic Tamil minority has periodically called on India (with its larger number of Tamils) to guarantee their protection from the Sinhala majority. In practice, however, many of the extremely violent terrorist assaults have been perpetrated by the Tamils themselves. A state of emergency has been in force for many years. Relations with India have stabilised following that country's intervention in the mid-1980s to quell the growing violence.

Economy   Sri Lanka's economy has been badly damaged by the civil war. Although the growth of GDP has been strong in recent years, the Colombo bombing will pose several serious problems. The explosion destroyed most of the records of the central bank, which took the full force of the bomb, and the country's privatisation plans may be held up as a result. The Finance ministry had expected to realise $390 million through the sale of state assets in 1996. Even if the loss of the central bank's records can be overcome, possible buyers may be deterred by fears about security despite the inclusion in the 1996 budget of generous tax and duty concessions. Adding to the government's woes is the need to increase the military budget. The end result could be a deficit of 15-16% of GDP in 1996, compared with a forecast of 7.8% before the bombing.

Main Industries   Farming - especially tea, rubber, cotton, spices and copra - is the backbone of the export economy. Sugar cane, fruit and vegetables are grown for the domestic market. The government wishes to encourage a wider spread of crops, but the country's periodic droughts make this difficult. Manufacturing centres largely on the processing of raw materials, although there is also some heavy industry and a petroleum refinery. Minerals exist in abundance but are still underdeveloped. Ilmenite, graphite, dolomite, kaolin, feldspar, phosphates and others are known to be present.

Energy   Sri Lanka has very little indigenous energy resources, except for its abundant hydro-electric capacity, and it relies on imports for nearly all its requirements.

	1993	1994	1995
Inflation (% change)	11.7	8.4	7.7
Exchange rate (per US$)	48.32	49.42	50.76
Interest rate (% per annum)	16.4	13.0	
GDP (% real growth)	6.2	6.8	2.5
GDP (Million units of national currency)	499,760.0	578,795.0	638,946.3
GDP (US$ million)	10,342.7	11,711.8	12,587.6
GDP per capita (US$)	587.0	655.8	696.3
Consumption (Million units of national currency)	369,776.0	415,673.0	445,390.8
Consumption (US$ million)	7,652.6	8,411.0	8,774.4
Consumption per capita (US$)	434.3	470.9	485.4
Population, mid-year ('000)	17,620.0	17,860.0	18,078.6
Birth rate (per '000)	19.9		
Death rate (per '000)	5.3		
No. of households ('000)	3,178.9	3,234.3	3,294.0
Total exports (US$ million)	2,859.0	3,208.0	3,798.0
Total imports (US$ million)			5,185.2
Tourism receipts (US$ million)	207.0	214.0	
Tourist spending (US$ million)	117.0	128.0	133.5

Average household size 1995 (persons)	5.21				
Urban population 1995 (%)	22.4				
Age analysis (%) (1992)	*0-14*	28.2	*15-64*	64.3	*65+* 7.6
Population by sex (%) (1992)	*Male*	49.8	*Female*	50.2	
Life expectancy (years) (1992)	*Male*	69.4	*Female*	73.6	
Infant mortality (deaths per '000 live births) (1991)	25.0				
Adult literacy (%) (1995)	90.2				

TRADING PARTNERS

Major export destinations 1995 (% share)		Major import sources 1995 (% share)	
USA	32.1	Japan	9.1
Germany	8.9	India	8.7
United Kingdom	7.8	Hong Kong	7.7
Japan	5.5	South Korea	6.5

St Kitts

Area (km²)   261

Currency   East Caribbean dollar (EC$ = 100 cents)

Location   St Kitts and Nevis comprises the islands of St Christopher and Nevis, situated in the northern Leeward Islands, in the Eastern Caribbean. The two are separated by a three-kilometre maritime strait, and are mountainous and densely forested. The climate is equable, although subject to storms in the autumn months. The capital is Basseterre.

Head of State   HM Queen Elizabeth II

Head of Government   Dr Kennedy Alphonse Simmonds

Ruling Party   People's Action Movement

Political Structure   St Kitts (St Christopher and Nevis) has been a fully independent member of the Commonwealth since 1983. The Crown is represented by a Governor-General who appoints the Prime Minister and Cabinet in accordance with the wishes of Parliament. The unicameral National Assembly consists of a speaker, three senators appointed by the Governor-General, and 11 members who are elected by universal suffrage for a term of five years. The island of Nevis has a separate eight-member legislature and a Cabinet with certain internal powers.

Last Elections   In the inconclusive November 1993 elections to the National Assembly, the People's Action Movement obtained four of the 11 elected seats, while the St Kitts-Nevis Labour Party won four, the Nevis Reformation Party one, and the Concerned Citizens' Movement two seats. The result was seen as a disappointment to the island of Nevis where support for secession from the federation is relatively strong. Dissatisfaction reached a peak in early 1994 when the Governor-General announced a state of emergency.

Political Risk   The existing political system has proved itself capable of surviving internal political disagreements, but the possibility of a secession by Nevis - which is entirely within the constitutional powers of the Nevis Cabinet - could create major problems. St. Kitts's dependence on the UK for almost all its exports and foreign exchange earnings makes its economy vulnerable to conditions in the latter country.

International Disputes   Agriculture contributes more than half of GDP, and is centred on the coastal areas. Sugar cane, bananas, copra and cotton are the main export products. Manufacturing consists mainly of light goods industries, with an emphasis on textiles. Tourism, although only marginally developed, has considerable potential, and is currently growing at up to 20% per annum.

Economy   The country has no indigenous fuels except timber, and relies on imports from Venezuela and/or Mexico for most of its requirements.

Main Industries   St Kitts has recently been trying to diversify its economy away from the traditional reliance on farming, with an effort to develop the tourism sector and the cotton textiles industry. The government has approved legislation designed to encourage development of an offshore financial services. Living standards, however, are still low in comparison with those in neighbouring countries.

	1993	1994	1995
Inflation (% change)	1.8	1.5	4.0
Exchange rate (per US$)	2.70	2.70	2.70
Interest rate (% per annum)	13.0	13.0	13.0
GDP (% real growth)	-1.8	7.0	2.0
GDP (Million units of national currency)	514.9	559.3	593.3
GDP (US$ million)	190.7	207.1	219.7
GDP per capita (US$)	4,767.6	5,178.7	5,493.6
Consumption (Million units of national currency)	337.5	346.2	346.8
Consumption (US$ million)	125.0	128.2	128.4
Consumption per capita (US$)	3,125.0	3,205.6	3,211.2
Population, mid-year ('000)	40.0	40.0	40.0
Birth rate (per '000)			
Death rate (per '000)			
No. of households ('000)	8.7	8.7	8.8
Total exports (US$ million)	211.0	24.0	
Total imports (US$ million)	70.6	80.0	
Tourism receipts (US$ million)	69.0	71.9	
Tourist spending (US$ million)	5.0	5.2	5.2

Average household size 1995 (persons)	4.34				
Urban population 1995 (%)	42.4				
Age analysis (%) (1988)	*0-14*	33.3	*15-64*	57.4	*65+* 9.2
Population by sex (%) (1988)	*Male*	51.1	*Female*	48.9	
Life expectancy (years) (1988)	*Male*	65.9	*Female*	71.0	
Infant mortality (deaths per '000 live births) (1992)	24.1				
Adult literacy (%) (1980)	97.3				

St Lucia

Area (km²) 616

Currency East Caribbean dollar (EC$ = 100 cents)

Location St Lucia, situated in the Windward Islands of the Eastern Caribbean some 32 km north of St Vincent and 40 km south of Martinique, is no more than 40 km long at its greatest extent, yet its important strategic role has made it much sought after over the years. This is due partly to its record as a safe harbour during the annual hurricane season which afflicts other parts of the region. The capital is Castries.

Head of State HM Queen Elizabeth II

Head of Government John G M Compton

Ruling Party United Workers' Party (UWP)

Political Structure St Lucia, a member of the Commonwealth, is one of the Windward Islands group which favours political integration with Dominica, Grenada and St Vincent and the Grenadines. The 17-member legislature is elected by universal suffrage for a term of five years. In recent years the Compton Administration has been criticised for what its political opponents have called "benevolent dictatorship" or "clientism". Compton was, however, comfortably returned to his post in 1992, and appeared to be gaining in popularity.

Last Elections The April 1992 elections to the 17-member Parliament produced a clear win for the UWP which won 11 seats compared with only nine in 1987. The St Lucia Labour Party won the remaining six seats, with the Progressive Labour Party none.

Political Risk The reassuring vote of confidence for Prime Minister Compton in 1992 appeared to indicate that the chances of an overturn are slim. More serious, perhaps, will be the impact on its economy of the EU's changes in its banana import regime. The proximity of Grenada and Dominica, with which it has many affinities, could conceivably result in further external complications in the future, although at present there is no reason to fear this.

Economy St Lucia is trying, like many other Caribbean islands, to diversify its economy. Standards of living are modest, and tourism is seen as one of the main opportunities for wider employment. A free trade zone has been established at Vieux Fort.

Main Industries Farming is the dominant activity, with bananas, coconuts, cocoa, breadfruit, mangoes and avocados being grown for export while cassava, yams, fruit and vegetables fulfil most domestic needs. Industry centres on the processing of farm products for the domestic market, and most other products are imported. Tourism is growing rapidly and attracts over 200,000 visitors a year, mainly from the USA. The growth, however, is restricted only to the larger resorts and its benefits have been spread unevenly.

Energy The country has no indigenous energy resources and relies on imports for all fuel requirements.

	1993	1994	1995
Inflation (% change)	0.8	2.7	7.0
Exchange rate (per US$)	2.70	2.70	2.70
Interest rate (% per annum)	10.2	10.1	10.0
GDP (% real growth)	4.2	-0.3	1.0
GDP (Million units of national currency)	1,342.6	1,375.3	1,486.3
GDP (US$ million)	497.3	509.4	550.5
GDP per capita (US$)	3,551.9	3,638.4	3,932.0
Consumption (Million units of national currency)	278.4	289.0	316.5
Consumption (US$ million)	103.1	107.0	117.2
Consumption per capita (US$)	736.5	764.6	837.3
Population, mid-year ('000)	140.0	140.0	140.0
Birth rate (per '000)			
Death rate (per '000)			
No. of households ('000)	28.5	28.6	28.8
Total exports (US$ million)	106.4	100.0	
Total imports (US$ million)	291.5	300.0	
Tourism receipts (US$ million)	221.0	232.2	
Tourist spending (US$ million)	22.9	24.1	26.4

Average household size 1995 (persons)	4.62				
Urban population 1995 (%)	48.1				
Age analysis (%) (1989)	*0-14* 44.5	*15-64* 49.9	*65+* 5.6
Population by sex (%) (1989)	*Male* 48.6	*Female* 51.4	
Life expectancy (years) (1986)	*Male* 68.0	*Female* 74.8	
Infant mortality (deaths per '000 live births) (1992)	18.5		
Adult literacy (%) (1970)	81.7		

St Vincent & the Grenadines

Area (km²)   389

Currency   East Caribbean dollar (EC$ = 100 cents)

Location   St Vincent, a 30-kilometre island, is the main island in a group of some 100 islets which extend for more than 60 km through the Grenadines group in the Windward Islands. Other islands in the Grenadines are part of the state of Grenada. St Vincent itself is about 160 km west of Barbados and 34 km south-west of St Lucia. The capital is Kingstown.

Head of State   HM Queen Elizabeth II

Head of Government   James F Mitchell

Ruling Party   New Democratic Party

Political Structure   St Vincent and the Grenadines has been a Commonwealth member since gaining independence from the UK in 1979. The Crown is represented by a Governor-General who appoints the Prime Minister in accordance with the wishes of Parliament. The unicameral National Assembly consists of six appointed senators and 15 members who are elected by universal suffrage for a term of five years. The country is one of the Windward group which is considering formal political integration at some time in the future.

Last Elections   Elections to the National Assembly were held in February 1994, when the New Democratic Party won 12 of the 15 elected seats, with more than 55% of the votes cast. The opposition Labour Party regained the three of the seats which it had held before the 1989 election, while the Movement for National Unity and the United People's Movement failed to elect any candidates.

Political Risk   The 1994 elections marked a mild trend away from the consensus politics which have characterised the country in recent years. The country will make no significant changes in course, however.

Economy   The pace of growth has been slow in recent years and the standard of living is only moderate in comparison with other countries in the region. Government officials emphasise the need to diversify the country's product range and farm output.

Main Industries   The traditional mainstay of the economy is farming which accounts for more than half of total GDP. Bananas, arrowroot, coconuts, cocoa and spices are the main export crops, while cassava and vegetables are grown for the domestic market. Manufacturing centres on the processing of raw materials for domestic use, but a range of light activities are being encouraged. Tourism is still fairly limited but growing rapidly.

Energy   St Vincent and the Grenadines have no indigenous fuels except for firewood, and the country imports nearly all its requirements. However, hydro-electric power accounts for three-quarters of all electricity generation.

	1993	1994	1995
Inflation (% change)	4.3	1.0	1.9
Exchange rate (per US$)	2.70	2.70	2.70
Interest rate (% per annum)	11.2	11.0	11.0
GDP (% real growth)	2.0	1.5	1.3
GDP (Million units of national currency)	596.0	611.0	630.7
GDP (US$ million)	220.7	226.3	233.6
GDP per capita (US$)	2,006.7	2,057.2	2,123.5
Consumption (Million units of national currency)	142.0	154.9	170.1
Consumption (US$ million)	52.6	57.4	63.0
Consumption per capita (US$)	478.1	521.5	572.9
Population, mid-year ('000)	110.0	110.0	110.0
Birth rate (per '000)			22.4
Death rate (per '000)			6.6
No. of households ('000)	24.8	25.1	25.5
Total exports (US$ million)	57.7	50.0	
Total imports (US$ million)	134.0	135.0	134.0
Tourism receipts (US$ million)	55.0	60.3	
Tourist spending (US$ million)	4.8	5.3	5.8

Average household size 1995 (persons)	4.10				
Urban population 1995 (%)	47.0				
Age analysis (%) (1980)	*0-14*	43.8	*15-64*	50.4	*65+* 5.8
Population by sex (%) (1991)	*Male*	49.9	*Female*	50.1	
Life expectancy (years) (1986)	*Male*	67.8	*Female*	71.3	
Infant mortality (deaths per '000 live births) (1992)	17.3				
Adult literacy (%) (1970)	95.6				

Sudan

Area (km²)   2,505,815

Currency   Sudanese pound (S£ = 100 piastres)

Location   Sudan, the largest country in Africa, lies in central north-east Africa where it shares borders to the north with Egypt, to the east with Eritrea and Ethiopia, to the south with Kenya, Uganda and Zaire, and to the west with the Central African Republic, Chad, and to a small extent Libya. Very little of its terrain is suitable for cultivation, except for a limited area around the River Nile and its tributaries the Atbara, the Blue Nile and the White Nile. The capital is Khartoum.

Head of State   President Omar Hassan Ahmad Al-Bashir

Head of Government   President Omar Hassan Ahmad Al-Bashir

Ruling Party   All parties are banned, but the National Islamic Front is influential.

Political Structure   The elected regime was overthrown in 1989 and the leaders have dominated Sudanese politics since then. Led by Gen. Al-Bashir, the military rulers dissolved the National Assembly and instituted what amounted to rule by decree in order to enforce drastic austerity measures. In 1992 and 1993, public protests forced them to create a 300-member Transitional National Assembly and dissolve the ruling Revolutionary Command Council in favour of a new civilian government. The country's nine existing regions were later divided into 26 in order to facilitate administration and allow better regional development. The overriding problem is the bloody civil war which has been waged by separatist guerrillas in the south of the country since the 1980s.

Last Elections   A general election, the first since the suspension of the Constitution in 1989, was held in March 1996. President Al-Bashir and most of his cabinet were re-elected.

Political Risk   War between the Arabic-speaking, Islamic north and the African and Christian south has been waged off and on for decades. The rebels, known as the Sudan People's Liberation Army (SPLA) have several times been near defeat. Now, they have regrouped and rearmed and could be on their way to success. Isolated by the international community, the government's own coffers are empty and it is having difficulty keeping its ragtag army in the field. The worst public disturbances in the lifetime of the fundamentalist regime occurred in Khartoum in late 1995. The riots grew out of student-led, anti-government protests against rises in food prices.

International Disputes   The SPLA is being supported by Uganda, Kenya, Ethiopia, Eritrea and Egypt, all of whom have become increasingly fearful of Sudanese support for armed Islamic movements. Only Kenya maintains relations with the National Islamic Front (NIF) in Khartoum. Other countries further afield, including the USA, take an equally dim view of the NIF's support for what they see as terrorism. Sudan may soon face UN sanctions for harbouring men suspected of trying to assassinate Egypt's president in 1995.

Economy   Sudan's economy has suffered badly owing to recurrent droughts, a slump in the world prices of its main exports and the resumption of the civil war.

Main Industries   Farming is the main source of income for the great majority of the population, with sugar, wheat, millet and sorghum grown for domestic consumption, while groundnuts and oilseeds are some of the main export crops. Cattle are herded, mainly by nomads, in the desert. Agricultural production has reached new lows as the economy is ground down and farmers are excluded from large portions of the country while the war rages. Manufacturing accounts for only about 5% of GDP. with cement, timber processing, textiles and leather goods being the main products.

Energy   The country has almost adequate supplies of oil and natural gas, and some hydro-electric potential but its energy-producing facilities have been ravaged in the war.

	1993	1994	1995
Inflation (% change)	101.4	127.7	
Exchange rate (per US$)	153.85	277.78	53.13
Interest rate			
GDP (% real growth)			
GDP (Million units of national currency)	1,246,410.1	3,008,360.3	
GDP (US$ million)	28,130.0	28,936.0	28,302.6
GDP per capita (US$)	1,000.0	999.5	950.0
Consumption (Million units of national currency)	902,773.7	2,178,952.7	
Consumption (US$ million)	5,867.9	7,844.2	7,448.1
Consumption per capita (US$)	208.6	271.0	250.0
Population, mid-year ('000)	28,130.0	28,950.0	29,792.2
Birth rate (per '000)	39.8	42.0	
Death rate (per '000)	13.1	13.9	
No. of households ('000)	4,555.5	4,709.5	4,864.0
Total exports (US$ million)	200.0	229.2	
Total imports (US$ million)	850.0	1,240.8	
Tourism receipts (US$ million)	3.0	4.0	
Tourist spending (US$ million)	31.8	42.0	39.9

Average household size 1995 (persons)	5.82				
Urban population 1995 (%)	24.6				
Age analysis (%) (1983)	*0-14* 44.0		*15-64* 53.0		*65+* 3.0
Population by sex (%) (1993)	*Male* 50.2		*Female* 49.8		
Life expectancy (years) (1990-95)	*Male* 51.6		*Female* 54.4		
Infant mortality (deaths per '000 live births) (1993)	78.1				
Adult literacy (%) (1995)	46.1				

TRADING PARTNERS

Major export destinations 1995 (% share)		Major import sources 1995 (% share)	
Saudi Arabia	15.5	Libya	17.2
China	12.5	Saudi Arabia	8.8
Italy	11.8	Egypt	6.4
Japan	6.5	France	6.2

Suriname

Area (km²)   163,820

Currency   Suriname guilder (Sf = 100 cents)

Location   Suriname is located on the north-eastern Atlantic coast of South America, where it is flanked in the west by Guyana, in the east by French Guiana and in the south by Brazil. The major settlements are on the coast. Further inland, the dense jungle gives way to a high sierra where the only cultivable crop is balata, a rubbery sap obtained from certain trees. The capital is Paramaribo.

Head of State   President Ronald Venetiaan (September 1991)

Head of Government   Jules Adjodhia

Ruling Party   The New Front for Democracy and Development is the ruling coalition.

Political Structure   The Republic of Suriname gained its independence from the Netherlands in 1975, and continued for some years to receive aid. In the late 1970s, however, a corrupt government plunged the country into a protracted civil war, against which background a succession of coups and counter-coups took place. The situation had eased by 1993, following another military coup, and since then the politicians have been attempting to dilute the influence of the armed forces. The executive President is chosen by an electoral college, as is a Prime Minister who answers to a 51-member National Assembly elected by popular vote for a five-year term.

Last Elections   In general elections held in May 1996, the incumbent president, Ronald Venetiaan, and his New Front coalition narrowly defeated the National Democratic Party (NDP), which is led by the former military strongman, Desi Bouterse. Despite charges of election fraud, Venetiaan's New Front took a majority of the 51 seats in the National Assembly while the NDP captured only 11.

Political Risk   The comparative political peace in recent years has revived hopes that the country, with its substantial mineral resources, can achieve a high degree of economic activity. Guerrilla hostilities have theoretically been suspended since 1992, although opposition to the Government remains at a high level in the bush.

International Disputes   Suriname has outstanding territorial claims against its two neighbours, Guyana and French Guiana, although neither claim is being pressed hard at present. In both cases the disputes arise from nineteenth-century uncertainties as to the course of rivers through impenetrable jungle; Suriname is claiming about 8,000 sq km from French Guiana and some 20,000 sq km from Guyana.

Economy   Suriname's economy has been damaged, though not entirely devastated, by the ongoing civil disturbances and by the periodic drops in the world price for bauxite, its chief export product. With the restoration of political calm, some improvement has occurred and the gains should be sustainable in the 1990s. In 1993, the country's currency, the guilder, was decoupled from the US dollar.

Main Industries   Bauxite and low-grade iron ore are present in massive quantities, and are exported in both crude and processed form. The drawback is that the country depends crucially on these mining operations; a three-month mining strike in 1993 almost wrecked the economy. Agriculture is limited to the coastal regions, where the terrain is more accessible and products range from sugar and banana plantations to rice (the staple crop) and vegetables. Further inland, timber and forestry are important, and a huge and controversial timber extraction project was announced in early 1994. In the high sierras, balata (a form of ersatz rubber) is extracted from trees. Manufacturing is limited to the fulfilment of basic local needs; most consumer products are imported.

Energy   Suriname has immense and largely realised hydro-electric potential in its upland jungle areas, as well as some oil resources offshore.

	1993	1994	1995
Inflation (% change)	143.5	368.5	235.9
Exchange rate (per US$)	1.79	409.50	435.80
Interest rate			
GDP (% real growth)			
GDP (Million units of national currency)	11,862.2		
GDP (US$ million)	6,626.9	2,001.5	1,817.3
GDP per capita (US$)	16,163.2	15,778.4	4,300.0
Consumption			
Consumption (US$ million)	961.3	1,040.8	1,105.6
Consumption per capita (US$)	2,345.0	2,478.1	2,616.0
Population, mid-year ('000)	410.0	420.0	422.6
Birth rate (per '000)	25.7	25.3	
Death rate (per '000)	6.0	6.0	
No. of households ('000)	82.7	83.1	83.4
Total exports (US$ million)	351.0	450.8	
Total imports (US$ million)	300.0	427.3	
Tourism receipts (US$ million)	11.0	12.1	
Tourist spending (US$ million)	12.7	14.0	14.9

Average household size 1995 (persons)	4.81				
Urban population 1995 (%)	50.4				
Age analysis (%) (1990)	*0-14* 41.7		*15-64* 54.2		*65+* 4.1
Population by sex (%) (1990)	*Male* 47.9		*Female* 52.1		
Life expectancy (years) (1990-95)	*Male* 67.8		*Female* 71.3		
Infant mortality (deaths per '000 live births) (1993)	27.9				
Adult literacy (%) (1995)	93.0				

TRADING PARTNERS

Major export destinations 1995 (% share)		Major import sources 1995 (% share)	
Norway	26.3	USA	37.3
USA	18.9	Netherlands	5.9
Netherlands	13.6	Trinidad and Tobago	4.3
Brazil	5.0	Netherlands Antilles	3.8

Swaziland

Area (km²) 17,365

Currency Lilangeni (L = 100 cents)

Location Swaziland is a landlocked state in southern Africa, bordered in the east by Mozambique and on all other sides by South Africa. Four rivers ensure a satisfactory flow of irrigation to the lowlands; higher up the land turns to mountain ranges. The climate is tropical but pleasant. The capital is Mbabane.

Head of State HM King Mswati III (1986)

Head of Government Prince Jameson Mbilini Dlamini (1994)

Ruling Party All political parties are banned under the 1978 constitutional amendments.

Political Structure The Kingdom of Swaziland, an independent member of the Commonwealth, is the only absolute monarchy in sub-Saharan Africa. All political activity has been banned since 1973, when King Sobhuza II took "supreme power". His successor, the current king, has relaxed the rules a bit. He appoints the Prime Minister and Cabinet directly and they answer to him rather than to the 65-member House of Assembly or the 30-member Senate. Current practice is for 55 members of the House of Assembly and 10 Senators to be elected by the 40 traditional tribal communities, with the King appointing all the others. Evidence of mild dissatisfaction with the monarchy and calls for greater democratisation are becoming more frequent.

Last Elections The first non-party elections took place in August and November 1993, to the House of Assembly in which the former Prime Minister, Obed Dlamini was removed from office and replaced with the conservative Mbilini Dlamini.

Political Risk Swaziland remains one of the few societies outside the Middle East which is entirely dominated by tribal loyalties, as distinct from political debate. There is little evidence of any trend toward multi-party democracy. Opponents of the current regime, who are led by Swaziland's Federation of Trade Unions, do not seek to overthrow the monarchy but merely turn it into a figurehead. Only the most dedicated revolutionaries want free politics and multi-party elections.

International Disputes Swaziland has been accused of harbouring refugees from neighbouring Mozambique in violation of a repatriation agreement was reached in late 1993.

Economy With a per capita GDP of around US$800, Swaziland ranks among the more prosperous countries of the region. Thanks to its well-diversified economy, it has proved fairly robust in the face of collapsing commodity prices, though recent instabilities have brought difficulties.

Main Industries The agricultural sector is still the most important area of the economy for most of the population, supporting subsistence crops such as sugar cane, cereals and fruit as well as cash crops such as pineapples and cotton. Manufacturing contributes 25% of GDP, although the country's output is mainly destined only for domestic consumption. Specialities include brewing, timber products, textiles and various crafts. The country earns much of its foreign exchange from the weekend visits of South Africans who come for gambling and the wildlife and from remittances by Swazis working in South Africa's mines and factories.

Energy Swaziland has an ample supply of hydro-electric power, but otherwise few natural energy resources, all of which have to be imported.

	1993	1994	1995
Inflation (% change)	17.0	14.3	14.7
Exchange rate (per US$)	3.26	3.55	3.63
Interest rate (% per annum)	14.0	15.0	18.0
GDP (% real growth)	0.3	-8.0	2.0
GDP (Million units of national currency)	2,501.3	2,630.0	3,076.9
GDP (US$ million)	767.3	740.8	847.6
GDP per capita (US$)	902.7	841.9	931.5
Consumption (Million units of national currency)	1,478.6	1,659.7	2,072.9
Consumption (US$ million)	453.6	467.5	571.1
Consumption per capita (US$)	533.6	531.3	627.5
Population, mid-year ('000)	850.0	880.0	910.0
Birth rate (per '000)	46.2	43.1	
Death rate (per '000)	10.5	11.1	
No. of households ('000)	137.9	141.5	145.2
Total exports (US$ million)	738.0	742.0	833.0
Total imports (US$ million)	874.0	937.0	1,060.0
Tourism receipts (US$ million)	30.0	31.8	
Tourist spending (US$ million)	17.0	18.0	22.0

Average household size 1995 (persons)	5.95				
Urban population 1995 (%)	31.2				
Age analysis (%) (1986)	*0-14* 47.4		*15-64* 48.8		*65+* 3.8
Population by sex (%) (1986)	*Male* 47.2		*Female* 52.8		
Life expectancy (years) (1990-95)	*Male* 55.2		*Female* 59.8		
Infant mortality (deaths per '000 live births) (1993)	75.2				
Adult literacy (%) (1995)	76.7				

Sweden

Area (km²)   449,790

Currency   Swedish kronor (Skr = 100 öre)

Location   Sweden occupies the eastern and southern section of the Scandinavian peninsula which runs south-west from the Arctic Circle to meet with Denmark across the narrow sea channel which gives access to the Baltic from the North Sea. With a predominantly hilly and mountainous terrain, but without oil resources like Norway, it relies heavily on its heavily forested hills for much of its revenues. The main population centres are in the south and east. The capital is Stockholm.

Head of State   HM King Carl XVI Gustaf (1973)

Head of Government   Goran Persson (1996)

Ruling Party   Sveriges Socialdemokratiska Arbetareparti leads a coalition with the Left Party and the Environment Party

Political Structure   Sweden is a constitutional monarchy in which the King appoints the Prime Minister on the basis of parliamentary advice. Legislative authority is vested in a unicameral 394-seat Parliament (Riksdag), which is elected by universal suffrage for a term of only three years. Sweden became a full member of the EU in January 1995 - having been in the European Monetary System for many years.

Last Elections   General elections in September 1994 produced a rout for the centre-right coalition of Moderates, Liberals and Centre Party delegates which had governed since 1989. Although the three ruling parties won 80, 26 and 27 seats, respectively, they were unable to hold their majority against the Sveriges Socialdemokratiska Arbetareparti, which had ruled for 51 of the last 62 years, and which increased its representation from 132 seats to 162. The Left Party, meanwhile, improved from 16 seats in 1989 to 22 seats, and the Miljöpartiet de Grona (Green Party) regained 18 seats, having lost all its seats in 1989 after failing to reach the 4% threshold needed for parliamentary representation. Instead the Ny Demokrati lost all its 25 seats under the same electoral provision.

Political Risk   Despite the economic difficulties of the moment, the Swedish political system is in no danger whatever of affording a significant political risk in terms of either consumer markets or investment. Indeed, the removal of long-standing obstacles to foreign share ownership may be taken as a token of good faith. Membership in the EU was expected to bring other benefits but a majority of the population are now anti-EU and oppose European Monetary Union (EMU). Although Sweden remains technically neutral in defence terms, it joined the United States' "Partnership for Peace" operation in May 1994.

International Disputes   Finland and Sweden disagree over the ownership of a group of islands in the Gulf of Bothnia, which Finland, the current owner, calls Ahvenanmaa and Sweden calls the Aaland Islands. The issue will not sour bilateral relations, however. Of more immediate interest has been the controversy surrounding Sweden's proposed road link with Copenhagen in Denmark, which has aroused fierce opposition among environmentalists, although construction is now well underway.

Economy   Sweden's per capita income was the highest in the world during most of the past quarter of a century but by 1995 the country's ranking had fallen to 17th. In the same period, Sweden's direct and indirect taxes rose to 56% and public spending reached 72% of GDP - by far the highest of any OECD country. Throughout the 1980s Sweden also managed to keep unemployment down but now the country is falling behind by that measure as well; as the economy shrinks, the number of jobless has reached 8%. The country continues to be one of the richest markets in Europe but this combination of slow growth and high debt will force the new government to scale back on Sweden's vaunted welfare system. That will inevitably cause public dissatisfaction but no economy can long sustain levels of public spending exceeding 70% of GDP.

Main Industries   The manufacturing sector dominates the Swedish economy and includes major industries which range from motor vehicles to aerospace, chemicals, pharmaceuticals, timber processing and pulp and paper. Farming is the main livelihood in large parts of the country, especially in the north; but elsewhere forestry is still the mainstay of the local economy. The services sector, which includes a range of banks, insurance companies and related institutions, suffered a sharp decline in the early 1990s but has now recovered and is highly developed.

Energy   Sweden has no indigenous fuels except for its hydro-electric energy and has pledged to shut its nuclear power plants by the year 2010. There are objections to this move, and it could eventually be rejected. If the pledge is withdrawn, Sweden's businesses would be much relieved since the stations currently supply 45% of Sweden's electricity. It is not yet clear what alternative power sources would be used if nuclear power is phased out.

	1993	1994	1995
Inflation (% change)	4.6	2.2	2.5
Exchange rate (per US$)	7.78	7.72	7.14
Interest rate (% per annum)	11.4	10.6	12.6
GDP (% real growth)	-2.7	2.9	1.0
GDP (Billion units of national currency)	1,442.0	1,517.0	1,570.4
GDP (US$ million)	185,347.0	196,496.1	219,947.1
GDP per capita (US$)	21,255.4	22,354.5	24,909.1
Consumption (Billion units of national currency)	770.8	798.2	825.9
Consumption (US$ million)	99,074.6	103,393.8	115,672.3
Consumption per capita (US$)	11,361.8	11,762.7	13,099.9
Population, mid-year ('000)	8,720.0	8,790.0	8,830.0
Birth rate (per '000)	13.5	12.8	11.6
Death rate (per '000)	11.1	10.3	11.0
No. of households ('000)	3,832.0	3,856.2	3,880.0
Total exports (US$ million)	49,857.0	61,292.0	79,908.0
Total imports (US$ million)	42,681.0	51,725.0	64,438.0
Tourism receipts (US$ million)	2,650.0	2,821.2	
Tourist spending (US$ million)	4,484.0	4,752.4	5,316.8

Average household size 1995 (persons)	2.16				
Urban population 1995 (%)	83.1				
Age analysis (%) (1995)	*0-14* 20.0		*15-64* 62.0		*65+* 18.0
Population by sex (%) (1995)	*Male* 49.4		*Female* 50.6		
Life expectancy (years) (1994)	*Male* 76.1		*Female* 81.9		
Infant mortality (deaths per '000 live births) (1994)	3.4				
Adult literacy (%) (1982)	99.0				

TRADING PARTNERS

Major export destinations 1995 (% share)		Major import sources 1995 (% share)	
Germany	10.9	Germany	20.5
United Kingdom	7.8	United Kingdom	10.1
USA	7.4	France	7.5
Denmark	6.2	Norway	6.9

Switzerland

Area (km²)   41,285

Currency   Swiss franc (SFr = 100 centimes/rappen)

Location   Centrally located in southern Europe, Switzerland's three official languages (French, German and Italian) reflect its three most important neighbours - although Austria to the east is also a major trade partner. Switzerland represents Liechtenstein at diplomatic level. The capital is Berne.

Head of State   President Jean-Pascal Delamuraz (1996)

Head of Government   Jean-Pascal Delamuraz (1996)

Ruling Party   Power is shared by the Christian Democrats (CVP), Radical Democrats (FDP), People's Party and the Social Democratic Party (SDP).

Political Structure   Switzerland is a federation of 20 cantons and 6 half-cantons which include German, French, Italian and Romansch speakers. The first three of these are official languages, while Romansch is a "semi-official" language. There is a high degree of political devolution. At the federal level, the executive President is elected every year from among the seven-member Cabinet. There is a 200-member Nationalrat (Lower House of Parliament). Although Switzerland is considering applying to join the United Nations, and the International Monetary Fund, it has decisively rejected membership of the EU.

Last Elections   Elections to the Nationalrat in October 1995 produced a clear polarisation within the four-party coalition that has ruled the country since 1959. The left-wing SDP and the right-wing People's Party both recorded advances at the expense of the two centrist parties. Curiously, the two big winners advocate markedly different approaches on major issues. The People's party strongly opposes membership in the EU, it rejects liberalised distribution of hard drugs and supports big spending cuts to balance the federal budget. The SDP intends to fight equally hard for the preservation of social entitlements and for Switzerland's participation in European integration. The net result of this outcome is likely to be a political paralysis which satisfies very few voters.

Political Risk   Famous for its legendary political stability and its principled refusal to align with any other world movement, Switzerland now faces somewhat of an identity crisis. Since 1995 the country has become an island totally surrounded by the EU. The country's new status penalises some industries which produce components and parts in EU countries and then assemble these in Switzerland. Big contractors to the public sector have been hurt by public procurement rules of the EU or the European Economic Area. Switzerland's economic backbone, the financial services sector, has also come under great competitive pressure not only from within the EU but also from rival offshore banking centres.

International Disputes   Switzerland voted, in a referendum in February 1994, for a measure banning foreign lorries from transit travel with effect from 2004; it also voted to ban the construction or enlargement of motorways intended to facilitate transit travel. The decision is a severe blow to the EU, which has registered protests at what it sees as an unwelcome precedent.

Economy   The Swiss economy was transformed in the 1960s by the influx of financial services, which quickly replaced the fading agricultural system as a source of revenue. A well-developed industrial structure contributed to an all-round stability which proved attractive to foreign investors. Yet the country faces possible isolation after its refusals to join the European Economic Area and the EU. Economic growth in 1994 and 1995 was less than 3%, following a real contraction of 2.3% in 1993. Because exports account for more than a third of Swiss GDP, each 5% rise in the external value of the franc is estimated to cut 0.5% off the economic growth rate. Thus the gradual rise in the country's currency is proving a real drag on growth.

Main Industries   The financial services sector, which owes its prominence to the country's liberal tax laws and banking secrecy rules, has suffered owing to the growing strength of rival markets and the international community's demands to relax bank secrecy laws in order to combat money laundering. Industry includes a wide range of precision engineering, electronic, pharmaceutical and textile products, as well as wood manufactures and construction. However, farming relies on heavy subsidies and is maintained more out of a sense of heritage than for reasons of economic efficiency. Tourism, especially winter sports, is an important part of the economy. It employs as much as a fifth of the workforce during some months of the year and is the country's third-largest earner of foreign exchange. The rise in the value of the Swiss franc and improvements in holiday facilities in Austria, Italy and France have led to a downturn in the country's tourist receipts, however.

Energy   Switzerland has no indigenous fuel sources whatever, apart from its hydro-electric potential and is forced to rely on nuclear power to an unusual degree. All other fuel must be imported.

	1993	1994	1995
Inflation (% change)	3.3	0.8	1.8
Exchange rate (per US$)	1.48	1.37	1.18
Interest rate (% per annum)	6.4	5.5	6.6
GDP (% real growth)	-2.3	2.8	2.7
GDP (Billion units of national currency)	343.0	356.0	360.6
GDP (US$ million)	231,756.8	259,854.0	305,593.2
GDP per capita (US$)	33,394.3	37,175.1	43,408.1
Consumption (Billion units of national currency)	202.3	206.5	210.8
Consumption (US$ million)	136,689.2	150,729.9	178,644.1
Consumption per capita (US$)	19,695.8	21,563.7	25,375.6
Population, mid-year ('000)	6,940.0	6,990.0	7,040.0
Birth rate (per '000)	12.1	11.9	11.7
Death rate (per '000)	9.0	8.9	8.7
No. of households ('000)	2,832.0	2,849.6	2,898.0
Total exports (US$ million)	58,687.0	66,227.0	77,649.0
Total imports (US$ million)	56,716.0	64,074.0	76,985.0
Tourism receipts (US$ million)	7,001.0	9,357.7	
Tourist spending (US$ million)	5,803.0	8,036.5	9,524.8

Average household size 1995 (persons)	2.31				
Urban population 1995 (%)	60.8				
Age analysis (%) (1995)	*0-14* 19.2		*15-64* 67.0		*65+* 13.8
Population by sex (%) (1995)	*Male* 48.9		*Female* 51.1		
Life expectancy (years) (1994)	*Male* 75.4		*Female* 81.6		
Infant mortality (deaths per '000 live births) (1994)	5.1				
Adult literacy (%) (1984)	100.0				

TRADING PARTNERS

Major export destinations 1995 (% share)		Major import sources 1995 (% share)	
Germany	24.5	Germany	35.1
France	10.0	France	11.8
USA	9.1	Italy	10.5
Italy	8.0	USA	6.6

Syria

Area (km²)   185,680

Currency   Syrian pound (£Syr = 100 piastres)

Location   Syria owes its unusual political influence to its position in the extreme north-east of the Mediterranean, where the Islamic Middle East meets with Israel on the one hand and secular Turkey on the other. Its Mediterranean coastline, in fact, is no more than 150 km. More important is the country's long eastern and south-eastern border with Iraq and Jordan, and that with Lebanon and Israel in the south-west. The climate is cool Middle Eastern, with occasional cold winters. The capital is Damascus.

Head of State   President Hafez al Assad (1971)

Head of Government   Mahmoud Zubi

Ruling Party   Ba'ath Party leads the National Progressive Front coalition.

Political Structure   The country's 1973 Constitution calls for an executive President who is formally elected by universal suffrage every seven years. In principle, the President answers to a People's Assembly of 250 members who are elected for four years. In practice, however, the Alawite group around President Assad has dominated Syrian politics since he seized power in 1970 and most decisions are taken by the ruling Ba'ath Arab Socialist Renaissance party.

Last Elections   The last elections to the Majlis (Parliament) took place in August 1994, when the Ba'ath Party and its allies won 167 of the 250 seats and went on to reform the existing coalition. Independents won the other 83 seats - one fewer than in the 1991 elections. Hafez al Assad was reconfirmed as president after being approved in an uncontested national referendum.

Political Risk   Syria's relations with the West have improved dramatically since the late 1980s, thanks to a gradual moderation of its anti-Israeli line, an active peacemaking policy in Lebanon and a firm stand in favour of Iran and against Iraq following the Iraqi invasion of Kuwait in August 1991. The Syrian-Israeli peace talks did not progress during the first half of 1996 but are still very much alive, despite the interruptions. Domestically, there is little open opposition to President Assad.

International Disputes   Syria's involvement in the Lebanon conflict initially led to a complete breakdown in its relations with Israel but, today, the Israelis probably prefer to have Syrian forces in Lebanon than to depend on the Lebanese. Syria's relations with Turkey are occasionally tense because it claims the Hatay Province lying south of the two countries' 1921-1939 boundary. Syria, however, co-operates with Turkey with regard to the substantial contingent of Kurds in its north-eastern corner. Like Turkey and Iraq, it rejects their demands for a separate Kurdish state, and has sometimes permitted Turkish forces to cross the border in "hot pursuit" operations.

Economy   Syria has been slowly reforming its centrally planned economy ever since it lost its main benefactor, the Soviet Union. A new investment law has brought in more than $5 billion in additional capital from Syrian expatriates and the wealthy of Damascus and Aleppo. The development of private enterprise has been concentrated mainly in import trade, retailing and tourism. Most of the government (including President Assad) is unenthusiastic about the emergence of a free market. They cite Russia's experience as an example to avoid and have no wish to anger the hundreds of thousands employed in state-run enterprises.

Main Industries   Farming, the main activity, is concentrated mainly on the Mediterranean coastline. Most of the eastern area of the country is arid uplands but there are extensive irrigation schemes in the north-east, along the Euphrates. Cotton and tobacco are cash crops, while wheat, barley and fruit are grown for the domestic market. Farmers hope their economic position will improve as a result of the government's promise to extend irrigation schemes and to pay them world prices for their crops. Industry tends to centre on raw materials processing, and includes textiles, soap making, glass, plastics and fertilisers. Development of the manufacturing sector is constrained by a host of obstacles including export taxes, a shortage of credit and a corrupt and sluggish bureaucracy. Phosphates and asphalt are mined but the country has ample deposits of other natural resources that have yet to be developed.

Energy   In the short term, the country is held together by its oil exports, which are worth $2 billion per year and equivalent to nearly 60% of total export earnings, and the last disbursements of Kuwait's and Saudi Arabia's financial reward for Syria's part in the Gulf war. Unfortunately, today's oil fields are expected to run dry within eight years, and tough terms give foreign companies little incentive to look for others.

	1993	1994	1995
Inflation (% change)	11.8	9.2	7.0
Exchange rate (per US$)	11.23	11.23	40.77
Interest rate			
GDP (% real growth)	-4.3	0.1	0.5
GDP (Million units of national currency)	413,755.0	496,504.0	
GDP (US$ million)	36,843.7	44,212.3	39,000.0
GDP per capita (US$)	2,751.6	3,194.5	2,725.4
Consumption (Million units of national currency)	294,417.0	318,730.0	
Consumption (US$ million)	26,217.0	28,382.0	28,630.0
Consumption per capita (US$)	1,958.0	2,050.7	2,000.7
Population, mid-year ('000)	13,390.0	13,840.0	14,310.0
Birth rate (per '000)	27.7	28.8	
Death rate (per '000)		3.3	
No. of households ('000)	2,692.6	2,822.0	2,950.0
Total exports (US$ million)	3,146.0	3,547.0	4,044.0
Total imports (US$ million)	4,140.0	5,467.0	4,480.0
Tourism receipts (US$ million)	700.0	742.0	
Tourist spending (US$ million)	300.0	318.0	320.8

Average household size 1995 (persons)	4.61				
Urban population 1995 (%)	52.4				
Age analysis (%) (1992)	*0-14* 49.2		*15-64* 46.4		*65+* 4.4
Population by sex (%) (1992)	*Male* 51.1		*Female* 48.9		
Life expectancy (years) (1981)	*Male* 64.4		*Female* 68.1		
Infant mortality (deaths per '000 live births) (1993)	10.9				
Adult literacy (%) (1995)	70.8				

TRADING PARTNERS

Major export destinations 1995 (% share)		Major import sources 1995 (% share)	
Italy	18.2	Italy	9.0
Lebanon	13.8	Germany	8.7
Germany	13.8	USA	4.3
Spain	9.0	France	4.0

Taiwan

Area (km²) 35,990

Currency New Taiwan dollar (NT$ = 100 cents)

Location Taiwan is principally located on what was formerly known as the island of Formosa, a territory no more than 400 km from north to south which lies between the South China Sea and the East China Sea about 200 km off the coast of mainland China and about 700 km north-east of Hong Kong. The capital is Taipei.

Head of State President Lee Teng-Hui (1988)

Head of Government Lien Chan (1993)

Ruling Party Kuomintang

Political Structure Taiwan, the self-styled Republic of China, has been governed continuously since its foundation in 1947 by the right-wing Kuomintang founded by the nationalist leader Chiang Kai-shek. The executive President had traditionally elected by an electoral college for a six-year term of office, but in 1996 the island held its first popular presidential elections.

Last Elections With 54% of all votes cast, President Lee Teng-Hui received unexpectedly strong support in the 1996 elections. His closet rival, Peng Ming-min, garnered only 21% of the vote. Ming later predicted that his Democratic Progressive Party may disband. With Lee's huge mandate, he will now cautiously begin to build a consensus on some common approach to the mainland question.

Political Risk China's pre-election demonstration of naval and military might in the Straits of Taiwan did nothing to intimidate Taiwanese voters. President Lee has hinted that Taiwan and the mainland might soon take action to ease tensions. At the same time, he has put China on notice that he will not give up his crusade to win a seat for Taiwan in the United Nations. Beijing bitterly opposes such thinking because it undermines the mainland's "one China" policy. Meanwhile, Taiwan has its own problem at home with its 350,000 aborigines, who are known as "mountain people". Immediately following the elections, the government announced a set of programmes to reduce the huge divide between these people and the Han Chinese.

International Disputes In the aftermath of Taiwan's 1996 elections, China has quieted its threats while the island's president has once again obliquely suggested the possibility of closer links with the mainland. The prospect of immediate confrontation has died down but the conflict between the entrenched nationalism of China and the nascent nationalism of Taiwan will persist. In addition, Taiwan is one of the many claimants (including China) for the sovereignty of the oil-rich Spratly islands in the South China Sea.

Economy Taiwan's highly diversified and successful economy has been created in the face of considerable obstacles, not all of which have yet been addressed. The Government's protectionist stance with regard to its major industries and financial markets is beginning to draw more criticism, not only from the United States but also from other major trading partners. Future prospects will depend heavily on conditions on the mainland and the performance of the Chinese economy. Trade between the two countries is flourishing (despite the tense political atmosphere) and Taiwanese investors are a major source of capital for Chinese industries.

Main Industries Taiwan's industrial sector is technologically sophisticated and highly advanced. The industrial base is unusual since it mainly depends on many small, economically nimble companies rather than a handful of very large ones. Prominent industries include: electronics, vehicle manufacturing, precision engineering, textiles and clothing, chemicals and pharmaceuticals. Agriculture still provides the major source of employment, with production of sugar, yams, rice, tea and bananas as well as vegetables and fruit for domestic consumption. Fishing is very important.

Energy Apart from coal and a small quantity of oil, Taiwan has no fuel resources of its own and is obliged to import all requirements, mostly from Indonesia. The country has its own petroleum processing facilities, however.

	1993	1994	1995
Inflation (% change)	3.6	3.8	3.7
Exchange rate (per US$)	26.63	26.46	26.49
Interest rate			
GDP (% real growth)	6.5	-0.6	0.2
GDP (Million units of national currency)	5,874,513.0	6,058,817.9	6,295,600.0
GDP (US$ million)	220,597.6	228,980.3	237,659.5
GDP per capita (US$)	10,605.7	10,903.8	11,210.4
Consumption (Million units of national currency)	3,345,885.0	3,515,183.4	3,720,644.4
Consumption (US$ million)	125,643.4	132,849.0	140,454.7
Consumption per capita (US$)	6,040.6	6,326.1	6,625.2
Population, mid-year ('000)	20,800.0	21,000.0	21,200.0
Birth rate (per '000)	14.5	15.6	
Death rate (per '000)	4.9	5.3	
No. of households ('000)	5,501.5	5,598.0	5,698.0
Total exports (US$ million)	84,678.0	89,900.0	
Total imports (US$ million)	77,087.0	80,500.0	
Tourism receipts (US$ million)	2,943.0	3,608.0	
Tourist spending (US$ million)	7,585.0	7,915.2	8,368.4

Average household size 1995 (persons)	3.53				
Urban population 1995 (%)	75.0				
Age analysis (%) (1992)	*0-14*	32.6	*15-64*	61.6	*65+* 5.8
Population by sex (%) (1992)	*Male*	51.7	*Female*	48.3	
Life expectancy (years) (1992)	*Male*	71.9	*Female*	77.2	
Infant mortality (deaths per '000 live births)					
Adult literacy (%) (1980)	88.0				

Tajikistan

Area (km²)   143,100

Currency   The Tajik rouble was introduced in May 1995: until then, all data were in Russian roubles

Location   Tajikistan, almost the southernmost point of the former Soviet Union, is a predominantly Moslem state which borders on Afghanistan and China in the south. But for the Hindu Kush, a narrow tongue of Afghan territory, it would also meet Pakistan. In the west it borders on Uzbekistan and in the north-east on Kyrgyzstan. With a mainly dry climate but with well-irrigated soil, it produces cotton and similar crops. The capital is Dushanbe.

Head of State   Imamali Sharipovich Rakhmonov

Head of Government   Jamshed Karimov (December 1994)

Ruling Party   Communist Party of Tajikistan

Political Structure   Tajikistan declared its independence from the Soviet Union in August 1991. A six-month civil war followed shortly afterwards. Ex-communists from the west of the country deposed an alliance of Islamists and secular democrats from the east. The ex-communists now run the government but sporadic violence continues. Tajikistan has seen fewer changes than most ex-Soviet states and is still watched closely by its former masters in Moscow. Nearly all opposition is from Islamic parties - four of which were banned in June 1993 after allegations of terrorism. There is a 230-member Parliament, elected by popular vote, and since 1994 the President has been directly elected: before this, he was appointed by the Parliament.

Last Elections   Presidential elections were held in November 1994, when Imamali Sharipovich Rahmonov, a former chairman of the Supreme Soviet, was re-elected as head of state. But the appointment proved controversial, as it had done in 1991. All Islamic parties and their supporters abstained from the vote. The last elections to the Supreme Soviet were held in March 1990, before independence, when the Communist Party scored an overwhelming victory.

Political Risk   The fifth round of peace talks, arranged by the UN, resumed in Turkmenistan in February 1996. The opposition Islamists and democrats want a share in government but, so far, the ex-communists have refused. Despite Russian pressure for a settlement based on power-sharing, the talks have made no progress so far. The government's opponents, especially in Kulyab and Khodent, continue to engage in armed resistance. In 1996, the mufti, or religious leader of the country, was gunned down. Similar killings of other leading political and religious figures have added to the tension. In April 1996, Tajikistan signed a political-military treaty with Russia, China, Kyrgyzstan and Kazakhstan intended to enhance mutual trust in the region.

International Disputes   Tajikistan has no major outstanding territorial claims at present. However, the country has a long history of involvement in war and unrest which links it to Afghanistan, Russia and China. The Russians regard the country as part of what they call their "near abroad". With their hands full in Chechnya, the Russians want an early peace settlement of Tajikistan's problems.

Economy   Political troubles have prevented Tajikistan from making any attempt to reform its moribund economy. Instead, the government relies on Russian handouts. Tajikistan has few significant economic activities other than farming, producing mainly livestock products. Food shortages are becoming serious, however. The prices of bread and grain have reached astronomical levels with many food processing activities being controlled by racketeers. Mercedes cars and other ostentatious forms of consumption are proliferating, though none of this wealth has been generated through the market economy.

Energy   Tajikistan has large but mainly untapped natural gas and oil supplies; efforts are under way to attract foreign investment in the sector. Hydro-electric power contributes to domestic supply.

	1993	1994	1995
Inflation (% change)	300.0	-80.0	
Exchange rate (per US$)			
Interest rate			
GDP (% real growth)	-17.2	-12.0	-20.5
GDP			
GDP (US$ million)	3,475.9	3,115.0	2,516.4
GDP per capita (US$)	616.3	541.7	430.9
Consumption			
Consumption (US$ million)			
Consumption per capita (US$)			
Population, mid-year ('000)	5,640.0	5,750.0	5,840.0
Birth rate (per '000)	33.1	34.8	
Death rate (per '000)		6.7	
No. of households ('000)	1,203.8	1,233.4	1,265.0
Total exports (US$ million)	173.3	274.0	
Total imports (US$ million)	103.3	174.0	
Tourism receipts (US$ million)			
Tourist spending (US$ million)			

Average household size 1995 (persons)	4.39				
Urban population 1995 (%)	32.2				
Age analysis (%) (1992, est)	*0-14* 48.6	*15-64* 47.1	*65+* 4.3
Population by sex (%) (1989)	*Male* 49.7	*Female* 50.3	
Life expectancy (years) (1989)	*Male* 66.8	*Female* 71.7	
Infant mortality (deaths per '000 live births) (1993)	47.0		
Adult literacy (%) (1989)	97.7		

TRADING PARTNERS

Major export destinations 1995 (% share)		Major import sources 1995 (% share)	
Russia	43.0	Russia	59.8
Italy	11.2	Germany	7.1
USA	10.4	China	4.6
Germany	6.6	USA	3.9

Tanzania

Area (km²) 939,760

Currency Tanzanian shilling (Tsh = 100 cents)

Location Tanzania is located on the central East African coast bordering the Indian Ocean, and comprises the mainland territory of Tanganyika and the islands of Zanzibar and Pemba. Tanganyika is bounded in the north by Uganda and Kenya, in the west by Rwanda, Burundi and Zaire, and in the south by Zambia, Malawi and Mozambique. The capital is Dar es Salaam.

Head of State President Benjamin Mkapa (1996)

Head of Government JCleopa D Msuya (December 1994)

Ruling Party CCM-Chama Cha Mapinduzi (Revolutionary Party of Tanzania)

Political Structure The Republic of Tanzania is an independent member of the Commonwealth, whose executive President is elected for a maximum of two five-year terms by direct popular vote. Legislative authority is vested in a unicameral National Assembly, which serves for a five-year term; 216 of its members are elected by universal suffrage and another 65 are nominated by the President. Until 1992 the CCM was the only legal political party. The question of national unity has dominated the political agenda since the start of 1993, with the island of Zanzibar seriously considering a move toward independence from Tanganyika on the mainland. Consequently, the National Assembly has approved a plan to investigate the possibility of creating three assemblies: one for the whole country, one for Tanganyika and one for Zanzibar.

Last Elections The elections held in October 1995 degenerated in chaos with voting in Dar es Salaam postponed until mid-November. Benjamin Mkapa was eventually declared the winner with 62% of the vote. Although it was always clear that the CCM would win, the opposition Civic United Front (CUF) charged that vote-rigging was widespread. The CUF draws much of its support from Muslim-dominated areas along the coast and now demands that the whole union, which was formed in 1964, be recast and that Zanzibar become independent.

Political Risk Tanzania's extreme poverty discourages donors, policy makers and businesses. Zanzibar's two islands are sharply divided from the mainland along political, religious and ethnic lines and there is a growing danger that a similar situation will develop on the mainland (Tanganyika). However, Tanzania is less divided by tribal disputes than its neighbour, Kenya, where politics have always been tribal.

International Disputes Tanzania's recent elections brought harsh criticism from the international community. Seventeen western states demanded a recount, all to no avail. Tanzania has a dispute with Malawi over the ownership of territorial water rights in Lake Nyasa (called Lake Malawi by Malawi) where their borders meet. The issue remains technical, however, and has not caused major strains in recent years.

Economy Tanzania's economy is struggling to reorganise after decades of centralist direction. The poor economic growth in recent decades owes at least as much to economic mismanagement as it does to the weak state of the commodity markets. Infrastructural shortcomings are likely to hamper progress over the next several years. Meanwhile, donors suspended their balance-of-payments aid to the country in 1994. These funds are extremely vital but are unlikely to be resumed swiftly.

Main Industries Agriculture is by far the most important economic activity, with the great majority of the population depending on subsistence farming. Coconuts, coffee, tea, cotton and groundnuts are also grown for export. Zanzibar is a major exporter of spices. Industrial activity is limited mainly to the fulfilment of local needs, and centres on raw materials processing, textiles, timber products and brewing. There is a small diamond mining industry, but otherwise minerals are unimportant.

Energy Apart from brushwood and a small amount of oil, Tanzania has no indigenous energy production facilities. It does, however, have a large hydro-electricity capacity which is now being used to good effect.

	1993	1994	1995
Inflation (% change)	23.5	34.1	27.4
Exchange rate (per US$)	405.27	509.63	555.18
Interest rate (% per annum)	31.0	39.0	39.3
GDP (% real growth)	-18.8	-3.2	-14.0
GDP (Million units of national currency)	1,404,369.0	1,822,570.0	1,996,880.6
GDP (US$ million)	3,465.3	3,576.3	3,596.8
GDP per capita (US$)	123.7	124.0	118.6
Consumption (Million units of national currency)	707,135.0	810,168.5	783,634.0
Consumption (US$ million)	1,744.8	1,589.7	1,411.5
Consumption per capita (US$)	62.3	55.1	46.5
Population, mid-year ('000)	28,019.0	28,850.0	30,340.0
Birth rate (per '000)	49.8	45.5	
Death rate (per '000)	13.6	14.4	
No. of households ('000)	5,521.4	5,586.3	5,655.0
Total exports (US$ million)	450.0	519.0	637.0
Total imports (US$ million)	1,497.0	1,505.0	1,404.0
Tourism receipts (US$ million)	147.0	159.2	
Tourist spending (US$ million)	102.0	110.4	98.0

Average household size 1995 (persons)	5.10		
Urban population 1995 (%)	24.4		
Age analysis (%) (1985)	*0-14* 47.8	*15-64* 49.0	*65+* 3.2
Population by sex (%) (1985)	*Male* 48.9	*Female* 51.1	
Life expectancy (years) (1985-90)	*Male* 51.3	*Female* 54.7	
Infant mortality (deaths per '000 live births) (1993)	84.9		
Adult literacy (%) (1995)	67.8		

TRADING PARTNERS

Major export destinations 1995 (% share)		Major import sources 1995 (% share)	
India	10.2	United Kingdom	11.4
Germany	10.1	Kenya	10.7
Japan	9.2	Japan	8.4
Belgium/Luxembourg	7.5	India	6.7

Thailand

Area (km²) 514,000

Currency Baht (= 100 satangs)

Location Thailand, although the largest state in the Indo-Chinese peninsula, has access to the sea only in the far south. With Myanmar accounting for almost all of its shoreline with the Bay of Bengal, its access to that sea is limited to a long but narrow (150-kilometre wide) isthmus to the south which eventually links up with Malaysia. Its more extensive coastline is on the Gulf of Thailand, where it borders Cambodia in the east. In the north-east it shares a border with Laos. The capital is Bangkok.

Head of State HM King Bhumibol Adulyadej (1946)

Head of Government Banharn Silpa-archa (July 1995)

Ruling Party Chart Thai (Thai Nation) leads a seven-party coalition.

Political Structure Thailand's political system has been dominated for decades by the armed forces. In 1991, the military initiated a full-scale coup against Gen. Chatichai Choonhavan and dissolved the National Assembly, reopening it 13 months later after new elections. The military junta was dissolved shortly afterwards. In mid-1995, the government lost the support of one of the four coalition partners and resigned. It was replaced in a full election by the opposition Chart Thai party.

Last Elections General elections to the House of Representatives were held in July 1995, producing a surprise defeat of the ruling Democrat Party at the hands of the Chart Thai party.

Political Risk The 1995 elections were the source of some anxiety abroad following charges of drug smuggling. The result was a major departure from the 1992 poll, which had revealed a solid degree of popular support for the military. Despite its erratic political history, Thailand has done much to contribute to the stability of the region, participating in various Pacific and South East Asian political fora. Government officials are growing increasingly concerned about the rapid inflow of illegal workers which they regard as a threat to security. Estimates made in mid-1996 put the figure at over 2 million unregistered workers (four times the number in mid-1994). Most come from Burma, Cambodia, Laos and China and are blamed for a rise in crime and disease.

International Disputes Thailand's relations with Laos and Cambodia have been severely strained as a result of the latter's accommodation of the Khmer Rouge rebels, who continue to fight a rearguard campaign in Cambodia today. The country's vehemently anti-drug position has done little to limit the flourishing opium trade along the Lao and Myanmar borders, where traffickers move freely thanks to their own private armies.

Economy Although Thailand is still regarded as a "developing" country, industrialisation is bringing many material benefits to its 60 million people, making it one of Asia's most remarkable success stories. Japanese companies, seeking to escape from the high costs of the strong yen, regard Thailand as their favoured site for new investments. Aside from foreign investment, exports are proving to be an especially important growth stimulus. Government officials still fear that the country would lose its competitive edge to lower cost manufacturers in China, Vietnam or Indonesia, but so far that has not occurred. More importantly, Thailand's exports of high-tech or sunrise industries have begun to exceed those of low-tech industries for the first time. However, the country must soon find some way to move companies out of labour-intensive industries and into more capital-intensive and R&D intensive operations. This transformation will be essential since labour shortages are gradually pushing up manufacturing costs and could eventually make Thailand uncompetitive relative to some of its less developed neighbours.

Main Industries Most of the Thai population rely on agriculture, largely in a subsistence capacity. Rice, sugar, maize and vegetables are grown for the home market, while palm oil, fishing and (until the recent ban) timber extraction have been the main export crops. Industry is rapidly developing with construction, textiles, clothing and electronics among the leaders. The sector also includes a number of more capital-intensive industries such as steel, bulk chemicals and metal fabrication. Mining also accounts for a large portion of GDP and exports, thanks to the country's abundant deposits of tin, lead, iron, tungsten, antimony and lignite. There is a small and growing tourist industry (outside Bangkok) but the country's facilities generally lag behind those of regional rivals.

Energy Thailand has fairly substantial oil and gas deposits which are being explored, and which already provide more than half of its requirements. There is large but mainly untapped hydro-electric potential.

	1993	1994	1995
Inflation (% change)	3.8	4.8	5.7
Exchange rate (per US$)	25.32	25.15	24.92
Interest rate (% per annum)	15.6	14.4	15.3
GDP (% real growth)	9.4	8.4	9.0
GDP (Million units of national currency)	3,170,000.5	3,601,000.7	4,148,680.0
GDP (US$ million)	125,197.5	143,180.9	166,479.9
GDP per capita (US$)	2,137.2	2,410.5	2,765.0
Consumption (Million units of national currency)	1,999,792.0	2,271,688.0	2,617,190.9
Consumption (US$ million)	78,980.7	90,325.6	105,023.7
Consumption per capita (US$)	1,348.3	1,520.6	1,744.3
Population, mid-year ('000)	58,580.0	59,400.0	60,210.0
Birth rate (per '000)	20.1	20.0	
Death rate (per '000)	6.5	6.5	
No. of households ('000)	12,689.1	12,851.0	13,014.0
Total exports (US$ million)	37,168.0	45,261.0	
Total imports (US$ million)	46,208.0	54,459.0	
Tourism receipts (US$ million)	6,205.0		
Tourist spending (US$ million)	2,173.0	2,395.0	2,784.7

Average household size 1995 (persons)	4.40		
Urban population 1995 (%)	20.1		
Age analysis (%) (1992)	*0-14* 31.3	*15-64* 64.7	*65+* 4.1
Population by sex (%) (1992)	*Male* 50.1	*Female* 49.9	
Life expectancy (years) (1992)	*Male* 65.7	*Female* 70.4	
Infant mortality (deaths per '000 live births) (1993)	36.6		
Adult literacy (%) (1995)	93.8		

TRADING PARTNERS

Major export destinations 1995 (% share)		Major import sources 1995 (% share)	
USA	18.1	Japan	29.7
Japan	16.8	USA	11.1
Singapore	11.6	Singapore	4.8
Hong Kong	5.0	Malaysia	4.4

Togo

Area (km²)   56,785

Currency   CFA franc (= 100 centimes)

Location   Togo is a narrow strip of land stretching north from the Atlantic coast of West Africa. It meets the Gulf of Guinea between Ghana in the west and Benin in the east. With a tropical climate, but with lower elevation than either Benin or Burkina Faso, the country has substantial agricultural capabilities. The capital is Lomé.

Head of State   President Gnassingbé Eyadéma (1967)

Head of Government   Edem Kodjo (April 1994)

Ruling Party   The Action Committee for Renewal and the Togolese Union for Democracy form a coalition.

Political Structure   Although Togo has a non-executive President, he has retained significant powers during recent periods of unrest. Recent years have been dominated by the growing split between President Eyadéma and the former Premier Joseph Koffigoh, who enjoyed wider public backing but was effectively barred from standing for President as a result of constitutional amendments. The overthrow of Eyadéma's party in the 1994 elections appeared to herald a change of tack.

Last Elections   The country's first parliamentary elections were held in February 1994, when the Togolese People's Assembly of President Eyadéma secured only 38 of the 81 seats, compared with 43 for the opposition group comprising the Action Committee for Renewal and the Togolese Union for Democracy. The first presidential elections took place after long delays in August 1993, when President Eyadéma had been returned to office.

Political Risk   The growth of public opposition to President Eyadéma, and his determination to dig in for a long battle, have become difficult to ignore in recent years. The possibility of conflict should certainly be taken into account by any potential exporter of consumer goods. With a low level of personal spending power, but with substantial natural resources and commodities, Togo remains a high-risk but potentially high-reward market for importers.

International Disputes   Togo's relations with its neighbours are frequently tense. The country demands the return of two areas of Ghana, the northern reaches of the Volta River in the east of the country and the southern coastal area around Lomé, which formed part of the former German Togoland. These areas were awarded to Ghana in 1919 in a partition between France and the UK, the two major colonial powers. The issue remains unresolved despite UN mediation and there have recently been accusations of maltreatment of minorities on both sides. However, the countries reopened their mutual borders in December 1994, in what appeared to be a conciliation.

Economy   The recovery of world prices for cocoa and other primary products has provided a much-needed boost to Togo's economy. Although no precise figures are available, French analysts estimate that GDP grew by 5-6% in 1995. The country's prospects remain fragile, however, with economic and political mismanagement hindering growth of domestic markets. Togo badly needs to develop a more diversified economy which does not depend on world prices for a very few commodities.

Main Industries   Togo's main industry is still farming, despite the growth in mineral exports. The great majority of the population depend on subsistence cultivation of crops such as cassava, manioc and vegetables. Palm kernels, cocoa and copra are grown for export. Industry is limited to the processing of agricultural raw materials. Phosphate mining is the country's biggest export earner, although production in the state-owned mines has declined in recent years.

Energy   Togo has limited domestic fuel resources, apart from firewood, and is forced to import nearly all of its requirements from abroad. Electricity generation is of a low order and there is little exploitation of the country's hydro-electric potential.

	1993	1994	1995
Inflation (% change)	-1.0	36.0	7.0
Exchange rate (per US$)	283.16	555.20	498.70
Interest rate (% per annum)	17.5	17.5	16.0
GDP (% real growth)			
GDP (Million units of national currency)	473,114.0	960,468.7	1,027,701.5
GDP (US$ million)	1,670.8	1,730.0	2,060.8
GDP per capita (US$)	430.6	440.2	510.5
Consumption (Million units of national currency)	270,913.4	549,981.3	588,480.0
Consumption (US$ million)	956.8	990.6	1,180.0
Consumption per capita (US$)	246.6	252.1	292.3
Population, mid-year ('000)	3,880.0	3,930.0	4,036.7
Birth rate (per '000)	44.5	47.3	
Death rate (per '000)	12.8	12.6	
No. of households ('000)	641.3	652.8	663.0
Total exports (US$ million)	136.0	162.0	209.0
Total imports (US$ million)	179.0	222.0	384.0
Tourism receipts (US$ million)	36.3	37.7	
Tourist spending (US$ million)	44.7	46.4	50.0

Average household size 1995 (persons)	5.78		
Urban population 1995 (%)	30.8		
Age analysis (%) (1992, est)	*0-14* 45.4	*15-64* 51.4	*65+* 3.2
Population by sex (%)			
Life expectancy (years) (1990-95)	*Male* 53.2	*Female* 56.8	
Infant mortality (deaths per '000 live births) (1993)	85.3		
Adult literacy (%) (1995)	51.7		

TRADING PARTNERS

Major export destinations 1995 (% share)		Major import sources 1995 (% share)	
Canada	9.4	Ghana	17.7
USA	8.1	China	13.5
France	6.4	France	12.7
Burkina Faso	3.1	Cameroon	6.2

Tonga

Area (km²) 699

Currency Pa'anga (T$ = 100 seniti)

Location Tonga lies in the south-east of the important South Pacific Group which also includes Vanuatu, Fiji and the Solomon Islands. Its nearest major neighbour is New Zealand, more than 1,500 km to the south. The capital is Nuku'alofa.

Head of State HM King Taufa'ahau Tupou IV

Head of Government Baron Vaea

Ruling Party There are no official political parties in Tonga at present, although unofficial groupings exist.

Political Structure The Kingdom of Tonga is a constitutional monarchy and an independent member of the Commonwealth. The King, who exercises full executive powers, is assisted by a 10-member Privy Council, or Cabinet. Legislative powers are held by a 30-member unicameral Legislative Assembly. Apart from the King, the Privy Council and nine hereditary nobles, the Assembly includes nine members elected by universal adult suffrage for a term of three years. The issue of constitutional reform sharply divides members of the Assembly.

Last Elections Elections to the nine available seats in the National Assembly were held in February 1993, when members of the pro-democracy movement won six seats. The movement's political prospects were effectively blocked, however, by the heavy parliamentary weighting in favour of hereditary and nominated members.

Political Risk Popular support for constitutional reform has periodically received a boost as instances of misconduct and corruption in the administration have become public. Concern over the health of the monarch, and growing dissatisfaction over the slumping economy, raise the level of political risk.

Economy Tonga's political uncertainties come at a time when the economy is actually starting to grow, albeit hesitantly. The economy remains primitive and undiversified, however, and there is little likelihood of rapid change.

Main Industries Farming is by far the largest sector of the economy, with copra, bananas, vanilla and various fruits being grown for export while fish, coconuts, yams and cassava form the bulk of the domestic diet. Manufacturing is limited to the processing of agricultural raw materials and all but the simplest consumer goods are imported. The Government decided in the 1980s to resist moves for a development of the tourist industry, on the grounds that this would damage its local culture.

Energy All of Tonga's fuel requirements, except for fuelwood, have to be imported at present.

	1993	1994	1995
Inflation (% change)	1.0	1.0	1.0
Exchange rate (per US$)	1.38	1.32	1.32
Interest rate (% per annum)	9.9	9.4	
GDP (% real growth)	0.4	5.9	3.0
GDP (Million units of national currency)	201.0	215.0	223.7
GDP (US$ million)	145.7	162.9	169.4
GDP per capita (US$)	1,456.5	1,628.8	1,729.0
Consumption (Million units of national currency)	59.9	64.1	66.7
Consumption (US$ million)	43.4	48.6	50.5
Consumption per capita (US$)	434.1	485.6	515.7
Population, mid-year ('000)	100.0	100.0	98.0
Birth rate (per '000)	15.0	14.8	
Death rate (per '000)	6.9	6.8	
No. of households ('000)	19.5	19.6	19.8
Total exports (US$ million)	16.0	14.0	14.0
Total imports (US$ million)	61.0	69.0	76.0
Tourism receipts (US$ million)	10.0	11.4	
Tourist spending (US$ million)	3.0	3.4	3.5

Average household size 1995 (persons)	4.71				
Urban population 1995 (%)	41.1				
Age analysis (%) (1990)	*0-14* 40.9		*15-64* 54.1		*65+* 5.0
Population by sex (%) (1990)	*Male* 49.7		*Female* 50.3		
Life expectancy (years)					
Infant mortality (deaths per '000 live births)					
Adult literacy (%) (1976)	99.6				

Trinidad and Tobago

Area (km²)   5,130

Currency   Trinidad and Tobago dollar (T$ = 100 cents)

Location   Trinidad is the most southerly island in the West Indies group, and lies just off the northern coast of Venezuela. Tobago, 32 km north-east of Trinidad, is the more popular area for tourism, but there are also numerous small islands. The climate is warm, with a dry spring and a wet and often stormy autumn. The capital is Port-of-Spain.

Head of State   President HE Noor Mohammed Hassan-Ali

Head of Government   Basdeo Panday

Ruling Party   The United National Congress (UNC) leads a coalition with Tobago's two representatives of the People's National Movement (PNM)

Political Structure   The Republic of Trinidad and Tobago is an independent member of the Commonwealth. The executive President is elected by Parliament for a term of five years. Legislative power rests with the bicameral Parliament which consists of a 31-member Senate and a 36-member House of Representatives. The House is elected by universal suffrage for five years while the Senate is appointed - 16 members by the Prime Minister, six by the Leader of the Opposition and nine by the President. Tobago, the smaller of the two islands, has been independent from the UK since 1987 and has its own 12-member House of Assembly with some autonomous powers. In Tobago, politics run to quite a different agenda from those of Trinidad and the political complexion is very different.

Last Elections   General elections were held in November 1995, when the Indian-based United National Congress (UNC) raised its share of the vote from 29% in the last election to 45% and won 17 seats. This is nearly as many as the mainly black, and nearly always ruling, People's National Movement (PNM). Although the PNM lost three seats to the UNC, it, too, raised its share from 45% to almost 50% when the vote for the third party, the National Alliance for Reconstruction (NAR), collapsed. The NAR won only the two seats allocated to Tobago.

Political Risk   The latest election has caused concern among outsiders because of the broadly ethnic split in the vote. Indians support the UNC and now account for about 40% of the country's population, roughly the same as blacks who support the PNM. Trinidadians, however, reject this possibility. They point out that the PNM draws votes for the 20% of people of mixed origin and from non-Hindu Indians while the UNC now has the backing of black Christians. Apart from a would-be coup by Muslim extremists in 1990, the islands have enjoyed a long period of calm since independence 33 years ago.

Economy   With one of the highest per capita incomes in the Caribbean, Trinidad and Tobago has a diversified economy with strengths in oil, farming, manufacturing and tourism. In recent years the government has invested large sums to encourage economic development. To stimulate exports, officials are attempting to negotiate bilateral trade agreements with other countries in the region. A preliminary government report claims that the economy grew by 3.5% in 1995, down from 4.2% in the previous year. Higher rates of growth are forecast for 1996. The country needs to maintain its impressive rates of growth since unemployment, although falling, is still too high at 16.5%.

Main Industries   The oil refining industry is only one of the beneficiaries of Trinidad's petroleum finds. There is also a range of other heavy industries, including steel, petrochemicals and rubber processing which owe their existence to crude oil. A range of manufacturing industries cater for local consumer needs, including textiles, food products, textiles and clothing. Performance of the manufacturing sector is mixed, however, with petrochemicals, tobacco and beverages all suffering in recent years. Farming is still extremely important in the economy. Trinidad has a pleasant and fertile soil in which sugar, citrus fruits and copra are grown for export, as well as rice, coconuts, yams and bananas for the domestic market. Timber extraction is growing.

Energy   Trinidad's economy was transformed in the 1970s and 1980s by the discovery of crude oil, and the country now has a range of downstream processing facilities aimed at producing oil products for export.

	1993	1994	1995
Inflation (% change)	10.7	8.8	5.3
Exchange rate (per US$)	5.35	5.92	5.65
Interest rate (% per annum)	15.5	16.0	15.2
GDP (% real growth)	-1.4	4.2	3.5
GDP (Million units of national currency)	24,883.0	28,680.0	31,257.0
GDP (US$ million)	4,651.0	4,844.6	5,532.2
GDP per capita (US$)	3,720.8	3,844.9	4,356.1
Consumption (Million units of national currency)	15,230.0	19,006.5	22,428.3
Consumption (US$ million)	2,846.7	3,210.6	3,969.6
Consumption per capita (US$)	2,277.4	2,548.1	3,125.7
Population, mid-year ('000)	1,250.0	1,260.0	1,270.0
Birth rate (per '000)	16.9	19.6	
Death rate (per '000)	7.1	6.0	
No. of households ('000)	265.9	265.3	265.0
Total exports (US$ million)	1,612.0	1,867.0	2,514.0
Total imports (US$ million)	1,448.0	1,131.0	1,606.0
Tourism receipts (US$ million)	80.0	83.4	
Tourist spending (US$ million)	115.0	119.9	135.0

Average household size 1995 (persons)	4.55				
Urban population 1995 (%)	71.8				
Age analysis (%) (1990)	*0-14* 31.3		*15-64* 63.3		*65+* 5.5
Population by sex (%) (1990)	*Male* 53.2		*Female* 46.8		
Life expectancy (years) (1985-90)	*Male* 68.5		*Female* 73.5		
Infant mortality (deaths per '000 live births) (1993)	10.5				
Adult literacy (%) (1995)	97.9				

TRADING PARTNERS

Major export destinations 1995 (% share)		Major import sources 1995 (% share)	
USA	41.2	USA	40.2
Jamaica	4.7	United Kingdom	9.4
Barbados	4.5	Germany	4.6
Guyana	3.6	Brazil	4.0

Tunisia

Area (km²)   164,150

Currency   Tunisian dinar (TD = 1,000 millimes)

Location   Tunisia, one of the smaller but more influential states in North Africa, lies on the Mediterranean coast with Algeria to its west and Libya to the east. Equally important, however, is its proximity to Italy (a sea voyage of only 200 km from Tunis to Sicily) or to France, the governing power until 1956. The country's fertile northern soil enjoys adequate irrigation from numerous rivers; in the south, however, it gives way to desert terrain. The capital is Tunis.

Head of State   President Gen. Zine el-Abidine Ben-Ali (1987)

Head of Government   Hamed Karoui

Ruling Party   Rassemblement Constitutionnel Démocratique (RCD)

Political Structure   The Republic of Tunisia became independent from France in 1957 and was ruled until 1981 as a one-party state by the Parti Socialiste Destour. Now known as the Rassemblement Constitutionnel Démocratique, the party still rules the country with little opposition. The executive President is elected for a maximum of three five-year terms by universal suffrage, although in practice he has always stood unopposed. The 163 members of the unicameral National Assembly are also elected by popular vote.

Last Elections   Presidential elections were held in March 1994, when Gen. Ben-Ali was re-elected with 99% of the vote. His party holds 88% of the seats in parliament and controls all municipalities. The six legal opposition parties are virtually weightless compared with Ben Ali's RCD.

Political Risk   Tunisia's political risks stem not from economics but from the threat of Islamic fundamentalism. The government is extremely aware of events in Algeria and takes every precaution not to follow in that country's footsteps. Tunisians enjoy their economic prosperity; most support Ben Ali's intolerance of Islamists and agree with his assertion that Tunisia is not ready for full democracy. But with no real political opposition, no free press and no dissent, many wonder how the country will ever mature democratically. Meanwhile, popular disquiet has been fuelled by the Government's heavy handling of a number of assaults committed by the Islamic extremists of the Nahda movement. The international community has begun to press for a cessation of the human rights abuses allegedly being committed. Relations with Sudan, Egypt, Saudi Arabia and Kuwait are extremely poor, in the light of Tunisia's espousal of the Iraqi cause during the 1991 Gulf War.

International Disputes   Tunisia's proximity to the militantly Islamic states of Algeria and Libya has often placed it in a difficult position. The rise of Islamic fundamentalism has resulted in strains to the country's bilateral relationships.

Economy   Though per capita income is only $2,000, Tunisia does not have the serious income inequalities that exist in other north African countries. Home ownership is high and only one in 20 lives below the poverty line. Unemployment, at 14%, is too high but falling. Growth has been averaging 4% a year, despite the droughts that have plagued farmers, and inflation has averaged under 5%.

Main Industries   Much of the country's population depends on farming, which occurs mainly along the northern coasts and valleys. Cereals such as wheat and barley, and olives, vines and citrus fruits produce heavy exportable crops. Further inland, the scope is reduced to cattle herding. Manufacturing is still small-scale and commodity-oriented and the bulk of consumer goods are imported.

Energy   Tunisia's energy sector is modest in relation to its neighbours, but the country is self-sufficient in oil and has gas deposits which may or may not be viable.

	1993	1994	1995
Inflation (% change)	4.0	4.7	6.2
Exchange rate (per US$)	1.00	1.01	0.95
Interest rate (% per annum)	10.5		
GDP (% real growth)	2.8	3.4	2.2
GDP (Million units of national currency)	14,688.0	15,904.0	17,256.0
GDP (US$ million)	14,688.0	15,746.5	18,164.2
GDP per capita (US$)	1,713.9	1,787.3	2,021.7
Consumption (Million units of national currency)	9,079.0	9,860.0	10,730.2
Consumption (US$ million)	9,079.0	9,762.4	11,294.9
Consumption per capita (US$)	1,059.4	1,108.1	1,257.1
Population, mid-year ('000)	8,570.0	8,810.0	8,984.7
Birth rate (per '000)	24.1	22.5	
Death rate (per '000)	6.4	5.5	
No. of households ('000)	1,338.0	1,370.0	1,403.0
Total exports (US$ million)	3,802.0	4,657.0	5,475.0
Total imports (US$ million)	6,214.0	6,581.0	7,903.0
Tourism receipts (US$ million)	1,114.0	1,211.8	
Tourist spending (US$ million)	203.0	220.8	255.5

Average household size 1995 (persons)	6.08				
Urban population 1995 (%)	57.3				
Age analysis (%) (1989)	*0-14* 37.9		*15-64* 57.2		*65+* 4.9
Population by sex (%) (1989)	*Male* 50.7		*Female* 49.3		
Life expectancy (years) (1990-95)	*Male* 66.8		*Female* 68.7		
Infant mortality (deaths per '000 live births) (1993)	43.0				
Adult literacy (%) (1995)	66.7				

TRADING PARTNERS

Major export destinations 1995 (% share)		Major import sources 1995 (% share)	
France	28.1	France	37.0
Italy	22.3	Italy	22.1
Germany	15.7	Germany	18.0
Spain	4.1	USA	7.1

Turkey

Area (km²) 779,450

Currency Turkish lira

Location With control over both banks of the Bosporus, Turkey controls access to the Black Sea. The country has a land border with Greece and Bulgaria to the west. In the south-east it meets with Syria and Iraq, while the eastern border meets with Iran and in the north-east it borders Georgia and Armenia. The capital is Ankara.

Head of State President Süleyman Demirel (May 1993)

Head of Government Mesut Yilmaz (March to June 1996)

Ruling Party A centre-right coalition between Mesut Yilmaz's Motherland Party and Tansu Ciller's True Path Party was formed in March 1996 but lasted only three months. In-fighting between the two parties eventually forced Prime Minister Mesut Yilmaz to resign. Politicians are now exploring the possibility of other coalitions which might include the pro-Islamic Welfare Party.

Political Structure Turkey's president is elected by popular vote for seven years. The country has a unicameral 450-seat Grand National Assembly (Parliament) elected by universal suffrage for a term of five years. Turkey submitted an application for membership of the EU in 1992. Although Islam is dominant, the country has been secular since 1919. The Kurdish Democracy Party was banned in 1994 after a series of terrorist attacks.

Last Elections In the 1996 elections to the Grand National Assembly the opposition (pro-Islamic) Welfare Party received only a fifth of the seats but gained the largest share in the Assembly. Both the Motherland Party and True Path Parties got slightly less than a fifth of the seats, respectively. Eventually, they formed a new coalition keeping the Welfare Party from power, but this foundered in June after only three months.

Political Risk Despite a firm commitment to the democratic process, bitter political divisions complicate Turkish politics. Kurdish insurgents in the east and around the western coastal resorts have attracted punitive actions from the armed forces, while the revolutionary Dev-Sol and Dev-Yol terrorists remain active. The present coalition remains 15 seats short of a majority and may not last long. Opposition from the Islamic Welfare Party will make management of the economy difficult.

International Disputes Turkey has a number of disputes with other countries in the region. In the Aegean, Turkey claims half the sea bed that divides it from Greece, while the Greeks argue that each of their hundreds of islands (many within 15 kilometres of Turkey's coast) should enjoy a 12-mile territorial limit. In Cyprus, the creation of the Turkish Republic of Northern Cyprus after the 1974 invasion has brought hostility from Athens and a snub from other countries. Turkey's ongoing battle against the Kurdish militants has led to disputes with Iraq, Iran and Syria, each of which has its own Kurdish minority. Syria also demands the return of Hatay Province, Turkey's southernmost province. In 1995 Turkish authorities launched a renewed campaign against Kurdish insurgents which prompted a wave of international protests. The European Parliament's approval of the EU's customs union with Turkey was delayed until December 1995 because of concerns about the country's human rights record.

Economy GDP grew by 8.1% in 1995, more than making up for the 6.1% contraction in 1994 when the country slid into its worst recession on record. The recovery, which followed a 28% devaluation of the currency in April 1995, should help the country deal with its high levels of unemployment. Inflation remains a serious problem. Prices rose 78% in 1995, down from 126% in 1994. A more aggressive anti-inflation policy will be essential as the pace of economic growth accelerates. Per capita income rose by over 20% in 1995 to $2,685. However, economists emphasise that the black economy may now be as large as the official economy, making government data for growth and income unreliable.

Main Industries Industry is the largest sector of the Turkish economy, with most of the major companies being under state control. A wide range of consumer goods are manufactured, as well as heavy goods such as steel and cement, transport goods and chemicals. Much of the population relies on agriculture. In the lowlands, a fertile soil allows the cultivation of grapes, fruit, barley, cotton and other products. In the uplands, cattle herding and forestry are more common.

Energy Turkey has significant coal and lignite deposits, and small oil and gas fields, but the country still depends heavily on imports of oil. It does have easy access to hydrocarbons, thanks to its role as an entrepôt for Black sea traffic. Until the Gulf war of 1991, it was also the operator of Iraq's biggest oil export pipeline. Electricity supply capacity has almost doubled since 1989, but shortages still represent a major constraint on industrial development in 1995.

	1993	1994	1995
Inflation (% change)	66.1	126.0	78.0
Exchange rate (per US$)	10,984.60	29,833.27	46,010.00
Interest rate		88.0	88.0
GDP (% real growth)	15.2	-6.1	8.1
GDP (Billion units of national currency)	1,981,900.0	4,205,869.3	8,092,849.5
GDP (US$ million)	180,425.3	140,979.2	175,893.3
GDP per capita (US$)	3,013.7	2,304.3	2,853.6
Consumption (Billion units of national currency)	1,289,008.0	2,517,756.0	4,961,237.1
Consumption (US$ million)	117,346.8	84,394.2	107,829.5
Consumption per capita (US$)	1,960.1	1,379.4	1,749.3
Population, mid-year ('000)	59,869.0	61,180.0	61,640.0
Birth rate (per '000)	27.2		22.4
Death rate (per '000)			6.6
No. of households ('000)	13,897.0	14,272.3	14,655.0
Total exports (US$ million)	15,343.0	18,106.0	20,280.0
Total imports (US$ million)	22,872.0	29,174.0	23,270.0
Tourism receipts (US$ million)	3,959.0	2,858.8	
Tourist spending (US$ million)	934.0	674.4	861.7

Average household size 1995 (persons)	4.00				
Urban population 1995 (%)	68.8				
Age analysis (%) (1995)	*0-14* 37.5		*15-64* 56.3		*65+* 6.2
Population by sex (%) (1994)	*Male* 50.7		*Female* 49.3		
Life expectancy (years) (1991)	*Male* 62.5		*Female* 65.8		
Infant mortality (deaths per '000 live births) (1993)	52.6				
Adult literacy (%) (1995)	82.3				

TRADING PARTNERS

Major export destinations 1995 (% share)		Major import sources 1995 (% share)	
Germany	23.1	Germany	15.0
USA	8.0	USA	10.8
Italy	6.8	Italy	9.5
United Kingdom	5.6	United Kingdom	5.7

Turkmenistan

Area (km²)   488,100

Currency   Manat (introduced November 1993). Russian roubles are also used.

Location   Turkmenistan is located in the far south of the former Soviet empire, bordering Iran and Afghanistan in the south and the Caspian Sea in the west, with Uzbekistan and Kazakhstan to the north. The terrain is dominated by the Kara-Kum desert, and the climate is accordingly arid for most of the year. The capital is Ashkhabad.

Head of State   President Saparmurat Niyazov (October 1990)

Head of Government   Khan Akhmedov

Ruling Party   Democratic Party of Turkmenistan

Political Structure   Turkmenistan declared its independence from the Soviet Union in October 1991. Like Tajikistan, it is still ruled by the Communist Party, albeit under the new name of the Democratic Party of Turkmenistan. The 1991 Constitution allows for an executive President, who is the Chairman of the Supreme Soviet, and who was first elected by that body, although he was subsequently confirmed by popular vote. In practice, the country is a one-party state. The 175-member Supreme Soviet, headed by a Supreme Council, exercises legislative power, and is elected for five years.

Last Elections   The future of Turkmenistan's electoral system is in doubt, after a referendum held in January 1994 decided to abolish the 1997 elections in accordance with the wishes of President Niyazov. Ominously, the official reports of the poll declared that 99% of the electorate had voted in favour. The last elections to the Majlis were held in November-December 1992, when the Democratic Party of Turkmenistan won most of the seats. President Niyazov was re-elected unopposed in June 1992, obtaining 99% of the vote. The new People's Council was set up as a new supervisory body under the new Constitution and held its first election in December 1994 but, to general dismay, all candidates were returned.

Political Risk   A coup attempt against Niyazov was unsuccessfully launched in 1994. Although a predominantly Muslim country, Turkmenistan has seen little of the militant Islamic politics which have surfaced in other ex-Soviet republics.

Economy   In spite of its rich natural resource base, Turkmenistan is a low-income country compared with Russia, Ukraine and other central Asian republics. The government pursues an independent economic policy and has little difficulty in attracting foreign investment, thanks to its abundant resource base. The country has embarked on a privatisation programme with all enterprises having less than 500 employees scheduled to be sold off before the end of 1999. Medium-sized firms with 500 to 1,000 employees will be only partly privatised. Development of the economy suffers owing to an occasionally severe shortage of water. Turkmenistan and Uzbekistan are trying to co-ordinate water usage on the Amu Darya river.

Main Industries   Turkmenistan not only has substantial energy resources (primarily natural gas and oil) but offers considerable potential for diversification into mineral-resource-based industries. Current economic activity is predominately agricultural, however. Farming accounts for 40% of GDP and approximately the same proportion of employment. Cotton, grain, fruits and vegetables are the main crops. Industry contributes about a fifth of GDP and the construction sector accounts for another 25%, mainly due to the construction of a new airport and a number of large, modern hotels.

Energy   Natural gas is the major export item and the main source of foreign currency. In the past, these exports went to countries in the former Soviet Union and were sold below world market prices. The government now intends to expand its energy exports to Western Europe and other parts of the world. Turkmenistan's abundance of oil and natural gas is such that it is able to offer free electricity and gas to all its residents.

	1993	1994	1995
Inflation (% change)	300.0		
Exchange rate (per US$)	1,080.10		
Interest rate			
GDP (% real growth)	10.0	-18.0	-5.0
GDP			
GDP (US$ million)	5,020.0	5,927.0	5,631.0
GDP per capita (US$)	1,280.6	1,478.1	1,373.5
Consumption			
Consumption (US$ million)			
Consumption per capita (US$)			
Population, mid-year ('000)	3,920.0	4,010.0	4,099.7
Birth rate (per '000)	36.8	30.4	
Death rate (per '000)		7.4	
No. of households ('000)	711.4	731.3	750.0
Total exports (US$ million)			809.1
Total imports (US$ million)			537.6
Tourism receipts (US$ million)			
Tourist spending (US$ million)			

Average household size 1995 (persons)	5.19				
Urban population 1995 (%)	44.9				
Age analysis (%) (1992, est)	*0-14*	48.6	*15-64*	47.1	*65+* 4.3
Population by sex (%) (1989)	*Male*	49.3	*Female*	50.7	
Life expectancy (years) (1989)	*Male*	61.8	*Female*	68.4	
Infant mortality (deaths per '000 live births)					
Adult literacy (%) (1989)	97.2				

TRADING PARTNERS

Major export destinations 1995 (% share)		Major import sources 1995 (% share)	
Azerbaijan	44.0	Russia	19.1
Russia	11.5	Germany	17.3
Italy	10.6	USA	7.0
Germany	5.6	Azerbaijan	7.0

Tuvalu

Area (km²) 25

Currency Australian dollar (A$ = 100 cents)

Location Tuvalu is a group of nine coral islands and atolls formerly known as the Ellice Islands and located in the South Pacific to the north of Fiji, south of Kiribati and east of the Solomon Islands. With a total land area of just 25 square km, and with hardly any of its land reaching more than four metres above sea level, the islands are mainly suitable only for coconut growing. The capital is Funafuti.

Head of State HM Queen Elizabeth II

Head of Government Kamuta Laatasi

Ruling Party There are no political parties in Tuvalu.

Political Structure Tuvalu, an independent special member of the Commonwealth since 1978, is formally ruled by the British monarch acting through a Governor-General. In practice, all executive power is exercised by a Prime Minister and Cabinet who are elected from among the 12 members of the unicameral Parliament. The Parliament in turn is elected by universal adult suffrage for a term of up to four years.

Last Elections An inconclusive election was held in September 1993, when the two main parties emerged with six seats each.

Political Risk Tuvalu's political structure appears well able to cope with quite severe disagreements without needing to resort to drastic political action. However, the tiny economy continues to be vulnerable to external factors and this may eventually feed into the political sphere.

International Disputes Tuvalu has a compensation claim for £2 million against the United Kingdom. If paid, this sum would represent 29 years' worth of foreign exchange revenues.

Economy Tuvalu's economy remains in a depressed state with few prospects for stronger growth. The country is heavily dependent on foreign assistance.

Main Industries Most islanders depend on agriculture for their living. Coconuts, bananas, copra and some fish are exported, but most people live on cereals, fruit and vegetables, largely on a self-sufficiency basis. Manufacturing is small-scale and tends to centre on the processing of raw materials for local use. There are no major producers of consumer goods.

Energy Tuvalu has no oil or gas, and apart from firewood all energy requirements are imported.

	1993	1994	1995
Inflation (% change)	1.8	5.0	2.0
Exchange rate (per US$)	1.52	1.29	1.35
Interest rate			
GDP (% real growth)	2.0	-9.3	-1.0
GDP (Million units of national currency)	8.2	7.8	7.9
GDP (US$ million)	5.4	6.0	5.8
GDP per capita (US$)	599.4	604.7	525.1
Consumption (Million units of national currency)	5.4	5.2	5.3
Consumption (US$ million)	3.6	4.0	3.9
Consumption per capita (US$)	394.7	403.1	354.4
Population, mid-year ('000)	9.0	10.0	11.1
Birth rate (per '000)	32.6	25.7	
Death rate (per '000)	10.5	9.2	
No. of households ('000)	1.4	1.4	1.5
Total exports (US$ million)			
Total imports (US$ million)			
Tourism receipts (US$ million)	0.3	0.3	
Tourist spending (US$ million)			

Average household size 1995 (persons)	6.60				
Urban population 1995 (%)	46.0				
Age analysis (%) (1992, est)	*0-14* 42.0		*15-64* 54.0		*65+* 4.0
Population by sex (%)					
Life expectancy (years)					
Infant mortality (deaths per '000 live births)					
Adult literacy (%)					

Uganda

Area (km²) 236,580

Currency New Uganda shilling (Ush = 100 cents)

Location Uganda is a landlocked country in central East Africa, bordered in the east by Kenya, in the south by Rwanda, Tanzania, and the shore of Lake Victoria, in the north by Sudan and in the west by Zaire. The country has a mountainous terrain with ample rainfall, and has numerous large rivers which converge in the Lake Victoria complex to the south. The capital is Kampala.

Head of State President Yoweri Museveni (1986)

Head of Government Kintu Musoke (1994)

Ruling Party The National Resistance Movement is the political wing of the pro-Museveni National Resistance Army.

Political Structure An independent member of the Commonwealth, Uganda is ruled by an executive President who is assisted by a Cabinet. A 284-member Constituent Assembly was established in 1994, of which 214 members were elected, 10 nominated by the President and 56 nominated by special interest groups. The current President, Yoweri Museveni, came to power in the military coup of 1986 and suspended all political parties. Western donors, seeking a more democratic form of government as a condition for continued aid, have now forced the government to reconsider. If all goes according to plan, a referendum in the year 2000 will allow Ugandans to decide if they want to return to multi-party politics.

Last Elections The country's first direct elections were held in May 1996. Museveni, who had won an overwhelmingly victory in the previous elections in 1994, was returned to office but with a smaller majority. A surprising number of voters in the north of the country rejected Museveni's "no-party" system but his margin of victory was still comfortable.

Political Risk The president is generally regarded as a benevolent dictator who has acted positively to eliminate the aftermath of his often corrupt predecessors. However, violent opposition from a cult-like rebel group known as the Lord's Resistance Army has laid waste to the north of the country. Museveni, who is from the south of the country, enjoys little support in the north which is the poorest part of the country. No one believes that the rebels have the resources to overthrow the government but the country's hold on its northern provinces is tenuous. More violence erupted during the 1996 elections, suggesting that the tribal tensions which tore Uganda apart under dictators Idi Amin and Milton Obote is still not far from the surface.

International Disputes Uganda's relations with Kenya have been tense since the start of 1995, when Kenya accused Uganda of harbouring rebels. Sudan severed its diplomatic relations with Uganda in April 1995, for similar reasons and is suspected of supporting the Ugandan rebels in the north of the country.

Economy Uganda's economy has been disrupted by internal dissent and woefully inadequate infrastructure in the past but has performed impressively in the 1990s. The rate of growth in GDP has averaged 6% per year since 1987 and was probably much higher in 1995. Meanwhile, the country has been steadily revamping its policy environment and, today, has replaced Ghana as the model reformer in Africa. Infrastructure remains dilapidated and the country can ill afford improvements in this area. International aid presently accounts for 80% of all public investment and a substantial share of other public outlays. The major threat to the country's future comes from a different and more insidious source: large numbers of Uganda's workers and businessmen are being killed off by AIDS. Between 1980 and 1994, life expectancy fell from 52 to 42 years, one of the lowest in the world. Most businesses now require a blood test and few are willing to hire anyone under 35 years (under the assumption that middle-aged workers have better health prospects).

Main Industries The economy depends to a substantial degree on coffee, tea and cotton, the three main export crops. For domestic consumption, the main crops are plantains, bananas, cassava, sweet potatoes, potatoes, sorghum and maize. Many farmers operate on a subsistence basis. A surge in coffee prices in 1995 fuelled a small economic boom, prompting the government to place a tax on the commodity. Prices have now fallen but coffee should still account for 65% of GDP in 1996. The industrial sector is much smaller. Apart from the area around Entebbe, most manufacturers are engaged in the processing of raw materials for the domestic market. There are a few heavy industrial manufacturers producing steel and cement.

Energy Uganda has no indigenous oil or gas resources, although its hydro-electric capability is considerable.

	1993	1994	1995
Inflation (% change)	6.1	9.7	8.5
Exchange rate (per US$)	1,195.00	979.40	959.40
Interest rate (% per annum)	45.8		
GDP (% real growth)	4.6	16.6	8.0
GDP (Million units of national currency)	3,735,002.0	4,775,685.0	5,596,147.7
GDP (US$ million)	3,125.5	4,876.1	5,833.0
GDP per capita (US$)	156.7	236.5	273.3
Consumption (Million units of national currency)	3,733,693.0	4,473,997.0	5,142,301.0
Consumption (US$ million)	3,124.4	4,568.1	5,359.9
Consumption per capita (US$)	156.7	221.5	251.1
Population, mid-year ('000)	19,940.0	20,620.0	21,343.0
Birth rate (per '000)	50.1	48.8	
Death rate (per '000)	19.2	18.9	
No. of households ('000)	3,628.4	3,770.3	3,914.0
Total exports (US$ million)	179.0	424.0	461.0
Total imports (US$ million)	604.8	870.0	1,051.0
Tourism receipts (US$ million)	50.0	70.4	
Tourist spending (US$ million)	40.0	56.3	66.1

Average household size 1995 (persons)	5.18				
Urban population 1995 (%)	12.5				
Age analysis (%) (1992, est)	*0-14*	49.6	*15-64*	47.9	*65+* 2.5
Population by sex (%) (1991)	*Male*	49.1	*Female*	50.9	
Life expectancy (years) (1990-95)	*Male*	43.6	*Female*	46.2	
Infant mortality (deaths per '000 live births) (1993)	115.4				
Adult literacy (%) (1995)	61.8				

TRADING PARTNERS

Major export destinations 1995 (% share)		Major import sources 1995 (% share)	
Spain	23.1	Kenya	17.7
Germany	16.6	United Kingdom	8.4
France	14.8	Japan	5.4
Italy	10.5	France	5.4

Ukraine

Area (km²) 603,700

Currency Karbovanets

Location Ukraine, although far from being the largest of the former Soviet states, nevertheless contains a large part of its finest agricultural land. Situated to the west of the former empire, it borders on Poland, Slovakia and northern Romania in the west, on Belarus in the north, and on Russia in the east and south, where it meets the Black Sea. There are innumerable rivers, including the Dnepr and its tributaries. The capital is Kiev.

Head of State President Leonid Kuchma (July 1994)

Head of Government Pavlo Lazarenko (May 1996)

Ruling Party Rukh (The People's Movement) and the reformed Communist Party are the most powerful political groupings.

Political Structure Since declaring its independence from the former USSR in August 1991, the Ukraine has worked consistently within the Confederation of Independent States - except in the field of defence, where it bitterly opposes Moscow. In the process it has often found itself at odds with Russia, whose influence it has repudiated even in its predominantly Russian areas. The country has an executive President who is elected by universal suffrage, and a 450-member National Assembly (Parliament), also popularly elected for a five-year term. Hard-line communist elements have stepped up their pressure on Kuchma to adopt an anti-Western position since he won stronger executive powers in mid-1995, and he may have no choice but to comply.

Last Elections The last elections to the Supreme Soviet were held in March 1994. The second round produced 86 seats for the Communist Party, 18 for the Peasant's Party, 14 for the Socialist Party, 20 for Rukh and 163 seats for independents. 112 seats were still undecided after the second round, and several dozen went to small splinter parties.

Political Risk The growing tensions between Ukraine and Russia have given some cause for concern in recent years. Political violence in ethnic Russian communities and calls for Kuchma's resignation have become commonplace. The Ukraine is understandably ambiguous about NATO's eastern expansion and does not seek membership itself (partly because that might strengthen the pro-Russian camp in Ukraine's already heavily Russified Ukrainian army). Another danger is that the Ukraine may eventually be drawn into the Russian-dominated CIS defence pact, a move which it has managed to avoid so far. In the Crimean, a Russian Nationalist, Yuri Meshkov, was elected president in 1994 and has called for independence. Kuchma's abrupt replacement of his popular prime minister, Evhen Marchuk, with Pavlo Lazarenko in May 1996 has heightened the degree of political uncertainty. The move comes at a crucial time as Kuchma is simultaneously trying to pass a draft constitution, stabilise the economy and manage relations with Russia.

International Disputes Ukraine was remodelled so extensively under Josef Stalin, that it retains a large number of political and ethnic anomalies. While relations with Poland, from which a large part of its territory was snatched, remain fair, it has been plunged into deep disagreement with Russia over territorial, defence and ethnic issues.

Economy The Ukraine was the second largest economic power in the Soviet Union before its breakup. But since gaining independence, the economy has steadily contracted. GDP fell by 23% in 1994 and another 11% in 1995. Forecasts for 1996 suggest another small decline, although the worst of the recession may now be over. The Government is attempted to steer the country towards a market economy by cutting the public deficit, restricting industrial subsidies and promoting private business. So far, these plans have not been effective though the government has announced a new programme of spending cuts which would reduce the deficit to 4% of GDP by the end of 1997.

Main Industries With its rich agricultural land, the Ukraine accounted for nearly half of all farm output in the Soviet Union before its breakup. Now, however, the sector is in disarray. Poor harvests in 1994 and 1995 have aroused fears about the country's political stability. Other important industries include coal mining, iron and steel, oil, chemicals, machine tools and food-processing, all of which are experiencing serious difficulties both in buying raw materials and in finding external markets for their goods. In general, the country is split between an industrialised (and Russified) east and a more rural west. This dichotomy hinders growth, fragments the country's markets and makes it difficult to resolve problems of unemployment and improvement in transportation infrastructure.

Energy One of the major preoccupations of the government and its western advisors is the Ukraine's energy crisis. Supplies of gas, oil and coal sometimes reach dangerously low levels. The crisis is largely due to domestic energy policies. The country must now pay world market prices for energy supplies (purchased mainly from Russia). Yet it continues to subsidise oil and gas deliveries to domestic power plants and industries.

	1993	1994	1995
Inflation (% change)	4,194.0	114.4	
Exchange rate (per US$)	25,000.00	60,750.00	104,160.00
Interest rate			
GDP (% real growth)	-14.1	-23.0	-11.4
GDP			
GDP (US$ million)	132,271.0	101,745.0	90,370.0
GDP per capita (US$)	2,534.9	1,960.0	1,750.0
Consumption			
Consumption (US$ million)	97,484.0	75,062.0	66,740.0
Consumption per capita (US$)	1,868.2	1,446.0	1,292.4
Population, mid-year ('000)	52,180.0	51,910.0	51,640.0
Birth rate (per '000)	10.7		
Death rate (per '000)	11.2		
No. of households ('000)	8,800.0	8,947.4	9,100.0
Total exports (US$ million)	7,817.0	9,708.2	12,754.0
Total imports (US$ million)	9,533.0	9,989.2	13,922.1
Tourism receipts (US$ million)			
Tourist spending (US$ million)			

Average household size 1995 (persons)	5.39		
Urban population 1995 (%)	70.3		
Age analysis (%) (1995)	*0-14* 21.4	*15-64* 66.4	*65+* 12.3
Population by sex (%) (1995)	*Male* 46.3	*Female* 53.7	
Life expectancy (years) (1991)	*Male* 65.9	*Female* 75.0	
Infant mortality (deaths per '000 live births) (1993)	15.1		
Adult literacy (%) (1989)	98.4		

TRADING PARTNERS

Major export destinations 1995 (% share)		Major import sources 1995 (% share)	
Russia	47.2	Russia	54.5
Bulgaria	8.3	Germany	10.7
Italy	5.9	Poland	5.9
China	3.9	USA	1.8

United Arab Emirates

Area (km²) 75,150

Currency UAE dirham (= 100 fils)

Location The United Arab Emirates is a confederation of nominally independent states which form a crescent running along the southern Persian (Arabian) Gulf coast of Saudi Arabia - although its eastern edge also incorporates an access to the Gulf of Oman. With the main land area of Oman to the east, and with the enclave which is the urban capital of Oman lying at its extreme eastern tip (in the Straits of Hormuz), the country occupies a position of immense strategic importance. The capital is Abu Dhabi.

Head of State Shaikh Zaid bin Sultan Zayed (President)

Head of Government Shaikh Maktoum bin Rashid al-Maktoum

Ruling Party There are no legal political parties in the United Arab Emirates.

Political Structure The United Arab Emirates is a federation of seven Emirates (Abu Dhabi, Dubai, Sharjah, Ras al-Khaimah, Fujairah, Umm al-Qaiwain and Ajman), each a monarchy in its own right. The seven monarchs together comprise the Supreme Council and elect the President and Vice-President from among their members; the President then appoints his Cabinet. The 40-member Federal National Council is appointed indirectly by the seven Emirates. Different laws apply in each of the Emirates. For example, Sharjah but not Dubai has a ban on alcohol. However, in 1994 the Sharia law was extended to all seven Emirates, apparently in a move to end violent crime and to prevent drug-related offences.

Last Elections There have been no elections to any of the UAE's bodies in recent decades.

Political Risk The apparently contradictory needs of the seven Emirates has proved no obstacle to their political co-operation in recent years. However, developments in the oil sector still have the power to divide them. The UAE's geographical position means that it faces less threat from Iran than its northern neighbours. Religious extremism is of great concern but the government treats these critics carefully, locking up only a few and admonishing the rest.

International Disputes The UAE has outstanding territorial issues only with Saudi Arabia, Oman and among its own member states. The majority remain in abeyance at present, however. Iran has an active claim to three islands belonging to the United Arab Emirates and strategically located in the Straits of Hormuz. Iran invaded the islands in 1971, arousing condemnation from the Arab League, but has been allowed since then to maintain troops on one of the three islands.

Economy With a per capita income of more than US$20,000, the United Arab Emirates ranks among the richest states in the Middle East. Its access to a variety of sea routes has proved strategically convenient during hostilities in the Gulf region, so that it has proved immune to many setbacks.

Main Industries Apart from its activities as an oil producer, the UAE acts as a downstream processor of petroleum products and a conduit and transhipment centre for producers elsewhere in the region. Abu Dhabi is the main centre of petrochemical activity. Industrial development is strongest at Abu Dhabi and in the much smaller Dubai area. Dubai is the country's main port.

Energy The UAE is fully self-sufficient in terms of all energy resources.

	1993	1994	1995
Inflation (% change)	6.0	0.0	0.5
Exchange rate (per US$)	3.67	3.67	3.67
Interest rate			
GDP (% real growth)	-0.8	2.9	2.0
GDP (Million units of national currency)	129,200.0	133,000.0	136,338.3
GDP (US$ million)	35,204.4	36,239.8	37,149.4
GDP per capita (US$)	19,396.3	19,483.8	16,082.0
Consumption (Million units of national currency)	57,005.0	57,421.9	57,599.6
Consumption (US$ million)	15,532.7	15,646.3	15,694.7
Consumption per capita (US$)	8,558.0	8,412.0	6,794.2
Population, mid-year ('000)	1,815.0	1,860.0	2,310.0
Birth rate (per '000)	23.2	28.3	
Death rate (per '000)	2.7	2.5	
No. of households ('000)	432.0	446.0	461.0
Total exports (US$ million)			
Total imports (US$ million)			
Tourism receipts (US$ million)			
Tourist spending (US$ million)			

Average household size 1995 (persons)	4.76				
Urban population 1995 (%)	84.0				
Age analysis (%) (1977)	*0-14*	26.3	*15-64*	72.1	*65+* 1.6
Population by sex (%) (1977)	*Male*	71.2	*Female*	28.8	
Life expectancy (years) (1990-95)	*Male*	73.0	*Female*	75.3	
Infant mortality (deaths per '000 live births) (1993)	18.8				
Adult literacy (%) (1995)	79.2				

TRADING PARTNERS

Major export destinations 1995 (% share)		Major import sources 1995 (% share)	
Japan	39.4	Japan	8.6
South Korea	5.9	USA	8.2
India	5.7	United Kingdom	7.5
Singapore	5.6	Italy	7.0

United Kingdom

Area (km²) 244,755

Currency Pound sterling (£ = 100 pence)

Location Lying off the coast of western continental Europe between the Atlantic Ocean and the North Sea, the United Kingdom comprises mainly two distinct land masses - the larger incorporating England, Scotland and the Principality of Wales, and the smaller consisting of Northern Ireland - actually, the north-western part of the island of Ireland. The capital is London.

Head of State HM Queen Elizabeth II

Head of Government John Major (1990)

Ruling Party Conservative Party

Political Structure The United Kingdom is considered to be a constitutional monarchy even though it has no written constitution. The non-executive monarch rules through an elected House of Commons (Lower House of Parliament), and this is supplemented in an advisory capacity by a House of Lords (Upper House). Northern Ireland has been ruled directly from London since the abolition of the Stormont Parliament there in the early 1970s. However, English laws are not automatically applicable in Northern Ireland or in Scotland, where other rules sometimes apply.

Last Elections The April 1992 elections to the House of Commons produced a reduced majority of 21 for the Conservative Party, which obtained only 336 of the 651 seats, and 42% of the vote, compared with 375 in 1987. The Labour Party obtained 271 seats (34% of the vote), while the Liberal Democrats won only 20 seats despite winning 18% of the vote. The Scottish National Party won three seats, the Welsh nationalist Plaid Cymru four, the Official Ulster Unionists nine, the Democratic Unionists three, the Ulster Popular Unionists one and the (Northern Ireland) Social Democratic and Labour Party four seats. The Conservatives lost more seats through defections and by-elections and by mid-1996 clung to the slimmest of majorities in the House of Commons.

Political Risk A steady decline in the popularity of John Major and his Conservative Party since mid-1995 has been matched by a gradual increase in the influence of Tony Blair's Labour Party. A change in the ruling party could have important implications for the UK's role in the EU as many in the current administration strongly oppose the organisation's major goals - in particular, the policy of monetary union.

International Disputes For the last 25 years the main territorial issue in the UK has revolved around the often violent attempts of Irish nationalists to force the Government to return the province of Northern Ireland to the Republic of Ireland. Although Republican militants have, for the first time, announced their intention to abandon the armed struggle, talks have floundered following a scaled-back campaign of bombings and violence. Ireland officially condemns the attacks, though its own Constitution calls for the return of Northern Ireland. The only intra-EU territorial dispute concerns Spain's demand for the return of Gibraltar.

Economy The UK's economy did not turn in an impressive performance in 1995. Manufacturing output showed little growth and the rate of increase in GDP slowed to 1.5% during the fourth quarter of the year. The government hopes to boost growth by cutting taxes and interest rates in an effort to boost consumer spending. That component already accounts for more than half the increase in GDP in a typical quarter and could rise further as these measures take affect. However, the pattern of consumer spending today appears to differ from that at the beginning of this decade. The greater amounts that households now have no longer translates into more retail sales. Instead, extra spending appears to be going into other services such as entertainment, restaurant meals, health and recreation, travel and other leisure activities. Unemployment, though not high by the standards of France or Belgium, remains at levels which are politically sensitive.

Main Industries Manufacturing encompasses a wide range of activities including both consumer and heavy industrial goods, aerospace and information technology. Oil production continues to be an important earner of foreign exchange. The services sector is the strongest area of the economy, with banking and insurance being internationally competitive. Agriculture is fairly limited in importance, despite the fact that the country is fully self-sufficient in most basic products. Farms tend to be larger than the European average.

Energy The UK is self-sufficient in crude oil and gas, but prefers to export some of its higher-grade crudes and import coarser grades for use as feedstock for chemicals. Total production reached a new high of 130 million tons in 1995. Meanwhile, new discoveries raised the volume of reserves to 3.3 billion tonnes, confounding predictions that the oil and gas industry would decline by the end of the 1990s.

	1993	1994	1995
Inflation (% change)	1.6	2.5	3.4
Exchange rate (per US$)	0.67	0.65	0.63
Interest rate (% per annum)	5.9	5.5	6.7
GDP (% real growth)	4.1	3.3	1.3
GDP (Billion units of national currency)	631.0	667.8	699.6
GDP (US$ million)	947,874.4	1,022,821.3	1,103,945.1
GDP per capita (US$)	16,289.0	17,515.7	18,846.4
Consumption (Billion units of national currency)	395.4	418.0	441.0
Consumption (US$ million)	593,961.2	640,220.6	695,912.9
Consumption per capita (US$)	10,207.1	10,963.7	11,880.5
Population, mid-year ('000)	58,191.0	58,394.6	58,576.0
Birth rate (per '000)	13.1	12.9	13.4
Death rate (per '000)	11.3	10.7	10.6
No. of households ('000)	21,337.0	21,394.9	21,453.0
Total exports (US$ million)	180,180.0	204,923.0	237,365.3
Total imports (US$ million)	205,390.0	227,000.0	261,061.3
Tourism receipts (US$ million)	13,451.0	14,728.0	
Tourist spending (US$ million)	17,431.0	19,085.8	20,746.1

Average household size 1995 (persons)	2.59		
Urban population 1995 (%)	89.5		
Age analysis (%) (1995)	*0-14* 19.5	*15-64* 64.8	*65+* 15.8
Population by sex (%) (1995)	*Male* 49.1	*Female* 50.9	
Life expectancy (years) (1993-94)	*Male* 73.6	*Female* 78.9	
Infant mortality (deaths per '000 live births) (1993)	6.3		
Adult literacy (%) (1984)	99.0		

TRADING PARTNERS

Major export destinations 1995 (% share)		Major import sources 1995 (% share)	
Germany	12.3	Germany	14.6
USA	12.1	USA	12.3
France	9.2	France	9.0
Netherlands	7.2	Netherlands	6.1

Uruguay

Area (km^2)   186,925

Currency   New Uruguayan peso (= 100 centésimos)

Location   Uruguay, the smallest republic in South America, lies on the central Atlantic coast between Argentina in the south and west, and Brazil in the north. With an equable climate and with generally adequate rainfall despite occasional droughts, the area consists largely of grassy plains with lush forests in some parts. The capital is Montevideo.

Head of State   President Julio Maria Sanguinetti (March 1995)

Head of Government   President Julio Maria Sanguinetti

Ruling Party   Colorado Party leads a four-party coalition with the National (Blanco) Party.

Political Structure   Uruguay has an executive President who is elected every five years, together with a 99-member House of Deputies and a 31-member Senate. The political system was effectively suspended from 1973, when a military dictatorship took over the country, until 1985, when civilian rule was restored.

Last Elections   The November 1994 elections, whose results were not published until January 1995, produced a narrow victory for the Colorado Party (11 seats) over the ruling National (Blanco) Party (10 seats) and the Progressive Encounter (9 seats) - which proved an unsuitable basis for single-party government. Accordingly, the three parties formed a coalition in January 1995 with the New Space Party which had won the remaining parliamentary seat, under the Colorado leader Sangionetti.

Political Risk   Uruguay's commitment to political reform has been clear since the end of the 1980s, and there seems little reason to expect a return to military rule. In the economic sphere, however, the situation is somewhat different. For years Uruguay traded on its role as an island of stability and certainty in a continent of chaos. Critics say this is not enough in a tumultuous South American decade of change. As other countries slim the state, and reshape and open their economies, Uruguay's determined inertia looks less admirable and less sustainable.

Economy   Uruguay has never suffered the economic mayhem that has afflicted some of its neighbours. Inflation, at over 40%, is high but hyperinflation has never emerged. The peso is weak and is periodically depreciated but the decline is a graduated one and not a free fall. External debt has been steadily reduced and the current-account deficit is down to about 2% of GDP. However, the country's generous welfare system is a growing cause for concern among economists. Education, health and social welfare have benefited greatly from this system, but government spending now accounts for over 30% of GDP. The president points to measures taken to tighten public-sector management and allow more competition, but businesses increasingly complain about the bureaucracy and regulations.

Main Industries   Agriculture is the dominant sector, with cattle herding the main farming activity and the biggest single source of foreign exchange. Wheat, barley, maize, rice, oilseeds and vegetables are also produced for the domestic market. Manufacturing includes not only various agro-processing industries but also production of a range of more sophisticated consumer goods. Other industries manufacture industrial components and industrial intermediates such as vehicle tyres, cement, plywood and petroleum products. Mineral extraction is of little significance in comparison with most other South American economies. Uruguay has iron ore, dolomite, marble and granite.

Energy   Uruguay has no significant oil resources and is dependent on imports for all its needs - although it has massive hydro-electric potential. The high cost and low quality of the output of state monopolies in oil and electricity are a constant target of criticism for business.

	1993	1994	1995
Inflation (% change)	54.1	44.7	42.2
Exchange rate (per US$)	3.95	5.05	6.28
Interest rate (% per annum)	97.3	95.1	99.1
GDP (% real growth)	4.0	2.2	-11.1
GDP (Billion units of national currency)	53.1	78.5	99.3
GDP (US$ million)	13,452.8	15,539.0	15,796.1
GDP per capita (US$)	4,270.7	4,901.9	4,951.7
Consumption (Billion units of national currency)	37.1	52.6	63.8
Consumption (US$ million)	9,400.0	10,409.9	10,145.6
Consumption per capita (US$)	2,984.1	3,283.9	3,180.4
Population, mid-year ('000)	3,150.0	3,170.0	3,190.0
Birth rate (per '000)	17.9	17.7	
Death rate (per '000)	9.8	9.4	
No. of households ('000)	667.5	675.1	683.0
Total exports (US$ million)	1,645.0	1,913.0	2,089.0
Total imports (US$ million)	2,326.0	2,786.0	2,867.0
Tourism receipts (US$ million)	447.0	473.4	
Tourist spending (US$ million)	129.0	136.6	133.1

Average household size 1995 (persons)	4.44				
Urban population 1995 (%)	90.3				
Age analysis (%) (1990)	*0-14* 25.8		*15-64* 62.6		*65+* 11.6
Population by sex (%) (1990)	*Male* 48.8		*Female* 51.3		
Life expectancy (years) (1985-90)	*Male* 68.9		*Female* 75.3		
Infant mortality (deaths per '000 live births) (1992)	18.6				
Adult literacy (%) (1995)	97.3				

TRADING PARTNERS

Major export destinations 1995 (% share)		Major import sources 1995 (% share)	
Brazil	26.9	Brazil	28.4
Argentina	12.3	Argentina	24.7
USA	7.7	USA	15.6
Germany	4.9	Italy	8.8

USA

Area (km^2) 9,363,130

Currency US dollar (US$ = 100 cents)

Location The United States is a federation of 50 states which spans the land mass between the Pacific Ocean and the northern Atlantic. As such, it occupies most of the North American continent, extending from the Alaskan enclave in the far west to Maine in the extreme north-east. In the north it borders on Canada, and in the south with Mexico. The west and south-west consist mainly of mountain ranges. The capital is Washington, DC.

Head of State President Bill Clinton (January 1993)

Head of Government President Bill Clinton

Ruling Party Democratic Party controls the government; Republicans hold a majority in both the House of Representatives and Senate.

Political Structure The United States has an executive President, elected for a four-year term of office by universal suffrage, who then selects and directs his own Cabinet ("Administration"). The US Congress comprises a 435-member House of Representatives, half of whom are elected every two years, and a 100-member Senate, which serves for six years but a third of which is re-elected every two years. The country has a strong federal structure, and devolves its legal and fiscal system to a considerable extent.

Last Elections At the presidential elections held in November 1992, the Democrat candidate Bill Clinton defeated the incumbent George Bush, receiving 43% of the popular vote and 370 electoral college votes. The Democrats maintained control of both chambers of Congress in the 1992 election, winning 259 seats in the House of Representatives and 57 in the Senate. However, the mid-term elections in November 1994 produced a devastating setback for the Clinton administration. The Democrats lost control of both houses of Congress, when the Republicans won 227 seats in the House of Representatives and 53 seats in the Senate.

Political Risk The USA is by far the most wealthy democracy in the developed world. Its Constitution offers an effective guarantee of open government. Minor risks are sometimes posed by abrupt swings in the value of the US dollar and the tendency of domestic producers to lobby for mandatory restraints against imported goods.

International Disputes With the conclusion of the Cold War and the dissolution of the Soviet Union, US foreign policy is no longer dominated by the superpower tensions of the past. As its post-war protecting role in Europe has become obsolete, its attention has shifted more towards the opportunities in South America and Asia. The USA continues to be vitally concerned with developments in the Middle East which is a major source of its future oil supplies.

Economy The US economy performed much better than most competitors over the past two years but weakened in the last quarter of 1995. That development now appears to be an aberration as the rate of growth resumed during the second quarter of 1996. Inflation remains low, despite a fall in unemployment and a rise in manufacturers' orders. Meanwhile, the Clinton Administration's desire to expand on its trade agreements in Latin America and Asia has been stymied by resistance in Congress. A number of compromises between Republican and Democratic leaders has belatedly resulted in agreement on a 1996 budget but an even more acrimonious battle can be expected when negotiations on the 1997 budget begins.

Main Industries The country's diversified manufacturing activities range from heavy goods such as steel and motor vehicles to high-technology, aircraft, light engineering and consumer products which, by popular consent, rank among the best in the world. The USA also has a highly developed chemical and biotechnology industry. Many older industries are less competitive, however. Agriculture is predominately large scale and generally efficient, making the country a major exporter of foodstuffs and processed foods. Services is the largest sector in the economy and many of these activities (for example, banking) are rapidly undergoing a consolidation at present.

Energy Although a substantial producer of oil in its own right, the USA is gradually becoming an even larger importer of oil and gas, much of this from Mexico and Venezuela, to make up the perennial supply shortfall. The country's nuclear facilities presently account for 20% of all its electricity needs.

	1993	1994	1995
Inflation (% change)	3.0	2.6	2.8
Exchange rate (per US$)	1.00	1.00	1.00
Interest rate (% per annum)	6.0	7.1	8.8
GDP (% real growth)	2.3	3.5	2.2
GDP (Million units of national currency)	6,343,300.0	6,738,400.0	7,080,000.0
GDP (US$ million)	6,343,300.0	6,738,400.0	7,080,000.0
GDP per capita (US$)	24,573.1	25,851.3	26,917.1
Consumption (Million units of national currency)	4,378,200.0	4,627,000.0	4,893,000.0
Consumption (US$ million)	4,378,200.0	4,627,000.0	4,893,000.0
Consumption per capita (US$)	16,960.6	17,751.1	18,602.4
Population, mid-year ('000)	258,140.0	260,660.0	263,030.0
Birth rate (per '000)	15.8	15.6	15.3
Death rate (per '000)	8.3	8.4	8.4
No. of households ('000)	97,946.0	99,111.0	100,308.0
Total exports (US$ million)	464,773.0	512,521.0	583,863.0
Total imports (US$ million)	603,438.0	689,215.0	771,272.0
Tourism receipts (US$ million)	74,171.0	75,060.0	74,010.0
Tourist spending (US$ million)	51,980.0	53,085.0	58,445.0

Average household size 1995 (persons)	2.49				
Urban population 1995 (%)	76.2				
Age analysis (%) (1992)	*0-14*	21.9	*15-64*	65.4	*65+* 12.7
Population by sex (%) (1992)	*Male*	48.8	*Female*	51.2	
Life expectancy (years) (1991)	*Male*	72.0	*Female*	78.9	
Infant mortality (deaths per '000 live births) (1993)	8.3				
Adult literacy (%) (1985)	99.5				

TRADING PARTNERS

Major export destinations 1995 (% share)		Major import sources 1995 (% share)	
Canada	21.6	Canada	25.4
Japan	11.0	Japan	21.8
Mexico	7.8	Mexico	10.8
United Kingdom	4.9	Germany	6.5

Uzbekistan

Area (km²)   447,400

Currency   Som

Location   Uzbekistan, one of the southernmost of the former Soviet republics, runs south-east in a broad sweep, from the dried-out Aral Sea to the Afghan border in the south and the Tajikistan border in the east. Kazakhstan remains to the north; a further finger of land extends eastward to meet Kyrgyzstan. The land is mostly desert or at best plain, and the climate is warm and mainly dry. The capital is Tashkent.

Head of State   President Islam Karimov (1990)

Head of Government   Abdulkhashim Mulatov (May 1993)

Ruling Party   People's Democratic Party (PDP)

Political Structure   Uzbekistan, a predominantly Sunni Muslim state within the former USSR, has an executive President who is directly elected by universal suffrage for a term of eight years (recently extended from five years). He answers to a 500-seat Supreme Soviet. Uzbek politics have changed less than those of many other republics, since the outgoing communist administration has effectively been re-elected in its entirety, with religious groups offering the only serious organised competition.

Last Elections   The last full elections to the Supreme Soviet were in March 1990, before independence, when the ruling Communist Party (now reformed as the PDP) was generally unopposed. By December 1991, when free presidential elections were held, the Communist Party chairman Islam Karimov still won 86% of the vote - a move on which he sought to capitalise by having his term extended by three years, so as to serve until 1999. Islamic groups are important in Uzbek politics.

Political Risk   Street demonstrations for greater democracy have attracted media attention in recent years, but the protests are generally unfocused and the Government has exerted a firm grip on the domestic security situation. A severe clampdown on the freedom of the press was initiated in January 1994. But Uzbekistan has been surprisingly successful in attracting foreign investors, mainly to its energy sector.

Economy   Organisation of the economy has changed very little since the breakup of the Soviet Union. Most decisions are still taken by planners rather than the market and few moves to introduce reform have been made. The loss of many of the subsidies from Moscow means that short-term growth prospects are poor. Although inflation is being brought under control, the country's real GDP shrank by 4% in 1995 following a contraction of 3% in 1994. Uzbekistan's economy is desperate for water for irrigation and this shortage seriously affects its agricultural performance. In January 1994 the country entered into an economic union with Kyrgyzstan and Kazakhstan and the prospect of agreement on water sharing between the countries could alleviate this constraint.

Main Industries   Uzbekistan has significant mineral resources, and mining plays a central role in the economy, notably of coal, gold, copper, tungsten and aluminium ore. In addition there are large deposits of oil and natural gas. Agriculture is an important part of the economy, based on livestock (mainly pigs and sheep), and the cultivation of cotton, grain, fruit and vegetables. Established industries include chemicals, iron and steel, as well as others based on the country's mineral resources.

Energy   The country has substantial deposits of oil and natural gas, which represent its biggest attraction to foreign investors at present. Power generation is one of the main established industries, with export potential.

	1993	1994	1995
Inflation (% change)	534.0	746.0	325.0
Exchange rate (per US$)			1,150.00
Interest rate			
GDP (% real growth)	-2.4	-3.0	-4.0
GDP (Million units of national currency)	1,200,800.0		
GDP (US$ million)	24,420.1	24,218.5	23,060.0
GDP per capita (US$)	1,117.1	1,083.6	1,009.2
Consumption			
Consumption (US$ million)	18,521.0	17,921.8	16,911.0
Consumption per capita (US$)	847.3	801.9	740.1
Population, mid-year ('000)	21,860.0	22,350.0	22,850.0
Birth rate (per '000)	33.8	29.0	28.2
Death rate (per '000)	6.7	6.5	
No. of households ('000)	3,775.1	3,821.6	3,870.0
Total exports (US$ million)	1,231.1	1,624.6	
Total imports (US$ million)			
Tourism receipts (US$ million)			
Tourist spending (US$ million)			

Average household size 1995 (persons)	5.61				
Urban population 1995 (%)	41.3				
Age analysis (%) (1992, est)	*0-14* 49.6		*15-64* 48.1		*65+* 2.3
Population by sex (%) (1989)	*Male* 49.4		*Female* 50.6		
Life expectancy (years) (1989)	*Male* 66.0		*Female* 72.1		
Infant mortality (deaths per '000 live births)					
Adult literacy (%) (1989)	97.2				

TRADING PARTNERS

Major export destinations 1995 (% share)		Major import sources 1995 (% share)	
Russia	40.9	Russia	39.0
Germany	10.1	Germany	21.6
Italy	9.6	South Korea	10.4
France	6.0	Japan	3.9

Vanuatu

Area (km²) 14,765

Currency Vatu (V = 100 centimes)

Location Vanuatu, which was formerly run as an Anglo-French condominium under the name New Hebrides, consists of about 80 islands in the south-west Pacific located about 1,000 km west of Fiji. Most of the islands are uninhabited and many are active volcanoes. The country has a moderate tropical climate, and is occasionally susceptible to cyclones. The capital is Port Vila.

Head of State President Jean-Marie Leye (March 1994)

Head of Government Maxime Carlot Korman

Ruling Party Union of Moderate Parties (UMP) rules with the support of the Vanuatu National United Party (VNUP).

Political Structure The Republic of Vanuatu is an independent member of the Commonwealth. The executive President is elected for a five-year term by an electoral college which includes not only the Parliament but also the presidents of the numerous Regional Councils. These Councils enjoy a considerable degree of regional autonomy. The 46 members of the unicameral national Parliament are elected by universal adult suffrage for a four-year term.

Last Elections Elections were held in December 1991 to the Parliament when the administration of Walter Lini was overturned as the UMP won 19 of the 46 seats. Lini's Vanua'aku Pati, which had governed since independence, had been split just prior to the election following his forced removal from the Premiership. He launched his own party, the Vanuatu National United Party, which won 10 seats in the election as did the Vanua'aku Pati. The Melanesian Progressive Party won four seats, the Fren Melanesia won one and independents won two seats. Afterwards, the VNUP agreed to support the UMP.

Political Risk The unexpectedly strong level of political infighting and political fragmentation in recent years reflects a deep distrust between the many ethnic and regional communities. Language is an issue: Carlot's party is predominantly French-speaking, while the ousted Lini was an English speaker. However, the country's democratic mechanisms appear to have stood up well to the recent strains.

Economy Although far from poor by the standards of the region, Vanuatu has seen little growth in its economy during recent years and is looking to the service sector for dynamism. Meanwhile, the country remains heavily dependent on copra exports and is vulnerable to any wide swings in the price of this commodity.

Main Industries Farming, mainly on a subsistence basis, accounts for much more than half of the country's national economy and feeds more than three-quarters of the population. Copra, cocoa and coffee are grown for export, while most residents live on cassava, yams, mangoes, sweet potatoes, taro and breadfruit. Cattle raising is widespread, and fishing is an important source of proteins. Manufacturing tends to centre on the processing of food products, notably canned or frozen meat, or timber products. All other manufactures are imported. Tourism, although potentially lucrative, has been slow to take root in Vanuatu. On the other hand, the opening of the economy to international financial services, via tax concessions and secrecy laws, has been more successful.

Energy Vanuatu has no indigenous oil, gas or coal resources and will remain dependent for the foreseeable future on imports for its energy requirements.

	1993	1994	1995
Inflation (% change)	5.4	2.3	2.2
Exchange rate (per US$)	121.58	116.01	111.28
Interest rate (% per annum)	16.0	16.0	16.0
GDP (% real growth)	1.6	-3.6	-1.8
GDP (Million units of national currency)	21,959.0	21,644.4	21,726.2
GDP (US$ million)	180.6	186.6	195.2
GDP per capita (US$)	1,128.8	1,151.7	1,183.3
Consumption (Million units of national currency)	11,701.0	11,650.0	11,812.3
Consumption (US$ million)	96.2	100.4	106.1
Consumption per capita (US$)	601.5	619.9	643.3
Population, mid-year ('000)	160.0	162.0	165.0
Birth rate (per '000)	35.2	32.2	
Death rate (per '000)	7.2	7.8	
No. of households ('000)	26.6	27.1	27.9
Total exports (US$ million)	23.7	25.0	28.0
Total imports (US$ million)	79.0	89.0	93.3
Tourism receipts (US$ million)	30.0	31.1	31.2
Tourist spending (US$ million)	1.2	1.2	1.2

Average household size 1995 (persons)	5.62				
Urban population 1995 (%)	19.3				
Age analysis (%) (1989)	*0-14* 45.6	*15-64* 51.8	*65+* 2.6
Population by sex (%) (1989)	*Male* 52.1	*Female* 47.9	
Life expectancy (years) (1990-95)	*Male* 63.5	*Female* 67.3	
Infant mortality (deaths per '000 live births)			
Adult literacy (%) (1979)	52.9		

Venezuela

Area (km²)   912,045

Currency   Bólivar (= 100 céntimos)

Location   Venezuela, perhaps the most oil-rich state in South America, lies on the north-east Atlantic and Caribbean coast of the continent, with Brazil to the south, Colombia to the west, and Guyana to the east. Much of the south and west of the country comprises the high sierras of the Guiana highlands, and in the north-west the land rises again to the Sierra Nevada. Elsewhere, there are low forested areas, especially along the Orinoco River which winds slowly north-east through the country. The capital is Caracas.

Head of State   President Rafael Caldera Rodriguez (February 1994)

Head of Government   President Rafael Caldera Rodriguez

Ruling Party   National Convergence Party

Political Structure   Venezuelan politics have been complicated by continuous dissent and uncertainty. In 1993, the country elected its third president in three years. The President is directly elected for a five-year executive term and answers to a 49-member Senate and a 201-member Chamber of Deputies, also elected for five years. The country has an extensively devolved political structure, with 20 autonomous states and 72 dependencies. In recent years the government's failure to address the country's economic problems has generated widespread discontent and, occasionally, violence.

Last Elections   Presidential elections were held in December 1993, when Rafael Caldera Rodriguez was appointed to replace Ramón José Velasquez, who held the post for less than a year. Local elections in December 1995 revealed little enthusiasm for Caldera's new Convergence Movement. Instead, voters strongly supported the old, centre-left Democratic Action party.

Political Risk   Dissatisfaction with the country's 80-year-old president is widespread. Venezuelans get little benefit from the $18 billion in annual oil income that the country earns. Opposition parties reorganised in 1996 when the Democratic Action formed a loose alliance with the Radical Cause and the conservative Social Christians and then secured leadership in both houses. The slow pace of agricultural reform and a tendency toward government intervention in prices and retail legislation are further problems. The country's strained relations with international lending institutions have improved, leading to a $2.5 billion in emergency loans from the IMF and the IADB in April 1996. This fact, coupled with the recent rise in oil prices, may provide the government some relief by the end of 1996.

International Disputes   Venezuela has an outstanding territorial dispute with Guyana over an area of land deep in its interior, but this is largely dormant. There have been tensions in the country's relationship with Colombia, which claims that Venezuela has aided Colombian rebels trying to bring down the Colombian government.

Economy   Once considered one of the wealthiest and most developed countries in Latin America, Venezuela is today struggling to jump-start its economy and avoid defaulting on nearly one-third of its $26 billion in foreign debt. A banking crisis in 1994 cost the state nearly $5 billion, strained government coffers and plunged the economy into a prolonged recession. Rather than turning to international capital markets, the government started printing money to meet its needs. Inflation, which was over 100% per annum in early 1996, was the result. The country's GDP shrank by around 5% in 1994 and growth was negligible in 1995. One ominous result is that the distribution of income is worsening, with the richest 10% of the population now receiving 40% of annual income while the middle class shrinks. In April 1996, the president announced a sweeping new programme for economic adjustment that will be implemented in conjunction with the recent IMF loan. It calls for a quick return to free convertibility of the currency and freely floating interest rates. And in order to cut the budget deficit, there will be an increase in sales taxes (from 12.5% to 16.5%) along with a fivefold increase in the country's heavily subsidised petrol prices.

Main Industries   Oil is the mainstay of the Venezuelan economy, accounting for 80% of foreign exchange revenues in a typical year. The sector feeds a variety of downstream industries based on oil. Agriculture, on the other hand, is fragmented and lacking in investment. Many of the country's farmers produce only subsistence crops, although cotton, coffee, cocoa, rice, sugar, tobacco and bananas are produced for export. Meat production is of an unusually high order.

Energy   Venezuela is fully self-sufficient in oil, gas and electricity, with an exportable surplus of all three commodities. Total export earnings in 1995 were $18 billion.

	1993	1994	1995
Inflation (% change)	38.1	60.8	59.9
Exchange rate (per US$)	90.83	147.75	174.94
Interest rate (% per annum)	48.9	46.6	32.2
GDP (% real growth)	-2.5	-1.3	-4.1
GDP (Million units of national currency)	5,449,100.0	8,651,300.0	13,265,900.0
GDP (US$ million)	59,992.3	58,553.6	75,831.1
GDP per capita (US$)	2,896.8	2,738.7	3,504.5
Consumption (Million units of national currency)	3,989,100.0	6,039,100.0	8,830,153.9
Consumption (US$ million)	43,918.3	40,873.8	50,475.3
Consumption per capita (US$)	2,120.6	1,911.8	2,332.7
Population, mid-year ('000)	20,710.0	21,380.0	21,638.0
Birth rate (per '000)	28.1	25.6	
Death rate (per '000)	4.7	4.5	
No. of households ('000)	3,723.3	3,805.6	3,888.0
Total exports (US$ million)	14,066.0	15,756.0	18,543.0
Total imports (US$ million)	12,200.0	8,921.0	11,977.0
Tourism receipts (US$ million)	554.0	512.9	
Tourist spending (US$ million)	2,083.0		

Average household size 1995 (persons)	5.29				
Urban population 1995 (%)	92.9				
Age analysis (%) (1992)	*0-14* 36.2		*15-64* 59.9		*65+* 3.9
Population by sex (%) (1995)	*Male* 50.4		*Female* 49.6		
Life expectancy (years) (1990)	*Male* 66.8		*Female* 72.8		
Infant mortality (deaths per '000 live births) (1994)	23.4				
Adult literacy (%) (1995)	91.1				

TRADING PARTNERS

Major export destinations 1995 (% share)		Major import sources 1995 (% share)	
USA	51.1	USA	43.1
Colombia	8.8	Colombia	7.8
Brazil	4.0	Germany	4.6
Germany	3.0	Brazil	4.1

Vietnam

Area (km²) 329,565

Currency New dông (= 10 hào = 100 xu)

Location Vietnam is located on the South China Sea coast of the Indo-Chinese peninsula. The country follows the coast for more than 2,000 km from the Chinese border in the north to the far south where it joins Cambodia on the Gulf of Thailand. There is also a western border with Laos. The climate is tropical and extremely humid. The capital is Hanoi.

Head of State President Do Muoi

Head of Government Senior Gen. Vo Van Kiet

Ruling Party Communist Party of Vietnam (CPV)

Political Structure Vietnam's economic and political reforms have not diminished the Communist Party's hold on power. The country has a semi-executive President who has until recently been elected from single-candidate lists, and a 395-member National Assembly which is formally vested with all legislative power. In practice, the CPV controls the armed forces and the judiciary. In 1995, Vietnam became the first communist member of the ASEAN group.

Last Elections The CPV won all but two of the 395 seats at the ninth National Assembly election in 1992. A few non-communists stood for office but none were elected and the system is effectively stacked against them.

Political Risk Some expect Vietnam to be the next of Asia's "little dragons". Its 70 million people clearly represent a huge potential market. Government officials, however, are especially cautious about these prospects. They have made clear that they intend "to maintain a socialist ideology" - a phrase which suggests a fear that emerging market forces can undermine the party's grip on the economy. Nor do the country's leaders intend to let foreign investment chip away at state control. True political risks appear to be minimal but Hanoi's caution will cramp economic growth. Aid donors are concerned about Vietnam's unwillingness to make policy changes while economic performance is satisfactory. The failure to do so could mean that the country is unable to create the 1 million new jobs needed to keep pace with a growing population.

International Disputes Vietnam's war against the United States left scars on its relations with that country which are only now starting to heal. Meanwhile, Vietnam is still confronting the hostility of China, following its Soviet-backed invasion of Cambodia (then called Kampuchea) from 1980 to 1990. The country is one of many claimants for the sovereignty of the Spratly Islands in the South China Sea, which are thought to be rich in oil.

Economy During 1990-1995 Vietnam's industry grew at an annual rate of 13.6%. The eighth national party congress in 1996 set a new five-year plan that would lead to industrial growth of 15% a year between 1996 and 2001. Vietnam clearly aims to be one of the region's "super-achievers" by the end of the decade. However, there is a troublesome side effect to all this success: economic progress is proving to be very uneven. For example, growth in the south-east region around Ho Chi Minh City averaged 17.5% in the first half of this decade but in the poor, south-central coast region it was only 1.7%. The government's efforts to ensure that the benefits of growth are widely dispersed are handicapped by the weak provincial infrastructure and the fact that most rural workers lack the necessary skills. Vietnam must also develop more small and medium-sized businesses (as China has done) but has no programmes to do so. Finally, funding for health, education and infrastructure has been neglected but is desperately needed in the countryside. Spending in these areas pays off slowly but is essential for sustainable growth.

Main Industries At least three-quarters of the population are engaged in subsistence farming. Cultivation of rice is widespread and the country is self-sufficient. Fruit, vegetables and tobacco are also grown. Fishing is particularly important; the government plans to double the level of seafood exports by 2000 in a further attempt to attract foreign capital. Industrial development has been slow, but a growing range of consumer products are now being manufactured by the private sector. About 7,000 state-owned enterprises are remain in operation (down from 12,000 in 1990) but the government claims that in 1995 only 8% were making losses. Since these firms are not audited, the figure is hard to check but the firms do provide around 40% of government revenues. Most new foreign joint-venture firms are set up with state-owned partners, meaning that the inflow of foreign capital is actually strengthening the state's grip. In 1995, plans were announced for a massive new port complex in the north of the country which will be the largest investment project yet.

Energy Vietnam is self-sufficient in coal, but imports most of its fuels. In 1993, however, a massive gas field was discovered in Vietnamese territorial waters and other discoveries have followed. The country currently derives about a third of its electricity from hydro-electric sources.

	1993	1994	1995
Inflation (% change)	5.3	14.4	15.3
Exchange rate (per US$)	14,500.00	11,072.90	11,104.00
Interest rate			
GDP (% real growth)	7.2	6.5	11.0
GDP (Billion units of national currency)	186,223.5	226,887.3	290,377.1
GDP (US$ million)	12,843.0	20,490.3	26,150.7
GDP per capita (US$)	180.9	282.6	355.1
Consumption (Billion units of national currency)	190,000.0	193,286.0	206,549.4
Consumption (US$ million)	13,103.4	17,455.8	18,601.3
Consumption per capita (US$)	184.6	240.7	252.6
Population, mid-year ('000)	70,980.0	72,510.0	73,648.9
Birth rate (per '000)	30.7		
Death rate (per '000)	8.0		
No. of households ('000)	15,283.5	15,524.0	15,760.0
Total exports (US$ million)	2,870.0	3,500.0	
Total imports (US$ million)	3,140.0	3,300.0	
Tourism receipts (US$ million)			
Tourist spending (US$ million)			

Average household size 1995 (persons)	4.44				
Urban population 1995 (%)	20.8				
Age analysis (%) (1989)	*0-14*	39.0	*15-64*	56.3	*65+* 4.8
Population by sex (%) (1989)	*Male*	48.7	*Female*	51.3	
Life expectancy (years) (1990)	*Male*	59.2	*Female*	63.6	
Infant mortality (deaths per '000 live births) (1993)	42.0				
Adult literacy (%) (1995)	93.7				

Western Samoa

Area (km²) 2,840

Currency   Tala (W$ = 100 sene)

Location Western Samoa consists of nine islands, of which the two largest are Savai'i and Upolu, lying in the South Pacific north of Tonga and some 2,400 km north of New Zealand. The country has a pleasant climate, although it is susceptible to cyclones. The capital is Apia.

Head of State HH King Susuga Malietoa Tanumafili II

Head of Government Tofilau eti Alesana

Ruling Party Human Rights Protection Party (HRPP)

Political Structure Western Samoa, an independent member of the Commonwealth, has a constitutional monarch who may dissolve the 49-member Fono (Parliament) at any time and who appoints the Prime Minister on the recommendation of the Fono. A system of full universal voting was introduced in December 1990, prior to the country's first fully franchised elections. However, the voting mechanism was changed in 1993 to extend the life of the Parliament from three years to five.

Last Elections During the general election of April 1991, the ruling Human Rights Protection Party of Tofilau eti Alesana was returned with 30 of the 47 seats in the Fono, while the Samoan National Development Party obtained 16 and the remaining seat went to an independent. Elections to two additional seats were won by the HRPP in early 1992.

Political Risk Western Samoa has been working vigorously to attract foreign investment, and offers tax incentives and freeport facilities. The country has a well developed infrastructure and is reasonably stable in political terms.

Economy With a per capita income of around US$600, Western Samoa represents only a small consumer market. An improvement in the world prices for several of the country's major exports (for example, cocoa) have provided a much-needed boost to the economy. Upon the advice of international lending institutions, the government has introduced a 10% sales tax in an effort to diversify the tax base away from direct taxation.

Main Industries Farming, largely on a subsistence basis, occupies the greater part of the workforce. Coconuts and copra, cocoa, bananas, coffee and tropical fruits are grown for export, while cassava, fruit and vegetables are destined for the domestic market. Farmers have occasionally suffered since 1993 from outbreaks of taro-leaf blight which severely affect exports. Industry is small scale and caters only for the local market but officials are trying to encourage diversification. Tourism is growing, but is still limited in scale.

Energy Apart from firewood, the country is entirely dependent on imports for its fuel requirements.

	1993	1994	1995
Inflation (% change)	1.7	18.3	1.1
Exchange rate (per US$)	2.57	2.53	2.48
Interest rate (% per annum)	12.0	12.0	12.0
GDP (% real growth)	4.2	-1.3	2.0
GDP (Million units of national currency)	275.2	321.3	331.3
GDP (US$ million)	107.1	127.0	133.6
GDP per capita (US$)	645.2	739.0	763.5
Consumption (Million units of national currency)	214.1	250.0	257.8
Consumption (US$ million)	83.3	98.8	103.9
Consumption per capita (US$)	502.0	575.0	594.0
Population, mid-year ('000)	165.9	171.9	175.0
Birth rate (per '000)	32.0	32.4	
Death rate (per '000)	6.7	6.0	
No. of households ('000)	32.9	34.2	35.6
Total exports (US$ million)	6.0	4.0	9.0
Total imports (US$ million)	105.0	82.0	95.0
Tourism receipts (US$ million)	19.6	22.7	
Tourist spending (US$ million)	2.1	2.4	2.5

Average household size 1995 (persons)	4.67		
Urban population 1994 (%)	21.0		
Age analysis (%) (1981)	*0-14* 44.3	*15-64* 52.7	*65+* 3.0
Population by sex (%) (1981)	*Male* 51.8	*Female* 48.2	
Life expectancy (years) (1976)	*Male* 61.0	*Female* 64.3	
Infant mortality (deaths per '000 live births) (1991)	45.6		
Adult literacy (%) (1971)	87.9		

TRADING PARTNERS

Major export destinations 1995 (% share)		Major import sources 1995 (% share)	
Australia	86.8	New Zealand	35.6
New Zealand	6.4	Japan	21.0
Japan	1.8	Australia	19.4
American Samoa	1.4	Fiji	8.5

Yemen

Area (km²)   527,968

Currency   Yemeni riyal (= 100 fils)

Location   The Republic of Yemen, which took its present form in 1990, occupies the entire southern tip of the Arabian Peninsula, and effectively controls the strategically important access from the Arabian sea through the Gulf of Aden, to the Red Sea. With Saudi Arabia to its north and Oman to the north-east, it faces Djibouti, Ethiopia and Somalia across the Gulf of Aden. The capital is Sana'a.

Head of State   President Ali Abdullah Saleh

Head of Government   Abdel Aziz Abdel-Ghani (June 1994)

Ruling Party   Coalition of the General People's Congress, the Yemeni Islah Party and the Yemen Socialist Party.

Political Structure   The current state of Yemen was the result of a federation in May 1990, when the Republic of Yemen was formed by the union of the Yemen Arab Republic (North Yemen) with the People's Democratic Republic of Yemen (South Yemen). The North Yemeni President, Lt-Gen. Ali Abdullah Saleh, became national President and a transitional government was formed. But differences between the two regional groups soon arose, and in 1994 the southern states declared their own secession from the federation, with Gen. Ali Salem Al-Beidh claiming to be president of the South. The north soon crushed the rebellion and by mid-1995 the country appeared to be stabilising. Technically, Yemen's unified House of Representatives comprises 301 members, and a 45-member Advisory Council supports the executive President and his Cabinet. In practice, this system is in abeyance.

Last Elections   Elections were held for the first time in April 1993, when the General People's Congress won 121 of the 301 seats in the House of Representatives, the Yemen Alliance for Reform won 62 and the Yemen Socialist Party 56 seats. The Arab Socialist Ba'ath Party (the old communist administration) won seven seats, independents took 47 seats, and other parties obtained eight seats.

Political Risk   The unification of North and South Yemen was marred by both internal and external problems which culminated in the outbreak of civil war in 1994. Internally, the economy has been upset by the forced return of 800,000 Yemeni expatriate workers who were removed by Saudi Arabia when that country was grappling with fierce opposition from Islamic fundamentalists who wanted to enforce the Sharia. Externally, Yemen has been shunned by much of the Arab world after supporting Iraq in its military occupation of Kuwait in 1990-1991.

International Disputes   Very few of Yemen's external boundaries have ever been adequately designated. Armed confrontations with Saudi Arabia occurred in the 1980s. In 1996, Eritrea came close to war with Yemen over the Dahlak Islands in the Red Sea but peace talks have now been opened to resolve that issue.

Economy   Yemen has a moderately diversified economy, with oil revenues, farming production and entrepôt and transhipment fees all contributing to the general wealth. However, incomes are still low - about half of the average in Syria, for example. The economy was also badly damaged by the political and internal disruption which has persisted since 1993. In an effort to boost the pace of growth, the government has launched a programme to attract 35 billion riyals in foreign investment and has followed this up with a 50% devaluation of the riyal and steep price increases at home.

Main Industries   The oil industry has the potential to become a driving force behind a newly influential state. Refineries are coming on line and free trade zones are being introduced in an attempt to regain the country's industrial importance within the region. Nevertheless, most of the population is still engaged in subsistence agriculture, with sorghum, millet, sesame and other cereals being the most popular crops. The climate is too dry for agriculture in the far north of the country, where desert prevails.

Energy   Yemen has been producing oil since 1987 and has several new wells under exploration. During the first half of the 1990s production capacity was estimated to be around 400,000 barrels per day but the country potential output was thought to be much higher.

	1993	1994	1995
Inflation (% change)	45.0		
Exchange rate (per US$)	12.01	12.01	47.45
Interest rate			
GDP (% real growth)			
GDP (Million units of national currency)	116,601.4	64,237.7	
GDP (US$ million)	9,708.7	5,348.7	
GDP per capita (US$)	789.3	422.2	
Consumption (Million units of national currency)	109,541.0	60,348.1	
Consumption (US$ million)	9,120.8	5,024.8	
Consumption per capita (US$)	741.5	396.6	
Population, mid-year ('000)	12,300.0	12,670.0	13,058.0
Birth rate (per '000)	49.5	50.7	
Death rate (per '000)		14.9	
No. of households ('000)	2,131.7	2,206.8	2,283.0
Total exports (US$ million)	800.0	1,032.0	
Total imports (US$ million)	2,400.0	2,012.0	
Tourism receipts (US$ million)	45.0	48.9	
Tourist spending (US$ million)			

Average household size 1995 (persons)	5.43		
Urban population 1995 (%)	34.0		
Age analysis (%) (1987)	*0-14* 47.5	*15-64* 47.5	*65+* 5.0
Population by sex (%) (1987)	*Male* 49.5	*Female* 50.5	
Life expectancy (years) (1990-95)	*Male* 49.9	*Female* 50.4	
Infant mortality (deaths per '000 live births)			
Adult literacy (%) (1995)	38.5		

TRADING PARTNERS

Major export destinations 1995 (% share)		Major import sources 1995 (% share)	
South Korea	22.5	United Arab Emirates	10.6
China	10.5	Saudi Arabia	10.4
Japan	16.1	USA	8.8
Singapore	11.5	France	6.6

Yugoslavia (former)

Area (km²) 255,805

Currency Yugoslav Dinar

Location Until 1991 the Republic of Yugoslavia comprised all the land lying along the eastern Adriatic coast from Italy down to Albania and Greece in the south, and extending inland as far as Hungary, Romania and Bulgaria. However, the map changed with the independence of Slovenia, Macedonia and Croatia, so that it now consists only of Serbia (still the largest republic) and Montenegro. The capital is Belgrade.

Head of Government Led by President Slobodan Milosevic of Serbia

Political Structure The former state of Yugoslavia consisted not only of the republics of Serbia and Montenegro, which make up the new Yugoslav state, but also Slovenia, Croatia, Bosnia-Herzegovina and Macedonia. Under the old system, the state was a federation of the republics, together with the autonomous Serbian provinces of Kosovo and Vojvodina. The new system has yet to gain international recognition. Legislative elections were held in December 1992 for the 250-seat Serbian Republican Assembly, when the SPS won 101 seats. In the separate Montenegrin Republican Assembly the Democratic Party of Socialists of Montenegro won the majority of seats, with 43% of the vote.

Political Risk Under UN sanctions for 41 months and hit by the cost of the wars in neighbouring Bosnia and Croatia, conditions in the former Yugoslavia are deteriorating rapidly.

International Disputes The bitter fighting between the former states of Yugoslavia has alienated the former Yugoslavia from almost every country in Western Europe. It has also led to sharp deterioration in relations with Albania, which fears a Serbian invasion after the clampdown in the Serbian-owned but Albanian-dominated autonomous province of Kosovo.

Economy The economy has been plunged into chaos by the continuing hostilities in the country, as tourism and other foreign revenues on which the two rump republics have depended have abruptly stopped. By 1996, production in the former Yugoslavia had fallen to the level prevailing in 1968. Most factories have closed. Metal workers have threatened to strike and pensions are delayed for several months. A dispute between the president of the central bank, Milosevic and the IMF threatens to hold up an injection of capital which is desperately needed.

Main Industries Although devastated by the fighting in neighbouring countries, Yugoslavia retains the potential to be a major agricultural producer. The favourable climate in most parts of the country allows productive farming of fruits and vegetables. Over 80% of land in Serbia and Macedonia is privately rather than collectively owned. Industry is moderately developed, with a wide range of heavy and consumer goods, including cars and electrical goods, being manufactured. Finally, mining - for chrome, limestone, lead, zinc and other metals - remains an important potential source of income when peace is restored to the region.

	1993	1994	1995
Inflation (% change)	3,000.0		
Exchange rate (per US$)			
Interest rate			
GDP (% real growth)			
GDP			
GDP (US$ million)	12,200.0		
GDP per capita (US$)	508.8		
Consumption			
Consumption (US$ million)			
Consumption per capita (US$)			
Population, mid-year ('000)	23,977.7	24,005.3	
Birth rate (per '000)	13.4	13.2	13.2
Death rate (per '000)	10.0	10.1	10.2
No. of households ('000)	7,499.9	7,546.1	7,592.3
Total exports (US$ million)			
Total imports (US$ million)			
Tourism receipts (US$ million)			
Tourist spending (US$ million)	23.0		

Average household size 1995 (persons)					
Urban population 1995 (%)	56.5				
Age analysis (%) (1989)	*0-14* 23.8	*15-64* 67.1	*65+* 9.2
Population by sex (%) (1994)	*Male* 49.4	*Female* 50.6	
Life expectancy (years) (1989-90)	*Male* 69.1	*Female* 74.9	
Infant mortality (deaths per '000 live births) (1993)	18.4		
Adult literacy (%) (1990)	92.7		

TRADING PARTNERS

Major export destinations 1995 (% share)		Major import sources 1995 (% share)	
Germany	38.8	Germany	41.9
Italy	35.6	Switzerland	12.0
India	7.8	Italy	11.8
Japan	1.0	United Kingdom	6.7

Zaire

Area (km²) 2,345,410

Currency New Zaïre (Z = 100 makuta)

Location Zaire, the largest country in Central Africa, extends from the Central African Republic and Sudan in the north to Zambia and Angola in the south, with Tanzania, Uganda and the tiny states of Rwanda and Burundi to the east and Congo to the west. Despite its size, it has only one coastal access, a channel running to the Atlantic between Congo and Angola. The terrain ranges from the vast plains of the north and far south to the dry Zaire River valley in the west. The capital is Kinshasa.

Head of State President Mobutu Sésé Seko (1965)

Head of Government Léon Kengo Wa Dondo (July 1994)

Ruling Party Mouvement populaire de la révolution (MPR)

Political Structure Zaire, or the Republic of the Congo as it is also known, has a nominally executive President who is elected for a seven-year term by universal vote and is the de facto head of the ruling Mouvement populaire de la révolution. Yet President Mobutu Sésé Seko, who seized power in 1972, has found his role under attack from the 310-member Legislative Council (Parliament), and by 1994 he had been reduced almost to a figurehead as plans were laid for the country's first multi-party elections since 1972. Mobutu fought back by appointing his own, unrecognised, government under Faustin Birindwa, and by mid-1995 the procedural differences over the status of the Prime Minister had all but privatised the political system.

Last Elections Legislative elections were last held in September 1987, when the MPR was the only legal contestant. Although fresh elections were promised for July 1995, they were postponed by President Mobutu. Mobutu had also stopped the planned presidential election in December 1991, having last been formally re-elected in July 1984. Kengo Wa Dondo was elected Prime Minister by the transitional government in July 1994.

Political Risk There are serious doubts in the international community about the quality of Mobutu's leadership. Not only his political opponents but also the influential bishops have been inveighing against him. His removal would open the way to more aid and co-operation from France and Belgium, which is seriously embarrassed by its links with Mobutu. In 1993 riots and an army mutiny led to the arrival of French troops, and foreigners were evacuated, underlining the country's extreme instability. Highly-publicised outbreaks of the deadly Ebola virus, which kills virtually all its victims, occurred in 1995 and 1996. The influx of Rwandan refugees around the Lake Kivu area has become a burning political issue, prompting Mobutu to postpone elections.

International Disputes The most recent disputes in Zaire have arisen over the country's desire to expel almost 100,000 Hutu refugees from Rwanda, some of them forced at gunpoint to return to their homeland despite the threat of attacks from their Tutsi countrymen. The UN Security Council's resolution lifting the arms embargo on the current Rwandan government heighten tensions between the two countries. Zaire and Zambia have also differed over their mutual border in the area of Lake Mweru, leading Zaire to establish border posts within what Zambia regarded as its territory. The issue remains unresolved, although an interim agreement was reached in 1987.

Economy Zaire's economy continues to deteriorate. Declining commodity prices for diamonds, gold and other products have sometimes been the culprit but economic mismanagement may be an even more important contributor. Per capita spending power is only about $200 per annum and the country's currency, the zaïre, continues to depreciate. The total lack of any coherent monetary policy is suggested by the fact that three successive governors of the central bank were dismissed within a year for allegedly failing to contain inflation. In late 1994 the International Monetary Fund suspended Zaire's membership of the IMF.

Main Industries Mining, especially for diamonds, gold, copper, zinc, cobalt and uranium, contributes the largest share of the national economy, although even here there is thought to be scope for further growth. Farming, often on a subsistence basis, is the dominant sector, however. Oil palms, coffee, rubber, cocoa and timber are grown for export, while cassava, cereals, fruit and tobacco are grown for the domestic market. Cattle are herded in the grassland areas. Manufacturing is limited to the processing of raw materials, except for a small number of basic consumer products.

Energy Zaire has a limited amount of oil located offshore, and some gas, but in the main it is obliged to import its requirements from abroad. There is substantial hydro-electric potential.

	1993	1994	1995
Inflation (% change)	1,986.9	23,773.0	542.0
Exchange rate (per US$)	2.51	1,194.12	4,968.30
Interest rate (% per annum)	95.0		
GDP (% real growth)	-10.0		
GDP		10,855,393.7	
GDP (US$ million)	10,302.8	9,090.7	8,500.0
GDP per capita (US$)	249.9	213.6	191.1
Consumption		9,096,820.0	
Consumption (US$ million)		7,618.0	
Consumption per capita (US$)		179.0	
Population, mid-year ('000)	41,230.0	42,550.0	44,469.8
Birth rate (per '000)	44.0	48.4	
Death rate (per '000)	14.5	14.8	
No. of households ('000)	10,992.2	11,391.4	11,800.0
Total exports (US$ million)	368.0	419.0	436.0
Total imports (US$ million)	372.0	382.0	388.0
Tourism receipts (US$ million)			
Tourist spending (US$ million)			

Average household size 1995 (persons)	3.58				
Urban population 1995 (%)	29.0				
Age analysis (%) (1985)	*0-14* 46.6		*15-64* 50.8		*65+* 2.6
Population by sex (%) (1985)	*Male* 49.5		*Female* 50.5		
Life expectancy (years) (1990-95)	*Male* 50.4		*Female* 53.7		
Infant mortality (deaths per '000 live births) (1993)	92.6				
Adult literacy (%) (1995)	77.3				

TRADING PARTNERS

Major export destinations 1995 (% share)		Major import sources 1995 (% share)	
Belgium/Luxembourg	36.1	Belgium/Luxembourg	15.5
USA	16.8	South Africa	10.8
Italy	9.8	Hong Kong	8.6
South Africa	8.3	Germany	7.1

Zambia

Area (km²)   752,615

Currency   Zambian kwacha (Kw = 100 ngee)

Location   Zambia is a landlocked country lying in the centre of Central Southern Africa. It borders in the south on Zimbabwe, Botswana and Namibia. In the north are Zaire and Tanzania, in the west is Angola and in the east is Malawi. The country has a varied terrain, ranging from mountain ranges to the lowlands of the Zambezi, Luapula, Kafue and Luangwa rivers. The climate is sub-tropical, but humidity is not excessive. The capital is Lusaka.

Head of State   President Frederick Chiluba (1991)

Head of Government   President Frederick Chiluba (1991)

Ruling Party   Movement for Multi-Party Democracy (MMD)

Political Structure   From 1972 to 1991 Zambia was run as a single-party state, in which the United National Independence Party (UNIP) stood unopposed at every level. In 1991 a new multi-party Constitution was introduced, leading in October 1991 to multi-party elections in which UNIP was beaten. A week later the 27-year state of emergency was ended. The executive President is elected by universal suffrage for a five-year term, and answers to a 150-member National Assembly which sits also for five years. In March 1993 President Chiluba declared an indefinite state of emergency after reports of an attempted coup against him. A series of political purges in 1994 followed a major escalation of corruption allegations.

Last Elections   The country's first multi-party elections took place in October 1991, when the Movement for Multi-Party Democracy defeated the UNIP of President Kenneth Kaunda, who had ruled since 1964. The MMD gained 125 of the 150 seats in the National Assembly, against UNIP's 25 seats. Only four of the 20 UNIP Cabinet ministers were returned to their parliamentary seats. However, it was reported that over half of the electorate had not voted.

Political Risk   Zambia's initially peaceful transition to multi-party democracy was marred by the reintroduction of state of emergency in 1993. Foreign investors, who were at first attracted by Kaunda's unexpectedly graceful departure from power, have grown cautious once again. Since then, the government has worked, with some success, to stabilise the situation. Aid continues to flood into the country and the country enjoys a relatively good reputation within the international community. The situation could deteriorate rapidly, but for the time being, Zambia is one of the more stable and attractive markets in the region.

International Disputes   Zambia and Zaire are unable to agree on their mutual border in the area of Lake Mweru. The issue remains unresolved, despite an interim agreement reached in 1987. Zambia has also had shaky relations in the past with neighbouring Mozambique, but most of the underlying problems have been smoothed over for now.

Economy   Zambia's economy, although basically dependent on commodity exports, has made considerable progress over the past two decades. Growth of both agriculture and manufacturing has reduced the country's dependence on mining. Meanwhile, the government has implemented a modest programme of privatisation and economic reform which has boosted efficiency. Most of the work force is still engaged in some sort of subsistence activity and enjoys a standard of living which is above average for southern Africa.

Main Industries   Farming centres on maize, vegetables and livestock raising, mainly for domestic consumption. Sugar, tobacco and cotton are produced for export. The agricultural sector suffers from underinvestment, although poor weather has added to its worries in recent years. Mineral extraction involves mainly copper, the single most abundant deposit in Africa, which generally provides more than 90% of all foreign exchange revenues. There is no significant tourist sector.

Energy   Zambia has no indigenous oil or gas reserves, though it has some coal. The country is obliged to depend on imports for most of its fuel needs. The vast bulk of its electricity derives from hydro-electric sources.

	1993	1994	1995
Inflation (% change)	189.0	53.7	
Exchange rate (per US$)	434.78	769.23	845.20
Interest rate			
GDP (% real growth)			
GDP (Million units of national currency)	1,440,663.0	2,607,689.7	2,915,940.0
GDP (US$ million)	3,313.5	3,390.0	3,450.0
GDP per capita (US$)	370.6	368.5	368.2
Consumption (Million units of national currency)	1,173,588.0	2,029,587.3	2,168,348.0
Consumption (US$ million)	2,699.3	2,638.5	2,565.5
Consumption per capita (US$)	301.9	286.8	273.8
Population, mid-year ('000)	8,940.0	9,200.0	9,370.0
Birth rate (per '000)	49.0	46.0	
Death rate (per '000)	15.1	15.0	
No. of households ('000)	2,134.9	2,210.0	2,285.0
Total exports (US$ million)	1,500.0	1,060.0	
Total imports (US$ million)	1,450.0	921.0	
Tourism receipts (US$ million)	44.0	44.4	
Tourist spending (US$ million)	51.9	52.3	50.9

Average household size 1995 (persons)	3.90				
Urban population 1995 (%)	43.1				
Age analysis (%) (1990)	*0-14* 47.3		*15-64* 50.0		*65+* 2.6
Population by sex (%) (1990)	*Male* 49.2		*Female* 50.8		
Life expectancy (years) (1985-90)	*Male* 52.4		*Female* 54.5		
Infant mortality (deaths per '000 live births) (1993)	104.0				
Adult literacy (%) (1995)	78.2				

TRADING PARTNERS

Major export destinations 1995 (% share)		Major import sources 1995 (% share)	
Japan	17.9	South Africa	28.5
Saudi Arabia	12.9	United Kingdom	12.0
Thailand	11.8	Zimbabwe	9.4
India	6.1	Japan	8.8

Zimbabwe

Area (km²) 390,310

Currency Zimbabwe dollar (Z$ = 100 cents)

Location Zimbabwe is a landlocked country lying in east-central Southern Africa. It is separated from the Indian Ocean by Mozambique - a factor which proved crucially awkward during the decades of civil war in that country. In the north it borders on Zambia, in the south-west on Botswana, and in the south on South Africa. The climate is dry and tropical, yet there is usually enough water thanks to the numerous large rivers which flow through the country. The capital is Harare.

Head of State President Robert G. Mugabe (1987)

Head of Government President Robert G. Mugabe

Ruling Party Zimbabwe African National Union-Patriotic Front (ZANU-PF)

Political Structure Zimbabwe, an independent member of the Commonwealth, has an executive President who is elected by universal suffrage for a six-year term and presides over a single-chamber House of Assembly. The Assembly's 150 members, who also serve for six years, include 120 elected members, 10 tribal chiefs, eight provincial governors appointed by the President, and 12 other presidential appointees. Since 1991 the Government has sought to break with its colonial past through controversial land appropriations, which remove farm lands from white ownership.

Last Elections President Mugabe was re-elected in March 1996 for another six years. He took 93% of the vote, although the turnout was only 32%. Mugabe's party, the ZANU-PF coalition, controls 147 of the 150 parliamentary seats and runs almost all local government. ZANU's dominance of the political scene, coupled with its long political rein, means that the traditional distinctions between the state, the government and the party have all be disappeared in Zimbabwe.

Political Risk Despite appearances, Zimbabwe is still a one-party state whose leadership aspires to a Marxist-Leninist establishment. The country's programme of land appropriations raises some doubts about the security of foreign investments in Zimbabwe under any but the most securely guaranteed conditions. Corruption is also becoming a serious problem; virtually all government contracts require some form of kickback or "commission" to those with political influence or to the bureaucrats who stand guard over regulations. Yet aid continues to flow and international creditors remain sympathetic. Meanwhile, President Mugabe has embarked on a painful but necessary restructuring programme which underlines his confidence in the support of the electorate.

International Disputes Zimbabwe is accused of harbouring refugees from neighbouring Mozambique with which a repatriation agreement was reached in late 1993.

Economy Zimbabwe's economy has deteriorated in recent years, mainly due to poor financial management. The budget for 1994-1995 called for a deficit of 6.7% of GDP but the outcome was a public spending programme which exceeded 13%. No spending cuts were scheduled in the 1996 budget, a fact which has made the IMF and western donors extremely uneasy. There is pressure to reduce the swollen civil service, privatise loss-making state corporations, the grain marketing board and other farming boards as well as railways, telephones and electricity. Most government officials strongly oppose these views; in part, because state-owned firms offer a handy source of patronage. Several years of drought, accompanied by a period of poor government management, have complicated the picture. Tobacco and mineral exports could alleviate the country's financial crunch in 1996 if world prices remain strong.

Main Industries With its fertile lands, Zimbabwe is the breadbasket of southern Africa. Many farms are small, however, and the bulk of production is intended for subsistence purposes. Maize, wheat, fruit and vegetables are grown for domestic consumption, and tobacco, cotton, sugar and beef cattle are raised for export. The country's agricultural sector is vulnerable to drought and output has been severely reduced in recent years. The Government has attracted criticism since 1992 for its decision to confiscate some 190,000 hectares of land owned by white farmers and to distribute it to blacks. The mineral sector centres on gold, silver, asbestos and copper and makes a major contribution to GDP so long as world commodity prices are strong. Manufacturing is of a limited significance, catering mainly for domestic rather than export requirements.

Energy Zimbabwe has coal but no oil, and the bulk of its petroleum needs have to be imported. The country derives about a third of its electricity from hydro-electric resources.

	1993	1994	1995
Inflation (% change)	27.6	22.3	22.6
Exchange rate (per US$)	6.47	8.15	8.67
Interest rate (% per annum)	36.3	34.9	34.7
GDP (% real growth)	3.2	2.3	-9.0
GDP (Million units of national currency)	37,928.8	47,453.8	52,942.3
GDP (US$ million)	5,862.3	5,822.6	6,106.4
GDP per capita (US$)	543.8	522.3	529.6
Consumption (Million units of national currency)	13,561.9	16,967.7	18,930.2
Consumption (US$ million)	2,096.1	2,081.9	2,183.4
Consumption per capita (US$)	194.4	186.8	189.4
Population, mid-year ('000)	10,780.0	11,148.2	11,530.0
Birth rate (per '000)	39.1	37.2	
Death rate (per '000)	12.0	12.0	
No. of households ('000)	2,797.3	2,907.3	3,018.0
Total exports (US$ million)	1,568.0	1,885.0	2,104.3
Total imports (US$ million)	1,820.0	2,241.0	2,749.7
Tourism receipts (US$ million)	103.0	100.4	
Tourist spending (US$ million)	97.0	94.6	99.2

Average household size 1995 (persons)	3.63		
Urban population 1995 (%)	42.0		
Age analysis (%) (1987)	*0-14* 47.7	*15-64* 49.1	*65+* 3.1
Population by sex (%) (1992)	*Male* 48.8	*Female* 51.2	
Life expectancy (years) (1990-95)	*Male* 52.4	*Female* 55.1	
Infant mortality (deaths per '000 live births) (1993)	67.0		
Adult literacy (%) (1995)	85.1		

TRADING PARTNERS

Major export destinations 1995 (% share)		Major import sources 1995 (% share)	
South Africa	17.6	South Africa	40.0
United Kingdom	10.8	United Kingdom	6.7
Germany	8.1	USA	5.7
Japan	8.1	Japan	5.7